WESTMAR COLLEGE LIBRARY

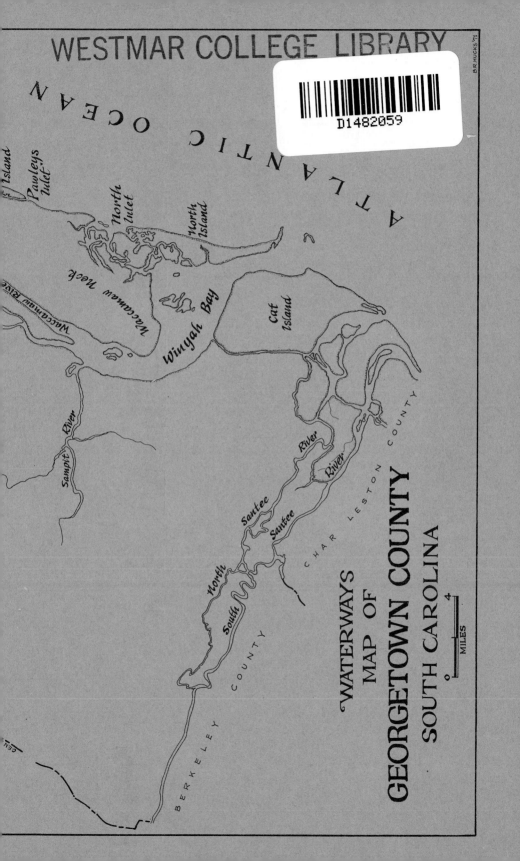

WATERWAYS
MAP OF
GEORGETOWN COUNTY
SOUTH CAROLINA

ATLANTIC OCEAN

Pawleys Inlet

North Inlet

North Island

Waccamaw Neck

Waccamaw River

Winyah Bay

Cat Island

Sampit River

Santee River

River

North Santee

South Santee

CHARLESTON COUNTY

BERKELEY COUNTY

MILES

B.R. HUCKS '71

About the author

A native of Charleston, South Carolina, George C. Rogers, Jr., is a graduate of the College of Charleston. He received his M.A. and Ph.D. degrees from the University of Chicago and studied at Edinburgh University on a Rotary Fellowship. His published books include *Evolution of a Federalist: William Loughton Smith of Charleston (1758–1812)* and *Charleston in the Age of the Pinckneys.* One of the leading authorities on South Carolina history, Dr. Rogers is currently professor of history at the University of South Carolina.

THE HISTORY OF GEORGETOWN COUNTY, SOUTH CAROLINA

THE PUBLISHER GRATEFULLY ACKNOWLEDGES THE RECEIPT

OF A GRANT TOWARD THE MANUFACTURING COST OF THIS

BOOK FROM THE GEORGETOWN COUNTY BOARD OF EDUCATION.

THE HISTORY OF GEORGE-TOWN COUNTY, SOUTH CAROLINA/GEORGE C. ROGERS, JR.

UNIVERSITY OF SOUTH CAROLINA PRESS/COLUMBIA, SOUTH CAROLINA

975.789
R726

F
277
.G-35
R6

Copyright © 1970 by
The University of South Carolina Press

Published in Columbia, S.C., by the
UNIVERSITY OF SOUTH CAROLINA PRESS

First Printing, August 1970
Second Printing, July 1971

International Standard Book Number: 0-87249-143-9
Library of Congress Catalog Card Number: 70-95260

Suggested Library of Congress classification
furnished by
McKissick Memorial Library of the
University of South Carolina:
F277.G35R

84793

To
Betty and Bernard

ACKNOWLEDGMENTS

The late Joseph Laurie Bull, Jr., of Georgetown, Chairman of the Georgetown County Board of Education, conceived the idea of this history of Georgetown County. The idea was endorsed by the Georgetown County Board of Education and an author sought. In November 1962 I agreed to undertake the task of writing such a work. My principal interest has been an exploration of local sources that might be used in writing the history of South Carolina. Local history must be based upon the most thorough survey of the facts; and fortunately, in South Carolina there is a wealth of material.

The South Carolina Department of Archives and History houses one of the finest, if not the finest, collections of colonial and state documents. Charles E. Lee, who so ably directs that institution and who has spent such fruitful time in arranging the materials so that scholars can use them, has given his advice at every step of the way. His staff, consisting of William L. McDowell, Miss Wylma A. Wates, Miss Ruth S. Green, R. Nicholas Olsberg, Mrs. Florence M. Law, Mrs. Isobel Kirkwood, and Mrs. Ruth Trice have been helpful. At the Caroliniana Library of the University of South Carolina, E. L. Inabinett and Mrs. Clara Mae Jacobs have opened up the great collections of personal papers to this author. Kenneth E. Toombs, Librarian of the University of South Carolina, J. Mitchell Reames, Mrs. Davy-Jo Ridge, Mrs. Elizabeth LaBruce Pugh, Mrs. Evelyn S. Barron, Mrs. Mary E. Goolsby, Miss Mary Timberlake, and Mrs. Estelle Boulware of the McKissick Library staff have made working easier and looked up innumerable details.

In Charleston, the wealth of material at the South Carolina Historical Society contains much about Georgetown. Mrs. Mary Elizabeth Prior and Miss Helen McCormack have been unfailing guides to these facts. At the Charleston Library Society, Miss Virginia Rugheimer has brought out the Georgetown newspapers.

In Georgetown the County Library contains some information on the county in manuscript form, principally the items preserved there belonging to the Winyah Indigo Society. Mrs. Mary S. Bonds and Mrs. Janet F. Paris have in turn given assistance to the author.

Miss Wylma A. Wates and Robert M. Weir have read chapters of the manuscript and commented upon them. The late William A. Foran read the chapters on the Civil War and Reconstruction and challenged in his provocative way many of my assumptions. Most particularly, Daniel W. Hollis has gone over every line to comment upon form and content. This manuscript is better for their help. Robert D. Ochs, as always, provides a happy working climate for the members of his department.

The person who has given the most assistance throughout this project has been William C. Young, Superintendent of Education for Georgetown County. Mr. Young has watched over the project on behalf of the Georgetown Board of Education. His patience with an author who seemed to prolong the project endlessly has been notable. But, being an historian himself, he always understood the exact demands upon the author and eased the long and difficult path.

Mrs. Charlotte Kaminski Prevost, Mrs. Sarah Parker Lumpkin, and Mrs. Katherine Fraser Overton of Georgetown have read the entire manuscript and made valuable comments, always directed at preventing errors which only the dedicated local person can help the author avoid.

There are so many people to thank in writing a book of this scope. Each of the following persons has contributed something to this book, be it facts, ideas, or helpful suggestions: Miss Susan Lowndes Allston, William F. Allston, Miss Augusta M. Bailey, C. B. Berry, Mrs. Bessie F. Betancourt, Mrs. Carol Rothrock Bleser, Mrs. Mary S. Bonds, Wallace Brown, Mrs. Henry DeSaussure Bull, Mrs. Joseph L. Bull, Jr., Alan Calmes, Jonathan Daniels, Chalmers Davidson, Thomas P. Davis, Alston

Deas, William W. Doar, Arthur H. Doyle, John Duncan, Miss Florence Epps, Mrs. Frederick W. Ford, Philip M. Hamer, Samuel M. Harper, Mrs. Margaret H. Harrison, W. Edwin Hemphill, Oliver W. Holmes, Mrs. Sarah Jackson, Newton Jones, Charles W. Lawrimore, Mrs. Paul H. Leonard, Mrs. Mildred Weston Lewis, Roy Merrens, John Hammond Moore, William Patterson, Mrs. Jesse C. Quattlebaum, Mrs. Alice H. Quinn, Mrs. Emily Bellinger Reynolds, Miss Katherine Drayton Mayrant Simons, L. C. Sloan, Mrs. Ellen Ford Steinhart, Richard Taylor, George B. Tindall, Edward Weldon, and Mrs. Richard G. White.

Particular mention should also be made of Miss Helen McCormack, who has selected many of the illustrations used in the book.

On this occasion a very special mention must be made of Mrs. Nina F. Brooks, who has typed and retyped this manuscript with a patience and a skill deserving of the highest praise.

I have dedicated this book to Elizabeth and Bernard Manning whose abiding interest in all of my historical work can only be recognized in this small but grateful way.

LIST OF ABBREVIATIONS

Abstracts of the Wills of the State of South Carolina, 1670-1740, will be cited for *Abstracts of the Wills of the State of South Carolina, 1670-1740,* ed. Caroline T. Moore and Agatha Aimar Simmons (Columbia, S. C., 1960).

BPRO for transcripts of the records in the British Public Record Office, London, in the S. C. Archives.

CLS for Charleston Library Society, Charleston, South Carolina

CO for Colonial Office records in the BPRO

DAB for *Dictionary of American Biography*

DUL for Duke University Library, Durham, North Carolina

Gazette for the *South-Carolina Gazette*

Mass. Hist. Soc. for the Massachusetts Historical Society, Boston, Mass.

LC for the Library of Congress, Washington, D. C.

New York Hist. Soc. for the New York Historical Society, New York, N. Y.

N.S. for New Series

NYPL for the New York Public Library, New York, N. Y.

O. R. Army for *Official Records of the Union and Confederate Armies in the War of the Rebellion.*

O. R. Navy for *Official Records of the Union and Confederate Navies in the War of the Rebellion.*

Penn. Hist. Soc. for the Pennsylvania Historical Society, Philadelphia, Penn.

PRO for the Public Record Office, London, England

Reynolds and Faunt, Biographical Directory of the South Carolina Senate for Emily Bellinger Reynolds and Joan Reynolds Faunt, *Biographical Directory of the Senate of South Carolina, 1776-1964* (Columbia, S. C., 1964).

S. C. Archives for the Department of Archives and History, Columbia, S. C.

S. C. Hist. Soc. for the South Carolina Historical Society, Charleston, S. C.

SCHM for the *South Carolina Historical Magazine*

SCL for the South Caroliniana Library, Univ. of S. C., Columbia, S. C.

S. C. Statutes for *The Statutes at Large of South Carolina,* ed. Thomas Cooper and David J. McCord (Columbia, S. C., 1837-1841).

SHC for the Southern Historical Collection, Univ. of N. C., Chapel Hill, N. C.

WLCL for the William L. Clements Library, Univ. of Michigan, Ann Arbor, Mich.

CONTENTS

ILLUSTRATIONS

(following page 270)

ENDPAPERS

THE HISTORY OF GEORGETOWN

COUNTY, SOUTH CAROLINA

I

THE LIMITS OF GEORGETOWN COUNTY

This is a history of the people who have lived in the geographic region which is now Georgetown County, South Carolina. This land has been a part of many divisions of the province and of the state—counties, parishes, judicial districts, as well as a bewildering array of smaller administrative units. A chronological survey of these divisions will provide a framework within which to tell the story of the people who lived around Winyah Bay.[1]

In 1629 Carolina was granted to Sir Robert Heath, but his charter was superseded by that granted in 1663, and regranted in 1665, to the eight Lords Proprietors. Winyah Bay was in the center of the 1665 grant which extended from St. Mary's River on the south to Virginia on the north. An abortive settlement on the Cape Fear River in the

---

[1] The fullest account of the evolution of local divisions of South Carolina is in William C. Harllee, *Kinfolks* (New Orleans, La., 1934), I, 41–62. The best brief account is [Charles E. Lee] "Archives News," *SCHM*, LXIX (1968), 154–157. According to A. S. Salley, Jr., "Winyah" is correct. The pronunciation should not have the "yaw" sound. Wineau, Winea, and Winee were early phonetic spellings of this Indian word. David Doar, *Rice and Rice Planting in the South Carolina Low Country* (Charleston, S. C., 1936), p. 57n. After the demise of the *Winyaw Intelligencer* in the 1830's, the *Winyah Observer* began publishing on March 10, 1841, which would indicate that the change in spelling accepted by the local people took place about 1840.

1660's was followed by a successful one at Charleston in 1670.[2] As the configuration of the land as it meets the water around Wilmington, Georgetown,[3] Charleston, and Beaufort is similar, the success of Charleston had some elements of accident. There was much exploring and more hesitation before Charleston emerged as the center of this new attempt at English colonization.

In 1682 the Lords Proprietors gave directions for laying out three counties: Berkeley County was in the center and included Charleston; Colleton was to the south; Craven to the north. Craven County originally lay between the Seewee River (now Awendaw Creek) and the Santee River, extending inland thirty-five miles. By custom, which the law later endorsed, Craven County eventually included the area north and east of the Santee-Congaree-Broad river system, as well as the original area, which was subsequently divided into the parishes of St. James Santee (French Santee) and St. Stephens (English Santee).

Although these counties functioned as administrative, judicial, and militia units, few records have been preserved. In fact, few ever existed. Sheriffs, coroners, justices of the peace, and militia officers were appointed for these counties, but much of their work was summary and unrecorded. County courts did function for awhile in the 1720's.[4] From the first election for members to the Commons House of Assembly until 1716 the counties served as election districts.[5] Colleton had ten members; Berkeley and Craven together elected twenty members. But these elections were held in Charleston, not in the outlying districts. These counties, along with the parishes, provided the territorial basis for the militia until the Revolution.[6]

[2] Charles Town became Charleston in 1783, but Charleston is the spelling used throughout this book.

[3] George Town became Georgetown in 1798, but Georgetown is the spelling used throughout this book. S. C. *Statutes*, VII, 283–289.

[4] M. Eugene Sirmans, *Colonial South Carolina, A Political History, 1663–1763* (Chapel Hill, N. C., 1966), pp. 142–144, 154, 166.

[5] The law of Dec. 15, 1716, was repealed by the Lords Proprietors July 22, 1718, and by section 24 of the election act of Sept. 15, 1721. S. C. *Statutes*, II, 683–691; Act No. 365 (1716), S. C. Archives. The 1721 law again made the parish the election unit. S. C. *Statutes*, III, 135–140.

[6] S. C. *Statutes*, IX, 645–663.

In 1706 the Anglican Church was established and the colony divided into ten parishes.[7] In each parish a church was to be built, a minister to be provided, and a register of births, christenings, marriages, and burials to be kept. None of the first ten parishes specifically embraced the Winyah region. St. James Santee, which at first was merely Craven County, was definitely limited by the Santee River on the north in 1708.[8] In 1720 the inhabitants at Winyah petitioned the Assembly, asking to be formed into a separate parish as the nearest church in Craven County was too distant to benefit them. On March 10, 1721/1722, "An act for erecting the settlement at Winyaw, in Craven County, into a distinct parish from St. James Santee, in the said County" was passed. The new parish, Prince George Winyah, named after George Prince of Wales (who became George II of England in 1727), was "bounded to the south-west on Santee river, and to the north-east on Cape Fear river, to the eastward on the ocean, and to the westward as far as it shall be inhabited by his Majesty's subjects."[9] As the parishes of colonial South Carolina had civil as well as religious functions, a measure of local self-government was thereby brought to the first settlers at Winyah. Henceforth the people of the parish would elect assemblymen, church wardens, vestrymen, and overseers of the poor. All important judicial business, however, had to be transacted at Charleston until the eve of the Revolution.

Because of the spread of population inland the Assembly divided Prince George Winyah on April 9, 1734. The new parish was named Prince Frederick after the then Prince of Wales, who (as he died before his father) never became king of England, although his son did as George III. The old parish was divided as follows:

beginning at the southwesternmost part of the plantation of John Du Bose, on Santee river, from thence on a line to the head of John Green's Creek,

[7] S. C. Statutes, II, 282–294.
[8] S. C. Statutes, II, 330.
[9] S. C. Statutes, III, 171–172. The traditional date for the establishment of this parish is 1721; actually it was 1721 by the old style calendar. In 1752 the first of the year was moved from March 25 to Jan. 1. In this work all dates are written as though they were new style. Instead of writing March 10, 1721/1722, the author will write March 10, 1722.

and down the said creek till you come to Black river, and from thence over Black river to the plantation of John Bogg, and from the said plantation of John Bogg, to be included in the town parish, in a due north line, till you come to Pedee river; and that part of the said parish wherein the parish church now is, shall and is hereby declared to be a distinct parish by itself, separate from the other part of the Parish of Prince George Winyaw, and for ever hereafter shall be called and known by the name of Prince Frederick; and the other part of the parish, where Georgetown lies, shall be called and for ever hereafter be known by the name of Prince George Winyaw.[10]

In 1735 the parish line was extended due north from the Pee Dee River to the "utmost bounds of the province." [11] Since the first parish church of Prince George had been built on the Black River in what was henceforth to be Prince Frederick Parish, the new church would be built in the parish of Prince George. Both parishes, however, would be entitled to two members in the Assembly.

In 1757 the parish of St. Mark's was carved out of Prince Frederick, and in 1768 the parish of St. David's was formed from parts of both St. Mark's and Prince Frederick. St. Mark's and St. David's were outside the area that eventually became Georgetown County. By an act of May 23, 1767, a third parish, All Saints, which included "all the lands which lie between the sea and the Waccamaw River, as far as the boundary line of North Carolina" was created out of Prince George. Although the King disallowed the act on December 9, 1770, the new state government re-established the parish on March 16, 1778.[12]

In 1769 the royal province was divided into seven judicial districts, each district to have a circuit court presided over by the justices of the common law courts riding circuit out of Charleston.[13] A courthouse and

---

[10] "An act for dividing the parishes of St. Paul's in Colleton County, and Prince George Winyaw, in Craven County," dated April 9, 1734. S. C. Statutes, III, 374–376.

[11] S. C. Statutes, IX, 87–88. For the difficulties that still ensued from drawing the line due north from the Pee Dee River, see Alexander Gregg, History of the Old Cheraws (Baltimore, Md., 1967), pp. 33–37. Peedee is the old spelling; Pee Dee is the newer spelling and the form used in this book. Susan L. Allston regretted the change. Susan L. Allston, "The Peedee," Names in South Carolina, VI (1959), 6–8. The Georgetown newspaper of the 1850's was the Pee Dee Times.

[12] S. C. Statutes, IV, 266–268, 407–408; Frances H. Porcher, "Royal Review of South Carolina Law, 1719–1776" (MA thesis, Univ. of S. C., 1962), pp. 76, 112.

[13] "An act for establishing courts, building goals and appointing sheriffs and other officers, for the more convenient administration of justice in this province," signed on July 29, 1769, contained the following definition of the new judicial district:

a jail would be built in each district, and for the Georgetown judicial district they were located in Georgetown. This district included what are now the counties of Georgetown, Horry, Marion, Dillon, Williamsburg, and part of Florence.

On March 12, 1785, the legislature divided each of the seven judicial districts into judicial subdivisions which were to be known as counties and to have county courts. Four counties were carved out of the Georgetown judicial circuit: Winyaw, Liberty, Kingston, and Williamsburg. Winyaw County was described as beginning

at Linud's ferry, on Santee river, thence along the road to Potatoe ferry [on Black River], to Shepherd's ferry on Black Mingo, to Britton's ferry on Great Pedee, thence along the said river and Big Bull's creek to Waccamaw river, thence along the said river to the lower end of Shad's Island, and from thence by a direct course over the said river to the sea, thence along the sea coast to the mouth of North Santee, and thence along the north branch thereof to the beginning. . . .[14]

Each county was to have seven justices of the peace, of whom three would be a quorum for holding the county court, which had a civil and criminal jurisdiction over minor causes.[15] In the lowcountry county courts were not set up, so that Georgetown in practice continued under the jurisdiction of the 1769 Georgetown judicial circuit.[16]

On December 21, 1798, the state legislature passed "an act to establish an uniform and more convenient system of judicature" by which all judicial divisions then existing were abolished and the state freshly

---

"The said courts at George Town of all such pleas criminal and civil within George Town Precinct or District which shall include all places between Santee River aforesaid the Sea and the Line which divides the parish of Saint Mark from the Parish of Prince Frederick which shall be continued in the same course across Pedee to the North Carolina Boundary." This act, although neither printed nor mentioned in S. C. Statutes, may be found in Richard Maxwell Brown, The South Carolina Regulators (Cambridge, Mass., Mass., 1963), pp. 148–158. The original act is in S. C. Archives.

[14] S. C. Statutes, IV, 661–666.

[15] The basic law for the county courts was that of March 24, 1785, entitled "an act for establishing County Courts, and for regulating the proceedings therein." S. C. Statutes, VII, 211–242.

[16] One proof that Georgetown did not have a county court is an act, dated March 7, 1789, concerning Charleston, Georgetown, and Beaufort, which was entitled: "An act to remedy the defects of the courts of ordinary in the several districts where there are no county courts. . . ." S. C. Statutes, VII, 249–250.

divided. At this time the three counties of Winyaw, Kingston, and Williamsburg, as laid out in 1785, were joined into a new judicial district. Liberty County became Marion District. Georgetown, Charleston, Colleton, and Beaufort districts were grouped into an eastern judicial circuit, one of four circuits established at this time in the state.[17] In 1801 Kingston County was cut off from Georgetown District, renamed Horry, and made a special district.[18] In 1804 Williamsburg County became Williamsburg District.[19] Georgetown District after 1804 merely embraced the area that had been delineated as Winyaw County in 1785.

Georgetown District remained the local administrative and judicial division while Prince George Winyah and All Saints parishes continued to serve as election units until after the Civil War.[20] The constitutional convention of 1865 abolished the parishes as election units. The constitutional convention of 1868 transformed the districts into counties. Georgetown County in its present extent and area dates from 1868.

Modern Georgetown County comprises 517,120 acres or 808 square miles.[21] Its average length, considering the county to be a rectangle with its longest side resting on the coast, is thirty-five miles; its average width perpendicular to the coast is twenty-four miles. The eastern boundary is a "smooth, slightly incurved beach" which is broken by a few inlets: Murrell's, Midway, Pawley's, North, Winyah Bay, North Santee, and South Santee, with the principal opening being that into Winyah Bay.

[17] S. C. Statutes, VII, 283–289.
[18] In this act the town of Kingston was renamed Conwayborough. S. C. Statutes, V, 407–408.
[19] This act is listed in S. C. Statutes, V, 478; the original is Act No. 1826 (1804), S. C. Archives.
[20] Under the Constitution of 1790 the parish of Prince Frederick disappeared as an election unit. At that time All Saints (including its ancient boundaries) was to have one member in the House of Representatives and Winyaw (not including any part of All Saints) was to have three. In the Senate All Saints had one member and Winyaw and Williamsburg combined had one member. An act of Feb. 19, 1791, redefined Prince George Parish as "bounded northwardly by a line beginning at Lenud's Ferry, on Santee river, thence along the road to Potatoe ferry, to Shepherd's ferry on Black Mingo, to Briton's ferry on Great Pedee, thence along the said river and Big Bull's creek; any law, custom or usage to the contrary notwithstanding." S. C. Statutes, V, 179. After 1791 the representation continued as above but for "Winyaw" one had to read "Prince George Winyah." Under the constitutional amendment of 1808, Williamsburg was separated from Prince George Winyah.
[21] The following description is drawn from W. E. McLendon, G. A. Crabb, M. Earl Carr, and F. S. Welsh, Soil Survey of Georgetown County, South Carolina (Washington, D. C., 1912).

Winyah Bay extends twelve miles north, west, and north into the county and receives the drainage of the Waccamaw, Pee Dee, Black, and Sampit rivers. "Paralleling the Waccamaw River to the Horry County line, the Pee Dee swings more to the west and forms over half of the northern boundary. The Santee River, with its lower prong, the South Santee, flows along the entire southern boundary. The Black River crosses the county almost centrally from west to east, although very crooked in detail, and the Sampit, a deep tidal stream of local origin, extends nearly due west from the head of Winyah Bay."[22] Each river is subject to tidal action beyond the western limits of the county. The Santee and Pee Dee are navigable as far as the Piedmont, the Black to Kingstree, the Black Mingo (a northern tributary of the Black) to Rhems, the Waccamaw above Conway, and the Sampit for ten miles.

Thomas P. Lockwood divided the region into "light sandy lands," "rich rice swamp," and "pine barren lands of various qualities."[23] McLendon, Crabb, Carr, and Welsh in *Soil Survey of Georgetown County, South Carolina*, written in 1912, described the county as wholly in "the flat, pin[e]y-woods region of the state."[24] The elevation on the western boundary reaches a height of forty feet, and the land slopes imperceptibly toward the coast about one to two feet to the mile. Within the gently sloping region there are a number of slightly depressed areas known as bays which are in a semi-swampy condition, heavily timbered with water-loving trees, shrubs, and vines. Carver's Bay lies between the Pee Dee and the Black; Gapway Bay between the Black and the Sampit; and Big and Little Kilsock bays south of the Sampit.[25]

The climate of the entire county is affected by the nearness of the ocean, particularly by the presence of the Gulf Stream just fifty miles offshore. The cabbage palmetto grows along the coast, the live oak throughout the area, the magnolia around the bays. Most of the wet areas were filled with cypresses and gums, the dry lands by longleaf

[22] *Ibid.*, pp. 5–6.
[23] Thomas P. Lockwood, *A Geography of South-Carolina* (Charleston, S. C., 1832), p. 32.
[24] McLendon et al., *op. cit.*
[25] B. W. Wells and Steve G. Boyce, "Carolina Bays: Additional Data on their Origin, Age and History," *Journal of the Elisha Mitchell Scientific Society*, LXIX (1953), 133; W. F. Prouty, "Carolina Bays and Their Origin," *Bulletin of the Geological Society of America*, LXIII (1952), 170.

pine. The mean winter temperature is about fifty-one degrees; the summer about eighty. The rainfall annually averages fifty inches, which is well distributed throughout the year although slightly more falls in the summer. The growing season is nine months long.

The natural products first exploited were the timber resources: pitch, turpentine, tar, and staves. Then rice was found to do well, first in the river swamps and flat areas near creek bottoms and later in the tidal lands. Indigo was a crop for the drier lands. Drainage has always been a problem in the county, both for agricultural and health reasons.

The soil of this part of the coastal plain, or "lowcountry," was unconsolidated materials which had been deposited in an ancient sea, supplemented by alluvial deposits on the edges of the narrow streams. These alluvial deposits had been washed from upland soils and deposited in times of overflow. The most important soil is Georgetown clay, which was sought out by the early rice planters for its low, wet condition, inexhaustible fertility, and proximity to the tidal flow that drained and irrigated it. All that was needed originally was to remove the cypress and gum trees and then to dike and ditch the land, which was done by slave labor. These prime agricultural lands during the years of extensive rice culture were five to ten miles from the coast, beyond the reaches of the salt water, and up all the rivers within the county—on the Pee Dee and the Waccamaw at least to Sandy Island.

II

THE INDIANS

The Indians were the first occupants of the area surrounding Winyah Bay; the Spaniards probed the region at times; the English finally dominated. The Indians who inhabited what is now South Carolina belonged, according to the ethnologists, to three linguistic stocks: the Iroquoian, the Muskhogean ,and the Eastern Siouan.[1] The Iroquoian stock had come from the north and were represented by the Cherokees, who spread like a blanket over the Southern Appalachians, and by the Tuscaroras, who occupied the middle course of the Cape Fear River. The Muskhogean came from the southwest and occupied the region south and west of the Santee, Broad, and Congaree rivers. The Eastern Siouan were indigenous to the Carolinas and Virginia, having been pushed back and hemmed in by the more warlike Iroquoian and Muskhogean stocks. In South Carolina the Eastern Siouan inhabited the lands north of the Santee, with the exception of the Seewees who were wedged between Awendaw Creek and the south bank of the Santee.

Of the seventeen Eastern Siouan tribes in eastern Carolina listed by David D. Wallace, the following had some definite connection with

[1] The following description is based upon James Mooney, *The Siouan Tribes of the East* (Washington, D. C., 1894); John R. Swanton, *The Indians of the Southeastern United States* (Washington, D. C., 1946); and Chapman J. Milling, *Red Carolinians* (Chapel Hill, N. C., 1940).

present-day Georgetown County: Seewees, Santees, Sampits (Sampas), Winyaws (Weenees), Peedees, and Waccamaws.² The most lasting evidence of their presence remains in the names of the rivers along which the tribes lived: the Seewee (later the Awendaw), Santee, Sampit, Weenee (later the Black), Pee Dee, and Waccamaw. These tribes had lost their separate identities by 1720 and had completely disappeared by 1755.

Wars among the Indian tribes partly explain their depletion. The Siouan and Iroquoian stocks were old enemies, and in the Carolinas the contests between the Catawbas and the Cherokees and between the Tuscaroras and the Eastern Siouan groups were traditional. The tribes living on the coast between the Santee and the Cape Fear rivers might have escaped extinction at an earlier date due to the inaccessibility of that region. When John Lawson made his tour of this area he went from Charleston through the Seewee country to the Santee River, then up that river to its headwaters in North Carolina, from which point he moved eastward to the coast, completely circumscribing the Indians living around Winyah Bay.³ When the South Carolinians marched under Colonel John Barnwell against the Tuscaroras in 1711–1712 and when Colonel James Moore in 1712 and Colonel Maurice Moore in 1713 led other expeditions, they took the same circuitous route, because of the greater ease of movement along the traders' path. Colonel Barnwell took Winyah and Pee Dee Indians with him; Colonel James Moore a contingent from the larger tribes. In both instances the victorious Indians brought back the defeated Indians for sale as slaves.⁴

It was slavery more than war or disease that destroyed these small coastal tribes. As early as 1683 the Proprietors had heard that the settlers were making war on the Indians around Winyah Bay in order to obtain slaves.⁵ Since the Proprietors had given permission to sell Indian captives in the West Indies, the trade in slaves was stimulated and

² David Duncan Wallace, *South Carolina, A Short History, 1520–1948* (Chapel Hill, N. C., 1951), p. 13.

³ *A New Voyage to Carolina by John Lawson*, ed. Hugh T. Lefler (Chapel Hill, N. C., 1967).

⁴ Verner W. Crane, *The Southern Frontier, 1670–1732* (Ann Arbor, Mich., 1956), pp. 158–161. See map attached to Joseph W. Barnwell, "The Second Tuscarora Expedition," *SCHM*, X (1909), between 32 and 33.

⁵ Milling, *op. cit.*, pp. 220–221.

soon the colonists could not distinguish between Indians taken in war and those acquired in other ways.[6] Although a 1703 law placed a duty of twenty shillings on each Indian slave exported, more Indian slaves were exported from South Carolina than from any other continental colony.[7] Those that were shipped to the West Indies died rapidly. But even those retained in South Carolina did not flourish, for the Indians, being hunters and fishers, did not adjust to agricultural labor.[8] Undoubtedly, it was the trade in Indian slaves that decimated the tribes around Winyah Bay.

Lawson in 1700 noted that the Seewees, once a large nation, had shrunk in numbers since the coming of the English. Smallpox and drink had taken a toll, but a naive attempt to sail to England with their furs and skins wiped out the tribe. Having noted the passage of ships from England along their coast, they assembled a great fleet of large canoes and sailed off, hoping to by-pass the Charleston middlemen, only to be dispersed by a storm. Those picked up by passing ships were sold into slavery.[9] In 1715 there were only fifty-seven left.[10]

By 1715 the Santees had only 43 warriors. After a contest with the white men in 1717, those surviving were sold into slavery in the West Indies. About the Sampits little is known. The Waccamaws, who were listed as most numerous in the 1715 Indian census, having six villages with 610 inhabitants on Waccamaw Neck, were destroyed in 1720. In that year 100 warriors made war on the settlers; at least 60 of these were captured and sent into West Indian slavery.[11] Although the Winyahs had been reduced to one village and 106 souls by 1715, they sided with the white men in 1720 against the Waccamaws and therefore survived somewhat longer.

[6] Almon Wheeler Lauber, *Indian Slavery in Colonial Times within the Present Limits of the United States* (New York, 1913), p. 174.

[7] *Ibid.*, pp. 240–241; *S. C. Statutes*, II, 201.

[8] Elkins in discussing why Negro slavery lasted and Indian slavery did not bases his explanation upon "simple primitivism"—that the Negroes were accustomed to agriculture, the Indians of North America were not. Stanley M. Elkins, *Slavery, A Problem in American Institutional and Intellectual Life* (Chicago, Ill., 1959), p. 94n.

[9] Lefler, *op. cit.*, pp. 18–19; Anne King Gregorie, *Notes on Sewee Indians and Indian Remains of Christ Church Parish* (Charleston, S. C., 1925), pp. 10–11.

[10] For the figures for the Indian census of 1715 see Milling, *op. cit.*, p. 222n.

[11] A letter to Mr. Boone, June 24, 1720, *Calendar of State Papers, Colonial Series, 1720–1721*, ed. Cecil Headlam (London, 1933), p. 58.

The Pee Dees, because of their remoteness, endured the longest, although in 1716 they were considered smaller and less important than the Waccamaws. In 1717 some of their leaders came down from their town near present-day Cheraw to Charleston to make a treaty of friendship. Although the laws of 1712, 1722, and 1735 recognized the children of Indian slaves to be slaves, they also recognized as free those Indians in friendship and amity with the provincial government. The presumption of the law of 1740, which continued Indian slavery, was in favor of freedom and placed the burden of proof upon those who claimed Indians as slaves. The presumption in the case of Negroes was that they were slaves.[12] Yet, large planters invariably had a few Indian slaves. When Elias Foissin, a Georgetown planter, died in 1739, he owned forty-two Negro slaves and five Indian slaves: Toney, Tamey, Jupitor, wench Catey, and boy Tom.[13]

The pressure to enslave Indians continued, as did inter-tribal wars. When the Pee Dees were harassed by the Catawbas in 1744, they asked for protection. In 1752 the Catawbas urged Governor James Glen to link the remaining Pee Dees with them, for, as they said, it would be "a great Addition of Strength to us." [14] The Pee Dees must have embraced the Catawbas, for there is no mention of any of these Georgetown Indian tribes in the colonial records after 1753. After the Eastern Siouan tribes on the coast fell away in numbers, they coalesced with the Catawbas, the last tribe to maintain its own cultural identity and separate existence on South Carolina soil.

Trade with the Indians drew the first white settlers to the region of Winyah Bay. From 1710 to 1724 the Indian trade was managed by a Board of Indian Commissioners, appointed by the Assembly. By a law

[12] Lauber, *op. cit.*, pp. 207–208, 315–316. A 1739 act forbad trade with any Indian tribe except by license. Among the "settlement" Indians excluded from the scope of the act were the Winyaws and the Pedees, which would indicate that these tribes were still in existence at that date but no longer numerous enough to be feared. S. C. *Statutes*, III, 517.

[13] "Inventory of the estate of Elias Foissin," Inventories, KK (1739–1744), pp. 87–94, S. C. Archives. On Dec. 22, 1741, Gedion and Elizabeth Ellis of Craven County freed Titus, their Indian slave. Miscellaneous Records, EE (1741–1743), pp. 156–157, S. C. Archives.

[14] Milling, *op. cit.*, pp. 227–230; *Documents relating to Indian Affairs, May 21, 1750–August 7, 1754*, ed. William L. McDowell, Jr. (Columbia, S. C., 1958), p. 362. The Catawbas were themselves reduced to 100 gunmen by 1760 by rum, war, and smallpox. *Gazette*, May 3, 1760.

of June 30, 1716, three factories were established in South Carolina for trading with the Indians: at Savano Town, at the Congarees, and at Winneau. Winneau thereby became the center of the trade to the north of Charleston.[15] On July 11, 1716, the board appointed William Waties, Sr., factor for the Indian trade to the north, instructing him to establish a factory at "the old Cassikey's House on Black River." [16] From this point the trade with the Indians who lived in "love and amity" with the government was controlled. Public stores (coats, blankets, shirts, knives, buttons, beads, tools, arms, ammunition, liquor, rum) were sent to Winneau from Charleston and there traded for skins and furs. On one occasion 600 skins were sent to Charleston; on another, 119 raw deer skins and 422 "drest." [17] The factor also dealt in Indian slaves for one of his intructions read: "You are not to buy knowingly any free Indian for a Slave, or make a Slave of any Indian, that ought to be free, that is to say, Indians of any Nation that is in Amity and under the Protection of this Government." [18]

The line of trade between Winneau and Charleston followed the Black River into Winyah Bay, then into the Atlantic Ocean past the mouth of the Santee to Seewee Bay, whence by Awendaw Creek the Wando River and Charleston were reached. Letters and stores passed to and fro along this route. When corn was scarce among the Indians in August 1716, Waties was instructed to send for some at Benjamin Webb's at Salt Ponds near Seewee. On another occasion corn was to be had at either Seewee, Santee, or Weenee. The pettiauger, the principal means of transportation, was somewhat larger than a canoe; it had a rudder, oars, a sail, and a tarpaulin to cover the skins, of which it could carry 600 at one time.[19] These vessels hugged the shore and navigated the inland waters in order to avoid pirate ships or Spanish *guarda costas*.

In September 1716, in order to increase the scope of the trade, Waties was ordered to establish a post at "Uauenee" (otherwise called the

[15] *Journals of the Commissioners of the Indian Trade, September 20, 1710–August 29, 1718*, ed. W. L. McDowell, Jr. (Columbia, S. C., 1955), p. 328.
[16] *Ibid.*, pp. 74–75.
[17] *Ibid.*, p. 160.
[18] *Ibid.*, p. 95.
[19] *Ibid.*, pp. 105–106, 137, 202.

Great Bluff), which would be nearer the Pee Dees. Waties, having secured a carpenter from Charleston, built a log house twelve feet by ten. In these early days such posts were in dangerously exposed positions. The Cheraws, higher up the Pee Dee, were not in amity with the government and posed a threat from the northwest. The Waccamaws were not averse to stealing cattle from settlers on the Black River. Since the Santees indulged in treachery in 1716, only the Winyahs could be trusted. The fact that some white traders illicitly supplied the Indians with arms and ammunition only made the situation worse. It was more than Waties could contend with; he resigned in February 1717. His place was taken by his assistant Meredith Hughes, who, being warned against the Cheraws, decided in the summer of 1717 to give up the post at "YourEnee" as being too exposed so long as the Cheraws had not made peace with the government. After the Santees were crushed in 1717, Hughes appeared in Charleston with Johnny, king of the Winneaus, and some of the chief men of the Waccamaws, in order to settle matters of war and peace, as well as trade. The Wineaus and the Waccamaws wanted a trading post at Andrew Collins's plantation at Black River.[20] Hughes wanted to get the Waccamaws to move back to their home on the Neck, for they had settled on the south side of Black River, and the Black River settlers were fearful that they would be caught between the Cheraws and the Waccamaws. In order to stop the illicit trading, Hughes, armed with a warrant and attended by a constable, searched the home of Lewis John, one of the traders suspected.[21] This uneasiness among the settlers no doubt was one of the causes of the war in 1720 in which the Waccamaws were destroyed. This war marked the end of the threat from these Eastern Siouan tribes.[22] It also brought to an end the Indian trade in the area.

[20] There is no plat or grant for Andrew Collins on the Black River. There is a plat for Andrew Collings, dated Feb. 20, 1732, for 400 acres on south side of Pee Dee River. "Andrew Collings," Pre-Revolutionary Plats, S. C. Archives. This land was granted on Feb. 17, 1736. Grants, GG (1735–1737), p. 313, S. C. Archives.

[21] McDowell, Jr., *Journals of the Commissioners, op. cit.,* pp. 132–137, 161–163, 208–210, 232, 264–265, 275.

[22] Hugh Meredith who resided in 1731 both at Cape Fear and at Black River stated that by that time both Carolinas were safe from Indian wars. Hugh Meredith, *An Account of the Cape Fear Country, 1731,* ed. Earl G. Swem (Perth Amboy, N. J., 1922), pp. 27–29.

Colonel George Chicken, who was sole Indian Commissioner from 1724 to 1727, was also commander of the Northward Regiment of Foot (the Craven County militia). The captain of the Winyah company was Meredith Hughes. Control of Indian trade and military duty went hand in hand.[23] But in the 1720's Indian trade gave way to the preparation of naval stores as the principal mode of livelihood for the settlers.

[23] Crane, *op. cit.*, p. 200; Council Journal, May 29, 1721–June 10, 1721, p. 12, S. C. Archives.

III

THE LAND AND THE PEOPLE

The Spaniards were presumably the first white men to settle along Winyah Bay. Paul Quattlebaum has told the story of the first settlement, that of San Miguel de Gualdape, which he and others have located on the east bank of the Waccamaw—near where the house on Hobcaw Barony stands today. His book, *The Land Called Chicora*, marshals the evidence that is proof of Spanish settlement. Presumably, a group of Spaniards landed along the Cape Fear River and then marched southwest until they came to a river where they established a settlement. The evidence, however, is not absolutely convincing, and, as the Spaniards did not remain, they left no marks or traces upon the later history of the region.[1]

The first English settlers were the Indian traders. No *Mayflower* sailed into Winyah Bay, nor did any small fleet such as that which brought the first families to Charleston. The movement of the first residents, however, can be gleaned from the records. There were a number of grants of land which were made at Winyah in the year 1705, three being for 500, 200, and 100 acres to John Perry of Antigua for land lying

[1] Paul Quattlebaum, *The Land Called Chicora, The Carolinas under Spanish Rule with French Intrusions, 1520–1670* (Gainesville, Fla., 1956). Also see J. G. Johnson, "A Spanish Settlement in Carolina, 1526," *Georgia Historical Quarterly*, VII (1923), 339–345.

between "Sampeet Creek" and "Weenea River."[2] These grants had been obtained by John Abraham Motte, Perry's agent, who improved the lands, for in December 1710 he sold all of his horses, cattle, sheep, hogs, and plantation tools to the Reverend William Screven. Motte had earlier, on September 2, 1710, sold Perry's three plantations to Screven with the proviso that he would secure a deed of conveyance from Perry within twelve months.[3] Whether Screven ever obtained title to these lands is not known. Perhaps because of the uncertainty Screven secured a warrant from Governor Robert Gibbes for 200 acres on Sampit Creek on November 3, 1710, which were surveyed early in 1711 as the plat was returned on May 9, 1711. This grant was registered on August 6, 1711.[4] Screven died on October 10, 1713, in the house that he had built on the site of present-day Georgetown.[5] His wife willed in 1717 to her son Elisha these lands on which he in 1729 laid out a town.[6] Later, the Perry family successfully re-established their rights to this property.

Percival Pawley secured thirteen grants to 2,500 acres on the Pee Dee, Sampit, and Waccamaw rivers between June 18 and August 4, 1711. One of the Pawley grants extended from the Waccamaw River to the "sea marsh," establishing thereby the pattern for long, narrow

[2] The three grants were dated Sept. 15, 1705. Proprietary Grants, XXXVIII, 516–517, S. C. Archives. Job Howe wrote John Archdale on Jan. 15, 1706, to advise on the possible location for a new group of Carolina settlers. Howe stated that sufficient room could only be found either on the Port Royal or "Winneau River" as the Ashley, Cooper, Edisto, and Santee rivers had been settled. Since there was a war with Spain, it would be dangerous to settle on the Port Royal. "Therefore I advise them to Winneau which is a good harbour the channel better than Ashley River & land good and sufficient to encourage a settlemt and ye mouth of ye said River lyeth noe more than A league to ye Northward of ye mouth of Santee." Archdale Papers, LC.

[3] Both deeds were signed and sealed in the presence of Chief Justice Nicholas Trott on May 7, 1711, and registered on May 28, 1711. Miscellaneous Records, F (1707–1711), pp. 220–223, S. C. Archives. William Screven was a Baptist minister who had come from Maine to Carolina in 1698 and served as pastor of the First Baptist Church of Charleston until about 1706. Leah Townsend, South Carolina Baptists, 1670–1805 (Florence, S. C., 1935), pp. 5–12.

[4] Proprietary Grants, XXXIX, 286–287, S. C. Archives. The return of the plat is given as of Oct. 26, 1711, when this grant was recorded in the Memorial Book on July 24, 1733. Memorial Book, II, 195, S. C. Archives.

[5] [Elizabeth Anne Poyas] The Olden Time of Carolina (Charleston, S. C., 1855), p. 112. He was buried on what became Lot 66 on Prince St. "The Burial Place of the Reverend William Screven," SCHM, XVI (1915), 93–95.

[6] Henry A. M. Smith, "Georgetown—The Original Plan and the Earliest Settlers," SCHM, IX (1910), 88.

plantations which stretched from river to ocean across Waccamaw Neck.[7] The Pawley lands were among the first to be improved. By December 1717 Percival Pawley had surplus cattle with which to supply the Indian post at Winneau.[8] A packer to inspect exports from Winyah was appointed in 1714. The appointment was a sure sign of developing trade.[9]

Captain Thomas Lynch (1675–1752), who had a plantation on the Wando River in Christ Church Parish and acted as a courier between Charleston and the Indian trading post, carrying a letter to William Waties, Sr., in 1716 and another to Meredith Hughes in 1718, obviously explored the possibilities of the country as he went and returned.[10] In 1718 he took out grants for 3,000 acres on the North Santee River.[11]

The parish records, which go back beyond the establishment of Prince George, state that Peter Lane, the son of John and Sarah Lane, was born on Black River November 5, 1713. Children of three families were recorded in this parish record prior to 1722: those of John and Sarah Lane, John and Martha Bell, and Peter and Susannah Sanders.[12] An act of September 15, 1721, to empower commissioners to alter and lay out high roads, private paths, bridges, creeks, causeways and to clear water-passages named commissioners for different parts of St. James Santee. John Lane, John Bell, Sr., and John Bell, Jr., were appointed by the governor as commissioners "for the north east side of the northermost branch of Santee River" while Captain William Furbush, Elisha Scriven, Captain Meredith Hughes, John Haze, and Nathaniel Ford were named "for that part of the parish called Winyaw."[13]

[7] Proprietary Grants, XXXIX, 111–113, 166–167, 498, S. C. Archives.

[8] *Journals of the Commissioners of the Indian Trade, September 20, 1710–August 29, 1718,* ed. W. L. McDowell (Columbia, S. C., 1955), p. 273.

[9] S. C. *Statutes,* II, 615–617. The growth of the region should not be overemphasized, however. George Hunter wrote on his 1730 map that "about 18 years ago [1712] there were not above 5 families on the Northward of Sante River." "George Hunter's Map of the Cherokee Country and the Path thereto in 1730," *Bulletin No. 4 of the Historical Commission of South Carolina* (Columbia, S. C., 1917).

[10] McDowell, *op. cit.,* pp. 105, 297; Frampton E. Ellis, *Some Historic Families of South Carolina* (Atlanta, Ga., 1905), pp. 29–30.

[11] Memorial Book, III (1733–1739), 415, S. C. Archives.

[12] *The Register Book for the Parish Prince Frederick Winyaw,* ed. Elizabeth W. Allston Pringle (Baltimore, Md., 1916), p. 1.

[13] S. C. *Statutes,* IX, 51.

As the above persons lived very far from the parish church of St. James Santee, they petitioned in 1720 for a new parish. In March 1722 in the act to establish the parish of Prince George, Captain Meredith Hughes, John Lane, and John Haze were designated commissioners to supervise the building of the church.[14] These records indicate that by the time of the revolution which overthrew the Proprietors (1719–1721), a permanent settlement had been established at Winyah.

There were in fact two communities, for there was some doubt whether the new church should be built on Black River or at Winyah. A petition of 1723 requesting that the church be built on Black River stated that "above one hundred and sixty souls [were] settled on the said river and above one sixth part at Sam Pitt."[15] As the church was built up Black River, the above numbers must prove that the Black River settlement at that time was the largest. In ten years the settlement at Winyah would outgrow the one up the Black River and would be demanding its own church. As the planting of rice became more important than the Indian trade, the focus of settlement shifted from the Black to the Sampit.[16] The Black River bluff was nearer the Indians and more easily defensible; yet the mouth of the Sampit was more convenient for marshaling the rice as commerce swung in a new direction.

The names of the first settlers can be taken from the parish registers, the land grants, the commercial documents, the court papers, the town records, and the advertisements in the *South-Carolina Gazette*.[17] The following names appear most often and could be considered the family names of the first settlers and landowners: Abercromby, Allston, Atkinson, Baxter, Beauchamp, Belin, Bell, Blythe, Bonneau, Broughton, Chardon, Cleland, Coachman, Cogdell, Collins, Commander, Croft, Cuttino, Foissin, Ford, Furbush, Fyffe, Godfrey, Gourdin, Hambleton, Hasell, Haze, Henning, Heriot, Horry, Huggins, Hughes, Hume, Johnston, Keith, Kinloch, LaBruce, Lane, LaRoche, Lenud, Lesesne, Lewis, Lynch, May-

---

[14] S. C. *Statutes*, III, 171–172.

[15] Commons House Journal, No. 6 (1722–1724), pp. 307–308, S. C. Archives.

[16] The production of pitch and tar was much more important than the growing of rice in the 1720's. *The Statistical History of the United States from Colonial Times to the Present* (Stamford, Conn. [1966]), p. 770.

[17] Pringle, *op. cit.*; Pre-Revolutionary War Plats, Grant Books, Memorial Books, S. C. Archives; Judgment Rolls, Court of Common Pleas, S. C. Archives; *SCHM*, IX (1908), 95–101; *Gazette*, 1732–1750.

rant, Michau, Mitchell, Morrall, Murray, Ouldfield, Pawley, Poole, Postell, Pyatt, Robertson, Romsey, Screven, Smith, Snow, Stewart, Swinton, Toomer, Trapier, Tregagle, Tucker, Vereen, Waties, White, Whiteside, Wilson, Withers, Wragg, and Young.

An analysis of these names reveals three fairly well-defined groups: the French, the English, and the Scots. None of these settlers, however, came in groups; they came as individuals. Some were sons of men who had settled in Colleton or Berkeley counties, the second generation making a new start on a new frontier. Others were men who held public office or engaged in trade in Charleston and were investing their profits in the newly developing region. Later, the lands that they had acquired would draw them and their families as permanent residents. Although to the north and not the west, this was the frontier of the Carolinas in the 1730's, the decade in which Winyah Bay was finally encircled by land grants.

Beauchamp, Belin, Bonneau, Chardon, Cuttino, Foissin, Gourdin, Horry, LaBruce, LaRoche, Lenud, Lesesne, Michau, Postell, Vereen, and Trapier were French names, representing Huguenot families who reached Carolina before 1700. The French Huguenots had originally settled in the region between the Cooper and the Santee rivers, forming in 1706 the parishes of St. Denis (within St. Thomas) and St. James Santee (French Santee), both of which were permitted to use the Book of Common Prayer in its French version.[18] The south bank of the lower Santee had been almost entirely settled by the Huguenots. As Prince George Winyah was to the north of St. James Santee, it was natural that the settlement of the former should have taken place in large numbers by men moving out of the latter. The French Huguenots who settled around Georgetown were eager to follow their successful fathers as rice planters, first on the North Santee and then on the Waccamaw and the Pee Dee. The French were mainly planters, although the LaRoches and Paul Trapier were merchants.

The English names were Allston, Atkinson, Baxter, Bell, Blythe, Broughton, Coachman, Cogdell, Collins, Croft, Ford, Furbush, Godfrey,

---

[18] For the early Huguenots see Arthur Henry Hirsch, *The Huguenots of Colonial South Carolina* (Durham, N. C., 1928). The authorized translation was by Dr. John Durrell, executed at the command of Charles II for use in the Islands of Jersey and Guernsey. S. C. *Statutes*, II, 288.

Hambleton, Hasell, Haze, Henning, Lane, Ouldfield, Poole, Pyatt, Snow, Toomer, White, Whiteside, Wragg, and Young. These men had come to Georgetown as opportunity had beckoned. John and William Allston left their father's place in St. John's Berkeley to take out grants on the Waccamaw.[19] John Ouldfield, Jr., left the family home on Goose Creek to make a start on his own near Georgetown.[20]

The Scots gave a distinct flavor to the community. Abercromby, Cleland, Fyffe, Heriot, Hume, Johnston, Keith, Kinloch, Murray, Robertson, Romsey, Stewart, Swinton, and Wilson were examples of Scotsmen taking advantage of the Union of 1707. Before 1707 the Scots were forbidden by the Navigation Acts to trade with the English colonies; after that date they could share in the trade of the British Empire on equal terms with the English. The Scots were, therefore, by 1730 a prominent part of the mercantile community of Charleston, and the development of Georgetown coincided with their coming of age in the new colony. Some were landholders (such as James Kinloch) who were seeking additional lands;[21] some were officeholders (such as Attorney-General James Abercromby) investing the fruits of their offices;[22] but most were merchants who in time would either return to Scotland or settle down in Carolina as planters.

All desired land—or possibly, in the case of the Scots, trade first and land second. But there could be no trade (other than that with the Indians) until the land had been taken up and a surplus produced for export. The land was originally granted to the eight Lords Proprietors, who remained the supreme landlords until the crown bought their rights in 1729.[23] It had been the intention of the Proprietors to set up a balanced agrarian society—one-fifth of the land to be held by the Propri-

[19] The lands were surveyed in 1732. Grant Book, AA (1731–1734), pp. 63, 124, 298–299, 333–334, S. C. Archives.
[20] Caldwell Woodruff, "Heriots of Scotland and South Carolina" (Linthicum Heights, Md., 1939), p. 145, typed copy in S. C. Hist. Soc.
[21] James Kinloch's plantation was 27 miles from Charleston, where the road forked for Strawberry, the French Church, and Winyah Bay. "George Hunter's Map of the Cherokee Country and the Path Thereto in 1730," *Bulletin No. 4 of the Historical Commission of South Carolina* (Columbia, S. C., 1917).
[22] James Abercromby was attorney-general, 1731–1732, 1733–1742. W. Roy Smith, *South Carolina as a Royal Province, 1719–1776* (New York, 1903), p. 412.
[23] Robert K. Ackerman, "South Carolina Colonial Land Policies" (PhD dissertation, Univ. of S. C., 1965).

etors, one-fifth by the local nobility (landgraves and caciques were to be created), and three-fifths by the people. The society was to have feudal (quit-rents were to be paid) and aristocratic (a local nobility would flourish) characteristics. The Proprietors would have seigniories, the local nobility baronies, and the people plantations and farms.

Under the Proprietors there did grow up a system by which land was granted, a system which, with few changes, was used later by the royal authorities. A person desiring a grant of land would appear before the governor and council, make his request, and receive from them a warrant to the surveyor-general, ordering him to have the land surveyed. After the land had been surveyed, the surveyor-general submitted the warrant with a certificate of the survey (a plat) to the register of the province for recording. Then the would-be grantee swore allegiance to the king and fidelity and submission to the Proprietors. Only then did the governor in the presence of the council sign, seal, and deliver the grant to the grantee. There were thus three sets of documents—warrants, certificates of survey (or plats), and grants. Patents for baronies were usually considered orders from the Proprietors to the governor and council to issue warrants for the survey of 12,000 acres. The grantee, therefore, had to convert his patent into a grant.

The system of granting land was the same under the royal authority with the king taking the place after 1729 of the Proprietors as original grantor, with the exception, however, that no more patents for baronies were to be issued. Quit-rents were retained, henceforth to be paid to the crown. In order to ascertain who owed quit-rents in 1731, all possessors of land were required by the new royal officials to register their patents, grants, or conveyances, by which they claimed land in the office of the auditor-general or his deputy. The memorials thus drawn up are a valuable source for the study of the land system.[24]

Two baronies were laid out near Georgetown during the proprietary period. On June 18, 1711, Winyah Barony on the bay was granted to Landgrave Robert Daniel, who sold it the following day to the second Landgrave Thomas Smith. Nothing is known of the history of this grant until 1732 when Landgrave Thomas Smith laid off a part of this barony,

[24] Memorial Books, I–XVI (1731–1776), S. C. Archives; also see *SCHM*, LXVIII (1967), 46–49.

Smith's Barony as it was then called, as a second town, a few miles to
the southeast of Georgetown. From 1732 until his death in 1738 he tried
to sell lots in the town, but he was not successful. Georgetown was
already growing, and two towns on Winyah Bay were not needed. At
his death the land passed to his heirs, but the largest portion eventually
passed by deed in 1756 to Elias Horry.[25]

The history of the other barony begins with a formal grant of 12,000
acres to John Lord Carteret on December 5, 1718. This barony, or seigni-
ory as it might more properly be called since it was originally granted
to one of the Proprietors, passed by deed on February 18, 19, 1730, to
John Roberts of London for £500, presumably without any improvements having been made. As a resurvey indicated that there were 13,970
acres, a new grant of September 30, 1736, included the overplus. This
barony, known as Hobcaw Barony, passed at some later date to three
Londoners, the first sale of the land in smaller quantities being made as
late as 1766, when it was carved into plantations under the direction of
Paul Trapier as agent for the owners.[26] Both baronies were ultimately,
therefore, divided into plantations.

The common mode of securing land under the royal grants was by
the headright system of family grants. The head of a family received
150 acres for himself and lesser amounts for each member of his family.
Since a slave was considered a member of the family for this purpose,
it was possible to receive a large grant of land. Thomas Lynch received
three grants in 1733 for 1,400, 2,100, and 4,500 acres, and five grants for
500 acres each in 1736.[27] In this fashion he built up his holdings on
Lynch's Island and the North Santee, establishing the basis for the
famous plantation of Hopsewee. Smith's Barony was more extensive
originally, but, since it had been granted before the value of the marsh
lands for growing rice was fully understood, the Lynch lands were to
be more productive. Lynch before 1740 built a home which still stands

[25] Henry A. M. Smith, "The Baronies of South Carolina," *SCHM*, XIII (1912),
3–12.

[26] The three London merchants were Sir William Baker, Nicholas Linwood, and
Brice Fisher. Henry A. M. Smith, "The Baronies of South Carolina," *SCHM*, XIV
(1913), 61–80.

[27] Grant Books, AA (1731–1734), pp. 112–114; BB (1734–1737), pp. 533–552,
S. C. Archives; Council Journal, PRO Photostats, No. 1 (June 28, 1734–Dec. 17,
1737), under date of Nov. 11, 1736, S. C. Archives.

on the banks of the North Santee,[28] a man without a barony or a title, but a grandee in the new land nonetheless.

The change from proprietary control to royal control meant a change to a more efficient system of government. The administration of Governor Robert Johnson (1731–1735) was a time for putting the province in order.[29] With the new officials appointed—the surveyor-general, the auditor-general, the secretary, the receiver-general of quit-rents—and with the new books opened to record business, the colony moved forward. It was fortunate that the strength of the new government was put behind the opening of the Winyah lands. The earliest settlers clinched their position by securing additional grants of land.

William Waties, Jr., received grants of 2,369 acres in 1735, 646 in 1736, 624 in 1737, 300 in 1739, and 350 in 1740.[30] George Pawley, son of Major Percival Pawley, received grants of 1,155 acres in 1734, 176 in 1735, and 941 in 1737.[31] The Waties and Pawley grants were mainly on the Waccamaw River. Meredith Hughes received grants on the Black River of 350 acres in 1735 and 700 acres in 1738.[32] John Lane took grants for 570 acres on the Sampit River in 1734 and for 150 acres on the Black River in 1735.[33] Elisha Screven had grants of 500 acres in 1735 and of 300 acres in 1737, partly lying on Black River.[34] Nathaniel Ford had 350 acres surveyed in 1737 on the west side of the Little Pee Dee River, which land was granted in 1742.[35]

The surveyor was a principal figure in this new community. To some extent each man was his own surveyor, as almost every inventory listed the instruments used in marking off the land. James St. John, the sur-

---

[28] This is the oldest plantation home still standing in Georgetown County. Alberta Morel Lachicotte, *Georgetown Rice Plantations* (Columbia, S. C., 1955), p. 191.

[29] Richard P. Sherman, *Robert Johnson, Proprietary & Royal Governor of South Carolina* (Columbia, S. C., 1966).

[30] "William Waties," Pre-Revolutionary War Plats and Index to Grants, S. C. Archives.

[31] "George Pawley," Pre-Revolutionary War Plats and Index to Grants, S. C. Archives.

[32] "Meredith Hughes," Pre-Revolutionary War Plats and Index to Grants, S. C. Archives.

[33] "John Lane," Pre-Revolutionary War Plats and Index to Grants, S. C. Archives.

[34] "Elisha Screven," Pre-Revolutionary War Plats and Index to Grants, S. C. Archives.

[35] "Nathaniel Ford," Pre-Revolutionary War Plats and Index to Grants, S. C. Archives.

veyor-general of the province, designated local men as deputy surveyors and sent to them the precepts authorizing surveys. He appointed Peter Lane, the first native-born Georgetonian, as a deputy surveyor on May 6, 1733. One of his instructions was that all lands on navigable rivers should be laid out with "only one fourth fronting on the said river." [36]

The collection of plats and grants in the archives reveals that the Georgetown men took out their first royal grants in 1732 or shortly thereafter. This does not mean that these men had squatted upon the land until 1732 and then took out royal grants. They already had land by proprietary grant or by purchase from those who had received grants from the Proprietors. Peter Sanders, the Black River planter, who died February 2, 1724, left by will 1,000 acres to his wife and six children. [37] John Haze (Hayes), a planter of Craven County, who apparently took out no royal grants and died prior to September 1733, left his property to John Wallis. [38] The new receiver-general of quit-rents, John Hammerton, or his deputy visited Winyah every year after 1732 to have the lands recorded in the new memorial books so that the quit-rents due to the crown could be collected. [39] Thomas Lynch stated on April 4, 1733, that he held land by mesne conveyance which stemmed from a grant of 1705. He had himself been granted 3,000 acres on the North Santee in 1718. He held all his land under a quit-rent of twelve pence per hundred acres. [40] William Waties, Jr., registered a memorial on January 29, 1732, to 500 acres on the Waccamaw River granted to him in 1717 at twelve pence per hundred acres. On February 15, 1732, Waites registered 1,300 acres granted originally to Robert Daniel and then sold first to Thomas Smith, then to Samuel Eveleigh, and finally to himself. This plantation, already called "Lorrill Hill" on the Waccamaw, bore

[36] James St. John was surveyor-general of lands, 1731–1743. W. Roy Smith, *op. cit.*, p. 413. Peter Lane's appointment and instructions are in Miscellaneous Records, DD (1732–1742), pp. 13–15, S. C. Archives. His name appears as the surveyor on most of the above plats.

[37] "Will of Peter Sanders," dated Aug. 30, 1727, recorded July 25, 1730, Charleston County Wills, II (1729–1731), 22–23, S. C. Archives.

[38] "Will of John Hayes," dated April 17, 1733, recorded Sept. 13, 1733, Charleston County Wills, III (1731–1737), 69, S. C. Archives.

[39] *South-Carolina Gazette*, May 27, Sept. 2, Oct. 14, 1732, and subsequent issues. The first issue of this newspaper was Jan. 8, 1732.

[40] Memorial Book, III (1733–1739), 415–417, S. C. Archives.

a quit-rent of twelve pence per hundred acres.[41] A great deal of Pawley land was put down as having been granted originally to Major Percival Pawley in 1711.[42] John Lane registered land which he had bought from Meredith Hughes.[43] Although the 1730's was the decade in which most of the land in present-day Georgetown County was first granted (plats of the 1730's frequently note that the grants bounded on vacant lands), there had been grants certainly as early as 1705.

Advertisements in the *South-Carolina Gazette* provide a glimpse of improvements. On July 14, 1733, a plantation of 150 acres of land on the Black River was advertised as having a house, a tanyard with five large vats, large troughs, and six cords of bark. On November 6, 1736, a 500-acre plantation was advertised with a good dwelling house, out houses, corn field, pasturage, cleared rice swamps, and all within a good fence. On May 12, 1739, William Whiteside advertised 1,000 acres on the Sampit, four miles from Georgetown, with 200 acres cleared, a dwelling house and all convenient buildings, "a parcel of neat cattle," and Negroes valuable as coopers, sawyers, smiths, and sailors as well as house and plantation slaves.

In the 1730's there was one significant addition to land policy. Governor Robert Johnson instituted the township system.[44] Ten townships were to be planted along a semi-circle from the Savannah River to the North Carolina line, all about equally distant from Charleston. They were established for the purposes of defense, partly against the external enemy, the Indian, and partly against the internal enemy, the slave. As the slave population had been advancing rapidly, the townships were reserved for white Protestants who would be given bounties as inducements for settling the land.

Three townships lay to the west and north of Georgetown: one on the Black River (Williamsburg), one on the Pee Dee (Queensboro), and one on the Waccamaw (Kingston). The settlement of the Welsh Tract, which was to extend from Queensboro in a northwesterly direc-

[41] Memorial Book, I (1731–1732), 422–423; II, Part 1, 42; IV (1732–1733), 42–43, S. C. Archives.

[42] Memorial Book, V (1733–1742), 59, 66–68, S. C. Archives.

[43] Memorial Book, III (1733–1739), 434, S. C. Archives.

[44] The best description of the township scheme is in Robert L. Meriwether, *The Expansion of South Carolina, 1729–1765* (Kingsport, Tenn., 1940).

tion to the North Carolina line, with the Pee Dee River as its backbone, was another phase of this general scheme. In October 1735 the townships east of the Santee were thrown open by Lieutenant Governor Thomas Broughton and the council to inhabitants of the colony.[45] Both immigrants and natives could henceforth receive grants in these eastern townships.

Some settlement was made in Williamsburg Township prior to 1735 by Scotch Irish from Belfast, and the cultural tone of the region dates from that settlement.[46] Queensboro and Kingston were located where land was poor, and they did not flourish because South Carolinians, who were nonresidents, received grants. Williamsburg was the most successful township, because it soon found a good crop in indigo. In the case of the Welsh Tract, the settlers began arriving in 1737 from the north and continued to come from Pennsylvania, giving the region around Mars Bluff a special coloration. Maurice Lewis, judge of the vice-admiralty court in Charleston and a native of Anglesea in Wales, made an effort to bring some of his countrymen through Charleston to the Welsh Tract.[47]

These new people were drawn into the Georgetown world by the water routes. From Williamsburg down the Black River, from Queensboro and the Welsh Tract down the Pee Dee, and from Kingston down the Waccamaw they soon shipped their surplus provisions to feed the slave populations of the rice plantations. Georgetown stood between them and Charleston. Immigrants and goods flowed in and up the rivers; crops flowed down and out. Kingstree, Black Mingo, Britton's Neck, and Little River sprang up as communities with stores to serve these new farming areas.

The land system itself had been shaped by the importance of access to water. It had always been the policy in granting lands to narrow the frontage on rivers in order to give as many settlers as possible an opening on them. Each plantation, each farm, had its landing. This policy

---

[45] *Ibid.*, p. 86.

[46] R. J. Dickson, *Ulster Emigration to Colonial America, 1718–1775* (London, 1966), pp. 49–52.

[47] Meriwether, *op. cit.*, p. 91. "Will of Maurice Lewis," dated Sept. 15, 1739, recorded Nov. 7, 1739, Charleston County Wills, IV (1736–1740), 203–204, S. C. Archives. Lewis was judge of the vice-admiralty court from 1736 until his death in 1739. W. Rcy Smith, *op. cit.*, p. 414.

emphasized the fact that land without an access to a waterway was of little value.[48] Although the land was divided by the rivers, the people themselves were drawn back together by the water. It is only in the twentieth century that the waterways have lost their importance; the hardpaved road and the plentitude of bridges permitted the automobile to open up what the boat previously could not. In the twentieth century the differences between Georgetown and the rest of the state are being wiped out. In the eighteenth and nineteenth centuries Georgetown was drawn inward by her waters, which flowed together into Winyah Bay. It was the bay with its tributaries, the Sampit, the Black, the Pee Dee, and the Waccamaw (with the Santee world just to the south) which gave it a unity and made it possible for a distinct society to develop, at the center of which until 1910 was the rice plantation.

As rice culture demanded frequent floodings, water was first obtained in sufficient quantities by damming up small streams and creating reserves. By the end of the eighteenth century tidal action was used to flood the fields. At first, rice was grown more up the rivers; later it was brought down into the broad tidal estuaries.[49] The importance of tidal action was known quite early. William Swinton in advertising two tracts of land in the *Gazette* on January 19, 1738, said "each contains as much River Swamp, as will make two Fields for 20 Negroes, which is over flow'd with fresh water, every high tide, and of consequence not subject to the Droughts." Present-day Georgetown County is the historic rice-growing area. With the exception of the Cape Fear River, this was also the northernmost limit of rice culture.[50] This fact makes the history of Georgetown County far more important than a mere local history, for in this county a unique story in American history was played out. Only around Beaufort might a similar story be told, but there, as in Georgia, rice met sea island cotton.[51] Charleston was always set apart

[48] For a discussion of the importance of water frontage see Ackerman, *op. cit.*, pp. 48–49.

[49] There has been a great debate over who first used the tidal action in flooding the rice fields. Apparently, the value of tidal floodings was known quite early. The system was perfected later.

[50] For a good account of the Cape Fear region to the north with references to rice culture there see Lawrence Lee, *The Lower Cape Fear in Colonial Days* (Chapel Hill, N. C., 1965), pp. 147–149.

[51] The best history of rice culture in the neighborhood of Beaufort is Duncan Clinch Heyward, *Seed from Madagascar* (Chapel Hill, N. C., 1937).

from Georgetown and Beaufort by her vast commercial interests. So the history of Georgetown County is the history of the rise, flourishing, and decline of two of the great staples of the colonial and early American period. Rice, indigo, sugar, and tobacco were the great colonial staples, and the history of Georgetown County is the history of two of these.

Rice was grown in South Carolina as early as the 1690's, but the period of its great expansion was in the 1730's. South Carolina on the average exported 71,514 hundredweight of rice during the 1720's; during the 1730's the average exported was 142,850. In the year 1740 she exported 308,178 hundredweight, a figure not to be reached again until 1765.[52] Quite naturally, this was also the decade of greatly increased importations of slaves. From 1720 through 1726 the average annual importation was 616 slaves. The average for the years 1731–1738 was 2,089.[53] The opening up of the lands around Georgetown was one of the chief reasons for the increase.

There was a fortunate combination of circumstances at work in the 1730's which helped to launch the Georgetown story. The early years of experimentation in the cultivation of rice had been passed, and a labor supply was at hand. The new royal government gave stability and security of land titles, and royal policy did not prevent the accumulation of tracts of land large enough for the plantation system to develop. There were also able men ready to exploit the possibilities: Thomas Lynch on North Santee and John and William Allston on the Waccamaw.

With the production of rice on such a scale, a central gathering place was needed and a mercantile group, to handle trade. Georgetown on the banks of the Sampit became a better assembly point for export than did Wineau up the Black River. The change from Wineau to Georgetown was a change from Indian trade and naval stores to rice. Georgetown emerged in the 1730's as the focal point of the new trade. For the first time it was to be a port of entry with its own set of royal officials.

[52] *The Statistical History of the United States from Colonial Times to the Present* (Stamford, Conn. [1966]), pp. 767–768.
[53] *Ibid.*, p. 770.

IV

THE FOUNDING OF GEORGETOWN

As early as 1723 the people of Winyah had petitioned for a port of entry, for on February 9, 1723, the Assembly urged its committee of correspondence to write the South Carolina agent in London to secure such a designation for Winyah.[1] If Winyah were made a port of entry, local produce could be shipped directly to a foreign destination and the shippers would be free of freight charges to Charleston. The production of naval stores had reached a peak in 1725, having been stimulated by a parliamentary bounty. This bounty was removed by 1726, which made the freight charges to Charleston appear more burdensome.[2] Slaves had been bought in 1725 in anticipation of profits, but with the ensuing downturn in trade the producers of naval stores were in debt. The new precinct courts had failed to protect the Charleston merchants for country juries would not sell out their neighbors.[3] By 1727 the men of Winyah

---

[1] Commons House Journal, No. 6 (1722–1724), p. 171, S. C. Archives.

[2] Lawrence Lee, *The Lower Cape Fear in Colonial Days* (Chapel Hill, N. C., 1965), p. 97. The decline in the export of pitch from Charleston was as follows: 57,422 barrels in 1725; 29,776 in 1726; 13,654 in 1727; 3,186 in 1728; and 8,377 in 1729. *The Statistical History of the United States from Colonial Times to the Present* (Stamford, Conn. [1966]), p. 770.

[3] M. Eugene Sirmans, *Colonial South Carolina, A Political History, 1663–1763* (Chapel Hill, N. C., 1966), pp. 143–144; BPRO, XII (1725–1727), 201–206, S. C. Archives.

were refusing to pay their taxes as well as their debts. The region was in rebellion. Arthur Middleton, acting as governor, issued a proclamation on April 21, 1727, calling upon all officers of the crown to disperse the rioters.[4]

The inhabitants of Santee and Winyah petitioned the Assembly: "tho we have paid so many taxes yet none of it is applied to our services in order to make a port. 'Tho' we have the best conveniency in the province for trade, a Fresh water River no Worms and also the conveniency for vessels which damages us for want thereof Ten Thousand pounds a year by carrying our produce to Town all which makes it the harder for us to pay Tax."[5] In order to back up their petition the disgruntled men met at Dorchester on the Ashley River early in May 1727 with their leaders: Landgrave Thomas Smith, George Pawley, and William Waties, Jr. Arthur Middleton went to confer with them, but they insisted on marching into town and threatening the members of the Council, whom they particularly blamed for their troubles. Middleton was only able to quell the disturbance by using men from Captain George Anson's ship to apprehend Landgrave Thomas Smith on charges of treason. When Middleton convened a session of the legislature, the outlying parishes sent riotous persons to town who prevented the Assembly from passing a new tax act until their grievances were satisfied. And this was at a time when there was a rumor of a war with Spain. The situation to the north of Santee River was one of the principal causes of chaos in the province.[6]

Robert Johnson, the new royal governor, who was determined to solve these problems, had a number of talks with high British officials before he left London. On January 2, 1730, he wrote a memorandum for the British government: "First as there are many people now settled upon the River of Wynieah I conceive it to be necessary to lay out a Town, make it a Port of Entry and appoint a Collector there."[7] These concessions would be to the people to the north, but the Charleston mer-

---

[4] BPRO, XII (1725–1727), 196–197, S. C. Archives.
[5] BPRO, XII (1725–1727), 211–214, S. C. Archives.
[6] BPRO, XIII (1728–1729), 31, 44–47, 292–300, S. C. Archives.
[7] BPRO, XIV (1730), 29 S. C. Archives; Richard P. Sherman, *Robert Johnson, Proprietary & Royal Governor of South Carolina* (Columbia, S. C., 1966), pp. 119–120.

chants would also be appeased by confining the dispensation of justice to the common law courts that sat at Charleston. Johnson urged these measures, or otherwise, he said, the debtors would continue to fly to the Cape Fear.[8]

George Hunter, later surveyor-general of the province, had visited Winyah to ascertain its qualifications for a port. He wrote on his map, dated May 21, 1730: "At Wineaw Bar I sounded the Channel and at Low Water neap Tides found 10 foot water. At High Water Spring Tides there rise 16½ feet. And the same water, has at Georges Town on Sampit Creek 4 fathom. Georges Town was laid out in Lots & sold last year [1729] to people who are obliged to build a House in 15 Months. They expect there a port of Entry to ease them of the freight to Charles Town. They have one foot less water or there abouts than Charles Town."[9] Therefore, when Robert Johnson arrived in South Carolina in December 1730, Georgetown was already laid out. The royal authorities must have acted in 1731 to make Georgetown a port of entry, since the *Gazette* for April 1, 1732, reported a rumor that Georgetown had been made a free port and on June 24 added that Peter Goudett had been appointed collector and naval officer there.[10]

The land upon which Georgetown now stands was originally granted on September 15, 1705, to John Perry, who with his brother and sister obtained six grants at that time for 3,300 acres.[11] Perry, a man of wealth and position in the island of Antigua, planned to make a settlement in South Carolina under the direction of an agent, John Abraham Motte. By 1708 the six grants were owned by John Perry since he willed them in that year to his daughter Mary. Perry died in 1713, presumably without ever having come to Carolina. In 1728 his daughter Mary married

[8] BPRO, XIII (1728–1729), 421–426; XIV (1730), 39–40, S. C. Archives.

[9] "George Hunter's Map of the Cherokee Country and the Path thereto in 1730," *Bulletin No. 4 of the Historical Commission of South Carolina* (Columbia, S. C., 1917). George Hunter was surveyor-general of lands from 1743 to 1756. W. Roy Smith, *South Carolina as a Royal Province, 1719–1776* (New York, 1903), p. 413.

[10] Brunswick on the Cape Fear River was made a port of entry in 1731. Lee, *op. cit.*, pp. 119, 161.

[11] The following description is based upon Henry A. M. Smith, "Georgetown—The Original Plan and the Earliest Settlers," *SCHM*, IX (1908), 85–101. Also see Proprietary Grants, XXXVIII, 492–493, 516–517, S. C. Archives; Indenture of John and Mary Cleland with Archibald Baird and Richard Gough, dated Feb. 6, 1750, Miscellaneous Records, 00, Part 1 (1767–1771), pp. 59–64, S. C. Archives.

John Cleland of the Parish of St. Peter le Poor in the City of London. By her marriage settlement her Carolina lands were settled upon herself and her husband with remainder to their children. When Mary and John Cleland arrived in the province in 1735, they found that her lands were already in the possession of others.

Elisha and Hannah Commander Screven were in possession of these lands in 1735. Elisha Screven could have claimed these lands under a deed of 1710 by which John Abraham Motte had conveyed three of John Perry's plantations to William Screven, father of Elisha, but the records do not show whether the terms of this conveyance were carried out.[12] Elisha might have also claimed under a grant of 1711 which was recorded in the Memorial Book in 1733.[13] Certainly in 1729 Elisha Screven felt he was the possessor of the land for he had William Swinton, a surveyor, lay off the town. Lots were sold soon after the laying out of the town. On October 21, 1732, Elias Horry advertised for sale in the *Gazette* "Lot No. 23, at *Georgetown*, Winyaw, Fronting the Bay; Front 50 Foot, 217 Foot or thereabouts in Depth."

Elisha Screven had married Hannah Commander, the daughter of Samuel Commander, Sr., who had a right of dower or thirds to these Georgetown lots.[14] Some lot owners had taken a separate renunciation of dower from Hannah Screven. According to an advertisement in the *Gazette*, November 30, 1734, the plan to place the lots in the hands of trustees was projected in order to permit a general renunciation of dower rights by Hannah Screven. In February 1735 she swore before commissioners that she had made the renunciation freely, voluntarily, and without any fear of compulsion from her husband.[15]

On January 15, 16, 1735, Elisha and Hannah Screven conveyed the town to three trustees: George Pawley, William Swinton, and Daniel

[12] Miscellaneous Records, F (1707–1711), pp. 220–222, S. C. Archives.

[13] Memorial Book, II, Part 1, 195, S. C. Archives. Ramsay in 1808, after receiving information from three Georgetown men, wrote: "The ground on which Georgetown stands was originally granted to Mr. Perry. . . . It was through mistake granted a second time to the Rev. William Screven. . . ." David Ramsay, *History of South Carolina* (Newberry, S. C., 1858), II, 302.

[14] Hannah Commander was the eldest daughter of Samuel Commander, Sr., and sister of Samuel, John, and Joseph Commander. "Will of Samuel Commander, Sr.," dated Sept. 17, 1733, recorded March 15, 1736, Charleston County Wills, III (1731–1737), 238–239, S. C. Archives.

[15] Miscellaneous Records, II, Part I (1751–1754), 280–281, S. C. Archives.

LaRoche.[16] Attached to this deed was a plan of the town, the first plan to have been preserved. The indenture states that Elisha Screven's original intentions had been to provide a place for trade and defense as well as for churches and a school. For these purposes he had set aside 174½ acres for a town and 100 acres for a commons.

The town acreage had been divided into blocks by five streets running parallel to the Georgetown River (Sampit River) and seven streets running at right angles to the river. The blocks contained a total of 230 lots. The lots on the north side of Front Street facing the river were quarter-acre lots; the others were half-acre lots. The next two streets on the deed were not named but the fourth and fifth streets were Duke and Church. The streets at right angles to Front Street from west to east were Wood, King, Orange, Broad, Screven, Queen, and Common (Cannon). Lot 230 was reserved for a fort and was on the south side of Front Street to the east. Lots 225, 226, 227, 228, and 229, each to be one acre except 227 which was two acres, were on the north side of Church Street with their backs to the commons. Lot 225 was for a grammar school, the master of which must be licensed by the Bishop of London. Lot 226 was for a Presbyterian church of the doctrine and discipline of the Church of Scotland. The minister would be selected by the Scottish and English Presbyterians in town. Lot 227 was for an Anglican church. The Church of England townspeople were given the privilege of electing the minister. Lot 228 was for a Baptist church. Lot 229 was for a house of correction. Lots 149 and 150 were for a courthouse and prison when the King should incorporate the town. The market was to be in Broad Street. The lots were to be sold for £7.10 current money, with the owners having the right of pasturage on the commons for one horse and one cow. After five years the lots would sell for £10; after seven more years for £15; and after another seven for whatever the trustees should decide. Money obtained from the sales was to be paid to Elisha Screven or his heirs. The vacant land between Front Street ("commonly called the Bay") and low water was to be left open, but owners of lots on the north side of Front Street could build wharves on the south side. Those who bought lots had to build within eighteen months a house twenty-two by sixteen feet with brick chimneys

[16] Miscellaneous Records, II (1751–1754), 262–275, S. C. Archives.

or forfeit their lots. The trustees began to advertise the vacant lots in the *Gazette* of January 25, 1735.

It was on July 10, 1735, that Mary and John Cleland advertised in the *Gazette* that no lawful authority had approved the sale of any of these lots. Some adjustment was then made between the Screven and Cleland claimants, and on June 29, 30, 1737, a deed was recorded in which the titles to all of the lots sold were confirmed upon payment of £18 currency for each lot.[17] The lots for public purposes were still reserved, with lots 202 and 203 being set aside for a parsonage and a glebe for the rector of the parish church. The lands lying between Front Street and low-water mark were declared to belong to the owners of the lots fronting on such lands. The commons of 100 acres was returned to the Clelands, who then set aside, with the approval of the trustees, 130 acres to the west of the town for the common pasturage. The Clelands then added eighty-eight lots to the town, part on the west between Wood and a new street named Cleland and part on the east between Cannon Street and a new street named St. James. No plan was attached to this deed.

A list of lot owners was attached to the deed of June 29, 30, 1737.[18] Those listed were not necessarily residents, as many of the names were of men high in the provincial government who lived in Charleston. Othniel Beale, Nicholas Trott, James Abercromby, Charles Pinckney, and Benjamin Whitaker, all provincial officerholders, and Nathaniel and Andrew Broughton, sons of Lieutenant Governor Thomas Broughton, were men obviously speculating in real estate values. Screven, Cleland, Swinton, LaRoche, and Pawley were more likely to have built homes, as perhaps did the early Indian traders Meredith Hughes and William Waties, Jr., and the early Black River settler John Lane. The list also contained the names of many men whose families would long be associated with the town and the county: John and William Allston, William Anderson, Anthony Atkinson, Thomas Blythe, John Coachman, John and Joseph Commander, Elias Foissin, Thomas Henning, Alexander Nisbet, John Ouldfield, John Richardson, Alexander Robertson, William Romsey, Alexander Skene, Henry Toomer, and Anthony White. These

---

[17] Miscellaneous Records, II (1751–1754), 276–279, S. C. Archives.
[18] Henry A. M. Smith, *op. cit.*, pp. 95–101.

men were natives of the region, but also speculators. Anthony White owned fourteen lots.[19]

Houses were built soon after the lots were surveyed; a few undoubtedly existed before the survey. The first Georgetown house advertised for sale in the *Gazette* (August 7, 1736) was described as being twenty-three by sixteen feet with a double chimney, stable, and hen house. When Thomas Bolem died at Georgetown in August 1737, he was the owner of a tavern "provided with all conveniences." [20] The buying and selling of lots and houses was often at public vendue. A public sale was recorded as having been held at the home of Jonathan Skrine.[21] These advertisements give little information about the style of the houses, but these facts can be added to what is known concerning houses standing till very recent times. A picture emerges of a small town with comfortable wooden houses, long sloping roof lines pierced by slender chimneys, piazzas along one side with additional buildings strung out in the yards. In 1765 Lord Adam Gordon called it "a pretty little Town" and John Bartram found "a lovely shade in many parts of ye town." [22] Most significant at first was the total absence of public buildings. Not until the construction of the Episcopal church in the 1740's was there a principal structure in the town. The focus of the town life was in the homes of the planters, merchants, and local officeholders.

There were two sets of officials connected with Georgetown as a port, one set appointed by the provincial government in Charleston and the other by the royal government in London. The first provincial official to be appointed was the packer, who was responsible for the quality of exports. An act of December 14, 1714, called for one packer to be situated at Winyah; later there were two.[23] In Charleston, after the

[19] Anthony White advertised in the *Gazette*, Nov. 9, 1734, sundry lots and tracts of land for sale at Georgetown.

[20] *Gazette*, Aug. 6, 1737.

[21] *Gazette*, April 6, 1738.

[22] [Lord Adam Gordon] "Journal of an Officer's Travels in America and the West Indies," *Travels in the American Colonies*, ed. Newton D. Mereness (New York, 1916), p. 398; John Bartram, "Diary of a Journey through the Carolinas, Georgia, and Florida, 1765–66," *Transactions of the American Philosophical Society*, N. S., XXXIII, Part 1 (Philadelphia, Penn., 1942), 19. An illustrated article, written by C. S. Murray, on the "small quaint houses" of Georgetown appeared in the Charleston *News and Courier*, Jan. 27, 1929.

[23] *S. C. Statutes*, II, 615–617.

original appointment by the Commons House of Assembly, packers were elected by the townspeople; for Georgetown there is no record of any elections although the packers, according to the law of 1746, were to be chosen annually at the time of parish elections by the freeholders of the parish in which the port was located.[24] The packer was to inspect beef, pork, pitch, tar, rosin, turpentine, and rice before these articles were exported to see that they were properly packed and of sufficient quality. In Charleston packers were always coopers. Coopering was an important ancillary trade in an exporting community.[25] Indigo, the new and financially exciting crop of the 1740's, was certified as to its quality by the planters themselves, swearing before their neighborhood justices of the peace.

The customs officials appointed by the province were the receiver, comptroller, and country waiter. These were appointed by the Commons House of Assembly to collect the export and import duties levied by that body, and they served during good behavior. The receiver collected and gathered the country duties (those levied by the province); the comptroller granted landing permits; the country waiter watched over the shipping of exports and certified the prescribed forms. William Whiteside and Archibald Baird were receivers; Thomas Blythe, Thomas Hasell, Maurice Simons, and Job Rothmahler, comptrollers; Jonathan Skrine and Joseph Dubourdieu, country waiters.[26]

The royal customs officials were appointed by the crown. At a port of entry the customs collector was the chief official. By October 14, 1732, Peter Goudett was certainly collector, for John Hammerton, receiver-general of the quit-rents, made Goudett, whom he called collector of customs, his deputy at Georgetown to collect the quit-rents that were due to the crown from Craven County.[27] Archibald Baird, who probably

---

[24] S. C. Statutes, III, 689.

[25] The author is preparing an article on the packers of Charleston.

[26] S. C. Statutes, III, 597–598, 776–777; IV, 44; Miscellaneous Records, GG (1746–1749), p. 243, S. C. Archives. William Whiteside was appointed notary public in 1743 at the port of Georgetown to dispatch public business in that harbor. Miscellaneous Records, FF (1743–1746), pp. 359–360, S. C. Archives. For Maurice Simons see Miscellaneous Records, MM, Part 2 (1763–1767), pp. 663–664, S. C. Archives. For Job Rothmahler see Miscellaneous Records, RR, Part 1 (1774–1779), p. 46, S. C. Archives.

[27] Gazette, Oct. 14, 1732.

replaced Goudett, served as collector at Georgetown from 1740 to the Revolution.[28] James Cassells was deputy collector for a short time in the 1770's.[29]

The naval officer was responsible for keeping a register of the vessels that arrived and departed at his port, sending a copy of this register to Charleston quarterly. William Swinton, the first deputy naval officer at Georgetown, sent his initial report for the quarter ending at Michaelmas (November) 1733.[30] James Fox, naval officer in Charleston, sent home this report on May 20, 1734, with a covering letter to the Lords Commissioners for Trade and Plantations: "On my visitation of the Port of George Town Wyniaw, I found the Quarterly Accounts by my predecessor had not been duly returned, so ordered imediately Mr. William Swinton (whom I have appointed my Deputy at that Port,) to make out the same; which he having performed to Lady day last [March 25], I now humbly transmit them to your Lordships, and beg leave to assure you, they shall for the future regularly come with those of the Port of Charles Town. . . ."[31] Such reports, which henceforth were regularly received from Georgetown, were occasionally printed in the *Gazette* before being sent to England. The summation for the first full year (November 1, 1733, to November 1, 1734), which was printed in the *Gazette*, gave a picture of Georgetown trade which was typical of the early years.[32] During that period three sloops cleared for Charleston, five sloops, a schooner, and a brigantine for Philadelphia, three sloops for Boston, and one for Bermuda. Rice and fruit were carried to Charleston while pitch, tar, and turpentine were cargoes for the other ports. Sailing directly for London were three ships and three snows, and one brigantine sailed for Poole and one for Bristol. These carried pitch and

[28] Memorial of Archibald Baird, May 5, 1774, Treasury Papers, In-Letters, 511/436, PRO, London. Baird was the nephew of John Cleland. "Will of John Cleland," dated May 17, 1760, proved May 30, 1760, Charleston County Wills, VIII (1757–1763), 489, S. C. Archives.

[29] Loyalist Transcripts, LV, 107–121, on microfilm, S. C. Archives.

[30] CO/5/509, f. 124, PRO, London.

[31] CO/5/509, f. 127, PRO. London.

[32] The records for the four quarters of 1735 are given in CO/5/509, ff. 142–145, PRO, London. A snow sailed from Georgetown to Dover, Eng., in 38 days in 1762. *Gazette*, May 14, 1763.

turpentine. The principal export was still naval stores; only 322 barrels of rice were shipped to Charleston.[33]

During the colonial period local government for the towns was in the hands of the Commons House of Assembly, as neither Charleston nor Georgetown was incorporated. The indenture of January 15, 16, 1735, did mention the possibility of incorporation by the crown, but two post-Revolutionary documents reveal that this possibility was never realized. In 1787 "Sundry Inhabitants of Georgetown" sent a memorial to the South Carolina Senate in which they stated: "That in the Charter for Laying out the Town of George Town into Lots, three Trustees were appointed to carry the Plan into Execution, All of whom have been dead these several years past, and their Representatives (who live at a considerable distance from Town) decline acting, by which means, the Inhabitants suffer much inconvenience, on account of the regulations for Erecting Buildings, opening Streets etc. not being adhered to." [34] The other document is a report of the case *The Commissioners of the Streets of Georgetown* v. *Archibald Taylor,* in which there is a statement by one of the lawyers for the defense that Georgetown

never was laid out by any public authority, nor had it even the semblance of a corporation till a very late period; therefore, as members of a corporate body, they cannot maintain this action. The first notice taken of *Georgetown* by the legislature after the revolution, was in an act passed in 1787, authorizing the public market, regulating the streets, and for other purposes of police mentioned in the said act. By this act, the commissioners of the streets are empowered to keep them clear and in good repair, and to cause annoyances to be removed, and all obstructions, under certain penalties therein mentioned; and the same powers were also given them, as had been given to the trustees mentioned in *Cleeland's* deed. By another act, passed in 1791, the commissioners are authorized to assess the inhabitants in a sum sufficient to keep the streets and causeys in repair, etc. but neither of these acts gave, or could give, any thing like a *freehold* to the commissioners.

Since the judges decided unanimously in this case that the petitioners could not support their action "as the right of freehold was never in

[33] CO/5/509, ff. 142–145, PRO, London.

[34] "The Memorial of Sundry Inhabitants of Georgetown" to the President of the Senate [1787], SCL.

them," the above argument and facts were apparently true.[35] The power to govern the town had been in the three trustees and their heirs forever. They could have appointed commissioners to lay out streets, to erect buildings and keep them in repair, to establish a market, and provide police, which must also imply the right to tax. In practice, with the passage of time and the dispersal of the heirs of the original trustees, this system broke down. The Revolution finished it off and made necessary the reforms of the post-Revolutionary period, in 1787 the legislature for the first time began to regulate the affairs of the town.

The Assembly did set up one commission for the port in April 1735 when it named Captain Meredith Hughes, Major George Pawley, Daniel LaRoche, William Swinton, and Captain Anthony White as commissioners of the pilots for the port of Georgetown. They were authorized to lay buoys and erect beacons, build one or more pilot boats, and nominate pilots for appointment by the governor. They also had the power to assess and tax property in the two parishes of Prince George and Prince Frederick for carrying out their duties, although they could not raise more than £1,000 per annum. The pilot fees were set by law. Vessels arriving from abroad paid the same powder money that would be paid by vessels arriving in Charleston; vessels arriving from Charleston paid only half-fees. These commissioners were appointed for three-year terms, and others were to be appointed by the Assembly in the future.[36] Through this agency of local government beacons were placed at the entrance to Winyah Bay.

Ferries and high roads were also established and designated under the watchful eye of the Assembly. Ferry rights were vested in individuals who received fees for maintaining a public service. On April 17, 1725, the Assembly vested the rights to a ferry over the Black River in Alexander Montgomery. The law noted that the inhabitants of Winyah had become numerous and that a ferry over the Black River would be highly beneficial in keeping open communications in times of alarm.[37]

[35] *Reports of Cases Argued and Determined in the Superior Courts of Law in the State of South Carolina, Since the Revolution,* ed. Elihu Hall Bay (New York, 1811), II, 290.

[36] S. C. *Statutes,* III, 406–408. This commission was extended by laws of 1746, 1752, and 1761. S. C. *Statutes,* III, 678–680, 760–762; IV, 597–598. In 1766 the commissioners advertised for a pilot for the port of Winyah. *Gazette,* Sept. 8, 1766.

[37] S. C. *Statutes,* IX, 62–63.

On August 20, 1731, three additional ferries were established in the Parish of Prince George Winyah. The right to one, which joined Waccamaw Neck to Georgetown, was vested in Samuel Masters and to another, which crossed the Sampit River from Elisha Screven's plantation on the north side to Robert Screven's on the south side, in Robert Screven. One was provided for crossing the Santee, which was vested in Jonathan Skrine.[38] These ferry rights were granted for a term of years. The Assembly was, therefore, called upon from time to time to pass additional legislation.

Because of the extent of water to be crossed, the ferry from Waccamaw Neck to Georgetown was often difficult to operate, particularly in windy weather. In 1756 the principal point of crossing was moved up the Neck and two ferries established, one across the Waccamaw from George Threadcraft's plantation to Elias Foissin's island, the other across the Pee Dee from John Glen's plantation to the west side of the river.[39] The route to Georgetown then passed over the Black River Ferry. In 1770 and 1771, because of the complaints that those who traveled from Waccamaw to Charleston must pass over so many ferries, new services were established from the Neck to Georgetown and to the south side of Sampit River, these being vested in William Allston, Sr., and John Cogdell, who must have supplied complementary services.[40]

The main barrier was the Santee River, which had four principal ferry crossings by the eve of the Revolution. These can be easily identified on Henry Mouzon's map of 1775.[41] The crossing nearest the mouth of the river was by Lynch's Causeway and connecting ferries, a route open by 1741. The second ferry crossing up the river and the one that must have been in use at the earliest time became known as Lenud's Ferry. The rights were first granted to Jonathan Skrine in 1731. In 1739 the ferry from the south side was vested in James Kinloch while that

[38] S. C. *Statutes*, IX, 69–70.

[39] S. C. *Statutes*, IX, 180–183.

[40] S. C. *Statutes*, IX, 241–245. This was William Allston, Sr., who continued to run his ferries through the Revolution, collecting £27.15.11 sterling after the Revolution for ferriages. "William Allston, Sr.," Audited Accounts, S. C. Archives. It may have been during these years that the plantation at the southern tip of Waccamaw Neck was named Calais and one south of the Sampit on Winyah Bay named Dover.

[41] Henry Mouzon's map of North and South Carolina, 1775, S. C. Archives.

from the north side was vested in Abraham Michau. In 1750, Kinloch's ferry rights passed to Alexander Dupont.[42] Abraham Michau's rights must have passed to the family of his brother-in-law, Nicholas Lenud, for the Michau and Lenud lands adjoined on the north Santee. Nicholas' son Albert was a saddler's apprentice in Charleston prior to June 22, 1745. This ferry was operated by Albert Lenud and his brothers down to the Revolution.[43]

In 1741 the ferry rights on the road from Moncks Corner to Kingstree were vested in James Murray. After his death in 1754 James Hunter applied for these rights in 1758 as trustee for Joseph Murray, the son of James Murray and a minor. Theodore Gaillard, who had obtained in 1756 ferry rights on the south side of the Santee, used the ferry landing at Murray's Causeway on the north side of the river. Hunter successfully maintained the rights of his ward and Murray's Ferry continued to operate.[44] The fourth ferry upstream was James Beard's Ferry, later Nelson's, on the road from Charleston to Camden.[45]

The basic law establishing a system of roads for this region was passed in 1721. By that act the governor appointed a group of commissioners of the high roads who were to serve for life.[46] In 1741 commissioners were permitted to resign after three years service if they so desired. These commissioners (five of whom constituted a quorum) were required to meet twice a year at the parish church. Usually, the legislature designated the route and the commissioners supervised the work.[47] On June 7, 1733, the legislature called for a public road to be laid out from Robert Screven's plantation on the Sampit to the Santee River.[48]

[42] S. C. Statutes, IX, 108–110, 153–154.

[43] "Will of Madelaine Rembert," dated Feb. 4, 1734, proved March 21, 1734, Abstracts of the Wills of the State of South Carolina, 1670–1740, I, 194–195. "Albert Lenud" and "Nicholas Lenud," Pre-Revolutionary Plats, S. C. Archives. Albert Lenud, "an Apprentice Lad . . . Santee born," ran away from John Laurens in 1745. Gazette, June 22, 1745.

[44] S. C. Statutes, IX, 121–124, 187–188, 195–197; "Will of Joseph Murray," dated Feb. 22, 1754, proved April 11, 1754, Charleston County Wills, VII (1752–1756), 162–163, S. C. Archives; Journal of the Commons House, XXXII (Oct. 23, 1758–April 7, 1759), 98, 127, 184, S. C. Archives:

[45] S. C. Statutes, IX, 184–186, 200. A 1755 plat for James Beard shows the road to the ferry. Bound Plats, VI, 186, S. C. Archives.

[46] S. C. Statutes, IX, 51.

[47] S. C. Statutes, IX, 129.

[48] S. C. Statutes, IX, 74–75.

After the formation of the new parish of Prince Frederick, the Assembly supplied two boards for this area, one a board of commissioners of the high roads for Waccamaw Neck (which was one of the first attempts to treat the Neck as a separate jurisdiction) and another for the remainder of the parish of Prince George and for Prince Frederick.[49] These boards had the power to assess the lands and slaves of planters in order to raise funds to build and repair the roads.

In 1744 commissioners to build a bridge "over the north branch of the Black river, opposite to the landing of John Wallis, Esq., deceased" were appointed.[50] In 1745 the Assembly ordered the cutting and clearing of water courses in the swamps at the head of Black Mingo Creek, beginning at the plantation of Anthony White on that creek.[51] In 1747 five new boards were established for the upper regions of Prince Frederick parish.[52] In this fashion the interior was opened to the immigrant and traveler. In 1756 a new board was appointed for Waccamaw Neck to lay out a road from the Waccamaw ferry established that year to the Cape Fear.[53] This was the road that followed the eight-mile swash along the coast and became the main north-south road.

The biggest internal improvement scheme was the building of a causeway over Lynches Island, lying between the North and South Santee and owned by Thomas Lynch. This causeway on the direct line of travel between Georgetown and Charleston was always managed by a separate board of commissioners. The plan, set forth in an act of March 11, 1737, called for a ferry to be kept on the south side of South Santee at Isaac Mazyck's plantation and another on the north side of North Santee at William Buchanan's plantation. Mazyck and Buchanan were required to keep one substantial canoe and ferry boat with two or more able-bodied men to serve travelers at all times.[54] On May 3, 1739, the

---

[49] S. C. Statutes, IX, 87–88.

[50] Anthony White, Edward Handlin, John White, William Fleming, and John McKever were named commissioners. S. C. Statutes, IX, 135. Anthony White advertised in 1748 that his home was near "Black-mingo Bridge." Gazette, Feb. 8, 1748.

[51] S. C. Statutes, IX, 136–138.

[52] S. C. Statutes, IX, 144–147.

[53] The names were William Allston, John Clark, Archibald Johnston, John Waties, Alexander McDowell, Charles Lewis, and Josias Allston. S. C. Statutes, IX, 182.

[54] William Whiteside, George Pawley, William Buchanan, Jonah Collins, and Daniel Horry were named commissioners. S. C. Statutes, IX, 104–108.

commissioners advertised that the assessment would be two pence per acre and five shillings per head for slaves for building the causeway. They advertised on July 28 that those who did not pay immediately would be subject to a double tax.[55] The causeway which ran from ferry-landing to ferry-landing, was completed by March 1741, for at that time plans were initiated for keeping the causeway in repair. The inhabitants of both Prince George and St. James Santee were assessed for this purpose.[56] However, in 1753, the inhabitants of St. James Santee were relieved of this tax burden, as an act of 1737 had placed all of the islands between the North and South Santee in the parish of Prince George.[57] In 1771 it was necessary to rebuild the causeway, and Thomas Lynch contracted to do the work.[58]

In 1739 a post was set up from Charleston to the northern colonies via Georgetown and the Cape Fear. The Assembly appropriated £200, which the Charleston merchants supplemented in order to provide this service.[59] In 1756 this service was improved by the establishment of two new ferries and the road to Cape Fear.[60]

Today no one needs to pause as one enters the county. In the colonial period the ferry-crossings were important breaks in the journey. The provincial government took advantage of these necessary pauses to inspect travelers, in order to apprehend runaway slaves and indentured servants or deserting seamen. One white man had to be present on each ferry to inspect the papers of travelers. If a man were not well-known, he might carry a ticket of identity obtained from a justice of the peace. Since Isaac Mazyck, Thomas Lynch, and William Buchanan were justices of the peace, certificates could easily be made out for returning runaways to their owners or to Charleston. The ferries, therefore, served a double purpose. The ferries increased the mobility of some but hedged

[55] *Gazette*, May 3, July 28, 1739.
[56] S. C. *Statutes*. IX, 119–120.
[57] S. C. *Statutes*, IX, 164.
[58] S. C. *Statutes*, IX, 243.
[59] *Gazette*, April 26, 1739.
[60] Henry Laurens wrote Meyler and Hall, Oct. 2, 1756: "Letters will now come pretty expeditiously from any part of North America as a Post is lately establish'd that bring Letters all the way from New England." Laurens Papers, S. C. Hist. Soc. In 1771 the post boy carrying mail northward was robbed five miles beyond Georgetown. Proclamation of Lt. Gov. William Bull, March 25, 1771, Miscellaneous Records, 00, Part 2 (1767–1771), p. 537, S. C. Archives.

in the freedom of others. The ferries were the gates to the Georgetown rice kingdom.[61]

The main eighteenth-century highway was the sea. All produce went by water to market, and most of the passengers between Georgetown and Charleston traveled by water in spite of the dangers from privateers and storms. During the War of Jenkins' Ear, 1739–1748, the coast between Georgetown and Charleston was particularly beset by Spanish privateers based in Cuba. In August 1745 after a schooner carrying Percival Pawley and Colonel George Pawley's son was captured, the militia was called out, since the people feared an invasion from the sea.[62] In November 1747 Isaac Mazyck's schooner was taken by a Spanish privateer.[63] But the most exciting episode involved the schooner *Molley*, Zachariah Brazier, master, which was owned by James Wright, a merchant of Georgetown. The *Gazette* of August 24, 1747, gave this dramatic account: "Capt. *Brazier* sail'd from hence for *Winyaw*, and was chas'd soon after he got over this Bar by a *Spanish* Privateer; but, being well acquainted with the coast, he ran his Vessel ashore, and retir'd with his crew unseen by the Enemy; saw the Privateer's Boat come on board his Schooner, and (upon a hard Gale of Wind coming on) go off again, upon which he immediately retook Possession, got her off and sail'd her into *Bull's Island* Inlet, off which Place he was again chas'd." Peace did not bring an end to dangers from the sea, for the two great hurricanes of 1752 were more terrifying than any Spanish privateer.[64]

[61] William Simpson, *The Practical Justice of the Peace and Parish-Officer, of His Majesty's Province of South-Carolina* (Charlestown, S. C., 1761), pp. 224, 233. For a list of the justices of the peace see *Gazette*, Nov. 4, 1756. The *Gazette*, Jan. 10, 1743, announced that there were deserters from the British men-of-war in Charleston who were making their way to North Carolina and Virginia by way of Winyah and that they had certificates permitting them to cross the ferries.

[62] *Gazette*, Aug. 19, 1745.

[63] *Gazette*, Nov. 2, 1747.

[64] The *Molley* had been built at Winyah in 1746. Ship Register, 1734–1765, p. 11, S. C. Archives. Two hurricanes hit South Carolina on Sept. 15 and 30, 1752. The second was more damaging in the Georgetown region. David M. Ludlum, *Early American Hurricanes, 1492–1870* (Boston, Mass., 1963), pp. 44–48. A French privateer with a Spanish crew seized the pilot's house on North Island in Dec. 1762. *Gazette*, Dec. 11, 1762. Privateers apparently blockaded Georgetown during the winter of 1762–1763. *Gazette*, Jan. 1, Feb. 26, 1763. In 1767 a schooner from Winyah broke up on Charleston bar with a loss of 20,000 lbs. of indigo. *Gazette*, Feb. 9, 1767.

The vessels engaged in the Georgetown trade were schooners, sloops, brigantines, and snows; a ship rarely entered Winyah Bay. The schooners and sloops were built in New England; the larger vessels in England. Since few of the latter came to Georgetown, most of the vessels in the Georgetown trade were built to the north. Georgetown herself, however, had a shipbuilding industry during the colonial period, particularly between 1745 and 1756. This industry brought to Georgetown a number of New Englanders, a small but important group who made a lasting impression upon the local society, providing important elements to the community, men who were sea captains and shopkeepers, a middle class quite distinct from the farming and planting elements, a group whose descendants came into power in Georgetown after 1876.

An examination of the South Carolina Ship Register, 1734–1774, reveals that at least thirty-three vessels were built in and around Georgetown during the pre-Revolutionary period. A sloop was built at Georgetown in 1738 for Daniel LaRoche, a merchant, and a schooner was built on the Santee in 1741 for Noah Serré, a planter.[65] Each used his vessel to carry goods to Charleston; LaRoche to take crops and bring back goods for sale and Serré to deliver his own crop and to bring back necessities for his five Santee River plantations.

A brigantine was built at Georgetown in 1745; two schooners in 1746; a schooner and a snow (Waccamaw River) in 1748; a schooner (Santee River), two brigantines, and two snows in 1749; two schooners and a snow (Waccamaw River) in 1750; a ship in 1751; a snow and a schooner in 1752; a sloop, two schooners (one of them built at Little River), and a brigantine in 1753; three schooners in 1754; a sloop and two schooners in 1755; a brigantine in 1756; a sloop in 1759; a schooner in 1760; and a schooner in 1761. Only one vessel was built in Georgetown between 1761 and the Revolution, a schooner in 1773.[66]

If these figures can be taken as nearly complete, the greatest shipbuilding period in Georgetown corresponded with the boom in indigo. As indigo production leveled off, shipbuilding waned. When the merchants James Jamieson of Charleston and Anthony Bonneau of Georgetown wanted to buy a brigantine of 100 tons in 1774 (which they named

[65] Ship Register, 1734–1765, pp. 298, 315–316, S. C. Archives.
[66] Ship Register, 1734–1765 and 1765–1780, passim, S. C. Archives.

George Town), they bought one that had been constructed in Beaufort.[67]

The *Gazette* also provides evidence that Georgetown was a shipbuilding center. On July 9, 1748, it announced the launching of the *Mary Ann* of 200 tons and twelve guns built by Benjamin Darling, a New Englander. The frame was of live oak and was thought by good judges "to be the compleatest Vessel ever built in America. . . ." On April 2, 1750, a new vessel just off the stocks, of 110 tons, its frame of live oak and finished of all ship carpenters' work with a complete set of rigging, was advertised for sale. These two announcements prove that sizable vessels were built in Georgetown by New Englanders drawn to Georgetown by the excellent timber resources. The largest vessel constructed in Georgetown was the ship *Francis,* of 180 tons, registered on October 14, 1751, by Thomas Shubrick, Charleston merchant, as having been built at Winyah in 1751.[68] Benjamin Darling may have had the principal shipyard; he most probably built the brigantine *Darling,* of 40 tons, which Christopher Gadsden registered in Georgetown on February 17, 1756.[69]

The group that took advantage of Georgetown as a part of entry were the merchants who were the principal inhabitants of the town. They cannot be identified by reference to the newspapers, for Georgetown did not have a colonial newspaper and her merchants seldom advertised in the Charleston newspaper. However, many of them can be identified by a search of the ship register, as the larger merchants owned their own vessels or at least held shares in vessels, often with their Charleston correspondents. A 1738 entry stated that William Romsey and Company and Daniel and Thomas LaRoche, all of Georgetown, owned the schooner *Charleston* along with Peter Horry of Charleston, merchant. Peter Horry, until his death in 1739, was the Charleston

[67] Beaufort replaced Georgetown as a secondary shipbuilding center on the eve of the Revolution. Ship Register, 1765–1780, p. 195, S. C. Archives.

[68] Ship Register, 1734–1765, pp. 62, 81, 95–96, S. C. Archives.

[69] Ship Register, 1734–1765, pp. 146–147, S. C. Archives. On Nov. 16, 1753, John and Mary Cleland sold Benjamin Darling, shipwright, Lots 230, 231, and 232 in Georgetown for £750 currency. These lots, which had been set aside for a fort, were on the Sampit River in the southeastern corner of the town. Charleston County Deeds, OO (1753–1754), pp. 11–21, S. C. Archives.

agent of the Romseys and the LaRoches.[70] Other firms can be identified in the Judgment Rolls of the Court of Common Pleas. From this source it is known that in 1746 the firm of Andrew Johnston and Company consisted of William Fleming, Archibald Baird, and Andrew Johnston.[71]

Daniel LaRoche held shares in a greater number of vessels than did any other Georgetown merchant. On November 28, 1745, LaRoche with Edward Croft and Paul Trapier registered a vessel as joint owners, but it was with Andrew Delavillette and David Montaigut that Daniel LaRoche worked most closely. The firm of LaRoche, Delavillette, and Montaigut registered a sloop, a schooner, and three brigantines between 1747 and 1750.[72] By owning their own vessels these merchants could cut the cost of freight to Charleston and provide services that other merchants could not. On March 12, 1741, Daniel and Thomas LaRoche made a contract with two Charleston merchants promising to deliver between the first and last of the ensuing August 600 barrels of turpentine, 400 barrels of pitch, and 200 barrels of tar, all to be delivered at prices agreed upon in March.[73] The assembling of such a cargo was easier if the merchant owned his own vessels. Daniel LaRoche was speculating on his own efficiency by promising future delivery at stated prices. When funds were needed to finance this trade, money could be borrowed in Charleston. The Reverend Alexander Garden loaned LaRoche £1,200 and LaRoche, Delavillette, and Montaigut £3,000.[74] That these men were willing to borrow these sums at 10 percent interest indicates the boom conditions of the 1740's. Daniel LaRoche

[70] Ship Register, 1734–1765, p. 289, S. C. Archives. William Romsey of Georgetown and Samuel and William Baker of London were among the executors of the "Will of Peter Horry," dated May 20, 1738, proved Dec. 7, 1739, Charleston County Wills, IV (1736–1740), 257–258, S. C. Archives. There are a number of letters from Robert Ellis of Philadelphia to Messrs. Daniel and Thomas LaRoche, Romsey and Trapier, and Peter Horry which prove that Ellis sent his vessels southward when the northern rivers were frozen to transport naval stores and rice to market. Robert Ellis Letter Book, 1736–1748, Penn. Hist. Soc. Advertisements that give further evidence of these relationships can be found in *Gazette*, Nov. 29, 1735, July 31, 1736.

[71] Judgment Rolls, 1760, No. 167A, S. C. Archives. A master of a London vessel promised to pay William Fleming & Co. £1,000 for outfit of a vessel in 1741. Miscellaneous Records, EE (1741–1743), pp. 39–42, S. C. Archives.

[72] Ship Register, 1734–1765, pp. 23–24, 36, 55–57, 64, S. C. Archives.

[73] Miscellaneous Records, EE (1741–1743), pp. 418–419, S. C. Archives.

[74] Miscellaneous Records, II, Part 1 (1751–1754), 230–231, 235, S. C. Archives.

eventually overextended himself, went bankrupt, and fled the province in 1753.[75]

Paul Trapier surpassed Daniel LaRoche. Trapier began in a small way with a store at Georgetown, where he sold goods on commission for Joseph Wragg of Charleston. As Wragg had assumed the risks, the profits for Trapier were relatively small. In 1741 Trapier decided to go to London to secure credit and goods that would permit him to expand his operations. Wragg wrote Thomas Smith of Spittlefields in London that Trapier wanted "to establish things on a new footing." As Trapier would be a complete stranger in London, Wragg was willing to pledge £2,000 sterling that Trapier would make punctual payments on his debts.[76] Trapier went to London, secured credit and goods, and returned to Georgetown to trade on his own. However, he continued in close association with Joseph Wragg.[77]

In a place the size of Georgetown it was natural for trade to gravitate into the hands of a few merchants. The leading merchants would cooperate with each other in order to establish an ascendancy over the others. LaRoche and Trapier shared the ownership of one vessel, an indication that they cooperated in trade until the failure of LaRoche in 1753.[78] The same type of evidence shows that Paul Trapier was associated with almost every important Georgetown merchant down to the Revolution. In succession he shared the ownership of schooners with

[75] In Jan. 1752 LaRoche had turned over to George Saxby and Elias Foissin his property. Charleston County Deeds, KK (1751–1752), pp. 74–79, 85–94, S. C. Archives. Foissin and Saxby advertised for sale on March 19, 1753, 10,000 acres, eight town lots, and 130 slaves belonging to Daniel LaRoche. *Gazette,* Jan. 22, 1753; John Guerard to Alexander Hume, Jan. 24, 1754, John Guerard Letterbook, 1752–1754, S. C. Hist. Soc. Delavillette fled the province in 1753 with thirty slaves for St. Eustatius, owing Austin and Laurens several thousand pounds. Henry Laurens to Robert Stuart, April 28, 1756, Laurens Papers, S. C. Hist. Soc.

[76] Joseph Wragg to Thomas Smith of Spittlefields, Feb. 18, 1741, Miscellaneous Records, II, Part 2 (1751–1754), 612–613, 623, S. C. Archives. Also see Miscellaneous Records, LL, Part 1 (1758–1763), pp. 158–162, S. C. Archives. For a debt of Trapier and Romsey to John Laurens see *The Papers of Henry Laurens,* ed. P. M. Hamer and G. C. Rogers, Jr. (Columbia, S. C., 1968), I, 29, 380.

[77] On Aug. 28, 1746, Joseph Wragg, Paul Trapier, and Benjamin Romsey registered a 40-ton schooner; on April 19, 1748, Paul Trapier, Benjamin Romsey, Joseph Wragg, Samuel Wragg, Jr., and Thomas Tucker, master, registered a 25-ton schooner. Ship Register, 1734–1765, pp. 9, 35, S. C. Archives.

[78] Ship Register, 1734–1765, p. 91, S. C. Archives.

William Poole, Samuel Wragg, Jr., Job Rothmahler, and John Forbes. As Trapier owned a store in Charleston by the middle of the 1740's and as several of his Georgetown associates moved to Charleston later (Benjamin Romsey becoming a country factor there and John Forbes a merchant), he was a rare example of a country merchant invading the commercial metropolis. As Trapier was often in Charleston attending sessions of the Assembly and appearing as litigant in the court of common pleas, he could keep a close scrutiny on affairs in that port.[79] Paul Trapier earned, according to tradition, the title "king of Georgetown."

It was more natural for Charleston merchants to be drawn to Georgetown as was Samuel Wragg, Jr., the son of Joseph Wragg, who by 1748 was looking after his father's Georgetown interests. He married Judith, the sister of Job Rothmahler, with whom he traded in the 1750's.[80]

Another Charleston merchant drawn to Georgetown was Christopher Gadsden. Gadsden had a store in Georgetown and another at the Cheraws.[81] Between 1753 and 1756 he registered three vessels; on the last occasion he listed himself as a merchant of Georgetown.[82] On December 29, 1755, he married his second wife, Mary Hasell, whose brother Thomas was comptroller of the customs in Georgetown.[83] As Gadsden bought Lot 66 in Georgetown in 1756 and received a grant of 1,300 acres on the Pee Dee River in 1757, it looked as though he was settling permanently.[84]

A few planters owned schooners, especially those along the Santee River such as Noah Serré, Isaac Mazyck, and John Mayrant, who while planting on a large scale had no marshaling point like Georgetown

[79] See "Paul Trapier," Judgment Rolls, Court of Common Pleas, S. C. Archives. For terms of co-partnership with William Poole in 1749 see Miscellaneous Records, LL, Part 1 (1758–1763), pp. 129–130, S. C. Archives. Ship Register, 1734–1765, pp. 79, 104, 137, S. C. Archives; Gazette, Jan. 8, 1750, Oct. 18, 1760.

[80] Gazette, May 21, 1753.

[81] The Writings of Christopher Gadsden, 1746–1805, ed. Richard Walsh (Columbia, S. C., 1966), p. xvii.

[82] Ship Register, 1734–1765, pp. 112–113, 121, 146–147, S. C. Archives.

[83] SCHM, XX (1919), 61. Gadsden and Paul Trapier were executors of the estate of Thomas Hasell. "Will of Thomas Hasell," dated July 14, 1756, proved Sept. 20, 1756, Charleston County Wills, VII (1752–1756), 556–557, S. C. Archives.

[84] "The Burial Place of the Reverend William Screven," SCHM, XVI (1915), 93–95. Christopher's father, Thomas Gadsden, had received grants of land on the Black River in 1734 and 1739. Grant Books, I, 273; III, 336; VIII, 45, S. C. Archives.

through which to send their crops to Charleston.[85] The most important Santee River planter was Thomas Lynch, who owned in 1749 a twenty-ton schooner with the merchant Kenneth Michie of Charleston and one-fourth interest in another schooner.[86] Daniel Horry, whose land lay on the South Santee, shared a schooner with Paul Trapier in 1764. Thomas Horry shared a sloop with Philip Tidyman, the Charleston jeweler, who had invested his profits in Santee lands.[87]

Mariners often owned their own schooners. Joseph Cox, who carried letters for Henry Laurens, did so.[88] On occasion an enterprising master of these coasting vessels moved into the planter or merchant class. In 1761 John Cogdell was master of William Shackelford's schooner *Good Intent*. In 1765 he acquired an island in Winyah Bay. And in 1771 he was given the ferry rights from his plantation on Waccamaw Neck to Georgetown and Sampit.[89]

Front Street with stores on the north side and wharves extending into the Sampit on the south side was the center of this commercial bustle. On April 15, 1751, Paul Trapier sold at public vendue in Georgetown two lots on the bay convenient for trade. One had a storehouse on the front of the lot and a well-built house on the back, thirty feet square with a dry cellar, six feet high, underneath. The other had a salt house, a large store, and a good wharf the full breadth of the lot.[90] Among the stores were a number of taverns. The Charleston paper in 1746 announced that goods might be found "at Mr. Tregagles," a reference to the well-known tavern kept by Nathaniel Tregagle.[91] In October 1745 William Logan on his arrival from the north "put up at Tho' Blythe's

---

[85] Ship Register, 1734–1765, p. 211, S. C. Archives.

[86] Ship Register, 1734–1765, pp. 51–52, S. C. Archives.

[87] Ship Register, 1734–1765, p. 233, S. C. Archives.

[88] Durozel Villepontoux, Albertus Albertson, Thomas Mace, and Joseph Cox were masters who owned vessels. Charles Minor, a shipwright, owned a 20-ton schooner built on Little River. Ship Register, 1734–1765, pp. 15, 119–121, 144, 159, S. C. Archives. Capt. Cox carried a letter from Henry Laurens to John Cleland, William Fleming, and Andrew Johnston, dated Sept. 7, 1747. Hamer and Rogers, *op. cit.*, I, 54–55.

[89] Ship Register, 1734–1765, p. 203, S. C. Archives; Grant Books, XIII, 155, S. C. Archives; S. C. *Statutes*, IX, 243–246.

[90] *Gazette*, April 15, 1751.

[91] *Gazette*, July 21, 1746. Some of Nathaniel Tregagle's commercial correspondence has survived. Papers relating to Nathaniel Tregagle, 1742–1764, Aswarby Muniments, 1/23, Lincolnshire Archives Office, Lincoln, Eng.

in George Town" which he described as "a very nice house" where he "had good entertainment & good Lodgings." [92] As Thomas Blythe was a deputy surveyor, comptroller of the customs, and a justice of the peace, a great deal of business could have been transacted in his tavern.[93]

The Georgetown trade was highly profitable during the 1740's and 1750's. Fortunes were made. Some merchants became planters; others withdrew to Charleston or retired to England. Andrew and Archibald Johnston invested in plantations; Andrew Johnston later withdrew to Charleston for reasons of health, advertising for sale his two Georgetown plantations in October 1756.[94] By 1760 Nathaniel Tregagle had accumulated enough to retire to England, turning over his debts to Austin, Laurens, and Appleby for collection.[95] Paul Trapier bought Windsor plantation in 1762.[96]

These men had grown rich on the export trade in naval stores, rice, and indigo, particularly the latter. The export figures at Charleston for pitch, tar, and turpentine were at their peak in the years from 1732 through 1738, much of which still came from the neighborhood of Georgetown. The figures for the export of rice from Beaufort and Georgetown begin in the year 1732, the amount exported increasing to 4,785 barrels in 1740. The amount exported from these two ports did not surpass this figure, except in 1755, until 1761, after which date there was an increase. The decline in rice between 1740 and 1761 was due first to an increase in wartime freight rates and then to the shift to indigo. Indigo is the crop that made Georgetown rich and famous, for the indigo produced along Black River in what is now Williamsburg County was the finest produced in South Carolina. The export figures for Charleston indicate the growth of this crop.

[92] William Logan's Journal of a Journey to Georgia, 1745," *Pennsylvania Magazine of History and Biography*, XXXVI (1912), 16.

[93] George Hunter appointed Thomas Blythe deputy surveyor on May 7, 1743. Miscellaneous Records, EE (1741–1743), pp. 337–340, S. C. Archives. He became comptroller by an ordinance of May 7, 1743. *S. C. Statutes*, III, 577–578. He was justice of the peace in 1755. *Gazette*, Oct. 9, 1755. Peter Horry described his apprenticeship to Scottish merchants in Georgetown in "Memoir of Peter Horry," Guignard Papers, SCL.

[94] *Gazette*, Oct. 21, 1756.

[95] Tregagle's accounts and letters of George Appleby to Nathaniel Tregagle, Aswarby Muniments 1/23 and 10/67, Lincolnshire Archives Office, Lincoln, Eng.

[96] Alberta M. Lachicotte, *Georgetown Rice Plantations* (Columbia, S. C., 1955), p. 72.

Year	Pounds of Indigo
1747	138,334
1748	62,195
1749	138,299
1750	63,102
1751	19,891
1752	3,787
1753	28,474
1754	129,645
1755	303,531
1756	222,805
1757	876,393
1758	563,025
1759	695,661
1760	507,584 [97]

After 1760 there was a leveling-off in the production of indigo, as French West Indian indigo again became available in England and rice was once more a lucrative crop in Carolina. The peak years of indigo culture were during the French and Indian War, except for three fabulous years on the eve of the American Revolution.

Slaves were not imported into Georgetown directly. Duties were paid on slaves brought into Georgetown in the years 1755, 1764, 1765, 1769, 1771, 1772, and 1774, but these were small lots.[98] The overwhelming number of slaves brought into Georgetown were bought in Charleston. The letters of Henry Laurens describe how the indigo planters during the boom days were drawn to Charleston during the late spring and summer in order to purchase more hands for the additional acres of indigo that they had planted. The firm of Austin and Laurens would advertise their sales in the interior by circulating handbills. When a large cargo of slaves was to be sold, planters would come from as far as 100 miles. If they came that far, they would be most reluctant to

[97] *The Statistical History of the United States from Colonial Times to the Present* (Stamford, Conn., [1966]), p. 762.

[98] Public Treasurer, Journal B: Duties, 1748–1765, pp. 136, 440; Public Treasurer, Journal C: Duties, 1765–1776, pp. 571, 654, 691, 797, S. C. Archives. The largest number of slaves imported was 112 in 1774. See also Robert Higgins, "The Negro Duty Act" (MA thesis, Univ. of S. C., 1967).

return without a purchase. On these occasions the bidding was keen.[99] In this fashion slaves from James Fort on the Gambia River, Sierra Leone, Cape Mount, the Windward and Gold Coasts, Calabar, the Cameroons, and Angola were brought to the area around Winyah Bay. An important new element was thereby added to the local population.

[99] Hamer and Rogers. *op. cit.*, *II*, passim. Shackelford and Luptan in 1761 advertised 25 slaves for sale in Georgetown and George Pawley, Jr., 40 slaves in 1762. *Gazette*, Dec. 26, 1761, Feb. 20, 1762. These were undoubtedly sales of local slaves.

V

THE PARISH LEADERS

A society seldom embodies itself at one place and at one time so that it can be easily studied and observed by the historian. In those few instances when a society does come together, it usually leaves no record of its assembling. The people of the Georgetown parishes did assemble from time to time on market days, on election days, on the muster field, in church congregations, but descriptions of such assemblages do not exist. The documents that remain refer to the results of such meetings. There are lists of assemblymen, of vestrymen, and of militia officers elected at these gatherings. The only way, therefore, to study this society is to study its leaders.

On election days the voters assembled at the doors of the parish churches to cast their ballots. Every free white man over twenty-one who professed the Christian religion and who possessed a freehold of fifty acres or had paid an annual tax of at least twenty shillings and had been a resident of the province for one year before the issuing of the writs could vote. As there was rarely in Carolina during the colonial period a grant of less than fifty acres of land, most heads of families must have been qualified to vote. However, in order to take a seat in the Assembly a man must be possessed of 500 acres and ten slaves or of a house and town lots worth more than £1,000.[1] Although the qualifications for voting were democratic, the qualifications for officeholding were not. The lesser folk had to vote for their betters. Law and custom created a deferential society.

Prince George Winyah elected two members to the Assembly from 1725 to 1736. After Prince Frederick was established in 1734, each parish sent two members to the Assembly until the Revolution.[2] The men who represented the parish of Prince George from 1725 to 1736 were the settlers who had gained prominence: the Indian traders, the militia leaders, and the largest planters.

James Nicholas Mayrant, who sat in the Assembly for St. James Santee before sitting for Prince George, was a Santee River planter. He was named a justice of the peace for Craven County in the commissions of 1721 and 1724. His wife Susannah Gaillard, the daughter of another Huguenot Santee River planter, bore him one son and two daughters before his death on February 20, 1728. His son John Mayrant (1726–1767) married successively daughters of two of the leading Charleston merchants, thereby establishing a family long connected with the Georgetown region.[3] As the possessor of a famous race horse, John Mayrant was the premier sportsman along the river.[4]

Richard Smith, a militia captain, owned plantations on Winyah Bay, the Sampit, Black, and Cape Fear rivers which he worked with forty-six "choice" slaves. Although he died in 1735, he had already begun to live on an elegant scale at his home on the Sampit near Georgetown. He left to his brother, as he did not have any children, his cutlass, his gun, his case of pistols, his "rideing horse Jolly Boy," his "scarlet suit of cloaths," and to a friend his silver watch and gold ring.[5]

---

[1] The £1,000 was undoubtedly computed in currency. S. C. Statutes, III, 135–140.

[2] A complete list of those elected from the two parishes from 1725 to the Revolution is printed in Appendix I. The first election after the forming of the parish of Prince George was in 1725.

[3] John Mayrant married first (1753) Anne Stone, the daughter of William Stone, and second (1758) Ann Wooddrop, the daughter of William Wooddrop. "The Mayrant Family," compiled by Mabel L. Webber, SCHM, XXVII (1926), 81–84.

[4] [John B. Irving] The South Carolina Jockey Club (Charleston, S. C., 1857), p. 37.

[5] "Will of Richard Smith," dated Jan. 20, 1725 [1735], recorded April 28, 1735, Charleston County Wills, III (1731–1737), 161–163, S. C. Archives; Gazette, Sept. 13, 1735.

William Waties, Jr., was the son of the Welshman and Indian trader, William Waties, Sr.[6] It is difficult to distinguish between the two in the land records, but the gentleman elected from St. James Santee in 1721 was William Waties, Jr. In March 1724 he asked to be excused as the representative on the basis that his plantation was so distant from Charleston that it was inconvenient for him to attend sessions.[7] In 1728 he accepted his election to the Third Assembly in order to represent the discontented in the region beyond the Santee. Although he spent most of the 1730's extending his properties, he did accept public service on three occasions. In the spring of 1731 after a few Tuscaroras had stolen slaves and cattle from planters around Winyah Bay, Waties followed them to North Carolina and held a parley with their chiefs. He once again accepted a seat in the Assembly in 1733. In 1734 he served as a commissioner to run the boundary line between North and South Carolina. When he died he left 123 slaves, sixteen horses, 109 head of cattle, fifty-five head of sheep, one pettiauger, one ferry boat, five canoes, one set of surveying instruments, half ownership in a sloop, and bonds and notes valued at £18,311 currency.[8] He was also rich in lands, for his three sons William, John, and Thomas and his daughter Ann (who married Andrew Johnston) had been established as principal landowners. Each of his three sons later sat in the Assembly.

George Pawley, the most prominent of Major Percival Pawley's sons,[9] was elected three times to the Assembly and also served his community as commissioner of the pilotage, commissioner of Lynch's Causeway, commissioner of the new parish church of Prince George, and commissioner of the high roads on Waccamaw Neck. In 1744 he wrote the *Gazette* that "As the Common Good of Mankind ought always to be our chief Consideration" he was recommending to his neighbors a chemical composition, "Rattle-Snake-Stones," which he had found to be a useful

[6] "The Waties Family of South Carolina," compiled by H. D. Bull, *SCHM*, XLV (1944), 12–16.

[7] Commons House Journal, No. 7, Part 1 (1723–1725), p. 162, S. C. Archives.

[8] "Inventory of the estate of William Waties," recorded July 30, 1743, Inventories, KK (1739–1744), pp. 264–268, S. C. Archives.

[9] Anthony (died 1741), Percival (died 1749), and George (died 1774) were the sons of Maj. Percival Pawley. Charleston County Wills, XII, Book B (1767–1771), 435; VI (1747–1752), 328; XVI (1774–1779), 48–53, S. C. Archives.

antidote against snake bite.[10] This quality of vigilance was recognized when Governor Glen sent Pawley as his personal agent to the Cherokees in 1746.[11] Later Governor Lyttelton made use of his services by appointing him adjutant-general of the provincial militia.[12]

There were six assemblies in 1728 and 1729, the period of governmental chaos before the arrival of Governor Robert Johnson. The more prominent Georgetown men apparently withdrew from public service at this time, only returning to their seats in the Assembly after Governor Johnson's arrival. Although Meredith Hughes was the important Indian trader and militia leader, John Tompson, James Brown, John Bullen, Thomas Bonny, and Tweedie Somerville were of a lesser rank. In 1731 Captain Richard Smith and Richard Pawley came forth. Smith had served before, and Pawley was a son or nephew of Major Percival Pawley. In 1733 Smith served with William Waties, Jr. When Smith died, William Swinton was selected to fill the remainder of his term.

The Scotsman William Swinton, who was elected on April 16, 1735, was the surveyor who laid out the town and one of the three original trustees of the town. As deputy naval officer, commissioner of the pilotage, justice of the peace, and overseer of the poor, he held royal, provincial, county, and parish offices. Among his little library of a dozen books were Shaw's *Justice*, the Bible, and *An Answer to Christianity as old as the Creation*, whence came no doubt his instructions on how to uphold the new society. When he died on September 27, 1742, he left five plantations and personal property valued at £14,335.10 currency, which included sixty-two slaves and 180 head of cattle. He had married Hannah Brown, the widow of Captain James Brown. He left his two sons and his daughter a respectable fortune.[13]

Between 1736 and 1750 Prince George and Prince Frederick were represented by Georgetown merchants and planters, Santee River

[10] *Gazette*, Sept. 10, 1744.

[11] Miscellaneous Records, GG (1746–1749), p. 48, S. C. Archives; Council Journal, No. 26 (1757–1758), p. 84, S. C. Archives.

[12] *Gazette*, July 21, 1757, Sept. 22, 1759. Pawley also served twice as a commissioner to settle the boundary with North Carolina. Marvin L. Skaggs, *North Carolina Boundary Disputes Concerning her Southern Line* (Chapel Hill, N. C., 1941), pp. 42n, 73n, 113.

[13] Mrs. Henry D. Bull, "William Swinton, Surveyor and Commissioner of George-Town," unpublished manuscript; "Inventory of estate of William Swinton," appraised Sept. 27, 1742, Inventories, 1740–1743, pp. 184–187, S. C. Archives.

planters, and Charleston officials. Prince Frederick, being more distant from Charleston, relied more frequently on nonresidents to represent the parish. Throughout this decade and a half, the burden was shared with no one specializing in the role of assemblyman.

Between 1736 and 1750 Prince Frederick was represented by Thomas Henning, Maurice Lewis, James Abercromby, John Bassnett, Noah Serré, Daniel Crawford, Isaac Mazyck, David Hext, Anthony White, and John White. Thomas Henning possessed lands on the Black, Pee Dee, and Waccamaw rivers, owned town lots in Georgetown, was master of a vessel that regularly sailed between Georgetown and Charleston, and had a store in Charleston.[14] Anthony White and his son John White, both of whom were justices of the peace, were the principal residents on Black Mingo Creek. When Anthony White died in 1747 he owned 290 head of cattle, five silver table spoons, and eight volumes of the *Spectator*.[15] In March 1750 John White advertised for sale a 300-acre plantation on Black River, fifteen miles from Georgetown, which contained a commodious two-story brick dwelling-house, convenient brick outhouses, landing, fine pasture, garden, and orchard.[16]

Noah Serré and Isaac Mazyck were among the wealthiest of the Santee River planters. Serré possessed five plantations and a town house in Charleston.[17] Isaac Mazyck not only owned several plantations on the Santee but also had stores in Charleston. His own schooner plied between the two places. At the time of his death in 1771 he owned a house in Georgetown.[18]

Maurice Lewis, James Abercromby, John Bassnett, and Daniel Crawford were officials who resided in Charleston. David Hext, who lived in Charleston and planted on the Edisto, had no connection with George-

---

[14] *SCHM*, IX (1908), 95; "Thomas Henning," Pre-Revolutionary Plats, S. C. Archives; *Gazette*, Oct. 10, 31, 1741, Oct. 27, 1746.

[15] "Inventory of estate of Col. Anthony White," appraised June 27, 1747, Inventories, MM (1746–1748), pp. 309–311, S. C. Archives.

[16] *Gazette*, March 26, 1750. Col. John White died in 1760. "Will of John White," dated Feb. 24, 1758, proved Jan. 7, 1761, Charleston County Wills, IX, Book A (1760–1767), 46–49, S. C. Archives.

[17] "Will of Noah Serré," dated Nov. 30, 1744, proved Feb. 11, 1745, Charleston County Wills, V (1740–1747), 500–503, S. C. Archives.

[18] "Will of Isaac Mazyck," dated May 25, 1769, proved Feb. 6, 1771, Charleston County Wills, XIV, Book A (1771–1774), 1–12, S. C. Archives.

town, either officially or unofficially.[19] Maurice Lewis, a Welshman from
Anglesea, was first master in chancery and then judge of the vice admiralty court. He was lieutenant in the town militia of Charleston and
justice of the peace for Berkeley County. He speculated in Queensboro
and Kingston township lands and assisted the migration of his countrymen to the Welsh tract. When he died in 1739, he owned ten slaves in
Charleston and five at Winyah.[20] James Abercromby, attorney-general
of South Carolina, owned a town lot in Georgetown, 1,800 acres in
Queensboro township, and a 980-acre plantation on the Pee Dee, which
his brother managed for him.[21] John Bassnett was master in chancery.[22]
Daniel Crawford, a Charleston merchant of Scottish descent, served
that city as vendue master.[23]

Between 1736 and 1750 Prince George was represented by William
Whiteside, William Poole, Robert Austin, Joseph Huggins, Isaac Mazyck,
James Abercromby, Elias Horry, Alexander Vander Dussen, John Ouldfield, George Pawley, William Waties III, Paul Trapier, and Elias Foissin. William Whiteside was a Sampit River planter who served in Georgetown as comptroller of the provincial duties, justice of the peace, deputy
receiver-general of quit-rents, and notary public.[24] William Poole, Georgetown merchant and planter, owned at his death in 1750 a personal estate

[19] "Will of David Hext," dated May 11, 1751, proved Dec. 6, 1754, Charleston
County Wills, VII (1752–1756), 265–268, S. C. Archives; "Inventory of estate of
David Hext," appraised Dec. 12 and 19, 1754, Inventories, R (2) (1753–1756),
pp. 292–296, S. C. Archives.

[20] SCHM, II (1901), 13n.; XI (1910), 188; XIII (1912), 219; Miscellaneous
Records, DD (1732–1742), pp. 210–212, S. C. Archives; "Will of Maurice Lewis,"
dated Sept. 15, 1739, proved Nov. 7, 1739, Charleston County Wills, IV (1736–
1740), 203–204, S. C. Archives; "Inventory of estate of Maurice Lewis," appraised
Nov. 14, 1739, Inventories, 1740–1743, pp. 53–55, S. C. Archives.

[21] SCHM, IX (1908), 100; XI (1910), 187; "James Abercromby," Pre-Revolution-
ary Plats, S. C. Archives. Mary Duff wrote to her daughter Helen, May 11, 1741:
"On May we had a letter from my son James in Carolina giving an account of
William's death—who was settled 60 miles to the north from his brother in the
overseers house and near a town they call Georgetown and as it is a new plantation
I am afraid he has taking discouragement in leaving his brother and has been ill
taking care of their business. . . ." Forglen Muniments, box 1, bundle 28, Scottish
Record Office, Edinburgh, Scotland.

[22] Miscellaneous Records, KK (1754–1758), pp. 269, 380, S. C. Archives.

[23] SCHM, IX (1908), 95, 97; X (1909), 160; "Will of Daniel Crawford," dated
May 30, 1760, proved June 20, 1760, Charleston County Wills, VIII (1757–1763),
491–493, S. C. Archives; Gazette, Aug. 3, 1747.

[24] "William Whiteside," Pre-Revolutionary Plats, S. C. Archives; Gazette, April
28, 1746.

valued at £22,950 currency and 100 slaves.[25] Paul Trapier, who first took his seat in 1748, was a political figure of the 1750's.

Joseph Huggins,[26] Isaac Mazyck, and Elias Horry were Santee River planters. Elias Horry (1707–1783) in 1737 had succeeded his father Elias Horry (1664–1736) as coroner of Craven County.[27] John Ouldfield (1706–1751) was the son of John Ouldfield, the immigrant from Chester, England, who had come to St. James Goose Creek and died on the Pee Dee. The son had married on March 20, 1740, Anne LaRoche, daughter of John LaRoche and Mary Horry. Their only child Mary Ouldfield, born August 13, 1743, became the region's first great heiress when her father died in 1751 leaving her several plantations and seventy-three slaves.[28] George Pawley planted on the Waccamaw. William Waties III (1717–1751) was the third generation of his family to serve the region beyond the Santee. Elias Foissin (died 1767) was the son of Elias Foissin (died 1739). The father had owned forty-two Negro slaves, five Indian slaves, and personal property worth £10,286.17.10; the son at his death, having been a planter and justice of the peace, owned plantations on the Wando, Black, Pee Dee, and Waccamaw rivers as well as houses in Georgetown, eighty-two slaves, and personal property worth £33,-591.2.1.[29]

Prince George relied less on Charleston officials, electing only Robert Austin, James Abercromby, and Alexander Vander Dussen. Austin, a

[25] "Inventory of estate of William Poole," appraised April 19, 1750, Inventories, B (1748–1751), pp. 287–288, S. C. Archives.

[26] "Will of Joseph Huggins," dated April 25, 1758, proved Dec. 14, 1761, Charleston County Wills, IX, Book A (1760–1767), 237–238, S. C. Archives.

[27] Notes on the Horry Family, S. C. Hist. Soc.; Miscellaneous Records, DD (1732–1742), pp. 227–228, S. C. Archives.

[28] Caldwell Woodruff, "Heriots of Scotland and South Carolina" (Linthicum Heights, Md., 1939), p. 145, typed copy in S. C. Hist. Soc.; "Inventory of estate of John Ouldfield," appraised March 15, 1753, Inventories, R (1) (1751–1753), pp. 527–530, S. C. Archives. Mary Ouldfield married Robert Heriot on Nov. 5, 1761. Robert Heriot (1739–1792), who had come from Scotland via Holland and Jamaica, wrote his mother on Aug. 30, 1762, that he had arrived in Georgetown three years previously to visit "our friend & relative" John Cleland and had there met Polly Ouldfield, heiress. Her guardian was Col. Thomas Middleton, under whom Heriot had served on the expedition against the Cherokees. Woodruff, op. cit., pp. 73–75.

[29] "Inventory of estate of Elias Foissin," recorded Sept. 3, 1739, Inventories, KK (1739–1744), pp. 87–94, S. C. Archives; "Inventory of estate of Elias Foissin," appraised April 29, 30, 1767, Inventories, X (1768–1769), pp. 68–76, S. C. Archives; "Will of Elias Foissin," dated Feb. 21, 1767, proved April 15, 1767, Charleston County Wills, XI, Book A (1767–1771), 14–18, S. C. Archives.

Charleston merchant and lawyer, was a judge of the common law courts, register of the province, and captain of the town militia. He resigned his seat in the Assembly on May 18, 1742, to become comptroller of the country duties.[30] Alexander Vander Dussen, the province's most prominent military figure, had served under Oglethorpe in 1740 as colonel of a South Carolina Regiment of Foot and in October 1745 had been made a brevet lieutenant colonel in the British army in order to become the commander of the three Independent Companies then being organized in South Carolina.[31]

During the 1740's political power was shared among the merchants and planters of the parishes, who sometimes called upon their Charleston acquaintances to assist them. But these groups were slowly being knit together by marriages. An elite was forming. In the 1750's two men emerged to lead this elite; one a merchant, Paul Trapier, and the other a planter, Thomas Lynch (1720–1776). Paul Trapier, who had married Magdalene Horry in 1743, was elected in 1748, 1751, and 1757.[32] Thomas Lynch, who took as his first wife Elizabeth Allston, was elected to every Assembly with only one exception from 1751 to the Revolution.[33] Trapier and Lynch were joined in the Assembly by William Buchanan, a Santee River planter,[34] William Allston, a Waccamaw River planter,[35]

---

[30] SCHM, II (1901), 134n; XI (1910), 188; Miscellaneous Records, DD (1732-1742), pp. 237, 253, S. C. Archives; Gazette, Sept. 26, 1754; Robert L. Meriwether, The Expansion of South Carolina, 1729–1765 (Kingsport, Tenn., 1940), p. 91. He succeeded John Hext as comptroller of the country duties. Commons House Journal, No. 17, Part 2 (1742), p. 352, S. C. Archives.

[31] SCHM, XXXIII (1932), 292.

[32] Transactions of the Huguenot Society of South Carolina, No. 33 (1928), p. 58.

[33] Thomas Lynch (1720–1776) was the son of Thomas Lynch (1675–1752) and Sabina Vanderhorst. The younger Lynch married first Elizabeth Allston, the daughter of William Allston, who died in 1744, and second Hannah Motte, the daughter of the provincial treasurer, Jacob Motte. Frampton E. Ellis, Some Historic Families of South Carolina (Atlanta, Ga., 1905), pp. 29–30. In 1753 Trapier and Lynch joined twenty-five of the richest and most influential men in the province to post bonds of £1,000 each for the new public treasurer, Jacob Motte. Miscellaneous Records, II, Part 2 (1751–1754), 685, 700, S. C. Archives.

[34] William Buchanan of North Santee, planter, died in 1757. His "esteemed friend Thomas Lynch" was one of his executors. "Will of William Buchanan," dated Oct. 19, 1756, proved April 1, 1757, Charleston County Wills, VIII (1757–1763), 49–52, S. C. Archives.

[35] This was William Allston, Sr., the son of William Allston, who died in 1744. His brothers were Joseph and John Allston. His brothers-in-law were Thomas and John Waties, Archibald Johnston, and Thomas Lynch. "Will of William Allston," dated

and John and Thomas Waties, the sons of William Waties, Jr., who themselves had married sisters, the daughters of William Allston, who had died in 1744.[36]

The only outsider was George Gabriel Powell, a Welsh adventurer. After being dismissed in 1743 as deputy governor of the island of St. Helena, he returned briefly to England and then came out to Carolina where he acquired a plantation near Georgetown. Because of his military reputation, he was appointed a colonel in the militia and in 1759 commanded the Craven County militia in Lyttelton's expedition.[37]

By 1754 the back parts of Prince Frederick could outvote the lower sections of the parish and sent Richard Richardson [38] and Joseph Cantey [39] to the Assembly. Richardson and Cantey continued to lead this region after it became in 1757 the parish of St. Mark's. Although the Cherokee campaigns of 1759, 1760, and 1761 kept the backcountry in turmoil, Richardson so successfully defended his section that his grateful fellow parishioners gave him a present of silver plate in 1762.[40] Prince Frederick also turned to militia leaders during these troublesome times, selecting in turn Colonel Powell, Dr. James Crockatt (who was captain of the Black River Church militia company),[41] and John and William Moultrie (officers in Colonel Thomas Middleton's regiment of provincial troops).[42] Actually, Prince Frederick found it difficult to fill her places in the Assemblies of 1760 and 1761.

Jan. 29, 1743, proved April 12, 1744, Charleston County Wills, V (1740–1747), 292–294, S. C. Archives.

[36] John Waties died in 1760 and Thomas Waties in 1762. "The Waties Family of South Carolina," compiled by H. D. Bull, SCHM, XLV (1944), 15–16.

[37] SCHM, XXXVI (1935), 34–35. Powell took out three grants in Craven County totaling 794½ acres between 1769 and 1771. Index to Grants, S. C. Archives.

[38] Col. Richard Richardson (1704–1780) owned a plantation on the Wateree, married in 1738 Mary Cantey, first cousin once removed of Joseph Cantey, and commanded a regiment in the Cherokee War in 1759. SCHM, XI (1910), 225–226.

[39] Capt. Joseph Cantey (1704–1763) bought "Mount Hope" on the Santee in 1739. He was a commissioner to build St. Mark's Church in 1757. He owned only three slaves. "Inventory of estate of Joseph Cantey," recorded Feb. 27, 1764, Inventories, 1763–1767, pp. 22–23, S. C. Archives; Joseph S. Ames, "The Cantey Family," SCHM, XI (1910), 216–217.

[40] Gazette, Oct. 2, 1762.

[41] Dr. Crockatt was a member of the Charleston Library Society in 1750; he died on April 14, 1765. Joseph Ioor Waring, A History of Medicine in South Carolina, 1670–1825 (Columbia, S. C., 1964), pp. 69, 385.

[42] Gazette, May 30, 1761.

The members of the Royal Council, drawn from the top of the society, were appointed by the crown on the recommendation of the governor. In the period of Georgetown's early and rapid growth, two men closely connected with the parish of Prince George were appointed to the Council. James Kinloch, a Scotsman, was appointed to the Council in 1720 and died in 1757. He had possessed lands in the parish of St. James Goose Creek at the juncture of the Indian path and the road to Winyah and had extended his planting interests by acquiring lands in Prince George. At his death he owned 13,081 acres.[43] John Cleland, also a Scotsman, was appointed a councilor in 1740 and served until his death in 1760. Cleland had arrived in the first half of 1735 from London with his wife, whose dowry included the site of Georgetown. He served as deputy naval officer in Charleston and pursued a career as merchant there until 1740 when he retired from trade.[44] These two families were joined in 1751 by the marriage of Kinloch's only surviving son Francis to Cleland's only child Nancy.[45]

The Council shared with the governor the power to appoint justices of the peace for each county. Therefore, Cleland and Kinloch undoubtedly suggested names for the list of Craven County justices. Almost all of those who sat in the Assembly from Prince George and Prince Frederick were justices of the peace, if not of Craven County, at least of Berkeley County. These justices were conservators of the peace appointed from "the most sufficient persons" dwelling in the counties. Their commissions, passed under the great seal of the province, were customarily read at the opening of the Court of General Sessions in Charleston. Lists were announced from time to time, not annually. There are known lists for 1721, 1724, 1734, 1737, 1756, 1761, and 1762. These justices were responsible for local government in the counties. William Simpson emphasized their importance by writing in 1761 in his handbook for the Carolina justice: "If this office be duly executed, the whole christian world hath not the like."[46]

[43] M. Eugene Sirmans, "The South Carolina Royal Council, 1720–1763," *William and Mary Quarterly*, XVIII (1961), 392; "James Kinloch," Pre-Revolutionary Plats, S. C. Archives.

[44] Miscellaneous Records, DD (1732–1742), pp. 180–181, S. C. Archives; *Gazette*, May 3, 1740.

[45] *Gazette*, Feb. 18, 1751.

[46] William Simpson, *The Practical Justice of the Peace and Parish-Officer, of His*

The justice had no power to hear or determine any breach of the peace whatever. In the case of assault and battery, burglary, homicide, larceny, rape, robbery, etc., he had only the power to examine, to bail (if the offense was bailable), or to bind over to the Court of General Sessions. If the last, he would turn over the person to the constable, who would take the prisoner to the jail in Charleston (for there was none in Georgetown before 1772) where he would be detained until the opening of the court.[47] The prisoner would then be tried upon a presentment upon the statute. The justices of the peace tried only causes "small and mean," which by the law of 1745 included only those cases involving less than £20 current money. Cases involving larger sums were heard in the Court of Common Pleas in Charleston. The justices, therefore, never determined any offenses wherein trial by jury was required.[48]

The common law courts were convened in Charleston. The juries were drawn from time to time from the annual lists of the provincial taxpayers. Jurors were fined if they failed to attend. The names of men from Craven County were often drawn, but few actually went to Charleston to sit on juries as the expense and time involved were both excessive. It was easier to pay the fine of £5 for failure to attend as a petit juror or £10 for failure to attend as a grand juror. Of the seventy-one men called from these two parishes between November 12, 1754, and April 5, 1763,

---

Majesty's Province of South-Carolina (Charleston, S. C., 1761), p. 126. The description of the work of the justice of the peace is drawn from this book. For the lists of the justices of the peace, see Council Journal, May 29, 1721–June 10, 1721 (under date June 1, 1721) and Probate Court Book, 1722–1724, p. 304, S. C. Archives; *Gazette*, June 15, 1734, April 2, 1737, Nov. 4, 1756, March 28, 1761, and April 3, 1762. The people who lived within the fork of Drowning Creek and Little Pee Dee River petitioned the governor in 1757 for a justice of the peace as there was not one within fifty or sixty miles of them. For want of a justice of the peace the place was "a harbour for all manner of ill disposed persons such as horse thieves cow stealers hog stealers sabbath brakers blasphemers such as leaves their own wives and takes other mens wives Nay in short the place is so settled with rogues that an honest man can scarce live among them." Petition from Craven County, June 16, 1757, Lyttelton Papers, WLCL.

[47] James Jenkins, constable, lost his prisoner (a counterfeiter) and his wallet at Santee on his way to Charleston in 1760. *Gazette*, Dec. 23, 1760. Another counterfeiter being sent by Charles Woodmason to Charleston from Black River escaped en route in 1762. *Gazette*, Sept. 25, 1762.

[48] Unless some were held in the precinct courts established by the act of Sept. 20, 1721. The original of this law has been lost. S. C. *Statutes*, III, 147.

only twelve attended.[49] As the *Gazette* usually published a list of those who refused to sit, the extent of this failure to serve was publicly known. Daniel LaRoche, Thomas Potts, and Pierce [Percival] Pawley were fined £5 each in 1752; John Pyatt was fined in 1754; Paul Trapier, Allard Belin, and Nathaniel Tregagle were fined in 1756; and Colonel George Pawley and Job Rothmahler were fined £10 each in 1762.[50] Just as the men of these parishes tended to turn over the problems of representation to men in Charleston, they also turned over to them their duties as jurormen. If less than twelve appeared to serve as jurors from throughout the province, the additional members of the jury were made up by drawing names from a box containing only Charleston names.[51] The right to trial by a jury of one's peers was presumably one of the rights that the patriots fought for in the Revolution!

The justices served their plantation society in a number of ways. If stray horses and cattle broke into fields (which by law were supposed to have fences six feet high), then the justice of the peace was required to advertise the animals in the *Gazette* or at a place of divine worship. The owners upon payment of a fee could recover their animals. Such advertisements signed by the justices of the peace frequently appeared in the *Gazette*.[52]

The role of the justice of the peace in the preservation of the institution of slavery was important. If slaves were discovered off their plantations without tickets or if an owner did not provide proper food and clothing or if an owner worked his slaves more than fifteen hours a day in the summer or fourteen hours in the winter, then the masters could be fined. If runaway slaves were discovered, and their owners were unknown, they could be sent to the work house in Charleston. If a slave had committed a crime, he was tried before a freeholders court which was composed in capital offenses of two justices of the peace and three freeholders. Justices might give the judgment and order the constables to carry out the sentence summarily. If the slave was

[49] Journal of the Court of Common Pleas, Nov. 12, 1754–April 5, 1763, passim, S. C. Archives.

[50] *Gazette*, April 6, 1752, March 26, 1754, Sept. 4, Dec. 23, 1756, Oct. 30, 1762.

[51] S. C. *Statutes*, III 274–287.

[52] *Gazette*, March 12, April 16, 1744, July 6, 1745, June 30, 1746.

executed, the justice of the peace valued the slave so that the owner could be reimbursed from the public treasury.[53]

The justice of the peace not only made out the original indenture for indentured servants but also certified the additional time that was due after a servant had run away and been retaken. At the time of the freeing of the indentured servant the justice of the peace endorsed the certificate of freedom. If there was any dispute concerning wages, indenture, or freedom, two justices of the peace decided, but appeal could be taken from their decision to the governor and Council, meeting together as the highest court of appeals in the colony. Runaway slaves, runaway servants, and deserting seamen were to be handled in much the same way. Since the latter two groups were white and therefore more difficult to discover, justices of the peace were permitted to issue traveling certificates to free men so that they might move about without hindrance. Servitude, indenture, apprenticeship were common; the state of freedom, at least for the ordinary man, less so. Thus, the need for internal passports. Indeed, every man needed a justice of the peace's license to travel on horseback on the Lord's day.

Justices were required to grant licenses to hawkers and peddlers. Anyone trading without a license was carried before the justice; anyone dealing directly with a slave was subject to punishment. Twice a year the justices of a county met together to grant tavern certificates to tavern-keepers, these certificates being exchanged for a license from the public treasurer.

The constables were lesser figures who carried out the warrants issued to them by the justices. It was the constable who might raise the power of the parish in hue and cry. All males sixteen to sixty were subject to appointment as constables. The selection was made by the chief justice and assistant judges at the annual meeting in Charleston in the spring of the Court of General Sessions. They served for a year or until discharged. Those appointed one year must attend the court the next year in order to make the presentments. This requirement demanded attendance once a year in Charleston.

---

[53] In 1739 two slaves owned by William Romsey and Co. were tried by a freeholders' court for attempting to run away to St. Augustine. One was executed and his body hung in chains at Hangman's Point in Charleston "in sight of all Negroes passing and repassing by Water." *Gazette*, April 12, 1739.

A great many of the assemblymen and the justices of the peace were also officers in the militia. The basic militia law of 1747 stated that all males sixteen to sixty were to be in the militia.[54] The governor could organize one or more regiment in each county and one or more company in each parish. The officers of each unit were appointed by the governor. Ordinary musters would be held in the parishes; general musters in the county. The captains of each company would be responsible for keeping a roll of all eligible males in his parish. As slaves could be included in the militia if the owners would certify to their good behavior, a list of slaves available for service would be kept. The commissioned officers had power to call out the militia to suppress pirates, sea rovers, Indians, and bands of runaway slaves. The governor might call out the militia in time of invasion or insurrection. The alarm would be sounded by the firing of guns. The captains appointed two sergeants who carried out the orders of the captains in much the same way as the constables carried out the orders of the justices of the peace.

The Council Journal for May 4, 1757, gives a complete organizational chart for the seven regiments and three troops of horse then organized in the province.[55] The officers of the Craven County Regiment were George Pawley, colonel, John White, lieutenant colonel, John Waties, adjutant, and Alexander McDowell, surgeon. Of the twenty-eight companies in this regiment, two were organized south of the Santee. Daniel Horry was captain of the St. James Santee company, and Charles Cantey was lieutenant of the St. Stephen's Fair Forest company. The North Side of Santee company was commanded by John Jennerett, captain, and Albert Lenud, lieutenant; the Lower District Santee had as its lieutenant John Horry.

In and around Georgetown there were six companies. Benjamin Trapier was captain, Thomas Blythe lieutenant, and William Shackelford ensign of the Georgetown company. Percival Pawley was captain, Josias Allston lieutenant, and Joseph Allston ensign of the company on Waccamaw Neck. Anthony White was captain of the Black River company. Dr.

---

[54] S. C. Statutes, IX, 645–663.

[55] Council Journal, No. 26 (1757–1758), pp. 84–86, S. C. Archives. Job Rothmahler was major according to the "List of Craven County Regiment under the command of Colonel George Pawley, 1756," in the Henry E. Huntington Library, San Marino, Calif.

James Crockatt was captain and Charles Woodmason lieutenant of the Black River Church company. Isaac Brunson was captain, Richard Richardson lieutenant, and Samuel Cantey ensign of the Black River Head Company. John Chessborough was captain and John Godfrey lieutenant of the Lower Pee Dee company. The other companies in Craven County were formed in the following areas: Williamsburg Township (two companies), Kings Township Waccamaw, Little Pee Dee, west of Wateree River, east of Wateree River, Britton's Neck, in the Congaree Forks, on Broad River, on west side of Wateree River (two companies), on Waxaws (two companies of which Andrew Pickens was the captain of one), on Wateree above the Catawba Towns, on the north branch of Lynches Creek, on the south branch of Lynches Creek, Indian Town company on the head of Black Mingo, and on the head of Black River and Lynches Creek. There were 61 officers, 1,809 men, 79 alarm men, and 2,271 slaves. This is an early census of the region, particularly of the slaves. There were more than 300 eligible slaves in St. James Santee and in St. Stephens; more than 200 each in Georgetown, Black River, and Lower Pee Dee; and more than 100 in North Santee, Waccamaw Neck, and Williamsburg Township; and almost none for the backcountry companies.

In colonial America there were several categories of troops. There were the regulars, regiments raised in England and paid by England; there were independents, regiments raised in America but paid by England; there were provincials, regiments raised in America and paid by the colonies; there were also volunteer elite companies, raised locally and serving without pay. The militia was at the bottom of this list in every way and was never considered an effective fighting force.[56] It was seldom called out except as in 1745 when a Spanish privateer threatened Georgetown from the sea.[57] Only in 1759, when Governor Lyttelton tried to organize an expedition against the Cherokees, was there a large-scale mobilization of the militia. On that occasion in October 1759 the alarm guns were fired in Charleston and echoed throughout the province.[58] The militia mustered. The regiment of the Upper Craven

---

[56] John Shy, *Toward Lexington, The Role of the British Army in the Coming of the American Revolution* (Princeton, N. J., 1965), pp. 3–44.

[57] *Gazette*, Aug. 19, 1745.

[58] *Gazette*, Oct. 13, 1759.

County militia assembled at Lynches Lake under the command of Colonel George Gabriel Powell, who had succeeded George Pawley. Powell in his letters to Lyttelton explained how difficult it was to gather the men together, secure supplies for them, and march them to the rendezvous at the Congarees.[59] Governor Lyttelton had tried to increase the efficiency of the militia by attending general musters throughout the province. He had reviewed the Craven County Regiment in April 1757 at Winyah.[60] Lyttelton appointed George Pawley adjutant general of the province, and Pawley had taken his duties seriously. In the fall of 1759 Pawley attended every muster: on October 2 "at Mr. Kinloch's Old Field on Santee," on October 4 at Georgetown, on October 8 at Black Mingo, and on October 11 at "Marr's Bluff" on the Pee Dee.[61] The expedition of 1759, however, was not a success.[62] Two expeditions manned by British regulars were necessary in 1760 and 1761 to quell the Indians. Clearly, the militia could be used near home, but at a distance it was not effective.[63] The titles of the officers. however, were greatly cherished and gave status to the holders in Southern society.

The patrol was drawn from the militia. Each parish was divided into patrol districts. At each muster day the captain of the militia company picked from the list a number of persons who would serve as a patrol until the next muster day, the patrol riding its rounds once a fortnight. The patrols might whip Negroes found out of their places.[64]

In contrast to the justices of the peace and the militia officers who were appointed by the governor and the Council, the church wardens and vestrymen were elected annually by the people on Easter Monday. There were two church wardens and seven vestrymen in each parish.

[59] *Gazette,* Nov. 10, 1759; George Gabriel Powell to William Henry Lyttelton, Oct. 20 and 29, 1759, Lyttelton Papers, WLCL.

[60] *Gazette,* April 14, 1757.

[61] *Gazette,* Sept. 22, 1759.

[62] Gadsden, James Coachman, Withers, Francis Marion, Robert Heriot, Alexander Fyffe, John Moultrie, and others had volunteered. Christopher Gadsden to Lyttelton, Oct. 31, 1759, Lyttelton Papers, WLCL.

[63] On Feb. 27, 1760, George Pawley wrote Governor Lyttelton from Georgetown saying that he had received a letter from Lt. Col. John White enclosing one from Thomas Potts, Jr., an inhabitant about twenty miles from Georgetown on the Black River. Both letters begged for help as the Indians were upon them. Pawley added that he was marching that night with one-half of the Georgetown company of militia. Lyttelton Papers, WLCL.

[64] Simpson, *op. cit.,* pp. 194–199.

The parish itself was a unit of local government, as much an administrative as an ecclesiastical division. Freeholders who were members of the Church of England were eligible to vote.

The vestries appointed registers, clerks, and sextons. The register kept a record of the births, baptisms, marriages, and deaths of everybody in the parish. There were fines for those who failed to record such events in their families. The clerk kept the minutes of the vestry meetings, acting as secretary to that body. Quite often the register and the clerk were the same person, as the remuneration for each job was small. The eighteenth-century register for the parish of Prince George has been lost, as have the minutes of the vestry meetings. The names of a few of the church wardens can be recovered from the *Gazette* from advertisements concerning church affairs placed in that newspaper.[65] Fortunately, both the register and vestry minutes for Prince Frederick survive, the latter providing an insight into the administrative aspects of parish work.

The church wardens and the vestrymen had to take three oaths and subscribe to one declaration, which were administered to them by a justice of the peace.[66] The vestry worked closely with the justices of the peace and militia officers. Poor apprentices might be bound by the church wardens, but the indentures had to be certified by a justice of the peace. On March 1, 1757, the church wardens at Prince Frederick apprenticed Shadrack MacCormack, a poor orphan, then seven years of age, to John Simpson, a cooper on Jeffrey's Creek, "till the sad Boy came of age." [67] In 1762, Drury Lane, an orphan child about ten years of age, was bound an apprentice to Jacob Burton, shoemaker, until he arrived at the age of twenty-one. Some certificates of apprenticeship have been recorded among the Miscellaneous Records of the secretary

[65] Thomas Godfrey and William Luptan were church wardens on April 7, 1759; Paul Trapier and John Withers on March 23, 1761; and Thomas Wright and Benjamin Perdriau on July 28, 1762. *Gazette*, May 12, 1759, May 9, 1761, Aug. 6 [7], 1762. Sometimes the names of the church wardens are given in the return of the writs in the journals of the Commons House of Assembly. The most complete list is to be found in [H. D. Bull], *Rectors, Wardens and Vestry, Prince George, Winyah, 1721–1953* (n.p., n.d.).

[66] Simpson, *op. cit.*, pp. 77–81.

[67] *The Register Book of the Parish Prince Frederick Winyaw*, ed. Elizabeth W. Allston Pringle (Baltimore, Md., 1916), p. 145. The following story of poor relief is drawn from this book. The names may be found in the index.

of the province, but none relating to these instances in Prince Frederick Parish have been discovered. Another duty of the church wardens was to inspect the arms of the parishioners on Sunday as a law required arms to be brought to church. The church door was in fact the local bulletin board, for it was presumably the spot seen most regularly by the people.

Overseers of the poor were parish officials, who were also elected annually on Easter Monday. They looked after the orphans, the aged, the blind, the mad, and buried the poor dead. They ascertained the amount needed to care for these unfortunates, set the poor rates for the year, collected the tax and distributed it, making sure that value was received for the money expended. Customarily, two overseers of the poor were elected. William Swinton and Robert Robinson, elected in 1730, were the first to appear in the records. Prince Frederick elected three in 1766 and four in 1774.

When an orphan child was taken on the parish at £30 per year, as the minutes might read, it meant that the child had been placed with a family who were allowed £30 for caring for the child. In 1757 Michael Carey, "an infirm and poor Person, an Object of Charity, and incapable of Labour having lost his Eye Sight," was taken on the poor rates and was maintained by the parish until 1779. Henry Yaw, who first agreed to maintain him, was instructed to find him sufficient "Meat, Drink, Washing, Lodging, Linen, and Cloaths." The cost of maintaining Carey varied from £51 to £110 a year. No institution was provided in the parish for the orphans, the old, and the blind, but families, for a small addition to their income, took this duty upon themselves.

Like all welfare systems, this system could be abused. The case of Mary Bonnell, taken on the parish in 1766, is a case in point. Since she was mad, the wardens asked a doctor to prescribe for her "toward the retreavend, her Sencess." John Godfrey boarded her first for £100 a year; then Charles Wilson offered to keep her for £69 per annum. In 1770 the vestry made a contract with Thomas Nowland and his wife to board Michael Carey and Mary Bonnell for a total sum of £94. The Nowlands were also to board Margarett Spencer for £55. These sums were below what others had charged to maintain these individuals, and Thomas Nowland was soon thereafter charged with the mistreatment of those in his care. On December 5, 1770, the vestry removed Carey and

Spencer from the care of the Nowlands, calling at the same time for an inquest into the death of Mary Bonnell, who had died on November 3. A jury of good and lawful men of the county of Craven were impaneled and ordered to dig up and view the body, which they did, but since it had been lying thirty-six days it was difficult to tell the cause of death. Depositions were then taken from the neighbors of the Nowlands on November 8 at Black Mingo and on the tenth at Black River church.

The depositions were taken before Samuel Nesmith, a justice of the peace. The most damning deposition was that given by Mary Williams, who said she had heard on the morning of November 3 a person at Thomas Nowland's house before sunrise crying: "O lord, O lord, murder, murder, and at same time heard Mrs. Lucretia Nowland Daming and Cursing & further she sath not." Michael Carey, the blind old man, testified that Mary Bonnell had taken a table out of the house to scour. A little later he had heard Mrs. Nowland disputing and then crying out to him to help her with Mary Bonnell, whom she believed to be dead. He helped Mrs. Nowland bring her into the house, but she died almost immediately. Thomas Nowland himself stated that he had gone to get some beef and that when he returned he met his wife at the door who said that Mary Bonnell had died suddenly. Mrs. Nowland's deposition stated: "before Sun Rise Mary Bonnell cared out the table to be scoured, then she Complin'd of her Stomack, and Everything looked dark before her Eyes, and fell down, against a post in the peach, then She and Michael help her to the bed and said Lucretia put on a Clean shift Emediately and let her lye till her husband came home."

Those who assisted in preparing the body for burial testified at Black Mingo on December 8. Cornelius Nelson said that Thomas Nowland came on the afternoon of the third of November for a coffin. Nelson had been much surprised at that time to learn that Mary Bonnell was dead, for she had been "very merry a singing" the Thursday before. In helping to put Mary Bonnell in the coffin he had seen two different bruised marks on each arm. Mrs. Hannah Nelson, who had helped prepare the body, said that she had seen "a small black spot on Mary Bonnell Breast." After securing these depositions and weighing the evidence, the jury were of the verdict that "Mary Bonnell did dy a hasty sudden death, but it does not appear to us to the Other ways than by the hand of God."

Another charge on the poor rate was for the burial of the poor. Thomas Cribb was allowed £10 for the burial "of a Traveller, who dy'd at his House." Richard Cockburn received at the same time £10 for the burial of a soldier. Obviously, those who died had to be buried quickly; remuneration must come after the deed. Occasionally the vestry might order a coffin; they paid 3s. 10d. for one in 1765.

Medical care was also provided. Dr. William Fyffe was paid for the medicines that he prescribed for Mary Bonnell. Dr. Andrew Burnett was paid 6s. 10d. for attendance on Rachel Downing in 1764. When Dr. Wood boarded Margaret Mathews in his own home while he treated her for a "Turrible disorder," he was paid £10 a month and an extra £50 upon her cure.

The poor themselves might apply for assistance. Mathew Orchard applied "for the Benefit of the Parrish as Being Unable to Get his Liveing for some time Past." When Daniel Fitzpatrick applied "as an object of charity," the vestry agreed to maintain him if he could find a place to board. Neighbors, of course, might speak in behalf of some unhappy person. On January 21, 1778, thirteen men signed a petition to the church wardens of Prince Frederick in behalf of Margret Marten, who had been reduced to want and poverty by the "Polsey." As she had been in the province upwards of thirty years and was of good reputation in the neighborhood, she deserved consideration from the parish.

There was always a conscious attempt to reduce the financial burden upon the parish. Contracts for maintaining the poor were let annually, and each year cheaper accommodations were sought. When there was a complaint that the widow Hughes and her two children were starving, the wardens took the two biggest children and put them out as apprentices in creditable houses and then insisted that the widow go to work to maintain herself and young child, as "she is verry Able & A Great deel of Spinning offerd her." On one occasion a man was paid £20 for carrying a child to Cape Fear to reduce the burden upon the parish. Mathew Orchard had suggested that if the parish would give him £20 he would go northward and "not be any further trouble to the parish."

The one attempt to bring in a large group of unfortunate people and place them upon the parish was a failure. Thirty-two Acadians were sent from Charleston in August 1756 to be lodged, maintained, and accommodated by the parish until otherwise provided for. The vestry said that they might live in the parsonage house but refused to provide any further for their reception. Dr. James Crockatt and Charles Woodmason (who were also justices of the peace and militia officers) were left to do what they could for these people. On August 10 they divided them out among the people of the parish, but most of them were taken in by Crockatt, Woodmason, Dr. Andrew Burnett, and Reverend John Baxter, the Presbyterian clergyman. They were in a truly deplorable state; six of them died by the first week of November.[68] Public-spirited citizens had stepped in when the parish officials had refused to cooperate. There may have been some distaste for these French Catholics, but undoubtedly the parish welfare organization was not strong enough to withstand burdens of this sort.

The parish expenditures varied from year to year. In 1762 the sum in Prince Frederick was £89.5; in 1774 it was £400.18.3. The annual figure was usually about £200 currency. These sums were raised by a rate placed on slaves, land, money out at interest, and stock in trade. The principal source of income was from the head tax on slaves which varied during these years between 1s. and 2s. 6d per slave. In the early years of the parish this might have been the only rate in the poor tax levied. In 1756 the vestry advertised for the inhabitants to turn in a list of their slaves to the collector of the poor tax.[69] A typical advertisement is that of Prince George Parish in the *Gazette* of August 6, 1762: the rates were 2s. 6d. per head on slaves, 2s. 6d. per 100 acres of land, and 1s. 3d. on each £100 at interest, stock in trade, value of town lots, faculties, professions, handicrafts, etc. The poor rate was an income tax on the rich for the benefit of the poor.

The provincial taxes were set by the Commons House of Assembly once a year in the general tax law. The annual law designated individuals in each parish to be the inquirers and collectors of the general tax. This was another duty the leading men must assume from time to time.

[68] Thirty-six Acadians were sent to Prince George and thirty-one to Prince Frederick, according to Chapman J. Milling, *Exile Without an End* (Columbia, S. C., 1943), pp. 39–40. According to the *Gazette*, eighty Acadians set out in canoes accompanied by scout boats for Winyah. *Gazette*, May 7, 1756.

[69] *Gazette*, Oct. 21, 1756.

As Charles Woodmason complained in 1762 when he was inquirer and collector, these officials should have been fixed permanently in their jobs in order that they might become acquainted with the procedure and also with those who customarily avoided paying their taxes.[70]

There was taxing, therefore, at many levels. Parliament itself did not tax the people, unless one considers the duties on certain imports collected by the royal officials as a form of taxation, rather than of regulation of trade. The crown demanded quit-rents, which were paid throughout this period, although perhaps not always collected in the most convenient fashion. Fees, of course, were paid to royal officials for making out land grants. Fees were also collected by the justices of the peace and the constables who were appointed by the governor. The assemblymen, who were elected, taxed the people directly in the general tax. The commissioners, who were appointed by the Assembly for local purposes (to supply pilots or to build Lynch's Causeway), sometimes taxed the people. The commissioners of the roads demanded service from each master's slaves usually in the fall after the corps were in. Although no evidence remains, the town trustees of Georgetown most probably taxed the townsmen. The church wardens, vestrymen, and overseers of the poor also taxed the people. In most instances, therefore, the people were taxed by their representatives.

Assemblymen, justices of the peace, militia officers, church wardens, vestrymen, overseers of the poor, commissioners for high roads, tax collectors—these were the officials who governed the community. Among these men there was a great deal of plural officeholding. The prominent were supposed to serve; it was their duty. If they did not serve, they could in some instances be fined. The eighteenth-century merchant and planter had a duty to the public that was almost impossible to avoid. The state rested upon such service.

This was not an aristocratic society in the European sense, for a privileged position was not passed on to the next generation by hereditary right. Francis Kinloch, although the son and son-in-law of royal councilors, never sat in the Royal Council of South Carolina. There were

---

[70] *Gazette*, March 26, 1753, March 20, 1762. For proof that the leading men served as inquirers, assessors, and collectors of the general tax in rotation see *S. C. Statutes*, III, 353, 385, 440, 475, 504, 529; IV, 56, 132, 192.

two corporate bodies within the parishes, but these did not become nuclei for privileged groups. The trustees of Georgetown were a self-perpetuating body, but it would have taken several generations for the original three to have spawned an aristocracy. The Winyah Indigo Society, established in 1757, was also too young. A Georgetown elite was emerging, but it was not buttressed by institutions; it was self-created and self-disciplined.

Charles S. Sydnor in *Gentlemen Freeholders*[71] has described eighteenth-century Virginia as a society characterized by the special training the gentry got for public affairs by holding numerous local offices. This training in local government served the gentry well when they went on to the House of Burgesses and to the Continental Congress. Sydnor's picture of Virginia is not inapplicable to South Carolina. The Georgetown gentry had much the same sort of training in local offices. Seldom did any man advance to the Assembly until he had served his community at home.

Robert and Katherine Brown have tried to refute Sydnor's view of a developing aristocracy by asserting that Virginia was essentially a democratic society since most men could vote and did vote.[72] But, as the critics of the Browns have pointed out, the men voted for their superiors; it was a deferential society. The Browns, admitting that there were some aristocratic overtones, ascribed them to the pull of British examples and institutions. There was, of course, a tug in the British direction in both Virginia and South Carolina and that tendency was toward aristocracy.

The entire Georgetown society was tied to the British crown by oaths. The assemblyman had to take oaths in order to serve in the Assembly. He took these oaths before the governor, the king's personal representative in the colony, and these oaths spelled out his duties of obedience to the royal family. Before any man could be commissioned a justice of the peace he had to take four oaths (the oaths of allegiance, of supremacy, of abjuration, and of justice of the peace) and sign a declaration against popery. The militia officers had their oaths, and the

[71] Charles S. Sydnor, *Gentlemen Freeholders: Political Practices in Washington's Virginia* (Chapel Hill, N. C., 1952).
[72] Robert E. and B. Katherine Brown, *Virginia, 1705–1786: Democracy or Aristocracy?* (East Lansing, Mich., 1964).

church wardens and vestrymen had theirs.[73] Each official took an oath to uphold the crown, and not Parliament. And sometimes these oaths were renewed. Governor Lyttelton shortly after his arrival issued a proclamation on June 4, 1756, ordering all oaths to be readministered "to all Judges, Justices, and other Persons that hold any Office of Trust or Profit within this Province." To make it easier for men distant from Charleston, he appointed deputies throughout the province before whom the oaths could be taken. Paul Trapier and George Pawley were to administer the oaths in Georgetown; Thomas Lynch and Tacitus Gaillard at Santee.[74] The tug of loyalty was great. This was a miniature England.

[73] See Simpson, *op. cit.*, pp. 1–7, 191–192.
[74] *Gazette,* June 5, 1756.

VI

THE CULTURE OF COLONIAL GEORGETOWN

The bustle of a frontier community provides little time for reflection, and without reflection there can be no culture. The people were engaged in getting and acquiring, not in thinking. The struggle with nature, the management of a raw labor force, the dangers of the sea and of the rivers, and the chaos of the backcountry kept each man tied to a daily routine that was more relentless and grinding than inspiring. Leisure did begin to appear by the 1740's, particularly among the planting families. Whether it was Noah Serré at his home in Charleston or John Ouldfield at his home in the parish, there were some who could quite early provide their children with books and musical instruments that would widen their horizons and lift their souls beyond the ordinary limits. Yet the culture acquired was largely transplanted, brought from Great Britain or in a few cases obliquely descending from France.

The chief civilizing agent in the early years was the church. The clergymen sent out by the Society for the Propagation of the Gospel in Foreign Parts to the new parishes were men who had been educated at Oxford or Cambridge or Trinity College, Dublin, and, no matter how poorly they performed, they brought something of their learning with them. The cultural center, though at best a meager one, was the parish church and the parsonage house.

A church was begun on Black River in Prince George parish in 1726, launched with a handsome subscription from Governor Francis Nicholson.[1] The Reverend Thomas Morritt, the first minister, had been sent out by the Society for the Propagation of the Gospel in Foreign Parts (S.P.G.), but through "inadvertency" had not been licensed to officiate. He had remained in Charleston as master of the free school until the pressing pleas of the new parish drew him to Prince George in 1728. When the new parish of Prince Frederick was formed in 1734, each of the parishes claimed his services, but by then he was being criticized for devoting too much of his time to trade and planting. When Commissary Alexander Garden cited him to answer complaints, he resigned.[2] Morritt unwittingly had set a pattern for the future clergymen by succumbing to the lure of riches. The society transformed the clergy more than the clergy transformed society, and this was to be true of Carolina clergymen for centuries.

Morritt's successor was the Reverend John Fordyce, who had been sent out by the S.P.G. first to Nova Scotia and then to Carolina. He served the parish of Prince Frederick longer than any clergyman served either of these parishes before the Revolution.[3] Fordyce must have been a very busy man, tending his flock on Black River, at the new town on Winyah Bay, and on Waccamaw Neck. It is difficult to draw a picture of these country parsons, but the inventory of the Reverend John Fordyce's estate gives a few hints of what that picture might be—of a parson writing a sermon at home, or circulating about his parish, or even tending his glebe.

There sits the Reverend John Fordyce with his spectacles on, his satin shoes with silver shoe-buckles pushed under the old desk, "a parcel of

[1] Frederick Dalcho, *An Historical Account of the Protestant Episcopal Church, in South-Carolina* (Charleston, S. C., 1820), pp. 303–304.

[2] *The Fulham Papers in the Lambeth Palace Library*, compiled by William Wilson Manross (Oxford, Eng., 1965), pp. 135–136, 140, 143, 146–148; Helen E. Livingston, "Thomas Morritt, Schoolmaster at the Charleston Free School, 1723–1728," *Historical Magazine of the Protestant Episcopal Church*, XIV (1945), 151–167.

[3] John Fordyce arrived March 4, 1736. He served the parish before being officially elected. The precept for his election was issued on May 22, 1741, to the parish of Prince Frederick by the church commissioners. The return of the precept signifying his election was dated March 9, 1742. The election was approved by the church commissioners on May 25, 1742. Church Commissioners Book, 1717–1742 [1743], pp. 63, 72, 77–78, S. C. Archives. Also see Dalcho, *op. cit.*, pp. 307, 319–320; Manross, *op. cit.*, p. 153.

books consisting of religious and prophane tracts" in his bookcase, ten quires of paper at hand, with a "fountain pin" or "steel pencil" with which to jot down his notes, perhaps a pinch from the silver snuff box or a drop from the liquor case to clear the head and keep the thoughts coming, and a silver watch to tell him of the passage of time. When he was done, he would pick up his "common prayer book old version" and go off to church. At the end of his life he had "about 20 lb. weight of Manuscript sermons" which the appraisers valued at one pound currency. What a judgment he might have thought that on his efforts! When he wished to pay a visit, he would put on his riding coat and grab his cane and call Beauhicket, his favorite horse. Or he summoned his slave to row his boat or paddle his canoe down the Black River to his destinations on the lower Pee Dee or across to Waccamaw Neck. In either case he would take along his pair of "neat silver mounted pistols." He loaned money to his friends, for twenty-eight persons owed him £109.-10 currency at his death; not much, but a sign of charity. His glebe produced a crop of corn, rice, and potatoes and within the six-foot fence required by law (if he obeyed the law), he kept three horses, sixteen head of cattle, and seventeen sheep. There were fifteen slaves (his male slaves were named Caesar, Jupiter, Dartmouth, and Oxford) to help in the field or at his home. The total value of his property, excluding real estate, was £4,361.7.0 currency. Such was one of the country parsons of Carolina.[4]

If the people of the parishes did not cherish these country parsons, they did cherish the church. The principal building erected in the three parishes prior to the Revolution was the parish church of Prince George Winyah. On this building much care was taken, much money spent. The subscription list of January 1, 1736, was headed by John Cleland and Daniel LaRoche and Company with £200 each. As Cleland was the principal landholder in the city and LaRoche and Company were his agents in Georgetown, these were booster contributions as much as testimonies to the Lord. The motives of those who contributed were undoubtedly mixed, some desiring an edifice worthy of their own expectations in this world, others desiring to glorify the Lord. Anthony White

---

[4] "Inventory of the estate of Rev. John Fordyce," appraised July 17, 1751, Inventories, R (1) (1751–1753), pp. 314–322, S. C. Archives.

gave £100, James Gordon, Maurice Lewis, George Pawley, and William Waties, Jr., £50 each. Among the contributors of smaller sums were William Allston, Joseph LaBruce, William Romsey, William Poole, and Thomas Belin.[5] This effort was pushed forward by Meredith Hughes's legacy of £100 in 1741, but even more by the 1742 church act which earmarked the income from import duties collected at Georgetown for the next five years for the construction of the church. George Pawley, Daniel LaRoche, and William Whiteside were named commissioners to handle the funds and to superintend the construction.[6] The cornerstone was laid on October 30, 1745, with the commissioners, church wardens, vestrymen, and many of the parishioners present. The *Gazette* reported that the building would be completed in nine months from that date and was then "carrying on" with great dispatch.[7] On Sunday August 16, 1747, the new church was opened with divine service performed by the Reverend Alexander Keith, who had assumed his duties in 1746 as the first pastor of the new parish.[8] The church was not yet completed, however. An act of April 21, 1753, authorized the selling of pews and commissioned work for the finishing and adorning of the church.[9] The *Gazette* of April 24, 1755, contained an advertisement signed by George Pawley, Thomas Mitchell, and Thomas Hasell, commissioners for finishing the church, asking for bids on joinery, carpentry, plastering, tiling, glazing, and painting. This church, which was built by the new rice and indigo profits, still stands, a living example of the aesthetic tastes of these newly emerging merchants and planters. It might be compared favorably with St. Michael's in Charleston, which was begun eight years after that of Prince George Winyah.[10]

This solid edifice of imported brick, with windows capped with roman arches and glass fanlights, a handsome example of colonial architecture, should have inspired the people of Georgetown in their religious

[5] Belin was written "Blein." Dalcho, *op. cit.*, p. 305. The LaRoches advertised Cleland's lots for sale. *Gazette*, July 30, 1737, June 1, 1738.
[6] Dalcho, *op. cit.*, p. 306; S. C. *Statutes*, III, 579–581. In 1752 another law earmarked the duty on slaves for this purpose. S. C. *Statutes*, III, 755–756.
[7] *Gazette*, Nov. 11, 1745.
[8] *Gazette*, Aug. 31, 1747.
[9] Dalcho, *op. cit.*, p. 307; S. C. *Statutes*, IV, 3–4. Contracts for the sale of pews in this church can be found in SCL and in S. C. Hist. Soc.
[10] For a description of the building of St. Michael's see George W. Williams, *St. Michael's, Charleston, 1751–1951* (Columbia, S. C., 1951), pp. 129–151.

zeal, but the story of the church in Prince George and the two neighboring parishes is a sad one. Some of the parishioners were truly devoted; many were not. George Pawley must be listed among the former since he not only superintended the construction of the church in Georgetown but also gave land and superintended the building of a chapel of ease on Waccamaw Neck.[11] This church in Georgetown, however, seemed a lonely achievement. The church at Prince Frederick was not rebuilt before the Revolution. Except for the chapel on Waccamaw Neck and another at Murray's Old Field near the Santee, no other church was constructed.[12]

The Anglican clergy did not provide strength. Alexander Keith served Prince George until late in 1749, when he resigned to become the assistant at St. Philip's in Charleston. Keith set down in his "Commonplace Book" his order of study. "We ought to study that which will be most useful in our proper Station," he wrote. He listed the best writers on the thirty-nine articles, the creed, the decalogue, the Lord's Prayer, the Protestant dissenters, and the Quakers. Each day he read three chapters in the Scriptures: one as soon as he arose, another after dinner, and a third "before I go to bed."[13] He was meticulous and studious but never happy at Georgetown. Alexander Garden wrote on December 5, 1749, that Keith had recently resigned a distant parish for "just reasons."[14]

[11] The earliest mention of a church building on Waccamaw Neck is in Rev. John Fordyce's letter of Feb. 1, 1739: "I generally preach at the Chapel of Wackamaw once per annum, being a part of George Town parish at a Distance and inconvenient for Traveling where I had a Large Congregation of Religious people and about 15 Communicants, upon the first day of Lent 1737–8. . . ." Quoted in Henry DeSaussure Bull, *All Saints' Church, Waccamaw, 1739–1948* (Columbia, S. C., 1949), pp. 3–4. George Pawley undoubtedly took a great interest in church affairs. On June 7, 1739, he had written Lt. Gov. William Bull suggesting that the dividing line between Prince George and Prince Frederick should be along the Great Pee Dee River. Church Commissioners Book, 1717–1742 [1743], pp. 70–72, S. C. Archives.

[12] Samuel Clegg, Theodore Gordine, Samuel Newman, William Michau, and John Perrit were named commissioners in the 1767 act to supervise the building of this chapel of ease near Murray's ferry. *S. C. Statutes*, IV, 268.

[13] Alexander Keith, "Common Place Book, c. 1730–1740," SCL.

[14] Dalcho, *op. cit.*, pp. 163, 307; Manross, *op. cit.*, p. 153. When Peter Manigault heard that his cousin might marry "Parson Keith," he wrote his mother, June 24, 1753: "If she likes him I can have no Objection to the Match, but I would have her consider, that Gentleman of his Cloth wear their Clothes longer than other Sort of People, & that there is no great diversion in sewing a Horsehair Button on a greazy

The parish of Prince George had four clergymen between Keith's resignation in 1749 and the Revolution: Michael Smith (1753), Samuel Fayerweather (June 1757–July 1760), Offspring Pearce (1761–June 1767), and James Stuart (November 10, 1772–1777). Michael Smith left Prince George for Prince Frederick.[15] Samuel Fayerweather was ordained in England in 1756, but he was a New Englander and spent a large portion of his time there. In 1760 the S.P.G. transferred him to Narragansett, Rhode Island.[16] Offspring Pearce came out in 1761. Because of his health he spent much of his time at North Island at the mouth of Winyah Bay where in 1762 he was almost carried off by a Spanish privateer. In 1767 he was transferred to the parish of St. George Dorchester.[17] James Stuart posted bond in London in 1766, served in Virginia and in Maryland, and was called to Prince George in 1772. Although he married Ann Allston Waties, the widow of Thomas Waties, he took the side of the crown in the Revolution and was driven out of his parish in 1777.[18]

There were three incumbents in Prince Frederick parish between the death of Fordyce in 1751 and the Revolution: Michael Smith (1753–1756), George Skeene (1762–1766), and John Villette (1772). Michael Smith reported to Bishop Thomas Sherlock in May 1753 that there were five dissenting preachers in his parish and that most of the inhabitants were dissenters. His problems, however, were of his own making. Because of his notorious immorality he was asked to leave.[19] Charles Woodmason, who was one of the church wardens, was asked by the vestry to read prayers and to deliver a sermon each Sunday, which he consented to do for six years. He visited all parts of the parish as collector of the poor tax, kept the vestry minutes, and corresponded with

---

black Waistcoat." *SCHM*, XXXII (1931), 179. When the parish of St. Stephen's was formed in 1754, Keith became its first rector; he continued to serve the parish until his death in 1772 at Newport, R. I., where he had gone for his health. *SCHM*, X (1909), 167; XVII (1916), 49.

15 Dalcho, *op. cit.*, p. 307.

16 Dalcho, *op. cit.*, p. 307; Manross, *op. cit.*, pp. 303, 326. Copley painted him in Boston. Jules D. Prown, *John Singleton Copley in America, 1738–1774* (Cambridge, Mass., 1966), pp. 105, 214.

17 Dalcho, *op. cit.*, pp. 307–308; Manross, *op. cit.*, p. 329.

18 Dalcho, *op. cit.*, p. 308; Manross, *op. cit.*, pp. 309, 330; "A Note on James Stuart, Loyalist Clergyman in South Carolina," ed. Henry D. Bull, *Journal of Southern History*, XII (1946), 571–575.

19 Dalcho, *op. cit.*, p. 320; Manross, *op. cit.*, p. 153.

those interested in coming to the parish as clergyman. Later, Woodmason himself went to England for ordination.[20] George Skeene was
elected in June 1762, having come out well-recommended and with an
"open mission." He was dead by December 30, 1766.[21] John Villette
came out in 1771 but evidently stayed less than a year. On February
10, 1775, the vestry was writing for a clergyman, saying that Villette
had left over three years before.[22]

The S.P.G. failed to keep these parishes continuously supplied with
clergymen. The search for applicants was time-consuming. Even when
a man was secured, there was a long voyage, a period of adjustment to
the climate (failure to adjust could be fatal), and finally the lure of
better cures nearer Charleston. Naturally, the parishes were often without clergymen. When the parish did secure a resident minister, he might
lapse into the pattern of a planting life.

The most forceful clergyman to work in the region was Charles
Woodmason. He had been a merchant, planter, church warden, vestryman, justice of the peace, constable, coroner, and collector of the general tax. He knew local government; he knew the people. When he
decided to go to England in 1765 to be ordained as a Church of England clergyman, he must have felt that the dissenters who flourished
in the parish of Prince Frederick should be won back to the church.
The people he had known were from upper Prince Frederick, the part
that became St. Mark's. It was to St. Mark's that he returned as a clergyman. There he faced the turmoil of a people in transition to new re-
ligions, for the backcountry was infested by Baptist emissaries from the
North. These were not the Baptists of William Screven; these were
unchurched folk converted by men who came down from the north in
the 1740's and 1750's to preach a new religion of the heart. The strong
and uncomplimentary picture that Woodmason painted in his journal
was of a people on the fringes of society, lacking a culture, but in search
of one. These were the people whom the Canteys and the Richardsons
had to control. The Canteys and Richardsons were no different from

<hr>

[20] *The Carolina Backcountry on the Eve of the Revolution, The Journal and Other
Writings of Charles Woodmason, Anglican Itinerant,* ed. Richard J. Hooker (Chapel
Hill, N. C., 1953), p. xv.
[21] Dalcho, *op. cit.,* p. 320; Manross, *op. cit.,* pp. 154–155, 306, 329.
[22] Dalcho, *op. cit.,* p. 321; Manross, *op. cit.,* p. 157.

the Lynches, the Horrys, and the Trapiers in their desires, but the low-country magnates had forms available, parishes and courts, to control society and to keep the people working. The creation of a backcountry parish was not enough; there was still a need for courts and jails. If Georgetown society was less polished than that of Charleston, it was because it was always in danger of crumbling into such groups as those that plagued Woodmason. In the final analysis, the Georgetown region was always nearer Charleston than the headwaters of either the Pee Dee or of the Wateree. A man like Woodmason wanted to create in the backcountry what he knew existed on the coast. This was the aim of all of the clergymen in the country parishes, but Woodmason, the strongest, was only able to announce his failure very loudly.[23]

There were Presbyterians in Prince Frederick who were served by the Reverend John Baxter. His register of sermon texts, commenced in 1733, indicates that he preached at Colonel Lynch's on the Santee, at Winyah, at Black River, on Waccamaw Neck, and at Mrs. Britton's on the Pee Dee. Since he was granted in 1737 1,100 acres in Williamsburg Township, he must have settled there about that date. The old Presbyterian church, marked on the 1820 map of Georgetown District, was located on the road from Murray's ferry on the Santee to Potatoe Ferry on the Black River.[24]

Culture seeped in from Charleston, brought by the merchants and planters who wished to improve their social status. Culture came not as a by-product of a search for salvation, but as a by-product of an intense desire for advancement in this world. The church which had tried through the Society for the Promotion of Christian Knowledge to provide libraries in the colonies had not provided one for Georgetown. The men of Charleston, having realized that a society without books and without conversation about books is devoid of intellectual leadership, formed in 1748 the Charleston Library Society. This Library Society was a forum for the province as much as for the city for its initial membership included men from all parts of the colony. John Cleland, Elias Foissin, Andrew Johnston, Thomas Lynch, John Ouldfield, Dr. Charles Fyffe, George Gabriel Powell, William Waties III, and the Rev-

[23] Hooker, *op. cit.*, passim.
[24] George Howe, *History of the Presbyterian Church in South Carolina* (Columbia, S. C., 1870), I, 204, 255, 288; Grant Books, XLI, 165, S. C. Archives.

erend Alexander Keith were members in 1750.[25] When these same gentlemen were in Georgetown, they met and conversed in their own homes
and in the taverns of the town. In November 1742 Nathaniel Tregagle,
with the financial backing of Jonathan Skrine, had opened a public house
or tavern which was a gathering place.[26] William Logan, the Philadelphia Quaker, who stopped in Georgetown in October 1745 on his way to
Charleston, wrote in his diary after a night's lodging at Thomas Blythe's:
"We Were Well Entertained here & spent the Day in Co with many
Gent of the Town, who were Very kind & Curt's and dined at this House
mostly in a Clubb." [27]

These groups discussed the latest news from London, the prospects
for indigo, and the religious ferment stirred by George Whitefield or
read the latest issues of the *South-Carolina Gazette*, for although
Georgetown had no colonial newspaper, the men of rank read the
Charleston paper.[28] In the 1760's there were agents for distribution of
the *Gazette* in both Prince Frederick and Prince George parishes.[29] Con-
viviality meant food and drink, and these were paid for by dues collected in the new crop of the day—indigo. Tradition says that the Winyah Indigo Society grew out of a convivial club which met monthly as
early as 1740 in the Old Oak Tavern on Bay Street.[30] The Winyah
Indigo Society, which sprang from the interest of the agricultural community in a new and exciting crop, was Georgetown's answer to the
Charleston Library Society. With the formation of the Winyah Indigo
Society there henceforth existed in Georgetown a library, a school, and
something of an intellectual center.

[25] *SCHM*, XXIII (1922), 169–170.

[26] Miscellaneous Records, EE (1741–1743), pp. 369–370, S. C. Archives; *Gazette*,
July 21, 1746.

[27] "William Logan's Journal of a Journey to Georgia, 1745," *Pennsylvania Magazine
of History and Biography*, XXVI (1912), 16, 162.

[28] The *Gazette* carried much news of the Garden-Whitefield controversy in 1740
and 1741 and the Cato Letters in March 1749.

[29] Charles Cantey, Albert Lenud, Joseph Anderson, and Robert Byers were the
agents at Santee; Henry Cassells, David Anderson, and James Bradley for the North
Side Black River; George Gabriel Powell, Paul Trapier, Joseph Brown, Thomas
Godfrey, William Shackelford, and William Smith at Georgetown; William Allston
at Waccamaw. *Gazette*, March 31–August 25, 1764.

[30] [William D. Morgan] *A Short History of the Winyah Indigo Society* (n.p., n.d.),
p. 3; *Pee Dee Times*, April 25, 1855.

It was natural that the Winyah Indigo Society should emerge out of the ferment over the new staple. As early as February 6, 1755, Christopher Gadsden and Archibald Johnston advertised in the *Gazette* that they would receive subscriptions for a society to spread information on "Indico-making, from the cutting to the barrelling." The more information on indigo, the more profit; the more profit, the more money for education. Thus, the crop would be the basis for a higher culture. The society was organized in May 1755, but in order to accept gifts and provide for a school the Winyah Indigo Society was incorporated by an act of the Assembly on May 21, 1757. Thomas Lynch was first president, Joseph Poole senior warden, Samuel Wragg, Jr., junior warden, Nathaniel Tregagle treasurer, Joseph Dubourdieu clerk, and Dr. Charles Fyffe and William Shackelford, Jr., stewards.[31]

There had been experimentation with wild indigo in the early years of Carolina, but not until the 1740's when there was a decline in the prosperity of the rice planters and a war with France, which cut off imports of indigo from the French West Indies, did indigo make a successful entrance on the Carolina agricultural scene. Indigo required "a high loose soil, tolerably rich" which was found in the forks between many South Carolina rivers, the high land behind the rice fields.[32] Indigo actually grew better in the tropics, but the cheapness of South

[31] *S. C. Statutes*, VIII, 110–112. This act was ratified by the King in Council at the Court of St. James on Jan. 27, 1758. Miscellaneous Records, LL (1758–1763), pp. 43–45, S. C. Archives. The King in Council on Jan. 15, 1772, approved an act of the South Carolina Assembly, dated April 6, 1765, which amended the earlier act to reduce the quorum necessary for business from 25 to 15 at annual meetings and to 9 at other times. Miscellaneous Records, PP, Part 1 (1771–1774), pp. 209–211, S. C. Archives. The anniversary address was always given on the first Friday in May and numbered from 1755. In the original act the spelling was "Winyaw Indico Society" but throughout this volume the modern form "Winyah Indigo Society" has been used.

[32] The following works describe the growing and production of indigo: Lewis Cecil Gray, *History of Agriculture in the Southern United States to 1860* (New York, 1941), I, 290–297; *Colonial South Carolina, Two Contemporary Descriptions by Governor James Glen and Doctor George Milligen-Johnston*, ed. Chapman J. Milling (Columbia, S. C., 1951), pp. 17–18, 139–140, 203–206; William Partridge, "On the Manufacturing of Indigo in this Country," *American Journal*, XVIII (1830), 237–240; Mary H. Leonard, "An Old Industry," *The Popular Science Monthly*, XLVI (1895), 649–658; Dwight Jackson Huneycutt, "The Economics of the Indigo Industry in South Carolina" (MA thesis, Univ. of S. C., 1949); "Mr. Thomas Mellichamp's Directions for making Indico of the different kinds, equal to the best French," *Gazette*, Aug. 23, 1760.

Carolina land made up for the failure of Carolina indigo to yield more than two cuttings a year as compared to four or five in the tropics. The best indigo was grown in Spanish Guatemala; the next best in the French West Indies. In Carolina the Guatemala seeds were highly prized.[33]

Seeds were planted by hand during a moist period. Weeding was necessary to prevent the indigo plant from being choked out. Within two months the first cutting could be made. The skill of the indigo planter was exercised after the cutting, in the process by which the dye was extracted from the stalk and leaves of the plant. Three vats were needed, placed in a line, each succeeding vat being slightly lower than the preceding one: a steeper, a battery, and a settler. The plants were placed in the steeper and pressed down slightly to keep them under water. About twenty hours of fermentation were needed. The vagaries of the weather had to be watched for heat was "the grand Agent, the *sine qua non,* in the whole process of *Indigo.*" This was the heat generated by the fermenting process which might be speeded up or retarded by the weather—never by fires. After steeping, the liquor was drained off into the battery where slaves continually agitated the liquor until it changed into "a purpleish high Mazarine Tincture." The three colors to be obtained were "the Fine Copper," "the Fine Purple," and "the Fine Flora" ("which is the highest of our ambition," as Thomas Mellichamp wrote). The beating must stop at exactly the right moment. Tests of the fluid were continuously made in an essay cup. After the beating the liquid was drained into the settler for four to twelve hours. Lime was frequently used to precipitate the indigo particles. The residue was hung up in bags or placed in trays. Ultimately, the indigo was cut into cubes which were then shipped to market. One slave might take care of two acres; and one acre would produce about fifty pounds of indigo, the amount depending upon the cuttings obtained. This indigo would sell for about twenty shillings currency per pound.

There was much interest in the growing and processing of indigo. Two letters in the *Gazettes* of October 22 and 29, 1744, described the culture of indigo for the first time; other letters appeared later.[34] Peter Sanders of the Black River family advertised in 1746 that he had

---

[33] "Guatimala" indigo seed were advertised in the *Gazette* March 23, 1752.
[34] *Gazette,* Oct. 22, 29, 1744, Dec. 1, 1746, Jan. 19, 26, 1747.

discovered the best way to prevent the leaking of indigo vats.[35] The most important contribution was made by Thomas Mellichamp of St. Andrew's Parish who, after publishing a treatise on the subject in 1757, was granted a bounty by the Assembly. In the same issue that announced the publication of Mellichamp's treatise there also appeared the first verses of the poem entitled "Indigo," which began: "The Means and Arts that to Perfection bring,/The richer dye of Indico, I sing." A local Vergil thus glorified the new agricultural revolution. And in Georgetown there were patrons ready to further his work: Joseph Brown and Dr. Charles Fyffe offered to take subscriptions so that the entire poem might be published.[36]

The British Parliament, however, gave more concrete assistance to the new industry by its act of 1748 granting a bounty of six pence sterling per pound.[37] This act had been obtained through the earnest solicitations of James Crokatt, South Carolina's agent in London.[38] The bounty was to be paid for a period of seven years to the English importer by the collector of the port through which the indigo arrived in England, but only if the indigo sold for more than three shillings sterling per pound. The act was designed to stimulate quality production. The Carolina factor loading the indigo had to produce for customs in Carolina a certificate sworn before a justice of the peace by the planter who had produced the indigo. The certificate was sent to the English importer,

[35] *Gazette,* July 7, 1746. On April 16, 1746, the provincial bounty on indigo was repealed because there was a great probability that much would be grown that year. *S. C. Statutes,* III, 670–671.

[36] *Gazette,* Aug. 25, 1757. For Eliza Lucas Pinckney's contribution to the indigo industry see Harriott Horry Ravenel, *Eliza Pinckney* (New York, 1896), pp. 102–107. Charles Woodmason wrote an article which was published in the *Gentleman's Magazine,* but Henry Laurens, who identified the author in one of his letters, thought the author had gotten some of his facts wrong. Woodmason said an acre would produce 60 to 80 pounds; Laurens not more than 50. C. W., "Method of Raising, Improving, and Manufacturing Indigo in Carolina," *Gentleman's Magazine,* XXV (May and June, 1755), 201–203, 256-259; Henry Laurens to Richard Pattison, Sept. 16, Oct. 23, 1756, Laurens Papers, S. C. Hist. Soc.

[37] An extract of "an act for encouraging the making of Indico in the British Plantations in America," passed May 13, 1748, was printed in the *Gazette,* Aug. 27, 1748.

[38] He may have been a relative of Dr. James Crockatt, even though they did not spell their name in the same way.

who collected the bounty from the English customs.[39] The South Carolina Assembly passed an act in 1749 to prevent fraud.[40] However, although much of the Carolina indigo was of inferior quality and should not have received the bounty, most of the indigo shipped to market did receive it. The bounty was continued until 1770, when it was decreased to four pence per pound, at which level it remained until 1777.[41] This was an important subsidy for the indigo planters of the Georgetown District.

The boom in indigo production drew to Carolina in November 1756 Moses Lindo, a skilled indigo sorter of London, who offered to class, sort, and pack indigo for the foreign market and in 1757 promised the planters of Winyah, among others, that he would not let the indigo of the first class fall in price below twenty shillings currency per pound. Lindo's judgment was respected in the London indigo market, and his systematizing of the trade brought profits for the planters. In 1762 he was publicly thanked by a host of important Carolina indigo planters including Thomas Lynch, Dr. John Murray, Andrew Johnston, John Moultrie, Jr., and John Mayrant. Governor Thomas Boone made him "Surveyor and Inspector General of the Indico" in order to increase his prestige abroad. In 1763 he was able to secure forty shillings currency per pound for George Saxby's indigo. Lindo continued to serve the Carolina indigo planters until his death in 1774, but in the later years a combination in London of importers of foreign indigo discriminated against the Carolina crop.[42] The profits of the 1757–1759 period were not repeated.[43]

The Winyah Indigo Society established a school where pupils might be taught the use of letters and the principles of religion. In May 1755

[39] Indigo certificates (the forms) were advertised for sale in the *Gazette*, Nov. 20, 1755.

[40] "An act to prevent frauds in making, packing and exporting indigo," assented to June 1, 1749. *S. C. Statutes*, III, 718–720. Concerning such frauds see "Memo of Thomas Lowndes," April 13, 1748, Newcastle Papers, Add. Ms. No. 32,714, f. 482, British Museum.

[41] Gray, *op. cit.*, I, 292.

[42] Barnett A. Elzas, *The Jews of South Carolina* (Philadelphia, Penn., 1905), pp. 47–67. Hugh Swinton was appointed on May 2, 1774, to replace Moses Lindo as "Inspector of Indigo." Miscellaneous Records, RR, Part 1 (1774–1779), p. 62, S. C. Archives.

[43] Gray gives the range in price before the Revolution as 2s. 6d. to 6s. 6d. sterling per lb. Gray, *op. cit.*, I, 293. Huneycutt, gives the range from 2s. 6d. to 5s. 8d. per lb. Huneycutt, *op. cit.*, p. 31.

the society announced that twelve poor children would be educated on the bounty of the society. They sought subscriptions and a master who could teach reading, writing, arithmetic, the English tongue, and Latin. Money was contributed. In October the clerk of the society, Joseph Dubourdieu, advertised that the society had £1,000 to be let out at interest. Those who wished to borrow might see the clerk in Georgetown or George Austin in Charleston. The school was functioning before the charter was obtained, but it could not have flourished as it was trying in January 1760 to fill ten vacancies in the school. As each of these children received his education, books, pens, ink, paper, firewood, and two suits of outside clothes each year, one wonders why there was a vacancy at all.[44]

The society school provided only a beginning education. For those who wished to be trained for commerce or for the professions or to be a gentleman, it was necessary to go elsewhere. The counting houses of Charleston would provide an apprenticeship for commerce. To be a professional man or to acquire an education befitting a gentleman it was necessary to go to England.

Of the four professions—teaching, the church, the law, and medicine —only medicine appealed greatly to the fathers of the Georgetown boys as a future career for their sons. Teaching, being only of a rudimentary sort in the colony, was not a proper profession for the sons of merchants and planters. The church did not appeal. Almost all those who served the Georgetown parishes both before and after the Revolution were young men who came out from England. In colonial Georgetown there was not much room for a lawyer since all of the courts in the colony were in Charleston. To practice law would mean to change one's residence. However, doctors were needed, particularly on the plantations.

The early Georgetown doctors were not native-born; many were Scotsmen. They were trained elsewhere and came to Georgetown to follow their profession. Dr. Robert Brown, who died in 1741, "late of Winyaw," was one of the earliest doctors.[45] Dr. Charles Fyffe came out from Dundee in 1748; his brother Dr. William Fyffe probably came

[44] *Gazette*, May 22, Oct. 16, 1755, Jan. 5, 1760.
[45] For a list of Georgetown doctors see Joseph Ioor Waring, *A History of Medicine in South Carolina, 1670–1825* (Columbia, S. C., 1964), pp. 384–385.

out at the same time. Dr. William Fyffe, writing in 1771, felt that "physick" was perhaps the least profitable business in Georgetown.[46] He held gloomy views on the prospects for a young doctor. "Physick" was a "genteel business" that required no capital, but, if a young man followed that line, "he will barely make a fortune by it unless by marriage . . . if he designs this latter business whether he has learning or not let him have assurance and a large share of that small talk so taking with the weakest part of our sex. You may depend on it I'm not against his knowing his business well but I know from experience that the getting a run of practice depends more upon art and assurance than real skill. The prejudice my natural bashfulness has done me is incredible. . . ."[47] Dr. Charles Fyffe told a different story after the war when he was trying to secure reimbursements from the British authorities for the estate that had been confiscated by South Carolina. At that time he said that he had made between £150 to £200 sterling before the war from his own practice. Dr. Charles Fyffe was in a position where he would have exaggerated, but perhaps his brother had not been as successful. Certainly both made enough to acquire plantations and slaves.[48]

Another Scotsman, Dr. Robert Gibb, who had studied medicine in his native Edinburgh, came to Georgetown in 1754. By the time of his death in 1777 he had acquired a fortune of £4,300 sterling, which included an 800-acre plantation on the Pee Dee, a house and lots in Georgetown, and fifty-six Negroes. But, as his sister later wrote, "for some years preceeding his death he applied himself more to the culture of his estate than to the Practice of Physic."[49] Doctors like clergymen succumbed to the pull of the land. Dr. John Moultrie, Jr.,[50] Dr. John

[46] William Fyffe to his sister Elizabeth, May 17, 1771, Fyffe Papers, WLCL.
[47] William Fyffe to his sister Elizabeth, Dec. 17, 1768, Fyffe Papers, WLCL.
[48] "Petition of Charles Fyffe," Loyalist Transcripts, LV, 428–447, on microfilm, S. C. Archives. William had died in 1771 at the age of forty-three. Waring, *op. cit.*, p. 384.
[49] "Dr. Robert Gibb," Loyalist Transcripts, LVI, 168–186, on microfilm, S. C. Archives.
[50] Dr. John Moultrie, Jr., was the first native-born American to graduate in medicine from Edinburgh. He married the daughter of George Austin, acquiring thereby indigo lands on the Pee Dee and later accepted an appointment as lieutenant governor of East Florida. Waring, *op. cit.*, pp. 269–270.

Murray,[51] and Dr. James Crockatt (died April 14, 1765) were all
figures of the Georgetown scene, but each was more a planter than a
doctor.

The doctors who came to Georgetown not only brought medical knowledge with them but also a great deal of general knowledge. Their membership in the Winyah Indigo Society, their meetings with the planters
on their rounds, and their attendance at the taverns of the town must
have helped somewhat to enlighten the Georgetown mind. Dr. Charles
Fyffe was one of the original members of the Charleston Library Society,
one of the first stewards of the Winyah Indigo Society, a patron of poets,
and owner of a library of 700 books. Dr. James Crockatt's library contained the works of Boerhaave (his Chemistry in Latin), Ovid, Vergil,
Cicero, Swift and Dryden, Tillotson, Montesquieu and Puffendorf, a
French grammar, and many other volumes.[52] The doctors may have
given more tone to the society than the clergy.

The finest education was reserved for those who were to become
gentlemen. Such an education is usually reserved for the third generation of the new rich, but in Georgetown some of the second generation
had this opportunity. The *Gazette* of August 31, 1738, reporting the
death of James Kinloch's twenty-year-old son from a violent fever, said
that he had arrived in the province only fifteen months before after
having been five years in several parts of Europe for his education. His
younger brother Francis was educated in the same style, but the finest
education was reserved for Francis and Cleland Kinloch, of the third
generation, who were placed in 1767 at Eton by their guardian, the
former royal Governor Thomas Boone. Francis Kinloch continued his
education at Geneva, then made a grand tour of Europe before returning to study at Lincoln's Inn. His brother Cleland continued his
own education in the same manner, even during the Revolution, not returning to America until after the war was over.[53] This style of

---

[51] Murray became an assistant judge of the province and owned lands in many
parts of the state. Waring, *op. cit.*, p. 272. He was instrumental in passing on information concerning indigo to the British Society in London. *Gazette*, April 1, 1757.

[52] Dr. Robert Gibb showed these items to S. Wragg, C. Fyffe, and J. Gordon on
Oct. 29, 1765. Miscellaneous Records, Y (1769–1771), pp. 13–18, S. C. Archives.

[53] For the education of Francis and Cleland Kinloch see George C. Rogers, Jr.,
Evolution of a Federalist, William Loughton Smith of Charleston, 1758–1812 (Columbia, S. C., 1962), pp. 56–96.

education became the model for the sons of the wealthiest planters. Paul Trapier, Jr., was educated at Eton, St John's College, Cambridge, and the Inner Temple. Thomas Lynch, Jr., was educated at Eton, Caius College, Cambridge, and the Middle Temple. Daniel Horry sent his son to Westminster and the Middle Temple.[54] These men were not being trained, however, for the practice of law in country courthouses, nor perhaps even in Charleston; they were being trained for the public world that family riches opened to them.

For the children of the lesser folk there was very little formal education. There were twelve poor scholars at the Winyah Indigo Society, but even those places were not always filled. The educational story reveals a division in society between the polished and the untutored. Society was solidifying with a ruling elite at the top and with men of lesser rank excluded from participation in provincial affairs. The Kinlochs, the Lynches, the Trapiers, and the Horrys were the richest, the best educated, and the most prominent in affairs of state.

The lesser folk did have their fairs and market days. They enjoyed cock-fighting, bear-baiting, contests of skill such as foot racing and contests of absurdity such as chasing a greased pig, the coarse pleasures of the country.[55] The elite, on the other hand, were beginning to frequent the balls and races of Charleston. A race was held at Georgetown as early as March 2, 1743, when "a very fashionable Piece of Silver Plate" valued at £150 currency was "to be run for." [56] In 1766 Thomas Lynch's Havannah won a subscription purse of £350 by defeating John Allston's Tristram Shandy, John Mayrant's Dutchess, and Captain Gardner's Spark. The following day Lynch's colt Noble walked over the course and collected the prize since no one dared to enter a horse against him.[57] The Georgetown horses were so good that they dominated the racing in Charleston. Dr. John Murray's Skim won one race at Charleston

[54] J. G. de Roulhac Hamilton, "Southern Members of the Inns of Court," *North Carolina Historical Review*, X (1933), 279–280, 285–286; SCHM, VII (1906), 170.

[55] In June 1775 Paul Trapier, Samuel Wragg, Job Rothmahler, Robert Heriot, and Anthony Bonneau were authorized to hold two fairs annually at Georgetown, on the third Monday in November and the first Monday in June. A director, who would have power to hold a "Court of Pipowder," and a clerk were to be appointed. Miscellaneous Records, RR, Part 1 (1774–1779), pp. 188–189, S. C. Archives.

[56] *Gazette*, Feb. 28, 1743.

[57] *South Carolina Gazette and Country Journal*, Jan. 21, 1766.

in 1765 and Lynch's Havana another. In 1769 William Allston's Tryal won.[58] The Georgetown Race Week became more formal. In 1744 the Georgetown Jockey Club members were notified that the races would be held on the first Tuesday and Wednesday in December and that the members must notify the steward of the colors in which they intended to dress their riders.[59] The races were discontinued when Revolutionary fervor demanded an end to these idle pastimes.[60]

What must have kept the society together was a love of the outdoors. The hunting and fishing equipment mentioned in the inventories of the rich were matched in the inventories of the poor. But it was on the muster-field that the male population of the parishes was drawn together. The officers were appointed from the well-to-do, but all males sixteen to sixty were liable for militia service. It was the Cherokee War that galvanized this society. The manual exercise of arms became a part of polite education for all schoolboys. The *Gazette* wrote that "at George Town in particular, we are told, the Indico Society's scholars perform to admiration." [61] The men of Williamsburg were complimented for their zeal in drilling.[62] These preparations brought out the colonels and the captains, elevating George Pawley and George Gabriel Powell to a place beside the Lynches and the Trapiers.[63] Military glory bolstered the new elite.

[58] *Gazette,* March 2, 1765, Feb. 9, 1769.
[59] *Gazette,* Sept. 19, 1774.
[60] *Gazette,* Nov. 21, 1774.
[61] *Gazette,* May 12, 1757.
[62] *Gazette,* Feb. 24, 1757.
[63] Christopher Gadsden to Governor Lyttelton, Oct. 31, 1759, Lyttelton Papers, WLCL.

VII

REVOLUTIONARY ASPIRATIONS

By the 1760's the parish of Prince George was essentially a planting community. Even the doctors and the clergymen soon found themselves giving up the practice of their professions for the greater profit to be obtained from planting indigo and rice. The Georgetown merchants who had made profits out of the transportation of indigo to market during the boom years had turned planters too. In 1763, when Andrew Johnston was shifting his place of residence to Charleston, he offered four plantations for sale, including one on the Pee Dee where he had made so much indigo.[1] Although the Georgetown merchants had controlled the carrying of the indigo and rice to market in the 1740's and 1750's, this was less true in the years just prior to the Revolution. The know-how of the Charleston merchants was used to squeeze the Georgetown men out of commerce. The Charleston merchants undermined the Georgetown merchants in the 1760's in the same way that New York merchants undermined those of Charleston in the 1820's.

Georgetown was a port of entry, but in the year ending March 1, 1765, 360 vessels cleared from Charleston for a non-South Carolina destination,

---

[1] Alberta Morel Lachicotte, *Georgetown Rice Plantations* (Columbia, S. C., 1955), p. 155; *Gazette,* Feb. 7, 1761, Oct. 15, 1763.

while only 40 cleared from Georgetown and 24 from Beaufort.[2] A royal inspection of colonial ports in 1768 revealed that at Georgetown the duties received never amounted to the expense of management, the reason being "that the chief of such as would arise here is collected at Charlestown the Emporium of this Province." The majority of what was produced was shipped "in the Province Schooners, which are subject to no kind of inspection, to Charlestown the market, and appear in the Exports from thence." The decline of Georgetown as a port may have been due to the silting up of the harbor mouth, for the same report stated that "the water on the Bar at the Entrance of Wynyaw Harbour is so Shoal that no Vessels of Burthen can get in."[3] In 1770 Lieutenant Governor William Bull stated that "The shallow Bar at Winyaw is the best and only defense for George Town."[4] These descriptions were far different from George Hunter's of 1730. The absence of shipbuilding in the Winyah Bay area by the 1760's reflects this mercantile decline. What remained of vast importance to the planters was the coastal trade to Charleston.

Political power consequently fell into the hands of the planters. This fact is revealed by an analysis of the men who represented these parishes in the seven assemblies elected from 1765 until the Revolution. During the 1740's power had been equally shared between the merchants and the planters, but with the appearance of Thomas Lynch in the Assembly in 1751 a change had taken place. Lynch was elected to every Assembly except one from 1751 until the Revolution. In the 1750's his principal colleague was Paul Trapier; in the 1760's he was joined first by Daniel Horry and then by Elias Horry, Jr. From 1768 to the Revolution Thomas Lynch and Elias Horry, Jr.. represented Prince George in every Assembly. Daniel Horry and Elias Horry, Jr., were first cousins and, as was Lynch, Santee River planters. Paul Trapier, who had turned planter in 1762, was by his marriage to Magdalene Horry the uncle of both of

[2] CO 5/511, f. 110, PRO, London.

[3] "Extracts from Mr. Mills Reports of the inspection of the ports and districts in the Provinces of North and South Carolina, Georgia, East & West Florida," n.d. but after 1768, Clinton Papers, WLCL.

[4] Bull to Hillsborough, Nov. 30, 1770, BPRO, XXXII (1768–1770), 388, S. C. Archives.

these young men. Elias Horry, Jr., married Margaret Lynch, the first cousin of Thomas Lynch. The Lynches, the Trapiers, and the Horrys dominated Georgetown politics.

In 1768 and 1769 the Georgetown planters received an increase of political influence when All Saints was created a parish with two representatives in the Assembly.[5] Since the backcountry needed additional representation more than the lowcountry, this step seems an odd one until it is noted that it exemplified the emergence of the Allston family, the most powerful family in the entire history of Georgetown County. In 1768 All Saints elected Thomas Lynch and Joseph Allston; in 1769 the parish chose Joseph Allston and Benjamin Young. Joseph Allston (1733–1784) was the son of William Allston and Esther LaBrosse de Marboeuf.[6] Josiah Quincy in 1773 described his visit with Joseph Allston at The Oaks as follows:

Spent this night with Mr. Joseph Allston, a gentleman of immense income all of his own acquisition. He is a person between thirty-nine and forty, and a very few years ago begun the world with only five negroes— has now five, plantations with an hundred slaves on each. He told me his neat income was but about five or six thousand pounds sterling a year, he is reputed much richer. His plantation, negroes, gardens, etc., are in the best order of any I have seen! He has propagated the Lisbon and Wine-Island grapes with great success. I was entertained with more true hospitality and benevolence by this family than any I had met with. His good lady filled a wallet, with bread, biscuit, wine, fowl, and tongue, and presented it next morning. The wine I declined, but gladly received the rest. At about twelve o'clock in a sandy pine desert I enjoyed a fine regalement, and having met with a refreshing spring, I remembered the worthy Mr. Allston and Lady with more warmth of affection and hearty benizons, than ever I toasted King or Queen, Saint or Hero.[7]

Benjamin Young (1733–1782) was the son of a Charleston house carpenter who established himself first as a merchant in Georgetown and

---

[5] Created May 23, 1767. S. C. *Statutes*, IV, 266–268.

[6] See William Allston (died 1744) chart in Appendix II.

[7] "Journal of Josiah Quincy, Junior, 1773," *Proceedings of the Massachusetts Historical Society*, XLIX (1915–1916), 453. Joseph Allston was married to Charlotte Rothmahler.

84793

then as a planter at Youngville on the Waccamaw River.[8] This was only a temporary accession of power, however, as the parish act was disallowed in 1770.[9]

Even in Prince Frederick the interest of the largest planters was to the fore. In 1765 Prince Frederick chose William Moultrie (who would later marry the widow of Thomas Lynch) and Samuel Clegg. Clegg, a Prince Frederick man, bought over 3,000 acres of Hobcaw Barony in 1767, the part that was to be known as Calais and Michau's Point.[10] From 1768 to the Revolution there were only three men who sat for Prince Frederick. Theodore Gaillard, who consistently held one seat, was the brother-in-law of Daniel Horry, having also married a daughter of Noah Serré.[11] Charles Cantey (1718–1780) was a planter of St. Stephen's Parish.[12] Benjamin Farar was a Regulator and therefore might be considered outside the governing elite. Yet he and his father-in-law, Tacitus Gaillard, also a Regulator, were merely the men in the backcountry who wished to restore order in their sections so that they might imitate the lowcountry planters.[13]

That which was needed to cap off this planting society was a seat for one of its members in the Royal Council of South Carolina. The obvious choice would have been Francis Kinloch, who owned Kensington and Weehaw plantations on the Black River and Rice Hope on the Santee. At the time of his death in 1767 his personal estate was valued at £133,131.5.6 currency, which included 338 slaves and a mansion house in Charleston. His home in Charleston was filled with marble

[8] *Register of St. Philip's Parish, 1720–1758*, p. 72; "Will of Archibald Young," dated March 15, 1748, proved June 23, 1749, Charleston County Wills, VI (1747–1752), 177–179, S. C. Archives. He bought lot 37 for £500 from George Saxby in 1758. Register of Mesne Conveyance, V-V, pp. 211–215, S. C. Archives. For Youngville see *SCHM*, XXIV (1923), 79. Benjamin Young died in 1782. See petition of his son Thomas in "Benjamin Young," Audited Accounts, S. C. Archives.

[9] Frances H. Porcher, "Royal Review of South Carolina Law, 1719–1776," (MA thesis, Univ. of S. C., 1962), pp. 76, 112.

[10] Inventories, B. (1748–1751), p. 150, S. C. Archives; Lachicotte, *op. cit.*, pp. 11–12.

[11] He was a planter of St. James Santee and died in 1781. "Will of Theodore Gaillard," dated March 16, 1781, proved July 7, 1781, Charleston County Wills, XIX (1780–1783), 187–188; XX, Book A (1783–1786), 135–137, S. C. Archives.

[12] Joseph S. Ames, "The Cantey Family," *SCHM*, XI (1910), 219–221.

[13] Richard Maxwell Brown, *The South Carolina Regulators* (Cambridge, Mass.. 1963), pp. 194, passim.

tables, glass lanthorns, and mahogany furniture. There were twenty-one table cloths, twelve pair pillow cases, five "pavillions" (mosquito nets), two flower china vases worth £40, prints worth £70, and in his stables a £600 chariot, a £150 phaeton, and £60 chair, besides plate on his sideboard valued at £1,148.14. Yet this opulent Georgetown planter was never asked to be a member of the Royal Council. He died at Rice Hope on June 2, 1767, "one of the most considerable and successful Indico planters in this province."[14]

The aspirations of the Georgetown planters were thwarted by the disallowance of the All Saints Parish act and by the failure of any of their men to receive a place on the Council. As Josiah Quincy commented: "Compose the Council of the first planters, fill all the Public Offices with them, give them the honours of the State, and though they don't want them, give them it and emoluments also: introduce Baronies and Lordships—their enormous estates will bear it"—if all this were done, South Carolina would be safe for the crown.[15]

Although these planters were self-made men, they were not unread. Noah Serré, the father-in-law of both Daniel Horry and Theodore Gaillard, had a fine library at his Santee River plantation at the time of his death in 1745.[16] In 1751 John Ouldfield, Jr., left an even larger library in his Craven County home.[17] Both gentlemen owned the standard guides for the justice of the peace. Serré possessed Moliere's plays, Dryden's *Juvenal*, Potter's *Antiquities of Greece*, as well as works on English history. John Ouldfield's taste was reflected in his seven damask table cloths, twenty-six dozen bottles of Madeira, five maps of the world, violin, and flute. His library exceeded eighty listed titles. The libraries of the Georgetown men generally reflected the background of each. The Huguenot Elias Foissin had many works on the persecution of French Protestants.[18] The Scotsman Andrew Johnston owned "twelve goof sticks

---

[14] Inventories, X (1768–1769), pp. 295–301, S. C. Archives; *Gazette,* June 15, 1767. On information of Francis Kinloch, Esq., the grand jury indicted T. Mitchell, P. Trapier, E. Horry, G. G. Powell, W. Jamieson, Joseph Allston, and Josias Allston for not keeping Lynches Causeway in repair. *Gazette,* June 2, 1766.

[15] "Journal of Josiah Quincy, Junior, 1773," *op. cit.,* p. 455.

[16] Inventories, LL (1744–1746), pp. 223–229, S. C. Archives.

[17] Inventories, R (1) (1751–1753), pp. 527–530, S. C. Archives.

[18] Inventories, X (1768–1769), pp. 71–72, S. C. Archives.

and balls" as well as Robertson's *History of Scotland*.[19] Thomas Blythe must have come from Yorkshire as his *Antiquities of York, History of Yorkshire,* and a work on the Yorkshire cathedral attest.[20] These men were aware of the history of their own family groups. But what emerges from an examination of these libraries is not so much the differences between them but the similarities, no matter what the national background had been.[21]

What they shared in common was a dissenting tradition. They were men whose fathers and grandfathers, if not themselves, had suffered in the cause of liberty. Histories of the persecution of the French Huguenots would be expected, but it was the story of the English civil wars of the seventeenth century that dominated the lists. Elias Foissin owned a French history of the revolution in England. Rapin's *History of England* was listed in almost every inventory. But even more important were the works that had kept alive the seventeenth-century ideas in the eighteenth century.[22] Andrew Johnston and John Ouldfield both had four-volume sets of *Cato's Letters.* The English opposition writers in the early eighteenth century presented the story of the devouring nature of tyranny, the fact that liberty had continually been on the defensive. The histories of Turkey were enthralling for in them were all the variations on the theme that power was evil.

The contents of the libraries of Lynch, Horry, Trapier, Allston, Gaillard are not known, but they most assuredly must have been of the same description. Among themselves the story of George Gabriel Powell's family was not unusual. As William Dillwyn wrote in 1772: "This Gentlemans Grandfather John Powell (a Welshman) by adhering to the Cause of the Seven Bishops in the Reign of James 2d. rendered

---

[19] Inventories, 1763–1767, pp. 66–71, S. C. Archives.

[20] Inventories, Y (1769–1771), pp. 39–42, S. C. Archives.

[21] Also see "Inventories of the estates of Maurice Lewis, Thomas LaRoche, and John Cleland," Inventories, 1740–1743, pp. 53–55; KK (1739–1744), pp. 347–348; T (1758–1761), p. 353, S. C. Archives.

[22] An analysis of these inventories supports the general thesis of Caroline Robbins, *The Eighteenth-Century Commonwealthman, Studies in the Transmission, Development and Circumstances of English Liberal Thought from the Restoration of Charles II until the War with the Thirteen Colonies* (Cambridge, Mass., 1961). Also see Walter B. Edgar, "The Libraries of Colonial South Carolina" (PhD dissertation, Univ. of S. C., 1969).

himself so obnoxious to the Court, that he was obliged to leave his Country and after some Stay in the Netherlands went to the Cape of Good Hope and afterwards settled at St. Helena" where his son was born.[23] The Reverend John Baxter's favorite sermon as he preached here and there to his listeners of Scottish descent was "Tryals to Presbytery."[24]

Thus these men had a general view of history. Although they had come from diverse backgrounds, they all knew of conspiracies against their ancestors, against themselves, and therefore against liberty itself. They forged a new unity out of past adversities. As the blows rained upon them during the 1760's and the 1770's, they dragged from their family experiences and from their reading certain ideas which they developed into a political philosophy.

When Governor Thomas Boone refused to administer the oath to Christopher Gadsden, which was required for him to take his seat in the Assembly, the Governor created a crisis in South Carolina. When Parliament passed the Stamp Act, Parliament raised a crisis in all thirteen colonies. Thomas Lynch joined Christopher Gadsden and John Rutledge in the South Carolina delegation to the Stamp Act Congress in New York. There Lynch helped to draw up the address to the English House of Commons.[25] It was the first time that Southerners had cooperated with Northerners in a common opposition to British authority. On their return to Charleston each member of the delegation was honored by having a street named after him and jointly by a request for their portraits.[26]

The calm brought on by the repeal of the Stamp Act did not last long. It was broken by the attempt to enforce the new trade regulations which struck at the coastal trade and at the interests of Georgetown. All coasting vessels henceforth had to secure a registration and go through the formality of clearing in and out of Charleston and Georgetown,

[23] "Diary of William Dillwyn During a Visit to Charles Town in 1772," ed. A. S. Salley, *SCHM*, XXXVI (1935), 34–35.

[24] George Howe, *History of the Presbyterian Church in South Carolina* (Columbia, S. C., 1870), I, 204.

[25] "Journal of the Stamp Act Congress, 1765," printed in *The Weekly Register* (published by H. Niles), II, 337 (Baltimore, Md., 1812).

[26] Lynch Street has been renamed Ashley Avenue, but Rutledge and Gadsden remain. Edward McCrady, *The History of South Carolina under the Royal Government, 1719–1776* (New York, 1899), p. 586; *Gazette*, June 9, 1766.

when for over forty years there had been no interference with this trade.[27] In May 1767 the schooner *Active,* owned by James Gordon, a merchant of Georgetown, loaded with pitch, tar, and pork, was seized in Charleston harbor by Captain James Hawker of HMS *Sardoine.*[28] Upon the news of the seizure there was a rush to register. Before the end of May nineteen coasting schooners were registered, four from the Santee, one of these belonging to Daniel Horry and another to Isaac Mazyck.[29] In the final decree in the case of the *Active* on June 19, 1767, Judge Egerton Leigh decided in favor of Gordon—that vessels going from one point to another within the same province did not have to clear and and give bonds. Yet Gordon was forced to pay the costs of the trial, and, since Leigh stated that there had been "probable cause" for the prosecution, Gordon could not sue the officials responsible for the seizure. The cases involving the coasting vessels of Henry Laurens are better known,[30] but the seizure of the *Active* was more threatening to the Charleston-Winyah trade. If these new trade regulations helped to impel Laurens toward revolution, they also helped to push the big Santee and Winyah planters in the same direction.

Before South Carolina could revolt she must unify the province. Ever since the Cherokee War of 1759–1761 the backcountry had been in turmoil. Restless and lawless, it needed courts.[31] In 1757 the men on the edge of Craven County had wanted a justice of the peace;[32] by 1767 the leading men of the backcountry wanted courts. Tacitus Gaillard and Benjamin Farar helped to push through the Assembly in 1768 a circuit court act, but it was disallowed by the King in Council.[33] The need to buy out Richard Cumberland, the holder of the patent as provost marshal, plus the disallowance, alienated more South Carolinians. However,

[27] For what has been called "customs racketeering" see Oliver M. Dickerson, *The Navigation Acts and the American Revolution* (Philadelphia, Penn., 1951), pp. 208–256.

[28] This case is fully discussed in *Gazette,* June 22, 1767. The charge against the *Active* was that she had not entered, cleared, given bonds, carried cockets, etc. Dickerson, *op. cit.,* pp. 225–226.

[29] For the Santee River vessels see Ship Register, 1765–1780, pp. 55, 59, 60, 63, S. C. Archives.

[30] Dickerson, *op. cit.,* pp. 224–231.

[31] For the Regulator Movement and the passing of the two circuit courts acts see Brown, *op. cit.*

[32] Petition from Craven County, 1757, Lyttelton Papers, WLCL.

[33] Brown, *op. cit.,* p. 75.

in 1769 a second Circuit Court Act was passed; it divided the backcountry into judicial districts, each of which was henceforth to have a jail and a courthouse with the common law judges in Charleston riding circuit. The northern circuit consisted of Georgetown, Cheraw, and Camden districts. The parishes of Prince George and Prince Frederick composed Georgetown District. Thomas Lynch. Elias Horry, Jr., Paul Trapier, Joseph Allston, George Grabiel Powell, Thomas Godfrey, and Samuel Wragg were named commissioners for superintending the building of a jail and courthouse in Georgetown. These new courts began to function in 1772 and thereby brought greater order to each district.[34] The Circuit Court Act of 1769 helped to unify the state on the eve of Revolution.

George Gabriel Powell played a conspicuous part in bringing law and order to the backcountry. In 1761 he had been elected to the Assembly by both Prince Frederick and Prince George. Later he was the choice of St. David's. During the Regulation he used his power to support the government.[35] On August 10, 1769, he was appointed an assistant judge, which meant that after the Circuit Court Act of that year (which he had helped to write) he would be riding the northern circuit. In December 1770 Bull wrote of him as one who had subscribed the nonimportation agreements "and is strongly influenced by factious connections and unconstitutional prejudices, which he propagates with zeal, as well as his two brethren [the other assistant judges] in his charges to the Grand Jury, instead of discouraging them." [36] Therefore, although he upheld the laws of the province, he also gave countenance to the protests against England. When he was removed as an assistant judge on April 23, 1772, in order to make way for a placeman coming out from England, he must have veered more toward the patriot side, no doubt re-

[34] This act was not printed in *S. C. Statutes* but has been printed from the original copy in the S. C. Archives in Brown, *op. cit.*, pp. 148–158. The presentments of the Georgetown grand jury, Benjamin Young, foreman, dated April 26, 1775, were printed in Crouch's *South-Carolina Gazette*, Extraordinary, June 23, 1775. The grand jury complained of the insufficiency of the laws relating to white persons dealing with slaves, the lack of a public school and of a public market under proper regulation, and of a justice of the peace who was a drunkard.

[35] Brown, *op. cit.*, pp. 56–58, 96–97.

[36] Bull to Hillsborough, Dec. 5, 1770, BPRO, XXXII (1768–1770), 409, S. C. Archives.

calling all of the injustices heaped on his ancestors.[37] He was destined to preside over the first general meetings of the people to be held in Charleston on the eve of the Revolution.[38]

It was Lynch, however, who more truly represented the planters of Georgetown. He was one of the biggest indigo planters. In 1765 he advertised for a man thoroughly acquainted with "indigo making" to manage seven or eight sets of vats on his plantation.[39] He was not only among "the noble twenty-six" of November 1768, but also of the committee of three with Gadsden and John Rutledge to draw up the address to the king.[40] In December 1770 Bull wrote of him: "The first movers in the grand machine are Mr. Thomas Lynch who, tho' a man of sense, is very obstinate in urging to extremity any opinion he has once adopted." [41] In March 1773 Josiah Quincy, who had attended the sessions of the Assembly, noted that Lynch "spoke like a man of sense and a patriot—with dignity, fire, and laconism." [42] His purpose seemed fixed. Thus, although a calm existed after the repeal of the Townshend duties and the breaking through of the nonimportation agreements in 1770, some men kept the cause alive. Thomas Lynch may have been able to do this better than anyone else in Prince George, for he had a Charleston home where he resided part of the year. However, his son Thomas Lynch, Jr.. was defeated early in 1774 for a seat in the Assembly from Charleston.[43] The conservative Charlestonians were apparently not ready to follow the radicals from the banks of the Santee. In October 1772 the royal governor had selected Beaufort rather than Georgetown as a proper place for the Assembly to meet. If Georgetown were radical, Beaufort was conservative with Charleston in between.

[37] Montagu to Hillsborough, April 27, 1772, BPRO, XXXIII (1771–1773), 141, S. C. Archives; Miscellaneous Records, PP, Part 1 (1771–1774), pp. 175–176, S. C. Archives.

[38] *Gazette*, July 11, 1774.

[39] *Gazette*, July 6, 1765.

[40] The vote in the Assembly to consider the Massachusetts Circular Letter had been 26 to 0. Commons House Journal, No. 37, Part 2 (1767–1768), pp. 20–21. S. C. Archives. The Assembly was dissolved before the address could be written.

[41] Bull to Hillsborough, Dec. 5, 1770, BPRQ, XXXII (1768–1770), 416, S. C. Archives.

[42] "Journal of Josiah Quincy, Junior, 1773," *op. cit.*, pp. 451-452.

[43] George C. Rogers, Jr., *Evolution of a Federalist, William Loughton Smith of Charleston, 1758–1812* (Columbia, S. C., 1962), p. 76.

The third Anglo-American crisis which led directly toward the American Revolution began with the Boston Tea Party. The people of Georgetown resented the Intolerable Acts, designed to coerce Boston, as strongly as any group in America. The planters understood clearly what hardships were involved in closing a port of entry, which they had struggled to win in the 1720's and maintain ever since. They therefore willingly contributed to the relief of Boston. Daniel Horry, Thomas Lynch, and Paul Trapier headed a committee of citizens in Charleston to receive supplies for Boston.[44] On July 6, 1774, Paul Trapier, Jr., turned over to Christopher Gadsden £732.5, which had been contributed by thirty-six persons in the two parishes; contributors included William Allston, Jr., Joseph Allston, John Allston, Josias Allston, and Francis Allston. These men were the leading planters.[45]

The assemblymen from Prince George and Prince Frederick attended the great three-day meeting of the people held in Charleston early in July; Colonel George Gabriel Powell presided. The purpose was to decide what should be done in the face of this new threat of parliamentary tyranny. The most important decision of this extra-legal body was the selection of the more radical ticket to represent South Carolina in the first Continental Congress, which had been called by Massachusetts to meet in Philadelphia in September. Henry Middleton and John Rutledge had the support of all, but Thomas Lynch, Christopher Gadsden, and Edward Rutledge defeated Miles Brewton, Charles Pinckney, and Rawlins Lowndes. With Lynch and Gadsden on the delegation, it could be said that Charleston and Prince George Parish, not South Carolina, were directly represented in the Continental Congress.[46]

The general meeting also established a committee of ninety-nine to put the resolutions of the meeting into execution, to correspond with the other colonies—in general, to act as an interim executive body. This was the first time that upcountry areas, by this time known as districts, were permitted representation. However, the parishes were generally represented by esquires, whereas the upcountry districts were represented by plain misters. Thomas Lynch, Elias Horry, Jr., and Benjamin Huger, all esquires, represented Prince George; Theodore Gaillard, Jr.,

[44] *South-Carolina Gazette; and Country Journal,* July 12, 1774.
[45] McCrady, *op. cit.,* pp. 743–744.
[46] *Gazette,* July 11, 1774.

Adam MacDonald, both esquires, and Mr. William Martin represented Prince Frederick.[47]

Thomas Lynch represented the dominant group in his parish. He spoke for one of the centers of the lowcountry elite. Why did such a wealthy man, whose son had just returned from a period of study in England, who had extensive estates and much to lose by revolution, take the side of revolution? Why did the Horrys and the Allstons? It is difficult to perceive any economic motive. Would the indigo planters not lose their parliamentary bounty? It could well be, as Jack Greene has said in *The Quest for Power*, that Lynch was one of those men fighting to preserve the rights that the members of the Assembly had won over a period of years.[48] No one had served longer in the Assembly than had Lynch. It was certainly more in behalf of the rights of that body than of the rights of all men that he fought. Leonard Levy has pointed out that these assemblies were jealous of their own right of freedom of speech, but not so careful of those who dared to criticize them.[49] (In South Carolina the case of printer Thomas Powell was a *cause célèbre*.) [50] Mixed, however, with this defense of the rights of the Assembly was a desire for status. It was the blending of two things that brought Lynch and his fellow planters into the Revolutionary camp originally—a desire to defend what they had won in their Assembly and a desire to be respected for what they themselves had achieved in three generations in America. The motives were more political, constitutional, and psychological, than economic. Yet, the course contained risks for the future. Lynch was not fighting to remove property qualifications for holding a seat in the Assembly, nor for the right of representation for the upcountry, nor was he fighting to free the slaves. In a sense, he was fighting for his planting class. But like any revolutionary, he spent little time at first thinking about the consequences of his

[47] *South-Carolina Gazette; and Country Journal*, July 12, 1774.

[48] Jack P. Greene, *The Quest for Power, The Lower Houses of Assembly in the Southern Royal Colonies, 1689–1776* (Chapel Hill, N. C., 1963), passim.

[49] Leonard W. Levy, *Legacy of Suppression, Freedom of Speech and Press in Early American History* (Cambridge, Mass., 1964), passim.

[50] The Council had placed the printer under arrest for contempt. Two justices of the peace, who were members of the Assembly, released him on the ground that the Council was not a house of the legislature and therefore had no right to punish for contempt. The justices were upheld by the Assembly. McCrady, *op. cit.*, pp. 715–721; Levy, *op. cit.*, pp. 76–78.

actions. However, there would be hesitations, second thoughts, before the path of revolution had been traveled very far. The fervor with which these planters embraced the Revolutionary cause should not obscure the qualifications in their own minds with which the men of Georgetown and of South Carolina went into the crisis. Their descendants would have to deal with the risks and the implications involved in these acts for more than two centuries.

When Thomas Lynch appeared in Philadelphia the following September, he was a man already known throughout the colonies. He had attended the Stamp Act Congress in New York in 1765; he had met the Northern men, like Josiah Quincy, who had visited Carolina; and in the summer of 1773 he had traveled in the North meeting others, such as John Adams and the proprietary leaders of Pennsylvania.[51] On this occasion the initial impression that he made was most favorable. On August 31, 1774, John Adams confided to his diary after renewing his acquaintance with Lynch: "We were all vastly pleased with Mr. Lynch. He is a solid, firm, judicious Man." [52] On September 7, Silas Deane wrote his wife: "Mr. Lynch is a gentleman about sixty . . . wears the manufacture of this country, is plain, sensible, above ceremony, and carries with him more force in his very appearance than most powdered folks in their conversation. He wears his hair strait, his clothes in the plainest order, and is highly esteemed." [53] The Northern leaders, who were pleased with his puritan bearing, were greatly interested in the South Carolina delegation for, as John Dickinson told Adams in May 1775, the balance in the convention "lay with South Carolina." [54] Since Thomas Lynch stood somewhere between Gadsden on one side and the Rutledges and Middleton on the other, he was a key figure in a key delegation.

Lynch's purpose in attending the convention in Philadelphia was to secure a redress of grievances, not a separation from Great Britain. In his view, Parliament did not have power to regulate trade. He was will-

[51] *Diary and Autobiography of John Adams,* ed. L. H. Butterfield *et al.* (Cambridge, Mass., 1961), II, 85.

[52] *Ibid.,* II, 117.

[53] *Letters of Members of the Continental Congress,* ed. Edmund C. Burnett (Washington, D. C., 1921), I, 18.

[54] Butterfield *et al., op. cit.,* III, 316.

ing, therefore, to adopt every means that he could adopt "with a good conscience" in order to make that position clear.[55] He desired a cessation of trade with the Mother Country so that pressure would be put upon the British merchants, forcing them to petition for relief as they had done in the previous crises. He felt that Parliament would grant relief, as bankruptcy would threaten many British merchants if they did not. Such a policy was not agreeable to the correspondents of these British merchants in Charleston and that may be the reason why they did not vote for him in the great meeting in July. When the first Continental Congress agreed to a nonimportation, nonexportation, and nonconsumption agreement, Lynch was in full accord with Congress. This association of the colonies could only be successful if it was enforced everywhere at the local level. It was necessary, therefore, for the delegates to return to their respective colonies and work for enforcement. It was in order to accomplish this purpose that the South Carolina Provincial Congress was called into being.

Those elected to the first Provincial Congress, which met in January 1775, from Prince George Winyah were Thomas Lynch, Sr., Elias Horry, Jr., Benjamin Huger, Joseph Allston, Benjamin Young, and Paul Trapier, Jr.; from Prince Frederick Theodore Gaillard, Thomas Port, Captain Adam McDonald, Anthony White, Samuel Richbourg, and Benjamin Screven. Thomas Lynch, Jr., represented St. James Santee. As these gentlemen were also elected to the second South Carolina Provincial Congress (with the exceptions of Samuel Richbourg who was replaced by John James, Sr.; Captain Adam McDonald by Archibald McDonald; and Thomas Lynch, Sr., by his son), which met in November 1775, they represent the men in Georgetown who endorsed the position that Lynch had taken in Philadelphia.[56]

The first Provincial Congress assembled in Charleston for eight days in January 1775. This body approved of what had been done in Philadelphia and elected the same delegation to represent the state in the second Continental Congress. A system of committees of observation and inspection was established for each parish and district throughout

---

[55] John Adams recorded his views. *Ibid.*, II, 138, 148.

[56] *Extracts from the Journals of the Provincial Congresses of South Carolina, 1775–1776*, ed. W. E. Hemphill and W. A. Wates (Columbia, S. C., 1960), pp. 5, 74.

the state in order to enforce the nonimportation, nonexportation, and nonconsumption agreements. Before these local committees could begin to function, however, events at the national level had moved the united colonies closer to revolution.[57] On April 19 blood was shed at Lexington and Concord; on May 10 the second Continental Congress assembled at Philadelphia.

At the second Continental Congress Thomas Lynch played a conspicuous part in the organization of the continental army, designed to invest the British army in Boston. In June, Congress appointed George Washington commander-in-chief. Throughout the summer Washington tried to weld the men into a fighting unit. On October 3, 1775, when Lynch at the request of Congress set out with Benjamin Franklin and Colonel Benjamin Harrison to confer with Washington before Boston, Samuel Adams wrote James Warren that Lynch was "a Man of Sense and Virtue," implying that he was a man working diligently to strengthen the forces in Massachusetts.[58] On his return to Philadelphia, although Lynch devoted his efforts to sustaining the continental army, there was in the back of his mind a hope that a show of force, a few successes, would bring peace. He wrote Washington on November 13 that he had letters stating that the destruction of the British army in Boston and the seizing of Quebec would force the British to make peace. He therefore approved of Washington's policy of hovering before Boston "like an Eagle over your Prey, always ready to Pounce it when the proper Time comes."[59] It was obvious, however, that as soon as Boston and Quebec should fall, Lynch would move for peace proposals through channels to his British friends, which still remained open.

After news arrived of the failure of Richard Montgomery and Benedict Arnold to take Quebec, Lynch began to sound out official British opinion through a dubious character, Lord Drummond, who appeared in New York City. On January 20, 1776, Lynch wrote Philip Schuyler: "I had before we heard of our Misfortune resolved to move for a Mode of Application for Peace, being assured by Ld Drummond that Ministry were very desirous of it on very generous terms such indeed as I

[57] *Ibid.*, pp. 11–30.
[58] Burnett, *op. cit.*, I, 214.
[59] *Ibid.*, I, 253. Also see Thomas Lynch to George Washington, Jan. 16, 1776, *ibid.*, I, 314–315.

would have dictated had I them, as they wished to have us. . . ." [60] In February 1776, while on a visit to inspect the defense of New York, he quizzed the more moderate men. In a private conversation he told William Smith, chief justice of New York: "If we separate from England, we shall be obliged to set up a republic; and that is a form of government some people are fond of which I think reads better than it works. It is best in idea, bad in experiment." [61] To some extent he was hoodwinked by Lord Drummond, but his sympathy for a settlement short of separation was leading him along the road of conciliation. He was unable to pursue this course further, for in March he suffered a stroke. On March 23, 1776, the South Carolina Provincial Congress appointed Thomas Lynch, Jr., to the South Carolina delegation to take care of his father and to remove some of the burdens from his father's shoulders, even though the son himself had been suffering from ill health ever since his expedition to North Carolina to raise troops for the patriot cause.[62] Dr. James Clitherall, who was in Philadelphia early in the summer, wrote: "I there saw Mr. Lynch whose situation struck me deeply with the feebleness of human nature. He was greatly recovered could keep on a conversation very well but now & then his Memory seemed to fail him. It was indeed shocking to see a man whose opinion at one moment swayed Millions & the next he himself under the direction of Doctors & Nurses." [63]

It was on the same March 23, 1776, that the Provincial Congress adopted a resolution authorizing their delegates to join with the others in every measure which "they shall judge necessary, for the defense, security, interest or welfare of this colony in particular, and of America in general." [64] It was now within the discretion of the delegation to commit the state to independence. If the Provincial Congress had sent the younger Lynch at this time to strengthen the father's backbone in the cause of independence, the father may have influenced the son, for John Adams noted that the Lynches wavered. They were drawn

[60] *Ibid.*, I, 322.
[61] William B. Willcox, *Portrait of a General, Sir Henry Clinton in the War of Independence* (New York, 1964), pp. 71–75.
[62] Hemphill and Wates, *op. cit.*, pp. 250-251.
[63] "Diary of Dr. James Clitherall, 1776," typed copy in SHC.
[64] Hemphill and Wates, *op. cit.*, p. 248.

to the side of the Rutledges, who were reluctant to take the giant step.[65] South Carolina at last consented, and on July 9, both father and son signed a letter to the president of South Carolina which enclosed "a very important Declaration which the King of Great-Britain has at last reduced us to the necessity of making." [66] When that document was engrossed and signed, only the son placed his name upon the document. The father was too ill to attend.

Independence implied a new form of government. The father had not been in favor of a republic, but that was the form discussed during the summer of 1776. In 1774 Thomas Lynch, Sr., already fearing that majority rule might threaten property rights, had challenged Patrick Henry's view that numbers alone should determine the weight of the colonies in the councils. Lynch, before Calhoun, saw the danger in King Numbers. "I think that property ought to be considered, and that it ought to be a compound of Numbers and Property, that should determine the Weight of the Colonies." [67] But it was the younger Lynch who on July 30, 1776, linked this fear of numbers with the fear that the majority might interfere with property in slaves. He would countenance no question concerning the right to own slaves. Both father and son assumed it was not in the ability or in the inclination of free men to work the lands of the South. Slaves were absolutely necessary, and they should not be taxed any more than land or sheep or cattle or horses.[68] These positions already made clear the type of new nation that the Lynches wanted, if there must be a new nation—a republic based on property as well as numbers, with property in slaves clearly protected. The new nation must provide protection for that society which then flourished on the banks of the Santee and the Waccamaw.

Was it uneasiness over the form of government which caused the Lynches and the Rutledges to speak in favor of an embassy to Sir William Howe after his defeat of Washington at the battle of Long Island late in August? Although the radicals in Congress were against such a

[65] Butterfield, op. cit., III, 317. Gadsden did not attend after Jan. 17, 1776. Burnett, op. cit., I, lxii. Lynch had written Philip Schuyler, Jan. 20, 1776: "my Colleague Gadsden is gone home, to Command our Troops, God save them. . . ." Ibid., I, 323.

[66] Ibid., II, 6–7.

[67] Butterfield, op. cit., II, 125.

[68] Ibid., II, 246.

mission, Congress endorsed the idea and appointed a committee composed of Benjamin Franklin, Edward Rutledge, and John Adams. The mission failed, but perhaps it was good that the decision in favor of independence had already been taken or such sentiment as that which sponsored the mission might have blocked any move to establish a new nation.

In December, while the British chased Washington through New Jersey, the two Lynches made their way home, but the father died in Maryland and was buried in Annapolis. Although the son reached Carolina, he was himself henceforth an invalid and saw little further public service. Late in 1779 he sailed for France via the West Indies on a ship that was lost at sea.[69] Had the Lynches possessed stronger constitutions they might have become as famous as the Rutledges, for their politics were similar. They were evidently not out of touch with their constituents, for their views concerning the new nation fitted well with the views later held by the Kinlochs and the Horrys. These planters wanted to command and to be respected, and for these reasons they were willing to break with Britain. They wanted to be free of excessive tax burdens placed upon them by an alien authority. They wanted a republic ruled by a planter elite of free white men, an elite that rested upon black slave labor. Yet the Lynches had made a commitment to independence and to freedom, and the Georgetown planter society would have to take the risks involved in the victory of such a cause.

With the ties with Great Britain snapping, new forms of government would emerge at every level. Such is the natural course of revolutions. Thus, while the Continental Congress was assuming the power of the nation and the Provincial Congress was assuming the power of the state, the local committees of observation and inspection were assuming the power of the parishes. The local committees, which began to enforce the nonimportation, nonexportation, and nonconsumption agreements, assumed the reins of local government and filled the vacuum which was created by the departure of royal officials. After news of Lexington and Concord had reached South Carolina, the first Provincial Congress reassembled and adopted an association on June 3, 1775.[70] By signing

[69] John G. Van Deusen, "Thomas Lynch, Sr.," and "Thomas Lynch, Jr.," *DAB*.
[70] Hemphill and Wates, *op. cit.*, p. 36.

this document the Carolinians bound themselves to fight, if so ordered by Congress, until the differences with England were reconciled. To sign such a document was to disavow one's oath to the King, which every vestryman, justice of the peace, and militia officer had taken. When these local committees of observation and inspection demanded adherence to the continental association and to the provincial association, they were demanding a commitment to the new cause.

Paul Trapier, Samuel Wragg, Paul Trapier, Jr., Benjamin Young, Joseph Allston, Thomas Godfrey, Anthony Bonneau, John Withers, Hugh Horry, Daniel Tucker, and Robert Heriot were the committee for Prince George to put into execution the continental association. Josias Allston, Samuel Dwight, Dennis Hankins, Francis Allston, and John Allston, Jr., were the committee for Little River. John James, Hugh Giles, Anthony White, Jr., William Gamble, Robert M'Cottery, John Witherspoon, Thomas Potts, Francis Britton, William Michau, William Thompson, and William Snow were the committee for Prince Frederick.[71] The striking fact about the membership of these committees, when contrasted with the delegations sent to the Assembly from these parishes in the past, is that all of the members were residents, none Charlestonians. It would, of course, have been foolish to appoint men who lived in Charleston to enforce the association in the outlying parishes. Men on the spot were needed. True representation was the result of this practical need. Particularly in the case of Prince Frederick, these were the natural local leaders, the men who would swarm around Francis Marion. The crisis forced the oligarchy to share leadership with the local men.

These committees found it difficult to watch every river and landing to prevent importations and exportations. The case of Captain Ellis is a good example. The captain was loading his vessel in December 1775 at Georgetown for a voyage to the Turks Islands for salt when he was

---

[71] *Ibid.*, p. 23. On Sept. 13, 1775, the committee for Little River wrote to the committee of intelligence in Charleston asking what should be done with two individuals who would not sign the Association. Thomas Port wrote the council of safety, July 21, 1775, from the Pee Dee that every man in his district who had been assembled to sign the Association had done so "without one Dissenting Voice." Thomas Port mentioned that he had been elected captain of a company to defend the country against foreign and domestic enemies and that Hugh Giles was elected first lieutenant and Thomas Potts second lieutenant. Miscellaneous Letters received by the Council of Safety, Henry Laurens Papers, S. C. Hist. Soc.

stopped by the Georgetown committee. After he explained that he was preparing for a voyage to the Edisto River, a destination that was within the state and therefore not forbidden, the committee let him depart. A few days later, however, Captain Ellis was discovered on the Santee River loading his ship for a foreign destination. In this instance, the Georgetown committee felt that the committee in the parish of St. James Santee had not been vigilant. The association demanded not only vigilance, but also cooperation. Through cooperation the people were united in a common cause.[72]

John Rutledge had secured at Philadelphia an exception to the non-exportation agreement in favor of rice. This was a distinct concession to South Carolina; the Northerners consented to a compromise in order to win the support of a state they feared might not join the cause. Rice, therefore, could be exported from South Carolina, but control over the shipment of rice was placed in the hands of another committee, which in Georgetown was composed of the members of the committee of observation and inspection with the addition of five local merchants: Samuel Smith, George Croft, James Gordon, George Heriot, and Thomas Mitchell.[73] As indigo was not excepted, the indigo planters complained to the Provincial Congress, which then worked out a system whereby planters might exchange their indigo for rice, which could then be exported. This committee supervised the exchanges in order to even out the burdens. Later, a control on the sale of salt was established with Anthony Bonneau and George Croft as commissioners for Georgetown.[74]

In the same way that the Provincial Congress delegated control over trade to the local committees, it also delegated authority over defense matters. The committee of observation was also the committee of safety. Authority was granted for raising a battery of artillery, of which Paul Trapier, Jr., became the commanding officer. They were ordered to secure a sloop and to arm it. Powder was shipped to them.[75]

In the period of preparations before June 1776, Georgetown played a very minor role, although in one instance a very important one. As the

---

[72] Georgetown Committee of Safety to Council of Safety in Charleston, Dec. 14 and 28, 1775, "South Carolina Council of Safety, 1775–1779," NYPL.

[73] Hemphill and Wates, op. cit., p. 26.

[74] Ibid., p. 238.

[75] Ibid., pp. 142, 208, 232.

British navy began to watch the entrances to Charleston harbor, Georgetown became an important entrepot for vessels carrying powder and
weapons, the importation of which had been excepted from the general
rule. Georgetown because of these imports soon had a surplus of powder
and began to supply neighboring areas. In January 1776 the committee
sent some powder up the Pee Dee to St. David's Parish. More urgent
was the request that came in the same month from Cornelius Hartnett,
president of the Wilmington committee. He had written Paul Trapier,
president of the Georgetown committee, for two or three thousand
pounds of powder since loyalists were known to be rallying at that time
in Guilford County in preparation for marching on Wilmington and
joining with North Carolina's royal governor, Josiah Martin, who was
still at Fort Johnston at the mouth of the Cape Fear River. This was
the beginning of the movement that was to end disastrously for the
North Carolina loyalists at Moore's Creek Bridge in February. Trapier,
after consulting with the leaders in Charleston, shipped 700 pounds of
powder to Captain William Allston's Brookgreen plantation on the Waccamaw, to which place the Wilmington committee sent a detachment
of men to receive the powder. In this way the Georgetown committee
helped the patriots to the north of them keep the loyalists in check.[76]

At the time that the Provincial Congress in June 1775 had drawn up
the Association, that body also organized the first and second South
Carolina regiments, which were later incorporated into the continental
army. Christopher Gadsden was elected colonel, Isaac Huger lieutenant
colonel, and Owen Roberts major of the first regiment. William Moultrie
was elected colonel, Isaac Motte lieutenant colonel, and Alexander Mc-
Intosh major of the second regiment. It is in the election of the twenty
captains that the strength of the Georgetown war party is revealed. The
first eight captains elected were Charles Cotesworth Pinckney, Barnard
Elliott, Francis Marion, William Cattell, Peter Horry, Daniel Horry,
Adam McDonald, and Thomas Lynch, Jr.[77] As William Cattell was
Lynch's son-in-law, all but the first two were from the Georgetown

---

[76] Georgetown Committee of Safety to Council of Safety in Charleston, Jan. 20,
29, Feb. 12, 1776, to Committee of Safety in Wilmington, Feb. 20, 1776, "South
Carolina Council of Safety, 1775–1779," NYPL.
[77] Hemphill and Wates, op. cit., pp. 45–46.

party.[78] When one recalls both Gadsden's and Moultrie's connections with this area, it can be seen that the Georgetown area was the heart of militancy in the state.

When news arrived in the spring of 1776 that the British intended to attack Charleston, the men of Georgetown made additional efforts to help their sister city. Although Captain George Heriot, the engineer in charge of building fortifications in Georgetown, could not be spared, Captain George Cogdell and Captain Robert Heriot and their two companies of volunteers marched over Lynch's Causeway and down to Haddrell's Point where they assisted on June 28, 1776, in repulsing the British.[79] The victory at Fort Moultrie gave South Carolina three years before the state was called upon to defend itself again.

The second Provincial Congress had drawn up a constitution in March 1776 under which an election was held in the following October. The first state legislature, consisting of house and senate, in turn drew up in 1777 and 1778 a new state constitution under which elections were held on the last day of November 1778. The only important electoral change was the recreation of All Saints Parish.[80] The men who represented the parishes were from the same ranks as those who had attended the provincial congresses.[81]

During the four-year period from the Battle of Fort Moultrie to the surrender of Charleston, Georgetown flourished on wartime trade. Markets were easy to find and profits high, but the dangers of the sea had increased. Henry Laurens wrote letters for Georgetown merchants to open up a trade with French ports. In March 1777 he wrote letters in behalf of George Croft to merchants at Nantes and Rochelle. Croft's vessel, the schooner *Freeman,* captained by Alexander Boyd of Connecticut and laden with rice and indigo, was, however, captured in the Bay

[78] William Cattell married Sabina Lynch on March 8, 1767. *The South-Carolina and American General Gazette,* March 13, 1767.

[79] Georgetown Committee of Safety to Council of Safety in Charleston, Jan. 16, 1776, "South Carolina Council of Safety, 1775–1779," NYPL. On June 28, 1776, Mary Heriot wrote to her husband Capt. Robert Heriot at Haddrell's Point that when Capt. Postell's company goes "there will be scarce a white man left in this part of the country." Caldwell Woodruff, "Heriots of Scotland and South Carolina" (Linthicum Heights, Md., 1939), p. 81, typed copy in S. C. Hist. Soc.

[80] Recreated on March 16, 1778. *S. C. Statutes,* IV, 407–408.

[81] Notes of Miss Wylma Wates, S. C. Archives; *Gazette,* Dec. 8, 1779.

of Biscay and taken into Portsmouth, England.[82] In July 1777 Edward Weyman, marshal of the vice-admiralty court for South Carolina, seized the brigantine *Success* in Georgetown harbor for illegal importations of goods from England.[83] In February 1778 Peter Norris, prize master, brought in the prize schooner *Polly and Nancy*, which he immediately libeled although the owners of the privateer *Rutledge* eventually made good their claim to the vessel and cargo.[84] Amid such disruptions the war afforded, fortunes could be made. Those who profited from the wartime trade invested their funds in loans to the state.[85]

Georgetown was relatively safe compared to Charleston. When General Augustine Prevost threatened Charleston in May 1779 the treasury and the records of the state were removed temporarily (from May 12 to July 1) to "Georgetown & Waccamaw." [86] The British did raid the coast occasionally for provisions. Paul Trapier wrote Henry Laurens in October 1779 to secure his aid in recovering slaves stolen from Waccamaw Neck and sold in Boston. Trapier was writing in behalf of Anthony Pawley, Percival Pawley, Jr., William Vereen, and William Henry Lewis, all of whom Laurens knew: "They are very honest worthy men, and in general possessed of considerable property." [87] The beaches were patrolled. Alexander Dunn, for example, spent 165 days on patrol during the winter of 1779–1780.[88]

Many passed through on their way to and from the wars. Gabriel Manigault arrived from the West Indies and England on his way to Charleston.[89] But the most famous arrival was that of the young Marquis de Lafayette with the Baron de Kalb on June 13, 1777. They landed "on lonely North Island, outside the solitary summer residence

[82] These documents are in the case file of the *Freeman* in the High Court of Admiralty records. HCA 32/335/11, PRO, London.

[83] "Arthur v. Weyman," Revolutionary War Prize Cases, Court of Appeals, 1776–1787, Case No. 24, microfilm, Roll 2, S. C. Archives.

[84] "Norris v. the Schooner Polly and Nancy," Revolutionary War Prize Cases, 1776–1787, Case No. 25, microfilm, Roll 3, S. C. Archives.

[85] "William Allston, Jr.," "Joseph Brown," "Benjamin Coachman," "Thomas Horry," "Benjamin Huger," and "Paul Trapier," Audited Accounts, S. C. Archives.

[86] Auditor General, Schedule of Accounts Passed, April 12, 1778–Feb. 9, 1780, pp. 143, 147, S. C. Archives.

[87] Trapier to Laurens, Oct. 7, 1779, Charles Francis Jenkins Collection, Penn. Hist. Soc.

[88] "Alexander Dunn," Audited Accounts, S. C. Archives.

[89] Rogers, *op. cit.*, pp. 85–86.

of Major Benjamin Huger, South Carolina militia." The watchdogs barked; the Huger family prepared for British raiders. Lafayette knocked on the door and explained they had come from Bordeaux and were seeking a pilot. After fifty-four days at sea and two days of Huger hospitality, Lafayette wrote his wife: "The customs of this world are simple, honest, and altogether worthy of the country where everything re-echoes the beautiful name of *liberty*." There on North Island Lafayette swore to conquer or die in the American cause.[90]

[90] The most authoritative account (even high tide for early morning June 14, 1777, was computed) is in Louis Gottschalk, *Lafayette Joins the American Army* (Chicago, Ill., 1937), pp. 1–3.

VIII

GEORGETOWN IN THE AMERICAN REVOLUTION

The complacency of the early war years was shattered by the surrender of Charleston on May 12, 1780. Sir Henry Clinton realized that the capture of Charleston was of little importance unless the backcountry could also be controlled. His task was threefold: to conquer the country, to pacify the people, and to organize loyal militia units. Clinton left these problems for Lord Cornwallis to solve, since he was eager to return to New York before a French fleet could cut him off. Clinton sent Cornwallis toward the Santee and ordered Admiral Mariot Arbuthnot to send galleys into Winyah Bay, hoping to trap the patriots in Georgetown as they had been trapped in Charleston.[1] Admiral Arbuthnot, as so often before, did not cooperate, and the entrance of the British into Georgetown by sea did not take place until July 1.[2]

Governor John Rutledge, who fled Charleston before the surrender, was in Georgetown on May 5 to rally the people to defend the ferry landings along the Santee.[3] Colonel Banastre Tarleton, however, de-

---

[1] Clinton to Cornwallis, May 18, 1780, Cornwallis Papers, PRO, 30/11/2.

[2] For Clinton's failures in cooperation with Cornwallis and Arbuthnot see William B. Willcox, *Portrait of a General, Sir Henry Clinton in the War of Independence* (New York, 1964), pp. 513-514.

[3] John Rutledge to Colonel Kershaw, George Town, May 5, 1780, Rutledge Papers, SCL.

feated Captain Anthony White shortly thereafter at the approaches to Lenud's Ferry, which Cornwallis and Tarleton both crossed by May 22. Colonel Tarleton was dispatched by Cornwallis in a lightening chase of Colonel Abraham Buford's continentals, whom he caught and massacred on May 29 at the Waxhaws. Cornwallis fixed himself at Camden, whence he could slowly bring under his control the region to the east and also oppose any re-entry into South Carolina of a continental army.[4]

Captain John Plumer Ardesoif captured Georgetown from the sea on the first of July, seizing the vessels in the harbor with their cargoes as prizes of war. He sent sailors in armed barges up the rivers to plunder the plantations. Although he did not stay long enough to ravage the countryside completely, he alienated Major John James in a stormy interview and thereby set in motion a new rebellion among those who would be Marion's men.[5] On July 11 Major James Wemyss arrived with the 63rd Royal Regiment. He seized the rice on the nearby plantations, stating that these crops were part of public stores and therefore legitimate prizes of war.[6]

Clinton before he departed for New York had instituted a policy of pardon and amnesty. By his proclamations of May 22 and June 1 he held out the prospect of a pardon to all who would take oaths of allegiance to the crown. He undermined this policy, however, by another proclamation of June 3 which implied that those who took protection would also be expected to take up arms against the rebels. The British planned to intern high public officials and "prominent obnoxious persons" on the sea islands south of Charleston; lesser persons, after being disarmed, would be permitted to stay on their plantations. On June 1 Clinton had written Cornwallis that the country from the Pee Dee to the Savannah had accepted the proclamation but noted that "they seem to

[4] According to McCrady, Tarleton proceeded to Georgetown and dispersed the rebels there while Cornwallis was moving his army across the Santee. Edward McCrady, *The History of South Carolina in the Revolution, 1775–1780* (New York, 1901), pp. 494, 516-517.

[5] William Dobein James, *A Sketch of the Life of Brig. Gen. Francis Marion and a History of his Brigade from its Rise in June 1780 until Disbanded in December 1782* (Marietta, Ga., 1948), pp. 42–43.

[6] Wemyss wrote that he arrived on Saturday morning (prior to July 11). Wemyss to Cornwallis, July 11 and 25, 1780, Cornwallis Papers, PRO, 30/11/2.

have some scruple about carrying arms against the Congress. . . ." [7] The proclamation of June 3 was designed to remove this scruple by dint of a British order. Here was the crux of the problem: many patriots were willing to come in and swear allegiance to the crown, but they were not willing to take up arms against their friends. The first was a simple measure of expediency to protect their property; the second, a moral question that touched their consciences.[8]

On July 14 Major Wemyss sent Cornwallis the following representation that he had received from the leading citizens of Georgetown:

We Inhabitants in and about George Town Winyah beg leave to represent to Major Wemyss, that as the original cause of the disputes between Great Britain and her colonies was our being taxed without being represented—and as by a Proclamation of the 1st June last issued by His Excellency Sir Henry Clinton Knight of the Bath General and Commander in Chief of his Majesty's Forces in America, and Mariot Arbuthnot Esquire Vice Admiral of the Blue and Commander in Chief of his Majesty's Ships, We are assured that we shall not be taxed but by our representatives in General Assembly, We are therefore desirous of becoming British Subjects in which capacity we promise to behave ourselves with all becoming fidelity and loyalty.

Among the signers were Daniel Tucker, William and George Heriot, Thomas and Edward Mitchell, Paul Trapier, Samuel Wragg, George Croft, Benjamin Young, and John Allston, Jr., men, as Wemyss explained, who had been "chairmen of committees, sheriffs, and magistrates." [9] Wemyss had written three days earlier that the "principal inhabitants," many of whom had been "most violent and persecuting rebels," had been coming in to save their estates. He thought that if "ten or twelve of the leading people" should be sent to the sea islands that "the Friends of Government, who are much inferior to the other

---

[7] Clinton to Cornwallis, July 1, 1780, Memorandum of Cornwallis, June 4, 1780, Cornwallis Papers, PRO, 30/11/2.

[8] For a discussion of this crucial mistake see McCrady, op. cit., pp. 549–558.

[9] Others who signed were Christopher Taylor, John Vieran, Thomas Smith, Joseph Brown, Randolph Theus, Simeon Theus, Jr., John Wilson, Abraham Cohen, Edward Martin, Thomas Hasell, Peter Sanders, Francis Marshall, Peter Lesesne, John Porter, Thomas Burnham, Mordecai Myers, Thomas Hendley, John Hawkins, Andrew Debay, Solomon Cohen, Jesse Ballard, Richard Brooks, and John Goff. The date of Aug. 1, 1780, was added later to this document. Cornwallis Papers, PRO, 30/11/2.

party both in numbers and in consequence will be pleased and will be roused to take every method of carrying on the purpose of Government." If the leading men stayed in Georgetown on parole, "I think [they] will (as they have been used to command) discountenance the raising the militia much." Cornwallis must have given his permission, for on July 22 Wemyss wrote that the most dangerous would be paroled to the sea islands and "those that are looked upon in a lesser degree criminal" would be sent to their plantations. This harsh policy paved the way for organizing the loyal militia.[10]

Yet the policy of both Cornwallis and Wemyss was tempered with mercy. Robert Heriot had appeared at Cornwallis's headquarters in Camden on July 1 and had given his parole. It was recorded and, with signature attached, reads as follows:

I, Robert Harriott of the Province of South Carolina, acknowledge myself to be prisoner to His Majesty's Forces, and hereby promise upon my parole of honour, that I will repair to James Island, John's Island, Edisto Island, Edings's Island, St. Helena in the said Province, on or before the twentieth day of July Inst., (notifying the place of my residence to the commissary of prisoners at Charlestown, within two days after my arrival) & there remain until regularly exchanged, or permitted or ordered to remove; and that while prisoner I will not write, speak or act directly or indirectly against His Majesty's interest, and that I will surrender myself at any time & at any place when ordered by the Commander in Chief or any other of His Majesty's officers.[11]

Cornwallis, however, gave Heriot permission to go to Georgetown instead of the sea islands in order to visit the ailing members of his family. Before Wemyss left Georgetown on August 8 he voluntarily extended Heriot's leave because his daughter had died the day before and his son and wife were both seriously ill.[12]

During July Wemyss tried to raise a loyal militia. Clinton had outlined his program in a memorandum of May 22 for Major Patrick Ferguson, whom he had appointed inspector of the militia. All the young and unmarried men of Georgia and the two Carolinas were to be organ-

[10] Wemyss to Cornwallis, July 11, 14, 17 (two letters of this date), and 22, 1780, Cornwallis Papers, PRO, 30/11/2.

[11] Cornwallis Papers, PRO, 30/11/2.

[12] Wemyss to Cornwallis, Aug. 8, 1780, Cornwallis Papers, PRO, 30/11/2.

ized into companies of fifty to a hundred men to serve under the orders of Cornwallis. Each company would be commanded by a lieutenant chosen by the men. An ensign of the regular army would be assigned each company to provide discipline and order, "which however must be done with great caution, so as not to disgust the Men, or mortify unnecessarily their love of freedom." Officers during actual service would receive army pay. The service of the men was to be precisely limited; written certificates stating the inclusive times of service would be given, and pay of six pence sterling a day with provisions granted. These companies were not to serve beyond the borders of Georgia and the Carolinas. They would be furnished "oznaburgs for a rifle shirt" and ammunition and arms for those who had none. Major Ferguson was to restrain the militia from offering violence to innocent and inoffensive people "and by all means in your power protect the aged, the infirm, the women and children of every denomination from insult or outrage, endeavouring as much as possible to subsist your men and supply their wants at the expense of the known and obstinate enemys of the King and Constitution alone." If the admonitions contained in the plan had been obeyed to the letter, much of the difficulty that the British were to experience in South Carolina might have been avoided.[13]

Cornwallis intended to follow this plan. He did, however, on June 4 order that the estates of the prisoners on parole in the islands and those of the disaffected not embodied in the militia must contribute supplies for the support of the militia.[14]

Cornwallis had great difficulty in finding suitable officers. When Cornwallis asked Lieutenant Colonel Nisbet Balfour for names, Balfour replied that "all the leading men of property have been on the rebel side" and that it would be difficult to find men of rank and respect to serve as officers of the loyal militia.[15] The failure of the British to find leaders of the stature of Francis Marion lost them this region— or at least prevented them from holding it securely.

Wemyss, who felt it would be difficult to find sufficient officers for three regiments in his district, urged the formation of only two, one for

[13] Instructions to Major Ferguson, Inspector of Militia, from Clinton, May 22, 1780, Cornwallis Papers, PRO, 30/11/2.
[14] Memorandum of Cornwallis, June 4, 1780, Cornwallis Papers, PRO, 30/11/2.
[15] Balfour to Cornwallis [June 3 or 4, 1780,] Cornwallis Papers, PRO, 30/11/2.

the upper division to serve under Colonel Mills and one for the lower to serve under Colonel James Cassells, "a very sensible man, and a zealous friend to government." Wemyss was against using John Coming Ball as an officer because he was not respected by the people who lived north of the Santee. He was ready, however, to offer to Theodore Gaillard the colonelcy of the lower regiment if James Cassells should refuse. He warned Cornwallis, however, that due to quarrels among the loyalists it was difficult to ascertain the true character of the men on the British side. Wemyss acting upon his own advice sent off a messenger to Mills and wrote a letter to Cassells. This messenger to Mills did not get through. On July 25 he was still waiting for Cassells to arrive in Georgetown.[16]

The attempt of Wemyss to organize the militia was cut short by the advance into the northern portion of the Georgetown judicial district of the continental army under General Horatio Gates and the North Carolina militia under General Richard Caswell. This advance forced the 71st Royal Regiment to fall back from the Cheraws to Camden, permitting the North Carolina militia to break through to the Pee Dee and to disrupt the formation of Mills's militia, some of whom broke their parole and sided again with the rebels. The breaking of the parole, so recently given, infuriated the British and drove them to deeds of vengeance and retaliation. Mills himself barely reached Georgetown on July 28, having been pursued to within a few miles of the town. James Cassells was taken, and friends of government plundered of their Negroes. Although Wemyss felt himself safe in Georgetown, the plans for the loyal militia could not be carried forward: "should those Banditti be even dispersed soon, it will require a good deal of time to bring things to their former situation." [17]

Wemyss was severely pressed by the rebels, who now pursued a policy of harassment designed to make life as miserable as possible for the British. The heat and damp of Georgetown increased the problems of the British. On July 11 Wemyss had written Cornwallis for permission to station his men on North Island where the sea breezes would

---

[16] Wemyss to Cornwallis, July 14, 22, 25, and Aug. 2, 1780, Cornwallis Papers, PRO, 30/11/2.

[17] Wemyss to Cornwallis, July 28, 29, and 31, 1780, Cornwallis Papers, PRO, 30/11/2.

provide a more healthful climate, but Cornwallis, worried by the approach of Gates, wanted Wemyss to march his men to Camden. Wemyss was, however, immobilized. Early in August six of his men died within three days of putrid fever, while four sergeants and twenty-eight men were ill. Eighteen of these had to be sent to Charleston by water.[18]

The British were to be guilty over and over again during the Carolina campaign of extending their lines too far, forcing men to take protection, and then abandoning these unfortunates to the mercies of the patriots still fighting on the fringes of the British lines. Wemyss on this occasion wanted to leave a galley to guard the loyal people, but the loyalists thought this protection insufficient. The Reverend James Stuart, who had been forced to stop preaching at Prince George in December 1777 and whom even Wemyss found "exceedingly violent & disposed to persecute," judged it necessary for his own safety to proceed to Camden in advance of the British troops.[19] The merchant James Gordon and Dr. Charles Fyffe also thought it better to go to Camden.[20] Wemyss, therefore, sent the loyal to Camden and the sick to Charleston, but he was still delayed by the incessant rains which had flooded the country. Finally, on August 8, Wemyss marched to Gaillard's on the Santee, but he was too late to take part in Cornwallis's victory at Camden on August 16 and 17.[21]

In August as General Gates made plans to challenge the British control of South Carolina, he sent Francis Marion and Peter Horry to disrupt communications between Camden and Charleston. Francis Marion, although born in St. John's Berkeley, had grown up on the banks of Winyah Bay and was intimately acquainted with the terrain of Georgetown District.[22] Since he had had military experience against the Chero-

[18] Wemyss to Cornwallis, July 11, Aug. 2, and 4, 1780, Cornwallis Papers, PRO, 30/11/2.

[19] Frederick Dalcho, *An Historical Account of the Protestant Episcopal Church, in South-Carolina* (Charleston, S. C., 1820), p. 308; Wemyss to Cornwallis, July 14 and Aug. 4, 1780, Cornwallis Papers, PRO, 30/11/2.

[20] Wemyss to Cornwallis, July 23 and Aug. 4, 1780, Cornwallis Papers, PRO, 30/11/2. The tories of Georgetown were generally Scotsmen.

[21] Wemyss to Cornwallis, Aug. 4, 8, and 28, 1780, Cornwallis Papers, PRO, 30/11/2.

[22] "Dr. Anthony Cordes and Some of His Descendants," compiled by Emma B. Richardson, *SCHM*, XLIII (1942), 136, 142–145. Francis Marion's sister Esther had married John Allston (died 1751) and his brother Benjamin Marion married Martha Allston. William Allston of Brookgreen was the brother of John and Martha Allston.

kees, he was elected a captain in the 2nd South Carolina Regiment and saw service at the defense of Charleston in 1776. Henry Lee described him as "small in stature, hard in visage, healthy, abstemious, and taciturn . . . fertile in stratagem . . . a rigid disciplinarian . . . neither elated with prosperity, nor depressed by adversity, he preserved an equanimity which won the admiration of his friends, and exacted the respect of his enemies." [23] Because he was abstemious he refused to drink heavily at a Charleston party, dislocated his ankle trying to escape from an awkward social affair, and thereby was forced to leave Charleston before the surrender.[24] Because he was short and light, he could ride swiftly. Because of his character and abilities, he won the loyalty of his men. With Peter Horry he had made his way into North Carolina as Cornwallis advanced. These two were the heart of the resistance.

Marion began his famous operations against the British by taking command on Lynches Creek on August 10 or 12.[25] He was to burn boats on the middle Santee, and Horry on the lower Santee. Hugh Giles was to retake Georgetown.[26] After the defeat of Gates at Camden on August 16, the forces of Marion and Horry were in danger of being captured. Before taking flight Marion secured the escape of 150 Maryland continentals, who were being sent from Camden to Charleston. He then called upon Horry and Giles to meet him at Britton's Neck between the Great and Little Pee Dee rivers, and together they retreated into North Carolina.

Cornwallis sent Wemyss in pursuit of Marion. Wemyss swung down to Kingstree Bridge and then cut a wide swath through the country to Cheraw, from which he wrote on September 20: "altho I never could come up with them, yet I pushed them so hard, as in a great measure to break them up. The force that still continue together, have retreated over the Little Pedee." Marion demonstrated on this occasion, as he

[23] Quoted in McCrady, op. cit., pp. 570–571.
[24] Tradition says that Marion broke his ankle jumping out of a window on the second floor of the house that John Stuart had built on the corner of Tradd and Orange streets. He landed in Orange St.
[25] For Marion's career see James, op. cit., and Robert D. Bass, Swamp Fox, The Life and Campaigns of General Francis Marion ([New York,] 1959).
[26] Hugh Giles to General Gates, written between fork of Pee Dee and Lynches Creek, Aug. 12, 1780, Cornwallis Papers, PRO, 30/11/3. For Horry's description of these events see "Journal of General Peter Horry," ed. A. S. Salley, SCHM, XXXIX (1938), 127–128.

was to do repeatedly, his ability to outrun the enemy, for Wemyss noted that his own force had been well mounted and had on August 20 marched fifty-six miles without halting. The fact that Mills's earlier attempt to embody the militia at Cheraw had failed because his officers and men had broken their paroles, plus the fact that Marion was able to elude his grasp, intimidated Wemyss into waging a savage war. He reported that he had burnt and laid waste about fifty homes and plantations "mostly" belonging to people who had either broken their parole or oath of allegiance. Wemyss, who had British regulars plus fifty loyal militia with him, thereby broke Clinton's orders concerning the conduct of the militia in relation to the civilian population.[27] The war was moving into a more bitter phase. Tarleton had written Cornwallis on August 5 from Lenud's ferry: "many of the insurgents having taken certificates & paroles don't deserve lenity. None shall they experience. I have promised the young men who chuse to assist me in this expedition the plunder of the leaders of the faction. If warfare allows me I shall give these disturbers of the peace no quarter; If humanity obliges me to spare their lives: I shall carry them close prisoners to Camden."[28]

With Clinton in New York and Cornwallis at Camden, the command at Charleston fell to Lieutenant Colonel Nisbet Balfour of the 23rd Regiment. It was Balfour's responsibility to keep open the lines of communication to Cornwallis. As the provisions and arms destined for Cornwallis had to cross the Santee at Nelson's ferry, any rebel force hovering to the north of that river threatened the supply line. Balfour decided to use the loyal companies of Colonel John Coming Ball and Colonel Joseph Wigfall, organized in the parishes just south of the Santee, to guard the ferries across the Santee, and to send by sea Major James Moncrief of the engineers with the 7th Royal Fusiliers to construct Georgetown's defenses and support Colonel James Cassells in his attempt to keep the militia together.[29]

Moncrief, who had already built the defenses of Charleston, had been at Georgetown sometime when he wrote Balfour on September 20: "I have now done all I can to punish the People in the lower parts of this

[27] Wemyss to Cornwallis, Sept. 20, 1780, Cornwallis Papers, PRO, 30/11/3.
[28] Cornwallis Papers, PRO, 30/11/63.
[29] Balfour to Cornwallis, Aug. 31, Sept. 4, 8, and 20, 1780, Cornwallis Papers, PRO, 30/11/63–64.

Country." He enclosed a list of prisoners sent to Charleston and Johns Island and added: "The disposition of the people does not require so strict a guard, but, at all events, we cannot be too guarded at present. Have therefore weeded out the violent spirits." He also sent Negroes to work on the defenses of Charleston and 150 good horses to "my friend Tarleton." His principal suggestion for securing the region was the establishing of posts for the militia to occupy at strategic points. He wanted to push Colonel Cassells' regiment forward to Britton's Neck, an excellent post from which to watch Marion; he placed Colonel Ball at Shepherd's ferry over Black Mingo Creek near Patrick Dollard's tavern and Colonel Wigfall at Black River Church.[30]

Marion meanwhile had not been inactive. He marched against the Tories on Drowning Creek, a tributary of the Little Pee Dee, and defeated them. Some of these Tories under Major Micajah Ganey and Captain Jesse Barefield then made their way via Waccamaw Neck to Georgetown where Marion would again face them.[31] But with his rear protected Marion contemplated an assault on the loyal militia at Black Mingo Creek. After a four-day ride, Marion with Major Hugh Horry and Captains John James, Thomas Waties, and Henry Mouzon fell upon the loyal militia and routed them in fifteen minutes. Although the Tories had been forewarned by the clatter of the hooves of Marion's horses on the wooden bridge, they could not withstand the rebels, who had been aroused by Wemyss's depredations.

The presence of Marion on the Pee Dee worried the British. During October there was much discussion by the British command in Camden and in Charleston concerning the proper line of defense. Should it be the Black River, or the Pee Dee, or perhaps the Cape Fear? Moncrief, who had arrived in Camden on September 29, voted for the Black River. Wemyss did not believe that militia, without regulars, could hold the line. Lieutenant Colonel George Turnbull of the New York Volunteers thought that Balfour was "puffed up" by the number of loyal regiments available and did "not consider that our officers of militia in general are not near so active as the Rebells."

[30] Moncrief to Cornwallis, Sept. 20 and 28, 1780, Cornwallis Papers, PRO, 30/11/64.

[31] Alexander Gregg, *History of the Old Cheraws* (Baltimore, Md., reprinted 1967), p. 341.

At this point there began to creep into their correspondence a possible solution, one designed to eliminate the threat posed by the presence of Marion on the Pee Dee. Wemyss suggested that the Cape Fear River ought to be the frontier of this country; otherwise the rebels would remain masters of the Pee Dee. If the Cape Fear became the line of defense, then the Highlanders at Cross Creek and the Tories on Drowning Creek would again rally to the British cause. "If this plan should be try'd and succeed, the militia of Georgetown & the Cheraws (bad as they are), would under the direction of a prudent man, settle the whole of that country in a permanent manner." Lieutenant Colonel Robert Gray of the Cheraw militia wrote in the same vein to Cornwallis. Even Balfour, coming around to this point of view, began to doubt if the Pee Dee could be kept clear unless Cornwallis's operations could put a stop to "the inroads of small partys." It may have been this advice, placed in Cornwallis's mind at this time, which determined his march to Wilmington after the battle at Guilford Court House in March 1781. In October 1780 the Pee Dee was in the capable hands of Francis Marion, a man for whom the British already had great respect.[32]

Marion, who could not be inactive for very long, moved to cut the line of communications along the Santee. Lord Rawdon sent Tarleton from Camden on November 5 to chase Marion, but Tarleton could not find his enemy. He perceived that a general revolt had taken place below the Santee Hills, but, beyond that, he knew little for he was surrounded by a sea of silence. No one would lead him to Marion. The faces of the people were as "dark and mysterious" as their swamps. "Frustrated, he wrote Cornwallis: "Nothing will serve these people but fire and sword." The only treatment he could think of for the rebels was that prescribed "according to the ancient Scripture" to level all and sow the earth with salt. He was, therefore, satisfied to issue dire proclamations and return to Camden.[33]

Balfour wanted a post at Kingstree Bridge, garrisoned by regular

[32] Balfour to Cornwallis, Oct. 1, 5, and 10; Turnbull to Cornwallis, Oct. 1, 4, and 20; Wemyss to Cornwallis, Oct. 4; Gray to Cornwallis, Oct. 7, 1780, Cornwallis Papers, PRO, 30/11/3.

[33] Turnbull to Cornwallis, Nov. 5; Tarleton to "my dear sir," Nov. 5; Tarleton's proclamation, Nov. 11, 1780, Cornwallis Papers, PRO, 30/11/4.

troops.[34] Otherwise, Marion would merely return to that unfortunate area and the Santee would be unsafe again for the rum and salt then loading in Charleston for transportation to Camden. When Marion almost immediately appeared before Georgetown with 500 men, Balfour could not refrain from writing Cornwallis that in spite of Tarleton's "*dispersing* account" Marion had reappeared. "Marion's movement I beg Tarleton may be remembered of—it is no joke to us." Although Balfour must have felt as frustrated about Marion's movement as Tarleton had been, Balfour was still responsible for the supply lines along the Santee; he therefore sent Major McLeroth from Charleston to Kingstree with the 64th Royal Regiment.[35]

Although Lieutenant Bluke, who then commanded at Georgetown, was perfectly safe behind his new fortifications, Balfour had intended to reinforce him by sending militia companies from Charleston under the commands of Nicholas Lechmere and Robert Ballingall. When Balfour found it almost impossible to form militia groups in Charleston, he blamed the principal men of the city, who, although they had given their parole, were using their influence to prevent men from signing up. He, therefore, shipped off another group of prominent Charlestonians to St. Augustine. Balfour was acting out of a state of frustration brought on by his inability to cope with the Swamp Fox.[36]

With the appearance of Major McLeroth at Kingstree with the 64th, Marion quickly retreated behind the Pee Dee. Colonel James Cassells pressed Balfour to let him move up the Pee Dee so that he might protect those people on the Little Pee Dee, the Great Pee Dee, and Lynches River who had been offering to quit Marion "whom they all look upon only as a plunderer." Balfour was in favor of this move since Cassells was "by no means a man of chimera" as his behavior had always been "much more manly, & worthy of credit, than any other Col. of Militia, I have yet seen."[37] But McLeroth, although he had 300 British regulars, 300 mounted militia, and two cannon, abandoned Kingstree on Novem-

[34] Balfour to Rawdon, Nov. 1 and 5, 1780, Cornwallis Papers, PRO, 30/11/4.

[35] Balfour to Cornwallis, Nov. 10, 15, and 17; Rawdon to Cornwallis, Nov. 14, 1780, Cornwallis Papers, PRO, 30/11/4.

[36] Balfour to Cornwallis, Oct. 10, 16, and Nov. 15, 1780, Cornwallis Papers, PRO, 30/11/4. The names of those sent at this time to St. Augustine are listed in "Josiah Smith's Diary, 1780–1781," *SCHM*, XXXIII (1932), 100.

[37] Balfour to Cornwallis, Nov. 24, 1780, Cornwallis Papers, PRO, 30/11/4.

ber 22 and marched toward Murray's ferry on the Santee. Balfour hoped that McLeroth would stay on the north side of the Santee. If he moved to the south side or marched off to Camden, he would leave only militia to oppose Marion, who was "too formidable to trust so near the boats, and stores, without something better than militia." Under these circumstances, Balfour must strengthen Georgetown. On November 24, he decided to send Lieutenant John Wilson, an engineer, with a galley and two cannon to Georgetown where a week's work on the redoubts would make them "absolutely impregnable." [38] Since General Alexander Leslie arrived in Charleston with fresh troops in the middle of December, Balfour ordered Bluke to join the army, advising him to march his troops along the south side of the Santee to Camden, and replaced his force with Edmund Fanning's King's American Regiment and John Saunders' Queen's Rangers, a corps of 230 men fit for duty. As McLeroth had returned to Kingstree on December 6, Marion was temporarily immobilized. [39]

With all British eyes focused upon him, Marion needed a safe retreat. In early November he used Gapway Bay as a hiding place. It was from the camp in Gapway Bay that his nephew Gabriel Marion had sallied forth and had been killed. [40] In early December he picked the almost inaccessible Snow's Island, a ridge five miles long and two miles wide in the midst of the Pee Dee. "Along its eastern shore runs the Peedee. Lynches River lies on the north, and along the western and southern borders runs Clark's Creek, one of the mouths of Lynches. To the west lie Snow's Lake and the sloughs and morasses of Muddy Creek and Sockee Swamp." [41] To this base supplies were brought from the surrounding country.

Beyond the marching and the counter-marching, the ordinary life of the plantations and farms continued. Crops were planted, Negroes worked, and harvests gathered in—all quite often done under the management of women. Mrs. Robert Heriot managed her own plantation and

[38] Balfour to Cornwallis, Nov. 24, 29, 30, and Dec. 4, 1780, Cornwallis Papers, PRO, 30/11/4; Marion to Greene, Nov. 22, 1780, Greene Papers, WLCL.

[39] Balfour to Cornwallis, Dec. 15, 16, and 26, 1780, Cornwallis Papers, PRO, 30/11/4; Marion to Greene, Dec. 6, 1780, Greene Papers, WLCL.

[40] Bass, op. cit., pp. 88–90; Balfour to Cornwallis, Nov. 24, 1780, Cornwallis Papers, PRO, 30/11/4.

[41] Bass, op. cit., p. 104.

that of her brother-in-law William Heriot, while the two brothers were interned on the sea islands. Clothes for the slaves had to be secured, medical advice on smallpox considered, and a school for the children maintained. As Mrs. Heriot knew Colonel Cassells and was introduced to Lieutenant Bluke by Dr. Alexander Garden, she was able to ask for favors from both sides.[42] In February 1781 Robert Heriot was permitted a visit with his family.[43] There was much movement through the lines by those waiting out the struggle.

Under such circumstances food and supplies could be brought into the camp at Snow's Island. It took twelve days' work of Negroes using six large working oxen and a boat to carry salt from Plowden Weston's plantation to Snow's Island in February 1781. Alexander Tweed's Negro man worked five days in October 1781 carrying rum and necessarys to Marion's men. John Allston provided a mare and a horse, grain, rough rice, beef, oats, as well as the services of his ferry at Yauhany, Pee Dee, for the troops.[44]

Marion's strength ebbed and flowed in the fluid style of guerrilla warfare. W. W. Boddie estimated that 2,500 men served under Marion at one time or another.[45] Marion himself was promoted to brigadier general by Governor Rutledge at the end of December.[46] Some of the officers such as Colonels William Allston, Peter Horry, and Hugh Horry, and Captains Thomas Mitchell, John Allston, William Allston, and Thomas Waties were from the rice-planting class. But most of Marion's men were drawn from the small farmers who lived along the Black and Pee Dee rivers, or from among the Scotch-Irish of the Black Mingo region: Colonels Hezekiah Maham, Adam McDonald; Majors William Benison, Alexander Swinton, Hugh Giles, John James; and Captains Henry Lenud,

[42] Mary Heriot to Robert Heriot, Oct. 31, 1780, Caldwell Woodruff, "Heriots of Scotland and South Carolina" (Linthicum Heights, Md., 1939), pp. 87–91, typed copy in S. C. Hist. Soc.

[43] Pass dated Feb. 19, 1781, ibid., p. 92.

[44] "John Allston," "Alexander Tweed," and "Plowden Weston," Audited Accounts, S. C. Archives.

[45] William Willis Boddie, Marion's Men, A List of Twenty-five Hundred (n.p., 1938).

[46] John Rutledge to Delegates of South Carolina in Congress, Dec. 30, 1780, "Letters of John Rutledge," annotated by Joseph W. Barnwell, SCHM, XVIII (1917), 63.

Thomas Potts, John Baxter, William McCottry, Daniel Conyers, John McCauley, Henry Mouzon, John Postell.[47] Whatever their background, they rendezvoused from time to time at Snow's Island to commence another foray against the British. As Drayton Mayrant has poetically stated: on "moonlight nights in their buff-and-blue,/Stirrup to stirrup and two by two,/Marion's men came riding through."[48]

From the fastness of Snow's Island Marion rode forth to maul McLeroth at Kingstree.[49] McLeroth, the most humane of the British officers, was replaced by Lieutenant Colonel John Watson who constructed Fort Watson on Wright's Bluff five miles from Nelson's ferry on the Santee which, with Georgetown, continued to threaten Marion. Marion fixed his eyes on Georgetown, believing he could take it if Greene could spare him a force of continentals. He wrote Greene on December 28, 1780, that Georgetown had been reinforced. That post contained 300 men, including twenty well-mounted horse men, two galleys, and three nine-pounders for the redoubt which enclosed a brick building.[50]

Marion probed the defenses of Georgetown. On December 28, Colonel Peter Horry, Captain John Baxter, and Sergeant McDonald explored the Black River Ferry Road. In a skirmish with Tories, McDonald plunged his bayonet into the back of Major Ganey, who galloped back to town with blood gushing from his wounds.[51]

With Marion beginning to take offensive actions, Balfour warned Lieutenant Colonel George Campbell, who had replaced Edmund Fanning as commanding officer at Georgetown, that "it would be best not to attempt any onward movements, but to confine yourself to clearing the roads and communication, in your vicinity, of such lurking parties of the enemy as may infest them." Campbell should attend to the levying of cavalry "which are so essential in your part of the country, and, on this head, you will be pleased to assure Colonel Cassells that the raising of them has only the good of the province, and King's service for its

[47] McCrady, op. cit., pp. 577, 649, 699; Edward McCrady, The History of South Carolina in the Revolution, 1780–1783 (New York, 1902), pp. 82, 99–100.

[48] "Octaves on an Edisto Plantation," Drayton Mayrant, White Horse Leaping, (Columbia, S. C., 1951), p. 27.

[49] Bass, op. cit., pp. 107–112.

[50] Marion to Greene, Dec. 28, 1780, Greene Papers, WLCL.

[51] Bass, op. cit., pp. 120–123.

object." In order to strengthen his position, Campbell sent out detachments to secure horses at Black Mingo and salt on Waccamaw Neck.[52]

Marion bided his time. Early in January he described for Greene the changes that were taking place in front of him. By the ninth he knew that General Leslie had marched from Charleston to Camden, leaving Colonel Watson and 200 men at Wright's Bluff on the Santee to guard Nelson's ferry. Captain Bluke had finally departed Georgetown, taking eighty men with him. He had crossed to the south side of the Santee at Lenud's ferry, where he left twenty men as a guard and marched the rest to Nelson's ferry, which he was to cross in order to join Colonel Watson. Bluke's departure reduced the number of men in Georgetown to 200, which included fifteen regular horse and twenty mounted infantry. "They keep so close in their redoubt," Marion wrote, "that I have not had any opportunity to attack them. I keep parties of men constantly near them, to prevent forraging, or driving off stock."[53] Under such circumstances another clash was likely; it came on Waccamaw Neck.

Marion had sent Peter Horry to collect boats and drive off cattle near Colonel William Allston's Brookgreen plantation. Meeting with a body of twenty horse, Horry gave chase but came up against Campbell himself with about sixty men. Horry was obliged to retreat, but not before he captured two dragoons. Marion, who did not realize that the British were establishing a base at Wilmington, suspected Campbell of trying to cooperate with the Tories on Drowning Creek in order to encircle him.[54]

Balfour had written Cornwallis on January 7 that as soon as Major Craig, who was preparing an expedition for the Cape Fear, could reach Wilmington that the force at Georgetown should move up to Kingston on the Waccamaw and thereby open the door to the North Carolinians, who held both banks of the Cape Fear between Wilmington and Cross Creek.[55] Balfour wrote Lieutenant Colonel George Campbell on January 19: "As it will be necessary for you soon to make forward movements,

---

[52] Balfour to Campbell, Jan. 1, 1781, Cornwallis Papers, PRO, 30/11/109.
[53] Marion to Greene, Jan. 4 and 9, 1781, Greene Papers, WLCL.
[54] Marion to Greene, Jan. 14, 1781, Greene Papers, WLCL.
[55] Balfour to Cornwallis, Jan. 7, 1781, Cornwallis Papers, PRO, 30/11/109.

the Redoubt at George Town will consequently become a Rear work, and any additional strength to it, unnecessary. You will, therefore immediately dismiss all the Negroes etc. employed on it. 'Till such movements as I have mentioned, actually take place, you can have no occasion to retain many horse or carriages and may therefore return them to the owners, taking care, that they are in readiness, when such a call renders them necessary as by this means the country will be greatly eased, and a present saving accrue to government." Colonel Cassells was to be consulted in all dealings with the local population.[56] Major Craig sailed from Charleston for Wilmington on January 21.[57]

These British plans were disrupted by Marion's attack on Georgetown. The arrival of Light Horse Harry Lee and his continentals as reinforcements made the attack feasible. Since Captain John Postell had been gathering boats, Marion was able on January 23 to send Captains Carnes and Rudolph down the Pee Dee with the infantry to lie in wait a day among the rice fields. The plan of attack was based on the ease of landing in the water suburbs of the town inside the abbatis and palisades. Carnes was to head for the wharves and to capture Colonel Campbell, who resided near the parade ground. Rudolph was to seize anyone attempting to gain the redoubt. With the first shots, Marion's militia and Lee's legion would rush in to assist in the rounding up of the British troops. This plan was executed on the night of January 24. The surprise was great, and Colonel Campbell was captured, but most of the British troops remained barricaded in the brick redoubt, which, without battering and scaling equipment and without artillery, Marion could not assail. Lee thought the plan had been too complicated. If Rudolph, instead of intercepting fugitives, had been ordered to carry the fort by the bayonet, success might have been complete.[58] On January 25 Lee wrote Greene that the combined forces had been inadequate "to the assault of the enemy's enclosed works."[59] Marion, however, took the opportunity to send Captain John Postell south of the Santee and Colonel

[56] Balfour to Campbell, Jan. 19, 1781, Cornwallis Papers, PRO, 30/11/109.

[57] Balfour to Cornwallis, Jan. 25, 1781, Cornwallis Papers, PRO, 30/11/5.

[58] Bass, *op. cit.*, pp. 130–137; Henry Lee, *Memoirs of the War in the Southern Department of the United States* (New York, 1870), pp. 222–225.

[59] Lee to Greene, Jan. 25, 1781, Greene Papers, WLCL.

James Postell up the Santee toward Fort Watson to seize stores where possible.[60]

On the very day of Campbell's capture, Balfour was writing him of Tarleton's defeat at Cowpens on January 17. Balfour was dispatching the news of Tarleton's repulse so that Campbell might "provide against the evil effects which exaggerated and malevolent reports, of this transaction, may have on the minds of the country people, that if any rising amongst them shou'd be attempted, You may, by timely exertions frustrate such intentions: and, finally, by knowing, guard against any bad consequences which this affair might otherwise have on your post." [61] News of Cowpens coupled with Marion's exploit before Georgetown accomplished just what Balfour feared. The Santee was exposed to sudden incursions. Balfour rushed thirty regulars to Lenud's ferry and other reinforcements to the posts on the Santee and dispatched Saunders and the remainder of the Queen's Rangers to Georgetown.[62] On January 31 he summed up the situation for Clinton by pointing out that Greene was now using Lee and Marion, "two very enterprising officers," to distress the British east of Santee.[63]

While Marion was writing Greene that "Col. Lee's enterprising genius promises much," Lee was planning to return to Greene.[64] Greene was soon pressed back by Cornwallis into North Carolina and had to leave Marion to hold the region between the Santee and the Cape Fear rivers by himself. Although almost surrounded, Marion's men still harassed the British. On February 21 a small party from Marion's brigade captured Captain James De Peyster with twenty-five men of Fanning's Regiment, who had been detached on service a few miles from Georgetown.[65]

In March Colonel Watson, acting under orders from Lord Rawdon at Camden, marched down the Santee to engage Marion in a formal contest. Marion met him first at Wiboo swamp, then at the Lower Bridge on

[60] Bass, op. cit., pp. 137–138.

[61] Balfour to Campbell, Jan. 25, 1781, Cornwallis Papers, PRO, 30/11/109.

[62] Balfour to Wigfall, Jan. 25, 1781, Cornwallis Papers, PRO, 30/11/109.

[63] Balfour to Clinton, Jan. 25 and 31, 1781, Cornwallis Papers, PRO, 30/11/109.

[64] Marion to Greene, near Murray's Ferry, Jan. 27, 1781; Lee to Greene, near North (or Post) Ferry, Jan. 30, 1781, Greene Papers, WLCL.

[65] Balfour to Clinton, Feb. 24, 1781, Cornwallis Papers, PRO, 30/11/109. James places this episode in January. James, op. cit., p. 93.

Black River, where he parried Watson's attempt to reach Kingstree and finally caught him at the Sampit on March 20 as Watson ran for Georgetown. Marion was by this time pawing at the enemy like an angry tiger. Marion was enraged by the fact that Captain Saunders had illegally retained Captain John Postell, who had gone to Georgetown under a flag of truce.[66]

The events at Georgetown were never at the center of the stage. Whatever happened at Georgetown depended on what happened elsewhere—at Charleston, at Camden, at Guilford Court House, or at Wilmington. This was true throughout the Revolution, as it had been true when Barnwell led his troops in a broad circuit against the Tuscaroras and was to be true when Sherman, starting from Savannah, made a similar circuit through Columbia to his rendezvous with Johnston in North Carolina. The rivers and swamps of the lowcountry made such circuitous operations necessary. The terrain around Georgetown was suitable for the guerrilla activities of Marion and Lee, but not for the grand maneuvers of armies as large as those led by Cornwallis and Greene. Georgetown's fate was therefore being decided in North Carolina.

The battle of Guilford Court House was not a victory for either side, but that action did jolt Cornwallis's army and upset his plans. Cornwallis had to make a momentous decision: to return to South Carolina, or to march toward Wilmington and the coast, or to swing around Greene into Virginia. He decided upon Wilmington as his destination in order to rid himself of his sick and wounded and to refit his troops with supplies brought by sea from Charleston. He also hoped to rally the strength of the Tories along the Cape Fear River and Drowning Creek.[67]

Greene did not follow Cornwallis to Wilmington but turned his army southward and marched against Rawdon at Camden. Thomas Sumter and Andrew Pickens now moved on Greene's right toward Ninety-Six, while Marion, rejoined by Lee, once again threatened both Fort Watson and Georgetown. Balfour, facing this massive and coordinated reinvasion of South Carolina, had to keep open a possible escape route for Cornwallis along the coast as well as to sustain his interior posts. He there-

---

[66] Bass, *op. cit.*, pp. 143–153.
[67] Charles O'Hara to the Duke of Grafton, April 20, 1781, *SCHM*, LXV (1964), 173–179.

fore placed provisions at Georgetown in case Cornwallis should come that way and anxiously watched his posts.[68]

Colonel Lee rejoined Marion on April 14, and they invested Fort Watson the next day. The fort was situated on a small hill forty feet high; it was well stockaded with three rows of abbatis around it. No trees were near enough to the fort to cover the patriots from the fire of the British. The British could be forced to surrender, however, by cutting off their supply of water. So Marion and Lee placed riflemen between the fort and the lake from which they drew their water. But on the third day after investing Fort Watson, they found that a well had been sunk near the stockade, the sinking of which they could not prevent. The alternative to abandoning the siege was to build a platform which would dominate the fort and whence a fire could be directed at its interior. This arduous work was completed on the morning of April 23 under the direction of Major Hezekiah Maham. In this fashion the British were overawed and forced to surrender.[69] Lee was so pleased with Marion's talents in the reduction of Fort Watson that he wrote Greene: "I wish you would formally put me in true degree under General Marion's command. It will please him and I admire him." [70] Since jealousy among patriot officers was always rife, especially between the continental and militia officers, this was the highest praise for Marion, the partisan officer.

Greene already held Marion in high respect. Green wrote him on April 24, not yet knowing of his victory at Fort Watson:

When I consider how much you have done and suffered and under what disadvantages you have maintained your ground I am at a loss which to admire most your courage and fortitude or your address and management. Certain it is no man has a better claim to the public thanks or it more generally admired than you are. History affords no instance where in an officer has kept possession of a country under so many disadvantages as you have, surrounded on every side with a superior force, hunted from every quarter with veteran troops, you have found means to elude all their attempts, and to keep alive the expiring hopes of an oppressed militia, when all [safety] seemed to be cut off—To fight the enemy

[68] Balfour to Cornwallis, April 20, 1781, Cornwallis Papers, PRO, 30/11/5.
[69] Bass, *op. cit.*, pp. 169–178; Marion to Greene, April 23, 1781, Greene Papers, WLCL.
[70] Lee to Greene, April 23, 1781, Greene Papers, WLCL.

with a prospect of victory is nothing—but to fight with intrepidity under the constant impression of a defeat, and inspire irregular troops to do it is a talent peculiar to your self.[71]

With a notable victory and such praise to his credit, Marion was buoyed up to strike against Georgetown itself. Major Rudolph had been left to watch the British there while Marion and Lee concentrated on Fort Watson. But Cornwallis was still a question mark. Would he go off to Virginia or return to Charleston? Alexander Swinton wrote Marion on April 28 from the Pee Dee that he had heard that Tarleton was to move southward by way of Georgetown. Fearful of this possibility and knowing that Marion would want the first intelligence of such a move, Swinton sent men toward Wilmington to watch the movements of the troops there.[72] Greene advised Marion on May 1: "Keep a good look out for Tarleton." [73] When Cornwallis finally marched off for Virginia early in May, taking Tarleton with him, the war scene in eastern Carolina suddenly brightened. Georgetown seemed to be Marion's at last. And then, as it had happened so often before, Marion's men melted away, leaving him without the force necessary to achieve his long-hoped-for goal. Marion was despondent, shattered, frustrated; he wrote Greene on May 11:

I assure you I am very serious in my intention of relinquishing my militia command, not that I wish to shrink from fatigue or trouble, or for any private interest but because I found little is to be done with such men as I have, who leave me very often at the very point of executing a plan and their late infamous behaviour in quiting me at a time which required their service most[,] confirm me in my former intentions. If I cannot act in the militia I can[n]ot . . . remain in the state and I hope by going to the northward to fall in some employ where I may have an opertunity of serving the United States, in some way that I cannot be in this country.[74]

Marion, however, stayed on. During May he was in St. Stephen's parish on the south side of the Santee watching Rawdon, who had hastily re-

[71] Greene to Marion, April 24, 1781, Greene Papers, WLCL.
[72] Swinton to Marion, April 28, 1781, Greene Papers, WLCL.
[73] Greene to Marion, May 1 and 4, 1781, Greene Papers, WLCL.
[74] Marion to Greene, May 11, 1781, Greene Papers, WLCL.

treated from Camden to Moncks Corner. Marion still wanted to move against Georgetown, which had only 100 British troops, but waited for Greene's orders.[75] On May 26 Greene, besieging Ninety-Six himself, wrote Marion that if the British under the command of Rawdon were not intending to raise the siege of Ninety-Six and if Sumter would not feel too exposed, that Marion might then make an attempt to take Georgetown; but if Rawdon appeared to be making any preparations to raise the siege of Ninety-Six, then Marion was not to go for Georgetown for that was "but an inferior object."[76] Marion interpreted these orders as giving him the chance he had long been waiting for. He took Georgetown after that town had been in enemy hands almost a year.[77] His move, however, may have been premature and unnecessary, as the following letter of May 20 from Balfour to Captain Gray, then commanding at Georgetown, indicates:

I am favored with your three letters of the 17th Instant, and shou'd before this have given directions for your quitting George Town, but for the hope of learning something certain in respect of Lord Cornwallis and his intentions, as also whether Colonel Tarleton, with the dragoons, may not make your post the route here, in which case the retaining it is of the first moment—I therefore wish it held, if possible, 'till this point is determined. But shou'd you find yourself so press'd by the Enemy as to make a retreat necessary, you must execute it before it becomes unsafe, for which purpose you will retain the Vessel which take you this, and in such event to bring off with you all those whose principles may induce them to come with you.[78]

As Rawdon did march to the relief of Ninety-Six and as Georgetown may have been evacuated, Marion's move was a strategic error. Yet the long-awaited action was accomplished. Throughout the ten months of Marion's most famous period of activity, Georgetown had been the constant object of his intentions.

[75] Marion to Greene, May 16, 20, and 22; William Pierce (for Greene) to Marion, May 18, 1781, Greene Papers, WLCL.
[76] Greene to Marion, May 26, 1781, Greene Papers, WLCL.
[77] Mary Heriot wrote her husband on May 23, 1781, that the departing British galley fired a shot which passed through her house. Caldwell Woodruff, "Heriots of Scotland and South Carolina" (Linthicum Heights, Md., 1939), pp. 93–94, typed copy in S. C. Hist. Soc.
[78] Balfour to Gray, May 20, 1781, Cornwallis Papers, PRO, 30/11/109.

Marion leveled the fortifications at Georgetown, while the British hovered in sight at the mouth of the bay. Since the area round George-town was full of provisions, especially salt, Marion tarried north of the Santee.[79] On June 10 Greene urged Marion to join Sumter in order to watch the large number of British troops who had arrived in Charles-ton and might soon relieve Ninety-Six. Sumter wrote Greene the next day that "General Marion is about to return from George Town his force but inconsiderable." Greene was to say later that he could have faced Rawdon, who successfully raised the siege of Ninety-Six, if Sumter, Marion, and Pickens had joined him. This was a rebuke of the militia captains and especially of Marion, but Marion's defense was that all of the provisions that the army could hope for until the new crop came in were north of the Santee and that with the British lurking along the coast he could not leave these provisions to their mercy.[80]

Rawdon, although he broke the siege at Ninety-Six, could not remain in the upcountry. He, therefore, retreated first to Orangeburg and then to Dorchester and Moncks Corner. Again, Marion and Sumter were called upon to harass the British. On July 17, 1781, in their only joint action, they attacked Colonel Coats at Quinby Bridge. Sumter was in the center, Marion on the left, and Hugh Horry on the right. Since they ran out of ammunition during the engagement, their success was minor. Afterward Marion took up a position in St. Stephen's and Sumter in St. John's, both keeping an eye on Orangeburg.[81] During the rest of July Marion was busy trying to hold his force in the field and secure the necessary supplies from Georgetown for Greene. Although Captain James Withers was Marion's agent in Georgetown, Marion himself made a trip there to parry a thrust of the British. Since the British held the sea, it was almost impossible to stop the British from making these de-predations, and, though driven out of Georgetown, they could still cover the region south of the Santee from Haddrell's Point. Marion did estab-lish a post at Cainhoy to watch Haddrell's Point.[82]

[79] Marion to Greene, June 5 and 6, 1781, Greene Papers, WLCL.
[80] Greene to Marion, June 10 and 25; Sumter to Greene, June 11; Marion to Greene, June 16 and 25, 1781, Greene Papers, WLCL.
[81] Bass, *op. cit.*, pp. 205–210; Marion to Greene, July 19, 1781, Greene Papers, WLCL.
[82] Greene to Marion, July 21 and 30; Marion to Greene, July 24, 30, and Aug. 1, 1781, Greene Papers, WLCL.

August was a month of waiting on both sides. Rawdon had returned to England, leaving Balfour in command at Charleston.[83] The enemy out of fear and frustration had hung Colonel Isaac Hayne. They were driven to this measure to stop further erosion in their regiments of loyal militia, for many had begun to consider a change of side as the army of Greene drew near to Charleston. As the British still held Captain John Postell, one of Marion's officers, Marion feared that Postell might suffer the fate of Hayne. Greene, however, would not permit any retaliation against British officers in American hands.[84]

In September Greene tried to win a final victory, but the action at Eutaw Springs was inconclusive. Marion had been drawn in to help and afterward worried the British as they transported their wounded to Charleston. In pursuing the wounded Marion made his closest approach to Charleston, getting as far down the Cooper River as Henry Laurens' Mepkin plantation. General Greene, however, withdrew for a time to the High Hills of the Santee.[85]

In November General Alexander Leslie arrived in Charleston to assume command. He drew the British troops within a contracted perimeter around Charleston, with Moncks Corner and Dorchester as outposts. Wilmington was evacuated; the troops, tories, and slaves arrived in Charleston from Wilmington in fourteen vessels. At the end of November Greene moved his own army into the lowcountry, so that he might be able to watch this contraction closely, hoping that it would end eventually in the evacuation of Charleston. Greene expected a few good fights during the winter months, but no final evacuation until the spring. In this overall operation Marion's role was that of guardian of the South Santee, to parry sudden excursions from Charleston in search of rice and slaves.[86]

As the enemy had now been swept from the state except for an area within a twenty-mile radius of Charleston, Governor John Rutledge put

[83] Rawdon left on Aug. 21. Balfour to Clinton, Oct. 2, 1781, Cornwallis Papers, PRO, 30/11/109.

[84] [Robert Y. Hayne,] "The Execution of Colonel Isaac Hayne," *Southern Review,* I (1828), 70–106. Also see Greene to Marion, Aug. 10 and 20; Marion to Greene, Aug. 13 and 18, 1781, Greene Papers, WLCL.

[85] Marion to Greene, Sept. 6 and 13, 1781, Greene Papers, WLCL.

[86] Marion to Greene, Nov. 10, 18, 21, and 30; Greene to Marion, Nov. 11 and 15, 1781, Greene Papers, WLCL.

into operation his plan to re-establish civil government in South Carolina. This plan included the assembling of the legislature at Camden
or at some place nearer Charleston, if Greene could guarantee protection for the members. Jacksonborough was chosen as the site of the
meeting when Greene promised to move his army to that vicinity. The
election writs were sent to the generals, who were to supervise the elections. Marion wrote Greene on December 1 saying that he had the writs
but was "sorry to see this business so soon entered on, as I am clear
the election can not be full." [87] Although Marion knew that under existing conditions a proper election could not be held, he obeyed his instructions. He sent the writ for the parish of Prince Frederick to Anthony
White and William McCottry, who had been named election managers
for that parish. They supervised the voting that took place at William
Shepherd's tavern on Black Mingo Creek on December 17 and 18, 1781.
Elections were also held on the same days in Prince George and in All
Saints.[88]

Major John Baxter, Major John James, Captain John McCauley, Colonel William McCottry, Colonel James Postell, and Captain Thomas
Potts were elected from Prince Frederick. Major William Bennison, General Christopher Gadsden, Colonel Peter Horry, and Captain Thomas
Mitchell were elected from Prince George Winyah. Captain William
Allston, Jr., and Nathaniel Dwight were elected from All Saints. All were
officers with the exception of Nathaniel Dwight, who was one of Marion's
men. Although the names of Bennison, Horry, and Dwight appear in
some of the lists of members, they did not take their seats.[89] Horry, as
is apparent from his letters to Greene, was with the troops, as was
Major Bennison, who was killed in battle while the Assembly met. Horry
and Bennison may have been ordered to remain on duty. If all of Marion's officers who had been elected had attended the legislature, his
forces would have been stripped of officers.

Marion himself had been elected a senator from the parish of St.
John's Berkeley. Who would command his troops in his absence? It

[87] Marion to Greene, Dec. 1, 1781, Greene Papers, WLCL.
[88] *Journal of the House of Representatives of South Carolina, January 8, 1782–
February 26, 1782*, ed. A. S. Salley, Jr., (Columbia, S. C., 1916), p. 3; Writs of
Election for Jacksonborough Assembly, Legislative System, S. C. Archives.
[89] *Ibid.*, p. 132.

had become more and more difficult to hold his men together. If his troops melted away, how could the British be prevented from raiding the Santee River plantations? It was necessary, therefore, to leave Colonel Peter Horry in command while Marion was away.

The patriot heroes were a sensitive bunch. When the South Carolina Provincial Congress resolved to raise regular troops in June 1775, Peter Horry had been elected the fifth captain in the state's service. By January 1780 he was lieutenant colonel, commanding the 5th South Carolina Regiment. At that time it had been thought best to merge the 5th and 6th South Carolina regiments with the 1st and 2nd. While waiting for a decision concerning the supernumerary officers, Horry asked for leave and retired to his plantation. General Lincoln later informed him that the youngest officers in each grade would have to retire. Since he was then the youngest lieutenant colonel in the South Carolina line, he did not return to duty and was therefore not present at the surrender of Charleston. After Charleston fell, he went to Camden and offered his services to General Isaac Huger and Governor Rutledge, who advised him to go to North Carolina and to join the continentals. This he did, being the first South Carolinian to join de Kalb's troops. He remained with de Kalb until Gates ordered Marion to take command of the militia in the lowcountry. Horry, who accompanied Marion to Lynches Creek in August 1780, had been with Marion ever since in command of a regiment of horse. While sitting in front of Fort Watson on April 20, 1781, Horry wrote Greene saying that he had recently discovered that Lincoln had intended to relieve not the youngest in commission but the youngest in service. He should not have been relieved of his command and therefore wanted justice.[90]

It was somewhat later, in June 1781, that Greene signed on the same day commissions for Horry and Hezekiah Maham in the continental army. Horry wanted to refuse on the basis that he already held a commission in the South Carolina line of the continental army, but Greene's aide wrote: "the acceptance of the commission shall not invalidate any claim you may have to rank in the Federal Army." He was ordered to proceed in the organization of his corps, appoint officers, secure re-

[90] Horry to Greene, April 20, 1781, Greene Papers, WLCL.

cruits, and find supplies.[91] This he proceeded to do between July and October.[92] On October 23 he was ordered to place his men under the command of Marion and obey Marion's orders.[93] When Horry displayed some reluctance, Greene wrote him on November 6:

General Marion cannot wish to injure you after knowing how much you have done and suffered for the cause. It is your interest to be friends. It is the interest of the public that you should be so; and let me beg of you to endeavor to render things as agreeable as possible. The General is a good man. Few of us are without faults, let his virtues veil his if any he has. Let neither pride possession or resentment hurry you into anything that may widen the breach between you. Your bleeding country demands a sacrifice of little injuries and your own good sense will point out the best mode of avoiding them I beg leave to recommend harmony and concord between you. . . .[94]

This smoothed his ruffled feathers for a time.

This question of rank and precedence was reopened in January 1782 when Marion left for Jacksonborough, leaving Horry in command. Hezekiah Maham refused to submit to Horry's orders on the basis that he was not outranked by Horry in that their commissions were dated the same day. Horry immediately wrote to Greene on January 12 from Wambaw asking Greene to do him justice so that he would not for a second time be ill-used by his country. Maham defended his own position in a letter to Horry of January 20 which was, though tortuous in style, adamant in purpose: "I can not think, you have behaved well on this occasion you have been trying to get every advantage of the regiment." Marion knew Maham to be the better cavalry leader but thought Horry had the better claim to superior rank. Greene also thought that Horry should be upheld. Actually, Horry was wise enough to see that only Marion's presence would solve matters. On January 13 he informed Greene that Marion was greatly needed in camp, since he was sure that the militia would be more satisfied with Marion's command than his own. On the twentieth he wrote Marion to urge him to return, but Mar-

[91] Horry to Greene, June 28; I. Burnet (for Greene) to Horry, July 2; Greene to Horry, July 30, 1781, Greene Papers, WLCL.
[92] Horry to Greene, July 13, Aug. 26, Sept. 20 and 28; Pierce (for Greene) to Horry, Sept. 14, 1781, Greene Papers, WLCL.
[93] Greene to Horry, Oct. 23, 1781, Greene Papers, WLCL.
[94] Greene to Horry, Nov. 6, 1781, Greene Papers, WLCL.

ion, although wanting to leave, was quite busy with the work of the legislature and unable to secure permission for his departure as it would break up the legislature for lack of a quorum.[95]

The Jacksonborough Assembly was the first legislative body to meet in South Carolina since February 12, 1780. It contained many notable men, principally those who had maintained the fight against the British and those who had been exiled to St. Augustine by the British but who now had made their way home via Philadelphia. Marion was a good example of the first group and Gadsden of the second. In this body the conservative influence of the lowcountry had been reduced. The men of Williamsburg were, for example, more important than they had been, the men of Prince George less important than in the days before the war. This body should have devoted itself to driving the British out and to re-establishing the civil government. The legislature did select John Mathews as the new chief executive, thereby continuing civil government. But this body also punished the tories by banishment and confiscation of their property. The body was meeting too soon and too close to the enemy for revenge to be kept under control. It was quite natural to mark down prominent merchants and professional men such as James Gordon and Dr. Charles Fyffe, but the greatest passion was stirred when the names of those who had led the loyal militia were brought before the legislature. Marion's chieftains would have thought it right and fitting that Mills, Ball, Wigfall, Cassells, Brown, Ballingall, and Gray should be pricked. Here the motive of vengeance was at its height.[96]

Marion himself seemed more concerned for his men and his officers than with these larger questions. He wanted Colonel Campbell exchanged for Captain Postell. He wanted Greene to decide between Horry and Maham. Above all, he wanted to return to his command. On January 26 he said that if Rutledge would grant permission he would return to his troops after the election of the new governor on the morrow. Yet, on February 19 he was still at Jacksonborough, warning Greene on that date that he had heard the enemy was threatening Horry at Wambaw: "I should have returned to my brigade but going would brake

[95] Horry to Greene, Jan. 12, 13, 17; Maham to Horry, Jan. 20; Horry to Marion, Jan. 20, 1782, Greene Papers, WLCL.
[96] S. C. Statutes, VI 629–633.

the House and stop all business here." The enemy did strike at Horry while Horry was ill and Major William Bennison lost his life. Marion did return to his command by February 28.[97]

Early in February Greene had decided in favor of Horry over Maham as long as Marion was away. But after Marion's return to his troops, Greene decided to reduce Maham's corps and Horry's corps to one, which meant that another choice between the two had to be made. He asked Marion again for advice. Marion replied on March 23: "Col. Maham have taken such pains in mounting equipment and clothing his corps that it would be hard to dismiss him when that corps is so much superior to the other and can act with advantage without Horrys but the latter cannot without the former; it is the wish of most of Horrys officers to act with Col. Maham; and it is also their opinion that Horry is not so good a cavalry officer as the other." Since a great many of Horry's men had deserted, Greene decided in favor of Maham. He wrote Horry on March 27 saying that he was reducing the two corps to one: "I do not pretend to judge between you and Col. Maham. General Marion thinks Maham is better qualified for the cavalry service than you are and says if the public good and the condition of the corps and the wishes of the officers of both are to operate in the decision Col. Maham has an undoubted preference." The solution was for Marion to send Horry, whom he did consider the better infantry officer, back to Georgetown to garrison that town, which Colonel Christian Senf had begun to fortify.[98] This did not end the cooperation of Marion and Horry for it was henceforth their joint duty, Marion south of the Santee and Horry at Georgetown, to maintain a supply route from Georgetown across the Santee to Greene's army. This, in fact, became Greene's principal line of supply.

During the last phase of Greene's campaign, Georgetown played its most important role. Greene had established a line of supply along the great wagon road from Philadelphia to Camden, but a port of entry on the coast would permit speedier communication with the north. With

[97] Marion to Greene, Jan. 26, Feb. 19; Horry to Marion, Feb. 20; Horry to Greene, Feb. 28, 1782, Greene Papers, WLCL.

[98] Horry to Greene, Feb. 10 and April 8; Marion to Greene, March 23; Greene to Horry, March 27 and May 8; Greene to Marion, March 27, 1782, Greene Papers, WLCL.

Charleston still in enemy hands, Georgetown was the most obvious choice for this role. Between November 1781 and December 1782 it was a hive of activity. By November 1781 Greene was receiving from that place arms, ammunition, powder, bar iron, boots, military shoes, shirts, blankets, saddlery, cattle, salt, flour, coffee, sugar, wine, rum, claret, porter, cheese. A special request for writing paper could not be filled, however, as Governor Rutledge had taken all which the firm of Heriot and Tucker had, perhaps in preparation for issuing the writs for the then forthcoming elections to the Jacksonborough legislature. In August 1782 Greene wrote Anthony Wayne that the stores in Georgetown were "immence": "We draw all our supplies from that quarter. . . ."[99]

To regularize procurement in Georgetown Greene appointed John Waties, Jr., as a special agent to purchase and forward such stores as the army needed. Supplies immediately needed by the army were to be sent by wagons; goods kept on hand for future use were to be stored in the neighborhood of Black Mingo Creek, the haunt of Marion's men.[100] Stores must have been kept at plantations all along the Black River, as they were at Mrs. Trapier's.[101] Among the merchants in Georgetown from whom Greene purchased were Robert Heriot, Daniel Tucker, John Cogdell, William Wayne, Mordecai Myers, J. Ellis, John Dorsius, and Andrew Johnston.[102]

Salt, cattle, and shoes were supplied from local sources. Salt, of which the army used about twenty bushels a week, was a principal item always in short supply. Waties solved this problem by proposing that the salt-boilers upon Waccamaw Neck each contribute one day's boiling per week. As this scheme provided thirty bushels a week, Waties was able to write Greene on February 1, 1782, that henceforth he would be able to furnish the army on the shortest notice. Anthony Martin White, who lived up Black River, was to keep stock on hand.[103] In January Greene

[99] Robert Heriot to Greene, Nov. 12, Dec. 2; William Wayne to Greene, Nov. 13; Greene to Robert Heriot, Nov. 24, 1781, Greene Papers, WLCL; Greene to Anthony Wayne, Aug. 2, 1782, Wayne Papers, XVIII, 53, Penn. Hist. Soc. William Wayne was the nephew of Anthony Wayne.

[100] Greene to John Waites, Jr., Dec. 25, 1781, Greene Papers, WLCL.

[101] Robert Forsyth to Greene, Aug. 8, 1782, Greene Papers, WLCL.

[102] These names are mentioned in the correspondence between Greene and his Georgetown agents. See particularly Joseph Wragg to Greene, Aug. 24, 1782, Greene Papers, WLCL.

[103] Greene to John Waties, Jr., Feb. 1, 1782, Greene Papers, WLCL.

appointed John Gough superintendent of a factory to make shoes, giving him authority to impress Negroes to forward this business.[104]

As most items needed by the army had to be imported from the north, Greene gave Waties authority in December to import goods from North Carolina and Virginia. Articles of small bulk and great value had to be brought by land, but items of large bulk were to be imported by water. When this demand had driven up prices not only in Georgetown, but also in North Carolina and Virginia, Green authorized Waties to bring supplies from the head of the Chesapeake and from Philadelphia.[105]

The magnitude of this trade soon placed a burden upon the available shipping facilities. In April Greene was urging Waties to buy a "a fine freight boat" which drew little water, was a fine sailor, and carried forty casks of rice for the Georgetown–New Bern run. Greene and Waties also considered acquiring a vessel for the voyages to the head of the Chesapeake.[106] As sailors were also scarce, Richard Lushington, who had been an exile at St. Augustine but was then commander at Georgetown, asked Greene on June 26 for authority to exchange about sixty prisoners in the Georgetown jail for a like number of men from the prison ships in Charleston in order to secure sailors for the vessels then fitting out in Georgetown harbor.[107]

In order to pay for these goods, Greene drew bills on Robert Morris, secretary of the treasury to Congress, or on the states; if he drew on the former, he demanded a reduction in price for Morris' bills passed for the equivalent of specie.[108] In this effort to secure supplies for his troops, Greene eventually pledged his own credit to John Banks, an action which after the war was to bring Greene's personal fortune to the brink of ruin. On April 23, 1782, Greene accepted Banks's proposals for supplying the army with articles shipped to Georgetown by water "and I will from time to time send you or the partnership the necessary

[104] Greene to John Gough, Jan. 25, 1782, Greene Papers, WLCL. William Wayne sent 104 pairs of military shoes. Wayne to Greene, Feb. 14, 1782. Greene Papers, WLCL.

[105] Greene to John Waties, Jr., Dec. 25, 1782, Jan. 25, 1782, Greene Papers. WLCL.

[106] Greene to John Waties, Jr., April 23, 1782, Greene Papers, WLCL.

[107] Richard Lushington to Greene, June 26, 1782, Greene Papers, WLCL.

[108] John Waties, Jr., to Greene, April 14, 16, 1782; Greene to John Banks, April 23, 1782, Greene Papers, WLCL.

invoices and provide the means of payment either by bills upon Mr. Morris the Financier or upon any state in the southern department which ever may be the most agreeable." He wrote Waties the same day that these were the best terms that could be obtained this side of Philadelphia. Banks was soon bringing in European and British goods via the West Indies. On August 8 Banks asked Greene for a passport so that his vessel from the Danish island of St. Thomas might bring into America British goods, which were open to seizure under orders of Congress anywhere within three miles of the continent. As Banks explained to Greene, "Your passport will bear the appearance of countenancing or tolerating an illicit trade. . . ." [109] By such steps Greene was drawn into desperate measures. By February 1783 Greene was willing to take goods from Banks at high prices because of the distressed nature of the army and the inadequacy of the measures pursued by impressment.[110]

On occasion there were windfalls for the army. Rum was sent to Greene by Waties obtained from a vessel bound from the West Indies to Philadelphia which had been wrecked "on our bar." [111] A number of rebel privateers operated out of Georgetown during the spring and summer of 1782.[112] When three prizes were sent into Georgetown in June by a privateer in which Colonel Richard Lushington was interested, he offered the army the rum, sugar, and coffee found on the prizes. On June 29 Judge Hugh Rutledge asked General Greene for an escort so that he might proceed to Georgetown where several vessels were waiting with their cargoes, which could not be sold until the vessels were condemned at a session of the South Carolina vice-admiralty court.[113]

It was not unusual for the Americans at Georgetown to trade with the British at Charleston. Andrew Johnston, who had contacts in

[109] John Banks to Greene, July 22, Aug. 5 and 8, 1782, Greene Papers, WLCL.

[110] Edward Carrington wrote Hugh Rutledge, speaker of the House, for his advice on Feb. 4, 1783. Rutledge apparently had no advice. See Rutledge to Carrington, Feb. 7 or 14, 1783, Greene Papers, WLCL.

[111] John Waties, Jr., to Greene, Jan. 4, 1782, Greene Papers, WLCL.

[112] *Royal Gazette*, March 6, 1782.

[113] Richard Lushington to Greene, June 26, 1782, Greene Papers, WLCL; Hugh Rutledge to Greene, June 29, 1782, Hugh Rutledge Papers, SCL. For the capture of a Georgetown privateer and condemnation in Charleston by the British see "Memorial of William Kershaw, Jan. 6, 1783," "William Greenwood folder," Confiscated Estates, S. C. Archives.

Charleston, wrote Greene on December 18, 1781, asking if a merchant in Charleston lately from England "with a considerable cargo of dry goods" came into the American lines, whether his property would be protected. In October 1782 Johnston was desirous of sending some produce to Charleston in order to pay off a debt to a man who was shortly to leave for England. If Johnston were given this privilege, he would bring back some goods in his schooner.[114] Greene received a more direct request in April from a man who desired to go to Charleston with rice and tobacco in order to procure clothing for the army.[115] The British authorities in Charleston, who needed rice for the troops and slaves, permitted such exchanges. Greene as a rule disapproved of any trade in rice or other commodities that might strengthen the enemy and prolong their stay.

Boom conditions continued in Georgetown during the spring of 1782, in fact as long as Charleston was occupied by the British. This was a unique chance for the Georgetown merchants to recover from the interruptions of the war; they did not think that it was unpatriotic to recoup their fortunes. In June a correspondent of Greene wrote from Georgetown: "The traders here (in general) are possessed with the spirit of the times. They endeavour to make the most of every thing. Some I apprehend would extend it to a great degree had they the opportunity." [116] Greene, aware of these facts, had told Waties that if he could not get supplies at a moderate price he was not to "purchase for I will sooner suffer than bear such impositions as the people of Georgetown impose upon us." [117] Greene refused to make contracts for anything but absolute necessities as he hoped as soon as Charleston fell to buy more cheaply.

It was obvious that the British would soon attack Georgetown in order to disrupt this incessant flow of goods. On March 1, 1782, Greene

[114] See Andrew Johnston to Richard Call, Oct. 14, 1782; James Warington to Andrew Johnston, Oct. 10, 1782, Greene Papers, WLCL.

[115] Col. Peter Horry had given Maj. John McIver permission to go to Charleston to bring out some ladies. John Waties, Jr., to Greene, April 16; John McIver to Greene, April 27, 1782, Greene Papers, WLCL. Greene refused permission. Greene to John McIver, May 24, 1782, Greene Papers, WLCL. Mary Huger, the wife of Benjamin Huger, made a similar request of Greene in a letter of March 16, 1782. Greene Papers, WLCL.

[116] Robert Johnston to Greene, June 13, 1782, Greene Papers, WLCL.

[117] Greene to John Waties, Jr., Jan. 25, 1782, Greene Papers, WLCL.

warned the merchants of Georgetown of an impending attack and urged
Joseph Wragg, who was substituting for Waties while the latter was in
Wilmington and New Bern, to send all the government stores up the
Black River.[118] Greene also sent Colonel Christian Senf, the Hessian
engineer, to fortify Georgetown. Marion at first opposed this effort to
fortify the town on the basis that there were not enough troops to spare
for its garrison. He urged Senf to let the vessels take their cargoes up
to Black Mingo. The river was deep, the approach by land difficult, and
the spot inhabited "by our best citizens, my old first followers."[119]

Senf, however, commenced work immediately, impressing slaves from
the patriot planters and calling upon the commissioners of the confiscated estates to let him have slave carpenters and workers from the
plantations of the tories who had suffered penalties at Jacksonborough.[120] Many patriot Georgetown planters were later paid for slave
labor contributed from their own work forces from March to July, which
is the best evidence that Senf diligently pushed forward his work.[121] On
June 1 Marion surveyed the work and reported to Greene:

> I called at George Town and perceived the works at that port and
> found the fort on the point in forwardness. The Sampit river it com-
> mands within point blank shott[.] The channel leading up PD and Black
> River is a thousand yards which is rather to[o] far, but will certainly be
> a security to the trade in Geo. town, and the difficulty of removing,
> prejudice in traders, and carrying the trade higher up the country, made
> me permit the works to go on, but it is still my opinion that if a pas-
> sification do not take place, the works will be only a greater object to
> them as they may land at Newton and come round by Sampit bridge
> and enter the town on the back part which will take a thousand men to
> defend, and this they may effect in seven hours easy march, then embark
> and retreat. . . .[122]

Colonel Horry, who had been in charge at Georgetown since the end
of March, was not a spirited defender. Greene had sent him a company

[118] Greene to the merchants of Georgetown, March 1; Greene to Marion, March
1; Greene to Joseph Wragg, March 1, 1782, Greene Papers, WLCL.
[119] Marion to Greene, March 8, 1782, Greene Papers, WLCL.
[120] Christian Senf to Greene, March 28, 1782, Greene Papers, WLCL.
[121] "Joseph Allston," "Josias Allston," "William Allston, Jr.," "George Croft," "John
Goff," "John Postell," and "Plowden Weston," Audited Accounts, S. C. Archives.
[122] Marion to Greene, June 1, 1782, Greene Papers, WLCL. Newton may have been
the name, at that time, of a plantation on Winyah Bay south of the mouth of the
Sampit River.

of artillerymen from Camden, consisting of thirty men with one howitzer, but Horry was still full of complaints. His men were waiting for their bounty and their pay; they were nearly naked and deserting "very fast for want of cloathing."[123] In June, frustrated and indisposed, he retired temporarily and was replaced by Colonel John Baddeley, a member of the Jacksonborough Assembly from St. James Goose Creek.

Colonel Baddeley, who commanded at Georgetown for about a month, was most concerned about the health of his troops. He wrote Greene on June 22: "I flatter myself from the present prepared state of the fort and Gen. Marions being at hand, we shall be able to resist any naval armament that can be sent aginst us," but unless a hospital with proper medicines were secured there would be "fatal consequences."[124] Some medicines were procured in Georgetown, but it was not until late in July that Greene could permit Dr. David Olyphant to send medicines out of the army's chests. The problem was not solved until Lushington, who succeeded Baddeley, took it upon himself to secure medical supplies in Charleston from the enemy.[125]

Late in July the long-awaited attack by the British on Georgetown was launched. Greene warned Marion on July 27 that a large force had left Charleston for the Santee. By July 31 Colonel Lushington had been informed that the enemy had reached the mouth of the Santee with eleven transports, one armed brig, one armed schooner, 100 British troops, 100 Hessians, and 150 levies in search of rice and slaves. In spite of the fact that Greene's instructions of July 27 went astray, Marion got to Georgetown before the British.[126] Once again there was a hurried sending of precious stores up the Black River.[127]

[123] Greene to Horry, May 8 and June 8, 1782; Horry to Greene, May 14, 24, and 28, 1782, Greene Papers, WLCL.

[124] John Baddeley to Greene, June 22, 1782, Greene Papers, WLCL.

[125] Richard Lushington to Greene, July 24, Sept., 14; Greene to Lushington, July 27, 1782, Greene Papers, WLCL.

[126] Greene to Lushington, July 27, 28; Lushington to Greene, July 31, Aug. 4; Greene to Marion, July 27, 30, 1782, Greene Papers, WLCL.

[127] In the rush there was an unlucky accident. A white man and a Negro went into the hold of a brig using a candle to light their way in order to draw rum; they both perished when the boat caught fire and burned down to the water's edge; a great quantity of rum and sugar was lost. Robert Forsyth to Greene, Aug. 8, 1782, Greene Papers, WLCL.

The enemy did not attack Georgetown but they were still on August 5 at the mouth of the Santee, having been as high up as the Tidyman plantation. Greene pressed Marion to dislodge the British quickly and then return to the Cooper River, for he thought the British were planning to evacuate Charleston. By August 9 the British were gone from the Santee, having taken a lot of rice with them.[128] Alarms of this nature continued, for the British were trying to secure supplies for their departure and slaves as plunder. On August 23 Marion received another warning of a large force leaving Charleston. Lushington was still concerned about the safety of Georgetown as late as September 10.[129] These hit-and-run affairs were only minor irritations, yet in the course of one of them late in August to the south of Charleston Colonel John Laurens lost his life.

Marion spent September to December 1782 south of the Santee in the area bounded by Seewee Bay, the Wando River, Cainhoy, and Goose Creek, always on the lookout for other excursions by the British. Finally, on December 14, 1782, the British evacuated Charleston. Governor Mathews asked Marion and his men to march into the city with the victorious army of Greene, but Marion told Greene that his men would rather go home and that he himself had never had the smallpox "and it may be in town and I would not wish to take it naturally." [130] Sensible even on the day of victory, Marion ended his career in the cause of liberty.

[128] Pierce to Marion, Aug. 4; Greene to Marion, Aug. 9; Marion to Greene, Aug. 5 and 9, 1782, Greene Papers, WLCL.

[129] Burnet to Marion, Aug. 23; Marion to Greene, Sept. 10, 1782, Greene Papers, WLCL.

[130] Marion to Greene, Nov. 14 and 24, 1782, Greene Papers, WLCL.

IX

SOCIETY REFORMS

After the fighting was over the soldiers went home. In fact, the men who fought with Marion were continually going home. His men were "summer soldiers" in that they fought for short periods of time. The Audited Accounts are filled with requests for pay for terms of enlistment described in weeks and months, seldom in years.[1] It would be wrong to imply that with the departure of the British from Carolina the patriots went home in a body.

None of the Georgetown men had been sent to St. Augustine, nor were any imprisoned on ships in Charleston harbor. Some, however, had been sent to the islands south of Charleston. A few of the latter as well as other refugees eventually reached Philadelphia, the rendezvous of many displaced persons. On July 4, 1782, General George Washington wrote General Guy Carleton that South Carolina exiles in Philadelphia wanted transportation to Georgetown. On July 9 three vessels were dispatched from New York to Philadelphia to pick up the refugees. The British sent them south with provisions.[2]

---

[1] "John Allston," "Luke Barrot," "Thomas Frazer," "Joseph Greaves," "James McCracken," "Samuel Smith," and "William Wayne," Audited Accounts, S. C. Archives.

[2] There were 18 persons with 5 Negroes who wanted to go to Edenton, N. C., and then to Georgetown and 24 families (90 persons) with 46 Negroes who wanted to go to Georgetown. Washington said that 20 more families wished to go in the fall. British Headquarters Papers (American Revolution), XLIV, Nos. 5011, 5012 (1–2), 5049 (1–2), on microfilm, S. C. Archives. Also see "William Wayne," Audited Accounts, S. C. Archives.

J. Franklin Jameson in a celebrated book, *The American Revolution Considered as a Social Movement,* set forth the theme that there had been two revolutions, one to expel the British, the other to decide who should rule at home. The second had been an internal revolution in which the richest families, who had generally taken the British side, were driven out with lesser men taking their places. It was Jameson's contention that this second revolution had brought about a democratization of American society. The American Revolution had, therefore, followed the natural course of revolutions. When the waves of revolution begin to beat, Jameson wrote, one cannot tell where dislodgement will cease.[3] The question, therefore, arises for the historian: Did the returning whigs and tories merely settle down into their former places without objections from their neighbors, or had there been a true social revolution, an overturning of society? A close analysis of the Georgetown tories and of the sales of confiscated property will show that this thesis is not borne out when applied to Georgetown.

On August 1, 1782, lands belonging to Dr. James Crockatt, James Gordon, Theodore Gaillard, John and James Smyth, Dr. Charles Fyffe, and Dr. Robert Gibb were sold by the state of South Carolina at public auction in Georgetown. This real estate brought £406,371.1.6 currency. Yet it should be noted that the property sold was later restored except for the lands of Dr. Crockatt and Dr. Gibb and the town lots and movable property of Dr. Fyffe. Samuel Smith, William Parker, Paul Trapier, Anthony White, and William Allston were the purchasers of the six tracts of land confiscated from Dr. Crockatt. The largest tract of 483 acres was bought by William Allston. These purchasers were respectable figures who were adding to their already considerable properties. Lewis Dutarque bought Dr. Fyffe's lot with two dwelling-houses, John Allston his lot on the neck, William Heriot his sulky and mare, and Captain Harvey his twelve head of sheep, seventeen head of hogs, and four head of cattle. Changes of property-holding on this scale scarcely constituted a social revolution.[4]

[3] J. Franklin Jameson, *The American Revolution Considered as a Social Movement* (Boston, Mass., 1959), p. 9.

[4] "Advertisement of sale on Aug. 1," dated June 11, 1782, Confiscated Estates, Public Sales, 1782–1783, S. C. Archives; "Account Book of the Commissioners of Forfeited Estates, 1782–1783," S. C. Hist. Soc. For the restoration of the estates of

The only other sale of confiscated property in Georgetown was that of eighty-two Negroes on May 7, 1783, when £2,711.15.8 was realized. The purchasers were Joseph Allston, Arch. Mussen, John Rogers, Thomas O. Elliott, Anthony White, William Wayne, and Thomas Mitchell. Joseph Allston purchased half the Negroes, paying £1,527.6.8; the rest purchased a few slaves apiece.[5] In the sale of both land and slaves an Allston was the largest purchaser, and the Allstons even before the Revolution had been the richest family on Waccamaw River. These facts are proof that the Jameson thesis does not apply to Georgetown even if there might be some validity for the thesis when considering South Carolina as a whole.

For Jameson's thesis to have been true, the Kinlochs, Lynches, Horrys, and Trapiers should have lost their lands, for they represented, much more than those who suffered, the wealth and influence of pre-war Georgetown. As Thomas Lynch, Sr., and his son had both died, the Lynch plantations passed to the two daughters of the elder Lynch. Sabina, whose second husband was John Bowman, and Elizabeth, whose second husband was James Hamilton, Jr., carried the Lynch properties through the Revolution.[6] Although the younger Paul Trapier had died on July 8, 1778, he had left four children whom the elder Paul Trapier looked after until his own death in 1793. Paul Trapier did take protection in July 1780, but his lands did not suffer confiscation.[7]

Gordon, Gaillard, and the Smyths see act of March 26, 1784, where their names were taken off the confiscation list and marked down for an amercement of 12 percent. *S. C. Statutes*, IV, 624–626; VI, 634–635.

[5] These figures must be in sterling. "Account Book of the Commissioners of Forfeited Estates, 1782–1783," S. C. Hist. Soc.

[6] Frampton E. Ellis, *Some Historic Families of South Carolina* (Atlanta, Ga., 1905), pp. 29–30. John Bowman, a Scotsman, had come out from Glasgow prior to the Revolution to speculate in Florida lands. CO 5/563, pp. 258–259, PRO London; *The Provosts of Glasgow from 1609 to 1832*, ed. James Gourlay (Glasgow, Scotland [1942]), pp. 80–81. By marrying Sabina Lynch Cattell he came into possession of Peachtree plantation and the Lynch lands on the South Santee. According to the census of 1790 he owned 293 slaves in the parish of St. James Santee. James Hamilton was a Scotch-Irish Pennsylvanian who had fought with Greene in South Carolina during the Revolution. He became a citizen of the state on May 24, 1784, and married Elizabeth Lynch Harleston in June 1784. He came into possession of Hopsewee and the Lynch lands on the North Santee. He fought a duel with his brother-in-law John Bowman, who charged him with having sired several Northern children. Virginia L. Glenn, "James Hamilton, Jr. of South Carolina: A Biography" (PhD dissertation, Univ. of N. C., 1964), pp. 1–3.

[7] Notes on the Trapier Family, S. C. Hist. Soc.

The Horrys came very close to losing their land. Daniel Horry had gone to England in 1781 to take his son to school.[8] If his brothers-in-law, Charles Cotesworth and Thomas Pinckney, had not been so influential on the patriot side, he would have suffered. Elias Horry and Thomas Horry, the sons of Elias Horry, Jr., saved themselves by coming out of Charleston and throwing themselves upon the mercy of Governor John Rutledge just before the Jacksonborough Assembly met. Edward Rutledge wrote Arthur Middleton on February 14, 1782: "We shall extend Grace & Favor to E. & T. Horry young Manigault & such others as have signed the Address, & submitted themselves to the Mercy of this Country by imposing only a Fine of a few per Cent on their estates." On February 26, he wrote again: "The two young Horrys young Manigault & a few other Addressers, who have thrown themselves on the Mercy of their Country, are amerced on[ly] 10. p. Cent." [9] Ultimately, however, they escaped without any fines.

The Kinlochs did suffer for their failure to embrace the patriot cause with sufficient fervor. But even they only suffered in that Cleland Kinloch was amerced 12 percent of his estate; he did not lose his plantations. Francis and Cleland Kinloch had been in school in England and

[8] Mrs. Daniel Horry wrote General Greene on July 8, 1781, and on Jan. 12, 1782, asking permission to send rice from Santee to Charleston and then to England to pay for her son's education there. "She trusts, the education of American youth will appear a matter of sufficient importance to the general to excuse her giving him this trouble." Greene Papers, WLCL. Daniel Horry had commanded a state regiment of light dragoons until the surrender of Charleston. "Daniel Horry," Audited Accounts, S. C. Archives. Marion wrote Greene, March 13, 1782: "Mr. Daniel Horry is arrived from England but is kept in close observation and cannot come out—Mrs. Horry is gone to town, and hope in a few days to hear some thing certain, which I shall communicate to you." Greene Papers, WLCL.

[9] "Correspondence of Hon. Arthur Middleton, Signer of the Declaration of Independence," ed. Joseph W. Barnwell, *SCHM*, XXVII (1926), 5, 9. Rutledge had written Middleton on Dec. 12, 1781: "A short Time since E. & T. Horry came out to the Govr. they were met by Gervais & offered him their Hands, the little Fellow grew warm & told them he did not shake Hands wth. Rascals; well says E: we are come to give ourselves up, what do you think will be done to us? Done to you says G; why hang'd to be sure, & left them to acquaint the Govr. with their being there, as soon as he had turned his Back, they took fright, jumped upon their Horses, & dashed off; they were however sent after, were taken after they had got abt. 25 Miles & brought back. They have given security to appear when called for, & are with some others to wait the pleasure, or if you will, the Justice of their Country." *Ibid.*, XXVI (1925), 208.

Switzerland when the Revolution broke out. Their estates were administered for them by Thomas Boone, former Royal Governor of South Carolina. Francis returned home in the summer of 1778, was elected to the Continental Congress, and took up arms on the patriot side; Cleland did not. After Cleland's estate had been amerced, Francis petitioned the Senate of South Carolina in his brother's behalf, explaining that his brother had been sent by the executor of his father's will to England at an early age for his education. While still a minor he did return to Charleston when that city was still in British hands, but he did not take an oath to support the British government, nor did he sign any congratulatory address, nor subscribe any sums of money toward raising a loyal militia. He had remained a few months, but in order to reach a neutral port and return again to America he embarked for Europe. His ship was taken by an American privateer which was in turn taken by a British cruiser that landed him in Antigua. From there he went to England, where he had been ill ever since. Arthur Middleton and Edward Rutledge thought that Cleland Kinloch had gotten off lightly with only an amercement, which he paid. As the Horry and Kinloch families retained their properties, their influence was soon as great as it had been before the Revolution.[10]

The spirit of revenge was strong at Jacksonborough, but the legislatures that met after 1782 undid much of what that earlier body had done. If one examines the extent to which concessions were made by these later legislatures, it becomes obvious that confiscation in South Carolina had little effect upon the make-up of post-Revolutionary society. Even someone so remote from Georgetown as George Saxby found a person there willing to seek restitution of his property from the legislature. In 1785 John Cogdell said that Saxby had left the state before the commencement of the troubles and was at the time of his departure a person far advanced in age. His attorney had complied during the Revolution with every requisition made by the state upon his property,

---

[10] "Cleland Kinloch," Confiscated Estates, S. C. Archives; George C. Rogers, Jr., *Evolution of a Federalist: William Loughton Smith of Charleston, 1758–1812* (Columbia, S. C., 1962), pp. 71–73, 79–81, 83, 84, 89n, 106. Francis Kinloch, while serving in Virginia, asked and received permission from Gen. Greene to send Capt. Thomas Miller, a British prisoner, to Charleston to render "some of my nearest relations . . . essential services." Kinloch to Greene, March 6; Greene to Kinloch, April 28, 1781, WLCL.

paying a double tax required of nonresidents and furnishing forage to the army whenever requested. Should such a man be punished? [11]

Dr. Charles Fyffe petitioned the legislature on November 20, 1782, asking that the legislature be lenient to an old man who, if banished, would have to cross the tempestuous ocean and once more launch into a new career. He solemnly declared "that he never gave any information or accused any individual whatever, for the purpose of making him obnoxious to the British officers—on the contrary, many instances may be produced, where any influence he had with them, was used for the relief of those, who had fallen under their displeasure." After the fall of Georgetown, he had gone to Charleston to take charge of the refugee hospital there, where he had provided many services for wounded Americans. The legislature did not act in time to avoid the necessity of his sailing with the British fleet for England, but it did remove the edict of banishment later. Although Fyffe returned in December 1784, he was afraid to settle on his Pee Dee plantation and lived in Charleston. His estate eventually suffered only an amercement of 12 percent.[12]

James Gordon, although he admitted that he had accepted a commission in the loyal militia, petitioned the legislature on December 6, 1782, asking that he be restored to the rights and privileges of an American subject. He pleaded: "When the unfortunate event of the 12th of May 1780 reached that part of the country, where your petitioner resided; the inhabitants in general were struck with terror and amazement; and before this subsided, the conquering enemy was at their doors—No alternative was then left them (their town being defenseless) but that of surrendering themselves prisoners of war—And while on parole, not knowing what was to become of him and his property; the commission was offer'd him, which by the advice of his friends he accepted." He had never hurt any one and had rendered many services to the local people "particularly in procuring payment for their cattle, which had fallen into the hands of rapacious commissaries—that your

[11] George Saxby, Receiver General of Quit Rents, had owned Georgetown properties. He had been a partner of James Gordon. "George Saxby," Confiscated Estates, S. C. Archives.

[12] "Charles Fyffe," Confiscated Estates, S. C. Archives; Loyalist Transcripts, LV, 428–447, on microfilm, S. C. Archives; S. C. Statutes, VI, 634.

petitioner so early as August 1781, finding his interest and authority not sufficient to check the arbitrary views of some men—and if he continued to act as Lt. Col. of that district, he would be answerable for measures totally repugnant to his feelings; resigning his commission and lived as a private citizen in Chas. Town—where it was his study to render every service in his power to those in the country." The legislature accepted the story, restored his estate, and amerced it only 12 percent.[13]

James Cassells, the ablest of the British militia captains, did not fare as well as Fyffe and Gordon. He petitioned the legislature on December 10, 1783, from East Florida where he had gone after his banishment. He acknowledged that he had accepted a commission and had fought against the rebels, but he had only accepted the commission in July 1780 after the state had been entirely overrun by the British. He confessed "that he never used any power so put into his hands, to the hurt of any persons in the State but on the contrary used his endeavours to protect the persons and properties of his neighbours from violence and plunder." Paul Trapier and Samuel Smith petitioned the Senate in Cassells' behalf: "He acted as far as comes to the knowledge of your Memorialists with moderation towards the Inhabitants, and in frequent instances afforded them protection from the violence and plundering of the British Officers and Soldiery."

Although nothing was done for Cassells, something was done for his son. On January 8, 1788, Archibald Taylor, Mary Man Taylor, and Robert Heriot petitioned the legislature in behalf of John Cassells in order to prevent the commissioners of forfeited estates from seizing slaves that belonged to the son and not to the father. The son, born in 1770, was then in 1788 absent from the state, furthering his education. The slaves in question had belonged to his grandfather, Dr. John Man, who had willed them to his daughter who had died in 1770. When James Cassells left the state after the Revolution, he had taken his own slaves to East Florida with him, but he had left those slaves owned by his wife on the plantation that still belonged to the estate of Dr. Man. The petitioners, being next of kin (Mary Taylor having also been a daughter of Dr. Man), were asking relief on the basis that the slaves in question had not belonged to a tory. The petition was turned over to Thomas

---

[13] "James Gordon," Confiscated Estates, S. C. Archives; S. C. *Statutes*, VI, 635.

Waties, Francis Kinloch, and Edward Darrell, who recommended relief. The mere recommendation of the petition to a committee of which Kinloch was a member showed that the days of revenge were over.[14]

The best exhibit in the showcase of softening rancor is the petition of John Brockington of Black River and the document which accompanied it. John Brockington, a leading tory of Williamsburg District, had refused to leave with the departing British. By 1786 he was willing to admit that he had been misled in taking part with the enemies of the commonwealth. "He with contrition acknowledges the justice of the sentence passed against him by his country but at the same time, with heart-felt sorrow laments the situation of his unhappy wife and children reduced to the utmost distress, only for his crimes." Brockington's petition was supported by another, "the humble petition of the inhabitants of Black River and parts adjacent" who out of the goodness of their hearts "were willing to forget, and forgive, the injuries done by those who rendered themselves obnoxious to this commonwealth, by taking up arms in favour of the British, in the late war." Many of those who did "earnestly recommend the case of John Brockington's wife, and several small children," to the legislature's "favour, and humanity" were former soldiers of Marion. Among the eighty-two names were those of Anthony White, Jr., Alexander Swinton, Richard Green, Patrick Dollard, Francis Green, Stephen Ford, George Ford, Hugh Horry, Elisha Screven, George Heriot, Lewis Dutarque, and John Magill.[15] If these men could forgive and forget, so could the society as a whole. The treaty of peace with Great Britain in 1783 contained provisions designed to prevent further mistreatment of tories. The people of Georgetown lived up to the spirit of that treaty.

The British had rounded up many slaves and taken them off in December 1782 as plunder. It has been estimated that as many as 25,000 were spirited away, but what portion were Georgetown slaves is unknown. James Cassells did take his own slaves to East Florida. Certainly

[14] Petition of Trapier and Smith to President of Senate, n.d., Cassells Papers, SCL; "James Cassells," Confiscated Estates, S. C. Archives; Loyalist Transcripts, LV, 107–121, on microfilm, S. C. Archives. Richard Hampton owned Cassells' plantation in 1806. *Georgetown Gazette*, April 23, 1806.

[15] "John Brockington," Confiscated Estates, S. C. Archives; Robert D. Bass, *Swamp Fox* ([New York], 1959), p. 261.

some slaves were lost from the labor force in the three parishes. Those lost may have been replaced by new purchases, for slaves were imported after the Revolution until 1787. The patriots as well as Major James Moncrief had disrupted the labor force by sending many Georgetown slaves to Charleston to work on the fortifications there.[16] Even more were used on the fortifications of Georgetown in the spring of 1782.[17] Yet the pre-war labor force remained largely intact. There is no evidence that the slaves attempted to revolt during the Revolution. The British and Americans had fought surrounded by a passive slave population.

Production figures for rice and indigo for the three parishes do not exist; those for the state during the 1780's and 1790's show that the production of indigo fell off rapidly.[18] The lack of a bounty and the disruption of the trade were the principal factors. Great attention was, therefore, given to rice. The water culture, using the ebb and flow of the tide, was perfected. In 1787 Jonathan Lucas, Sr., built the first water mill for beating rice for John Bowman at his Peach Island plantation on the Santee. Soon after, Lucas built a mill for General Peter Horry at his Reserve plantation on Winyah Bay and another for Colonel William Allston at his Fairfield plantation on Waccamaw River. By 1792 he had built the first tide-operated mill at Millbrook on the North Santee for Andrew Johnston. Rice was henceforth the principal crop of the district[19].

By 1790 there were 430 white persons and 1,795 Negro slaves in All Saints Parish. In Prince George there were 5,111 whites and 6,651 slaves;

[16] "William Allston, Jr.," "William Heriot," "Percival Pawley," "Plowden Weston," Audited Accounts, S. C. Archives.

[17] "Joseph Allston," "Josias Allston," "George Croft," "George Ford," "Benjamin Huger," "John Postell," "Benjamin Trapier," and "Paul Trapier, Jr.," Audited Accounts, S. C. Archives.

[18] For figures for export of rice and indigo, 1780–1800, from S. C. see Lewis Cecil Gray, *History of Agriculture in the Southern United States to 1860* (Gloucester, Mass., 1958), II, 1024, 1036. According to the collectors at Georgetown: from Jan. 7, 1783, to Oct. 4, 1783, 2,568 barrels of rice were exported and 25 casks and 1,100 pounds of indigo; from Dec. 23, 1783, to June 25, 1785, 5,016 barrels of rice and 32,415 pounds of indigo; from Aug. 1, 1785, to Jan. 9, 1786, 5,262 barrels of rice and 42,163 pounds of indigo; from Jan. 16 to 18, 1786, 120 barrels of rice; and from March 21, 1786, to Feb. 7, 1787, 4,302 barrels and 442 half-barrels of rice and 24 casks and 616 pounds of indigo. Port and Town of Georgetown, Legislative System, Pre-1800, S. C. Archives. These were the amounts cleared for non-S. C. destinations but did not include the amounts shipped to Charleston.

[19] "A Lucas Memorandum," *SCHM*, LXIX (1968), 193.

in Prince Frederick there were 3,450 whites and 4,685 slaves. For the three parishes combined there were a total of 22,122 persons, of whom 13,131 were Negro slaves and 113 free persons of color. This was a slave-holding society with the slaves spread fairly evenly throughout the three parishes. The largest planters, however, were grouped in the coastal parishes. In All Saints William Allston owned 300 slaves, Thomas Allston 203, John Allston 156, Robert Heriot 128, and Joseph Allston 100. In Prince George Parish Cleland Kinloch had 300, Francis Kinloch 212, John Hume 210, Edward Mitchell 199, Archibald Taylor 166, Paul Trapier 137, Thomas Butler 137, John Pyatt 120, William Brailsford 120, Joseph Wragg 119, estate of Screven 115, Elizabeth Allston 112, James Hamilton 112. In Prince Frederick Parish only Theodore Gourdin with 150 had over 100 slaves.[20] The indigo planters of Prince Frederick who could not switch to rice were experimenting with tobacco before they turned to cotton.[21] During this period of disruption they may have sold some of their slaves to the rice planters on the coast.

It was easier for the countryside to recover than the town, which had been partially destroyed. On February 16, 1788, John Martin wrote from Georgetown to his son in England: "the Town was almost all Burnt by the British Troops when here, there are about 150 House's built since, the Church they made a Stable and then Burnt it, they have since got a Roof upon it and a Few Temperary Seats, but not half Finish'd." [22] Francisco de Miranda, arriving in Georgetown in July 1783, recorded his impressions: "The site is pretty and on slightly elevated terrain. The population appears to be decent and there are some very good houses, although some of these are burnt and others completely in ruins as a result of the last war." Of the country about, Miranda wrote: "The country houses here are handsome, comfortable,

[20] *Heads of Families at the First Census of the United States taken in the Year 1790, South Carolina* (Baltimore, Md., 1952), pp. 50–56.

[21] South Carolina established a tobacco inspection system in the 1780's. Job Rothmahler, John Cogdell, and Daniel Tucker were the commissioners for Georgetown. In 1789 Samuel Smith replaced Rothmahler. S. C. *Statutes*, IV, 604–607, 681–687; V, 113–121. The contraction of the rice-planting area to the tidal stretches of the rivers near the coast is described in Marjorie S. Mendenhall, "A History of Agriculture in South Carolina, 1790–1860" (PhD dissertation, Univ. of N. C., 1940), pp. 133–134.

[22] John Martin Papers, S. C. Hist. Soc.

and spacious, reflecting the wealth, sound taste, and love of rural life which characterize the inhabitants." [23]

Georgetown still possessed a merchant class, represented by hold-overs from the pre-war days (Job Rothmahler, Anthony Bonneau, Daniel Tucker, George and Robert Heriot, John Cogdell, Abraham Cohen, and Mordecai Myers), and by new men sucked in by the speculations of the 1781–1782 period (William Wayne). The old avenues of credit were opened again. John Cogdell ran a store in Georgetown for Smiths, DeSaussure, and Darrell of Charleston, who in turn were backed by the large Anglo-American firm in London of Bird, Savage, and Bird.[24] But with the export of indigo declining and rice planters becoming big enough to ship their produce from their own mills directly to Charleston, the Georgetown merchants were a less important group. When Washington paused in 1791 to look around the town, he saw five or six hundred people whose chief export was rice. Upon inquiry he was told that there was a bar "over which not more than 12 feet water can be brot," which "must ever be a considerable let to its importance." He observed that "Georgetown seems to be in the shade of Charleston." [25]

This shift in economic power from the Georgetown merchants and Prince Frederick indigo planters to the rice planters was paralleled by a similar shift in political power during the decade of the 1780's. Prince Frederick with six seats in the House of Representatives was the equal of All Saints with two and Prince George with four. Prince Frederick had one senator; All Saints and Prince George together had one senator. Actually, these delegations seemed in the mid-1780's to be dominated by the Prince Frederick men from Black River and Black

[23] The New Democracy in America: Travels of Francisco de Miranda in the United States, 1783–84, trans. Judson P. Wood and ed. John S. Ezell (Norman, Okla., 1963), pp. 16–17.

[24] John Cogdell's Waste Book, Dec. 1785–Feb. 1787, has been recently discovered among the records in the Office of Probate Judge, Georgetown, S. C. Although many pages are missing, this Waste Book records shipments of indigo, rice, pitch, tar, and turpentine to Bird, Savage, and Bird of London and receipt of English goods in return through the hands of Smiths, DeSaussure, and Darrell of Charleston. Retail sales of these goods are recorded to most of the principal figures in the Georgetown area, even to Robert Conway of Kingston and to Claudius Pegues and Benjamin Rogers from up the Pee Dee.

[25] Archibald Henderson, Washington's Southern Tour, 1791 (Boston, Mass., 1923), p. 137.

Mingo, the men who had fought the longest and the hardest during the Revolution. None of the really large rice planters was a member of any of these delegations except William Allston, who himself had fought with Marion.[26]

Another grand theme in American historiography, introduced by Charles A. Beard, states that the adoption of the new United States Constitution in 1788 was the culmination of a drive by the conservative interests in the country to recover some of the ground that had been lost to the more radical elements in American society during the Revolutionary period. One can think of the Beard thesis as dovetailing with the Jameson thesis. If the Revolution did bring about an internal revolution with a greater democratization of society, then the conservatives should have been on their guard waiting to recover what had been lost. If Marion's men from Black Mingo had captured the representation at the time of Jacksonborough and had held on to it, then the Kinlochs and the Horrys and the Trapiers should have been on their guard, waiting to build new institutions, new defenses against so many inroads on the old society. Beard said that the largest slaveholders joined with the commercial interests in Charleston in a conservative coalition and these in turn had joined with their Northern counterparts. The story of Georgetown lends much support to the Beard thesis.[27] There is some truth in saying that the lukewarm patriots were winning out at the expense of the truest patriots, that Santee was again emerging at the expense of Black Mingo.

In the 1780's the British merchants were trying to recover debts owed to them since before the Revolution. The ordinary citizens were opposed to paying off debts held by the former enemy. The culmination of the opposition in South Carolina came at Camden when the people of that district in 1785 prevented the court from sitting, much as Shays's men had done in Massachusetts.[28] As the court records for Georgetown district have been lost and advertisements in the Charleston newspapers

[26] *The Constitution of 1778,* ed. Robert L. Meriwether (Columbia, S. C., 1953).

[27] Charles A. Beard, *An Economic Interpretation of the Constitution of the United States* (New York, 1913).

[28] Thomas J. Kirkland and Robert M. Kennedy, *Historic Camden* (Columbia, S. C., 1926), II, 254–256; Rogers, *op. cit.,* pp. 109, 143.

give little evidence, it is difficult to say what the Georgetown story was. From an early law case it is known that Captain Anthony White in 1784 sued the tory plunderers of his plantation, who had taken articles worth £1,000 sterling from his house in September 1780. The jury awarded damages of £400 against one defendant, £200 against another, and £100 against a third trespasser. This decision would have been agreeable to the patriot elements in the region of Georgetown.[29] Perhaps there was not as much need for complaints against the courts in Georgetown as there was in Camden.

It is difficult to say anything about a movement in Georgetown for the constitutional convention which met in Philadelphia in 1787. However, when that document was sent to South Carolina and the state legislature voted in January 1788 whether South Carolina herself should convene a ratification convention, there was a definite expression of sentiment among the delegates from the three parishes. All Saints voted two for the convention, none against; Prince George two for and two against; and Prince Frederick none for and four against. The total vote for the three parishes was four for and six against with All Saints solidly for and Prince Frederick solidly against.[30] In this vote, Marion's men still prevailed over the grandees of the Waccamaw and the Santee.

The election of delegates to attend the ratification convention in Charleston was a vastly important election. All Saints elected Daniel Morral and Thomas Allston; Prince George elected Thomas Waties, Samuel Smith, Cleland Kinloch, and William Allston; Prince Frederick elected William Wilson, Alexander Tweed, William Frierson, James Pettigrew, Patrick Dollard, William Read, and John Burgess.[31]

[29] "White against M'Neily and Others," Elihu Hall Bay, *Reports of Cases . . . in the Superior Courts of Law in the State of South Carolina* (Charleston, S. C., 1798), I, 10–11. The principle of this case allowing allocation of damages among the wrongdoers was repudiated in 1968. Rourk v. Selvey, Opinion No. 18850, filed Dec. 12, 1968. Supreme Court of S. C. These cases were called to the attention of the author by Mr. Bernard Manning.

[30] *The Debates in the Several State Conventions on the Adoption of the Federal Constitution,* ed. Jonathan Elliot, (Philadelphia, Penn., 1941), IV, 317. Francis Kinloch, Plowden Weston, James Ladson, and Thomas Horry voted for calling a convention while representing other parishes.

[31] *Ibid.*, p. 333.

Aedanus Burke in a brilliant letter showed how the Charleston setting influenced the backcountry members who attended the convention.[32] Something of this influence was at work on the Prince Frederick delegation. The parish was almost unanimous against ratification; some even thought that the delegation itself had been instructed to vote against the constitution. Only two of the delegation spoke at the convention. Patrick Dollard was the man true to his constituents; Alexander Tweed a man swayed by the oratory of his convention colleagues.

Patrick Dollard, the respectable tavern-keeper, opposed the constitution because his constituents were against it. He had been one of Marion's men, "a sensible, hospitable man . . . comfortably settled near Blackmingo Creek," where Marion had defeated Ball. In his mind Dollard was still engaged in the age-old fight for liberty—"an American bosom is apt to glow at the sound" of that word. In this new constitution he saw something of the old tyranny, and he meant to warn the men of the convention. When he spoke, he spoke "with the greatest diffidence" knowing that the constitution had already been ably supported by "respectable gentlemen." Yet he felt it his duty to make known "the sense and language" of his constituents.

The people of Prince Frederick's Parish, whom I have the honor to represent, are a brave, honest, and industrious people. In the late bloody contest, they bore a conspicuous part, when they fought, bled, and conquered, in defence of their civil rights and privileges, which they expected to transmit untainted to their posterity. They are nearly all, to a man, opposed to this new Constitution, because, they say, they have omitted to insert a bill of rights therein, ascertaining and fundamentally establishing, the unalienable rights of men, without a full, free, and secure enjoyment of which there can be no liberty, and over which it is not necessary that a good government should have the control. They say that they are by no means against vesting Congress with ample and sufficient powers; but to make over to them, or any set of men, their birthright, comprised in Magna Charta, which this new Constitution absolutely does, they can never agree to.

He and his constituents had the highest opinion of the abilities of the gentlemen who represented the state ·in the convention, but he believed

[32] Aedanus Burke to John Lamb, June 23, 1788, printed in Rogers, *op. cit.*, pp. 156–157.

them to be mortal and "liable to err." He saw the majority in the convention leading the state first to "a moderate aristocracy" and then
under the dominion of "a corrupt and oppressive aristocracy."

My constituents are highly alarmed at the large and rapid strides which
this new government has taken towards despotism. They say it is big
with political mischiefs, and pregnant with a greater variety of impending woes to the good people of the Southern States, especially South
Carolina, than all the plagues supposed to issue from the poisonous box
of Pandora. They say it is particularly calculated for the meridian of
despotic aristocracy; that it evidently tends to promote the ambitious
views of a few able and designing men, and enslave the rest. . . . They
say they will resist against it; that they will not accept of it unless compelled by force of arms, which this new Constitution plainly threatens;
and then, they say, your standing army, like Turkish janizaries enforcing
despotic laws, must ram it down their throats with the points of bayonets.
They warn the gentlemen of this Convention, as the guardians of their
liberty, to beware how they will be accessory to the disposal of, or
rather sacrificing, their dear-bought rights and privileges. This is the
sense and language, Mr. President, of the people; and it is an old saying,
and I believe a very true one, that the general voice of the people is
the voice of God. The general voice of the people, to whom I am responsible, is against it. I shall never betray the trust reposed in me by
them; therefore, shall give my hearty dissent.[33]

Alexander Tweed also knew that his people were against the constitution but finally voted for it. He had heard it asserted that the representatives of Prince Frederick had been put under a promise to their
constituents by no means to approve the constitution. He denied that
such a restriction had been placed upon him, but, even if it had been
dictated to him, he would have spurned it. He had not come merely "to
echo the voice of my constituents" but to listen and to vote according
to his own conscience. He had been impressed by the men who had
spoken in behalf of the constitution, men "whose profound oratory and
elocution would, on the journals of a British House of Commons, stand
as lasting monuments of their great abilities." After having heard the
arguments on both sides, he said "that we very much stand in need of
a reform of government, as the very sinews of our present constitution
are relaxed." [34] Eventually he cast his vote with the majority in favor

[33] Elliot, op. cit., IV, 336–338.
[34] Ibid., pp. 332–333.

of ratification. Only Dollard, Read, and Burgess from Prince Frederick out of those sent from the three parishes voted against ratification.[35]

Among those from other parishes who voted in favor of ratification were Francis Kinloch, John Julius Pringle, Joseph Manigault, William Read, James Ladson, Ralph Izard, Jr., John Mayrant, and Thomas Horry. These men either owned land or their sons would very shortly own land near Georgetown. Both Cleland Kinloch and Thomas Horry, who had been threatened with confiscation, were among the group. Most remarkable of all was the fact that although Francis Marion had been elected from St. John's Berkeley and Peter Horry from Prince George, neither attended the convention. Were these two officers, heroes in their communities and in the state, unwilling to lead their men anymore, particularly against their own aspiring relatives? Or did they silently consent to the conservative revolution? That some believed that it was a revolution can be seen in Francis Kinloch's statement to ex-Governor Thomas Boone in a letter of May 26, 1788, at the close of the ratification convention. He was asking that Boone send him the Kinloch coat of arms: "As our steps towards monarchy are very obvious, I would wish my Children to have all the Rights to rank, & distinction, which is to be claimed from Ancestry." After a description of the new federal constitution, he added, "we are getting back fast to the system we destroyed some years ago." [36]

Washington's famous Southern tour in 1791 was used to enhance the popularity and prestige of those who had supported ratification. Washington entered South Carolina on April 27, 1791, breafasting at William Gause's, lunching at Cochran's, and dining at William Vereen's. Of April 28 Washington wrote: "Mr. Vareen piloted us across the Swash (which at high water is impassable, & at times, by the shifting of the Sands is dangerous) on the long Beach of the Ocean. . . ."[37] The entourage then lunched at Mr. Pawley's and after being met on the road with an invitation from Dr. Henry Collins Flagg, repaired to his home for the evening. Dr. Flagg, a Rhode Islander, who had come south before

[35] *Ibid.*, pp. 338–340.
[36] Francis Kinloch to Thomas Boone, May 26, 1788, "Letters of Francis Kinloch to Thomas Boone, 1782–1788," ed. Felix Gilbert, *Journal of Southern History*, VIII (1942), 103–105.
[37] Henderson, *op. cit.*, p. 125. The account which follows is drawn from this work.

the Revolution but had distinguished himself as chief surgeon in General Greene's army, had married after the Revolution Rachel Allston, the widow of Captain William Allston of Brookgreen.[38] From Brookgreen there was an early start the next morning for Colonel William Alston's home of Clifton which was "large, new, and elegantly furnished" standing "on a sandy hill, high for the Country" with the Colonel's rice fields below along the "Waggamau," as Washington spelled the river's name. Washington was duly impressed with the perfection of rice culture on the river. To a Charleston hostess he commented that it had "looked like fairyland."

At Colonel Alston's he was met by General William Moultrie, Colonel William Washington, and John Rutledge, Jr., who brought him a letter of welcome from Governor Charles Pinckney. The President with his welcomers were rowed down the river to Georgetown in an "elegant painted boat" manned by the captains of vessels in the harbor, who were dressed in "round hats trimmed with gold lace, blue coats, and white jackets." On arriving opposite the market, they were saluted by artillery fire from the foot of Broad Street. At the landing the "handsomely uniformed" Light Infantry Company stood with presented arms. The President was conducted to the home of Benjamin Allston, where he was read an address of welcome signed on behalf of the inhabitants by Hugh Horry, Dr. Joseph Blyth, Erasmus Rothmahler, Francis Kinloch, George Keith, Matthew Irvine, Dr. Robert Brownfield, and Samuel Smith. After responding to this address, a committee of masons from Prince George's Lodge, No. 16 (Moderns) of Georgetown, presented an address which was signed by L. White, R. Grant, A. Cohen, J. Blyth, and J. Carson. Then followed a public dinner with toasts to "The United States of America" and "The Federal Government," followed by others to "France," "Lafayette," "Greene," and ultimately "Our Illustrious President."

The next day Washington set out for the Santee accompanied now by Major Thomas Pinckney. A visit had been planned to the Lynch plantation, but John Bowman, the master, was ill with the measles.[39]

[38] Edgar Preston Richardson, *Washington Allston* (Chicago, Ill., 1948), p. 10.

[39] As John Bowman was the only lowcountry planter to vote against the ratification of the constitution, he may have been showing his displeasure. Elliot, *op. cit.*, IV, 339.

Their destination was Hampton, the home of Pinckney's sister, Mrs. Daniel Horry. From Hampton Washington continued his journey to Charleston. When Francis Kinloch eulogized Washington in 1800 in Georgetown, he, reflecting on Washington's visit to that place, noted: "It is proper in all nations that those who represent the majesty of the people should be at times encircled with the ensigns of authority, and that the splendour of the government they administer should be in some measure apparent in their persons. . . ."[40] The Georgetown Federalists were pleased with the first president for "the splendour of the government" obviously shown forth in Washington. The Pawleys, the Flaggs, the Alstons, the Kinlochs, the Horrys, and the Pinckneys had been happy to escort the great man through the parishes.

[40] Quoted in Henderson, *op. cit.,* pp. 142–143.

X

ARISTOCRATIC FACTIONS

The Federalist Party dominated South Carolina politics during the 1790's. The party was a coalition of aristocratic factions with the principal groups residing in Charleston. To these Charleston groups the Hugers of Georgetown and the Barnwells of Beaufort were allied. There had been four Huger brothers at the time of the Revolution: Daniel, Isaac, John, and Benjamin.[1] They were all patriots. Aedanus Burke, that staunch Republican, wrote that "The whole of them are a soldierly people, and good Republicans."[2] Daniel, the eldest, was not a very lovely person in his private life nor a very effective person in public life, but he was the head of the family. He was elected to represent the Georgetown and Cheraw District in the first United States Congress in 1788 and was re-elected in 1790.[3] William Loughton Smith believed that Huger alone among the members of the South Carolina delegation was close to his own Federalist point of view and regretted greatly Huger's continual absence from the sessions because of illness.[4]

[1] T. Tileston Wells, *The Hugers of South Carolina* (New York, 1931).

[2] Aedanus Burke to James Monroe, June 14, 1795, Gratz Collection, Penn. Hist. Soc.

[3] *Biographical Directory of the American Congress, 1774–1949* (Washington, D. C., 1950), pp. 1090–1091.

[4] George C. Rogers, Jr., *Evolution of a Federalist, William Loughton Smith of Charleston (1758–1812)* (Columbia, S. C., 1962), p. 168; "The Letters of William Loughton Smith to Edward Rutledge, June 6, 1789 to April 28, 1794," ed. George C. Rogers, Jr., *SCHM*, LXIX (1968), 11.

General Isaac Huger was the political head of the family; he was also the family's military chieftain. Although, as Major Alexander Garden has written, a "cloud of misfortune" obscured his fame "at one period" ("the disastrous surprise" of Huger's troops at Moncks Corner by Colonel Tarleton), he had fought to the end of the war.[5] General Huger was the first federal marshal in South Carolina and passed the position along to his son, Daniel Lionel Huger, when he retired. In 1794 John Hart was elected sheriff of Charleston District "by General Huger's interest." [6]

The youngest brother Benjamin was the hero of the family, an officer "of great gallantry, and high promise." He died while defending Charleston in 1779.[7] The Hugers had been settled on Cooper River for generations, but Benjamin Huger bought in 1767 a part of Hobcaw Barony and became a planter on Waccamaw Neck. It was to Major Benjamin Huger's summer house that Lafayette had come when he landed on North Island in 1777. By his first marriage Benjamin Huger had a daughter Mary, who married in 1788 Hugh Rutledge, brother of John and Edward Rutledge, and a son Benjamin, who married in 1796 Mary Allston, the daughter of Captain John Allston. Major Huger's second wife was the sister of Francis and Cleland Kinloch. Their son Francis Kinloch Huger married in 1802 a daughter of Thomas Pinckney.[8] The Hugers, therefore, supplied the link between the Georgetown aristocracy of Allstons and Kinlochs and the Charleston aristocracy of Rutledges and Pinckneys.

Benjamin Huger completed his education in 1789 and 1790 with a tour of France, Switzerland, Italy, and Portugal.[9] After his marriage and a summer's tour of New England with his bride he resided at Prospect Hill, his wife's property on the Waccamaw River.[10] He was a

[5] Alexander Garden, *Anecdotes of the Revolutionary War in America* (Charleston, S. C., 1822), p. 55.

[6] Rogers, *Evolution of a Federalist*, p. 183; John Brown Cutting to Thomas Pinckney, Dec. 19, 1794, Pinckney Papers, LC.

[7] Garden, *op. cit.*, p. 95.

[8] Genealogical notes on Huger Family, S. C. Hist. Soc.

[9] Thomas Jefferson to Benjamin Huger, July 26, 1789 with enclosed letter of introduction; Benjamin Huger to Thomas Jefferson, Aug. 11, 1790, Mass. Hist. Soc.

[10] John Drayton to Elbridge Gerry, May 30, 1796, Mass. Hist. Soc.; Isaac Huger to [Gen. Horatio Gates], May 28, 1796, Gratz Collection, Penn. Hist. Soc.; Marriage Settlements, No. 2 (1792–1796), pp. 499–503, S. C. Archives.

member of the South Carolina House of Representatives in 1798 and 1799 and in the years between 1808 and 1812. He served in the Sixth, Seventh, and Eighth Congresses of the United States (1799–1805) and in the Fourteenth (1815–1817). He ended his public service with a term in the South Carolina Senate (1818–1823) over which he presided as president from 1819 to 1822.[11] After he died on July 7, 1823, his fellow planters honored him by erecting a monument to his memory.[12] Many had named a child after him.[13] When President Monroe visited Georgetown in 1819, Benjamin Huger wrote the welcoming address and entertained him at Prospect Hill.[14]

The influence of Francis and Cleland Kinloch buttressed Benjamin Huger's political interest. Francis Kinloch, who in 1785 married Martha Rutledge, the daughter of John Rutledge,[15] had estates which if properly managed would have provided him the means not only for an opulent way of life but also a base for high public service. Yet, after his participation in the ratification convention of 1788 and the state constitutional convention of 1790, he never held a high public office or served in any legislative body. He seemed somewhat averse to the republicanism of his day. Like his father he may have thought himself worthy of a seat in a royal council but not in an elective assembly. If there had been "a little more of monarchy in the composition of our government," he confessed, there might have been things to which he might have aspired. But in America "I perceive no ambition in the world but that of getting rich & no idea of public virtue but that of saving the public money." [16] In March 1799 Kinloch had suggested himself for the mission to France.[17] In 1800 he was the obvious choice of the Georgetown gentlemen to deliver the oration on the occasion of Washington's death.[18] Having been

[11] *Biographical Directory of the American Congress, op. cit.,* p. 1090.

[12] Davison McDowell subscribed $20 on April 22, 1825. Mary James Richards, "Our McDowell Ancestry" (typed 1966), p. 23, McDowell Papers, SCL.

[13] Benjamin Huger Ward and Benjamin Huger Wilson.

[14] Huger recalled Washington's visit nearly thirty years before. It was Washington's object "to conciliate the feelings, and to reconcile the minds of his fellow citizens to the new Federal compact. . . . His success was complete." Address of Committee of Georgetown, S. C., to "Mr. President," [1819], Gratz Collection, Penn. Hist. Soc.

[15] *SCHM,* XXXI (1930), 17.

[16] Kinloch to ———, June 28, 1803, Gratz Collection, Penn. Hist. Soc.

[17] Kinloch to Timothy Pickering, March 1, 1799, Pickering Papers, Mass. Hist. Soc.

[18] Francis Kinloch, *Eulogy on George Washington* (Georgetown, S. C., 1800).

disappointed in his hope for an appointive office, he turned to travel. In June 1803, on the eve of his departure for four years in France and Switzerland, he wrote that he was a "disciple of Epicurus."[19]

Cleland Kinloch, equally rich, was more politically active than his older brother. Although he sat in the state legislature in the 1790's,[20] he soon became more concerned with his family, his homes, and his travels. He spent many summers in Newport and later built a home on the High Hills of the Santee where he resided most of the time.[21]

The Hugers, like the Rutledges and the Pinckneys, were moderate Federalists. They were aristocrats, but they had been patriots. Since the Hugers had always been a planting family, they possessed no mercantile allegiances, which were characteristics of the arch-Federalists of South Carolina. No doubt the aura of patriotism made the Huger name appealing to the voters of Black Mingo, and in the 1790's the name gained new luster. The romantic tie with Lafayette had drawn the Hugers close to France, as did their Huguenot background. Thus they were all aglow with the first flush of the French Revolution. In 1795 Francis Kinloch Huger made a dramatic attempt to rescue Lafayette from Olmutz prison. In this attempt he had the blessing of Washington and all Americans.[22]

Some might have thought that Benjamin Huger was a Jeffersonian

---

[19] Kinloch to ———, June 28, 1803, Gratz Collection, Penn. Hist. Soc. Kinloch's trip abroad burdened his properties so heavily that they never fully recovered their productivity. His *Letters from Geneva and France,* finished in 1808 and first published in the *Portfolio,* were his reminiscences, revealing him as a man observant of the romantic aspects of nature but not one sympathetic with the aspirations of the new men of his day. Kinloch's original manuscript and his personal copy with his own notations of *Letters from Geneva and France* (2 vols.; Boston, Mass., 1819) are in SCL.

[20] He was elected a member of the House of Representatives in Oct. 1790 and in Oct. 1798.

[21] In 1798 Cleland Kinloch and his family returned from Newport to Georgetown in the sloop *Aurora. Georgetown Gazette,* Nov. 9, 1798; John R. Sumter, *Stateburg and Its People* (Sumter, S. C., 1949), pp. 15, 109. He married in 1786 Harriet Simmons, daughter of Ebenezer Simmons. *SCHM,* XX (1919), 55.

[22] See Samuel Flagg Bemis, "George Washington and Lafayette, the Prisoner in Europe" in Samuel Flagg Bemis, *American Foreign Policy and the Blessings of Liberty and Other Essays* (New Haven, Conn., 1962), pp. 209–239; "Statement of the attempted rescue of General Lafayette from Olmutz," copy in Winyah Indigo Society Collection, Georgetown County Library; Garden, *op. cit.,* pp. 96–103.

because of his obvious French ties and also because he was the only member of the South Carolina delegation to vote for Jefferson at the time of the tie with Aaron Burr.[23] Yet Huger was unmistakably a Federalist. He stated on the floor of the House that he had been in 1800 "a warm, sincere, and zealous advocate of the two gentlemen [Adams and C. C. Pinckney] who were understood to be the Federal candidates." He had only voted for Jefferson because he had been preferred by his constituents.[24] At the time when Spain ceded Louisiana to France he explained that "He was not, it was true, one of the warm and enthusiastic devotees of the present administration, and he must honestly acknowledge that he should greatly prefer seeing the reins of Government, at this critical juncture, in the hands of WASHINGTON!"[25] Washington, not Jefferson, was his hero. Huger labored in Congress to secure a mausoleum befitting so illustrious a man.[26]

Huger knew that his family's influence did not extend very far into the backcountry. Backcountry opposition to the lowcountry aristocracy was a real threat in the 1790's. In February 1793 Lemuel Benton from the upper Pee Dee, who had been one of Marion's officers, defeated Daniel Huger and held the Georgetown congressional seat until 1798, when Benjamin Huger won.[27] In 1802 the state was gerrymandered in order to get rid of the Federalist Huger; yet he managed to win again in February 1803.[28] If the rice planters on the coast wanted to continue to rule, they would have to win the backcountry to their way of thinking.

There was, of course, some chance that the ideas released by the French Revolution might make an impression upon the community. For the first time in the 1790's the town had its own newspaper, a vehicle

[23] Huger was the only Federalist who voted for Jefferson. Henry S. Randall, *The Life of Thomas Jefferson* (New York, 1858), II, 595.

[24] *Annals* (8th Cong., 1st Sess.), pp. 532–533. Huger wrote Harrison Gray Otis, July 7, 1800, urging Otis to introduce young Josias Allston to President Adams. Huger feared that Josias Allston, who might be a member of the next S. C. legislature, was leaning in the Republican direction. This letter is in Mass. Hist. Soc.

[25] *Annals* (7th Cong., 2nd Sess.), pp. 488–489.

[26] *Annals* (6th Cong., 2nd Sess.), pp. 860–861; (14th Cong., 1st Sess.), pp. 672–674, 1007–1008.

[27] *Biographical Directory of the American Congress, op. cit.,* p. 546; Alexander Gregg, *History of the Old Cheraws* (Baltimore, Md., reprinted 1967), p. 377.

[28] Rogers, *Evolution of a Federalist,* pp. 354–355.

through which some of these ideas reached the people. James Carson began publishing the *South Carolina Independent Gazette* on April 2, 1791, with a quotation from "Junius" pinned to the masthead: "Let it be impressed upon your Mind, let it be instilled into your children, that the Liberty of the PRESS is the Palladium of all the Civil Political and Religious Rights of Free Men." Although scarcely a dozen copies of this newspaper remain, it is easy to discern that the tone of the sheet was Jeffersonian.[29]

The Methodists and to a lesser extent the Baptists were groups that brought revolutionary ideas to Georgetown. Francis Asbury recorded in his diary on February 23, 1785, his first impressions of Georgetown: "we met with a kind reception. I felt my mind solemn, and devoted to God, but was in great doubt of success. If God has not called us by his providence into these parts, I desire and pray that we may have no countenance from the people. . . ."[30] In January 1786 he preached twice in Georgetown, each time to about eighty people. In spite of his comment that "this is a poor place for religion,"[31] he kept returning—in 1787, 1790, 1791, 1792, 1794, 1795, 1796, 1799, 1802, 1804, and in following years. His first staunch supporter was the merchant William Wayne, nephew of General Anthony Wayne, who had settled in Georgetown during the prosperous year of 1782. He, whom "the Lord had brought . . . through deep exercises of soul," welcomed Asbury on each visit to his home.[32] But the people were not moved. In 1794 Asbury confided to his diary: "If a man-of-war is a 'floating hell', these [rice plantations] are standing ones: wicked masters, overseers, and Negroes—cursing, drinking—no Sabbaths, no sermons."[33] Asbury often wondered whether God had intended him to visit Georgetown.

On one visit he was riding down Waccamaw Neck and met a slave,

[29] The *South Carolina Independent Gazette* was published weekly by James Carson until March 22, 1796, when the name was changed to the *Georgetown Chronicle and South-Carolina Weekly Advertiser*. The newspaper was then printed by James Smylie, who in the summer of 1797 brought it out as a semi-weekly.

[30] *The Journal and Letters of Francis Asbury*, ed. Elmer T. Clark, et al. (London, Eng., and Nashville, Tenn., 1958), I, 483.

[31] *Ibid.*, p. 505.

[32] *Ibid.*, p. 483.

[33] *Ibid.*, II, 7.

Black Punch, whom he converted on the spot. The slave returned to his plantation and became an exhorter among the slaves, a work which might have had vast implications.[34] John Wesley in *Thoughts on Slavery* in 1774 had opposed slavery. Asbury held similar views during the first twenty years of his American ministry. Apparently, the appeal of his message was greater among the slaves than among the white population. After eleven years he could count nearly one hundred Africans and only seven or eight whites among his flock.[35] In 1795 the South Carolina Methodist preachers met in Charleston to exclude from among themselves those who persisted in owning slaves. Among those subscribing to the sentiment that they were "deeply sensible of the impropriety, & evil of Slavery" were a number of preachers who served the Santee or Pee Dee circuits. Thomas Humphries, William McDowell, John Simmons, and James King served Georgetown itself.[36] If this were the bent of the Methodists' ideas, the explanation for their lack of success is not difficult to discover. Asbury had noted the dilemma in his journal on March 10, 1794: "We held a little conference to provide for Charleston, Georgetown, Edisto, and Santee: some are afraid that if we retain none among us who trade in slaves, the preachers will not be supported, but my fear is that we shall not be able to supply this State with preachers."[37] Asbury and others continued to preach of the examples in the redemption and salvation of mankind by Jesus Christ, both in Georgetown and at Boone's chapel on an upper branch of the Sampit, but their message fell upon barren ground among the whites although upon rich soil among the slaves.

The story of the Baptists is similar to the Methodists, but with slightly more success in the 1790's due to the fact that they did not push their work with the slaves as much as did the Methodists. The early Georgetown Baptists clustered around William Cuttino, who had been converted

[34] W. P. Harrison, *The Gospel Among the Slaves, A Short Account of Missionary Operations among the African Slaves of the Southern States* (Nashville, Tenn., 1893), pp. 178–179.

[35] Clark, *op. cit.*, II, 70, 110.

[36] "Articles of Agreement Amongst the Preachers," 1795, Conference Papers, 1795, Methodist Papers, Wofford College; Albert Deems Betts, *History of South Carolina Methodism* (Columbia, S. C., 1952), pp. 60–76.

[37] Clark, *op. cit.*, II, 8.

in 1767 in Charleston by the Reverend Oliver Hart.[38] In July 1788 the Reverend Richard Furman wrote Hart: "There seems to be a work of grace begun in Georgetown. I have been twice there this spring; at the last visit baptized Mrs. Cuttino and her eldest son and administered the Lord's supper to twelve communicants. I received six more applicants, etc., before I left." [39] In June 1794, thirty-six members formed the Georgetown Church and were admitted to the Charleston Association. In 1801 Edmund Botsford, John Bossard, William Cuttino, Sr., Savage Smith, Cornelius Dupre, William Grant, William Cuttino, Jr., John Waldo, John Davis, John Evans, Jeremiah Cuttino, James Mackay, William H. Lide, William Murray, Samuel Blackwell, James Lane, Michael Blackwell, John P. Dunnan, and William B. Johnson petitioned for an act of incorporation which was secured from the legislature on December 19, 1801.[40] They built a "handsome and commodious wooden meeting-house" about sixty feet long on Lot 228, which had been reserved in the original plan for a Baptist church. John Waldo, who came to Georgetown in 1793 from New York, served as minister for awhile, but in 1796 Edmund Botsford, an immigrant indented carpenter who had been converted and then ordained by the Reverend Oliver Hart, began a long pastorate, which lasted until his death in 1819. Asbury was envious of the Baptists' success: they "have built an elegant church, planned for a steeple and organ: they take the rich; and the commonalty and the slaves fall to us. . . ." [41] The Baptists were actually not as successful as Asbury indicated. The charter for their church was renewed after ten years, but they did not secure permanent incorporation until December 19, 1827, as "The Baptist Church of Christ, in Georgetown, South Carolina." [42] Leah Townsend wrote that there were few additions

[38] Leah Townsend, *South Carolina Baptists, 1670–1805* (Florence, S. C., 1935), p. 58.

[39] *Ibid.*, p. 59.

[40] *Ibid.;* S. C. *Statutes*, V, 414; Petitions, Religion, 1800–1829, Legislative System, S. C. Archives.

[41] Clark, *op. cit.*, II, 423–424; Edmund Botsford, *The Spiritual Voyage, Performed in the Ship Convert, Under the Command of Capt. Godly-Fear, from the port of Repentance-unto-Life, to the haven of Felicity, on the Continent of Glory. An Allegory. To which is prefixed A sketch of the Life of the Author, by the late Rev. Richard Furman* (Charleston, S. C., 1828), pp. 3, 5, 6, 10, 11, 15, 17.

[42] S. C. *Statutes*, VIII, 353; Petitions, 1813, 1827, Religion, 1800–1829, Legislative System, S. C. Archives.

to the congregation during Botsford's long pastorate: "in fact, for years Mr. Waldo and Mr. Botsford were the only white male members."[43]

As the excesses of the French Revolution became known, the local gentry paused in their embracement of things French. The arrival of the refugees from the island of Santo Domingo strengthened the fears of slave insurrection. In Santo Domingo Toussaint L'Ouverture had led the blacks in a complete overturn of society. With this event and the knowledge that the French Revolution had spawned "Les Amis des Noirs," founded by Brissot de Warville, the Revolution lost its support among the slaveholding gentry. There might be a romantic episode to rescue Lafayette, but it was a Lafayette already left behind by the Revolution. Thus, when France insulted the United States by demanding bribes, the ruling group in Georgetown was ready to support the administration with money, men, and measures. A new newspaper, the *Georgetown Gazette*, appeared on May 8, 1798, published by Elliott and Burd.[44] As this paper evoked a warlike spirit by printing in an early issue Francis Hopkinson's patriotic anthem "Hail Columbia," it seemed to be an answer to the too-liberal Carson paper. A meeting of the citizens of Georgetown at Page's tavern on May 21, 1798, enthusiastically endorsed resolutions which stated confidence in the executive and a willingness to defend America.[45] During the summer of 1798 a committee was formed, headed by General Peter Horry, to raise funds for building a fort to defend the town.[46] Captain Benjamin Foissin Trapier and Lieutenant William Windham Trapier were both in Charleston, one in command at Fort Johnson and the other in the garrison at Castle Pinckney.[47] It was in the ensuing fall that Benjamin Huger was elected to Congress.[48]

In September 1799 "An Old Citizen" labeled a plan to educate the Negroes of Prince Frederick an absurd scheme. "As soon as slaves are educated they cease to be slaves, and will become masters the first

[43] Townsend, *op. cit.*, p. 59. Botsford went to Charleston in 1812 "to have a Second Attropfia on his Eye." He suffered greatly. "Journal of General Peter Horry," *SCHM*, XLIII (1944), 181.

[44] After Jan. 1, 1800, it was published by John Burd alone. Although Burd died on Oct. 23, 1801, the newspaper was continued until 1817 by a succession of publishers.

[45] *Georgetown Gazette*, May 22, 1798.

[46] *Georgetown Gazette*, Aug. 14, 1798.

[47] *Georgetown Gazette*, Aug. 21, 1799.

[48] Complete returns in *Georgetown Gazette*, Jan. 9, 1799.

opportunity, as in St. Domingo. . . ." Some had suggested that the French had emissaries in South Carolina who were trying to promote anarchy, but it should be known, continued this letter, that slavery was countenanced by divine revelation. The same principles that led Brissot to consider emancipation of the slaves led him also to the guillotine.[49] Only the state legislature could decide emancipation, and in 1800 the state, as if echoing this editorial, passed a new law which made it very difficult to emancipate a slave.[50]

Huger's speeches in Congress fully reveal his conception of the threats to the Union and, therefore, his conception of what that Union should be. As "a mere planter," [51] he spoke for his fellow rice-growers long before Calhoun pointed out the trends that would eventually disrupt the Union. It was the anarchy of the 1780's reinforced by the need "to provide against danger from abroad, and to insure protection at home" which had drawn the thirteen independent sovereignties together to form a nation.[52] The Constitution was "in its essence, a compact, a bargain, a perfect compromise of the interests, powers, influence, and rights of a number of independent societies, who have united for their common advantage, and who are no further bound or pledged to each other than by the articles and conditions in the written contract—the Constitution —which has been acceded to by them all." [53] Clashing interest had been resolved by compromise. Each would respect the needs of the others. When opposing an importation tax on slaves in 1804, Huger said: "The fair principle of taxation is, that every part of the Union should contribute equally. When any branch of trade is profitable in New York, I, though a Southern man, rejoice at it. When the fisheries of the Eastern States prosper, I feel highly gratified—not because those whom I represent are particularly interested in them, but because I consider myself as a part of the whole, and that whatever advances the interests of

[49] *Georgetown Gazette,* Sept. 11, 1799.
[50] *S. C. Statutes,* VII, 442–443.
[51] *Annals* (7th Cong., 1st Sess.), p. 1029.
[52] *Annals* (7th Cong., 1st Sess.), p. 690; (8th Cong., 1st Sess.), p. 522. Huger's speech in the House of Oct. 28, 1803, has recently been called "one of the truly great speeches of the early period." *A Second Federalist,* ed. C. S. Hyneman and G. W. Carey (New York, 1967), p. x.
[53] *Annals* (8th Cong., 1st Sess.), p. 522.

any part of this Union must promote the interests of every part of it."[54] This was the principal assumption made by the leaders of South Carolina when they entered the Union, that the other states would recognize her need for slavery on economic grounds, and, since the prosperity of South Carolina would strengthen the nation, the state would be left to make its own decisions.

But by 1803 Huger was already aware that in fourteen years the nation had changed. Innovation was sweeping through the nations of the world. The very success of America was undermining those principles upon which the nation was based.[55] Huger fought against the judiciary bill of 1802 and the twelfth amendment in the same way that Calhoun would fight against the tariff.[56] The separation of the powers and the independence of the judiciary were two of the great principles of the Constitution. Of the attempt to repeal the Judiciary Act of 1801, which had reorganized the federal judiciary system to make it more efficient (as Huger sincerely believed), he said: "I feel a strong conviction on my mind, that the most stable support, the main pillar of the noble fabric already totters on its foundation, and is about to be tumbled prostrate in the dust." [57] He looked upon the repeal as an attempt of the legislature to bring the judicial branch in line with its own thinking. Congress had an itch to become omnicompetent like the British Parliament. It was on the verge of confusing its legislative powers with those of a convention.[58] He already saw the executive and legislative powers combining "to construe the Constitution as might best suit their purposes, and all power would of course be in their hands." If the federal judiciary could not maintain its independence, civil war would follow.[59]

The Twelfth Amendment would also be "a deadly wound to the national compact" for by it a great principle would be sacrificed, the equality of the states.[60] Equality of the states was "the point upon which the whole business turned. . . ." [61] There had been a compromise in the

---

[54] *Annals* (8th Cong., 1st Sess.), p. 1005).
[55] *Annals* (8th Cong., 1st Sess.), pp. 519, 530.
[56] *Annals* (7th Cong., 1st Sess.), pp. 665–693; (8th Cong., 1st Sess.), pp. 518–535.
[57] *Annals* (7th Cong., 1st Sess.), p. 678.
[58] *Annals* (7th Cong., 1st Sess.), p. 687.
[59] *Annals* (7th Cong., 1st Sess.), p. 691.
[60] *Annals* (8th Cong., 1st Sess.), p. 520.
[61] *Annals* (8th Cong., 1st Sess.), p. 523.

convention between the large and small states in the setting up of the
national legislature. There had also been a compromise between the
large and small states in setting up the national executive. When it had
been decided to have a single executive and have him elected by the
people, this seemed to throw too much power into the hands of the
large states, who would have elected whom they pleased. Therefore, a
check to quiet the fears of the small states was sought. Huger had been
taught by those framers whom he had known that the provision obliging
the electors in each state to vote indiscriminately for two persons to fill
the offices of president and vice president was regarded as the best means
to quiet the fears of the smaller states. The fact that they must vote for
two (one from another state than their own), plus the fact that a tie in
the electoral college threw the vote into the House where the states
voted as equals, was a protection of the influence of the smaller states.
Therefore, the contemplated change would take away from the small
states and give to the large. It gives, he said:

a death-blow to that portion of the State sovereignties which has been
reserved to the several States, and that we thereby take a monstrous and
more than a gigantic stride, towards that very consolidation of the States
against which gentlemen have been wont of yore so bitterly to exclaim.
For we may boast as much as we please; we may say what we will of our
moderation, sincerity, and political virtue; we may give every security
which can be devised upon parchment or upon paper, and endeavor
to render it more sacred by seals, and even by oaths; still, so long as
human nature remains human nature—where power exists on the one
side and weakness on the other—there ever will arise ambition, and the
inclination to obtain additional power on the part of the most powerful; and consequently, in proportion as you add to the means . . . draw
us nearer to a consolidated government.[62]

What would this new stronger national government do with its power?
It would tax the agricultural interests for the benefit of the new manufacturing interests; it would tax the east for the benefit of the west.
Therefore, Huger opposed reduction of the excise taxes without a reduction of tariffs. He opposed a tax on the importation of slaves, not

---

[62] *Annals* (8th Cong., 1st Sess.), p. 530.

as a defender of slavery, but because it was a tax upon one interest unfairly placed.[63] Huger had, therefore, already seen that the country was "fearfully growing" and that as numbers controlled the national government the Constitution would be construed to add power to the center. Could the rice planters of South Carolina retain their place for long in such a union, which violated many of the compromises upon which it had been founded?

The Allstons were the richest of the Georgetown rice planting factions. Two brothers, John and William Allston, had secured royal grants in 1734 and 1735 on the Waccamaw river, thereby founding a dynasty.[64] John married Sarah Belin, leaving at his death in 1750 four sons (John, Josias of Turkey Hill, William of Brookgreen, and Samuel) and one daughter, the wife of Benjamin Marion.[65] Since John had only daughters and Josias ultimately moved to the Cape Fear,[66] William was the sire of the most famous of the double "l" Allstons. William used his wealth during the Revolution to support the patriots in North Carolina and at Snow's Island. William of Brookgreen, who died in 1781, was known as William Allston, the younger, or William Allston, Jr., to distinguish him from his uncle and his first cousin.

William Allston (1698–1744) married Esther LaBrosse de Marboeuf in 1721 and left three sons and six daughters at his death.[67] William, known as William Allston, Sr., and John, known as "Captain Jack," had many descendants, but the more famous progeny descended from Joseph, the fifth child. Joseph Allston (1733–1784), of The Oaks, who married Charlotte Rothmahler, successfully brought his fortune through the Revolution. At his death in 1784 he left his elder son Captain Wil-

---

[63] *Annals* (7th Cong., 1st Sess.), pp. 451–455, 1027–1032; (14th Cong., 1st Sess.), pp. 676, 1274.

[64] Index to Royal Grants, S. C. Archives. William Swinton surveyed 100 acres for John Allston on the Waccamaw River and signed the plat Aug. 15, 1732. "John Allston," Pre-Revolutionary War Plats, S. C. Archives.

[65] "Will of John Allston," dated March 24, 1750, proved May 11, 1750, Charleston County Wills, VI (1747–1752), 358–361, S. C. Archives. See Appendix II.

[66] "Will of Josias Allston," dated April 18, 1774, proved n.d., Charleston County Wills, XVII, Book B (1774–1779), 527–532, S. C. Archives.

[67] "Will of William Allston," dated Jan. 29, 1743, proved April 12, 1744, Charleston County Wills, V (1740–1747), 292–294, S. C. Archives.

ham Allston Clifton plantation and his younger son Thomas Prospect Hill.[68]

Captain William Allston had fought with Marion. In 1791, about the time he welcomed Washington to Clifton, he dropped an "l" from his name in order to distinguish himself from the other William Allstons. He married twice (Mary Ashe in 1777 and Mary Brewton Motte in 1791) and sired an enormous clan. During his long life he was referred to in awe as "King Billy."

Colonel William Alston's eldest son was Joseph, certainly the favored son of this sprawling cousinage. His grandfather had left him The Oaks, so that young Joseph was a rich man in his own right. His father had great ambition for him and planned his education accordingly. As Joseph himself wrote: "From my father's plan of education for me, I may properly be called a hot-bed plant. . . . Before seventeen I finished my college education; before twenty I was admitted to the bar." [69] Tutors, Princeton,[70] and travel had formed the young man.

When he made his appearance in Northern social circles at the end of the 1790's, he was an immensely rich and talented young man with the prospects of enormous political influence in his own state, which was at that time still one of the key states in the Union. Theodosia Burr must have fallen in love with his personal characteristics while her father undoubtedly itched to use his money and to control his political destiny. The young man no doubt enjoyed the admiration lavished upon him. The wedding took place in Albany in February 1801 while Aaron Burr was waiting to see if he might become President of the United States.

The Alston-Burr marriage had as many fatal flaws as the Union. Could the sophistication of New York flourish on the banks of the Waccamaw? Could a political union of New York and South Carolina be enduring? Joseph Alston was aware of the first problem and, in a marvelous letter designed to reassure Theodosia, portrayed the style of his society:

[68] "Will of Joseph Allston," Allston and LaBruce Family Records, SCL. Thomas Allston (1764–1794) married Mary (the daughter of his uncle Capt. Jack Allston), who later married Benjamin Huger. Marriage Settlements, No. 2 (1792–1796), pp. 499–503, S. C. Archives. William Allston apparently bought Belvoir from the Martin family in 1791 and renamed it Friendfield. John Martin Papers, S. C. Hist. Soc.

[69] Matthew L. Davis, *Memoirs of Aaron Burr* (New York, 1836), I, 425–426.

[70] J. H. Easterby, "Joseph Alston," *DAB*.

With regard to our manners; if there is any state which has a claim to superior refinement, it is certainly South Carolina. Generally speaking, we are divided into but two classes, very rich and very poor; which, if no advantage in a political view, is undoubtedly favourable to a polished state of society. Our gentlemen having large fortunes, and being very little disposed by the climate to the drudgery of business or professions, have full leisure for the attainment of polite literature, and what are usually called accomplishments; you therefore meet with few of them who are not tolerably well informed, agreeable companions, and completely well bred. The possession of slaves renders them proud, impatient of restraint, and gives them a haughtiness of manner which, to those unaccustomed to them, is disagreeable; but we find among them a high sense of honour, a delicacy of sentiment, and a liberality of mind, which we look for in vain in the more commercial citizens of the northern states. The genius of the Carolinian, like the inhabitants of all southern countries, is quick, lively, and acute; in steadiness and perseverance he is naturally inferior to the native of the north; but this defect of climate is often overcome by his ambition or necessity; and, whenever this happens, he seldom fails to distinguish himself. In his temper he is gay and fond of company, open, generous, and unsuspicious; easily irritated, and quick to resent even the appearance of insult; but his passion, like the fire of the flint, is lighted up and extinguished in the same moment. I do not mention his hospitality and kindness to strangers, for they are so common they are no longer esteemed virtues; like common honesty, they are noticed only when not possessed. Nor is it for the elegance of their manners only that the South Carolinians are distinguished; sound morality is equally conspicuous among them. Gaming, so far from being a fashionable vice, is confined entirely to the lower class of people; among gentlemen it is deemed disgraceful. Many of them, it is true, are fond of the turf; but they pursue the sports of it merely as an amusement and recreation, not a business. As to hunting, the country gentlemen occasionally engage in it, but surely there is nothing criminal in this! From my education and other pursuits I have seldom participated in it myself; but I consider it, above all exercises, the most manly and healthful.[71]

Theodosia tried to win her in-laws, and they to win her. She must have written enthusiastically of her welcome home after her first summer visit to the North, for her father replied: "Your reception has, indeed, been charming; it reads more like an extract from some romance than matter of fact happening in the nineteenth century within the

[71] Davis, *op. cit.*, pp. 430–432.

United States." [72] Of her two sisters-in-law Maria and Charlotte she seemed genuinely fond;[73] of her father-in-law and her brother-in-law William Algernon less so. After staying with them in Petersburg, Virginia, she wrote: "We travel in company with the two Alstons. Pray teach me how to write two *A's* without producing something like an *Ass.*" [74]

She lived with her other brother-in-law John Ashe Alston and his wife Sally at Hagley until the home at The Oaks was ready, but it was March 1804 before it was.[75] The birth of Aaron Burr Alston, however, inspired hope in both families for a lasting union. Grandfather Burr was soon insisting that young "ABA" learn his "ABC's." And Burr wrote Alston:

> Let me entreat you to stimulate and aid Theodosia in the cultivation of her mind. It is indispensable to her happiness and essential to yours. It is also of the utmost importance to your son. She would presently acquire a critical knowledge of Latin, English, and all branches of natural philosophy. All this would be poured into your son. If you should differ with me as to the importance of this measure, suffer me to ask it of you as a last favour. She will richly compensate your trouble. [76]

Of the Burr-Alston political union much was also rumored in the beginning. Maria Nicholson wrote her sister Mrs. Albert Gallatin on February 5, 1801:

> Report does not speak well of him [Alston]; it says that he is rich, but he is a great dasher, dissipated, ill-tempered, vain and silly. I know that he is ugly and of unprepossessing manners. Can it be that the father has sacrificed a daughter so lovely to affluence and influential connections? They say that it was Mr. A. who gained the 8 votes in Carolina at the present election, and that he is not yet relieved from pecuniary embarrassments. Is this the man, think ye? Has Mr. G. a favorable opinion of this man of talents, or not? He loves his child. Is he so devoted to the customs of the world as to encourage such a match? [77]

[72] *Ibid.*, II, 160.
[73] *Ibid.*, pp. 205–206.
[74] *Ibid.*, pp. 242–244.
[75] *Ibid.*, pp. 244, 253, 281.
[76] *Ibid.*, p. 326.
[77] Henry Adams, *The Life of Albert Gallatin* (New York, 1943), pp. 244–245.

Thomas R. Mitchell, writing in 1819, thought of Burr as a man who advanced by intrigue.[78] The Northern view of Burr at the beginning of the Burr-Alston connection was not much different from the Southern view at the end of that connection.

Burr did push Alston in November 1802 to proceed to Columbia in order that he might "be there two or three days before the commencement of the session," even though it meant missing Theodosia's return from the North. Burr thought it quite malicious that someone had implied that "the Alstons were of no consideration or influence in South Carolina."[79] In 1805 when Burr heard that Alston might "degenerate into a mere planter," he wrote: "If so, it is to be lamented that you have any thing above common sense, and that you have learned any thing more than to read and write, for all above common sense and school education spoils the planter."[80] Burr was eager to have Alston secure a summer residence in the South Carolina foothills, not only as a project with assurances of health for the family but as "an increase of your influence and connexions."[81] Did Burr tutor Alston in the need to unify the lowcountry and backcountry?

Alston did follow Burr's suggestions, although historians have said he had ambition enough of his own.[82] He kept in touch with Benjamin Huger; Theodosia could imagine while she was away in New York that "after all, it is more than probable that you have been smoking with Huger, entirely absorbed in your society and segar."[83] He shared Huger's state sovereignty views. In his Fourth of July oration of 1806 he stated that he would consider the United States Constitution "perfect" with "a

[78] Thomas R. Mitchell, *Thoughts on the Constitution of the State of South-Carolina* (Georgetown, S. C., 1819), p. 10.

[79] Davis, *op. cit.*, II, 215.

[80] *Ibid.*, p. 365.

[81] *Ibid.*, pp. 183–184.

[82] Easterby believed that Parton had overemphasized the influence of Burr upon Alston. J. H. Easterby, "Joseph Alston," *DAB*. Parton had written: "Colonel Burr fired him with his own ambition, stimulated his powers, urged and directed his studies, advised his occasional appearances in the courts, and induced him to enter the political arena." James Parton, *The Life and Times of Aaron Burr* (New York, 1857), I, 298. I have followed Parton. J. Motte Alston wrote that his uncle was "not an ambitious man, but Aaron Burr instilled into him some of that of which he, himself, was somewhat overstocked." *Rice Planter and Sportsman*, ed. Arney R. Childs (Columbia, S. C., 1953), p. 17.

[83] Davis, *op. cit.*, II, 182, 202, 207.

single alteration—the house of representatives formed like the senate—in other words, equal influence in the general government preserved to every state." [84]

Within the state he was a dominant figure in the movement to unite the lowcountry with the backcountry which culminated in the constitutional amendment of 1808. But Alston was helped by an economic transformation of the state. The backcountry had discovered cotton, and farmers soon became planters. Neither Francis Kinloch, nor Huger, nor Alston were in favor of reopening the slave trade, but the introduction of more slaves into the backcountry spread their style of life.[85] Alston argued in favor of more representation for the backcountry because he saw no reason to deny these people "when . . . they have assimilated so nearly to the privileged districts below. . . ." [86] In 1805 when Huger was replaced in Congress by David R. Williams, Williams was a planter more in the style of Huger than Lemuel Benton had ever been.[87]

These gentlemen were helped by the fact that the Methodists and Baptists had given up their crusade against slavery. The years 1803 and 1804 saw some new departures for the Methodists in the Georgetown community and in the South. A local schism had occurred among the South Carolina Methodists in 1793 when William Hammett, feeling that he was the true disciple of Wesley, repudiated the guidance of Asbury and Coke and formed the "Primitive Methodists." On December 21, 1793, the "Primitive Methodists of Ebenezer Church, Georgetown" was organized. This division was brought to an end with the death of Hammett in 1803. The property of the Primitive Methodists in Georgetown was taken over by Asbury's supporters.[88] The next year the national Methodists adopted two *Disciplines,* one for the churches

---

[84] *An Oration for The Fourth of July, 1806; Delivered by The hon. Joseph Alston, Esq. in the Episcopal Church . . . ,*" (Georgetown, S. C., 1806), p. 10.

[85] Francis Kinloch to Robert R. Livingston, Feb. 12, 1804, Robert R. Livingston Collection, New York Hist. Soc.; David D. Wallace, *History of South Carolina* (New York, 1934), II, 372.

[86] *Speech of Joseph Alston, Member of the House of Representatives, for Winyaw, in a Committee of the Whole, to which was referred the bill for amending the third and seventh sections of the first articles of the Constitution of this state* (Georgetown, S. C., 1808), p. 16.

[87] *Biographical Directory of the American Congress, op. cit.,* p. 1819; Harvey Toliver Cook, *The Life and Legacy of David Rogerson Williams* (New York, 1916).

[88] Betts, *op. cit.,* pp. 65–67; *S. C. Statutes,* VIII, 178; Clark, *op. cit.,* II, 423.

south of Virginia and one for those in Virginia and northward. The *Discipline* for the Southern Methodist churches played down opposition to the institution of slavery. This compromise permitted the Methodists to become a great church in the South, but it was a compromise with conscience.[89] To make the compromise work new leaders were needed, and such a one emerged from the Georgetown Methodist community in the figure of William Capers.

William Capers was born in 1790 at Cainhoy near the path that Asbury traveled yearly between Georgetown and Charleston. His father must have heard Asbury preach, for after moving his family in 1794 to a rice plantation on the Pee Dee, he helped to found the Methodist group in Georgetown. Although the family removed to Stateburg after 1800, the young William Capers was to return to the lowcountry (his step-mother was a daughter of Samuel Wragg of Georgetown).[90] In 1817, along with Samuel K. Hodges and Eleazer Waterman, he secured the incorporation of "The Methodist Episcopal Church of Georgetown." [91] Capers became the South's greatest slaveholding Methodist preacher. It was a career in which he tried to reconcile the teachings of Christ with the holding of slaves in bondage.

Edmund Botsford, the leading local Baptist, also adjusted to the existence of the institution of slavery. Botsford wrote *Sambo and Toney*, which was designed to teach Christian lessons to the slaves, or, as a Negro today would say, it taught the essence of Samboism. The message in Botsford's pamphlet was summed up in the words of a minister who was addressing slaves:

Let your master, the people of the world, and your fellow-servants see that you endeavor to live a pious, godly life, agreeably to your profession, in all honesty and sobriety. When you have an opportunity, talk to your fellow-servants about their souls' concerns, and pray daily for their conversion. Guard against self-conceit. Humility is a lovely virtue, and shines nowhere more than in a servant. Be careful to attend public worship when you have opportunity, and be regular and strict in secret and family prayer. Live in love with your wives, and keep to

[89] This is the theme of Donald G. Mathews, *Slavery and Methodism, A Chapter in American Morality, 1780–1845* (Princeton, N. J., 1965).

[90] William W. Wightman, *Life of William Capers* (Nashville, Tenn., 1858), pp. 11, 24–27.

[91] S. C. *Statutes*, VIII, 283.

them only. Be careful of your children, that they do not tell lies, use bad words, or steal. Learn to make home the most agreeable place to you, and then you will not want to ramble from one plantation to another, and so will be kept from many temptations and hurtful snares. Be attentive to your master's business, and obey him in all things; pray daily for him and his family.[92]

The Anglican church had been disestablished in 1778. Each Protestant congregation could thereafter incorporate itself in order to retain its property. The church wardens and the vestry of Prince George Winyah did not obtain an act of incorporation until February 29, 1788, which may indicate the slowness with which the Anglican church revived after the war.[93] Prince George did not elect a rector until April 16, 1787, when the Reverend Thomas Jones was called. He died on October 10, 1788, and was succeeded in turn by the Reverend Joseph White, the Reverend Stephen Sykes, the Reverend William Jones (son of the Reverend Thomas Jones), the Reverend George H. Spieren, the Reverend Samuel Lilly, and the Reverend Solomon Halling. The longest incumbency was that of the Reverend George H. Spieren, who served six and a half years.[94] It was not until 1806 and 1807 that the Episcopalians in South Carolina worked out a statewide organization and adhered to the national body of their church. This reinvigoration of the Episcopal church was accomplished at two conventions held in Charleston in February 1806 and February 1807, to which Prince George sent Francis Kinloch and Samuel Wragg, its two most prominent lay figures.[95] The conventions strengthened the Episcopal church in the state, but it was not until the arrival of the Reverend Maurice Harvey Lance in 1815 that a clergyman stayed long enough to make an impression upon the parish.[96] He secured an act of December 17, 1817, authorizing a lottery to raise $15,000 to improve the church and build an orphan house.[97] By the 1820's the tower had been added at the west end and the church of Prince George been refurbished.

[92] Rev. Edmund Botsford, *Sambo and Toney: A Dialogue between Two Servants* (New York, [1824]), p. 20.
[93] S. C. *Statutes*, VIII, 145–149.
[94] Frederick Dalcho, *An Historical Account of the Protestant Episcopal Church in South-Carolina* (Charleston, S. C., 1820), pp. 308–318.
[95] Rogers, *Evolution of a Federalist*, pp. 388–392.
[96] Dalcho, *op. cit.*, pp. 309–310.
[97] S. C. *Statutes*, VIII, 287.

Prince Frederick did not elect a clergyman until 1793, when that parish selected the Reverend Hugh Fraser, who remained as rector until 1810. He was, however, more a planter than a clergyman. This church was weakened by the fact that most of the Black River people had converted to the Methodist and Baptist persuasions.

Dalcho could discover only the Reverend John O'Donnell as an incumbent at All Saints in the years between the Revolution and 1812, when Hugh Fraser accepted the call to that parish. "The Episcopal Church of All Saints" was incorporated on December 20, 1820. This was the church of the largest rice planters and entered upon its most prosperous period in the decades before the Civil War.[98] None of the Episcopal clergymen opposed slavery.

With the opening in 1805 of the South Carolina College, it was no longer necessary to send a young man outside of the state for a higher education. To this college came the sons of the planters and farmers and small-town merchants whose minds were forged into a South Carolina mold. It was designed to cement the union between the backcountry and lowcountry; it also helped to mold the men of Georgetown. Before 1820 the college educated a succession of Georgetown boys: Stephen Ford, Jr., Benjamin Heriot, Sr., John and Joseph Pyatt, David Cuttino, John Futhey, Robert A. Taylor, William and Matthew Fleming, Francis Withers, Joseph M. Alston, Charles Huggins, John A. Keith, Joseph S. Bossard, Thomas F. Goddard, John D. Magill, Joshua Ward, M. H. Lance, Anthony Bonneau Shackelford, James A. Fleming, John A. L. Norman, Thomas House Taylor, Solomon Cohen, Jr., and Paul Trapier Keith.[99]

Would this growing unity at home be the base from which to extend a slave empire to the west? Francis Kinloch had been against the Louisiana Purchase. He wrote Robert R. Livingston on November 23, 1803: "surely we have territory enough, nor is it easy to say, what effect such an addition of senators and representatives, as will spring up in time from that extensive region, may have upon our publick counsels. I, as

[98] Dalcho, op. cit., pp. 319–322; S. C. Statutes, VIII, 318.
[99] Andrew Charles Moore, Roll of Students of South Carolina College, 1805–1905 (Columbia, S. C., 1905). General Horry entertained many of these students at his home in Columbia. "Journal of General Peter Horry," ed. A. S. Salley, SCHM, XXXVIII (1937)–XLIII (1947), passim.

a planter on the waters of the Atlantick, have the same objection to our possessing Louisiana, as the Jamaica Planters, have to their governments annexing any more sugar islands to the British dominions. . . ." [100] But Joseph Alston may have had different ideas. He certainly loaned his father-in-law money, traveled with him on the western waters during the summer of 1806, and publicly approved of his plans.[101] Those plans were to revolutionize Mexico and to settle the lands that Burr had acquired.[102] Undoubtedly, slavery would have followed in the wake of any successes.

Burr had a tendency to seek out Southern planters possessed of many slaves. Thomas Sumter and Wade Hampton, the latter with Mississippi interests, were his close friends.[103] Pierce Butler welcomed Burr after the duel to his sea-island kingdom.[104] And Andrew Jackson was his principal host in Tennessee. Above all, his son-in-law was Alston. Burr may not have aimed at treason, but an empire based on slavery would have disrupted the Union.

After Burr was apprehended, Alston wrote a public letter to Governor Charles Pinckney, dated February 6, 1807, denying that he was a conspirator and that Burr was toying with treason.[105] Did Alston abandon his father-in-law? Matthew Davis wrote that Alston during the crisis "seemed to shrink from the consequences of an intercourse with him [Burr]." [106] Did these events endanger Alston's marriage? Undoubtedly there were tensions which could only be eased by the future and the prospects for young Aaron Burr Alston. Burr's self-banishment and the child's death in June 1812 tightened still further the nerves of that tragic couple. Alston in July 1812 wrote Burr, who had just returned from Europe: "That boy, on whom all rested; our companion, our

[100] Robert R. Livingston Collection, New York Hist. Soc.

[101] Joseph Alston to Charles Pinckney, Feb. 6, 1807, Charleston *Courier*, Feb. 14, 1807.

[102] Davis, *op. cit.*, II, 379.

[103] *Ibid.*, pp. 147, 179, 242, 278.

[104] *Ibid.*, pp. 153, 236.

[105] Printed in Charleston *Courier*, Feb. 14, 1807.

[106] Davis, *op. cit.*, II, 383. On Dec. 26, 1807, Joseph Alston as speaker wrote Thomas Jefferson to convey the S. C. legislature's wishes that Jefferson run again. Alston added a personal touch to the letter, and Jefferson, replying on Jan. 23, 1808, thanked him for "the polite expressions of sentiment." Journal of the House of Representatives, 1807, pp. 154–155, S. C. Archives.

friend—he who was to have transmitted down the mingled blood of Theodosia and myself—he who was to have redeemed all your glory, and shed new lustre upon our families—that boy, at once our happiness and our pride, is taken from us—*is dead.*" [107]

These family tragedies had not ruined Alston's political position in South Carolina, for he was elected governor of the state in December 1812, albeit by only one or two votes.[108] Then came the truly tragic blow —the loss of Theodosia at sea while on her way to meet her father whom she had not seen in over four years. The anguish of those January days tied Burr to Alston once again.[109] Alston as brigadier general in the militia had sought service on the Canadian front,[110] a post which Wade Hampton secured, but Alston as governor could not leave the state. E. S. Thomas said that he had grown sour and touchy.[111] There had been no greatness for Burr in the west, and there was no greatness in this war for Alston. Burr was again teasing him into action, turning him against Monroe, the heir of the Virginia dynasty. In November 1815 Burr was whipping up Alston's flagging spirits, hoping that he would lead his state against the caucus that was preparing to nominate Monroe, a man whom Burr characterized as "dull and stupid . . . illiterate . . . indecisive . . . pusillanimous, and, of course, hypocritical. . . ." The only way "to break down this vile combination which rules and degrades the United States" was by pushing forward the name of Andrew Jackson.[112]

Alston, too ill to care, died during the late summer of 1816.[113] Yet the Allston-Alston dynasty had not passed away. It continued to extend

[107] Davis, *op. cit.*, II, 426. He died on June 30, 1812, at the age of ten. *SCHM*, XXXVII (1936), 157.

[108] Wallace, *op. cit.*, II, 372.

[109] Alston wrote Burr, Feb. 25, 1813: "This, then, is the end of all the hopes we had formed. . . . Oh, my friend, if there be such a thing as the sublime of misery, it is for us that it has been reserved." Davis, *op. cit.*, II, 428–432.

[110] *Ibid.*, p. 427.

[111] E. S. Thomas, *Reminiscences of the Last Sixty-Five Years* (Hartford, Conn., 1840). II, 69–82. Also see John Harold Wolfe, *Jeffersonian Democracy in South Carolina* (Chapel Hill, N. C., 1940), pp. 268–273.

[112] Davis, *op. cit.*, II, 433–436.

[113] Alston took his seat in Dec. 1814 as senator from All Saints and died on Sept. 10, 1816, *Charleston Times*, Sept. 16, 1816. Alston bequeathed Burr "all demands I may have against him. . . ." Davis, *op. cit.*, II, 438–439.

its tentacles into the life of the state through its ever-increasing rice profits, its many marriage alliances, and its political activities (the family produced two more governors before the Civil War). This dynasty was the supreme example of the power and influence of an aristocratic faction in the history of the state—that was to secede.

XI

LOCAL GOVERNMENT

By the 1820's South Carolina had reorganized her local government. The planters must feel secure at home as they faced opposition from abroad. The machinery of local government was worked out after the disruption of the American Revolution and was running smoothly by the time of the Missouri controversy and nullification crisis. Although the local office holders were quite often drawn from the small middle class, their offices with their functions had been described by a body which the planting elements controlled. There was a middle class in Georgetown with characteristics distinct from the planting class, but it was a group that had been brought into being by the rice interests and until the Civil War was a bulwark of the planting society.

Before the Revolution, control of local affairs had been in the hands of commissioners, justices of the peace, parish and county officers, and town trustees. This system had to be overhauled as the colony first became an independent state and then a member of the new federal union.

The reopening of the lines of communication was the first job. On March 12, 1783, the legislature stated that all commissioners of high roads and bridges who had been in commission on May 12, 1780 should continue in office until the following Easter Monday, when elections for new commissioners should be held. The freeholders in each parish were to elect the same number of commissioners as had formerly served.[1] On March 24, 1785 this system was placed on a firmer basis; freeholders would elect commissioners the first Monday in every April with the governor filling vacancies. The board of commissioners would meet at the parish church on the third Monday in April and the first Monday in August in order to assign work and to levy a tax when necessary.[2] In 1788 the boards were made self-perpetuating. Once elected on the first Monday in May 1788, the commissioners had to serve at least three years when they might resign if they so wished, and upon resigning they could name their successors if approved by the board. At this time the commissioners were given the power to grant licenses for taverns and billiard tables; the fees collected were used for the repair of bridges and roads.[3] Until the Civil War the commissioners of the high roads for the two parishes of Prince George Winyah and All Saints were responsible for the roads and bridges in their respective parishes. On December 21, 1792, the powers of the commissioners for Prince George were extended to cover that region which had been a part of Prince Frederick but which had not been included in Williamsburg County when it was formed in 1785.[4] In 1825 the basic antebellum road law was passed; it continued the life of these boards and stated that the roads were to be posted and numbered.[5] There were separate boards of commissioners for the bridge over Black Mingo Creek and for the road on South Island.[6] Ferries were still vested in individuals. J. R. Easterling in 1846 applied for a ferry over the Black River near his plantation.[7]

The number of commissioners appointed before the Revolution for keeping Lynch's Causeway in repair had been reduced by deaths. The heirs of Thomas Lynch sued the board for not having reimbursed the

[1] S. C. Statutes, IX, 274–275.
[2] S. C. Statutes, IX, 292–301.
[3] S. C. Statutes, IX, 307–319, 321–326.
[4] S. C. Statutes, IX, 347–359.
[5] S. C. Statutes, IX, 558–566. Also see Josiah J. Evans, A Digest of the Road-Law of the State of South Carolina (Columbia, S. C., 1852).
[6] The incumbents for all these commissions are given in Winyah Observer, Oct. 15, 1851. For bridge over Black Mingo Creek see Evans, op. cit., pp. 49–50.
[7] Winyah Observer, Aug. 19, 1846.

estate of Thomas Lynch, who under contract to the board had repaired the causeway.[8] Ebenezer Hazard, who crossed the causeway on January 27, 1778, had recorded the following story in his journal:

Thos. Lynch esqr. formerly Member of Congress, contracted with the Assembly to make a Road through this Island (which belongs to him) for £8500 So. Cara. Curry.—when he had finished it, as he thought, he offered it to the Commissioners who refused it as not being wide enough; he, in Resentment, cut Canals through it, but afterwards altered his Mind, & began to make a good Causeway, which he is now about. We saw a great Number of Negroes at Work upon it, throwing up Dirt &c.; but at present it is impassable, and the old one is very little better; Travellers frequently get their Horses swamped upon it, & if they attempt to walk, it is very probably they will be swamped too.[9]

Since Lynch's heirs won their court case, the legislature had to pass a law in 1791 appointing a special set of commissioners to raise a tax on the people of Prince George in order to reimburse the heirs.[10] The board of Lynch's Causeway, which had been reconstituted in 1788, continued as a separate body until the Civil War. In 1825 the causeway was again rebuilt.[11]

In 1778 Ebenezer Hazard had been making a survey for a post route and appointed Peter Lesesne as postmaster in Georgetown.[12] Even by 1786 Hazard, the new United States postmaster general, had only managed to extend the Southern stages to Wilmington, N. C., whence a packet boat carried the mail and passengers to Charleston.[13] There was a stage by 1797 from Georgetown to Charleston, for an announcement in the newspaper stated that there would be a five A.M. departure on Monday from Georgetown and arrival at Haddrell's Point opposite Charleston at nine Tuesday morning. In 1798 there was a regular two-way service between Charleston and Georgetown. On March 1, 1803, the route from Georgetown to Fayetteville, N. C., was opened. During

[8] S. C. Statutes, V, 194–195.
[9] Hazard was in South Carolina from Jan. 18 to March 6, 1778. Ebenezer Hazard's Journal, Penn. Hist. Soc.
[10] S. C. Statutes, V, 194–195.
[11] S. C. Statutes, IX, 312, 556–558; Evans, op. cit., pp. 48–49.
[12] Ebenezer Hazard's Journal, Penn. Hist. Soc.
[13] Oliver W. Holmes, "Shall Stagecoaches Carry the Mail?—A Debate of The Confederation Period," William and Mary Quarterly, XX (1963), 566–567.

the 1830's the stagecoach service reached the peak of its efficiency with daylight service between Georgetown and Charleston guaranteed.[14]

On March 21, 1784, the legislature appointed a new set of commissioners of the pilots for Georgetown from the local merchants: Job Rothmahler, Anthony Bonneau, John Cogdell, George Heriot, and Samuel Smith. These commissioners had the power to coopt new members. In order to secure funds for employing pilots and building pilot boats, as well as for keeping the harbor well-marked, an additional tonnage was levied of three pence per ton on every vessel at the port coming "from any place from without the limits of this state," a discrimination against the vessels of sister states as well as foreign vessels that was possible under the Articles of Confederation.[15] After the adoption of the new United States Constitution it was necessary for the state to pass a law depriving the commissioners of the pilots of their powers to levy and collect tonnage duties.[16] They did, however, continue to provide for the building of pilot boats and for establishing rules for pilots.[17] In 1805 these functions concerning pilots were assumed by the town council of Georgetown. A town ordinance for regulating pilots was printed in the *Georgetown Union*, September 30, 1837.

In 1789 the federal government asked the states to cede lands for lighthouses. Paul Trapier, who owned North Island, made a "gratuitous cession" of land on which a lighthouse was built. A superintendent of the lighthouse was appointed.[18]

The quarantine system was set up piecemeal. In 1783 Governor John Guerard appointed Paul Trapier, Thomas Mitchell and John Cogdell commissioners to build a pest house in Georgetown; its dimensions were to be twenty by forty-two feet.[19] The basic law of March 26, 1784 gave all power over quarantine policies to the governor,[20] but on De-

[14] *Georgetown Chronicle*, Sept. 23, 1797. Notes taken by Oliver W. Holmes from advertisements in S. C. newspapers.

[15] S. C. *Statutes*, IV, 597–598, 655–656.

[16] S. C. *Statutes*, V, 186–187.

[17] *Annals*, II (1st Cong.), 2160.

[18] S. C. *Statutes*, V, 255, 309; *Annals*, II (1st Cong.), 2160; IV (3rd Cong.), 1510; Port and Town of Georgetown, Legislative System, 1790–1799, S. C. Archives.

[19] Miscellaneous Records, UU, Part I (1783–1785), p. 55, S. C. Archives.

[20] S. C. *Statutes*, IV, 615–618.

cember 19, 1796 his power over the port of Georgetown was transferred to the commissioners of streets.[21] The federal laws of 1796 and 1799 permitted local authorities to continue to handle this matter.[22] In 1805 the town council assumed these powers. A town ordinance setting forth quarantine regulations was printed in the *Pee Dee Times,* August 20, 1856.

The South Carolina customs service, re-established by an act of March 24, 1785, designated Georgetown as the port of entry for the area from Little River to the South Santee. A collector of customs was appointed for Georgetown.[23] On July 31, 1789, the United States Congress established the federal system for collecting duties. The Georgetown District in South Carolina included "the shores, inlets, and rivers, from the boundary of North Carolina to Cape Roman [Romain]." The bond for the federal collector at Georgetown was set at $5,000.[24] On April 2, 1790, the federal government adopted the state system for inspecting exports.[25]

The Circuit Court Act of 1769 provided for annual sessions in Georgetown of the court of common pleas and general sessions to be held by judges of the province riding circuit. A jail and a courthouse had been erected before the war.[26] These courts resumed their sessions after the war with state judges in place of the royal judges. Judge William Drayton in his journal for April 1789 described his progress through the northern circuit from courthouse to courthouse.[27]

Georgetown District remained in the eastern judicial circuit. The court of general sessions and of common pleas was held in the spring and in the fall.[28] The clerk of court of general sessions and common pleas was elected after 1812 by joint ballot of the legislature for a four-

[21] S. C. *Statutes,* V, 284–285.
[22] *Annals,* V (4th Cong., 1st Sess.), 2916; IX (5th Cong.), 3802.
[23] S. C. *Statutes,* IV, 704–706.
[24] *Annals,* II (1st Cong.), 2133–2158, 2252–2295.
[25] *Annals,* II (1st Cong.), 2208.
[26] Jesse Ballard, contractor, and Charles Gee, bricklayer, were not fully paid for their work on the courthouse and jail until after the Revolution. "Jesse Ballard" and "Charles Gee," Audited Accounts, S. C. Archives.
[27] "Remarks in the Course of the Northern Circuit, April 1789," Journal of William Drayton, Charleston Museum.
[28] S. C. *Statutes,* VII, 283–289.

year term and after 1815 by the people.[29] Moses Myers, Thomas Heriot, T. L. Shaw, and W. J. Howard were clerks of court.[30] The court of equity met in Georgetown only in the spring. The commissioner in equity was elected after 1812 by joint ballot of the legislature for four-year terms.[31] Robert Heriot, John W. Coachman, and S. T. Atkinson served as commissioners in equity. Appeals could be taken from these courts to a higher state court.

By the Constitution of 1778 sheriffs were to be elected by the House and Senate for two-year terms; in 1790 the term was extended to four years. In 1808 the people of each district were to elect the sheriff annually, but in 1822 this was changed to a four-year term.[32] The coroner was selected in the same way as the sheriff but did not become an elected official in 1808. The coroner was appointed for a four-year term.[33] The offices of sheriff and coroner changed hands more frequently than other offices.

After the Revolution land was granted by the state instead of the crown. By an act of 1784 a commissioner of location was to be appointed by the legislature for each district.[34] Job Rothmahler was the first appointee for Georgetown District. [35] He was to issue warrants of survey, receive the plats from the surveyor, and transmit the original plat to the surveyor-general. In 1812 the commissioner of location was elected by the legislature for a four-year term and in 1815 elected by the people for a four-year term.[36] This office was abolished in 1839.[37] By that date little ungranted land remained.

The register of mesne conveyance was appointed for Georgetown on

[29] *Acts and Resolutions of the General Assembly of the State of South Carolina, Passed in December, 1839* (hereinafter *Acts, 1839*) (Columbia, S. C., 1839), pp. 22–37.

[30] The names of officeholders here and below are drawn from lists compiled by the author.

[31] S. *C. Statutes*, VII, 293–300.

[32] S. *C. Statutes*, VII, 223; V, 569–570; VI, 185–186; *Acts, 1839*, pp. 37–59.

[33] S. *C. Statutes*, VII, 242; V, 164; *Acts, 1839*, pp. 74–83.

[34] S. *C. Statutes*, IV, 590–593.

[35] Miscellaneous Records, UU, Part I (1783–1785), p. 78, S. C. Archives.

[36] S. *C. Statutes*. V, 12–13, 674.

[37] *Acts, 1839*, pp. 121–123. R. F. W. Allston was appointed surveyor general of the state in 1823 and served two terms. J. Harold Easterby, "R. F. W. Allston," *DAB*.

March 11, 1786. In 1812 he was to be elected by joint ballot of both houses for four-year terms.[38]

In 1776 the new office of ordinary was created, having been separated from the governorship. In 1778 an ordinary, who was to hold office during good behavior, was appointed by the legislature for each judicial district.[39] In 1799 at the time of administrative and judicial reorganization of the state, a court of ordinary was established in each judicial district. In 1812 the legislature made the term of office four years and in 1815 permitted the people of the judicial district to elect their ordinary.[40] Cornelius Dupre, Samuel Smith, and Eleazer Waterman served as ordinary from the 1790's to the Civil War.

The poor and needy still had to rely upon the parishes for support in the decade after the war. By an act of February 19, 1791, the duties of the church wardens and overseers of the poor were turned over to commissioners of the poor, lay officials who were elected each Easter Monday by the people. The job of poor commissioner was not one that could be shirked, for if elected and unwilling to serve a man must pay a fine.[41] In 1796 the commissioners levied a rate of 7d. on each slave, 1s. 2d. on each free person of color, and 1s. 2d. on every $100 of value of land and town lots.[42] In 1804 the rate was 15 cents on each slave, 30 cents on each free Negro, and 15 cents on every $100 of land and town lots.[43] The money collected was turned over to the treasurer of the Board of the Commissioners of the Poor. These sums were supplemented by

[38] S. C. Statutes, IV, 722; V, 674–675; Acts, 1839, pp. 104–123.

[39] Provisions of the 1776 and 1778 Constitutions.

[40] S. C. Statutes, VII, 294; V, 674–675; VI, 11–13; Acts, 1839, pp. 37–39, 59–74.

[41] S. C. Statutes, V, 175–176. In 1856 they were elected in October. Pee Dee Times, Oct. 22, 1856.

[42] Georgetown Chronicle and South-Carolina Weekly Advertiser, March 22, 1796.

[43] Georgetown Gazette, Feb. 15, 1804. Lists of the amount of poor tax paid in 1809, 1810, 1811, and 1816 exist for the Prince George Winyah election district. The lists provide a very quick way of deciding who were the wealthiest men. In 1809 the following men paid more than $20 in poor tax: John Hume ($57.83), Cleland Kinloch ($54.72), Robert F. Withers ($41.71), Thomas Horry ($40.00), Elias Lynch Horry ($38.00), Archibald Taylor ($31.95), Francis Kinloch ($30.78), Savage Smith ($29.67), Paul Trapier ($26.88), George Lockey ($23.90), Estate Edward Thomas ($23.60), Francis Withers ($22.80), Benjamin F. Trapier ($22.20), John Bossard ($21.87), Estate Allard Belin ($21.80), John Keith ($21.08). Poor Tax, Legislative System, 1800–1829, S. C. Archives.

an annual appropriation of $500 by the legislature for the transient poor. Money was often spent on burying the poor and helping them to move on to another place. In 1817 an Indian woman named Mary was buried at public expense. In 1826 a horse, boy, and cart were hired to assist Shadrack Wilson and his family to depart the district.[44] In 1821 the legislature gave the commissioners of the poor at Georgetown the power to purchase land and to build a poor house. In 1824 the commissioners petitioned for funds. In 1850 there was a special school being run at the poor farm by the commissioners of the free schools.[45]. In 1824 when the Georgetown ordinary was ordered to publish his notices in the newspaper rather than to post them on the church door, one of the last uses of the church as an administrative agency came to an end.[46]

The Georgetown Ladies Benevolent Society was incorporated on December 13, 1817, after Maria Eliza Heriot, Eliza Heriot, Margaret Ford, and other ladies petitioned the state legislature. This was a private organization designed for good works.[47]

On March 12, 1785, the legislature passed an act dividing the Georgetown judicial circuit into four counties: Winyaw, Williamsburg, Kingston, and Liberty. Winyaw began at "Lenud's ferry, on Santee river, thence along the road to Potatoe ferry [on Black River], to Shepherd's ferry on Black Mingo, to Britton's ferry on Great Pedee, thence along the said river to the lower end of Shad's Island, and from thence by direct course over the said river to the sea, thence along the sea coast to the mouth of the North Santee, and thence along the north branch thereof to the beginning."[48] Although Winyaw County was created in

[44] Reports of the Commissioners of the Poor, Georgetown, Legislative System, 1800–1829, S. C. Archives. A complete list of expenditures was published in *Winyah Observer*, April 27, 1844.

[45] Petitions, Public Buildings, Legislative System, 1800–1829, S. C. Archives; S. C. *Statutes*, VI, 159–160; Report of Commissioners of Free Schools, Georgetown, 1850, S. C. Archives.

[46] S. C. *Statutes*, VI, 236. On Dec. 26, 1825, the legislature vested in the commissioners of the poor the remaining powers that the vestries and church wardens had exercised relating to the government and removal of the poor in and from parishes. S. C. *Statutes*, VI, 283–284.

[47] S. C. *Statutes*, VIII, 284. The Petition of the ladies of the Georgetown Ladies Benevolent Society, 1817, Societies, 1800–1829, Legislative System, S. C. Archives.

[48] S. C. *Statutes*, IV, 662–663. The islands between the North and the South Santee were to have been a part of Washington County to the South.

1785, a county court was not organized.[49] The justices of the peace (since the Revolution nominated by the senate and house and commissioned by the governor) continued to function as before.[50] The 1791 law which limited the authority of the justices also provided for appointment by the legislature for a term of four years.[51] In Georgetown the magistrates were from the middle class; in the rural parts of the parishes the planters served.[52]

The taxes were collected by state and federal officials. The tax collector was elected by the legislature until 1836 when the office became elective by the people.[53] Federal surveyors collected the excise taxes. David Prior, as surveyor of the excise, advertised for payment of the carriage tax in the *Georgetown Chronicle,* September 23, 1797.

Since the Federal Militia Act of 1792 left the enrollment and organization of the men to the separate states, South Carolina in 1794 implemented the federal law. The state was divided into eight brigades. The Sixth Brigade composed of the 25th, 26th, and 27th Regiments was organized in the Georgetown judicial district. General Peter Horry was brigadier general, Colonel Robert Conway commanded the 25th Regiment, Colonel John Postell the 26th, and Colonel John Baxter the 27th.[54] When General Horry resigned in 1806, he was succeeded by Robert Conway, who in turn was followed by Joseph Alston.[55] In 1819 when the state was divided into ten brigades, the Georgetown District

[49] Since "An act to remedy the defects of the courts of ordinary in the several districts where there are no county courts . . . ," dated March 7, 1789, pertained to Charleston, Georgetown, and Beaufort, these were the districts where there were no county courts. S. C. Statutes, VII, 249–250.

[50] All commissions were abolished and new justices of the peace appointed in 1785. Those appointed for Georgetown District were: John Waties, Jr., Thomas Dunbar, Benjamin Davis, Jr., John Irvine, William Frierson, Samuel Price, William Withers, John Thompson Greene, Francis Greaves, John Dickey, Robert Dick, and William Thompson (of Black Mingo). Journal of House of Representatives, 1785, p. 388, S. C. Archives.

[51] S. C. Statutes, VII, 266. Another long list of Georgetown justices of the quorum and justices of the peace may be found in Journal of the House of Representatives, 1792, pp. 304–305, S. C. Archives.

[52] See directory of local offices in Winyah Observer, Oct. 15, 1851. In 1840 the justices became magistrates. Acts, 1839, pp. 22–37.

[53] S. C. Statutes, VI, 558–559.

[54] Jean Martin Flynn, "South Carolina's Compliance with the Militia Act of 1792," SCHM, LXIX (1968), 26–43.

[55] SCHM, XXXVIII (1937), 51; XL (1939), 144.

contained the 8th Brigade. Joseph Waties Allston and James M. Commander were commanders of the 8th Brigade.[56]

General Horry, Charles Brown, and David Pryor were made commissioners for obtaining land on which a magazine containing 100,000 lb. weight of powder and 1,000 stand of arms could be built.[57] In 1797 Major Samuel Wragg and Captain Benjamin Trapier were joined in the commission.[58] The militia was alerted in 1798 and in 1808 to ward off possible invasions from the West Indies.[59] During the War of 1812 the militia was posted on North Island and on Cat Island as well as in Fort Winyah.[60] It was, of course, from the militia that the patrols were selected who rode through the parishes to maintain order among the slaves. There were also several elite military organizations: the Georgetown Rifle Guards, the Columbian Blues, the Washington Greys, and the Wee Nee Dragoons.[61]

Sometime very early in 1785 forty-nine inhabitants of Georgetown (led by Paul Trapier, Samuel Wragg, Cleland Kinloch, Daniel Tucker, George, William, and Robert Heriot, John Cogdell, John Waties, Jr., Samuel Smith, Abraham Cohen, Patrick Dollard, and Thomas Henning) memorialized the South Carolina Senate asking for an ordinance autho-

[56] J. W. Allston had served in U. S. Army, 1813–1817. *The South Carolina Rice Plantation, as Revealed in the Papers of Robert F. W. Allston*, ed. J. H. Easterby (Chicago, Ill., 1945). p. 50.

[57] S. C. *Statutes*, V, 271–272.

[58] S. C. *Statutes*, V, 319. Maj. Samuel Wragg wrote Gov. Edward Rutledge, April 27, 1799, that Col. Senf had been in town and had objected to their plans for the magazine, but that too much had been spent to change their plans. Military Affairs, Legislative System, Pre-1800, S. C. Archives.

[59] Georgetown newspaper for 1798; Message of Charles Pinckney to the legislature Dec. 1807, Governors Messages, Legislative System, 1800–1829, S. C. Archives.

[60] "Journal of General Peter Horry," ed. A. S. Salley, *SCHM*, XXXVIII (1937) to XLIII (1942), passim. R. F. W. Allston wrote on Oct. 23, 1838, to J. R. Poinsett, then secretary of war, offering to buy the land upon which the fort had stood. He stated that the fort built "during the late war" on a few acres of rice land at the junction of the Sampit and Black rivers had long been abandoned. The tides had since taken away almost three-fourths of the original government purchase. RG 77, A 110, National Archives.

[61] The basic patrol law was passed in Dec. 1839. *Acts, 1839*, pp. 87–93. Georgetown Rifle Guards were incorporated on Dec. 20, 1826. S. C. *Statutes*, VIII, 349. On Dec. 18, 1829, the two beat companies of the lower battalion, thirty-first regiment, known as the upper and lower beats of Georgetown, were consolidated. S. C. *Statutes*, VIII, 555; *Winyah Observer*, May 8, 1841, July 6, 1844.

rizing the election of three commissioners annually to carry out the plan set forth in the original town charter for Georgetown. They stated:

That in the Charter for Laying out the Town of George Town into Lots, three Trustees were appointed to carry the Plan into Execution, All of whom have been dead these several years past, and their Representatives (who live at a Considerable distance from Town) decline acting, by which means, the Inhabitants suffer much inconvenience, on account of the regulations for Erecting Buildings, opening Streets &c. not being adhered to.[62]

The South Carolina legislature proceeded to supersede the power of the old trustees in two steps.

On March 17, 1785, the taxable inhabitants of Georgetown were given the privilege of voting for three commissioners on every Easter Monday who would be responsible for the repairing and cleaning of streets and preventing nuisances. Fines might be levied by the commissioners against those raising and keeping hogs in town, the funds going to the church wardens for the use of the poor.[63] The basic law, however, was that of March 27, 1787, which divested the trustees of their powers and vested these powers in five commissioners to be elected by the taxable inhabitants on the first Monday of every April. A clerk of the market would be elected at the same time. The elections were to be managed by the church wardens. The commissioners to be elected were instructed to place a new market in the center of Front (or Bay) Street at the end of Broad. The commissioners were to sell the old market lot (which was considered too far from the center of town), build a new market house, and let the stalls. No meat was to be sold anywhere else in town. No slave could sell anything at the market without a ticket from his master. The next year the legislature designated the end of Screven on Front (or Bay) Street as the site of the market.[64]

The commissioners of the streets would have the power to assess the

[62] "The Memorial of Sundry Inhabitants of Georgetown to the President of the Senate," wrongly dated 1787, "Georgetown," SCL.
[63] S. C. Statutes, IV, 673.
[64] S. C. Statutes, V, 21–24, 62.

people for funds to use in improving the streets, the causeways, and the ferries over the Sampit and Waccamaw rivers. They would be able to require a license of £5 for retailing liquor and of £50 for keeping a billiard table. These license fees were turned over to the commissioners of pilots and used to finance the building of pilot boats. The same commissioners would also have the power to regulate the assize and price of bread, to keep a regular account of all brands and marks of cattle brought to market, and to prevent persons from galloping through the streets, or letting goats and sheep meander through the streets, or trafficking with Negro slaves. Fines might be levied for any of these abuses.[65]

These changes did not completely satisfy the town leaders. After Charleston had been incorporated in 1783, there was a move to incorporate Georgetown. Many of the local people, however, thought that this would be a change in an undemocratic direction.[66] Carson printed in his new newspaper excerpts from John Wesley's works and Thomas Paine's *Rights of Man* which argued against incorporation, for by such an act a new privileged group was to be set up.[67] In 1796 sixty-five persons petitioned the legislature in favor of incorporation, and thirty-two signed a petition against. The legislative committee decided at that time that the commissioners of streets in Georgetown had sufficient powers to cope with town problems.[68] The battle for incorporation was not won until 1805.

The commissioners previously appointed for pilots, streets, and markets were replaced by one governing body by an act of December 19, 1805.[69] As the act itself stated, from the increase of trade and growing importance of the town it would have to be incorporated in order to preserve the health of the community, the security of property, and the maintenance of peace and good order. The new governing body was to be "the Town Council of Georgetown," composed of an intendant

[65] S. C. *Statutes*, V, 186–187.

[66] For a discussion of the same problem with reference to Charleston see George C. Rogers, Jr., *Evolution of a Federalist, William Loughton Smith of Charleston, 1758–1812* (Columbia, S. C., 1962), pp. 104–107.

[67] *South-Carolina Independent Gazette; and Georgetown Chronicle*, Sept. 15, 1792.

[68] Port and Town of Georgetown, Legislative System, Pre-1800, S. C. Archives.

[69] S. C. *Statutes*, VIII, 227–233.

and four wardens, who were to be residents and freeholders in the town. Each warden would represent one of the four wards established in the city. The area southeast of Queen Street was one ward; that between Queen and Screven was a second; that between Screven and Broad a third; and that on the other side of Broad the fourth. The intendant and wardens would be elected annually on the first Monday of each March, but no man would be re-eligible for these offices for more than five years in any seven. Every free white inhabitant of the state, a citizen of the United States, of the age of twenty-one or upward who had resided over one year within the town could cast a ballot in these elections. Free persons of color could not vote, nor were they apparently considered citizens of the United States by those who wrote this law.

The town council was to have a common seal and was permitted to own property, not exceeding fifty thousand dollars in value. They were to have power to make rules, by-laws, and ordinances

respecting the harbor, streets, lanes and alleys, public buildings, markets, weights and measures; the assize, prices and inspection of bread; the cordage and measuring of fire wood; the regulation of the docks and lots; the draining and filling up of low lands; the regulation of wharves, wharfage and storage; the landing and weighing of goods, wares and merchandize; public house, billiard tables, retailing of spirituous liquors; carriages, waggons, carts, drays, pumps, fire engines and buckets; the regulation of seamen, boatmen and disorderly people; slaves, free people of color; and in general, every other by-law and regulation, that shall appear to them requisite and necessary, for the health, security, welfare, good government and convenience of the said town.

These rules, however, could not be repugnant to the "laws of the land" and might be repealed by the state legislature.

The town council had the power to fine and punish. It also could exercise those powers which justices of the peace might exercise in the rest of the district. They could assess and levy a tax upon real property, although the tax could not rise above 1 percent of the value of the property. Three freeholders of the town would be appointed as tax assessors. A head tax of two dollars could be levied on each free male resident of the town who was not a freeholder. This tax could also be levied on free persons of color.

The town council could appoint a treasurer, clerk, clerk of the market, harbor master, fire masters, town constables, and other officers needed to carry out the by-laws and ordinances.[70] In case of a riot the intendant could summon the town officers and the inhabitants to assist him; those who refused would be fined. By an act of December 20, 1806, the town council was permitted to summon witnesses and the constables of the town were authorized to execute these summons.[71] The town council thereby had an investigatory power to help in its legislative work.

It was expressly stated in the 1805 law that the powers previously vested in the commissioners of the streets and markets and in the commissioners of the pilots were now vested in the town council. They were also to appoint one or more public packers or inspectors of rice, pitch, tar, rosin, turpentine, beef, pork, and timber, taking over power originally granted in 1746. By an act of December 19, 1810, this inspection, however, under state law was done away with.[72] The powers of the commissioners to inspect tobacco (granted on March 30, 1789) and of the commissioners to inspect flour (granted on December 19, 1796) were also vested in the new town council.

It was after the abortive Denmark Vesey insurrection in Charleston that Georgetown secured additional power from the state legislature in order to control the free Negroes in the community. On December 20, 1823, the town council secured the power to tax land within the limits of the town exclusively inhabited by a slave or by a free person of color which were not within an enclosure upon which a white person resided up to a figure which did not exceed $100 per annum. There was also to be an annual tax upon each free person of color who kept a store or shop of any kind, the sum not to exceed $100. Licenses might also be levied on itinerant peddlers.[73] Free persons of color were therefore discriminated against and watched.

[70] In 1827 a town marshal, harbor master, keeper of the engines, clerk, treasurer, scavengers, and repairer of the public pumps were all elected. *Winyaw Intelligencer,* June 6, 1827. A Board of Health was appointed later. *Georgetown Union,* July 7, 1838. There are two bound volumes of town records for the pre-Civil War years in the City Hall in Georgetown. One contains ordinances, 1806–1848, and the other minutes of the town council, 1851–1872.

[71] S. C. *Statutes,* V, 523–524.

[72] S. C. *Statutes,* V, 623.

[73] S. C. *Statutes,* VIII, 221–222.

The town was supplied with water from the town pumps which were repaired by town officials. Although there were firemasters to inspect ladders, buckets, etc., the fire-fighting equipment was held by private volunteer organizations. The Georgetown Fire Company was established in 1799.[74] By the 1850's there were three companies: the Salamander Fire Engine Company, the Winyah Fire Engine Company, and the Calhoun Hook and Ladder Company. The minute book of the Winyah Fire Engine Company gives the names of members, their assessments, and their attempts to improve service for the town. Since in 1861 they marched away to South Island, they could serve as a military organization if they were needed.[75]

When a state system of free schools was established by act of December 21, 1811, the election districts (the parishes in the case of Georgetown until 1865) were used as the organizing unit.[76] This law provided for a number of free schools in each election district equal to the number of members sent by each election district to the House of Representatives. The state would contribute three hundred dollars toward the support of each school. These sums with any that might come from private subscribers would be managed by the free school commissioners appointed for three-year terms by the state legislature. All Saints Parish had a board of three free school commissioners; Prince George Winyah had a board of nine. The boards had the power to appoint and to remove the school masters at will. The curriculum in these schools consisted of reading, writing, and arithmetic, plus whatever the boards might advise or the masters themselves could add. The child of any citizen might attend, but if there were a large number of applicants, the children of the poor were to be preferred. What started out as an exception, however, became the rule. These schools were always for the needy.

A brief history of the free public education provided by the act is found in the annual reports of the commissioners of the free schools.[77]

[74] On Dec. 21, 1798, William Heriot, Abraham Cohen, Paul Trapier, and others were incorporated as Georgetown Fire Company. S. C. Statutes, VIII, 203. The original petition is in Legislative File, Pre-1800, S. C. Archives.

[75] "Minute Book of the Winyah Fire Engine Company, Sept. 22, 1854–May 8, 1861," SCL; Pee Dee Times, May 13, 1857.

[76] S. C. Statutes, V, 639–641.

[77] The following account is drawn from the "Reports of the Commissioners of Free Schools for Prince George Winyaw and All Saints Parishes," S. C. Archives.

An early report of Robert Withers, chairman of the board of commissioners for the free schools in All Saints Parish, stated: "We are happy . . . that considerable advantage had accrued to this Parish from the establishment of Free-Schools. There are no Private Schools in this Parish, and a great number of Poor Children whose education would be totally neglected but for this Establishment." Savage Smith, chairman of the Prince George Winyah board, sent in a somewhat different verdict on November 16, 1813. There had been a general complaint from the teachers of the irregularity of attendance, particularly of those "who had not the means of obtaining education from their own resources from which circumstance the commissioners are of opinion that the Establishment of free schools have not been productive of the general benefit intended." The two reports represent two views that were held by local persons on the value of free public education. Some thought the schools were good, for without them the children of the poor would receive no education at all. Others believed that the parents of the children were not sufficiently interested to make the experiment worthwhile. In 1843 summer sessions were discontinued in the parish of Prince George Winyah, after the chairman reported the indifference of the parents throughout the year, but particularly in the summer. In spite of the latter view, however, these schools were run throughout the pre-war period.

In 1830 there were five schools (at Dogwood Neck, Bear Bluff, Honeyschook, Pigpen Bay, and Saucustere Bridge) with 81 scholars in All Saints parish. In 1840 there were five schools (with only three in operation) with 35 scholars. In 1850 there were nine schools with six in operation with a total of 159 scholars. In 1860 ten schools with eight in operation with 171 scholars. The story in Prince George Winyah was much the same. In 1830 there were five schools (on Pee Dee, near China Grove, on Sampit, at Georgetown, and near Withersville) with 108 scholars. In 1840 seven schools with 126 scholars. In 1850 eleven schools (two being special schools) with 183 scholars. In 1860 sixteen schools including three special schools with 232 scholars.

All Saints always had trouble in securing teachers, perhaps due to the isolated location of each of its schools. But small salaries made it difficult to secure teachers in both parishes. The salary for masters remained throughout the period at $100 per annum, a fact indicative of the static nature of this society. In 1838 Prince George discontinued all of her schools for lack of funds, but this was due to the unavailability of state funds that year. In 1858 Prince George had only five of its ten schools open because of a lack of teachers.

The level of education was low. Only reading, writing, and arithmetic were taught. The school year ran on an average for six months. The clearest comment came from Richard Dozier in 1853 who wrote that free schools did not work well in sparsely settled areas. There was little return for money expended on the schools in the parish outside George-town. Dozier could suggest no remedy except the appointment of a state superintendent of free schools to visit such schools and make a better plan for educating the "rising generation, who are now to a large extent growing up in profound ignorance."

When one considers that the total expenditure on sixteen schools in Prince George parish in 1860 was $1,828.15, one can imagine that little of substance was accomplished. One school at Soccasstee Bridge in All Saints was maintained during the 1850's by the "munificence of the Planters on Waccamaw Neck," but the sums added to the public funds by gift were undoubtedly small. Since masters were difficult to come by, they must have been either of very poor quality or merely householders of the neighborhood. In 1850 there were three women teachers in Prince George schools. The commissioners of All Saints did make a rule in 1851 that all masters must be examined by the board before being appointed. As a means of holding the masters to their jobs, they were asked to sign contracts "to deport themselves correctly for the quarter." If they did not, they were not paid. Northern teachers must have been excluded after an undetermined date. Peter Vaught reported: "A full set of South Carolina School Books is a great desideratum in our Free Schools—the great diversity of School Books . . . and most of them of Yankee Manufacture— is an evil, that should be corrected."

What percentage of the children had even this rudimentary education? In 1841 when a survey was taken in All Saints there were 65 children in five schools out of 153 poor children who are now fit for "edication"; the survey paid no regard to those too young to attend or to those who had already been in attendance. Although the children of the poor saw the inside of the school room for a few months each year, the education acquired must have been negligible. Of course, the children of the planters never attended these schools. There was something of a stigma attached to them, and this fact must have lessened still further the tendency to attend. In 1856 the author of an article, "Free School System of South Carolina," wrote: "The existing system, as actually administered, is a pauper system. . . . The act of 1811 was devised as the entering wedge of a comprehensive plan for general education; but, as a preference was justly and wisely given by the statute, while the provision was yet inadequate for all, to the children of the poor, the temporary exception has been converted into the rule, and an incidental concession into the determining principle of the act." [78]

Poor but promising boys were often transferred to the Winyah Indigo Society school, which they might attend on a charity scholarship. This school, which stood between Broad and Screven streets (summer sessions were held at North Inlet) flourished between 1809 and 1812 under the headship of John Waldo. R. F. W. Allston admitted that Waldo was an excellent teacher of Latin and Greek until his attentions become "too much engrossed by his pretensions as an author." He spent too much time on his English grammar. This school was then headed by William R. Theus.[79] Benjamin Huger Wilson, a self-made man, got his start from the training received in this school.[80] After Francis Withers left money in his will for a new building, the present Winyah Society Hall was erected on Prince Street in 1857 to serve as the school house.[81]

The public buildings that still grace Georgetown date principally from the decade of the 1820's, which fact must be indicative of strong urban pride during that period. The branch of the Bank of the State of South

[78] "Free School System of South Carolina," *Southern Quarterly Review*, N. S., II (1856), 130.

[79] "Journal of General Peter Horry," ed. A. S. Salley, *SCHM*, XLII (1941), 73; R. F. W. Allston, *Address before the Members and Pupils of the Winyah Indigo Society, Delivered in Georgetown, on the 5th of May, 1854* (Charleston, S. C., 1859), pp. 14–16. John Waldo's petition of 1817 asking the state to purchase his books is in S. C. Archives.

[80] "Minute Book of the Georgetown Rifle Guards Club," organized Aug. 20, 1874, pp. 96–100, SCL.

[81] "Will of Francis Withers," dated Nov. 24, 1841, proved Nov. 25, 1847, Charleston County Wills, XLIV, Book A (1845–1851), 268–284, S. C. Archives.

Carolina was housed in a new building after 1817.[82] The courthouse at Georgetown in 1820 was a large wooden building of two stories, upon a brick foundation,[83] but the storm of 1822 damaged it and the old market building. The new courthouse was erected by 1824 in the style of Robert Mills.[84] Prince George Winyah church was remodeled, with a tower being added to the western end of the church.[85] The March 9, 1825, issue of the *Winyah Intelligencer* noted that these civic improvements had been matched by the repair and painting of private dwellings. The Methodists after 1817 and the Baptists after 1827 were settled on a firm legal basis by acts of incorporation, which must have been followed by the repair of their buildings. The Jews had a congregation in Georgetown, but as yet no permanent home.[86] In 1827 the Masons dedicated their new hall.[87] And by 1835 a new market building had been erected with open stalls beneath and a room for the town council above. In 1842 a tower with clock and bell were added to the market house.[88] The state which had provided a Board of Commissioners for Public Buildings channeled some state funds into the upkeep of these buildings.[89] Before nullification the town had made significant civic advances.

A glimpse of the social life of the town in 1812 and 1813 can be seen in the journal of General Peter Horry, who occupied a town house rather than live at his plantation of Dover.[90] Entertainment consisted of dining with one's neighbors, riding out along the country roads ("as far as Mr. Kinloch's avenue"), and attending church in the Episcopal, Methodist, or Baptist houses. Banquets and cotillions were held at Page's Tavern or Whitehurst's Inn. In the early days of the nineteenth century, a number of the planters lived in town. Certainly many of them were in

[82] This was the first bank building in Georgetown.

[83] David Kohn and Bess Glenn, *Internal Improvement in South Carolina, 1817–1828* (Washington, D. C., 1938), p. 29.

[84] There is no proof that the courthouse was designed by Robert Mills.

[85] Register and Minutes of the Episcopal Church of Prince George Winyah, 1813–1916, on deposit in S. C. Hist. Soc.

[86] *The Jewish Cemetery at Georgetown, S. C.,* compiled by Barnett A. Elzas (Charleston, S. C., 1910).

[87] Albert G. Mackey, *The History of Freemasonry in South Carolina* (Columbia, S. C., 1861), pp. 226–227.

[88] Plaque on Market Building, which still stands.

[89] *Winyah Observer,* Oct. 15, 1851.

[90] Journal of General Peter Horry," ed. A. S. Salley, *SCHM,* XXXVIII (1937), 81–86

town during the periods when the courts sat. Later, when the gap between the planters and the townsmen was greater and when the richest planters had town houses in Charleston, the town decayed somewhat. This was after nullification. A letter in the *Winyah Observer,* October 20, 1841, written by one who had been absent for forty years, contrasted the commercial bustle of the 1790's with the quiet of 1841. It was the foreign trade that was missing. Another visitor in 1843 described the town as follows:

Georgetown District is the wealthiest portion of the State; but a more miserable collection of decayed wood domicils and filthy beer shops than are clustered together to make up the town, it would be difficult to find. Indeed, unlike the free States, the wealth of the South lies almost entirely in the country; the towns, unless Charleston form an exception, being made up of artizans and traders.[91]

And yet there was a significant town life, and during the first three decades of the century some attempts to raise the cultural level of town society. The local Masonic orders had served the purposes of unity and culture. The Masons were the first group to bring the Jews into the society of the town. In the 1790's Carson, the newspaper editor, was a member. When the new Masonic hall was dedicated in 1827, the inscription read "in the name of the supreme architect of heaven and earth . . . to religion, virtue, and science." [92] In the 1850's the Winyah Lodge, No. 40 of the Ancient York Masons and the Hayne Lodge, No. 11 of the Independent Order of Odd Fellows still furthered the goals of brotherhood.[93] The Fire Engine companies and the Winyah Indigo Society also served social purposes.

The Georgetown Library Society was founded on January 31, 1799.

[91] "Sketches of South-Carolina," *The Knickerbocker,* XXII (1843), 1–6. The census of 1850 lists 604 white persons, 924 slaves, and 100 free persons of color for the town. The town had obviously not grown since 1808. David Ramsay had written, after obtaining information in 1808 from three responsible Georgetown men, that "Georgetown contains about one hundred and twenty dwelling houses, in which there are between six and seven hundred white inhabitants; the negroes are in the proportion of two to one." David Ramsay, *History of South Carolina* (Newberry, S. C., 1858), II, 302.

[92] Mackey, *op. cit.,* pp. 226–227, 554. The Jews were present as early as 1762. Barnett A. Elzas, *The Jews of South Carolina* (Philadelphia, Penn., 1905), p. 241.

[93] *Winyah Observer,* Oct. 15, 1851.

Paul Trapier III and Robert Heriot drew up the rules. The society should take two newspapers from Boston, Philadephia, and Charleston, and one each from New York, Baltimore, Richmond, Wilmington, Savannah, Knoxville, and Lexington, as well as the local newspaper. They would also take two weekly papers from London, one of which would contain the debates of Parliament, the *London Magazine,* and the *Gazette of Leyden.* They would subscribe to critical and monthly reviews, together with all such periodicals and pamphlets worth the consideration of the society. Maps of the four quarters of the globe were to be obtained. The society must have carried out these plans if the books and papers that remain from the ravages of climate and worms are any proof.[94] Books were bought in Charleston, Philadelphia, and London, possibly through the medium of William Heriot, local bookseller.[95] The first rooms were rented from John Burd, the newspaper editor, who acted as librarian. The 1850 census listed 5,000 books in the public library and 13,800 in twelve private libraries.[96]

The *Georgetown Gazette,* the principal source of local news from 1798 to 1817, was published by a succession of editors: John Burd, Claudius Beleurgay, Andrew M'Farlan, Elisha Bowles, Francis M. Baxter, Thomas Tolman, Edward B. Cooke, and finally Eleazer Waterman.[97] Eleazer Waterman, a Connecticut Yankee who ran a variety of businesses in Georgetown, was the most influential member of the town middle class. He served the community in almost every capacity including intendant and kept the town supplied with newspapers whenever an editor stumbled.[98] In September 1817 he commenced publishing the *Winyaw Intelligencer,* which lasted until at least April 9, 1835. John A. Keith, James Smith, and William B. Toler assisted him.[99] T. C. Fay started a new

[94] "The Georgetown Library Society," *SCHM,* XXV (1924), 95–96. There are seven bound folders of manuscripts concerning the Georgetown Library Society, 1799–1832, in the Winyah Indigo Society Collection, in the Georgetown County Library.

[95] *Georgetown Gazette,* Dec. 1, 1802. Also see Catalogue of Books for sale at Georgetown Book Store in *Winyaw Intelligencer,* Aug. 18, 1819.

[96] Social Statistics, South Carolina, Census of 1850, S. C. Archives. A list of the books that had been in the library at the Trapier plantation of Windsor is in file 398, Office of Probate Judge, Georgetown, S. C.

[97] Clarence S. Brigham, *History and Bibliography of American Newspapers, 1690–1820* (Worcester, Mass., 1947), II, 1050–1051.

[98] Waterman told the story of his family in *Winyah Observer,* Feb. 11, 1846.

[99] Brigham, *op. cit.,* p. 1051.

Georgetown Gazette on October 13, 1823, but this lasted through 1826 only.[100] The *Georgetown Union*, published by John Matthews and Company, spanned the years 1830 to 1839. Published by Taylor and Matthews, it expired on August 31, 1839, with the issue of volume 10, number 15.[101]

The *Georgetown American* was successor to the *Union*. In its first edition of November 9, 1839, William Chapman, the editor, stated that all subjects except religion and abolitionism would be discussed. The *Georgetown American* expired on March 3, 1841, and William Chapman died the following August. Eleazer Waterman brought out the *Winyah Observer* on March 10, 1841, which he and his son Eleazer Waterman, Jr., and later J. W. Tarbox continued until the end of 1852. Leonard Dozier was the editor of the *True Republican*, which was launched in November 1849. By 1850, therefore, Georgetown had two papers, both of which were given the "character" of "political" in the census of that year.[102] Benjamin Huger Wilson editing the *Winyah Observer* during these crisis years until November 10, 1852. With the November 17, 1852, issue Richard Dozier became both editor and part owner of the *Observer*. Richard Dozier must have been the leading figure in the changes which took place at this time. On November 22, 1852, the *Pee Dee Times* began publication. The *Winyah Observer* apparently died at the end of the year and Richard Dozier with Eleazer Waterman, Jr., continued as proprietors of the *Pee Dee Times*. The Watermans, the Doziers, Wilson, and Tarbox, all of the Georgetown middle class, kept the newspapers alive.[103]

More books were published in Georgetown during the first three decades of the nineteenth century than at any other time of her history. Although Peter Horry tried unsuccessfully to get the Library Society to publish his biography of Marion before he turned to Parson Weems, local authors did find some support, particularly from the newspaper publishers.[104] Elliott and Burd published the first Georgetown imprint, Lewis Du Pré's *Observations on the Culture of Cotton*, in 1799. In 1800

[100] *Georgetown Gazette*, Oct. 13, 1823–1826.
[101] *Georgetown Union*, Aug. 31, 1839.
[102] Social Statistics, South Carolina, Census of 1850, S. C. Archives.
[103] Information obtained from respective issues of the newspapers.
[104] "The Georgetown Library Society," *SCHM*, XXV (1924), 97.

John Burd printed the orations of Francis Kinloch and Dr. Joseph Blyth on Washington. And then John Burd published what is today the rarest item (the first edition contained only six copies), an 1801 publication entitled *Correspondence between B. H. and F. K.* Next was Joseph Alston's Fourth of July oration of 1806. Francis M. Baxter published John Waldo's *Rudiments of English Grammar* in 1811; Eleazer Waterman published Waldo's *A Latin Grammar* in 1816 and *The Dictionary Spelling Book* in 1818. In 1818 the *Winyaw Intelligencer* press published Thomas R. Mitchell's *An Oration in Baptist Church,* and Waterman in the next year brought out the same author's *Thoughts on the Constitution of the State of South-Carolina.* Waterman printed John Lide Wilson's pamphlet on internal improvements in 1819. In 1822 John Singletary Capers had published *A Discourse* and William Capers *A Report before the Conference of Methodists.* In 1824 there appeared a publication *Relating to the Dispute between Governor Wilson and Henry A. Middleton.* In 1825 T. C. Fay printed T. Moore's *Marriage Customs.* An 1828 imprint was the *Memorial of the Citizens of Georgetown, South Carolina, adverse to the increase of the duty on coarse woolens,* which consisted of seven pages.[105]

The Georgetown urban middle class was made up of men from a variety of backgrounds. There were first of all the natives, who had not grown as rich as their more successful neighbors, the planters. Among these were the Heriots and the Shackelfords. A strong contingent of Jews organized much of the economic life of the town. The Cohens and the Myers held many of the local public offices in the 1790's and after. The Solomons family and Aaron Lopez had arrived by the 1820's; the Sampson family by 1840.[106] As important as the Jews were the Yankees, who had come in the coasting vessels at crop time to carry the produce to Charleston and to peddle their New England wares. From time to time some of the ship captains settled down. Benjamin Darling, the shipwright, had been an early example; Henry Buck who arrived by 1825 a recent example.[107] Eleazer Waterman from Connecticut, the Congdons

---

[105] "List of Georgetown Imprints," SCL. There were no imprints after 1828.

[106] Elzas, *The Jews of South Carolina,* pp. 241–244.

[107] Henry Buck, the grandson of Jonathan Buck, founder of Bucksport, Maine, established the Buck fortunes on the Waccamaw River. *Independent Republic Quarterly,* II (1969), No. 1, pp. 31–33.

from Rhode Island, and Richard Lathers from New York were additional examples. There were only a few foreign immigrants such as the Morgans from Ireland on the eve of the Civil War who contributed to the growth of the town. Finally, there were the young men who drifted down from the backcountry, like D. L. McKay who came from Cheraw. These were the men who held many of the offices described above. They were eager to be more important than they were, but until 1865 they were always overshadowed by the rice planters. Undoubtedly, they wished to become planters if luck and society would permit. Few if any made the step up. No Jew, no foreigner unless a relative had paved the way, no backcountry boy, only a couple of Yankees made the grade. Yet there was some merging of the two societies, as the *Reminiscences of Richard Lathers* reveals.[108]

This Georgetown society tried to imitate Charleston. The Georgetown Jockey Club was revived to put on a racing week to rival that of the metropolis. In February 1826 Lewis Siau and Company advertised a booth at the Georgetown race course where "relishes and dinners" would be available as well as the best assortment of liquors and "nick nacks." Another booth would serve "fresh fruit and confectionary." [109]

On Race Week and on public occasions the entire society of the district joined together to enjoy the present and to share memories of a common past. The threads that united classes were on display at the Fourth of July celebration in 1827. In Georgetown on that day the people and the dignitaries assembled at the Baptist Church at ten o'clock in the morning to begin the day with the singing of a hymn and the reading of a prayer. The Declaration of Independence was then read: the reading was followed by an oration. Afterward the Columbian Blues went through several military drills to the delight of the assembled townspeople. Later, there was a public dinner at Whitehurst's Traveller's Inn with many toasts. Among the toasts there was one for the South Americans—"May wisdom and virtue direct them in their hallowed course"—and one for the Greeks—"A Leonidas to her armies, a Solon to her Councils." The rhetoric of the hour and military pomp united

[108] *Reminiscences of Richard Lathers, Sixty Years of a Busy Life in South Carolina, Massachusetts and New York*, ed. Alvan F. Sanborn (New York, 1907).
[109] *Georgetown Gazette*, Feb. 24, March 3, 7, 1826.

the hearts of all; nor were the watching slaves untouched by such ceremonious occasions.[110]

The Yankee was still not out of place in such a setting. This was not yet 1851 when an embargo was placed upon the "Shaders" and "Duckers" who came annually from the North.[111] The editor of the *Georgetown Gazette* wrote on September 15, 1826, that the people of Georgetown were beginning to long earnestly for the "coming in" of the Yankee friends with their apples, onions, cabbages, cheese, codfish, potatoes, and bacon. Some had said that the Yankees came to take away "our money," but certainly, the editor argued, something was received in exchange: "The Barn-Yard Turkey is pleased to take the very centre of the dish, that the round Irish potatoes may flank and front him, and also bring up the rear; and the wild Duck that feeds and flutters in the fields, is never so comfortable as when under a hot press of Weathersfield onions." [112] The good things of the South and the North still went together to make one sumptuous feast.

[110] *Winyaw Intelligencer,* June 20, 1827.
[111] *Winyah Observer,* Nov. 16, 1850.
[112] *Georgetown Gazette,* Sept. 15, 1826.

XII

NULLIFICATION

The period 1820–1833 opened with two disastrous hurricanes and closed with the political storm of nullification. It was a violent decade. William W. Freehling has labeled it the most turmoil-ridden of those before the Civil War.[1] The slaves themselves were turbulent. George R. Ford, Black River planter, was murdered by slaves on May 26, 1821, and a detachment of militia, under Captain Huggins, had to chase the murderers through the Santee swamps.[2]

The great gale of 1804 with its flood tides brought the first major disaster from a tropical storm in almost fifteen years. The winds of the two coastal hurricanes of 1806 were greater, blowing down the lighthouse on North Island. Although Georgetown escaped the storms of 1810 and 1811 which hit the coast south of Charleston, she suffered more from the dreadful storm of August 27–28, 1813, than she did from those

[1] William W. Freehling, *Prelude to Civil War, The Nullification Controversy in South Carolina, 1816–1836* (New York, 1966), p. 64.

[2] George R. Ford "was murdered by Negroes May 26, 1821 but without doubt in heaven he rests from all trouble." Record of Members of Methodist Episcopal Church in Georgetown, Wofford Library. On Dec. 9, 1822, Gov Thomas Bennett told the legislature that it had cost the state $500 for a fortnight's duty for a militia detachment under Capt. Huggins. Governors' Messages, Legislative System, 1800–1829, S. C. Archives. Also see Herbert Aptheker, "Maroons within the Present Limits of the United States," *Journal of Negro History*, XXIV (1939), 175.

of 1752 and 1893.[3] Some of the Georgetown wharves were smashed; "two schooners, a sloop, and the hull of a brig, were driven onshore." [4] As the storm moved inland, swollen rivers swept away one-third of the rice crop. The hurricanes came so regularly that the phrase "September Gale" became a colloquialism. During the Winyah hurricane of 1820 the tide in the bay rose four feet above a normal spring tide. The *Winyaw Intelligencer* for September 13, 1820, described the destruction at North Inlet:

On 10th wind blew tempestuously all day fluctuating between points ENE and NE, but more generally blowing from NE. About sunset the scene became truly awful, the wind increasing in violence, and the tide running with frightful impetuosity. About this period, the church was blown from its foundations, and many of the inhabitants were seen removing from such houses as appeared most exposed to the dangerous tide and wind. After dark the gale continued to increase, and about 10 or 11 o'clock, there raged one of the most violent hurricanes that has ever been experienced here. At this hour the wind began to back (as it is called) to the N, blowing at times in squalls of incredible violence, bringing with them such floods of rain, that there was not a house in the village could entirely resist their fury. The wind about 1 o'clock appeared to have backed as far as NW from which quarter it continued to blow, but with decreasing violence until morning.[5]

The most memorable of all was the hurricane of September 27–28, 1822, which caught Georgetown in the dangerous right semi-circle of the storm. The tides were higher than in living memory; only a very small portion of North Island remained above water. The editor of the *Winyaw Intelligencer* estimated that more than 120 Negroes and 5 whites were drowned on North Island alone and that the total loss of life was near 300. The Robert Withers family had been swept away. Georgetown itself was seriously damaged. "The Court-House has sustained very serious injury, and many of the records of the Clerk's Office destroyed; the Sheriff's Office had every door and window blow in and the records and papers destroyed; the four chimnies of the Jail have been blown down and the building in other respects much injured;

---

[3] David M. Ludlum, *Early American Hurricanes, 1492–1870* (Boston, Mass., 1963), pp. 53–59.
[4] *Ibid.*, p. 59.
[5] *Ibid.*, p. 113.

many of the tiles have been blown from the roof of the Bank; the building over the Market, occupied by the Town Council, is nearly down, every pillar which supports it, being fractured." As a result of this tragedy a number of stormproof structures were built on North Island, South Island, and at the mouth of the Santee to afford protection for the slaves; some of these towers were still standing at the time of the hurricane of 1893.[6]

The political storms of the decade forced the planters to adopt nullification as a storm cellar, but the doctrine of nullification was more evanescent than the wooden towers.[7]

The new threat on the political horizon was positive legislation. The federal Congress, under the direction of Nationalists like Henry Clay, began to pass laws designed to unify the nation. There would be federal expenditures for roads and canals, a national bank to finance expansion, and a protective tariff to nurture new manufactures. Even more dangerous, if the powers of the central government had been stretched, would be laws interfering with the institution of slavery. Some South Carolinians, not yet focusing upon the slavery issue, were willing to follow a Nationalist such as John C. Calhoun, who as secretary of war, 1817–1823, worked to strengthen the union. But more were wedded to an independent course in which South Carolina would have her own road and canal-building program, her own state bank, and never desire to sustain local manufactories by a protective tariff. The leader of the state rights group during the Monroe years was William Smith, whose principal support came from the region east of the Santee-Wateree line. David R. Williams of Mars Bluff on the Pee Dee, Thomas R. Mitchell of Georgetown, and John Lide Wilson, who although a native of Williams' region made his name in Mitchell's district, were linked politically with William Smith.[8]

In the decade following 1817 South Carolina experimented with a

[6] *Ibid.*, pp. 114–116. Richard Standland of Kinloch plantation can still point out where these structures were located.

[7] "The group advocating state rights at any period have sought its shelter in much the same spirit that a western pioneer seeks his storm-cellar when a tornado is raging." Arthur M. Schlesinger, "The State Rights Fetish," *New Viewpoints in American History* (New York, 1922), p. 243.

[8] Freehling, *op. cit.*, pp. 98, 120, 216.

state-financed internal improvement scheme.[9] The central purpose was to improve the natural system of waterways throughout the state, particularly by building canals around the rapids on the major streams. The work of the Board of Public Works was, however, largely a failure. Where there had been some success it was due to the enterprise of a few men such as David R. Williams. By 1820 the Pee Dee had been cleared to Chatham, a distance of more than 100 miles up the river. One steamboat and two team boats were navigating the river with safety. The freight of cotton by water from Chatham to Georgetown had been reduced from $1.25 to seventy-five cents per bale. The team boat launched upon the river by General Williams was propelled by eight mules, navigated by five men, carried 300 bales of cotton, and took fifteen days to pass from Society Hill to Georgetown. Similar efforts to improve the navigation on the Black and Waccamaw rivers were made, but it was almost impossible to keep these rivers free of logs. These programs, however, had helped to run up the expenditures of the state. Since it was difficult by the end of the 1820's to secure state appropriations, the projects were left to private finance.[10]

The Santee Canal had been the great effort made by private capital in South Carolina, but it had never been a financial success for its sponsors.[11] To the extent that the Santee Canal had been successful, it had been a threat to Georgetown as a port, for the backcountry served by the Santee River system afterward looked to Charleston as the destination for its traffic. In 1816 there was an attempt to imitate the Santee scheme in order to benefit Georgetown. On December 19, 1816, the legislature passed an act to incorporate the Winyaw and Wando Canal Company, a company that hoped to join the waters of Winyah Bay and of Wando River, which flowed into Charleston harbor. A series of canals and locks were to join the Wando to the Santee, and then the Santee to

[9] *Internal Improvement in South Carolina, 1817–1828*, ed. David Kohn and Bess Glenn (Washington, D. C., 1938), pp. xiii–xiv.

[10] Harvey Toliver Cook, *The Life and Legacy of David Rogerson Williams* (New York, 1916), pp. 160–161. A picture of the trade between Cheraw and Charleston via Georgetown can be found in the papers of Moore and LaCoste of Cheraw, 1825–1826, SCL. Kohn and Glenn, *op. cit.*, pp. 58, 72, 85–86, 449–450.

[11] Ulrich B. Phillips, *A History of Transportation in the Eastern Cotton Belt to 1860* (New York, 1908), pp. 15–16, 34–43.

Winyah Bay, providing a safe intra-coastal route to market. According to the charter, work was to begin within two years and to be completed within seven. Lands not granted to individuals along the right of way would be vested in the company by the state. The company might purchase and own slaves. Upon completion of the waterway, the company could set rates that the traffic must pay. To this enterprise the state subscribed shares of stock. The principal figures, David R. Williams and Company, John Hume, Joel R. Poinsett, Wade Hampton, Hugh Rose, Frank Weston, John Gordon, Thomas Pinckney, Jr., and Charles Fitzsimons, were men with interests along the route that would be served from Charleston to Cheraw.[12]

Little or nothing was done. But on December 17, 1831, the legislature revived the charter of the company, which must begin work within three years on the part between Winyah Bay and the Santee and finish it within six years; on the southern part of the canal the company must begin work within seven and finish within ten years. But this revival of the charter brought no better results.[13]

If this project had been successful, it would not have helped the development of Georgetown as a port. It would have merely made it easier for the planters to get their crops to market. But the company also failed because canal building was giving way in the 1830's to railroad building.

Between 1828 and 1832 there was a successful effort to build a railroad from Charleston to Hamburg on the Savannah River.[14] The president of the company was Elias Horry IV, the only planter-industrialist that Georgetown District produced.[15] Horry had worked with Henry Deas, Alexander Hume, Robert Hume, and Joseph Manigault, Jr., to build a canal parallel to Lynch's Causeway between 1823 and 1825.[16]

[12] S. C. *Statutes* VIII, 277–279. The exact line of the canal is set forth in Kohn and Glenn, *op. cit.*, pp. A17–A18.

[13] S. C. *Statutes*, VIII, 370–371.

[14] Samuel M. Derrick, *Centennial History of South Carolina Railroad* (Columbia, S. C., 1930), pp. 11–98.

[15] *Ibid.*, pp. 57, 58, 80, 129, 130, 179; Elias Horry, *An Address Respecting the Charleston and Hamburg Railroad . . . Delivered in Charleston . . . the 2nd of October, 1833, on the Completion of the Road* (Charleston, S. C., 1833).

[16] S. C. *Statutes*, IX, 534, 556. In 1825 Abraham Blanding surveyed "Lynch's causey" and suggested some changes. "The causey had been formed by cutting two parallel ditches and raising the centre of the road by the stuff taken from them."

Although this was a local canal to serve the needs of the large planters on the Santee, it provided Horry with some experience in large operations. Amid this railroad interest some men got together and formed the Charleston, Georgetown, and All Saints Rail Road Company in 1838. This company was to build a railroad on the most practical route, from Charleston to Georgetown, and thence to some point to be determined on the line separating the parish of All Saints from the state of North Carolina. The company might build viaducts over the streams or use steamers to transport the cars as long as they did not obstruct navigation. This ambitious project also fell through.[17]

It was difficult to build a road along the coastal route; moreover, once built, it probably would not have paid for itself. The road that might have helped Georgetown would have been one into the backcountry. When Georgetown finally did obtain a railroad connection in the 1880's, it was of this nature. Before the war a railroad was built from Charleston to Darlington and Cheraw that cut across the Wilmington and Manchester Rail Road at Florence, that city thereby becoming the hub of the Pee Dee basin. This North-Eastern Railroad Company was a project of the latter half of the 1850's, but the lines came no nearer Georgetown than the crossing of the Black River at Kingstree. It brought rail transportation to the Pee Dee basin, but these were projects to help Charleston and Wilmington, not Georgetown.[18] The Georgetown planters could not have hoped for federal funds to support these projects, nor were they willing to vote federal funds for more national projects.[19]

There were two banks in Georgetown before the Civil War. The first, established in 1817, was a branch of the Bank of the State of South Carolina.[20] William Windham Trapier served as the first president of

---

The causeway was, however, not above the level of the water during freshes. After the water receded, the top of the causeway was boggy and slippery. He suggested that a canal be dug along the west side of the causeway which could be used at all times by boats and that the top of the causeway be timbered. Since his visit the commissioners had told him that the canal had been dug. Kohn and Glenn, *op. cit.*, pp. 394–395.

[17] *S. C. Statutes*, VIII, 472–480. Also see *Georgetown Union*, Sept. 15, 1838.

[18] Phillips, *op. cit.*, pp. 350–351, 354–355.

[19] Yet Huger voted for the Bonus Bill in 1816, and although T. R. Mitchell did not vote on the Cumberland Road Bill in 1822 he voted for the Maysville Road Bill in 1830. *Annals* (14th Cong., 2nd Sess.), pp. 934, 1062; (17th Cong., 1st Sess.), pp. 1734, 1875; *Congressional Debates* (21st Cong., 1st Sess.), p. 1147.

[20] *S. C. Statutes*, VI, 32.

the branch bank (1817–1832) and Joseph Waties Allston as the second (1832–1833).[21] The branch bank made loans to planters which were secured by their lands and slaves. These notes could not be liquidated quickly and brought little return to the bank.[22] In 1833 the president of the State Bank believed that the branch in Georgetown should be discontinued since "there is no longer any commerce in that place. . . . The Planters in that section of the State . . . send their produce to Charleston, and have Factors in town, who can always negotiate their Bank business." [23] The town did without a bank from 1833 until December 21, 1836, when the Bank of Georgetown was incorporated.[24] The private bank, which bought the branch bank's house,[25] sold its stock in South Carolina towns by commissioners who raised a capital of $200,000. The institution might discount bills of exchange and promissory notes but not at the rate of more than 1 percent for sixty days. Bills or notes of the bank would be receivable in payment of public taxes "as long as the said bank shall pay gold or silver, current coin, for their notes." [26] There were four presidents of the Bank of Georgetown: John Alexander Keith, John W. Coachman, Donald L. McKay, and James G. Henning.[27] All were natives except McKay, who had come from Cheraw to Georgetown to open a commission business, which he ran from October 1838 to August 1839. He became cashier of the bank in 1841. He was president from 1848 to 1854, when he resigned to move to Charleston where he became president of the Peoples Bank.[28] This second group of bank presidents was more intimately tied to the needs of the town than the first, who were planters. The bank, designed to foster the trade of Georgetown, appropriately engraved upon its bank notes a sheaf of

[21] W. A. Clark, *The History of the Banking Institutions Organized in South Carolina Prior to 1860* (Columbia. S. C., 1922), pp. 100–101; *Winyaw Intelligencer,* Nov. 17, 1832.

[22] George A. Trenholm to R. F. W. Allston, April 18, 1837, *The South Carolina Rice Plantation,* ed. J. H. Easterby (Chicago, Ill., 1945), pp. 69–73.

[23] *A Compilation of all the . . . Documents in relation to the Bank of the State of South Carolina* (Columbia, S. C., 1848), pp. 419–420.

[24] S. C. *Statutes,* VIII, 67, 91–96.

[25] *Bank Compilation, op. cit.,* p. 242.

[26] S. C. *Statutes,* VIII, 95.

[27] Clark, *op. cit.,* pp. 321–323.

[28] *Georgetown Union,* Oct. 13, 1838; Aug. 27, 1839. McKay was trying to sell his rice plantation on the Sampit before he moved to Charleston. *Winyah Observer,* Nov. 26, 1851.

rice.[29] There was no support among any of these men for a United States Bank.[30] The first issue of the *Georgetown American* in 1839 advocated the "total severance of all connection between the government and the banks." [31] The Georgetown planters were for Van Buren's independent treasury system.[32]

From 1789 until 1816 the tariff had been designed to raise money to support the expenses of government. In the latter year the principle of protection was introduced. Although John C. Calhoun had voted in favor, Benjamin Huger had voted against.[33] Huger had also opposed salary increases since there was no need to add to the expenses of government, thus creating a need for more revenue and an excuse for a higher tariff.[34] Georgetown remained overwhelmingly agricultural until the Civil War. In 1860 Georgetown District had two cooperage establishments, two saw mills, ten turpentine distilleries, and eleven rice mills.[35] There was never any support for a tariff in Georgetown District.

Thomas Rothmahler Mitchell, Georgetown's congressman,[36] delivered in the national House of Representatives on January 30, 1827, a full-scale attack upon Clay's American System.[37] The immediate occasion was the attempt of Congress to pass the woolens bill. Mitchell gave three reasons for his opposition to the bill. First, "it was unequal in

[29] Clark, *op. cit.*, pp. 321–323.

[30] J. I. Middleton expressed his views against U. S. Bank in *Georgetown Union*, Aug. 25, 1838.

[31] Nov. 9, 1839.

[32] Martin Van Buren, the architect of the subtreasury scheme, was made a member of the Planters Club on the Pee Dee in March 1842. R. F. W. Allston wrote him: "Recurring to the history of the administration of which you conducted so ably and upon principles so fully approved by those with whom you have this day been associated. . . ." In a letter of March 20, 1842, Van Buren accepted membership. "The Secretary's Record's of the Planters Club on the Pee Dee," Sparkman Mss., 2732, vol. 1, SHC.

[33] *Annals* (14th Cong., 1st Sess.), pp. 1274, 1352.

[34] *Annals* (14th Cong., 1st Sess.), pp. 1159–1169.

[35] "Products of Industry," South Carolina, Eighth Census, 1860, S. C. Archives.

[36] T. R. Mitchell (1783–1837), a great nephew of Francis Marion, defeated Benjamin Huger and John L. Wilson for Congress in 1820 and served in the Seventeenth (1821–1823), the Nineteenth and Twentieth (1825–1829), and Twenty-Second (1831–1833) Congresses. *SCHM*, XLIII (1942), 219; *Biographical Directory of the American Congress, 1774–1949* (Washington, D. C., 1950), p. 1574; Charleston *City Gazette*, Nov. 1, 1820.

[37] *Congressional Debates*, III (1826–1827), 871–878. The speech was printed in *Winyaw Intelligencer*, Feb. 14, 1827.

its operation;" second, it did not produce an increase in revenue; and third, "it established, as the policy of the government, the principles of the restrictive system—an odious and selfish system. . . ." The burden would fall on those "who till the earth; who navigate the sea; who conduct the fisheries; who build our cities and fortifications; who clear and improve our waste land; who form our armies, and who man our fleets." The burden would fall upon "the productive labor of the country," while the benefits would flow to "five hundred or a thousand rich capitalists, the owners of these manufactories." Mitchell thought the bill was part of a continuing program which stemmed from the ideas of Clay's American system. The *Winyaw Intelligencer* observed that "there was a universal feeling in our community against the inequitable system mis-called 'American'." [38]

Another opponent of the woolens bill was John Lide Wilson (1784–1849). Wilson had come to Georgetown to practice law with Joseph Alston, whose sister Charlotte he married on January 1, 1810.[39] With the death of his brother-in-law in 1816 he became the political leader of the Alston clan. He served in the Senate of South Carolina from 1818 until December 7, 1822, when he was elected governor of the state. As Wilson was again senator from Prince George Winyah in the period 1826 to 1830,[40] it was natural for the intendant to call upon Wilson to address a public meeting on July 10, 1827, on the woolens bill. Wilson reiterated the view that it was unconstitutional for the government "by partial legislation" to make one branch of industry "subsidiary to another." A committee of five was thereupon appointed to draw up a memorial addressed to Congress protesting the bill.[41]

The memorial, which appeared on August 11, gave a short history of the period since the War of 1812. During that war, although the products of the fields of Georgetown had been wasted due to the interruption of trade, there had been no complaints from the people of Georgetown District. During the War of 1812 the burdens had been shared;

[38] July 14, 1827.
[39] *Winyah Observer*, Feb. 21, 1849; SCHM, XXXIV (1933), 44; Gregg, *op. cit.*, pp. 77–78, 103. In 1825 Wilson married Rebecca Eden of Washington, D. C. *Georgetown Gazette*, Oct. 21, 1825.
[40] E. B. Reynolds and J. R. Faunt, *The Senate of the State of South Carolina, 1776–1962* (Columbia, S. C., 1962), p. 127.
[41] *Winyaw Intelligencer*, July 11, 14, 1827.

in 1827 they were not. Since the war there had been evidence of the stretching of federal power, and the Supreme Court by a broad interpretation of the Constitution had approved of this trend.[42] This emphasis upon positive legislation must be opposed by the people of South Carolina.

A revolutionary movement reminiscent of 1775 broke out. Meetings were held throughout the parishes early in August. On August 15 in Georgetown these groups joined together to call for a state convention of those opposed to the woolens bill. It was hoped that this convention would adopt a general nonconsumption agreement which would be enforced at the local level by committees such as those of the association of 1775.[43] But this movement ran upon resistance among those men who tried to hold to the traditional South Carolina attitude toward politics as a gentleman's game. Since party movements spawned demagogues, they should be shunned. The planters controlled the state through their personal influence and the deference paid to them by the other members of society. A writer in the *Georgetown Gazette,* September 26, 1826, opposed "paper nominations"; nominations should proceed from "you," meaning each individual. Electioneering was condemned because "real merit" was "unobtrusive." To have a political movement the rank-and-file must be appealed to on an emotional basis. But how could this be done without destroying the ideal of an aristocratic republic? Parties would lead to a scramble for patronage. As these gentlemen believed the American system to be a "general bribery system," should such a system be imitated on the local level? [44] In August 1827 the chief spokesman of the anti-convention men was Colonel John Porter, Jr. He opposed political conventions as bodies for disunion and rebellion. Had not the Hartford convention of 1814 and the Harrisburg convention of 1827 been designed to overawe the national councils? Porter merely wished

[42] *Winyaw Intelligencer,* Aug. 11, 1827.
[43] *Winyaw Intelligencer,* Aug. 18, 1827.
[44] *Winyaw Intelligencer,* May 12, 1830. Richard Lathers wrote that the rice planters "rarely sought the high and remunerative offices, but accepted without reluctance local appointments as school, charity, and road commissioners, and were ready to represent their district in the State legislature." But "there were no nominating conventions or political caucuses." *Reminiscences of Richard Lathers,* ed. Alvan F. Sanborn (New York, 1907), pp. 5–6,

gentlemen to sign the memorial; nothing more.[45] Porter prevailed momentarily, for he defeated Captain William Vereen at a special election late in August for a seat in the state legislature.[46]

The key political instrument in the South Carolina revolutionary movement was the convention. To attend the regular sessions of the legislature took a great deal of time. Therefore, the biggest men did not usually come forth for the legislature. When a convention was to be convened, however, the story was different. Instead of the convention representing the will of the people, it seemed to be a greater crystallization of the elite. Was it the revolutionary body of that elite? At this time Porter, John Harleston Read,[47] and Benjamin F. Dunkin [48] used the threat of the convention to scare some of the lowcountry planters by stating that at the next convention there would be a redistribution of seats in the legislature which would thereby diminish the influence of the lowcountry planters. For a while this argument made a point.

The issue that heightened tensions and permitted patrician politics to be swept aside was increased federal intervention in the slavery question. The decade opened with the Missouri Compromise, which legislated slavery out of the territory north of 36 degrees 30 minutes. Then the federal government asked South Carolina to repeal her seaman acts, which she had passed after the Denmark Vesey insurrection to guard against the entry of radical ideas. In 1824 Ohio had suggested a national movement to emancipate the slaves. Under the leadership of Governor John Lide Wilson, South Carolina had blocked both of these moves.[49] But the threat seemed larger when in 1827 the American Colonization Society petitioned Congress for funds to be used to send the slaves back to Africa. Robert Y. Hayne, who had defeated William Smith for the Senate in 1822 and who had been a supporter of Calhoun, now rose to speak against this scheme. Hayne, who had married Rebecca Alston in 1820, had very close connections with Georgetown Dis-

---

45 *Winyaw Intelligencer,* Aug. 25, 1827.

46 Election returns, Legislative System, 1830–1859, S. C. Archives.

47 *Winyaw Intelligencer,* Nov. 3, 1832.

48 Freehling, *op. cit.,* p. 154. There was some reason to fear a convention on this basis. See Chauncey S. Boucher, "Sectionalism, Representation, and the Electoral Question in Ante-Bellum South Carolina," *Washington University Studies,* IV (1916), 6–9.

49 Freehling, *op. cit.,* pp. 115–116.

trict.[50] The *Winyaw Intelligencer* on November 21 and 27, 1827, carried a story of the entire Hayne family being overturned in the dark seven miles from Georgetown when the wheel of their carriage went into a hole. When Colonel William Alston died in 1839, Hayne paid a great tribute to his father-in-law, one of the largest slaveholders in South Carolina.[51] Whether these associations strengthened in Hayne a new devotion to slavery or not, he spoke out against the Colonization Society in Congress in 1827.[52]

There was certainly no enthusiasm in Georgetown District for the American Colonization Movement. In November 1827 a schooner *Randolf* of Baltimore stopped at Georgetown by order of the society to pick up twenty-five colored persons who were to be transported to Liberia. They had been manumitted by Mr. McDearmid of Marlborough for this purpose, and had been sent down the Pee Dee to embark at Georgetown. The *Winyaw Intelligencer* tersely noted: "The subject admits of commentary, but we forbear." [53]

In 1827 the political lines were ragged. Mitchell and Wilson both held sway as defenders of the state, but they had made political enemies along the way.[54] The moderates as always were unorganized. Hayne, caught by the slavery question, was in transition from Nationalist to Nullifier. There was still some faith that Jackson and Calhoun might uphold South Carolina views. After all, Jackson was a native son whose exploits had been enthroned by Major Garden on the basis of Colonel Arthur Hayne's account in the South Carolina valhalla.[55] And Calhoun was at his side. Yet Calhoun's report on nullification, which after being cut down was published as the Exposition of 1828, was an anchor to

[50] *SCHM*, V (1904), 174.

[51] Theodore D. Jervey, *Robert Y. Hayne and His Times* (New York, 1909), p. 534. A. P. Hayne married Elizabeth Alston and planted for awhile at Marietta on the Waccamaw. *Rice Planter and Sportsman,* ed. Arney R. Childs (Columbia, S. C., 1953), pp. 38–39, 116, 136.

[52] Jervey, *op. cit.,* pp. 202–210.

[53] *Winyaw Intelligencer,* Dec. 5, 1827.

[54] R. B. Campbell defeated Mitchell in 1822. John Campbell defeated Mitchell in 1828. Philip F. Wild, "South Carolina Politics, 1816–1833" (PhD dissertation, Univ. of Penn., 1949), pp. 199, 369. Thomas L. Shaw had struck John L. Wilson in the face. *Winyaw Intelligencer,* Aug. 22, 1827. Also see *ibid.,* Aug. 25, 29, Sept. 1, 1827.

[55] Alexander Garden, *Anecdotes of the Revolutionary War in America* (Charleston, S. C., 1822), pp. 115–122.

leeward. When the split between Calhoun and Jackson came, there was only need to pull up the anchor and to set sail.

The event that prepared the planters psychologically for discarding patrician politics was the abortive slave insurrection of 1829. "An insurrectionary spirit" in the parishes was "accidentally discovered . . . barely in time to obviate the terrible consequences of contemplated insurrection." [56] On the night of July 23, 1829, Captain William Vaught of the Lower All Saints Beat Company heard rumors of an insurrection and dispatched his Sergeant Joseph Peake to raise the company. Peake later certified "that I rode her [Vaught's horse] extremely hard so much so that to my Knowledge she has not been able to do one days work since." [57] Two slaves were tried and hung for attempting to raise a rebellion. Wood, a slave of Francis Kinloch, was tried and sentenced on July 28, 1829, by a court of justices and freeholders (William S. Harvey and John R. Easterling were the justices and Eleazer Waterman, Thomas F. Goddard, W. W. Trapier, Joseph W. Allston, and Davison McDowell were the freeholders).[58] Charles, a slave of John Coachman, was tried by a similar court consisting of the same justices and of Stephen Ford, Eleazer Waterman, Edward T. Heriot, Thomas F. Goddard, and R. F. W. Allston as freeholders on September 16 and sentenced.[59] A third Negro, belonging to Hannah Tait, was executed for having assaulted a Negro woman who had discovered and reported the plan of insurrection.[60] The town council felt it necessary to petition the state legislature, asking to be reimbursed for money expended on the discovery and suppression of the insurrection. The cost of one officer and ten privates to stand guard over the jail and the gallows was $1,669.32. The town was too poor to raise the money by taxes. The intendant Eleazer Waterman and the wardens asked the legislature for a sum of $5,000 to

[56] Quoted in Freehling, op. cit., p. 62.

[57] "Petition of William Vaught," Legislative System, Slavery, Insurrection, S. C. Archives.

[58] "Petition of Francis Kinloch," Legislative System, Slavery, Insurrection, S. C. Archives.

[59] "Petition of John Coachman," Legislative System, Slavery, Insurrection, S. C. Archives.

[60] "Petition of Hannah Tait," Legislative System, Slavery, Insurrection, S. C. Archives.

support a town guard.[61] The military committee of the legislature rec-
omended approval: "The district of Georgetown, from its geographical
situation, and peculiar population, cannot but excite a deep interest in
the bosom of every one." [62] The money was appropriated in December
1829 and the town guard organized in March 1830. During the remainder of that year the town guard prevented improper groups of Negroes
from assembling and closely circumscribed the activities of all Northern trading people in town. "There is no question but many of these
people [Yankee visitors who came in the fall] make it their practice to
instil dangerous ideas into the minds of our coloured population." Yet
in December 1830 the legislature discontinued this appropriation.[63]

Georgetown with its overwhelming slave population stood to the state
in the same relation as the state had stood to the nation in 1787. Georgetown in 1829 needed the state to sustain her institutions, just as South
Carolina had needed the support of the nation in 1787 to maintain her
institutions. The nervousness of her population was due to the presence
of certain incendiary elements: "The existence of insubordination among
the slaves, the immense number of that class of population in the surrounding country, the sparseness of the White population, the extreme
sickliness of the climate in the summer season and consequently the
almost total desertion of the Town during that period." [64] She was ready
to be organized into a statewide movement.

William W. Freehling is correct that fears concerning the future of
slavery were etched deeply into the planters' mind.[65] Robert Y. Hayne's
reply to Webster in the spring of 1830 was suffused with these fears.[66]

[61] "Petition of Town Council of Georgetown," Nov. 16, 1829, Legislative System,
Slavery, Insurrection, S. C. Archives.

[62] Journal of the Senate, 1829, pp. 59–60, S. C. Archives.

[63] Journal of the House, 1830, pp. 222–226, Journal of the Senate, 1830, pp. 118–
119, S. C. Archives; Gov. Stephen D. Miller's message to the legislature, Dec. 3,
1830, Governors' Messages, Legislative System, 1830–1859, S. C. Archives; Statutes
at Large, VII, 451–460. In the fall of 1831 the presentment of the Georgetown grand
jury asked the state legislature to pass laws to prevent the circulation of the
Liberator and other subversive papers in their community. Presentments of the
Grand Jury, Georgetown District, Legislative System, 1830–1859, S. C. Archives.

[64] Quoted in Freehling, op. cit., p. 62.

[65] This is a major theme in Freehling's book.

[66] Jervey, op. cit., pp. 241–267.

The South Carolinians did not want a federal debate on slavery, for that might lead to interference. The *Winyaw Intelligencer* editorialized on May 12, 1830: "If it is not, it ought to be understood, that the Tariff is only one of the subjects of complaint at the South. The Internal Improvement, or general bribery system, and the interference with our domestic policy—most especially the latter—are things which . . . will, if necessary, be met with something more than words."

Between 1829 and the spring of 1833 the Nullifiers waged a relentless political campaign, which, although a departure from the traditional brand of patrician politics, was designed to make that system endure. Freehling has written that the 1830 campaign marked "an important period of transition in the changes from the old personal politics to the merging ideological parties." [67] The man who wrought the change was James Hamilton, Jr., the grandson of Thomas Lynch. James Hamilton, Jr., born at Rice Hope on the North Santee on May 8, 1786, had lived on the plantation in the winter and summered at Newport. Although the Santee lands had to be sold in 1811, his marriage on November 15, 1813, to Elizabeth Heyward recouped his own fortunes. [68] Hamilton by this marriage to Elizabeth Heyward joined the planters of the Santee with those of the Combahee. The strength of the Nullifiers was in the hands of the largest slaveholders, who from their almost feudal domains watched Georgetown and Beaufort and even Charleston. The nullification and secession movements were sparked by the great rural magnates. Hamilton was elected governor in December 1830 and under his management the State Rights Association organized associations in every part of the state.

Joseph Waties Allston and Robert F. W. Allston rallied the local Nullifiers and eventually routed the moderate planter leadership represented by men like William Bull Pringle and John Harleston Read I. In the fall elections of 1830 the strength of the Nullifiers increased. In All Saints Parish, J. W. Allston defeated W. B. Pringle for a seat in the state Senate by eleven votes. [69] Although John Harleston Read won the

[67] Freehling, *op. cit.*, p. 213.

[68] *Ibid.*, pp. 150–151; Virginia Glenn, "James Hamilton, A Biography" (PhD dissertation, Univ. of N. C., 1964), pp. 1, 4, 9.

[69] Election Returns, All Saints Parish, Legislative System, 1830–1859, S. C. Archives.

Senate seat for the parish of Prince George, the Nullifiers waged a long and successful battle to unseat him. As soon as the Senate convened Henry A. Middleton presented a memorial asking for an investigation into the election in Prince George. After counsel on both sides were heard, the seat was declared vacant. A new election was then held on December 13 and 14, 1830. The managers declared that Read had defeated R. F. W. Allston. When Read took his seat on December 18, J. W. Allston presented a memorial charging election irregularities.[70]

An investigation was not authorized until after the next session of the legislature convened in December 1831. According to the depositions taken at that time, the managers of the North Santee poll had refused to count the votes of John Hume, Sr. and Jr., John Butler, Frederick Rutledge, and Charles Cotesworth Pinckney on the basis that they had voted elsewhere at the preceding general election in October 1830. However, the election managers in Georgetown had permitted some twelve or thirteen persons to vote who generally summered in the North and had not returned until after the general election of October 1830. Since these men were for the most part Northern born, it was suspected that they had voted in the North. In their depositions they stated that they had not voted elsewhere. Henry Chace, Peter Chace, William Congdon, George B. Hall, Oliver Read, and Joseph G. Stevens had all been born in Rhode Island but were storekeepers in Georgetown during the winter. George T. and Jedediah Lathrop were saddlers from Connecticut; H. N. Johnson, shoemaker, was from Connecticut. John Dowdney, storekeeper, was from New Jersey. Alexis Menage, born in France, and William Brown, born in Scotland, were also storekeepers. It was apparent that Read had won because North Santee planters had been denied votes and Northern storekeepers had been allowed votes. No decision on the validity of the election was made at this time in December 1831.[71]

In March 1830 the *Georgetown Union* was founded by John Matthews to support the Anti-Nullifiers—the moderate planters, the Northern men,

[70] Election Returns and Contested Elections, Georgetown District, Legislative System, 1830–1859, S. C. Archives; Journal of the Senate, 1830, pp. 27, 30, 145, S. C. Archives.

[71] Contested Elections, Georgetown District, Legislative System, 1830–1859, S. C. Archives.

the immigrants, the Georgetown middle class.[72] The Unionists, however, lacked the organization, talents, and perhaps the vehement oratory needed to sustain them in the fight with the Nullifiers.

In 1831 the Nullifiers finally forced Calhoun to reveal his hand. In a series of essays written to the local newspapers he spelled out the nullification doctrine. The signals were up that the Nullifiers might win in 1832 in South Carolina. The *Winyaw Intelligencer,* which was the paper of the State Rights and Free Trade party, recorded the steps to victory.

The State Rights and Free Trade Association of Georgetown District held meetings throughout the year 1832. The first meeting of the year was held on January 31 at the Georgetown Court House. At this meeting Dr. Philip Tidyman made a report on what had transpired at the Free Trade meeting held in Philadelphia. Then there was a report on the state meeting held in Columbia, after which Colonel Thomas Pinckney Alston, Allard H. Belin, John A. Keith, Dr. Aaron Lopez, and J. Walter Phillips were selected to represent Georgetown at a forthcoming meeting in Charleston. The local organization was thereby tied into the statewide movement.[73]

Governor Hamilton, making militia inspections an excuse, toured the state in the spring in order to bolster the various local associations. In March, upon his arrival in Georgetown, he was given a dinner at the Winyaw Hotel which was attended by 150 persons. William W. Trapier presided at this gathering of the friends of Hamilton and Calhoun. The toasts reflected the absoluteness of their convictions. There was one to state sovereignty: "The Ararat which is to save this Union. . . ." To Calhoun: "The honest declaration of his sentiments may have injured him abroad but it has endeared him to all at home." To Calhoun's theory: "Our ark of safety—our constitutional defence—our rightful remedy—Nullification, Nullification, Nullification." Behind the constitutional stance there was a feeling that Carolinians were again embarked in a crusade against tyranny. According to the list of toasts, their heroes were Thomas Jefferson, Charles Cotesworth Pinckney, Thomas Sumter, and Francis Marion. The toast to Georgetown District was: "The scene of Marion's achievements—submission to oppression can never be the

[72] *Georgetown Union,* 1830–1839.
[73] *Winyaw Intelligencer,* Feb. 8, 1832.

doctrine of its inhabitants." Then, as a reminder of the parallels between 1832 and 1776, General Joseph Waties Allston, commander of the 8th Brigade, South Carolina militia, gave a toast to the father of the governor, James Hamilton, Sr., and to Keating Simons: "They fought together in the revolution, and are still found side by side, animating their countrymen in their struggle for freedom."[74]

As the spring wore on these men watched Congress for portents. If Congress should adjourn without lowering the tariff, then there should be immediate nullification of the existing tariff. A compromise would not be looked upon with favor, for, as the *Winyaw Intelligencer* said, compromise was a word "getting into bad odour."[75] A Southern convention was also "decidedly opposed," because to call it meant to delay. Such a convention, which would serve to let Southerners meet and know one another, should come later.[76]

By July 11 it was known in Georgetown that the tariff had passed and that it was similar to that of 1828.[77] The "principle of protection . . . is unequivocally upheld." When it was learned that three South Carolinians had voted for it, particularly Thomas R. Mitchell, who represented Georgetown District, they were marked for political death.[78] The Union Party, however, planned to give a dinner in Mitchell's honor at Black Mingo.[79]

At the next important meeting of the State Rights and Free Trade Association on August 15, the members stated that all their doubts about Congress were at an end. The tariff was a tax on Southern labor and a bounty to the Northern manufacturer. Although there were many from whom to pick candidates for the state legislature, the association selected as standard bearers in this contest Solomon Cohen, Jr., John Hays Allston, and R. F. W. Allston.[80] A committee was selected to draw up a statement concerning the best course of action, which was published in the *Winyaw Intelligencer* for August 25. The patience of the

[74] *Winyaw Intelligencer*, March 10, 1832. See Chapter 14, "Campaign Manager of Nullification, 1830–1832," in Virginia L. Glenn, *op. cit.*, pp. 166–168.
[75] April 28, 1832.
[76] *Winyaw Intelligencer*, May 16, 1832.
[77] *Winyaw Intelligencer*, July 11, 1832.
[78] *Winyaw Intelligencer*, Aug. 18, 1832.
[79] *Winyaw Intelligencer*, July 25, 1832.
[80] *Winyaw Intelligencer*, Aug. 18, 1832.

last ten years had gone. The aim was still to preserve the liberty, the constitution, and the union of the people, but this could now only be done by nullification, which was a peaceful and constitutional remedy. To postpone the assertion of state sovereignty was wrong. They must prove that "our threats were not mere gasconade," or no future battles could be fought. Knowing that Hampden and Russell, those seventeenth-century heroes, had not yielded to tyranny, and that the heroes of the American Revolution had not either, they advocated that a state convention assemble in order to decide whether nullification should be implemented or not.

The State Rights Party waged an active campaign. On August 30 there was a dinner at the Santee Muster Shed in honor of its three candidates. The indigenous North Santee planters, the Doars, the Atkinsons, and the Johnstons, headed by W. R. Maxwell, turned out in large numbers.[81]

The election held on October 8 and 9, 1832, for representatives to the state legislature was hotly contested, and the results were extremely close.

State Rights	George-town	Sampit	Santee	Black River	Carver's Bay	Pee Dee	Total
Solomon Cohen, Jr.	71	24	38	22	—	31	186
R. F. W. Allston	67	23	36	22	—	34	182
John H. Allston	67	21	36	18	—	35	177
Union							
P. W. Fraser	87	15	6	21	34	24	187
A. W. Dozier	85	13	6	22	34	23	183
E. T. Heriot	83	12	4	18	34	23	174

Fraser, Cohen, and Dozier were elected. R. F. W. Allston failed of election by only two votes. In All Saints Parish Joshua John Ward, the candidate of the State Rights Party, easily defeated William Bull Pringle, the Unionist candidate, by a vote of 162 to 34. If the vote of the two parishes is analyzed, it is apparent that the planters were strongly state rights. Waccamaw Neck and the North Santee were the planters' stronghold. They were weakest in Georgetown itself and in Carver's

---

[81] *Winyaw Intelligencer,* Sept. 5, 1832.

Bay, the latter being the home of the small farmers, a group far below the rank of the planters.[82]

In the state the Nullifiers had won a resounding victory. The legislature was quickly convened and a call for a convention issued. At this extra session J. W. Allston presented Solomon Cohen's petition asking that the investigation into election irregularities be continued and a decision reached. On October 25 the committee that looked into the matter reported: "It appearing that the Votes improperly rejected and received exceed the Majority on which the sitting Member was returned," the seat of J. H. Read should be declared vacant and a new election should be held. The Senate so resolved.[83]

The State Rights and Free Trade Association of Georgetown at a meeting on October 29 nominated Dr. P. Tidyman, Major A. H. Belin, Major J. A. Keith, and General J. W. Allston for the convention. Since Read's seat in the Senate had been declared vacant, R. F. W. Allston was nominated for the Senate. And in order to prepare for a clean sweep of those opposed to their views, they selected Stephen C. Ford to correspond with other associations in the congressional district to find someone to oppose Representative Thomas R. Mitchell, who must be punished for his vote in favor of the 1832 tariff.[84]

General J. W. Allston had to resign both his candidacy for a seat in the convention and his Senate seat in order to accept the presidency of the branch of the Bank of the State of South Carolina in Georgetown to succeed W. W. Trapier, who had recently died. So the four elected on November 12 and 13 to the convention from Georgetown were Tidyman, Belin, Keith, and Colonel J. Coggeshall; Peter Vaught and J. Walter Phillips were elected from All Saints.[85]

Although senators were elected every four years, there were contests that November in both Prince George and in All Saints. Read, like Porter before him, raised the possibility that at a convention the representatives of the lowcountry might be challenged since the state was

[82] Election Returns, All Saints Parish and Georgetown District, Legislative System, 1830–1859, S. C. Archives.
[83] Contested Elections, Georgetown District, Legislative System, 1830–1859, S. C. Archives.
[84] *Winyaw Intelligencer*, Nov. 3, 1832.
[85] *Winyaw Intelligencer*, Nov. 17, 1832.

not properly districted according to population. For opening up such a discussion he was condemned by the *Winyaw Intelligencer,* which pointed out that the representation of the parishes in the state legislature was like the representation of the states in the federal Senate, and in both instances were arrangements that should never be tampered with. Even with these views Read almost won, losing to Allston by a vote of 182 to 181. In the All Saints senatorial election Colonel Thomas Pinckney Alston easily defeated the Union man Cannon by a vote of 95 to 18.[86]

The convention of the people met in Columbia at the end of November and nullified the tariff acts of 1828 and 1832. The convention also issued addresses to the people of South Carolina and to the people of the United States. Furthermore, the convention requested the state legislature to reassemble and put the state in a posture of defense, to do what was necessary to carry out the intentions of the nullification convention.

There was still opposition within the state. The Georgetown Unionists (many of whom were of Scotch descent) selected Davison McDowell, the immigrant, to go to Columbia to the Union convention.[87] The *Winyaw Intelligencer* attempted to ridicule the group: "as curious observers of human nature, we would like to know what will be their business. Is it . . . to nullify the Nullifiers. . . . Or will they organize themselves and resist the authority of the State by force of arms! Or . . . like 'The King of France, with twice ten thousand men March [up] hill, and then—march down again?'" When the Unionists reminded their opponents of what had happened to the insurgents in the Whiskey Rebellion, the *Intelligencer* replied that a body of insurgents against the sovereignty of the state was a much fitter subject for executive coercion.[88] The attitude of the Nullifiers toward the Unionists was much the same as the attitude of Jackson toward South Carolina.

Jackson answered South Carolina on December 10 in his presidential proclamation, in which he denied the theory of nullification and secession and proclaimed the unity of the nation. The *Winyaw Intelligencer,*

[86] *Winyaw Intelligencer,* Nov. 3, 10, 17, 1832; Election Returns, All Saints Parish and Georgetown District, Legislative System, 1830–1859, S. C. Archives.

[87] McDowell left Georgetown on Dec. 4 and returned on Dec. 19. He wrote on the third: "I have no doubt our meeting will prove for the good of the State & the preservation of these United States." Mary James Richards, "Our McDowell Ancestry" (typed copy, 1966), p. 32, D. McDowell Papers, SCL.

[88] *Winyaw Intelligencer,* Dec. 8, 1832.

which had run at its masthead all fall a quotation from Jackson's message vetoing the bank bill, removed that quotation and with second thought pointed out that as early as July 1831 when he had written a letter to the Unionists Jackson had stood revealed as a tyrant. Suddenly, the president was depicted as a dictator with sword unsheathed, unfurling the "broad banner of CONSOLIDATION." [89]

During December Hayne resigned as senator to succeed Hamilton as governor of the state. He prepared the state to resist by ordering $100,-000 worth of arms and by organizing military forces. Hayne in his inaugural oration tried to inspire the people by an appeal to the state's historic path. "This is our own—our native land," stated Hayne, and he urged the people to "stand or fall with Carolina." [90] He was appealing to a strain which had already been fertilized by the writings of Major Alexander Garden. Garden's *Ancedotes of the American Revolution,* first published in 1822, but republished in 1828, had built a South Carolina hagiology. Marion, Horry, Maham, General Isaac Huger, and Major Benjamin Huger, the nobility of Rebecca Motte, the martyrdom of Isaac Hayne, were among the countless examples of God's support of Carolina's cause.[91] Lafayette's return had been a reminder, as were the contemporary struggles of the Greeks and the Irish. It was particularly galling that Jackson, a slaveholder who should have been their hope since he was fortune's child, was the leader who now opposed them.

On December 29 there was a large public meeting in Georgetown called by the State Rights and Free Trade Association to plan what should be done in the light of the President's proclamation. General J. W. Allston moved and Benjamin F. Dunkin seconded a set of resolutions stating that a union of legislative and judicial powers whether in king or Congress was the essence of despotism, that an attempt made by "a temporary servant of the people, to imitate the style of a hereditary monarch" by speaking of his "paternal feelings" was simply ridiculous, and that the power of a state to secede must be upheld.

Dunkin, Belin, and Coggeshall addressed the meeting, as did Henry A. Middleton. The latter's remarks revealed how men were drawn into

[89] *Winyaw Intelligencer,* Sept. 8, Dec. 19, 22, 29, 1832.
[90] Freehling, *op. cit.,* p. 264.
[91] Garden, *op. cit.,* passim.

the nullification movement. Middleton had originally opposed nullification not on grounds of its unconstitutionality, but on grounds of its impolicy. Now, however, the question was no longer what remedy, but whether this remedy would be supported. Believing the general government had only trust power and the state was fully sovereign, he had no alternative except to support nullification and the state's measures. He said some time later that he had attended not as a State Rights Party man but as a citizen.[92] The people of South Carolina had reacted toward Jackson's proclamation just as the people of Massachusetts had reacted to George III's demands that the General Court rescind the Circular Letter of 1768. The outside pressure forced men who had doubted the policy but who thought that the policy should be decided locally into the nullification camp.[93]

All the people of Georgetown still did not endorse this point of view. The editor of the *Intelligencer* had been present and had spoken to the effect that "any citizen appearing in arms against the State would be guilty of treason." After using such words he was "rudely attacked" in the street, and that night the office of the *Winyaw Intelligencer* was "brickbaited" and the doors and windows broken open.[94] The customs collector at Charleston had confidence in the collector at Georgetown "as regards his fidelity to the union and firmness to discharge his duty."[95]

The Unionists, still a sturdy clan, protested R. F. W. Allston's victory over Read. Benjamin King, Francis Withers, Anthony W. Dozier, John R. Easterling, Thomas L. Shaw, William Chapman, Henry Cuttino, and thirteen others signed a petition to the Senate, dated November 20, 1832, stating that the managers of the North Santee and Pee Dee polls had received as legal voters persons who admitted that they had voted elsewhere in October 1830 and October 1832. The managers of the Georgetown poll, however, had refused William Mayrant and Thomas Howe on the basis that they had voted elsewhere in the earlier elections; these men had stated that they would vote for Read. It was also

[92] *Winyaw Intelligencer*, Jan. 2, 1833. For Middleton's statement see *Winyaw Intelligencer*, Jan. 12, 1833.

[93] Jackson's proclamation had brought over the Pee Dee men. *Winyaw Intelligencer*, Jan. 5, 1833.

[94] *Winyaw Intelligencer*, Jan. 2, 1833.

[95] J. R. Pringle to Louis McLane, Nov. 26, 1832, "correspondence of treasury secretary with customs collectors," roll 32 of microcopy M-178, p. 45, S. C. Archives.

pointed out that the Santee poll stayed open two days while the other country polls stayed open only one day. John Lide Wilson argued Allston's case. The legislative committee, on the basis that the Georgetown managers had been correct and the Santee managers wrong, called for another election. The seat was declared vacant on December 19 and new elections called for.[96] R. F. W. Allston had been renominated at the December 29 meeting. At the election held on January 14 and 15, 1833, Allston received 200 votes to Read's 178.[97] This election showed a slight but important shift in support, men such as Henry A. Middleton perhaps changing their votes to Allston in the light of the December events.

The February 1 date at which time the customs was no longer to be collected was pushed back at a meeting of the convention in Charleston on January 21; the purpose was to give Congress more time to bring in a compromise measure. The *Winyaw Intelligencer* approved of this action even though it foreshadowed a compromise.[98] Calhoun, having returned to the United States Senate, was working for such a compromise. February was a month of waiting and preparation. The "Winyaw Volunteers," consisting of eighty men, met frequently at the back landing for drill. It was reported that the volunteers in the state ready to march on Charleston exceeded 20,000 men.[99]

Eventually, Congress passed Clay's compromise tariff measure and the force bill together, the latter constantly being referred to by the *Intelligencer* as the "bloody bill."[100] Obviously the convention would now have to reassemble. The *Intelligencer* felt that if only Clay's bill had been passed without the "bloody bill," then the convention could have easily accepted the compromise. After all, South Carolina's "Nullification has succeeded in procuring the surrender of the principle against which it was directed," for the new tariff bill had surrendered the principle of protection. But the "bloody bill" sanctioned the views of the presidential proclamation and that bill, therefore, should not be tol-

---

[96] Contested Elections, Georgetown District, Legislative System, 1830–1859, S. C. Archives.

[97] Election Returns, Georgetown District, Legislative System, 1830–1859, S. C. Archives.

[98] *Winyaw Intelligencer*, Jan. 25, 1833.

[99] *Winyaw Intelligencer*, Feb. 16, 1833.

[100] *Winyaw Intelligencer*, March 6, 1833.

erated. There would now be only an armistice instead of a peace with the President, who was now permanently armed with these new powers. Such arguments led to nullifying the force bill.

And yet the paper could emphasize that South Carolina had lost nothing by her posture of defense. There still might be ushered in an "era of amelioration." At least the Nullifiers knew now upon whom they could rely and "who of them will go with her through the dark valley of the shadow of death, while the false hearted are feasting and rejoicing with her foes." Perhaps this was the most important outcome of the crisis; it made unity in South Carolina obligatory. Those who had not stood with South Carolina in her hour of need were marked for oblivion.[101]

The chivalry now revealed its harsher, warlike side. When opposed, the ideal was to fight back. The Nullifiers were generally men who supported the use of the duel in personal affairs. John L. Wilson wrote a pamphlet, *The Code of Honor,* which he published in Charleston in 1838.[102] He believed that the duel was for personal settlements as nullification was for national ones. Freehling calls this "an intriguing example of the intimate rhetorical relationship between the code of individual duels and the rationale of state honor." [103] The Nullifiers desired to eliminate political opposition.

All Saints was already the Nullifiers' "rotten borough." Prince George must be made so. In the October elections of 1834 there was another bitter contest between the Unionists and the Nullifiers in the parish of Prince George. Thomas R. Mitchell wrote Joel R. Poinsett on September 19, 1834, that the Union Party "has raised an opposition ticket in All Saints to keep interlopers from the Georgetown poll." [104] In Prince George John W. Coachman, Solomon Cohen, Jr., and A. H. Belin opposed P. W. Fraser, James Green, and William Mayrant for the House, while R. F. W. Allston opposed A. W. Dozier for the Senate. In this election the managers returned the Unionist candidates as victors, but the Nullifiers protested when they learned that at least forty-seven men

---

[101] *Winyaw Intelligencer,* March 13, 1833.
[102] John L. Wilson, *The Code of Honor* (Charleston, S. C., 1838), pp. 1–4.
[103] Freehling, *op. cit.,* p. 235.
[104] *Calendar of Joel R. Poinsett Papers in the Henry D. Gilpin Collection,* ed. G. E. Heilman and B. S. Levin (Philadelphia, Penn., 1941), p. 54.

from Horry County had voted at the Small Hopes or Carver's Bay poll. At that poll Dozier got 104 votes, Allston 0. Allston therefore lodged a protest on December 2, 1834. He pointed out that there had been 368 votes cast in October 1832, 378 in January 1833, and 437 in October 1834. Of the 104 votes at Small Hopes some 47 were illegal. Witnesses were subpoenaed and traveled to Columbia to appear before the committee of privileges and elections. John W. Coachman explained to the committee how he had gone to Carver's Bay on election day with John Harrelson, the sheriff, and how he had had to defend himself at pistol point. He swore that the men who had arrived from Horry County had stated that "no Nullifier should be present" at the poll. Coachman and Harrelson had had to retreat amid hisses, threats, and curses. Eleazer Waterman, though a Unionist, had to confess that he had heard rumors that twenty-seven men were going to vote from Horry County. When the tax collector certified that thirty-eight of the Horry men had not paid taxes in Prince George, the committee decided that Dozier's poll must be reduced by thirty-eight and thereby vacated his seat in favor of Allston. Dozier on December 10 asked for a new election, surmising that he did not have a good case before the committee. On December 11 Coachman and Cohen were declared elected, on the twelfth Allston and Belin. This was the last of the turbulent elections and marked the final defeat of the Unionists.[105]

What was needed was a personal seal to the nullification campaign. The Nullifiers, therefore, forged a test oath which demanded undivided allegiance to the will of the sovereign convention. It was reminiscent of the oath of 1777, which forced almost one hundred people to leave the state. Those attending a Georgetown Unionist meeting on November 24 [1834] drew up a petition to the Senate of South Carolina which argued that the new oath "totally changes their political relations by forcing them to abjure all allegiance to the United States . . . convert them from the Citizens of a Republic into the subjects of a government in which they will have no agency or interest from freemen who have always enjoyed and exercised the right of self government into slaves

<hr />

[105] Contested Elections, Georgetown District, Legislative System, 1830–1859, S. C. Archives; Journal of the Senate, 1834, pp. 108–109, S. C. Archives.

whose only duty will be passive obedience." [106] This petition signed by Dr. Willis Wilkinson, president, and Thomas L. Shaw, secretary, perceived the truth of what Freehling has recently written: "In the end, the theory of nullification succeeded in establishing the majority despotism on the state level which it sought to destroy nationally." [107] In practice the test oath remained a threat rather than a reality, but it was there as a haunting reminder of a need for unity within the state—at almost any price.

The Unionists were now driven out of public life. The Withers, Read, Wilkinson family connections, the Scots (the Heriots, Frasers, McDowells), the Black River (the Greens) and the Black Mingo (the Doziers) men, the Methodists (Shaw and Waterman), and the Baptists (Cuttino) were not to provide the outstanding leaders of the next three decades. Joel Roberts Poinsett (with his Pringle in-laws) was too weak a rallying point. In order to oppose the power and influence of the large planters, the Unionists had to draw upon the support of the Northern men in the town of Georgetown and the small farmers of Horry County, but this crisis had eliminated the possibilities of support from these two directions. The big planters of the Waccamaw, the Pee Dee, and the North Santee, all Episcopalians, represented the bulk of nullification strength. The leaders of this group were able to dominate All Saints Parish with ease and Prince George with some difficulty throughout the remainder of the antebellum period.

Georgetown had not contributed any particular nullification leader of note, although both Hayne and Hamilton were closely associated with the district. However, a new figure had emerged who would lead Georgetown and the state in the next crisis—Robert Francis Withers Allston. Allston sat continuously in the state Senate, serving as president after 1850 for three terms, until he was elected governor of the state in 1856. In All Saints Parish Colonel Thomas Pinckney Alston sat until 1838, when he was succeeded by Dr. Edward Thomas Heriot for two terms. Beginning in 1842 All Saints sent Joshua John Ward to the Senate, where he remained until he was elected lieutenant governor of

---

[106] Petitions, Georgetown District, Legislative System, 1830–1859, S. C. Archives; *Camden Journal*, Dec. 6, 1834.

[107] Freehling, *op. cit.*, p. 171.

the state on December 7, 1850.[108] Allston on the Pee Dee and Ward on the Waccamaw were the principal planters and slaveholders of their regions. Their property was entirely within the district; nor were they absentee landlords living in Charleston. Because of their wealth they had immense status among their fellow planters in the state. They were of the very front rank among the men in South Carolina's most powerful body, the Senate. After the state legislature turned down the appropriations in December 1830 for a town guard for Georgetown, it was necessary for Georgetown's most powerful men to sit in the legislature. These were Allston and Ward. They and their fellow planters had as their ultimate storm cellar the doctrines of nullification and secession. Just after the meeting of the nullification convention Allston had written his wife: "Since the decision of the Convention there ought now to be but one party in the State, & that comprising *the whole state*—I would give all that I am worth—if by that means I could consummate this event." [109]

[108] E. B. Reynolds and J. R. Faunt, *The Senate of the State of South Carolina, 1776–1962* (Columbia, S. C., 1962), pp. 116, 127.

[109] R. F. W. Allston to Mrs. R. F. W. Allston, Dec. 5, 1832, Allston Papers, S. C. Hist. Soc.

XIII

THE RICE PLANTERS OF 1850

Between 1850 and 1860 the Georgetown rice planters reached the peak of their wealth, power, and influence. This was their golden decade, the culmination of 130 years of struggle. It was as though the entire Georgetown story led up to this summit, the brief halcyon period before the fall. By 1850 the system for the production of rice had been worked out; the slave labor force was stable and obedient; and the planters themselves had so intermarried that they formed one large family group. John Hyrne Tucker (1780–1859), William Algernon Alston (1782–1860), Francis Marion Weston (1783–1854), Edward Thomas Heriot (1793–1854), Thomas Pinckney Alston (1795–1861), and Joshua John Ward (1800–1853) were the grand old men, born just after the Revolution and dying before the catastrophe of the Civil War. If the history of this county is to be fully understood, it is this group which must be analyzed. Fortunately, the census of 1850 provides for the first time not only the name of each planter, the number in his family, and the number of his slaves, but also the size of his crops. Here at last the whole society is embodied in statistics.[1]

[1] Population, Slave, and Agriculture Schedules, Georgetown District, South Carolina, Seventh Census, 1850, S. C. Archives.

The total population of Georgetown District in 1850 was 20,647 persons. Of this total, 18,253 were Negro slaves, 201 free persons of color, and 2,193 free whites. The free persons of color and the whites were divided among 575 families; there were 575 dwellings in the county. Of the 2,193 white persons, 604 lived in the town of Georgetown. A little more than two-thirds of the white population was, therefore, spread through the rural portions of the county. For those who farmed or planted, the major crop was rice. In 1850 46,765,040 pounds of rice were produced in the county. Since those who harvested more than 100,000 pounds of rice a year produced 98 percent of the total crop, the planters were agriculturists on a large scale. Ninety-one persons produced more than 100,000 pounds of rice in 1850. By 1850 the small producers had disappeared.

Judge H. A. M. Smith in 1913 drew a map of the plantations of the Waccamaw River.[2] That map, with one or two minor changes, seems to be verified by the returns made to the census-takers in 1850. With a few additions by the author, as noted by asterisks, the list of plantations along the Waccamaw River from north to south would read as follows: On Sandy Island to the west of the Waccamaw:

Oak Hampton *	Holly Hill
Ruinville	Pipe Down *
Mount Arena	Grove Hill *
Sandy Knowe	Hasell Hill *
Oak Lawn *	

On the eastern shore of the Waccamaw River from the Horry county line to Fraser's Point:

Woodbourne	Oatland
Wachesaw	Willbrook *
Richmond Hill	Litchfield
Laurel Hill	Waverly
Springfield	Woodville *
Brookgreen	Caledonia
The Oaks	Midway
Turkey Hill	True Blue

2 Henry A. M. Smith, "Hobcaw Barony," *SCHM*, XIV (1913), map facing p. 61.

Weehawka	Alderly
Hagley	Oryzantia
Waterford	Youngville
Bannockburn	Bellefield
Oak Hill	Marietta
Fairfield	Friendfield
Prospect Hill	Strawberry Hill
Clifton	Calais or Fraser's Point
Forlorn Hope	Michau's
Rose Hill	

Captain William Percival Vaux and Dr. Edward Thomas Heriot were the only planters who actually made their homes on Sandy Island in 1850. Most of the plantations lying on that island were the properties of men who resided on the eastern bank of the Waccamaw or the western bank of the Pee Dee. The Belin family of Huguenot descent had planted for many years on Sandy Island. Three almanacs of 1792, 1797, and 1798, which belonged to Allard Belin, contain information on days of planting, hoeing, harvesting, and use of Negroes from other plantations.[3] This Allard Belin was a successful planter who left his estate to his son Colonel Allard H. Belin (1803–1871), who was in 1850 the head of the family. Although the estate had been mismanaged while he was a youth, Allard H. Belin was by the 1830's a wealthy man who "managed his affairs well, and was daily or rather yearly growing in wealth." [4] Colonel Belin married Virginia Wilkinson, daughter of Dr. Willis Wilkinson ("late of Georgetown") on May 26, 1842.[5] In 1850 he planted at Sandy Knowe but lived in Charleston.[6]

Joseph Pawley LaBruce and Mary Ann LaBruce, the children of John LaBruce and Martha Pawley, had inherited Sandy Island plantations. The widow of Joseph Pawley LaBruce lived at Oak Hill on the Waccamaw and visited the island infrequently. When Mary Ann LaBruce married Captain Thomas Petigru in 1829, she conveyed her plantations of Grove Hill and Hasell Hill in trust for her Petigru children. The

[3] S. C. Hist. Soc.
[4] "Memoirs of Frederick Augustus Porcher," ed. Samuel G. Stoney, SCHM, XLVII (1946), 45.
[5] Winyah Observer, June 4, 1842.
[6] RG 105, Box 525, National Archives.

Petigrus did reside on Sandy Island while Captain Petigru, commissioned midshipman in 1812, served in the United States Navy. He died in Washington, D. C., on March 6, 1857.[7]

Captain William Percival Vaux, who lived at Oakhampton, harvested in 1850 240,000 pounds of rice. He was a grandson of William Vaux, who after having been a master of an academy near London, came to South Carolina in 1763 and served as tutor in the Pawley family.[8] In February 1778 William Vaux married Ann Pawley, the daughter of Captain Percival Pawley.[9] The son Percival Edward Vaux (1782–1840), who married Sarah Richards in 1805,[10] had two sons. The elder was William Percival Vaux, who continued to plant on Sandy Island until the Civil War. The younger was Dr. Robert Withers Vaux (1822–1849), who married Catherine Ann Fitzsimons in 1845,[11] practiced medicine on the Waccamaw and Black rivers, died at the age of twenty-seven in 1849, and was buried at True Blue plantation, which had been a Pawley and Vaux property before passing into the hands of Colonel T. P. Alston. Both Percival Edward and Sarah Vaux had also been buried at True Blue.[12]

Dr. Edward Thomas Heriot was the son of William Heriot (1745–1807) and Mary Thomas (1771–1806).[13] Dr. Heriot's uncles, Robert and George Heriot, had been Georgetown merchants and active patriots. Although trained to the medical profession, Edward Thomas Heriot and his brother William Francis Heriot (1794–1841) had planted together. In 1850 Dr. Heriot lived at Mount Arena on Sandy Island but also owned Northampton on the Sampit and soon purchased Richfield on the Pee Dee from Benjamin Faneuil Hunt. He renamed Richfield, calling it Dirleton after the Scottish ancestral home of the Heriots. At

---

[7] Marriage Settlements, X, 210–214, S. C. Archives; James Petigru Carson, *Life, Letters and Speeches of James Louis Petigru* (Washington, D. C., 1920), pp. 74, 322. The Petigrus also owned Pipedown, which was sold to R. F. W. Allston in 1859. *The South Carolina Rice Plantation*, ed. J. H. Easterby (Chicago, Ill., 1945), p. 22.

[8] *Gazette*, Nov. 12, 1763.

[9] *SCHM*, XI (1910), 165.

[10] Marriage Settlements, V, 130–131, S. C. Archives.

[11] Marriage Settlements, XVI, 202–205, S. C. Archives.

[12] Henry DeSaussure Bull, *All Saints' Church Waccamaw* (Columbia, S. C., 1968), pp. 87–88; *Winyah Observer*, Oct. 3, 1849.

[13] The Heriot genealogy is found in Caldwell Woodruff, "Heriots of Scotland and South Carolina" (Linthicum Heights, Md., 1939), typed copy in S. C. Hist. Soc.

the time of his death, therefore, he possessed three plantations and a summer residence, Woodland, on Murrell's Inlet. Although he produced only 300,000 pounds of rice in 1850, he must have been planting on a larger scale in the following four years. In a letter written in April 1854 to a Scottish cousin, he stated that he had 115 Negroes at Mount Arena, 125 at Northhampton, 125 at Dirleton, and 4 at his summer retreat; a total of 369.[14] Dr. Heriot married Eliza Stark (1801–1866) of Columbia, South Carolina, on October 23, 1823. There were five children. The eldest son Francis Withers Heriot (1825–1873) succeeded his father as a planter and made his home at Mount Arena. The second son, Dr. Robert Stark Heriot (1830–1875), married Martha Helen Ford on November 6, 1855. The third son, Alexander Glennie Heriot (1840–1914), married on December 20, 1860, Anna Green Coachman. The two daughters, Mary Elizabeth (1827–1912) and Martha Emma (1842–1877), married Dr. James Ritchie Sparkman and William Ervin Sparkman, uncle and nephew.

The master of Wachesaw, the northernmost plantation in Georgetown District on the eastern side of the Waccamaw, was Dr. Allard Belin Flagg (1823–1901). His grandfather Dr. Henry Collins Flagg (1742–1801) of Rhode Island had served as surgeon in General Nathanael Greene's army and like a number of Greene's continental officers had married a South Carolina rice heiress at the end of the war. He married on December 5, 1784, Rachel Moore Allston, the widow of Colonel William Allston of Brookgreen. Their son, Dr. Ebenezer Flagg (1795–1838), married Margaret Elizabeth Belin (1801–1885) in 1817. Dr. Allard Belin Flagg, one of their nine children, was established as a planter by a gift of Wachesaw plantation from his uncle, the Reverend James L. Belin, on which property in 1850 Dr. Flagg produced 600,000 pounds of rice. He married on January 16, 1850, Penelope Bentley Ward, the eldest daughter of Joshua John Ward, the richest rice planter of his day.[15]

[14] Dr. Heriot to Miss Cunningham, April 1854, E. T. Heriot Letters, DUL.

[15] Alberta Morel Lachicotte, *Georgetown Rice Plantations* (Columbia, S. C., 1955), pp. 64–68; *Family Records of the Descendants of Gershom Flagg*, compiled by N. G. Flagg and L. C. S. Flagg (Quincy, Ill., 1907), pp. 122–128. The Rev. James Belin also gave his nephew The Hermitage, a summer home on the shore. Flagg also planted Oak Lawn on Sandy Island. RG 105, Box 525, National Archives.

Dr. John D. Magill (1795–1864) owned Richmond Hill, which contained 212 acres of rice land and 500 to 600 acres of uplands with a summer residence on the seashore. This plantation was worked by 116 slaves and produced 420,000 pounds of rice in 1850. Dr. Magill also owned Oregon plantation higher up the Waccamaw River in Horry County, which consisted of 248 acres of rice land and 4,000 acres of pine land. The Magills had been on the Waccamaw since the 1780's, but the family had come from the Black Mingo region, having contributed fighters to Marion's brigade. Dr. Magill, who had married Mary Eliza Vereen, the daughter of Captain William Vereen, on January 27, 1825, had two sons, John D. Magill, Jr., and William Joseph Magill, to whom he left at his death in 1863 Richmond Hill and Oregon respectively.[16]

Laurel Hill belonged to the Waties family until 1750, when it was bought by Gabriel Marion. Plowden Weston (1739–1827), who had come from Warwickshire and established himself in trade in Charleston first with Charles Atkins and then with Isaac Mazyck, bought Laurel Hill in 1775 from Gabriel Marion; in 1777 he bought lands adjoining Laurel Hill from William Allston of Brookgreen.[17] During the Revolution produce from the plantation supplied the troops of Peter Horry.[18] Plowden Weston by his first marriage on July 18, 1762 to Alice Hollybush had acquired plantations on the Wando River.[19] Charles Weston (died 1798) was the only child of this marriage.[20] Plowden Weston married March 26, 1775, Mary-Anne Mazyck, the daughter of his partner who owned lands on the Santee.[21] The Charleston firm of Weston and Mazyck served the Wando, Santee, and Waccamaw rice planters as

[16] Marriage Settlements, IX, 145, S. C. Archives; mortgage, dated March 31, 1866, in Richard Dozier Papers, SHC; *SCHM*, XXVI (1925), 153–155; *Winyaw Intelligencer*, Feb. 9, 1825.

[17] Register of Mesne Conveyance Records, A-5, pp. 449–453; P-4, pp. 246–250; T-4, pp. 261–264, S. C. Archives. Information on Weston family obtained from Weston Collection, S. C. Hist. Soc.

[18] "Plowden Weston," Audited Accounts, S. C. Archives.

[19] *Gazette*, July 24, 1762; "Will of John Hollybush," dated Nov. 17, 1749, proved June 22, 1750, Charleston County Wills, VI (1747–1752), 363–368, S. C. Archives.

[20] Alice Weston, the only daughter of Charles Weston, married Benjamin Huger Rutledge in 1824. Marriage Settlements, VIII, 549–552, S. C. Archives; *SCHM*, XXXI (1930), 96.

[21] *Gazette*, March 27, 1775.

factors for many years.²² Plowden Weston had accumulated by the time
of his death in 1827 a great fortune which he left to his two sons by
his second marriage, Francis Marion Weston (1783–1854) and Dr.
Paul Weston (1784–1837). Dr. Paul Weston inherited Pee Dee and
Wando lands, personal property worth $70,000, and 258 slaves. Francis
Marion Weston inherited Laurel Hill and an equal amount of personal
property and slaves.²³

The Westons always maintained close ties with their family in Warwickshire. Francis Marion Weston married in succession Mildred Weston (1774–1822) and Mary Weston (1779–1856), the daughters of his
uncle Charles Weston of Kursley in Warwickshire. Francis Marion Weston, who had bought Hagley from one of the Alstons,²⁴ produced 1,603,-
800 pounds of rice in 1850, although he is only listed as owning 196
slaves. At his death in 1854 ²⁵ his entire estate passed to his son by his
first marriage, Plowden Charles Jennet Weston.

Plowden Charles Jennet Weston was tutored at home by Alexander
Glennie before his parents took him to England and placed him at
Harrow. The fruits of his classical training are visible in *The Pleasures
of Music*, a poem which he published in England in 1836 and dedicated
to his "fellow Harrovian," William Clement Drake Esdaile. After attending Cambridge University ²⁶ Plowden Weston married Esdaile's
sister, Emily Frances Esdaile, on August 31. 1847.²⁷ During the 1850's
he rounded out his Waccamaw estates by selling Laurel Hill to Colonel
Daniel W. Jordan ²⁸ and by buying in 1858 True Blue and Weehawka

²² Plowden Weston's Record Book for his Waccamaw and Wando plantations,
1802–1820, College of Charleston Library.
²³ "Will of Plowden Weston," dated Sept. 18, 1819, proved Jan. 25, 1827, Charleston County Wills, XXXVII, Book A (1826–1834), 165–185, S. C. Archives; Mary
James Richards, "Our McDowell Ancestry," p. 27, typed copy in SCL.
²⁴ He purchased Hagley from either John Ashe Alston or from Joseph Alston.
²⁵ He died on Nov. 25, 1854, at Laurel Hill; his second wife died on April 19,
1856, at Hagley. *Pee Dee Times*, Nov. 29, 1854, April 23, 1856.
²⁶ *Rice Planter and Sportsman*, ed. Arney R. Childs (Columbia, S. C., 1953),
pp. 48, 111.
²⁷ *Winyah Observer*, Sept. 29, 1847. Her father was Edward Jeffries Esdaile of
Cothelestone House, Somerset. "Esdaile of Cothelestone," Sir Bernard Burke, *Landed
Gentry* (London, 1898), I, 467.
²⁸ Notes on Col. Daniel W. Jordan in possession of Mr. C. B. Berry, Crescent
Beach, S. C.

from Colonel T. P. Alston [29] and Waterford from R. F. W. Allston.[30] According to J. Motte Alston, Plowden Weston had "the interest on nearly, if not quite, $1,000,000 to live on." [31] The scholar-planter was a member of the South Carolina Historical Society, Maryland Historical Society, New York Historical Society, and in 1855 published in London a fine edition of documents on the early history of South Carolina. At his death his library was valued at $15,000 and his wine cellar contained 110 dozen bottles of wine.[32]

Joshua John Ward of Brookgreen was the king of the rice planters in Georgetown District. He produced 3,900,000 pounds of rice with 1,092 slaves on six plantations and adjacent lands in 1850. At the time of his death on February 27, 1853, he owned Longwood, Springfield, Brookgreen, Prospect Hill, Alderly, and Oryzantia plus Rose Hill Island, Clifton Island, and Mitchell's Island—all located along the reaches of the Waccamaw. There were 7,000 unimproved acres and 3,117 improved acres, the latter producing besides the rice 7,000 bushels of corn, 2,000 bushels of oats, 1,000 bushels of peas and beans, 66,000 bushels of sweet potatoes, 500 pounds of butter, and 600 pounds of wool. The cash value of his farm in 1850 was $527,050. The farm implements and machinery were worth $2,500. His 51 horses, 49 mules, 285 milch cows, 200 working oxen, 400 other cattle, 519 sheep, and 450 swine were valued at $34,808.

Ward was born at Brookgreen on November 24, 1800, the son of Joshua and Elizabeth Ward. His father Joshua Ward, of a family of Charleston merchants and lawyers, had married Elizabeth Cook, the widow of Charles Weston, who had died in 1798.[33] Joshua John Ward

---

[29] Deed, dated Dec. 30, 1858, Weston Papers, SCL.

[30] Easterby, *op. cit.*, pp. 140, 141, 143.

[31] Childs, *op. cit.*, pp. 110–111.

[32] These memberships are listed on the title page of Plowden C. J. Weston, *An Address Delivered in the Indigo Society Hall, Georgetown, South-Carolina, on the Fourth Day of May, 1860* (Charleston, S. C., 1860); *Documents Connected with the History of South Carolina*, ed. Plowden Charles Jennet Weston (London, 1856); Emily F. Weston to Ordinary, April 12 [1864], file 448, Office of Probate Judge, Georgetown, S. C.

[33] Joshua Ward (1769–1828) was the son of Col. John Ward (1732–1783), whose wife was a daughter of Peter Leger. In 1798 Joshua Ward had married as his second wife Elizabeth Cook Weston, who was a daughter of John Cook and Elizabeth Mayham. Ward Family Notes in possession of Mrs. Charlotte Prevost, Georgetown, S. C. For the story of Brookgreen see Lachicotte, *op. cit.*, pp. 55–63.

was a self-made man in the sense that he put together his own vast estate, although he started with at least one plantation to his name.[34] He consistently reinvested his profits in more land and slaves. Springfield had been the property of Washington Allston, who had sold it to Robert and Francis Withers, the latter selling it to Ward. Brookgreen had passed through the hands of the Allstons to the Withers and then to the Wards. Mrs. Benjamin Huger sold Prospect Hill to Ward after Huger's death in 1823. Alderly was purchased at a sale of the master in equity. Ward secured Rose Hill Island and Clifton Island from William Algernon Alston, Mitchell's Island from Dr. Francis S. Parker, Longwood from P. W. Fraser and John Green, and some Pee Dee lands from C. G. Memminger. Ward's career as a rice planter represented a process continually at work in the district from 1800 to 1850, the gradual accumulation of larger properties by the more skillful planters. There was a tendency for the big planter to round out his property, squeezing out the smaller men. Ward left all of his lands and all of his slaves to his three sons, neither land nor slaves to any of his seven daughters. Ward left his sons legally free to dispose of their lands as they should see fit, but he urged them in his will to follow the examples of their father and grandfather and keep the landed estates in the male line of the family

Ward, who had been educated in Scotland, married in 1825 Joanna Douglass Hasell (1805–1878), daughter of G. P. Bond Hasell of Edinburgh and first cousin of Dr. Andrew Hasell.[35] Ward left his wife his home at Brookgreen with the gardens, buildings, grounds, furniture, plate, carriage, and horses she might choose, house servants, and the summer residence on the shore called Magnolia, almost all of his personal property except his wines and liquors. To his eldest son Joshua Ward (died 1869) he left Springfield and Brookgreen and a summer place known as the Retreat, which the father had purchased from Mrs.

[34] His father's estate was appraised at $55,839, excluding $20,000 in bank stock. Richards, op. cit., p. 27. "Will of Joshua John Ward," dated Dec. 22, 1848, copy attached to bill filed in Court of Equity in Charleston on April 10, 1868, in the case of Arthur B. Flagg and wife et al. v. Joanna D. Ward et al., D. V. Richardson Papers, in private possession, Columbia, S. C.; Pee Dee Times, March 9, 1853.

[35] Marriage Settlements, IX, 142–145, S. C. Archives. G. P. B. Hasell (1781–1818) had married Penelope Bentley, Sept. 20, 1802, in Edinburgh. Wilson Genealogy, S. C. Hist. Soc.

Benjamin Huger. Mayham Ward (1837–1866) received Alderly, Oryzantia, 100 acres of Rose Hill Island. Benjamin Huger Ward (1841–1903), who was named for Ward's friend and neighbor, received Prospect Hill and Clifton Island. Mayham and Benjamin were jointly to own Longwood, the lands on the Pee Dee, and a lot of ten acres on Pawley's Island. The 1,000 slaves were divided equally among the three brothers. The property of each brother was valued at over $300,000 each. Each of the seven daughters was left a dowry of $40,000, to be paid out of Ward's estate. Joshua John Ward was a millionaire in a day when millionaires were rare indeed.

In spite of the fact that the seven daughters had neither lands nor slaves, they married well. Penelope, the eldest, married Dr. Allard Belin Flagg, the master of Wachesaw; Joanna married Joseph B. Pyatt, the master of Rosemont; Georgeanna married Arthur Belin Flagg, the brother of Allard; Catherine married her cousin Lewis Hasell;[36] and Alice married her cousin Bentley Weston. The two youngest daughters did not marry until after the Civil War.

Joseph Alston had owned The Oaks at the time of his death in 1816. This property passed to his namesake and nephew Joseph Alston, the eldest son of William Algernon Alston. This Joseph Alston, who married Helen Mason of New York, continued to plant at The Oaks until his death in 1855, after which his son William Algernon Alston planted until he died during the Civil War.[37]

Turkey Hill and Oatland were planted by the Pyatt family in 1850. The Pyatts, an English family, had been among the first settlers. John Pyatt I of Prince Frederick Parish married Hannah LaBruce in 1744.[38] John Pyatt II (1750–1795) married as his third wife Charlotte Withers, daughter of Francis Withers.[39] They had two sons. Captain Joseph Pyatt (1788-1819) died at his home on the seashore. John Francis Pyatt (1790–1820) married in 1812 Martha Allston (1789–1869), the daughter of Benjamin Allston, Sr.[40] She brought Turkey Hill and Oatland to add

[36] *Pee Dee Times*, March 31, 1858.
[37] Childs, *op. cit.*, p. 110. Joseph Alston also planted at Marietta. Account book of Dr. Andrew Hasell, S. C. Hist. Soc.
[38] *SCHM*, XIX (1918), 99.
[39] Pyatt Family Notes, S. C. Hist. Soc.
[40] *SCHM*, XXXI (1930), 202.

to the Pyatt plantations of Richmond and Rosemont near Georgetown. Although John Francis died at the age of twenty-nine he left three children: John Francis (1817–1884), Joseph Benjamin (1820–1910), and Charlotte. In 1850 Mrs. Martha Allston Pyatt and her two sons produced a family total of 2,010,000 pounds of rice with the labor of 768 slaves. Mrs. Pyatt managed Turkey Hill and Oatland while the two sons managed Richmond and Rosemont.[41]

The patriarch of Willbrook and Litchfield was John Hyrne Tucker, whose lands yielded 1,140,000 pounds of rice in 1850 by the hands of 201 slaves.[42] Tucker was born on July 19, 1780, while Major Wemyss was occupying Georgetown, and died on June 5, 1859.[43] His father was Daniel Tucker, a member of the Georgetown committee of safety, and his mother was Elizabeth, the daughter of Colonel Henry Hyrne. Both parents were of patriot families. Daniel Tucker had been a partner in the firm of Heriot and Tucker, trading for many years in Georgetown, but acquired Litchfield where he built before his death in 1797 a house, which still stands. John Hyrne Tucker, although "known as a very ugly man, very badly pitted from small-pox" with "an enormous nose full of blue veins and a knob on the end of it," married four times.[44] His first wife was Fanny Carolina, daughter of Colonel Charles Brown of Georgetown; she died in 1806 without leaving issue. His second wife was Elizabeth Ann Allston (1790–1822), a sister of R. F. W. Allston and Joseph Waties Allston. One daughter of this marriage married Francis Weston, nephew of Francis Marion Weston of Laurel Hill. The other daughter Anne remained a spinster. Tucker's third and fourth marriages were to sisters, nieces of the historian David Ramsay. From the third marriage to Susan Harriet Ramsay (died 1833) came seven children. Dr. John Hyrne Tucker II (1827–1865) inherited Willbrook in 1859; his younger brother Dr. Henry Massingberd Tucker (1831–1904) received Litchfield. One Charlestonian who met Tucker at the Charleston Library Society wrote that he cared nothing for books. "Rice planting was his

---

[41] *SCHM*, XXXI (1930), 201, 302.
[42] Lachicotte, *op. cit.*, pp. 46–54.
[43] Tucker notes, S. C. Hist. Soc.; a page was dedicated to him in the journal of the Winyaw and All Saints Agricultural Society, S. C. Hist. Soc.
[44] Childs, *op. cit.*, p. 34.

sole delight. He lived for and in rice. It was the first and the last thought of his mind." He loved his rice, his wine, and his grandchildren.[45] R. F. W. Allston wrote his own son Ben on June 10, 1859: "Last Monday we attended the funeral of Mr. Tucker who refused nourishment 2 days before, he said he wish'd to die. He has left Litchfield to Henry, Willbrook to Hyrne and some unclos'd land. The Pee Dee Settlement to John, Joe and Daniel and the House in Town [Charleston] to Mrs. Weston, his single daughters to live there always, to Anne 5 Negroes and $15,000, poor Anne has done her part very faithfully by him. . . ." [46]

Waverly plantation was managed between 1834 and 1857 by R. F. W. Allston for the estate of Joseph Waties Allston, his brother. In 1850 eighty-four slaves were producing 300,000 pounds of rice. Waverly had been the home plantation of their father, Benjamin Allston, Jr., at the time of his death in 1809. Their widowed mother continued to live at Waverly until 1819, when Joseph Waties Allston, the eldest son, came of age and took over his inheritance. The mother and the younger children then moved to Matanzas on the Pee Dee where the estates of the younger children were located.

Joseph Waties Allston was destined for a notable career in public life until his early death in 1834. He married three times, his third wife, Mary Allan, presenting him with two sons, Joseph Blyth Allston (1833–1904) and William Allan Allston (1834–1878). R. F. W. Allston, their uncle, managed this plantation until the property was divided in 1857 between the two sons. Joseph Blyth Allston received the plantation house, rice fields, and rice mill which had been rebuilt in 1837; William Allan Allston received the pine lands, which plantation was called Woodville.[47]

Caledonia was the home of the widow of Robert Nesbit, who had inherited the property from his uncle Dr. Robert Nesbit, who had married Elizabeth Pawley in 1797.[48] The nephew had been born at Berwick

[45] "Memoirs of Frederick Adolphus Porcher," ed. Samuel G. Stoney, *SCHM*, XLVII (1946), 47–48.
[46] Easterby, *op. cit.*, p. 158.
[47] Easterby, *op. cit.*, passim; Lachicotte, *op. cit.*, pp. 30–36.
[48] Robert Nesbit's Account Book, 1796–1804, SCL; Marriage Settlements, III, 208–211, S. C. Archives.

upon Tweed, Scotland, on November 17, 1799, and had resided in All Saints since 1808. When Major Robert Nesbit died on October 17, 1848, the members of the Hot and Hot Fish Club passed a resolution in memory of the native of Scotland who for more than thirty years had been "a practical planter" on the Waccamaw.[49] His wife Mary Hamilton Nesbit, the daughter of John Hamilton,[50] was managing the estate in 1850 when the crop of rice amounted to 540,000 pounds of rice. The property was later divided between their two sons, Robert Hamilton Nesbit and Ralph Nesbit.[51]

Benjamin Faneuil Dunkin (1792–1874), the absentee landlord of Midway, was a New Englander who at an early age had been drawn to Charleston by his cousin Benjamin Faneuil Hunt and later to the Georgetown District by military and legal connections. Dunkin's maternal ancestors were the Faneuils of Boston. After studying at Harvard he had joined his cousin Hunt in Charleston as a tutor. One of their acquaintances had been the tutor of young Aaron Burr Alston. For a time during the War of 1812 Dunkin served as adjutant to Colonel John Ashe Alston's regiment, whose headquarters were at Georgetown. Although the troops were encamped about a mile out of town on the Black River Ferry road, Colonel Alston and Dunkin had lodged in town at Whitehurst's Inn, where during the winter of 1814–1815 he made valuable friends, including Benjamin Huger and John Man Taylor. After the troops were disbanded Dunkin, who had read some law in Charleston, traveled the eastern judicial circuit picking up cases and fees. For the next seven years he made the eastern circuit each year, becoming an annual visitor in Georgetown. He later had a distinguished career at the bar, in the legislature of the state, and finally as chancellor of the court of equity (1837–1860) and chief justice of South Carolina (1865–1868). The fruits of his legal practice had been invested in Mid-

[49] Journal of the Hot and Hot Fish Club, Allston Papers, S. C. Hist. Soc.; *Winyah Observer,* Oct. 25, 1848.

[50] The marriage was on June 5, 1832. *Winyah Intelligencer,* June 13, 1832. John Hamilton died at the Nesbit house on Pawley's Island. *Winyah Observer,* June 28, 1842.

[51] Equity Proceedings, Jan. 14, 1867, Richard Dozier Papers, SHC. Mary Nesbit died in her forty-fifth year on June 4, 1857. *Pee Dee Times,* June 10, 1857.

way, which he purchased from Thomas Pinckney Alston. This plantation brought in 540,000 pounds of rice in 1850.[52]

Colonel Thomas Pinckney Alston (1795–1861) was the master of
Midway, True Blue, and Weehawka. He was the eldest son of the
second marriage of Colonel William Alston of Clifton. His mother, Mary
Brewton Motte, was the younger sister of the two wives of General
Thomas Pinckney. Not only was he the half-brother of Governor Joseph
Alston and half-brother-in-law of Governor John Lide Wilson, but his
eldest sister Rebecca married Senator Robert Y. Hayne, his sister
Elizabeth married Arthur P. Hayne, and his youngest sister Mary mar-
ried William Bull Pringle, one of the largest landholders on the North
Santee.

The 1850 census did not list the production of his fields, although
the same census recorded 274 slaves in his name. He had by 1850 already
sold Midway to Judge Dunkin, but the accounts of Dr. Andrew Hasell
show that the slaves on Colonel Alston's plantations of True Blue and
Weehawka were attended throughout the period 1843 to 1852.[53] He did
sell these two plantations to Plowden Weston in 1858 and auctioned off
his slaves in 1859.[54] He was apparently giving up an active planting
career and ultimately retired to "Ka-a," the 1,000 acre summer retreat
in Habersham County in the mountains of Georgia.[55]

Colonel T. P. Alston married first Jane Ladson Smith by whom
he had one child, J. Motte Alston (1821–1909), who has left in his
memoirs one of the most complete pictures of the rice-planting world.
The young Motte Alston was almost unique in this period in that he
secured virgin land from his grandfather's estate between the Waccamaw

---

[52] Judge Dunkin married Washington S. Prentiss on Jan. 18, 1820. "Diary of
Benjamin Faneuil Dunkin Begun 12 December 1861," S. C. Hist. Soc.; *In Memoriam.
Hon. Benjamin Faneuil Dunkin, Chief Justice of South Carolina. Proceedings of the
Meeting of the Charleston Bar, 18th December, 1874* [Charleston, S. C., 1874];
John A. May and Joan R. Faunt, *South Carolina Secedes* (Columbia, S. C., 1960),
pp. 137–138. Judge Dunkin about 1830 planted an extensive garden at Midway, one
feature of which was intricate mazes constructed of various concentric circles
bordered with hedges of cassena, wild orange, and box. Alice G. B. Lockwood,
Gardens of Colony and State (n.p., 1931), II, 230–231.

[53] Dr. Andrew Hasell's Account Book, S. C. Hist. Soc. He inherited Weehawka
and slaves thereon valued at $225,000. Childs, *op. cit.*, p. 27.

[54] Easterby, *op. cit.*, p. 414.

[55] Childs, *op. cit.*, pp. 71, 72, 96, 103, 118, 122.

and Bull Creek, where for fourteen years he carved out a new plantation. "The growth consisted of enormous cypress, gum, ash, etc., matted together with huge grape vines, and cane from fifteen to twenty feet high. . . ." Out of that jungle he forged a new rice plantation, Woodbourne, which was the northernmost plantation in the parish.[56] Colonel Alston by his second marriage to his sister-in-law Susan Smith had nine children.[57]

R. F. W. Allston, though a Pee Dee River planter, purchased 363 acres on the Waccamaw in 1847 from Miss Charlotte Pyatt. This was Waterford plantation with lands, as was the case with practically all of the Waccamaw plantations, on both sides of the river. Allston himself eventually sold it to Plowden C. J. Weston in 1858 at $200 an acre. It was thereupon added to the manificent estate of Hagley.[58]

Bannockburn had received its name from Colonel John Ashe Alston (1780–1832), the second son of "King Billy" by his first marriage. This Colonel Alston had married Sarah McPherson, and their only daughter was to inherit the estate. Sarah McPherson Alston married John Izard Middleton (1800–1877) on March 24, 1828. Although John I. Middleton was of an Ashley River family, the son of Governor Henry Middleton, he henceforth made his home in All Saints Parish, renaming the plantation Crowfield after the ancestral home of the Middletons. In 1850 his lands produced 750,000 pounds of rice; in 1860 he owned 318 slaves.[59]

Oak Hill was the home of the LaBruces, one of the oldest and best-connected families in the district. The first William Allston had married Esther LaBrosse de Marboeuf in 1721. The first Joseph LaBruce had married William Allston's sister. He secured royal grants on the Waccamaw in 1733 for 777 acres. In 1791 his descendant John LaBruce married Martha Pawley, daughter of Captain Percival Pawley.[60] John and

[56] Ibid., pp. 50–51.

[57] The second marriage was against his father's wishes. Ibid., p. 27. The names of the nine children, born between 1826 and 1843, are given in ibid., p. 144.

[58] Easterby, op. cit., pp. 43, 141, 143.

[59] Winyaw Intelligencer, Jan. 18, 1832; May and Faunt, op. cit., p. 185; SCHM, I (1900), 249. The 1850 census records 480,000 pounds of rice and 166 slaves for "A. J. Allston, Est." which lay apparently on the Pee Dee. The author guesses that this may have been the estate of John Ashe Alston, and therefore under the control of J. I. Middleton. This may account for the fact·that J. I. Middleton is not listed with any slaves in 1850.

[60] SCHM, XXI (1920), 79.

Martha LaBruce had two children: Joseph, who married in 1819 at Brookgreen Catherine Ward, the sister of Joshua John Ward, and Ann, who married Captain Thomas Petigru of Sandy Island. Joseph and Catherine Ward LaBruce had two sons and one daughter. Elizabeth Love LaBruce married Samuel H. Mortimer in 1840 at the LaBruce town house in Hampstead in Charleston. Joshua Ward LaBruce (1823–1844) married Elizabeth Hazlehurst of Charleston in 1845. John La-Bruce (1820–1877) married Selina Mortimer of Charleston in 1848. In 1850 John LaBruce and Joshua Ward LaBruce produced 570,000 pounds of rice with 150 slaves, part of this being produced on Sandy Island and part at Oak Hill.[61]

The master of Fairfield was Charles Cotesworth Pinckney Alston (1796–1881); known as Charles Alston, Sr., he was the younger brother of Colonel Thomas Pinckney Alston. Their father, "King Billy," had lived at Fairfield, after Clifton burned, until his death in 1839. Charles Alston, Sr., who also planted Bellefield, had a crop of 900,000 pounds of rice in 1850. He married Emma Pringle in 1824. Although three sons and one daughter survived the father, none of his children ever married.[62]

Clifton had been the principal residence of "King Billy" until it burned.[63] In 1850 the master of Clifton, and of Forlorn Hope and Rose Hill as well, was William Algernon Alston (1782–1860), who was the third son of the first marriage of "King Billy." Since the death of his elder brothers, Governor Joseph Alston and Colonel John Ashe Alston, he had been the foremost grandee on Waccamaw Neck, the central figure of a notable kinship group. He had married in 1806 Mary Allston Young, the sister of Washington Allston and the widow of Thomas Young. This marriage brought him Youngville. In the course of his life he also acquired Marietta, Friendfield, Strawberry Hill, and before 1860 the Fraser plantations of Calais and Michaux. In 1850 his lands

---

[61] Marriage Settlements, VIII, 34–37, S. C. Archives; Family Book of the LaBruces, in possession of Mrs. Elizabeth LaBruce Pugh, Columbia, S. C.; "Will of Catherine LaBruce," dated April 28, 1858, probated May 19, 1866, copy, Richard Dozier Papers, SHC. Joseph P. LaBruce died on March 13, 1827. *Winyaw Intelligencer,* March 14, 1827. "Col. Samuel Mortimer had a little place [on the South Santee] between Eldorado and Indianfield at one time called Mortimer Hill." David Doar, *A Sketch of the Agricultural Society of St. James, Santee* (Charleston, S. C., 1908), p. 44.

[62] Lachicotte, *op. cit.,* p. 25.

[63] *Ibid.,* p. 24.

yielded 1,800,000 pounds of rice, a crop second only to that of Joshua John Ward. The census shows him the owner, however, of only eighty-four slaves. Although he had four sons and five daughters, his list of descendants is short. All of his sons predeceased him. William Ashe Alston (1812–1842), who had just returned from a tour of Europe and from his marriage to a Louisiana sugar heiress, died on May 30, 1842.[64] Joseph Alston died in 1855. John Ashe Alston, who had married in 1838 Fanny Buford Fraser (1820–1897), the youngest daughter of the Reverend Hugh Fraser, died in 1856. When not in Charleston, John Ashe Alston's family resided at Strawberry Hill.[65] One daughter married Dr. Benjamin Burgh Smith, the brother of Colonel T. P. Alston's two wives, and lived at Rose Hill. Mary Ashe Alston married Dr. Seaman Deas, a planter on the North Santee. There were also Eliza Maria Alston Young and the twins, Anna Louise Alston and Charlotte Maria Alston.[66] At William Algernon Alston's death in 1860, his properties passed to his grandson (most probably the son of Joseph Alston, who died in 1855) William Algernon Alston, for the latter in a will dated November 14, 1860, left Marietta and Friendfield to Thomas P. Alston, Jr. (1832–1864), the son of Colonel Thomas Pinckney Alston, and left Strawberry Hill, Calais, and Michaux to his "cousins," Algernon Alston and Rowland Alston, the sons of John Ashe Alston, who had died in 1856.[67]

Calais or Fraser's Point and Michau's were at the southern tip of the Neck. Calais, which had been purchased before the Revolution by Samuel Clegg, passed to the Reverend Hugh Fraser at the time of his marriage in 1796 to Elizabeth Clegg Porter, the only child of Benjamin Porter.[68] Elizabeth Porter Fraser died in 1797 leaving one son, Benjamin Porter Fraser (1797–1829), who on April 6, 1819, married Agnes Kirkpatrick. Their son Hugh Fraser (1819–1852) married Margaret Jane

[64] Winyah Observer, June 18, 1842.

[65] Georgetown Union, March 31, 1838; Winyah Observer, July 5, 1845; Childs, op. cit., p. 106.

[66] "Will of Mary Ashe Deas," Judge of Probate, Georgetown County, Will Book A (1865–1912), pp. 14–16, WPA transcript, S. C. Archives; Childs, op. cit., p. 108.

[67] William Algernon Alston, aged seventy-eight years, was buried on Sept. 16, 1860. Bull, op. cit., p 89. "Will of William Algernon Alston," written in New York City and dated Nov. 14, 1860, proved Nov. 4, 1867, Charleston County Wills, LI (1862–1868), 762–764, S. C. Archives.

[68] Marriage Settlements, II, 509–513, S. C. Archives.

Bentley Weston, a daughter of Dr. Paul Weston. This grandson of the clergyman recorded a crop of 180,000 pounds of rice in 1850. He owned sixty-seven slaves. After his death in Richmond, Virginia, in 1852, these two plantations must have been sold to William Algernon Alston and the proceeds used to educate Benjamin Porter Fraser (1841–1930) and Paul Weston Fraser (1842–1878).[69]

These were the planters of Waccamaw Neck in 1850. They were a small group, set above the rest of society, but closely knit together by ties of blood and common interest. They were immensely rich for the Americans of their day; indeed, they were rich when compared with most of the planters of South Carolina. They lived with great style. The house servants of the Alston family wore "dark green broadcloth coats and vests trimmed in silver braid and red facings with trousers of green plush." Most of the festivities revolved around family occasions. Colonel Ward gave a party in 1849 at Brookgreen for his daughter, who married Dr. Flagg. To it came the Heriots, Petigrus, LaBruces, Vaux, and Belins from Sandy Island; the Allstons, Izards, Poinsetts, Reads, Westons, and Fords from the Pee Dee; as well as all of the Waccamaw families. "The party was kept up till the 'wee sma hours'," enjoying, as J. Motte Alston recalled it, a regular old-fashioned country dance to the music of sundry country fiddlers.[70]

In 1845 the gentlemen formed the Hot and Hot Fish Club for "convivial and social intercourse."[71] The clubhouse was built on land that originally belonged to Colonel T. P. Alston, but later was a part of B. F. Dunkin's Midway plantation, no doubt named for the fact that it was midway between the Horry county line and the tip of the peninsula, between Wachesaw and Fraser's Point. Here these men enjoyed, if one of their resolutions can be believed, "the happiest hours" of their lives. There was a race course, a billiard table, and a ten-pin alley, but the

[69] Fraser Family Chart, in possession of Mrs. Bessie F. Betancourt, Georgetown, S. C. Clegg's Point and Michaux had been advertised at the sale of Rev. Hugh Fraser's estate. *Georgetown American*, Jan. 8, 1840.

[70] Childs, *op. cit.*, pp. 12, 105.

[71] Journal of the Hot and Hot Fish Club, Allston Papers, S. C. Hist Soc.; Richard B. Harwell, "The Hot and Hot Fish Club of All Saints Parish," *SCHM*, XLVIII (1947), 40–47.

principal purpose of gathering was to enjoy good food, good wine, and good talk. J. Motte Alston summed up their good times succinctly:

> On Fridays—[we] met at [a] club at Midway, where we had a Club-house, large dining room, billiard and ten pin alley. . . . Here was, in the long ago, the training course of some of the finest racers in Carolina. . . . We presided by turns, and each member brought his own dish or dishes, wines, etc. . . . Each member brought his servant; and when all the good things had been discussed, interwoven with some politics and lots of rice talk, and the table cleared of all save the bottles of old wine, the thrice told anecdotes . . . would enliven the scene till night began to throw her kind mantle over the happy members of the Hot and Hot Fish Club.[72]

The original members of the club were Captain William Percival Vaux, Dr. Edward Thomas Heriot and his son Francis Withers Heriot from Sandy Island, Dr. John D. Magill, Joshua John Ward, Robert Nesbit, Colonel T. P. Alston and his son J. Motte Alston, John LaBruce and Joshua Ward LaBruce, John Ashe Alston and his brother-in-law Dr. Benjamin Burgh Smith, Hugh Fraser, and Dr. Andrew Hasell from Waccamaw Neck; and Francis Weston, Colonel Peter William Fraser, R. F. W. Allston, and John Harleston Read from the Pee Dee. All were planters with the exception of Dr. Hasell, who lived at Cedar Grove on the seashore and devoted his attention to his medical practice. His account books indicate that he attended the planters' families and slaves on practically every plantation up and down the river. Dr. Magill and Dr. Heriot had been trained in medicine but practiced only among their own people. At Dr. Heriot's death the club's resolution noted that he was first a doctor and then a planter "a pursuit more congenial to his views."

The members who joined the club between its founding and the Civil War were generally the sons or the relatives of members: Dr. A. B. Flagg, Dr. E. B. Flagg, Dr. W. J. Magill, Plowden C. J. Weston, Dr. Joseph R. Tucker, W. H. Tucker, Robert Nesbit, Joseph Alston, Jr., Charles Alston, William Allan Allston, Benjamin Allston, Mayham Ward, and Nathaniel Barnwell. The two new men were Colonel D. W. Jordan, who had bought Laurel Hill to add to his estates in Horry County, and Dr. W. W. Post. The latter was brought from Charleston by some of the

---

[72] Childs, op. cit., p. 60.

GEORGETOWN, S. C., 1901. Courtesy of Georgetown City Hall.

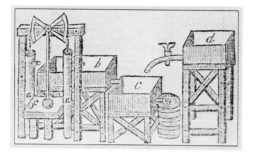

MACHINES USED IN MAKING INDIGO. *Gentleman's Magazine*, XXV (1755), 259.

EXPLANATION

aa Two pumps in a frame worked by a pendulum, to pump water into the steeper *b*.
c   The beater.
d   A vat of lime-water.
e   A tub set to receive the muddy water from the beater.
f   A stage whereon to work the pumps.

N. B. All this, except for the pumps, is necessary for every 6 or 7 acres you plant.

CHURCH OF PRINCE GEORGE WINYAH, 1747. W. D. Morgan Collection, Georgetown County Library.

GENERAL MARION INVITING A BRITISH OFFICER TO SHARE HIS MEAL, by John Blake White. Courtesy of the Architect of the Capitol, Washington, D. C.

HENRY MOUZON'S MAP OF NORTH AND SOUTH CAROLINA, 1775. Courtesy of S. C. Archives.

JAMES GORDON'S ADVERTISEMENT FOR "HIS STORE IN GEORGE-TOWN." *South Carolina Gazette,* December 24, 1762.

MARKET HALL, BEFORE 1841. W. D. Morgan Collection, Georgetown County Library.

PRE-REVOLUTIONARY GEORGETOWN HOUSE. W. D. Morgan Collection, Georgetown County Library.

COURTHOUSE, 1824. Photograph by Ernest Ferguson Winnsboro, S. C.

THEODOSIA BURR (MRS. JOSEPH ALSTON), by John Vanderlyn. Gift of Oliver Burr Jennings, 1917, in memory
of Annie Burr Jennings, from Yale University Art Gallery.

JOHN KEITH, by Pierre Henri. Courtesy of Mrs. Huger Sinkler and Frick Art Reference Library.

EDWARD THOMAS HERIOT, by William H. Sca
borough. Courtesy of Mrs. Hattie Sparkman Wit
print courtesy Frick Art Reference Library.

THE REVEREND ALEXANDER GLENNIE by Charles Fraser. Courtesy of the Carolina Art Association, Gibbes Art Gallery.

WILLIAM ALGERNON ALSTON (1782–1860),
J. F. Vallee. Collection of Carolina Art Associatio
print courtesy Frick Art Reference Library.

FRANCIS KINLOCH HUGER, by Charles Fraser.
Courtesy of Metropolitan Museum of Art, Rogers Fund,
1938.

MRS. MARTHA PAWLEY LABRUCE, by Samuel F. B.
Morse. Courtesy of Mr. and Mrs. Cuthbert B. Prevost,
Georgetown, S. C.

JOSEPH BENJAMIN PYATT, by Thomas Sully. Courtesy of Mrs. James R. Parker, Georgetown, S. C.

CHARLOTTE PYATT TRAPIER, by Thomas Sully.
Courtesy of Mrs. James R. Parker, Georgetown, S. C.

PLAN OF HOPSEWEE PLANTATION: McCrady Plats, Roll #408, Case 364, Book 13, page 1.

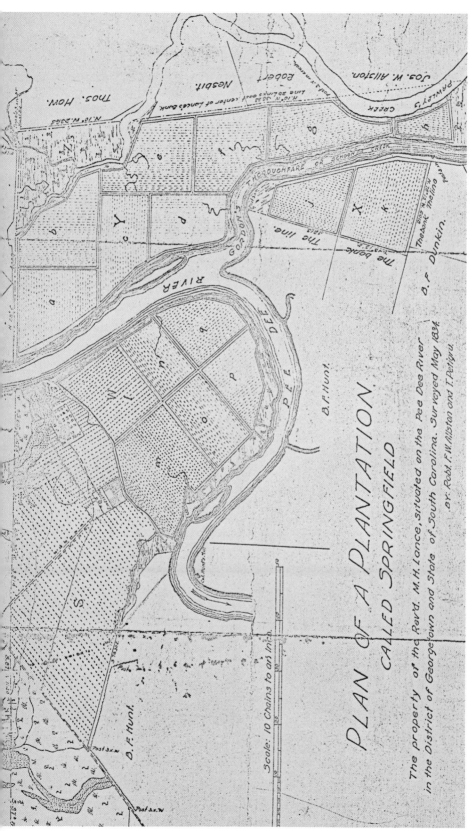

PLAN OF SPRINGFIELD PLANTATION. Courtesy of Dr. Richard N. Wrenn, Charlotte, N. C.

THE HOME OF THE JOSHUA JOHN WARD FAMILY
ON EAST BAY IN CHARLESTON (FORMERLY THE
FABER VILLA). Courtesy of Historic Charleston
Foundation.

JOSHUA JOHN WARD, by Charles Fraser. Courtesy
of Mrs. Robert L. Lumpkin, Georgetown, S. C.

ROBERT F. W. ALLSTON, by George Whiting Flagg.
Courtesy of Mr. William F. Allston of Miami, Florida.

THE HOME OF R. F. W. ALLSTON ON MEETING
STREET IN CHARLESTON. Courtesy of Historic
Charleston Foundation.

THE HOUSE AT DIRLETON PLANTATION. Courtesy of Mrs. Jesse C. Quattlebaum, Mount Pleasant, S. C.

THE HOUSE AT HOPSEWEE PLANTATION. Courtesy of Mrs. Jesse C. Quattlebaum, Mount Pleasant, S. C.

A SLAVE STREET. W. D. Morgan Collection, Georgetown County Library.

WOMEN FLAILING RICE. Courtesy of Belknap Press, Cambridge, Mass.

A ROOM AT FRIENDFIELD PLANTATION. W. D. Morgan Collection, Georgetown County Library.

CHURCH OF ALL SAINTS. Courtesy of Mrs. H. D. Bull, Georgetown, S. C.

MRS. R. F. W. ALLSTON, by George Whiting Flagg. Courtesy of Mr. William F. Allston of Miami, Florida.

WINYAH INDIGO SOCIETY HALL, 1857. W. D. Morgan Collection, Georgetown County Library.

UNITED STATES STEAMER *HARVEST MOON*. Official Records, Navy, XVI, facing page 282.

THE LYNAH C. KAMINSKI. Courtesy of Mr. and Mrs. Cuthbert B. Prevost.

ROBERT ANDERSON. Courtesy of South Caroliniana Library.

JOSEPH H. RAINEY. Courtesy of South Carolinian Library.

HEIMAN KAMINSKI. Courtesy of Mrs. Charlotte K. Prevost, Georgetown, S. C.

WILLIAM D. MORGAN. Courtesy of Georgetown Cit Hall.

PAWLEY'S ISLAND HOUSE. Courtesy of Mr. and Mrs. Cuthbert B. Prevost.

PAWLEY'S ISLAND RAILROAD; W. D. Morgan Collection, Georgetown County Library.

THE HOUSE AT ARCADIA PLANTATION. Courtesy
of Mrs. Jesse C. Quattlebaum, Mount Pleasant, S. C.

ATLANTIC COAST LUMBER COMPANY. Courtesy
of Katherine Fraser Overton.

INTERNATIONAL PAPER COMPANY. Courtesy of the International Paper Company.

planters. R. F. W. Allston wrote to his son Benjamin on June 3, 1858:
"The Doctor [Post] is very communicative and very insinuating and
deferential. You will find him and his wife both agreeable, but bear in
mind, he was raised in this city, is familiar with its street habits and is
the familiar and convenient friend and somewhat dependent on Charles
Alston, Mr. [Plowden] Weston and Mr. [John Izard] Middleton." [73] The
fact that Dr. Post was so tentatively accepted illustrates the exclusiveness
of this society. As three of the oldest and most prominent men on the
Neck were not members (John Hyrne Tucker, William Algernon Alston,
and Francis Marion Weston, all over sixty at the date of founding),
this must have been a club for somewhat younger men.

The history of the Episcopal church in All Saints Parish illustrates
how this society had grown richer, more tightly knit, and more exclusive
during the years that followed the Revolution.[74] In 1793 Captain Jack
Allston had had the first church taken down and a new one erected in
its place. Yet the parish was not reactivated until the Reverend Hugh
Fraser accepted a call in 1812. In 1813 this second church was fitted with
pews and on November 19, 1816, was consecrated by Bishop Theodore
Dehon. But the Reverend Hugh Fraser was not an energetic parson;
he was far more interested in becoming a great rice planter than a
saint in heaven. He had first served the parish of Prince Frederick, but
as early as 1806 he had been looking around for a more advantageous
post. On October 13, 1806, he had written from Black River to John
Hume, the North Santee planter, when he had heard that the vestry was
looking for a full-time minister yet was unable to bear the burden of a
full salary:

I am led to acquaint you & through your medium your respectable
neighbourhood—that could I be accomodated with lands either on lease
—or by reasonable personal purchase—(or in any other way the Vestry
& Wardens might see best to adopt)—sufficient to employ twenty five
or a greater number of field slaves—to advantage in the culture of rice—
I shou'd feel much pleasure in residing in your Neighbourhood at least
eight months in the year—say from Novr. to June—during which time
it wou'd be my pleasure & duty to discharge the function of my Office
at your Chh:

[73] Easterby, *op. cit.*, p. 141.
[74] Susan L. Allston, "All Saints', Waccamaw," Charleston *News and Courier*, Dec.
28, 1930; Bull, *op. cit.*, passim; Lachicotte, *op. cit.*, pp. 37–45.

Samuel Gaillard Stoney has commented on this letter: "After noting the graceful insinuation of his epistolary style, we are not surprised to find that he married thrice and always comfortably, and retired well before his death from his cure of souls to the care of his own fields." [75] It was therefore not until the beginning of 1832, with the pastorate of Alexander Glennie, that the truly great days of All Saints Parish began. The land had consistently taken its toll of the clergymen, but Glennie was made of sterner stuff.

Francis Marion Weston, who was the principal patron of the church, had brought Alexander Glennie over from England in 1828 as tutor for his son Plowden. When the Westons went abroad in 1831 for seven years, Glennie accepted a call to All Saints.[76] In 1838 after Mrs. Mary Huger, daughter of Captain John Allston, left $5,000 to the parish, the vestry decided to build a new brick church. The building committee was composed of F. M. Weston, Dr. E. T. Heriot, J. J. Ward, T. P. Alston, and J. H. Tucker. The new church was erected between December 1843 and October 1844 and was consecrated on April 8, 1845. This, the third church, was of colonial style, with massive columns in front and galleries on the side. Mrs. F. M. Weston gave the chancel chair and font, Plowden Weston the furniture, and Colonel Ward the organ. (The old church was re-erected on Tucker's Litchfield plantation as a Negro chapel.) The year of the consecration Colonel Peter W. Fraser, the earlier rector's son, gave a large lot on Pawley's Island for a summer rectory, where one was built in 1854 and is still in use.

Since this parish was thirty miles long, there grew up two chapels of ease. The lower church was built in 1817 on a site given by Joseph P. LaBruce on Oak Hill plantation. It had as its clergyman, first the Reverend Henry Gibbs, then Fraser, and finally Glennie. In 1855 another church was built eight miles north of the parish church on a spot near Wachesaw plantation given by the master of that plantation, Dr. Allard B. Flagg. This church, St. John the Evangelist, stood on a bluff overlooking the river and was for the benefit of the families who lived on Sandy Island. Each of the great plantations had a plantation chapel, the

[75] Samuel Gaillard Stoney, *Building a Church on the Santee, 1804–1807* (Charleston, S. C., 1945), p. 16.
[76] *Pee Dee Times*, Aug. 27, 1856.

most famous of these being the one at Hagley built and endowed by Plowden Weston. There was, therefore, a great revival of interest in the church, the chapels of ease, and the plantation chapels. These were to serve not only the masters but also the slaves.

The plantations along the Pee Dee starting at the district line and coming down to the point where the Pee Dee flows into the Black were:

Bates Hill	Arundel
Glenmore	Springfield
Holly Grove	Dirleton (formerly Richfield)
Hasty Point	Birdfield
Breakwater	Milton
Belle Rive (formerly Smurden)	Weymouth
Exchange (formerly Asylum)	Hickory Hill
Rose Bank (formerly Ditchfield)	Ingleside
Chicora Wood (formerly Matanzas)	Nightingale Hall
Enfield	Waterford
Guendalos	

And then, turning up the north side of the Black River, were White House, Keithfield, and Greenfield. The masters of these plantations were a second group of Georgetown District planters.[77]

John Hyrne Tucker at his death in 1859 owned Bates Hill, Glenmore, and Holly Grove. These plantations were known as the Pee Dee Settlement and were willed to Tucker's three youngest sons: John, Joe, and Daniel.[78]

Dr. Paul Weston (1784–1837) was the younger son of Plowden Weston, from whom he inherited in 1827 a town house in Hampstead and lands on the Wando River.[79] He purchased Asylum plantation in 1836.[80] While earning a medical degree from the University of Edinburgh,

[77] Mrs. Pringle gives a group portrait of these planters. Elizabeth W. Allston Pringle, *Chronicles of Chicora Wood* (Boston, Mass., 1940), pp. 156–158.

[78] Joseph received Bates Hill; John, Glenmore; and Daniel, Holly Grove. List of Pee Dee River plantations, in possession of Mrs. Charlotte K. Prevost, Georgetown, S. C.

[79] "Will of Plowden Weston," dated Sept. 18, 1819, proved Jan. 25, 1827, Charleston County Wills, XXXVII, Book A (1826–1834), 165–185, S. C. Archives.

[80] Weston Papers, S. C. Hist. Soc.

Scotland, which he received in 1803, he met his bride Antonia Bentley. As Antonia Bentley was the sister of Mrs. George Paddon Bond Hasell, she was the aunt of Mrs. Joshua John Ward.[81] Dr. Paul Weston's seven daughters bear names remarkably similar to the names of the seven daughters of Joshua John Ward. At the time of his death in 1837 two of his daughters were married. Joanna was the wife of her cousin Dr. Andrew Hasell; Penelope Bentley was the wife of Alexander Robertson, the Charleston rice factor. His only son Francis (1811–1890) inherited Asylum,[82] which he sold and bought Hasty Point and Breakwater, which in 1850 [83] yielded 600,000 pounds of rice from the work of 225 slaves. Francis Weston married in February 1833 Elizabeth Blyth Tucker, the eldest daughter of John Hyrne Tucker.[84] They had thirteen children.

Belle Rive was a plantation of the Read family, whose principal estates were at the mouth of the Sampit River across from Georgetown. John Harleston Read II, had changed the name of this plantation from Smurden to Belle Rive after having seen the lovely situation on Lake Geneva in Switzerland, where he had sent his sons to study.[85]

Davison McDowell (1783–1842) acquired Asylum plantation in 1819.[86] McDowell was an enterprising Irishman who put together many properties between his arrival in America in 1810 and his death in 1842.[87] His father James McDowell, who had come to Carolina in 1786, died

[81] Susan L. Allston, "Lives of Westons Sparkled with Adventure," newspaper clipping in possession of Mrs. Mildred Weston Lewis, Charleston, S. C. Mrs. Joanna Bentley, widow of Bentley Gordon Bentley, lived in Edinburgh from 1800 to 1815. R. Burnett, Superintendent of National Library of Scotland, to author, March 21, 1968.

[82] "Will of Paul Weston," dated March 31, 1837, proved April 7, 1837, Charleston County Wills, XLI, Book B (1834–1839), 601–603, S. C. Archives.

[83] Weston Papers, S. C. Hist. Soc. Mrs. Pringle was wrong in stating that Hasty Point was "named from Marion's hasty escape in a small boat from the British officers during the Revolution, and is a very beautiful point, overlooking the bold Thoroughfare and Peedee River." Patience Pennington [Elizabeth W. Allston Pringle], A Woman Rice Planter, ed. Cornelius O. Cathey (Cambridge, Mass., 1961), p. 53. The Gazette, of Sept. 6, 1760, had advertised Hasty Point plantation on the Pee Dee 16 miles from Georgetown for sale.

[84] Winyaw Intelligencer, Feb. 13, 1833.

[85] Lachicotte, op. cit., p. 141.

[86] Richards, op. cit., p. 39.

[87] Davison McDowell at Newry, Ireland, to his mother Mrs. Agnes Kirkpatrick at Stateburg, Aug. 18, 1810, D. McDowell Papers, SCL.

on the Pee Dee in 1787.[88] His mother arrived shortly after her husband's death without her son; she remained in Carolina and married Robert Kirkpatrick. Davison McDowell's two younger half-sisters married Robert O. Heriot and Benjamin Porter Fraser. Therefore, when Mc-Dowell arrived in Carolina for the first time, he was not friendless. He sold Asylum in 1836 to Dr. Paul Weston, who left it to his son Francis, who sold it in 1843 to R. F. W. Allston, who in turn sold it three years later to Cleland Kinloch Huger, who resold it in 1853 to R. F. W. Allston. Somewhere along the way this plantation was renamed Exchange plantation. Davison McDowell died on January 29, 1842, at Lucknow, "his residence" on the Pee Dee.[89]

Cleland Kinloch Huger (1818–1892) was the son of Colonel Francis Kinloch Huger. He married on January 18, 1842, Mary Dunkin (1825–1865), the daughter of Judge Dunkin of Midway plantation.[90] From 1846 to 1853 he planted at Exchange.[91] In 1850 he produced 180,000 pounds of rice with the help of sixty-four slaves.

McDowell sold the southern portion of Asylum plantation ("Ditch-field") to John Coachman (1769–1835).[92] John Coachman married five times.[93] By his second wife, Hannah Green, he had a son, John William Coachman (1807–1847). By his third wife, Mary Green, he had a daughter, Mary Jane Coachman, who married November 16, 1836, Donald L. McKay. By his fourth wife, Sarah Tyler, he had a son Benjamin Allston Coachman (born 1821). His fifth wife was Charlotte A. Allston, the sister of R. F. W. Allston. John W. Coachman married on March 15, 1838, Mary Helen Ford, the daughter of Stephen Ford. Benjamin A. Coachman married on December 13, 1843, Caroline Ford, another daughter of Stephen Ford. John W. Coachman resided on Black

[88] "Will of James McDowell," dated Jan. 9, 1787, proved Oct. 1, 1787, D. Mc-Dowell Papers, SCL.

[89] Richards, op. cit., passim; Lachicotte, op. cit., p. 126; Winyah Observer, Feb 2, 1842.

[90] Winyah Observer, March 30, 1842. On Feb. 7, 1867, he married Susan, a daughter of Col. T. P. Alston. SCHM, IV (1903), 114.

[91] He was elected a member of the Winyaw and All Saints Agricultural Society on Jan. 28, 1847, and resigned on April 28, 1859. Journal of Winyaw and All Saints Agricultural Society, S. C. Hist. Soc.

[92] Weston Papers, S. C. Hist. Soc.

[93] Coachman Genealogical Notes, S. C. Hist. Soc.

River until his death on June 19, 1847.[94] In 1850 Benjamin A. Coachman and Donald L. McKay produced 240,000 pounds of rice with forty slaves on Ditchfield, which R. F. W. Allston bought in 1851. Ditchfield was sometimes called Rose Bank.[95]

Matanzas had for many years been the property of Alexander Rose, Charleston merchant, when in 1806 Benjamin Allston, Jr., bought it. At his death in 1809 he left this plantation to his second son, Robert Francis Withers Allston (1801-1864). Mrs. Allston moved the younger children to Matanzas in 1819 so that she could tend it while young Robert was at West Point. Robert became responsible for the management of the plantation upon his mother's death in 1824 and assumed actual control in 1827. He became one of the most successful rice planters in the region, building up his own properties and those in the estate of his elder brother, Joseph Waties Allston. In 1846 he purchased Nightingale Hall from the estate of George Austin Moultrie and in 1847 Waterford, which extended from the Waccamaw to the Pee Dee. In 1850 he produced 840,000 pounds of rice with 401 slaves. During the next decade he added Exchange, Rose Bank, Guendalos, and Pipe Down on Sandy Island to his properties. He married in 1832 Adele Petigru (1810–1896), the sister of James L. Petigru of Charleston and of Captain Thomas Petigru of Sandy Island. His wife in 1853 changed the name of Matanzas to Chicora Wood. The house, built prior to 1819, still stands.[96]

The Reverend Hugh Fraser after the death of his first wife in 1797 had married first Mary Buford and then Frances Jane Buford. Colonel Peter William Fraser (1803–1849), the child of the second marriage, inherited his father's Pee Dee properties, Enfield and Guendalos. After his death on May 1, 1849, and his wife Mary Allston Fraser's death on October 1, 1849, these plantations passed to their only daughter, Jane Rose Fraser.[97] Her estate produced 480,000 pounds of rice in 1850. On July 1, 1852 she married Nathaniel Barnwell (1819–1857).[98] After his death on February 11, 1857,[99] Guendalos was sold to R. F. W. Allston.

[94] *Winyah Observer*, June 23, 1847; Register of Prince George Winyah Parish, 1813–1916, S. C. Hist. Soc.
[95] Allston paid $23,100 for Rose Bank. Easterby, *op. cit.*, pp. 21, 43.
[96] Lachicotte, *op. cit.*, pp. 99, 119–125; Easterby, *op. cit.*, pp. 19–23.
[97] *Winyah Observer*, May 9, Oct. 10, 1849.
[98] *Winyah Observer*, July 7, 1852.
[99] *Pee Dee Times*, Feb. 25, 1857.

Dr. William Allston (1772–1848) bought Arundel from John Julius Pringle in 1806.[100] In 1841 he sold it to Frederick Shaffer, one of the very few Northern men to acquire a Georgetown rice plantation. Shaffer designed for his plantation Gothic type buildings which still stand. In 1850 he grew 270,000 pounds of rice with the labor of ninety-seven slaves. After Shaffer's death in 1859, Charles Alston, Sr., bought this plantation for his son Charles Pringle Alston.[101]

It is not known who planted at Springfield in 1850. In the 1830's it had been in the possession of the Reverend Maurice Harvey Lance.[102]

Richfield belonged to Benjamin Faneuil Hunt (1792–1854), a Bostonian who had come south as a tutor and who had remained to become a leading lawyer of the state.[103] He purchased Richfield from Charles Brown; in 1850 he produced 600,000 pounds of rice with 234 slaves. Hunt sold Richfield to Dr. E. T. Heriot in 1854.[104] Dr. Heriot willed this plantation the same year to his daughter Mary, who had married in 1845 Dr. James R. Sparkman (1815–1897).[105] Dr. Sparkman, who was listed in 1850 with 190,000 pounds of rice and eighty-seven slaves, was already planting at Birdfield.[106]

Ralph Stead Izard, Jr. (1815–1858), was a scion of one of South Carolina's oldest rice-planting families, whose principal estates had been on the upper reaches of the Ashley River. His branch of the family, however, had been possessors of Milton, Weymouth, and Hickory Hill on

100 Lachicotte, op. cit., p. 111. Dr. William Allston had married in 1800 Mary Pyatt, daughter of the late John Pyatt. Marriage Settlements, III, 429–434, S. C. Archives. He died on Feb. 6, 1848, having stopped his medical practice twenty years before. Winyah Observer, Feb. 9, 1848.

101 Lachicotte, op. cit., pp. 109–111; "Will of Frederick Shaffer," dated June 13, 1859, proved June 17, 1859, Charleston County Wills, XLVIII (1856–1862), 473–474, S. C. Archives.

102 In 1834 it belonged to Lance, according to "Plan of a Plantation called Springfield," in the possession of Dr. Richard N. Wrenn, Charlotte, N. C. According to a note this is a copy of a plat recorded in Georgetown in 1853 when an exchange of property between R. O. Anderson and Charles Alston may have been made. The Rev. M. H. Lance wrote to R. F. W. Allston, Feb. 13, 1837, from Springfield. Allston Papers, S. C. Hist Soc.

103 John Belton O'Neall, Biographical Sketches of the Bench and Bar of South Carolina (Charleston, S. C., 1859), II, 436–440.

104 There was a rice mill on Richfield. Winyah Observer, Dec. 3, 1845; Pee Dee Times, Feb. 8, 1854. Hunt died in New York. Pee Dee Times, Dec. 13, 1854.

105 The wedding took place on Sandy Island. Winyah Observer, April 26, 1845.

106 E. P. Guerard wrote from Ramsay Grove, Feb. 23, 1857, to Dr. Sparkman, at Birdfield, Pee Dee, Sparkman Papers, 2791, SHC.

the Pee Dee for several generations before he inherited them in 1816 from his father. His maternal grandfather, Benjamin Stead, had made a fortune in the Charleston trade by 1759 when he retired to England. One of Benjamin Stead's daughters had married Ralph Izard, Jr., and the other had become the second wife of General Charles Cotesworth Pinckney. In 1839 Ralph Stead Izard, Jr., married his cousin Rosetta Ella Pinckney, a daughter of Colonel Thomas Pinckney, Jr., of the South Santee. His three plantations produced 844,000 pounds of rice from the tasks of 187 slaves.[107]

William Heyward Trapier (1805–1872) planted at Ingleside. He had married Charlotte Pyatt on December 31, 1846, at a wedding described by R. F. W. Allston as a "country fete." [108] Charlotte Pyatt had owned Waterford,[109] but that plantation was sold to R. F. W. Allston in 1847. In 1850 Trapier's lands yielded 510,000 pounds of rice from the work of 118 slaves.

Robert M. Collins (1813–1856) produced 240,000 pounds of rice on the Pee Dee in 1850, but the name of his plantation is unknown. The cash value of his farm was recorded at $1,600, which seems remarkably low and may be an error, although he owned only nineteen slaves. He married in 1837 Mary Jane Grier, the daughter of Samuel Grier, and died at the age of forty-three on January 29, 1856.[110]

John Julius Pringle I, who had acquired plantations on the Black River, left White House and Greenfield to his son John Julius Pringle II, who married in 1806 Mary Izard, the daughter of Senator Ralph Izard. In 1850 the widow of John Julius Pringle II, who had married Joel Roberts Poinsett in 1833, was living at White House, which plantation was worked by 103 slaves and yielded 300,000 pounds of rice. Her son John Julius Izard Pringle (1808–1864), who had married Jane Lynch of New York prior to 1842, lived at Greenfield, which produced 150,000 pounds of rice and had sixty-two slaves.[111]

[107] "Izard of South Carolina," *SCHM*, II (1901), 239–240.
[108] R. F. W. Allston to Mrs. Allston, Dec. 13, 1846, Allston Papers, S. C. Hist. Soc.
[109] Marriage Settlements, XVI, 371–377, S. C. Archives.
[110] *Georgetown Union*, Nov. 4, 1837; *Pee Dee Times,* Feb. 6, 1856; Bond of R. M. Collins, April 7, 1856, Richard Dozier Papers, SHC.
[111] Lachicotte, *op. cit.,* pp. 89–93; Mary Pringle Fenhagen, "Descendants of Judge Robert Pringle," *SCHM*, LXII (1961), 156, 221–222.

Keithfield, which had been the home of John Keith, was the principal plantation in the estate of Richard O. Anderson, whose lands accounted for 1,170,000 pounds of rice and supported 384 slaves. In 1853 Keithfield was bought by James Heyward Trapier.[112]

The planters along the Pee Dee had their homes on the west bank of the river. They were, therefore, not very far from the planters who resided on the north side of Black River, since all of their plantations lay within the fork of the two rivers. As the society in this fork became more stable, interrelated, and wealthier, there arose a demand for a neighborhood church. Prince Frederick Church was the oldest church in the neighborhood with a long service to those who lived along Black River. The Reverend Hugh Fraser had served this church from 1793 to 1810, but after the latter date the church had been without a rector. Many of the people on the stretch of Black River near the church had moved away, and the wooden church at the original site fell into ruin with only the graveyard as a reminder of its former prominence. The planters of the Pee Dee and the lower reaches of the Black River, therefore, decided to take over its name and to build a new church nearer their plantations. In 1827 Dr. William Allston, Davison McDowell, and R. O. Anderson met with Hugh Fraser to plan a new church. But not until after Hugh Fraser gave some land near Guendalos and a building committee consisting of Davison McDowell, R. F. W. Allston, and Francis Weston had been appointed in 1835 was a chapel built. Hugh Fraser served as minister until his death in December 1838. In 1848 a summer parsonage in Plantersville was given by Dr. James R. Sparkman. On November 17, 1859, after the vestry decided to build a more permanent structure out of brick, a cornerstone was laid at which ceremony R. F. W. Allston delivered the address. The building, designed in gothic style, was covered, but not finished, when the war began. The Reverend John Hunter, who came in November 1847, was responsible for building up the congregation and providing a mission to the slaves. Mrs. Ralph Stead Izard gave the paten; Mrs. John Harleston Read the silver cup;

---

[112] Lachicotte, *op. cit.*, pp. 94–96. Mrs. Charlotte K. [Keith?] Anderson, wife of R. O. Anderson, died at North Island on Oct. 19, 1826, at the age of eighteen. *SCHM*, XXXI (1930), 201.

and Mr. and Mrs. Joel Roberts Poinsett the silver alms plate and the Bible.[113]

There were a number of plantations along the north and south banks of the Black River above Pringle's ferry, but the relation of one to the other is difficult to place. Among these plantations were: [114]

Eastland	Vauxhall
Dunbar	Ramsay Grove
Oatland	Harmony Grove
Rural Hall	Waterford
Lark Hill	Campfield
Springwood	Inland
Millgrove	Peru
Poplar Hill	Rice Hope
Moss Dale	

The Greens were among the earliest settlers on the Black River. The 1734 parish line followed Green Creek, which flowed into Black River from the south side. John Green wrote to R. F. W. Allston from Vauxhall on January 7, 1837.[115] John J. Green advertised his steam rice mill opposite Georgetown for sale in the *Georgetown Union,* June 16, 1838, and stated that he was returning to the country. The issue of November 17, 1838, stated that he was on Black River. In 1850 J. J. Green on a farm worth $3,700 produced 154,000 pounds of rice with the aid of thirty-five slaves. Francis Green with forty-nine slaves produced 120,000 pounds of rice.

The Fords, another family long settled on the south side of Black River, planted at Rice Hope, Waterford, Peru, and Inland plantations. Stephen Ford (1748–1790) was the progenitor of the family. By his

---

[113] Lachicotte, *op. cit.,* pp. 114–118; "Church to Mark 200th Birthday," *Charleston News and Courier,* April 2, 1934; Albert S. Thomas, *A Historical Account of the Protestant Episcopal Church in South Carolina, 1820–1957* (Columbia, S. C., 1957), pp. 396–401.

[114] This list has been put together with difficulty from a list in possession of Mrs. Charlotte K. Prevost, Georgetown, S. C., and from the names of plantations mentioned in Rev. W. R. Pritchett, *There Is a River (Black River)* (n.p., n.d), copy in possession of Miss Wylma Wates, Columbia, S. C. Lark Hill was the residence of George W. Heriot before his death in 1846. *Winyah Observer,* Jan. 7, 1846. According to a contract made by E. P. Coachman with freedmen in 1865, he was planting at Oatland. RG 105, Box 525, National Archives.

[115] Allston Papers, S. C. Hist. Soc.

first marriage he had a son George Ford (1776–1821). George Ford was the father of Stephen Charles Ford (1803–1855), John Potts Ford (1812–1856), and James Rees Ford (1815–1889). Stephen Charles Ford, who may have been at Inland, had a crop of 150,000 pounds of rice from the hands of fifty-four slaves in 1850. John Potts Ford, who married Elizabeth Ann Vaux of Sandy Island on January 23, 1834, and who planted at Rice Hope, had 180,000 pounds of rice from ninety-eight hands. James Rees Ford, who married Martha Elizabeth Henning on January 31, 1839, and who planted at Waterford, had 132,000 pounds from fifty-four slaves.[116]

Stephen Ford (1786–1852), the younger brother of George Ford, raised 420,000 pounds of rice in 1850 with 140 slaves. Joseph Wragg Ford, a son of his second marriage, raised 108,000 pounds of rice with sixteen slaves. Either the father or the son was planting at Peru plantation.[117]

William E. Sparkman (1813–1846) planted at Springwood on the Black River.[118] He married Mary Ann Elizabeth Burgess on December 26, 1838, and died on February 1, 1846.[119] His estate yielded 300,000 pounds of rice from the labor of 101 slaves in 1850. William E. Sparkman, Jr., (1842–1891) married in 1867 Martha Emma Heriot, the younger sister of Mrs. James R. Sparkman.[120]

Sextus Tertius Gaillard planted at Campfield [121] and at Ramsay Grove. At Campfield there was a rice mill.[122] The two plantations produced 320,000 pounds of rice in 1850 from the labor of sixty-nine slaves. Gaillard had married Sarah B. Doughty in 1832 but had no children.[123] On

[116] Ford Family Notes in possession of Mrs. F. W. Ford, Georgetown, S. C.; Register of Prince George Winyah Parish, 1813–1916, S. C. Hist. Soc. Dr. Robert Withers Vaux lived at Rice Hope for a while. *Winyah Observer*, Dec. 6, 1845.

[117] According to a contract made with freedmen, J. W. Ford was planting at Peru in 1865. RG 105, Box 525, National Archives.

[118] Estate of W. E. Sparkman of Springwood, Black River, April 1846, Sparkman Papers, 2791, SHC.

[119] *Georgetown Union,* Jan. 5, 1839; *Winyah Observer,* Feb. 4, 1846.

[120] Woodruff, *op. cit.,* p. 175.

[121] Gaillard wrote R. F. W. Allston from Campfield in 1860, Allston Papers, S. C. Hist. Soc.

[122] Amount of rice pounded at Campfield mill each year to 1845, Sparkman Papers, 2791, Vol. 1, SHC.

[123] Marriage settlement dated June 19, 1832, in possession of Mrs. F. A. Witte, Columbia, S. C.

April 3, 1855 his niece Theodora Gaillard married Edward P. Guerard, and they made their home at Ramsay Grove thereafter.[124] Gaillard died in 1882.[125]

John Exum (1780–1859) planted at Millgrove.[126] In 1850 with the help of eighty-seven slaves he grew 300,000 pounds of rice. His only child Elizabeth Jane Exum married on July 2, 1846, Richard Dozier, a descendant of Anthony White who had been one of the first settlers on Black Mingo Creek.[127]

John R. Easterling produced 150,000 pounds of rice with sixty-five slaves on the Black River. He died on February 7, 1874, at the age of seventy-seven.[128]

William G. Linerieux (1784–1852) produced 120,000 pounds of rice with forty-eight slaves on Black River. He had run Benjamin F. Hunt's Richfield Mill in 1844.[129] He died on December 9, 1852 at the age of sixty-eight.[130]

Christopher J. Atkinson produced 180,000 pounds of rice with seventy slaves at Rural Hall.[131] He had married on October 6, 1831, but at his wife's death in 1858 there were no children.[132]

The plantations along the Black River from Pringle's ferry to Georgetown were:

Beneventum	Rosemont
Mansfield	Richmond
Wedgefield	Willow Bank
Windsor	Greenwich
Weehaw	Waties Point
Kensington	

---

[124] *Pee Dee Times,* April 11, 1855.

[125] "Will of S. T. Gaillard," proved Nov. 17, 1882, in possession of Mrs. F. A. Witte, Columbia, S. C.

[126] "Will of John Exum," dated Jan. 21, 1851, proved Oct. 20, 1859, Richard Dozier Papers, SHC; Mrs. Paul H. Leonard to author, Feb. 22, 1965.

[127] *Winyah Observer,* July 8, 1846. Richard Dozier owned Moss Dale and Poplar Hill according to contracts made with freedmen in 1865. RG 105, Box 525, National Archives.

[128] Tombstone inscription, Methodist churchyard, Georgetown, S. C.

[129] *Winyah Observer,* Dec. 4, 1844.

[130] *Winyah Observer,* Dec. 22, 1852.

[131] *For Love of a Rebel* (Charleston, S. C., 1964), pp. 138–139.

[132] *Pee Dee Times,* April 28, 1858. His wife died in 1858 at the age of seventy-one and was buried in the Methodist churchyard, Georgetown, S. C.

Beneventum had belonged to Christopher Gadsden until his death in 1805. Shortly thereafter it had been sold to John Julius Pringle I.[133] This may have been the plantation which Robert Pringle (1793–1860),[134] a son of John Julius Pringle I, planted in 1850, for he did harvest in that year 420,000 pounds of rice with the assistance of 142 slaves and it is known from the local newspapers that he was planting on Black River. Since Beneventum was opposite the other Pringle plantations, the Pringle ferry would have plied between one Pringle property and another.

Mansfield was named after Dr. John Man, who died in 1754.[135] His widow, Mrs. Susannah Man, brought up two daughters, one of whom married the tory James Cassells and the other the patriot Archibald Taylor. The estate of Dr. Man escaped confiscation and passed eventually to the children of Mary and Archibald Taylor. Their son John Man Taylor (1786–1823) resided at Mansfield until his death when the plantation passed to his sister, Anna Maria Taylor (1787–1851), who had married in 1816 the Reverend Maurice Harvey Lance (1792–1870), rector of Prince George.[136] The Reverend M. H. Lance, the son of Lambert Lance, came of a Charleston mercantile family and, in the manner of the Reverend Hugh Fraser, established a Georgetown dynasty.

The Lances had two daughters: Mary and Esther. Mary Lance (1818–1885) married in 1835 Dr. Francis S. Parker (1814–1865), a member of a well-known rice-planting family of Goose Creek, who bought Wedgefield in 1840 from the Wragg family. Dr. Parker traded Wedgefield to his father-in-law for Mansfield. He shortly thereafter acquired Greenwich. In 1850 Dr. Parker with 121 slaves grew a crop of 375,000 pounds of rice. By 1854 he had added Willowbank to his holdings.[137] The Reverend M. H. Lance in 1850 was himself planting at Wedgefield and at

---

[133] Lachicotte, op. cit., pp. 85–88.
[134] SCHM, LXII (1961), 153. Robert Pringle's plantation on Black River is mentioned in Pee Dee Times, Sept. 17, 1856.
[135] Lachicotte, op. cit., pp. 78–84.
[136] Marriage Settlements, VII, 123–126, S. C. Archives. Anna Maria Taylor had married first Josias Allston in 1804. Marriage Settlements, IV, 192–198, S. C. Archives; SCHM, XXXI (1930), 304.
[137] Plantation Records of Dr. F. S. Parker, 1846–1862, SCL; Lachicotte, op. cit., p. 75; May and Faunt, op. cit., pp. 191–192; "Will of Maurice H. Lance," dated July 23, 1868, proved Nov. 29, 1870, Judge of Probate, Georgetown County, Will Book A (1865–1912), pp. 59–62, WPA typescript, S. C. Archives.

Maurisina on the Sampit. His 262 slaves grew 660,000 pounds of rice. Esther Jane Lance (1822–1877) married John Harleston Read II of Belle Rive in 1840.

Windsor since 1762 had been the Trapier home. Paul Trapier (1716–1793), the first master of Windsor, had a son Paul Trapier (1749–1778), who had married Elizabeth Foissin in 1771.[138] There were four children of this marriage: Magdalene Elizabeth (who married John Keith in 1793),[139] Paul (who married Sarah Alicia Shubrick whose father Captain Thomas Shubrick had owned Greenfield),[140] Benjamin Foissin (who married in 1802 Hannah Shubrick Heyward),[141] and William Windham (who remained a bachelor). Paul Trapier (1806–1872) and Richard Shubrick Trapier, the sons of Paul and Sarah Trapier, did not reside in Georgetown District after they became clergymen in the Episcopal church. Benjamin Foissin Trapier (1774–1838) and Hannah Heyward (1783–1867) had at least eight children. William Heyward Trapier of Ingleside on the Pee Dee was the eldest son. Paul Horry Trapier was the second son. Benjamin Foissin Trapier, the third son, married in 1853 Julia E. Horry and thereby acquired North Santee lands at Mill Dam and Newland.[142] James Heyward Trapier (1814–1865), the fourth son, married on November 4, 1851, Elizabeth Heyward and bought Keithfield in 1853.[143] The estate of Benjamin Foissin Trapier (who had died in 1838) produced in 1850 540,000 pounds of rice by the labor of 207 slaves.[144]

Weehaw and Kensington were Kinloch plantations. Cleland Kinloch (died 1823), who had inherited them from his father, almost lost them during the confiscation of 1782. Cleland had only one child, a daughter Harriott. On January 20, 1819, she married at Kensington Henry Augus-

---

[138] Trapier Family Notes, S. C. Hist. Soc.; Lachicotte, op. cit., pp. 71–74. Elizabeth Trapier (1745–1817) married on Sept. 17, 1778, Edward Martin, sheriff of Georgetown District. They lived at Belvoir on the Waccamaw, which later passed to Edward Martin's brother John Martin. After John Martin's death in 1790, the plantation was sold. Belvoir was renamed Friendfield. John Martin Papers, S. C. Hist. Soc.; SCHM, XIV (1913), 66.

[139] Marriage Settlements, II, 113–116, S. C. Archives.

[140] Lachicotte, op. cit., p. 89.

[141] Marriage Settlements, IV, 278–281, S. C. Archives.

[142] Marriage Settlements, XVIII, 117–122, S. C. Archives.

[143] Lachicotte, op. cit., p. 94.

[144] He died at the age of sixty-five. Georgetown Union, Nov. 17, 1838.

tus Middleton (1793–1887), whose grandfather was Henry Middleton, president of the Continental Congress, and whose uncle was Arthur, the signer of the Declaration of Independence. He was, therefore, first-cousin-once-removed of John Izard Middleton, master of Bannockburn. In 1850 Weehaw and Kensington yielded 900,000 pounds of rice from the labor of 302 slaves. Since Henry A. Middleton also owned estates elsewhere in the state, he was one of the truly rich men of the district.[145]

Joseph Benjamin Pyatt produced 570,000 pounds of rice with 291 slaves at Rosemont in 1850. He, the younger son of Mrs. Martha Allston Pyatt of Oatland and Turkey Hill on the Waccamaw, married Colonel Ward's second daughter Joanna on April 18, 1850, at the upper church, Waccamaw.[146] John Francis Pyatt, the eldest son, produced 960,000 pounds of rice with 477 slaves in 1850 at Richmond. He married on December 8, 1857, Harriett Nowell, the daughter of a Charleston rice-mill owner.[147]

Waties Point, a plantation in the fork of the Black and the Sampit, was originally owned by Dr. Joseph Blyth; in 1840 it had been willed to R. F. W. Allston by his aunt Mrs. Blyth. Allston sold it for $9,000 in 1854 to David Risley, a lumber man from Philadelphia. Apparently, it had not been actively planted for some time prior to the sale to Risley, who intended to use it as a lumber yard.[148]

Another group of plantations was strung along the banks of the Sampit River and then down around the southern shore of Winyah Bay. They were as follows: [149]

Wedgefield	Mount Pleasant
Maurisina	Canaan
Friendfield	Midway
Northampton	Serenity

[145] *SCHM*, I (1900), 258.
[146] Family Bible of Joseph B. Pyatt, in possession of Mrs. Sarah P. Lumpkin, Georgetown, S. C. There was a magnificent garden at Rosemont with terraces of mimosas, sweet olives, jasmines, quince, gardenias, roses, oleanders. Lockwood, *op. cit.*, II, 228–229.
[147] Harriett Nowell Pyatt to ———, Jan. 18, 1864, Miscellaneous Manuscripts, S. C. Hist. Soc. This letter describes a trip from Charleston to Georgetown via Kingstree during the war.
[148] Easterby, *op. cit.*, pp. 21, 24, 118.
[149] List in possession of Mrs. Charlotte K. Prevost, Georgetown, S. C. Map printed in *SCHM*, XIII (1912), facing p. 1.

Hampstead   Maryville
Myrtle Grove   Belle Isle
Westfield   Mount Hope
Harmony   Prospect Hill
Bonnyneck   Dover
Silver Hill   Retreat
Oakley   Oakton
Lucerne   Estherville
Upton

The Sampit rice region was almost entirely the domain of the Withers family. James Withers, a Charleston bricklayer, had received a grant of 120 acres on Georgetown River on December 16, 1736. At his death in 1756 he left four sons: John, Richard, William, and Francis.[150] Between 1764 and 1770 the four sons and their mother received grants to 5,900 acres in the Georgetown region. The common practice of naming sons after uncles so complicated the Withers family picture that it is almost impossible to disentangle the family lines. Captain James Withers, who had fought with Marion, was successful as a planter and sent his son Francis to Harvard. Francis Withers (1769–1847), who inherited his father's properties, built the famous Withers home at Friendfield, on the north bank of the Sampit. Francis married twice but had no children by either marriage.[151] His nearest blood relation at the time of his death were members of the Wilkinson and Read families. His niece Eleanora had married Dr. Willis Wilkinson in 1806.[152] Another niece, Mary, had married in 1811 John Harleston Read I.[153] He had once possessed seven plantations but shortly before his death he sold Springfield on the Waccamaw to Colonel Ward, probably to round out his own properties and to help Colonel Ward round out his. He left his stock of wines at Springfield to his good neighbors, Dr. E. T. Heriot and Dr. A. B. Flagg. He left his widow the use of Friendfield, Mount Pleasant, Midway, and Canaan during her lifetime and then to his step-daughter, the daughter of his second wife. Elizabeth Hunt Warham married in

[150] "Will of James Withers," dated Feb. 17, 1756, proved July 9, 1756, Charleston County Wills, VII (1752–1756), 537–539, S. C. Archives.
[151] Lachicotte, op. cit., pp. 135–138.
[152] Marriage Settlements, V, 286–291, S. C. Archives.
[153] Marriage Settlements, VI, 57–61, S. C. Archives.

1845 Dr. Alexius Mador Forster (1815–1879).[154] To his grandnephews, John Harleston Read II and James Withers Read, he willed his Harmony plantation, and to his friend Dr. E. T. Heriot his Northampton plantation, both on the Sampit River. The will of Francis Withers does not mention Westfield, Bonnyneck, and Silver Hill, but these had been his plantations and may have been incorporated as part of the above plantations.[155] In 1850 the estates of Francis Withers yielded 720,000 pounds of rice from the work of 472 slaves.

The other planters on the Sampit were the Reverend M. H. Lance at Wedgefield and Maurisina, the Pyatts at Serenity, Hampstead, and Myrtle Grove,[156] and John Harleston Read I at Maryville. Read was of a Charleston patriot family. His grandfather had established the family fortunes with a ropewalk in Charleston. His father was Dr. William Read of General Greene's medical staff.[157] John Harleston Read I (1788–1859) married Mary Withers, the niece of Francis Withers in 1811, thereby inheriting Maryville at the mouth of the Sampit. Shortly thereafter he built a home which still stands. He married a second time in 1822 Emily Ann Huger, the adopted daughter of Major Benjamin Huger. John Harleston Read I purchased the neighboring plantations of Oakley, Lucerne, and Upton. John Harleston Read II (1815–1866) (who lived at Belle Rive on the Pee Dee and must have been managing his father's estates as well) produced 960,000 pounds of rice in 1850 with the help of 323 slaves.[158]

There were three plantations spread along the south shore of Winyah Bay that had a similar story. Belle Isle, Prospect Hill, and Dover were originally carved out of Landgrave Thomas Smith's barony. Elias Horry (1707–1783) had bought part of these lands in the 1750's. His nephew General Peter Horry, the Revolutionary hero, planted them after the war until his death in Columbia on February 28, 1815. General Horry

[154] May and Faunt, op. cit., p. 146.

[155] "Will of Francis Withers," dated Nov. 24, 1841, proved Nov. 25, 1847, Charleston County Wills, XLIV (1845–1851), 268–284, S. C. Archives; James Henry Rice, "Francis Withers," The State, Sept. 21, 1924; Winyah Observer, Dec. 1, 1847.

[156] Winyah Observer, Sept. 23, 1846; J. B. Pyatt's contracts of 1865, RG 105, Box 525, National Archives.

[157] George C. Rogers, Jr., Evolution of a Federalist, William Loughton Smith of Charleston (1758–1812) (Columbia, S. C., 1962), p. 404; SCHM, XXV (1924), 17–18.

[158] Lachicotte, op. cit., pp. 139–142; Charleston Courier, Sept. 3, 1866.

in 1801 began to call a part of Dover Belle Isle after Marion's birth-place. Leaving no children, he left Prospect Hill to his niece, Sarah Hall Horry Bay, and Belle Isle to his widow (Margaret Guignard of Colum-bia) and then to his niece. His niece married William Mayrant, Jr. (1792–1840). Their son, William Horry Mayrant (1821–1866), planted these plantations in 1850, which yielded 360,000 pounds of rice from the labor of 121 slaves. He acquired Retreat and Oakton, most proba-bly other segments of the original barony. Mount Hope was also a May-rant property.[159]

Estherville had been named after Esther Allston, who married Archi-bald Johnston in 1745. It was Archibald's great-grandson, Francis Withers Johnston, who planted at Estherville in 1850. He had ninety slaves who helped him harvest 300,000 pounds of rice.[160]

The planters along the Waccamaw, the Pee Dee, the Black, the Sam-pit, and Winyah Bay formed in November 1839 the Planters Club on the Pee Dee. The club lasted until the war. By 1844 a clubhouse had been built on land given by Colonel P. W. Fraser at the edge of his own Guendalos plantation. The meals were the center of interest at these convivial meetings. On one occasion ham, wild turkeys, venison, mutton, clams, oysters, shrimp, rice, brandy, madeira, and champagne were served. And the last entry in the club's records was on April 12, 1861, for two dozen plates, two dozen tumblers, and two dozen wine glasses. The original members of 1839 were the great planters of that era.[161]

> John Hays Allston, Pee Dee [162]
> R. F. W. Allston, Pee Dee
> Dr. William Allston, Pee Dee
> John Ashe Alston, Pee Dee
> Colonel Joseph Alston, Waccamaw
> Richard O. Anderson, Black River
> Colonel T. P. Alston, Waccamaw

[159] Lachicotte, *op. cit.*, pp. 143–154; "The Mayrant Family," compiled by Mabel L. Webber, *SCHM*, XXVII (1926), 88–89.

[160] Lachicotte, *op. cit.*, pp. 155–158.

[161] Records of Planters Club on Pee Dee, Sparkman Papers, 2732, Vol. 1, SHC.

[162] According to the *Winyah Observer*, Dec. 3, 1842, John Hays Allston resided at Breakwater. He was a son of Peter Allston of North Carolina, a native of Darling-ton District, a resident in Georgetown District for 36 years, and died at the age of sixty. *Winyah Observer*, Sept. 19, 1849.

John E. Allston, Pee Dee [163]

Colonel Allard H. Belin, Sandy Island

Colonel Thomas G. Carr, Georgetown [164]

John W. Coachman, Georgetown

Solomon Cohen, removed from Georgetown [165]

B. F. Dunkin, Waccamaw

A. W. Dozier, Georgetown (removed)

G. T. Ford, Black River [166]

Jas. R. Ford, Black River

John P. Ford, Black River

S. C. Ford, Black River

Colonel P. W. Fraser, Pee Dee

Hugh Fraser, Pee Dee

Dr. S. S. Gasque, Georgetown (deceased) [167]

E. T. Heriot, Sandy Island

B. F. Hunt, Pee Dee

Ralph S. Izard, Pee Dee

Major John A. Keith, Georgetown [168]

Dr. John D. Magill, Waccamaw

D. L. McKay, Georgetown

D. McDowell, Pee Dee (deceased)

Robert Nesbit, Waccamaw

John Izard Pringle, Pee Dee

[163] John E. Allston, aged thirty-six, died in Colleton County. *Pee Dee Times*, Feb. 13, 1856.

[164] Col. Thomas G. Carr was the son of Gen. Thomas Carr, who had died in 1827. *Winyaw Intelligencer*, July 11, 1827. Col. Carr died in Mexico at the age of thirty-six. *Winyah Observer*, Dec. 15, 1847. The Carrs were descended from the Pawleys. Pawley Family Chart in possession of Mrs. Charlotte K. Prevost, Georgetown, S. C.

[165] Solomon Cohen had been a leading Nullifier.

[166] George Thomas Ford, another son of Dr. George Ford, had married Mary Warham Toomer in April 1827. *Winyah Intelligencer*, April 28, 1827.

[167] Dr. Shadrack S. Gasque married Esther C. Rothmahler on March 4, 1824. Register of Prince George Winyah Parish, 1813–1916, S. C. Hist. Soc. Dr. Gasque made a survey of public health needs in Georgetown in 1832. *Winyaw Intelligencer*, July 21, 1832.

[168] A letter from Solomon Cohen, Jr., J. A. Keith, J. J. Ward, S. S. Gasque, and J. Smith had argued against the postponement of the assertion of state sovereignty. *Winyaw Intelligencer*, Aug. 25, 1832. John Alexander Keith married Sarah Brown on April 23, 1828. Register of Prince George Winyah Parish, 1813–1916, S. C. Hist. Soc.

Dr. F. S. Parker, Black River
Captain Thomas Petigru, Georgetown
J. R. Poinsett, Black River
Colonel J. H. Read, Jr., Sampit
W. E. Sparkman, Pee Dee
Dr. J. R. Sparkman, Pee Dee
John H. Tucker, Waccamaw
Major W. H. Trapier, Black River
W. Percival Vaux, Sandy Island
Dr. John Wragg, Black River [169]
Colonel J. J. Ward, Waccamaw
F. M. Weston, Waccamaw
P. C. J. Weston, Waccamaw
Dr. P. Weston, Pee Dee (deceased)
Francis Weston, Pee Dee

No new members were elected until 1854. Those admitted between 1854 and 1861 were mainly the sons or sons-in-law of members.

The planters of the North Santee were more closely linked to Charleston than their neighbors to the north of them around Winyah Bay. Along the Waccamaw and the Pee Dee the lands of each plantation were divided by the river, with the plantation home on the Waccamaw always on the high land to the east side of the river and on the Pee Dee on the high land to the west side. On the Santee River there were plantations lining both sides of the river, and, to make boundaries of plantations more difficult to discern, a series of islands lay between the North and the South Santee forming a delta in which were often located separate plantations. The delta plantations never contained a plantation house; they were usually working plantations of planters whose homes were on either the North or South Santee. Since Georgetown District extended to the South Santee, some of the planters whose homes lined the banks of the South Santee and were actually residents of the parish

[169] Dr. John Ashby Wragg, son of Samuel Wragg (1770–1844) married Caroline McDowell. Henry A. M. Smith, "Wragg of South Carolina," *SCHM*, XIX (1918), chart facing p. 121. Dr. Wragg must have resided at Wedgefield which the Wraggs sold to Dr. F. S. Parker in 1840. Lachicotte, *op. cit.*, p. 75.

of St. James Santee were listed in the census of 1850 as growing rice in Georgetown District. The following list gives the names of the plantations along the North Santee from east to west: [170]

Ford's Point	Pleasant Meadow
Cat Island	Richfield
Belle Island	Mill Dam
White Marsh	Camp Main
Hume's Cat Island	Newland
Daisy Bank	Woodside
Green Meadow	Rice Hope
Tidyman's	White Oak
Hopewell	Fawn Hill
Hope Land	LaGrange
Annandale	Hopsewee
The Marsh	Orkland
Pine Grove	Crow Hill
Wicklow Hall (The Strip)	The Oaks
Lynch Field	Commander's

The following is a list of the plantations south of those mentioned above, being the ones that were on the islands in the delta:

Crow Island	Tranquility
Fourmead	Blackwood
Midland	Indian Hill
Mottefield	Doar Point
Wicklow	Bear Hill
Moreland	

The following represent the plantations on the south bank of the South Santee that had lands lying in the delta:

Murphy's Island	Egremont
Indianfield	Woodville

[170] Based upon lists in the possession of Mrs. F. W. Ford and Mrs. Charlotte K. Prevost, Georgetown, S. C., and on the map, *SCHM*, XIII (1912), facing p. 1. Also see William F. Johnstone to J. R. Sparkman, June 20, 1871, in possession of Mrs. F. A. Witte, Columbia, S. C. David Doar describes the South Santee plantations in *A Sketch of the Agricultural Society of St. James, Santee, South Carolina* (Charleston, S. C., 1908), pp. 44–46.

Palo Alto	Peafield
Bellevue	Montgomery (Old Field)
Fairfield	Waterhorn (Wattahan)
Peachtree	Cedar Hill

The first plantation on the right as one came in from the ocean and began to move up the North Santee was Ford's Point. This was the home of Frederick Wentworth Ford (1817–1872) and possibly of his father Stephen Ford (1786–1852) as well.[171] F. W. Ford, the son of his father's first marriage, harvested 330,000 pounds of rice in 1850 with fifty-four slaves. He married on April 9, 1856, Mary Mazyck Hume, daughter of Dr. Alexander Hume of Hume's Cat Island.[172]

Cat Island plantation was the seat of Richard Henry Lowndes (1815–1905). The plantation had been the property of his father Thomas Lowndes, the son of Rawlins Lowndes, who was second president of the state of South Carolina during the Revolution. He produced 360,000 pounds in 1850 with 147 slaves. As Richard Henry Lowndes had married Susan Middleton Parker, both he and his wife were of Charleston families, unlike their neighbors the Fords who had come down from Black River.[173]

Hume's Cat Island and The Bluff belonged to the Hume family. Robert Hume had bought Hopsewee in 1762; his son John Hume (1763–1841)[174] had married Mary Mazyck, the daughter of a Santee River planter. Dr. Alexander Hume (1795–1848) married in April 1817 Mary Gadsden Morris, a granddaughter of Christopher Gadsden.[175] He died in Aiken, South Carolina, where he had a home near his Barnwell' and Edgefield plantations. His Santee estate yielded 600,000 pounds of rice in 1850 with 183 slaves, not yet having been divided among his five sons: Thomas Morris Hume, John Alexander Hume, Edward Gadsden Hume, Christo-

[171] Stephen Ford married first in 1816 Helen Marie Walter (1799–1822) and second on April 8, 1824 Jane Cogdell Thurston, who died at the age of fifty on Black River, June 14, 1850. *Winyah Observer*, June 19, 1850, July 28, 1852; Ford Family Chart, in possession of Mrs. F. W. Ford, Georgetown, S. C.

[172] *Pee Dee Times*, April 16, 1856.

[173] Lachicotte, *op. cit.*, pp. 161–163; *SCHM*, XL (1939), 53.

[174] John Hume, a soldier of Marion's, died March 28, 1841, on the North Santee. *Winyah Observer*, May 5, 1841.

[175] *SCHM*, II (1901), 44.

pher Gadsden Hume, and Robert William Hume.[176] Robert Hume, a brother of Dr. Alexander Hume, owned 135 slaves and produced 510,000 pounds of rice in 1850.[177]

William Rivers Maxwell (1794–1873) was the master of White Marsh. He married in 1819 Anna Maria, the sister of Francis Withers Johnston of Estherville, a plantation that lay to the north of his own. In 1850 his acres produced 600,000 pounds of rice with 137 slaves.[178]

Andrew Johnston (1805–1864) of Annandale was one of the most successful of the rice planters on the North Santee. His lands came from his great grandfather Archibald Johnston, who died in 1763. His grandfather Andrew (1748–1795) got Jonathan Lucas to build the first tide-operated rice mill at Mill Brook. His father William (1776–1840) was the progenitor of a large clan with many lands between Winyah Bay and the Santee. Francis Withers Johnston, the youngest son, was at Estherville; Anna Maria Maxwell was at White Marsh; another daughter married Simons Lucas, who planted to the west of Annandale. The head of the family, however, was Andrew, who after a visit to his ancestral home in Scotland renamed Mill Brook, Annandale, and built the home that still stands today. Perhaps at the same time they reintroduced the Scottish spelling of Johnstone. The lands were choice and the Scottish enterprise must have lasted long, for in 1850 there was a crop of 900,000 pounds of rice with 230 slaves. During the next decade

[176] "Will of Alexander Hume," dated May 19, 1848, proved June 10, 1848, Charleston County Wills, XLIV (1845–1851), 349–353, S. C. Archives. According to the will, Edward managed Cat Island and John managed The Bluff. In the Charleston *Mercury*, Oct. 17 (or 20), 1853, the entire estate was advertised for sale. Cat Island plantation contained 1,000 acres, of which 400 were prime tide swamp and 100 for provisions. There were a fine residence of 12 rooms, extensive kitchen, carriage house, overseer's house, stables, and accommodations for 150 slaves. The Bluff contained 220 acres of prime swamp. There was a summer residence on South Island four miles from Cat Island and ten miles from The Bluff. There were 120 slaves. Thomas M. Hume and Edward G. Hume bought in the North Santee properties. "Will of Thomas M. Hume," dated June 30, 1855, proved March 21, 1861, Charleston County Wills, XLIX (1856–1862), 812–816, S. C. Archives.

[177] At his death in 1841 John Hume, who had been in 1810 the largest landowner on the North Santee, left his estate equally to his seven children: Ann Simons, Catharine Simons, Charlotte Lucas, Robert, Alexander, John, and William. "Will of John Hume," dated Aug. 3, 1840, proved March 31, 1841, Charleston County Wills, XLII, Book A (1839–1845), 268.

[178] *SCHM*, XXXII (1931), 202; Lachicotte, *op. cit.*, p. 164.

Andrew added to his lands, a part of Estherville, Tidyman's Rush Land, and Lynch's.[179]

Rawlins Lowndes (1801–1877) of Wicklow Hall (sometimes called The Strip) was the elder brother of Richard Henry Lowndes of Cat Island. In 1850 540,000 pounds of rice and 190 slaves were listed in his own name, 300,000 pounds of rice and 195 slaves in the name of his father's estate. Having property elsewhere, Rawlins Lowndes resided only a portion of the year on the North Santee. In 1826 he had married a daughter of the New York Livingston clan and since that time had maintained a home in New York City and later had a small estate on the Hudson among the Livingston manors.[180]

William Bull Pringle (1800–1881) was the much younger brother of John Julius Pringle II, who had planted at White House on the Black River and whose widow had married Joel Roberts Poinsett. After his marriage in 1822 to Mary Motte Alston, daughter of Colonel William Alston of Clifton, William Bull Pringle spent a great deal of time in Georgetown District, representing this district for a number of terms in the legislature. His wife inherited the loveliest home in Charleston, the Motte-Alston home on King Street, where he resided most of the time and from which he managed all of his properties, which included far more than a few plantations on the North Santee. However, Pleasant Meadow and Richfield provided a portion of his princely income, 900,-000 pounds of rice from the work of 281 slaves.[181]

The grandee of the North Santee had been Elias Horry IV (1733–1834). His story illustrates the infinite complexity of family relationships in the rise of an aristocracy that was based as much upon marriage at it was upon wealth and achievement. Elias Horry I (1664–1736), the founder of the family, married Margaret Huger in 1704. He was coroner of Craven County and the owner of one of the original town lots in

[179] Andrew Johnstone married in 1826 Sophia Beaumont Clarkson (1808–1845) and in 1848 Mary Barnwell Elliott (1824–1909). Family Papers, William C. Johnstone, Louisville, Ky.; Johnstone Papers, SCL; Lachicotte, *op. cit.*, pp. 167–170. For a full description of Andrew Johnstone's estate, which he was willing to sell for more than $220,000, see Seaman Deas, Jr., to James K. Munnerlyn, Feb. 6, 1851, Cheves Collection, Middleton Papers, S. C. Hist. Soc.

[180] George B. Chase, *Lowndes of South Carolina* (Boston, Mass., 1876), pp. 39–40; Lachicotte, *op. cit.*, p. 178.

[181] *SCHM*, LXII (1961), 157–159.

Georgetown. His children were Daniel, Elias II, John, Margaret, and Madalene. It was Daniel's son Daniel who had married first Judith Serré, thus obtaining some of Noah Serré's extensive properties south of the Santee, and second Harriott Pinckney, the sister of Charles Cotesworth and Thomas Pinckney. Harriott Horry, the daughter of the second marriage, had become in 1797 the wife of Frederick Rutledge, a son of Governor John Rutledge. After her husband's death in 1821 Mrs. Rutledge managed the estates.[182] In 1850 she grew 660,000 pounds of rice with 301 slaves in Georgetown District. John Horry's two sons were Peter and Hugh, the Revolutionary heroes. The Mayrants on Winyah Bay were descendants in that line. Margaret had married Anthony Bonneau, and Magdalene had married Paul Trapier.

Elias Horry II (1707–1783) [183] had married a Lynch and had two sons, Elias Horry III (1753–1785) and Thomas Horry (1748–1820). It was Elias II who had begun to accumulate lands in the 1750's in the area of the North Santee. He and his son Elias III almost lost these lands at the time of the confiscation. Elias III and Thomas married sisters, the daughters of William Branford with plantations on the Ashley River and a lovely town house in Charleston.[184] Elias IV, the son of Thomas and Ann Branford Horry, inherited the family properties on the Santee and the Horry-Branford town house in Charleston. He was president of the South Carolina Railroad Company and a generous patron of the College of Charleston. Like so many of the wealthiest North Santee planters, he was an absentee landlord, living in Charleston.[185]

Elias Horry IV married twice, leaving a widow and seven children at his death in 1834. His plantations were the Bluff, Wattahan, Milldam, Jutland, Camp Main, Camp Island, Newland, Midland, and Millbrook, the latter two being on the South Santee. These were to be divided among his five sons, Thomas Lynch Horry, the eldest, and William

[182] *SCHM*, XXXI (1930), 17. Frederick Rutledge had planted at Waterhorn (Wattahan).

[183] "Will of Elias Horry," dated Jan. 13, 1781, proved Jan. 29, 1784, Charleston County Wills, XX (1783–1786), 325–328, S. C. Archives. He was living on a plantation at Wadhecan Creek near the Santee in Prince George Parish.

[184] *SCHM*, XX (1919), 86.

[185] Mr. Elias Horry, "who brought to the support of the already flagging enterprise a noble spirit, and the financial force of his large private fortune." W. L. Trenholm, "The History and Present Condition of Transportation in South Carolina," *South Carolina Handbook* (n.p., 1883), p. 631.

Branford Shubrick Horry, Elias Horry V, Edward Shubrick Horry, and Paul Trapier Horry. In 1850 the combined family estates yielded 1,020,-000 pounds of rice. Thomas Lynch Horry owned 101 slaves and the estate 150.[186]

One of the great figures of the South Carolina rice world had been Jonathan Lucas I, who had brought from England the mechanical know-how which he had applied to the construction of rice mills.[187] From engineering the family had turned to planting. His son Jonathan Lucas II had fourteen children, two of whom were rice planters on the North Santee in 1850.[188] Simons Lucas (1812–1890), who had married Emma Septima Johnston, planted at Rice Hope where he produced 300,000 pounds of rice with the assistance of seventy slaves. A younger brother, Henry Ewbank Lucas (1822–1900), planted at Woodside, which had been cut off from Rice Hope in the 1840's by Simons Lucas for his younger brother. In 1850 Woodside produced 360,000 pounds of rice from the labor of seventy-two slaves.[189]

The first Jonathan Lucas married a second time, and of this union there was a son, William (1790–1878), who married Charlotte, the sister of Dr. Alexander Hume of Cat Island.[190] William Lucas lived at the Wedge, south of the Santee, but the 1850 census listed him with a crop of 540,000 pounds of rice and seventy-two slaves in George-town District. William's son John Hume Lucas (died 1853) was the master of 178 slaves at Hopsewee, which produced 360,000 pounds of rice.[191]

Joseph Manigault had owned White Oak at the time of his death in 1843. The plantation, which contained 151 slaves and had a crop of 390,000 pounds of rice in 1850, had passed to his son Arthur Middleton

[186] "Will of Elias Horry," dated Aug. 16, 1833, proved Sept. 23, 1834, Charleston County Wills, XL (1834–1839), 88–108, S. C. Archives. The Bluff and Wattahan to his wife; Milldam and Jutland to W. B. S. Horry, Camp Main to E. H., Camp Island to E. S. H., and Newland to P. T. H., and Midland and Millbrook in St. James Santee to Julia E. Horry. His slaves were divided into six parcels after those for Thomas Lynch Horry were taken out—for the six children.

[187] Anne King Gregorie, "Jonathan Lucas," DAB.

[188] Notes on Lucas Family in Deas Genealogy, S. C. Hist. Soc.

[189] Lachicotte, op. cit., pp. 185–190.

[190] Simons, op. cit., pp. 145–146.

[191] Lachicotte, op. cit., p. 193; SCHM, XXXVII (1936), 148.

Manigault (1824–1886). The Manigaults, a Charleston family, had plantations in other parts of the state.[192]

Major James H. Ladson (1796–1868) was of another well-established Charleston family.[193] LaGrange and Fawn Hill in 1850 produced 600,000 pounds of rice from the work of 191 slaves.[194] His daughter Sarah Gilmer Ladson married James Reid Pringle (1813–1884), a first cousin-once-removed of William Bull Pringle. James Reid Pringle, a Charleston rice factor, had lands in Georgetown District which in 1850 were worked by 143 slaves and yielded 576,000 pounds of rice. Ravenel and Pringle, the rice factorage firm, owned seventy-six slaves and reaped 300,000 pounds of rice. Julius St. Julien Pringle (1820–1890), brother of James Reid Pringle, owned seventy-eight slaves and harvested 380,000 pounds of rice. He gave a lot of land in 1853 on which the new Church of the Messiah was to be built.[195]

Commander's was the last of the rice plantations on the North Santee. The Commander family, one of the oldest in the district, was represented in 1850 by James M. Commander, sheriff and brigadier general of the militia.[196] He grew 180,000 pounds of rice with thirty-six slaves.

The 1850 census states that Heriot Huggins owned sixty-one slaves and grew 300,000 pounds of rice. Colonel Charles Huggins, Santee River planter, had died on June 5, 1849, at the age of fifty-seven.[197] Heriot Huggins may have been a nephew of Colonel Huggins.[198] Since the Huggins had been particularly close to the Commander family, their lands may have been adjacent to the Commander estate.

Bear Hill and Crow Island were owned by the Deas family. Henry

---

[192] *Transactions of the Huguenot Society of South Carolina,* No. 4 (1897), pp. 82–83; Lachicotte, *op. cit.,* p. 190.

[193] "Will of James H. Ladson," dated Dec. 11, 1861, proved April 27, 1868, Charleston County Wills, LI (1862–1868), 816–817, S. C. Archives.

[194] J. H. Ladson's contract, 1865, RG 105, Box 525, National Archives.

[195] *SCHM,* LXII (1961), 162, 229–230; Minutes of the Vestry, S. C. Hist. Soc. The author has been unable to ascertain on what lands these Pringle harvests were grown.

[196] In 1812 Samuel Commander married Elizabeth Vereen, widow. The third party to the marriage settlement was Nathan and Robert Huggins. Marriage Settlements, VI, 121–123, S. C. Archives. These may have been the parents of J. M. Commander.

[197] *Winyah Observer,* June 27, 1849.

[198] The *Winyah Observer,* April 27, 1844, stated that on April 17 Nathan Huggins, the last son of Col. Charles Huggins of Santee, had died.

Deas, who had married in 1796 Margaret Horry, the daughter of Elias Horry II, had planted Richfield and Pleasant Meadow for awhile.[199] His brother Seaman Deas, Sr., produced 360,000 pounds of rice with 103 slaves and his son Dr. Seaman Deas produced 300,000 pounds with sixty-six slaves. In 1842 at Rose Hill plantation Dr. Seaman Deas had married Mary Ashe Alston, the daughter of William Algernon Alston.[200]

The first Philip Tidyman, a Charleston jeweler, had begun to invest his profits in Santee lands before the Revolution. He married in 1772 Hester Rose. the daughter of John Rose. Their son Philip Tidyman (1776–1850) planted the Tidyman lands at Marshfield and Cedar Hill. In 1850 the estate of Philip Tidyman, who had died that year, accounted for 130 slaves and 420,000 pounds of rice.[201] Philip Tidyman had resided in Charleston where he kept four liveried servants, entertained lavishly, and welcomed many foreign notables to his home.[202]

General Thomas Pinckney had accumulated a great property on the south Santee which he left to his sons Colonel Thomas Pinckney, Jr., and Charles Cotesworth Pinckney. The Pinckneys were planting Fannymede, Mottefield, Moreland, and Tranquility in the delta of the Santee in 1850. Colonel Thomas Pinckney, Jr., had married in 1803 Elizabeth Izard (1784–1862), the daughter of Ralph Stead Izard.[203] Mrs. Pinckney, a widow in 1850, grew 730,000 pounds of rice with eighty-four slaves in

---

[199] Alston Deas to author, Jan. 12, 1966.

[200] *Winyah Observer,* May 7, 1842. Seaman Deas, Sr., died in 1854. "Will of Seaman Deas," dated July 7, 1851, proved April 26, 1854, Charleston County Wills, XLVI (1851–1856), 430–434, S. C. Archives. Life at the North Santee plantations of Henry and Seaman Deas in 1826 and 1827 is described in William A. Deas to Edward Thomson, Dec. 17, 1826 and Edward Thomson to John Thomson, Feb. 3, 1827, Deas-Thomson Papers, Macquarie University, Australia.

[201] *SCHM,* XXV (1924), 18–20. The will of the father mentioned Cedar Hill on the Santee and the will of the mother Marshfield on the North Santee. Philip Tidyman's will mentioned Cedar Hill in St. James Santee and plantations on the North Santee. "Will of Philip Tidyman," dated March 18, 1780, proved Aug. 9, 1780; "Will of Hester Tidyman," dated June 20, 1838, proved May 10, 1841; "Will of Philip Tidyman," dated March 12, 1850, proved July 2, 1850, Charleston County Wills, XIX (1780–1783), 7–8; XLII (1839–1845), 275–280; XLV (1845–1851), 715–718, S. C. Archives.

[202] Bernhard, Duke of Saxe-Weimar Eisenach, *Travels through North America during the Years 1825 and 1826* (Philadelphia, Penn.; 1828), II, 11; James Stuart, *Three Years in North America* (New York, 1833), II, 69–71; Margaret H. Hall, *The Aristocratic Journey* (New York, 1931), pp. 213–214.

[203] *SCHM,* XXXIX (1938), 31–32; Pinckney Estate Papers, CLS.

1850. Charles Cotesworth Pinckney had a crop of 755,000 pounds of rice.[204]

Stephen Duvall Doar (1805–1872) owned ninety-seven slaves and had a crop of 360,000 pounds of rice from his Elmwood and Palo Alto plantations.[205] On February 25, 1835, S. D. Doar married Charlotte Ann Cordes, the sister of Alexander Watson Cordes.[206] In 1859 S. D. Doar bought Harrietta from Mrs. Rutledge's estate for $25,000.[207] His brother Elias M. Doar (1811–1851) had eighty-five slaves and a crop of 300,000 pounds, which must have been obtained from Doar lands on Cedar and Murphy's islands.[208]

John Gibbes Shoolbred (1796–1860) in 1850 produced 435,000 pounds of rice in Georgetown District with 121 slaves. He had married Emma Augusta Gibbes in 1820 and planted Woodville, Ashfield, and Millfield plantations.[209]

Thomas Lehre Bulow owned sixty-two slaves and harvested 210,000 pounds of rice in 1850 in Georgetown District, but the names of his plantations are not known.[210]

The planters of the North Santee banded together to build and maintain a church. In 1804 James Hamilton, John Hume, Elias Horry, Isaac Mazyck, Paul Mazyck, Thomas Horry, Esther Lynch, John Drayton, Seaman Deas, William Johnston, L. D. Wigfall, Benjamin Smith, Philip Tidyman, and Henry Deas signed a petition to the legislature, asking to be incorporated as "The North Santee Church in the Parish of Winyaw." Isaac Mazyck and John Hume while vacationing in Newport during July of 1804 made a contract with Abiel Waid of Taunton,

[204] SCHM, XXXIX (1938), 32–33.

[205] Doar, op. cit., pp. 44–46.

[206] SCHM, XLIV (1943), 21.

[207] Easterby, op. cit., p. 414.

[208] Elias M. Doar died at Cedar Island in his thirty-ninth year. Winyah Observer, Aug. 20, 1851. Josiah Doar, another brother, died at the age of forty-five on Nov. 2, 1851, at Murphy's Island. Winyah Observer, Nov. 12, 1851. The plantations of Midland, Peafield, Fairfield, Wicklow, and Morland are mentioned in the S. D. Doar Papers, SCL.

[209] SCHM, XII (1911), 90, 93; "Will of John Gibbes Shoolbred," dated Jan. 28, 1860, proved Feb. 7, 1860, Charleston County Wills, XLIX (1856–1862), 618–619, S. C. Archives.

[210] Bulow's will mentioned no plantation by name. "Will of T. L. Bulow," dated Jan. 29, 1855, proved July 18, 1857, Charleston County Wills, XLVIII (1856–1862), 119–121, S. C. Archives.

Massachusetts, to build what Dalcho called a "neat chapel." Waid
finished the job by February 1805, using cypress and pine furnished by
Alexander and Paul Mazyck.

Occasional services were held by clergymen, supplemented by lay
reading. It was very difficult, however, to secure a full-time clergyman
for the small salary. In 1835 the church secured the services of the
Reverend Charles Cotesworth Pinckney, and he served until he accepted
a call in 1838 to Christ Church in Greenville. In 1842 the church was
reorganized under the name of "The Church of the Messiah, North
Santee" at a meeting held at Millbrook. James H. Ladson was elected
warden; William R. Maxwell, Robert Hume, Rawlins Lowndes, and
Andrew Johnston vestrymen. Four clergymen then served the church
before the war. John H. Cornish, C. C. Pinckney (returning in 1847
and 1848), Edward C. Logan, and Thomas J. Girardeau. A new church
was begun under Logan in 1853 and finished under Girardeau in
1856. At the same time the congregation was building a summer chapel
and parsonage on South Island. This church on the North Santee served,
therefore, as a nucleus around which the Santee planters clustered, a
cohesive force just as were the churches of All Saints, Prince Frederick,
and Prince George.[211]

By 1850 the open, fluid society of many little men on the make which
characterized the decade of the 1740's or even the 1780's had been
replaced by a closed society of wealthy aristocrats. The town of Georgetown contained a small middle class, but that group was definitely inferior in status and wealth to the planters. There were now no Paul
Trapiers, Daniel Tuckers, or Robert Heriots, who as merchants stood
as high as the planting Allstons. In fact, most of the important Georgetown commercial families had passed into the planting class as had
the Trapiers, the Tuckers, and the Heriots. The disappearance of the
merchant class contributed to the static nature of Georgetown District
society. Yet even in the agricultural world new men found it impossible
to break through. A comparison of the crop returns recorded in the 1860

[211] Samuel Gaillard Stoney, *Building a Church on the Santee, 1804–1807* (Charleston, S. C., 1945; Register and Minutes of the Vestry, S. C. Hist. Soc.; Lachicotte,
op. cit., pp. 174–177; Thomas, *op. cit.,* pp. 350–354. There was also a North Santee
clubhouse. *Winyah Observer,* May 28, 1842.

census with those of 1850 reveals that the bigger planting families were producing more and that new men were unknown.

Dr. E. T. Heriot's two sons, Francis Withers Heriot and Dr. Robert Stark Heriot, were producing 360,000 and 450,000 pounds of rice respectively in 1860, both growing more than their father had grown in 1850. Plowden C. J. Weston, who had purchased additional properties during the decade, had emerged as the new grandee of the rice coast, his lands yielding 1,252,000 pounds of rice in 1860. Although Colonel J. J. Ward had died in 1853, his estate yielded the enormous crop of 4,410,000 pounds of rice in 1860, a crop larger than that grown by any other family in the entire district. The Pyatts had boosted their family total from 2,010,000 to 2,385,000 pounds of rice. John Hyrne Tucker, Jr., had replaced his father, pushing the family crop total from 1,140,000 in 1850 to 1,530,000 in 1860. Waverly, then in the hands of Joseph Blyth Allston, was producing 450,000 pounds of rice compared to 300,000 in 1850. Robert Nesbit at Caledonia got 720,000 pounds of rice in 1860 to his mother's 540,000 in 1850. Judge Dunkin's crop was up from 540,000 to 730,000 pounds of rice. John Izard Middleton had more than doubled his crop from 750,000 to 1,860,000. Both of the LaBruce brothers had done better: John Francis LaBruce up from 300,000 to 540,000 and Joshua Ward LaBruce from 270,000 to 540,000. Only William Algernon Alston, who was in the last year of his life, produced less—down to 1,450,000 pounds of rice.

Along the Pee Dee, although Francis Weston had increased his crop slightly, R. F. W. Allston had emerged as the most notable planter with an increase in rice from all of his lands from 840,000 to 1,500,000 pounds. Dr. James R. Sparkman had moved into the ranks of the big planters by raising his production from 190,000 to 945,000 pounds. The estate of Ralph Stead Izard, who died in 1858, yielded 1,250,000 pounds of rice.

Along the Black River four families dominated. John Julius Pringle, planting at Greenfield as well as at White House, raised his total from 150,000 to 720,000 pounds of rice. Dr. F. S. Parker increased the yield of his fields from 375,000 to 1,440,000. The Trapier family total was up from 960,000 to 2,100,000 in 1860. Henry A. Middleton increased his yield from 900,000 to 1,300,000.

Along the Sampit and Winyah Bay the Withers name had disappeared, but his step-daughter, who married Dr. Alexius M. Forster, was producing 658,000 pounds of rice on a part of the property that once belonged to Francis Withers. The Reads as a family had increased their yields from 960,000 to 1,575,000. William Horry Mayrant had improved his position with an advance from 360,000 to 607,000 pounds of rice.

On the North Santee, Frederick Wentworth Ford, now planting his father's lands as well as his own, had a crop of 1,860,000 pounds. The Lowndes family had increased their production from 360,000 to 810,000 pounds. Although Dr. Alexander Hume had been replaced by two of his sons, John Alexander Hume and Edward Gadsden Hume (1824–1889), the family production was down. The Johnstones, however, were up to 2,080,000 pounds of rice in 1860. William Rivers Maxwell, Andrew Johnstone's brother-in-law, had jumped his total from 600,000 to 1,485,000. William Bull Pringle was also a bigger planter. After Elias Horry IV's estate had been divided, William Branford Shubrick Horry (1818–1863) had apparently bought the plantations of his older brothers, for in 1860 his crop amounted to 1,035,000 pounds of rice. The eldest brother, Thomas Lynch Horry (1804–1871), produced only a bit more rice in 1860, 496,000 compared with 420,000 in 1850. Among the members of the Lucas family, William was no longer planting in Georgetown District, but Simons, Henry Ewbank, and John Hume all increased their yields slightly. Arthur Middleton Manigault had pushed production from 390,000 to 585,000 pounds. Major Ladson was up from 600,000 to 900,000. James Reid Pringle, his son-in-law, was also up from 576,000 to 900,000. The Tidyman estates were still intact and up. Neither Doar was listed in 1860, but Alexander Watson Cordes (1830–1878), the brother-in-law of S. D. Doar, was listed for 495,000 pounds of rice in 1860.[212]

The bigger planters had gotten bigger during the decade. The new names among the rice planters were either those of the sons of planters such as P. C. J. Weston, W. B. S. Horry, and F. W. Ford, or of husbands of Georgetown heiresses such as Nathaniel Barnwell and Dr. Alexius Mador Forster. The only new men with sizable crops were Philip

[212] SCHM, XLIV (1943), 21–22; Lachicotte, op. cit., p. 190; A. W. Cordes' contract, 1865, RG 105, Box 525, National Archives.

Porcher Mazyck (1792–1860) with 720,000, Alexander Mazyck (1801–1894) with 360,000, William Ravenel (1802–1888) with 315,000, Paul Fitzsimons with 270,000, Arthur Middleton with 270,000, and Dr. John Lascelles Nowell with 175,000. But none of these were self-made men. The Mazycks were an old Santee River family planting at Indianfield and Montgomery in the delta out of their base at Romney on the South Santee.[213] William Ravenel was a Charleston rice factor who had planted in partnership with J. R. Pringle in 1850.[214] Dr. Nowell had planted on the South Santee at Bellevue and Egremont; his daughter had married a Pyatt.[215] Both Fitzsimons [216] and Middleton [217]had estates elsewhere. Apparently, the only way to break into the rice-planting group was to have a fortune with which to purchase a plantation or to marry a heiress. In 1860 the Georgetown planters were a rich and powerful oligarchy that dominated their own district, and, to some extent, the state as well.

[213] Sons of William Mazyck and Elizabeth Porcher. Mazyck left South Santee lands to four sons. "Will of William Mazyck," dated Dec. 8, 1843, proved Nov. 19, 1845, Charleston County Wills, XLIII, Book B (1839–1845), 922–927, S. C. Archives. *Transactions of the Huguenot Society of South Carolina*, No. 3 (1894), p. 33; May and Faunt, *op. cit.*, pp. 179–180.

[214] William Ravenel married Eliza Butler Pringle, daughter of James Reid Pringle, on May 31, 1836. *SCHM*, XLIV (1943), 20–21; LXII (1961), 162. He was with Ravenel and Stevens, Charleston rice factors. Obituary, *The Sunday News* (Charleston *News and Courier*), Nov. 11, 1888; *Transactions of the Huguenot Society of South Carolina*, No. 1 (1889), pp. 49–50.

[215] Planted at Crow Hill and Auckland, according to 1865 contracts, RG 105, Box 525, National Archives.

[216] Paul Fitzsimons had married Martha S. Ford, daughter of John Potts Ford, the master of Rice Hope.

[217] Arthur Middleton (born 1832) planted at Daisy Bank. *SCHM*, I (1900), 255–256.

XIV

AN ARISTOCRATIC SOCIETY

Education, travel, and long sojourns in Charleston set the planters'
families apart from the rest of the people of the district. The sons
were trained to be planters and gentlemen; the daughters to be mis-
tresses of plantations. The children of the planters did not attend the
free schools, nor did they often attend the school of the Winyah Indigo
Society. They were educated by tutors in the home, or at schools in
Charleston, or sometimes at academies in other parts of the state. Rarely
were they sent abroad as they had been in the eighteenth century when
Francis and Cleland Kinloch and Thomas Lynch went to Eton. In the
eighteenth century it had not been unusual for the sons of planters to
be apprenticed to a mercantile firm in Charleston. By the middle of the
nineteenth century such an arrangement would have been most unusual.
Charlotte Ann Allston had considered putting her youngest son William
in a commercial house. On March 12, 1818, Charles Kershaw wrote her
that William was "certainly too young to be sent to Charleston to put to
Business, and besides it could not be done without a heavy Expence.
Merchants will not take lads into their Stores or Counting Houses, without their Parents find them in everything. . . ." [1] Alexander Robertson

[1] *The South Carolina Rice Plantation as Revealed in the Papers of Robert F. W.
Allston*, ed. J. H. Easterby (Chicago, Ill., 1945), p. 367.

was the only Georgetown boy who became a Charleston factor. As his Charleston rice-factorage firm of Robertson and Blacklock was a successor to that of Kershaw, he probably got his training in the manner that Kershaw described.[2] Anthony Toomer Porter was a clerk for a few years in the firm of Robertson and Blacklock, but in 1848 at the age of twenty-one he refused the offer of a junior partnership and returned to his planting affairs. Eventually he became a clergyman.[3]

The tutors were generally from England or from New England. William Vaux came out from England to be a tutor in the Pawley family.[4] Alexander Glennie came from Surrey in England to be Plowden Weston's tutor and remained to become the rector of All Saints.[5] When Anthony Toomer Porter decided to enter the ministry, he went to Glennie for guidance in his reading as preparation for entering a seminary.[6] Both Benjamin Faneuil Hunt and Benjamin Faneuil Dunkin had come south as tutors; they knew Aaron Burr Alston's tutor, a fellow New Englander. The Reverend John Pierpont of Boston, the grandfather of J. P. Morgan, was tutor in the family of Colonel William Alston of Clifton before taking the Alston boys to Litchfield, Connecticut, where he prepared them for Yale, which they all duly entered. Charles left; Pinckney and Motte graduated.[7]

The governesses were often French or German. Mrs. R. F. W. Allston had a German woman who had been "domesticated."[8] However, "a finish'd governess" was difficult to find.[9] In 1853 the Allstons had had a governess for two years who taught all the branches of an English education: music, drawing, French, Italian, and the rudiments of Latin for $500 per annum. "We chose her as a teacher on account of her ability

[2] Ibid., passim.

[3] A. Toomer Porter, Led On! Step by Step (New York, reprinted 1967), pp. 61–62.

[4] LaBruce Family Records, in possession of Mrs. Elizabeth LaBruce Pugh, Columbia, S. C.

[5] Henry DeSaussure Bull, All Saints' Church, Waccamaw (Columbia, S. C., 1949), p. 19.

[6] Porter, op. cit., pp. 81–87.

[7] Rice Planter and Sportsman, The Recollections of J. Motte Alston, 1821–1909, ed. Arney R. Childs (Columbia, S. C., 1953), p. 25; John K. Winkler, Morgan the Magnificent (New York, 1930), p. 27. The author has corrected these accounts after checking the lists of students at Yale. Col. Alston's sons by his first wife went to Princeton; those by his second wife went to Yale.

[8] Easterby, op. cit., p. 156.

[9] Ibid., p. 133.

to teach correctly what she pretends to teach. She is not a fast teacher, but is in the main a good one. She is withal a simple-minded honest-hearted woman." But she was fond of talking and "fond of good living, not exacting delicacies so much as a plenty of substantial fare, especially fond of hot cakes at breakfast." Although well-read, she rather liked to gossip about "the courtship and liaisons of the princes and princesses of Europe." [10]

Sometimes the planters pooled their resources to hire one tutor for the children of several families. R. F. W. Allston in 1838, acting on behalf of himself and Colonel Ward, Dr. Heriot, and Dr. Magill, hired in New York the Reverend C. B. Thummel, a former student of the universities of Halle and Tubingen. He was to teach English, French, German, Latin, Greek, music, drawing, painting, and dancing to some twelve or fifteen children of both sexes ranging from four to thirteen years of age. This school, the All Saints Academy, was under the direct supervision of the Reverend Alexander Glennie. Thummel received $2,000 a year, a house at Woodville plantation, and a summer home on the island, but he also had to take in boarders.[11] J. Motte Alston has left a description of this school.

About fifteen miles north of True Blue there was a school [in 1839] kept by a German, on the seashore, I engaged a room and board there, and when the Professor would have one or two spare hours, he would come to my room, where he would smoke his pipe and I would renew my acquaintance with Virgil, Horace, and such ancients as I thought would be pleasing, by way of rounding up the education of a rice planter. I also studied Spanish with much pleasure and talked on various subjects. I had a servant to wait on me and kept a thoroughbred mare in the stable to while away some tedious hours. A deep salt-water creek was in front of the house, and there I had a goodly supply of fine oysters; and in a stall next to my mare, I kept fenced in a full supply of partridges; and thus was I finely protected from boarding-house fare. I had two companions, somewhat older than myself but who had not dipped into college life, who were fine fellows who came to learn and

[10] *Ibid.*, p. 115; Elizabeth W. Allston Pringle, *Chronicles of Chicora Wood* (Boston, Mass., 1940), pp. 124–125.

[11] Easterby, *op. cit.*, pp. 80–81, 83, 86; *Georgetown American*, Dec. 4, 1839. The Academy was founded in 1830. The board sought incorporation in 1839 with capital of $50,000 pledged. Petition of E. T. Heriot, A. Glennie, and J. J. Ward to Senate and House, 1839; petition of F. M. Weston (president), E. T. Heriot (vice president), and A. Glennie (secretary) to Senate and House, 1844, S. C. Archives.

not play the undergraduate. Of course, I kept my dogs, varied in their accomplishments; and many a night would we, with light-wood torches brightly burning . . . sally out in hunt of the sly opossum, which was at this season finely flavored with the ripe persimmon. Then with a bag of this midnight game, we would sit around a live-oak fire on the shelly beach and sup on roasted oysters, freshly gathered from the deep creeks near by.[12]

Samuel Jones was principal in 1845.[13] David Delamer Rosa, who came from New York to teach in this school, was principal in the 1850's.[14]

A more rigorous schooling could be had at the Grammar School of the College of Charleston during the revival of that school between 1825 and 1836 under the headship of the Reverend Jasper Adams. The Grammar or English School was mainly preparatory; the curriculum embraced English, mathematics, themes, and declamations. There was also a classical and scientific school. Among the Georgetown boys in 1824 were William Heriot, M'Kewn Johnston; in 1825 Seaman Deas; in 1826 Francis Weston; in 1829 James H. Trapier; in 1830 William P. Vaux, John H. Read, James Withers Read; in 1831 John LaBruce, Richard Henry Lowndes; in 1832 J. Hume Lucas; in 1833 John Alexander Hume; in 1834 Daniel Tucker Heriot, John Hume Lucas, Jonathan Lucas, Robert H. Lucas, William Mayrant.[15]

More exclusive and nearer an English public school was the one kept by Christopher Coates on Wentworth Street in Charleston, which flourished between 1820 and 1850. Coates took about 100 boys a year; the fees totaled $100.[16] Anthony Toomer Porter in his autobiography has told how he was entered in the school.

It was an expensive school, and resorted to only by the sons of people of property and position, so that it was necessary to enter a boy's name for a vacancy a year or two ahead. Mr. Cotes, happening to come up to Georgetown to visit Mr. William Bull Pringle, at his plantation, some

---

[12] Childs, op. cit., p. 39.

[13] Winyah Observer, Dec. 31, 1845.

[14] Alberta Morel Lachicotte, Georgetown Rice Plantations (Columbia, S. C., 1955), p. 41; Pee Dee Times, Jan. 2, 1856.

[15] J. H. Easterby, A History of the College of Charleston (n.p., 1935), pp. 74–89, 278–289.

[16] Colyer Meriwether, A History of Higher Education in South Carolina (Washington, D. C., 1889), pp. 30–37. J. Motte Alston called it "the most celebrated school which Charleston ever boasted of." Childs, op. cit., p. 30.

six miles out of town, I was sent to him on my horse to have him enter my name. The old man had but one eye, and he struck me with terror the first time I saw him. I never did get over the terror and dislike with which the man inspired me. My name, however, was entered by him for the next year, and I rode off wishing most sincerely that he had said he had no place for me.[17]

In May 1842 young Porter went down to Charleston to enroll as a boarder. "In those days the school term was for the whole year, saving the holiday in December and April." Upon arriving Porter quickly learned two lessons.

I never can forget a lesson I received the second day at dinner. I had helped myself as usual, when Mr. Cotes, at the head of the table, asked me if I was going to eat all that was on my plate? Never having come in contact with such manners, I flushed up and felt indignant, and answered, I did not know whether I would or not. "Well," he said, "I will pass it over to-day, but henceforth help yourself to as much as you wish, but whatever you put on your plate you must eat." . . . The next lesson I learned was from seeing in an out-building walls covered with all manner of vile scribblings. Brought up with the greatest care by my mother, with my sisters as my principal companions, I was innocent of that form of evil. This writing and those drawings were new to me, and with the perversity of human nature I looked at things I ought not to have seen, and read, although a great deal of what I read I did not understand; but the effect was revolting to my moral sense.[18]

Dr. Gabriel E. Manigault outlined the curriculum:

The younger classes were practiced daily in spelling, arithmetic was carefully taught, geography was made more simple by the boys being obliged to prepare drawings of maps, and good handwriting was encouraged by the regular employment of a competent instructor; French was the only modern language for which there was a teacher, but he was always a native Frenchman; rhetoric, composition on some subject suitable to the capacity of each class, also occasionally a text book for the younger classes which gave them an insight into common everyday matters.[19]

Dr. Manigault thought that Mr. Coates weakened his program by his

[17] Porter, *op. cit.*, pp. 20–21.
[18] *Ibid.*, pp. 21–22.
[19] Quoted in Meriwether, *op. cit.*, p. 32.

indifference to elocution. Rhetoric, which was as important as the classics to the gentlemen of that day, was necessary in the age of patrician politics.[20]

R. F. W. Allston's daughters went to Madame R. Acelie Togno's in Charleston.[21] His son Charles was sent to the Willington Academy in Abbeville District.[22] Charles's letters to his sister during the Civil War emphasized the Christian education that he was receiving. They were also tinged with a longing for home; he missed his "gun and dog." [23] The sons of Davison McDowell attended Sumterville Academy.[24]

In the years after the Revolution the boys who were educated at home or at preparatory schools were sent to Northern colleges. John Hyrne Tucker graduated from Brown in 1800; his son John Hyrne Tucker II also attended Brown.[25] Paul Trapier, Benjamin Foissin Trapier, and Francis Withers attended Harvard in the 1780's.[26] Henry A. Middleton, Benjamin Huger, and Robert Pringle were in the class of 1813; Allard H. Belin of 1821, and John Harleston Read II of 1836. Thomas Pinckney Alston graduated from Yale in 1814, and his brother Jacob Motte Alston in 1815. John G. Shoolbred was there in 1816, and William Heyward Trapier in 1824. Princeton produced Robert Heriot in 1792, John Alston and William A. Alston in 1799, John I. Middleton in 1819, and Alexander Mazyck in 1820.[27]

West Point drew a number of young men for a training in engineering, which was valuable to the planter who was forever ditching his lands. Rawlins Lowndes graduated in 1820, R. F. W. Allston in 1821, James Heyward Trapier in 1836, and Benjamin Allston in 1853.[28]

[20] *Ibid.*, p. 35.
[21] Easterby, *Rice Plantation,* p. 135. Madame Togno wrote Mrs. Allston, July 17, 1854, that Adele was being trained in pencil and music and "in the English branches." Allston Papers, S. C. Hist. Soc. Also see Pringle, *op. cit.*, pp. 125–136.
[22] Pringle, *op. cit.*, p. 169.
[23] Allston Family Papers, SCL.
[24] Mary James Richards, "Our McDowell Ancestry" (typed copy, 1966), pp. 8, 37, Davison McDowell Papers, SCL.
[25] Lachicotte, *op. cit.*, pp. 47, 52.
[26] Gen. Peter Horry tells of his visit to the young Trapiers at Cambridge in "Journal of General Peter Horry," ed. A. S. Salley, *SCHM,* XXXIX (1938), 49.
[27] The lists of students at each school have been consulted.
[28] Easterby, *Rice Plantation,* pp. 13, 99; Ezra J. Warner, *Generals in Gray* (Baton Rouge, La., 1959), pp. 309–310.

The College of Charleston was the oldest college in South Carolina, but in the early decades of the nineteenth century it provided little more than a preparatory school education. The South Carolina College at Columbia which admitted its first class in 1805 was the more important collegiate training ground. Stephen Ford, Jr., in 1807 was the first Georgetown boy to graduate. Francis Withers finished in 1813, Joshua Ward in 1814, John D. Magill and M. H. Lance in 1815, Peter W. Fraser in 1822, Alexander H. Mazyck in 1826, Benjamin Foissin and James Heyward Trapier in 1833, John F. Pyatt in 1837, John St. Julien Pringle in 1839, John Gibbes Shoolbred in 1840, Alfred Huger Dunkin, Ebenezer B. Flagg, and William Alston Pringle in 1841, Joseph B. Pyatt and Frederick J. Shaffer in 1842, John Hyrne Tucker II in 1844, Charles Alston and Christopher Gadsden Hume in 1845, Charles E. B. Flagg in 1846, J. H. and Daniel Tucker in 1849, Simons Lucas, Joseph Blyth Allston, Robert Stark Heriot, and Henry M. Tucker in 1851, William Bull Pringle in 1852, John Izard Middleton in 1853, Thomas Allston Middleton in 1856, James Cordes Doar in 1860, and Bentley Weston in 1862.[29] In May 1854 R. F. W. Allston gave $12,000 to endow a scholarship, preferably for a young man who was preparing to study for the Episcopal ministry.[30] This school was more important than any other in molding the minds of South Carolina's planting class.

The Citadel, which opened in 1842, did not attract the sons of the planters. Only two Georgetown boys attended before the Civil War: Richard Green White and a Hemingway.[31]

The one profession that the sons of the planters sought with eagerness was that of medicine. R. F. W. Allston's mother had urged her son to study "physic," "as you can then save yourself the expense of doctors bills on your plantation, and in your Family." [32] Of very great importance, therefore, was the Medical College of the State of South Carolina.

[29] Andrew Charles Moore, *Roll of Students of South Carolina College, 1805–1905* (Columbia, S. C., 1905).

[30] Miscellaneous Records, X (1853–1855), 561–563, S. C. Archives.

[31] *Citadel Cadets, The Journal of Cadet Tom Law* (Clinton, S. C., 1941), p. 2. On May 14, 1852, William Allan Allston wrote Mrs. R. F. W. Allston of the death of Cadet William Henry Scriven, son of Colonel Belin's overseer. Also of Harris Gasque and Percy Prior. Allston Papers, S. C. Hist. Soc.

[32] Easterby, *Rice Plantation*, p. 13.

In the 1820's William G. Magill finished the Medical College; in the 1830's Seaman Deas, Ebenezer Flagg, James R. Sparkman, B. F. Trapier, and Francis S. Parker; in the 1840's E. B. Flagg, Allard Belin Flagg, R. W. Vaux, J. Maxwell Pringle, Benjamin Huger Read, and Alexius Forster; in the 1850's W. Magill, Arthur B. Flagg, Robert Stark Heriot, Daniel Tucker, J. R. Tucker, W. Alston, Jr., and B. C. Fishburne; and in 1860 S. D. Doar, Jr.[33]

The tradition of going abroad in the nineteenth century was not as important as it had been in the eighteenth century, although there is some indication that a revival of interest occurred in the 1850's as the wealth of a few mounted and education in the North became even more impossible. Philip Tidyman in 1800 was the first American to pass his doctoral examinations at Gottingen.[34] The University of Edinburgh always had an attraction for the descendants of Scotsmen. Paul Weston was there in 1803, Joseph Wragg in 1806, Cleland Kinloch in 1820, and Benjamin Porter Fraser, Paul Weston Fraser, George Bentley Weston, and Benjamin Huger Ward were all in attendance between 1858 and 1860.[35] Joshua John Ward was probably educated in Scotland. Plowden Charles Jennet Weston went to Harrow and then to Cambridge University. In 1841 three of the sons of William Bull Pringle were studying in England.[36] In 1845 William Heyward Trapier while visiting at New College, Oxford, presented a silver cup and a recipe for a mint julep; in addition, he also gave the college funds to endow an annual observance to be held each June 1. His generosity had been prompted by his discovery—upon being asked to name his drink—that this Southern specialty was unknown in Oxford.[37] In 1854 the sons of Ralph Stead Izard

[33] *Centennial Memorial of the Medical College of the State of South Carolina, 1824–1924* (Charleston, S. C., 1924), pp. 116–128. The SCL copy was owned by J. Ward Flagg of Brookgreen, who listed five of the Flagg family who had graduated from the Medical College. He was the fifth in 1881.

[34] His doctoral dissertation was entitled *De Orysa Sativa.* John T. Krumpelmann, *Southern Scholars in Goethe's Germany* (Chapel Hill, N. C., 1964), pp. 6–7.

[35] List supplied by Mr. A. B. Zahlan, Department of Physics, American University of Beirut, Lebanon.

[36] *SCHM*, LXII (1961), 223.

[37] David Ogg, "New College, Oxford, and South Carolina: A Personal Link," *SCHM*, LIX (1958), 61–63.

were at a school at Belle Rive on Lake Geneva.[38] In 1861 three sons of John Julius Izard Pringle were studying at Heidelberg.[39]

An annual summer sojourn in cooler climes also marked off the planting families from those unable to afford such changes of residence. During the eighteenth century it was not as necessary to leave the plantations, but with the general practice of tidal culture brought in after the Revolution, older fields were abandoned and became breeding grounds for mosquitoes. According to Lawrence F. Brewster, by the nineteenth century an annual summer removal was considered a necessity.[40] From May or June until October or November most planters took their families either to the shore or the sandhills or the mountains or the pine land communities that grew up later. The wealthiest traveled to Newport and Saratoga or, after the rise of abolitionism, to the Virginia springs.

Early May was usually the time of removal. Fredrika Bremer wrote on April 12, 1850, that she must hurry and pay a visit to Poinsett at his plantation on the Black River for all the planters leave their plantations "early in May." [41] David Doar has written that the return in the fall had to be carefully planned: "I heard one planter say that he would rather move to the plantation early in November without a frost than in October after a heavy frost because in the first instance, he said, vegetation died gradually and surely but in October it was killed suddenly and made sickness." [42] The exodus was almost total, as is evidenced by the fact that the Church of the Messiah, North Santee, never held services from June to November.[43]

---

[38] Angelica Singleton Van Buren described this school of over eighty English and American boys at Vevay, Switzerland, where they spoke French exclusively. Angelica Van Buren to Mrs. M. R. Singleton, July 12, 1854, Angelica Singleton Van Buren Journal, 1854–1855, Singleton Papers, SCL. She met Joseph Blyth Allston there. Same to same, Sept. 1, 1854. *Ibid.*

[39] Krumpelmann, *op. cit.*, p. 163; *SCHM*, LXII (1961), 221, 223. There is a long series of letters written from Vevay by the Pringle boys in the Allston Papers, S. C. Hist. Soc.

[40] Lawrence Fay Brewster, *Summer Migrations and Resorts of South Carolina Low-Country Planters* (Durham, N. C., 1947), pp. 3–6.

[41] *Ibid.*, p. 7.

[42] David Doar, *Rice and Rice Planting in the South Carolina Low Country* (Charleston, S. C., 1936), p. 37.

[43] Samuel Gaillard Stoney, *Building a Church on the Santee, 1804–1807* (Charleston, S. C., 1945), p. 16.

The sea islands were the nearest places of refuge. The Santee planters built summer homes on Murphy's Island, Cedar Island, and South Island, all situated at the mouth of the delta. On South Island Andrew Johnstone, Alexander Hume, and F. W. Ford had homes. David Doar, whose family lived on Murphy's Island and Cedar Island, in his book on the rice planters has given sketches of summer life on these islands. At Cedar Island there was a little village. Fishing parties and picnic dinners were the diversions. And from these islands the plantations could be easily reached. The planter could maintain a watchful eye on his slaves and the crop. Expeditions up the river to the plantations might partake of a race.[44]

North Island was a more familiar rendezvous. One summer gathering place was named Lafayette. The village at North Inlet was the largest of the summer communities, having 100 houses and a church. Although the settlement was swept away in the great hurricane of 1822, the resort was quickly rebuilt. R. S. Green advertised his school at North Inlet in 1825.[45] Lockwood in his geography of 1832 described these settlements as "equally delightful as to aspect, society and healthfulness." [46] The journal of General Peter Horry catches the easy pace of summer existence on North Island.[47]

General Horry moved over from his house in town and was supplied from Dover plantation with his carriage, mules, cow and calf, and servants. A boat was kept for fishing. The pigs ran wild. Fresh meat was obtained from the island's butcher; cattle lying on the beach was a not unusual sight. All sorts of vegetables could be brought from Dover— okra, snap beans, "see wee beans." If Mrs. Trapier got some pears she would share them with the General, as he would share his watermelons with her. The General apparently did not bathe in the sea since he had a large bathing tub. Eating, drinking, and driving on the beach were the diversions. There might be a julep before breakfast and shrimp at

[44] Doar, *op. cit.*, pp. 37–39.

[45] Brewster, *op. cit.*, p. 26.

[46] Thomas P. Lockwood, *A Geography of South-Carolina* (Charleston, S. C., 1832), p. 34.

[47] The following account of life on the beach is drawn from "Journal of General Peter Horry," ed. A. S. Salley, *SCHM*, XXXVIII (1937), 81–86, 116–119; XXXIX (1938), 46–49, 96–99, 125–128, 157–159; XL (1939), 11–14, 48–51, 91–96, 142–144; XLI (1940), 15–18; XLII (1941), 8–11, 72–75, 118–121.

breakfast. During the War of 1812 a visit to the officers stationed at the south end of the island was customary. Dinner often lasted from three to five in the afternoon. At one of these affairs the gentlemen drank two dozen bottles of wine. The morning and afternoon rides on the beach when the tide was low provided a chance for the General to see his friends: the Trapiers, Dr. Blyth, Mr. Michau and his two sons, Major Samuel Wragg, Hasell, John Man Taylor, Mr. Pyatt, Jr., John Waldo (the schoolmaster) and his assistant, Colonel Huggins, and Mr. Botsford.

The Waccamaw planters had only to move a few miles to the east, from the river side of the Neck to the ocean side. Their properties generally ran east and west from river to ocean so that it was quite easy to build a summer home on the eastern side of their estates. Some of these summer homes were notable: Dr. Heriot's Woodland at Murrell's Inlet, Colonel Ward's Magnolia and Retreat, J. Motte Alston's Sunnyside.[48] Dubourdieu Island and Pawley's Island were favorites. Reverend William Capers kept a school on Dubourdieu and preached there on every Sunday in 1817.[49]

The Black River and Pee Dee River planters came with their families, having to cross the rivers to reach the Neck and the shore. The Allston letters tell of the journeys back and forth from Matanzas.[50] Mrs. Allston could be rowed over and back in one day, shading herself with a large umbrella while the oarsmen sang in unison. On one trip she fell into the river: "I was wet up to my waist, and a good deal agitated, fortunately, I had a change of clothes at the house. . . ."[51]

Life on the shore could be strenuous or relaxing as each individual desired. Bathing in the surf or horseback riding on the beach were favorite diversions. Mrs. Allston feared that Carie North's routine would not improve her looks while sojourning on the beach as she continued to "give Adele 2 lessons in music of an hour each day," to practicing two hours herself, and then to give two hours to reading history and two hours to reading and writing French.[52] But such studying must have

[48] Childs, *op. cit.*, p. 125.
[49] Brewster, *op. cit.*, p. 27.
[50] Easterby, *Rice Plantation*, pp. 100–102.
[51] *Ibid.*, p. 121; Patience Pennington [Elizabeth W. Allston Pringle], *A Woman Rice Planter*, ed. Cornelius O. Cathey (Cambridge, Mass., 1961), p. 58.
[52] Easterby, *Rice Plantation*, p. 100.

been the exception. Mrs. Allston probably exemplified the pace when she wrote: "I walk the causeway every morning after breakfast, and stroll upon the beach and sandhills in the afternoon." [53]

After the turn of the century, when transportation was somewhat easier, a number of Georgetown men moved their families to the High Hills of the Santee for the summer. The High Hills, about eighty miles from Georgetown with no rivers to cross on the way, are a chain of hills about twenty-two miles long and five miles wide, which reach a height of 300 feet at Stateburg. Although Stateburg had not become the state's capital as its founder Thomas Sumter had hoped, it did become a summer capital. Many families found the region so attractive that they made a permanent change of residence. Judge Thomas Waties built Marden there in 1785. The father of William Capers sold his Waccamaw plantation in 1805 and erected Woodland. Cleland Kinloch lived at Acton in 1805, and Francis Kinloch Huger also built a home. Elihu Hall Bay and John Mayrant were migrants from the lowcountry, although some of their descendants returned to Winyah Bay. Mrs. Kirkpatrick, Davison McDowell's mother, was a resident. Just north of Stateburg was Bradford Springs, which the McDowells, Frasers, and Gaillards frequented in the 1820's.[54]

The first to go as far as the mountains was Joseph Alston, who had a home near the present site of Greenville before 1810. After 1833 Joel Poinsett was residing at the Homestead. In the 1830's Colonel William A. Alston and his twin daughters, the Misses Anna and Charlotte Alston, and Andrew Johnstone were also in Greenville. Benjamin Allston, Sr., made an annual pilgrimage during the last twenty years of his life. And the Reverend C. C. Pinckney, who had been pastor at the Church of the Messiah, North Santee, became the first permanent rector of Christ Church in Greenville, 1836–1846. Not too far away in Pendleton was Francis Kinloch Huger, who had moved up from Stateburg.[55]

[53] *Ibid.,* p. 102.

[54] Brewster, *op. cit.,* pp. 46–48, 74; Thomas S. Sumter, *Stateburg and Its People* (Sumter, S. C., 1926), p. 6; John R. Sumter, *Some Old Stateburg Homes* (Sumter, S. C., 1934), pp. 9–12; William W. Wightman, *Life of William Capers* (Nashville, Tenn., 1858), pp. 45, 47.

[55] Brewster, *op. cit.,* pp. 57–61. F. A. Porcher has left a compelling portrait of the entirely self-made, very rich, Benjamin Allston, "one of the distinguished habitués" of Greenville during the summer seasons. "His conversation was that of

The most famous of all of the Carolina mountain resorts was Flat Rock, North Carolina. Flat Rock was not accessible until the Saluda Gap Road, planned by the South Carolina Board of Public Works, was completed in 1825. Charles Baring and Mitchell King of Charleston, the pioneers of this resort in the late 1820's, were followed by the rice planters. John Izard Middleton was there by 1828. Thomas Lowndes, the father of Rawlins and Richard Henry, was in residence with his family by the mid-1830's; Andrew Johnstone, by 1839. The Dunkins and the Maxwells were there in the 1840's. After the Reverend C. C. Pinckney left Christ Church, Greenville, in 1846, he preached occasionally in Flat Rock. At Fletcher, not far away, Alexander Robertson built Struan, a white-columned mansion named after the Robertson ancestral estate in Scotland. In 1856 the Wards made a grand pilgrimage to Struan.[56] During the Civil War these summer homes provided ready-made refuges from the dangers on the coast.[57]

The Virginia springs had been popular from an early date. Colonel William Alston met Thomas Jefferson at Warm Springs in 1818. Joseph Waties Allston died at Red Sulphur Springs on August 13, 1834. Sextus Tertius Gaillard visited Salt Sulphur in July 1835; the Poinsetts were at Hot Springs in 1838. Mrs. William Bull Pringle stopped at White Sulphur in 1845; the John Izard Middletons at Rockbridge Alum Springs in 1858. The fashion was to make a circuit of the Virginia springs in order to enjoy the leisurely, rural, supposedly healthful life. Only the very rich could move so slowly and elegantly.[58]

Nearer home and far less pretentious were the pine land villages which began to attract a few families in the 1840's and 1850's. These were places safe enough for the family yet close enough for the fathers to ride over to their plantations during the day. They appealed to the planters who did not trust their entire planting operation to overseers.

---

an utterly uneducated man. His language was like a negro's, not only in pronunciation, but even in tone. He was deaf." But he was a man of character. "Memoirs of Frederick Adolphus Porcher," ed. Samuel G. Stoney, *SCHM*, XLVII (1946), 92–93.

[56] Brewster, *op. cit.*, pp. 63–69; Edward Read Memminger, *An Historical Sketch of Flat Rock* (Asheville, N. C., 1954); S. S. Patton, *A Condensed History of Flat Rock* (Asheville, N. C., n.d.).

[57] Rev. William Wyndham Malet, *An Errand to the South in the Summer of 1862* (London, 1863), pp. 213–252.

[58] Brewster, *op. cit.*, pp. 91–100.

Plantersville, the best example of such a rendezvous in Georgetown District, was advantageously located on slightly rising ground, midway between the Black and Pee Dee rivers. White's Bridge was a meeting place for the Sampit River planters.[59] What was needed was a healthy spot in the pine barrens at a distance from the swamps. Brewster has written: "To be safe in them it is necessary that the land be as barren as possible, and that not a tree be cut down except to leave room for the house. Even a little garden it's considered would entail some risk." [60] This community of summer houses was incorporated in 1852 by the state legislature.[61] After the Civil War, Plantersville became a more permanent rendezvous of the white population.

Those who could afford to hire good overseers might stay away longer and travel to more distant places. Newport had always been an attraction. The Flaggs had lived in Rhode Island. Two children of Elias Horry IV were born in Newport and one died at Newport.[62] Cleland Kinloch sailed home to Georgetown direct from Newport in 1799. John Hume and Alexander Mazyck made arrangements for the building of the Church of the Messiah while summering at Newport. Henry Augustus Middleton took his family there annually, acquiring extensive property holdings and becoming a continuing subscriber to the Redwood Library.[63] Saratoga was almost as popular as Newport. Rawlins Lowndes went to New York regularly. In 1838 R. F. W. Allston took his family

[59] *Ibid.*, p. 43; "Will of Maurice H. Lance," dated July 23, 1868, proved Nov. 29, 1870, Judge of Probate, Georgetown County, Will Book A (1865–1912), pp. 59–62, WPA typescript, S. C. Archives.

[60] Brewster, *op. cit.*, p. 35.

[61] S. C. Ford, S. T. Gaillard, J. R. Ford, J. P. Ford, J. R. Sparkman, G. T. Ford, and others were incorporated as the Plantersville Society on Dec. 16, 1852. *Acts of the General Assembly of the State of South Carolina, passed in December, 1852* (Columbia, S. C., 1853), p. 149. The petition of these gentlemen stated that in 1839 the Plantersville Co. had purchased 350 acres where they might enjoy health which the rice grounds did not provide. Petitions, Public Improvements, Legislative System, 1830–1859, S. C. Archives.

[62] William Branford Horry (April 30, 1799–May 26, 1808) was buried (after being killed by being thrown from his horse) in Trinity Churchyard, Newport, R. I. He had resided three years in the town.

[63] Alicia Hopton Middleton, *Life in Carolina and New England During the Nineteenth Century* (Bristol, R. I., 1929); George Champlin Mason, *Annals of the Redwood Library and Athenaeum, Newport, R. I.* (Newport, R. I., 1891), pp. 158, 186.

to Saratoga. Newport, and Boston.[64] In 1858 Robert Pringle visited Saratoga.[65]

The Georgetown planters also traveled abroad. Joel Roberts Poinsett and John Izard Middleton had served their country in diplomatic posts.[66] Andrew Johnstone and Dr. Heriot took their families to visit distant relatives in Scotland; the Heriots also viewed the Crystal Palace Exhibition in London in 1851. Ralph Stead Izard traveled to Switzerland to put his sons in school there. Joseph Blyth Allston visited the Izard boys in 1854 while making a grand tour after having graduated from the College in Columbia.[67] The next year R. F. W. Allston took his wife and eldest daughter on a tour of Europe.

With their ever-increasing wealth the Georgetown planters bought Charleston homes. By the 1850's there was scarcely a rich Georgetown planter who did not have a Charleston mansion.[68] Part of the Georgetown planters, particularly those from the Santee, were originally Charleston based. The Lowndes, the Horrys, the Humes, the Manigaults, the Middletons, the Pringles, the Ladsons, the Tidymans, the Deases, the Pinckneys, the Rutledges, and the Mazycks all had Charleston homes. Among these dwellings were some of the most famous of the Charleston mansions. There were no finer homes than the Branford-Horry house at the corner of Meeting and Tradd, the Miles Brewton home at No. 13 King in which William Bull Pringle lived, No. 4 Meeting Street where Major James H. Ladson resided, Philip Tidyman's Ladson's Court residence where his famous hospitality had been dispensed,[69] and Henry Augustus Middleton's home at No. 44 South Battery. These were, however, older homes than the ones that the Georgetown planters themselves built in the newer parts of town.

[64] Easterby, *Rice Plantation*, pp. 76–83.

[65] Brewster, *op. cit.*, p. 109.

[66] J. Fred Rippy, *Joel R. Poinsett, Versatile American* (Durham, N. C., 1935), passim; *SCHM*, I (1900), 249.

[67] Among an interesting series of letters he wrote to Mrs. R. F. W. Allston from Europe there is one of July 14, 1856, describing the history of the French Huguenots in Berlin. Allston Papers, S. C. Hist. Soc.

[68] The following account is based upon the Charleston directories for the two decades before the war.

[69] The Duke of Saxe-Weimar described such an entertainment. Bernhard, Duke of Saxe-Weimar Eisenach, *Travels Through North America during the Years 1825 and 1826* (Philadelphia, Penn., 1828), II, 11.

The most notable invasion of Charleston was by the Alston and Allston families. Colonel William Alston of Clifton purchased in April 1791 the Miles Brewton mansion after his marriage to Mary Brewton Motte. This house was willed to his daughter Mary, who married William Bull Pringle.[70] Colonel William Alston's sons also picked out the most handsome dwellings or selected the most conspicuous locations for the homes that they built. Colonel T. P. Alston lived at the corner of Society and Meeting. Charles Alston, Sr., owned No. 11 East Battery. William Algernon Alston's son Joseph was at No. 9 East Battery and later at No. 24 Pitt Street while another son John Ashe built on the northwest corner of Rutledge and Tradd a fine home that then overlooked the Ashley River and which contained a notable collection of paintings.[71]

Mrs. Benjamin Allston, Sr., lived in great style at 3 East Battery. She left at her death in 1859 great quantities of silver plate to her nieces and nephews, as well as diamond rings and a brooch to her step-daughter Mrs. Martha Pyatt, a French gold and white china dinner service to her step-granddaughter Charlotte Trapier, silver salt cellars to John F. Pyatt, fireplace furniture to Joseph B. Pyatt, the entry lamp to her home to Mary Coachman McKay, and brandy and wines to her executors Robertson and Blacklock.[72] Joseph Blyth Allston in 1859 was residing at No. 55 Tradd St. But it was R. F. W. Allston who tried to outdo all the other members of his family by purchasing in 1857 for $38,000 the show place No. 37 Meeting Street that had been built by Nathaniel Russell. The purchase price was a tremendous drain upon his finances even though he put up only $2,000.[73] Yet, since he was governor of the state and ready to launch his daughters into society, such a mansion was almost expected of him.

Even more noteworthy was the Georgetown colony in the newer parts of the city above Boundary Street. There was a cluster of Georgetown planters residing in the suburb of Hampstead. When the first Plowden Weston died in 1827 he left his home in Hampstead to his son

---

[70] Susan Pringle Frost, *Highlights of the Miles Brewton House* (Charleston, S. C., 1944), pp. 47, 51, 53.

[71] Childs, *op. cit.*, pp. 106–107.

[72] "Will of Mary Coachman Allston," dated May 1856, proved July 5, 1859, Charleston County Wills, XLVIII (1856–1862), 479–484, S. C. Archives.

[73] Easterby, *Rice Plantation*, pp. 23, 45, 136–139, 214, 230, 428.

Dr. Paul Weston. Every year the Westons moved from the Pee Dee to Charleston. Mrs. Weston once stated: "We have to take fifty individuals with us in the move, I mean children and all." When asked why, she replied: "We cannot possibly separate husband and wife for six months; so Harry, the coachman, has to have his wife and children, and the same with the cook, and the butler, and the laundress, until we are actually moving an army every time we move." [74] Francis Weston lived first on Drake and then No. 2 Columbus Street. The Wards bought the Faber villa on Bay Street at Amherst. John Hyrne Tucker was on the Bay near Blake. Mrs. Catherine LaBruce resided at No. 6 Drake Street overlooking the marsh of the Cooper River. Not very far away was Francis Withers' home on the corner of John and Meeting streets a new mansion of the 1840's. The Pyatt family was at the southeast corner of Meeting and Charlotte from 1849 to 1859. The Nowells lived at the corner of East Bay and Reid. The Reverend Maurice Lance resided on Charlotte Street. Benjamin Foissin Trapier had a home first on Drake Street and then at 53 Meeting. His son William Heyward Trapier lived on north Meeting and then at the corner of Meeting and Charlotte. Judge Dunkin, who had had a law office in Charleston, also had a home after 1840 in the house which still stands on the southeast corner of Smith and Warren streets. Not until 1859 did a Sparkman have a Charleston home when the widow of William Ervin Sparkman took a house on Pitt Street.

The planters resided in these homes during the social season in February after the crops were in and also during the summer months. They therefore sought homes on the tongues of land which stuck out into the Ashley and Cooper rivers. The lots were larger than in the older sections of the town, the gardens more extensive, and the piazzas broad. Besides the Alstons and Allstons on High Battery and the Westons and Wards in Hampstead there were other Georgetown planters strung along Rutledge and Lynch (later Ashley), particularly in the area that had been known as Harleston's Village. John Harleston Read lived at the corner of Wentworth and Rutledge from 1835 to 1859. In 1859 the

[74] Elizabeth W. Allston Pringle, *Chronicles of Chicora Wood* (Boston, Mass., 1940), pp. 158–159. With the building of the cotton factory in Hampstead, the Westons became unhappy. See E. B. Weston to Mrs. R. F. W. Allston, June 6, 1848, Aug. 14, 1849, July 9, 1850, Allston Papers, S. C. Hist. Soc.

Reads owned No. 29 Meeting Street and No. 10 Charlotte Street. Frederick Shaffer was at the corner of Calhoun and Pitt. John Hume was at 137 Wentworth in 1835; Robert Hume at 6 Lynch Street early in the 1850's. Jonathan Lucas was listed as of Cannonsborough in 1850. William Lucas and John Hume Lucas were on Rutledge, Simons Lucas on Pitt, and Henry Ewbank Lucas on Calhoun. S. D. Doar owned No. 30 Pitt Street.

Most of the Winyah planters attended the parish church of St. Paul's, Radcliffeborough. This spacious and elegant church, the largest in town, was built of brick and rough-cast on Coming Street, north of Boundary, between 1810 and 1815 and was known as the Third Church, being the third Episcopal congregation in the city, following St. Philip's and St. Michael's. Jonathan Lucas was on the original building committee. Jonathan Lucas, Jr., and Andrew Hasell were on the first vestry.[75] In the 1850's, when a fine new organ was bought by a subscription of $5,-000, the Pyatt brothers, Mrs. LaBruce, John Hyrne Tucker, the Reverend M. H. Lance, Alexander Robertson, and John Freer Blacklock contributed.[76] Francis Withers was a consistent contributor to the church, offering at one time to give $1,000 toward missions. Both E. C. Logan and T. J. Girardeau served St. Paul's as ministers in the 1850's, as well as the Church of the Messiah, North Santee. St. Paul's was known as "the planters' church."

This was the church in which many Georgetown folk were married, and in its graveyard many were buried. In 1854 the Reverend Maurice Harvey Lance married Sarah Laura, daughter of Samuel Smith of Georgetown.[77] Both the Withers and the Westons had cemetery lots according to a plat of July 1854, although no gravestones remain in the yard.[78] There are, however, many graves of Georgetown District planters

[75] Albert Sidney Thomas, A Historical Account of the Protestant Episcopal Church in South Carolina, 1820–1957 (Columbia, S. C., 1957), pp. 241–243, 350–352.
[76] "Resolution to raise $5,000 for an organ," framed document hanging in the church.
[77] Pee Dee Times, Aug. 2, 1854. See also Rev. Maurice H. Lance, An Address delivered in St. Paul's Church, Radcliffeborough, before the Charleston Protestant Episcopal Sunday School Society, on their Twelfth Anniversary, May 24, 1831 (Charleston, S. C., 1831).
[78] "Plat of a part of St. Paul's Churchyard, July 1854," framed document hanging in church. The remainder of the information comes from an examination of the graveyard by the author.

marked by gravestones. Jonathan Lucas, Sr., is buried in the church-yard, as are the wives of Jonathan Lucas, Jr., and William Lucas, as well as the master of Hopsewee, John Hume Lucas. There are many graves of the Lucas and Hume families, and a giant mausoleum of the Johnston family. Elias Horry IV, who died in 1834, was buried in the yard, as were many members of his family. Thomas Lowndes, the father of Rawlins and Richard Henry, was buried in 1843. John Harleston Read, who died in 1859, and John Harleston Read II, who died in 1866, were both interred here. Catherine Ward, wife of Dr. Lewis C. Hasell, has a stone dated 1862. The Tidymans, the Bulows, and the Nowells were also interred.

Upon the death of John Hyrne Tucker in 1859 a tribute of respect was adopted by the vestry of St. Paul's Church, Radcliffeborough: "Although the larger portion of each year was passed in attending to his planting interests on the Waccamaw and Pee Dee rivers, yet when he was with us, he ever manifested a deep and heartfelt interest in everything connected with the spiritual and temporal welfare of our Church, contributing always liberally, in every way, to its advancement." He and his fourth wife lie side-by-side in the churchyard.[79]

The Allstons and Alstons alone seemed to be lacking in their connection with this church. Governor John Lide Wilson died on February 13, 1849, in Charleston and was buried in St. Paul's.[80] There is also the grave of Charlotte Allston Jones, the orphan daughter of Mary Pyatt Allston Jones, the niece of R. F. W. Allston, who died at the age of four-teen while attending school in Charleston. Alexander Robertson, the rice factor who took care of so much Allston business in town including the supervision of children at school, wrote R. F. W. Allston on November 14, 1838: "I had every thing done as though she was my own, and discharged my last sad duty towards her by putting her in our private cemetery in St. Pauls church Yard."[81] Judge Dunkin, who lived around the corner on Warren and Smith, attended this church regularly. His daughter married an Alston and after the war this Alston family lived

[79] Harriette K. Leiding, *Historic Homes of South Carolina* (Philadelphia, Penn., 1921), p. 121.
[80] *Winyah Observer*, Feb. 21, 1849.
[81] Easterby, *Rice Plantation*, p. 411.

in the Dunkin home and attended St. Paul's.[82] Although situated in Charleston, St. Paul's was a Georgetown institution.

The Georgetown planters carried their ideas with them on their vacations and on their visits to Charleston. These gentlemen in the 1850's were the most ardent in favor of secession. With the rice planters from the Combahee and the cotton planters from the sea islands south of Charleston building summer homes in Hampstead, Radcliffeborough, Cannonsborough, and Harleston's Village, there was a chance for the planters to overawe the merchants and factors still residing in the older parts of the city. Charleston had a different mental climate in the 1850's from the city that had ushered in the American Revolution. The difference was marked by the presence of the planters from the Combahee, the Edisto, the Santee, and the Waccamaw. The power and influence of these planters was based upon their wealth derived from planting rice.

[82] Parish Register, Church Office, Cathedral of St. Luke and St. Paul, Radcliffeborough, Charleston, S. C.

XV

RICE PLANTING

Georgetown District was the principal rice-growing area in the United States. In 1840 the district produced 36,360,000 of a total national crop of 80,841,422 pounds of rice. In 1850 the district produced 46,765,040 of a total national crop of 215,313,497 pounds of rice. In 1860 the district produced 55,805,385 of a total national crop of 187,-167,032 pounds of rice. In 1840 Georgetown District came very close to producing one-half of the total rice crop of the United States.[1]

Cotton was not a Georgetown crop. After the Revolution some cotton was grown in the district, but in 1842 Anthony Toomer Porter, at the age of fourteen, having lived continuously in the district, could mistake a field of Irish potatoes for a field of cotton, so little was he accustomed to seeing the latter.[2] Robert Mills, when recording the statistics of the

[1] In 1840 Charleston District produced 11,938,750, Beaufort 5,629,402, and Colleton 5,483,533. In 1850 Charleston District produced 15,700,603, Beaufort 47,-230,082, and Colleton 45,308,660. In 1860 Charleston District produced 18,899,512, Beaufort 18,790,918, and Colleton 22,838,984. *Compendium of the . . . Sixth Census* (Washington, D. C., 1841), p. 192; *The Seventh Census of the United States: 1850* (Washington, D. C., 1853), pp. lxxxii, lxxxiv, 346; *Agriculture of the United States in 1860 . . . the Eighth Census* (Washington, D. C., 1864), pp. xciv, 128.

[2] A. Toomer Porter, *Led On! Step by Step* (New York, 1967), p. 4. Lewis Du Pré dedicated his 1799 pamphlet describing the way to cultivate cotton to Maj. Charles Brown, who had successfully experimented with the crop at "Rich-Land on Winyaw

state in 1826, observed that in Georgetown "every thing is fed on rice; horses and cattle eat the straw and bran; hogs, fowls, etc. are sustained by the refuse; and man subsists upon the marrow of the grain." [3]

The rice planters of Georgetown District depended upon overseers to manage their plantations. This was particularly true when the planters were growing rice on more than one plantation. The overseers came from the poorer class of whites who inhabited the pine lands of the district. Most of the surnames of R. F. W. Allston's overseers can be found in the Georgetown District census for 1790; his overseers, therefore, were generally natives. According to J. Harold Easterby, "their lot in life was hard; and they seldom overcame their handicaps." [4] In order to supplement their incomes the overseer often sold to the planter timber, shingles, and cooper stuff which they obtained from their native acres. When an overseer retired, he went back to the pine lands. R. F. W. Allston wrote of one overseer who, when he retired, "settled with his promising and thriving family in the pine lands of Georgetown District where, without anyone to say him nay, when disposed to roost a Turkey or trail the deer, he pass'd the remainder of his days, an honest independent and dutiful citizen, a faithful friend and good neighbour." [5]

According to Henry A. Middleton, one wanted in an overseer a temperate man who was good as a planter, a manager, and an attendant upon the sick.[6] The overseer began his career by making a written contract with the planter, usually in January. On January 15, 1822, Mrs.

Bay." Lewis Du Pré, *Observations on the Culture of Cotton* (Georgetown, S. C., 1799). In 1850 Georgetown District produced only 81 bales (400 pounds to the bale) of ginned cotton, of which R. W. Gourdin produced 67 bales.

[3] Robert Mills, *Statistics of South Carolina* (Charleston, S. C., 1826), p. 558. In 1850 Georgetown District produced 81 bales of cotton. Only Horry District produced less in South Carolina. *The Seventh Census of the United States: 1850, op. cit.,* p. 346.

[4] *The South Carolina Rice Plantation, as Revealed in the Papers of Robert F. W. Allston,* ed. J. H. Easterby (Chicago, 1945), p. 27. William K. Scarborough in making a statistical analysis of the 83 overseers in Georgetown District in 1860 discovered that their average age was 30.4 years, that only 12 percent were over forty years of age, that 58 percent were married, that none were illiterate, that 30 percent owned real property, that 18 percent owned substantial personal property, and that 22 percent owned slaves (the average number being 8.6). William K. Scarborough, *The Overseer: Plantation Management in the Old South* (Baton Rouge, La., 1966), p. 57.

[5] Easterby, *op. cit.,* p. 264.

[6] *Ibid.,* p. 261.

Elizabeth Frances Blyth made a contract with William T. Thompson to oversee Friendfield and Waties Point plantations "in a planter like manner, with care, skill, fidelity, sobriety, & ability, & more especially with moderation & humanity to the negroes." He was not to strike a Negro with a stick, nor exercise any severity without consulting Mrs. Blyth. He would be allowed a Negro woman to cook and wash for him and a Negro boy to wait upon him, and at the end of the term of one year he would be paid $500. An overseer often obtained the privilege to keep cattle for his own profit, but this privilege might be abused, as it was in Thompson's case.[7] Plowden Weston had three criteria by which to judge an overseer:

First—by the general well-being of all the negroes; their cleanly appearance, respectful manners, active and vigorous obedience; their completion of their tasks well and early; the small amount of punishment; the excess of births over deaths; the small number of persons in hospital, and the health of the children. *Secondly*—the condition and fatness of the cattle and mules; the good repair of all the fences and buildings, harness, boats, flats, and ploughs; more particularly the good order of the banks and trunks, and the freedom of the fields from grass and volunteer. *Thirdly*—the amount and quality of the rice and provision crops.[8]

The overseer's contract could be renewed if agreeable to both parties. During the forty years before the Civil War, salaries ranged from $250 to $1,200 a year. Thompson started at $500, since he was to manage two plantations. His salary rose until it reached $900 for the years 1833 to 1838. Jesse Bellflowers, who was R. F. W. Allston's most successful overseer, started with $300, but after 1852 he received $1,000 a year. With his savings, since he was single, Bellflowers bought slaves and made an additional $800 a year from their hire. Henry A. Middleton offered $1,200 to one of Allston's overseers in 1858.[9]

The overseer had complete management of the plantation. He was undoubtedly happier when the master and mistress were at a distance. Gabriel Ellis complained in 1838 that Mrs. Allston had divested him of

---

[7] *Ibid.*, pp. 24, 257–259.

[8] "Rules on the Rice Estate of P. C. Weston; South Carolina, 1856," *De Bow's Review*, XXI (January 1857), 38–44.

[9] Easterby, *op. cit.*, p. 27.

so much authority that he could not manage the Negroes.[10] The overseer often trained the planter's son. R. F. W. Allston wrote his son on January 28, 1856, that Bellflowers was getting old "and it would be well for you to profit some years by his experience whilst he is still active & capable." It was time, therefore, for young Ben to leave the army and become a planter. On the first of January each year the overseer made a full report of all property on the plantation, although he furnished other reports from time to time.[11]

Overseers might, of course, pick up and leave at any time, as James Kelly did during the California gold rush,[12] but they rarely moved up the economic and social ladder into the planter class, at least there is no example of this phenomenon in the decades just prior to the Civil War. J. A. Hemingway, who came to Allston in 1839 and worked for him for many years, was able in 1855 to offer Allston slaves valued at $10,000.[13] J. Motte Alston recorded the moderately successful story of Sam Kirton in these words:

Sam Kirton was one of the best men of his class I ever knew. When he came to me he was young and inexperienced and I only paid him $250 per annum. I increased his salary each year till he received $600 and then hearing that Pyatt of Georgetown would pay $1,000 for a good man I recommended Kirton to him. I had to make him leave me, though I regretted his so doing. He saved money and when the war broke out went into the Confederate army and afterwards was employed by my uncle Charles Alston, who told me he was the best overseer he ever knew. His health failing, he bought a farm on the Coosa River, near Rome, and when I was there in 1880 he came to see me, a married man and comfortably off.[14]

A successful overseer might be allowed to manage other plantations. Gabriel Ellis, who was hired by Allston in 1831, also managed in 1838 the estates of Dr. William Allston. This double burden may have been his undoing, for he was charged with cruelty to the slaves on Dr. Allston's plantations. Later, when serving with Henry A. Middleton at

[10] *Ibid.*, p. 255.
[11] *Ibid.*, p. 128; Scarborough, *op. cit.*, p. 163.
[12] Easterby, *op. cit.*, p. 127.
[13] *Ibid.*, p. 25
[14] *Rice Planter and Sportsman, The Recollections of J. Motte Alston, 1821–1909,* ed. Arney R. Childs (Columbia, S. C., 1953), p. 109.

Weehaw, he was described by Middleton as a "Bad Man."[15] Seldom, of course, was there the rapport which existed between R. F. W. Allston and Jesse Bellflowers. When Bellflowers was sick, Allston would visit him every evening "sitting a half hour or more" and "reading him a chapter and a Psalm."[16]

The laborers on the Georgetown rice plantations had been Negro slaves since the earliest days. Those present on the plantations in 1850 had been handed down generation after generation from father to son. After the decade of the 1780's very few slaves had been brought in from outside the district. It was said of Plowden Weston's slaves that "All the 350 negroes (except old Pemba, about 70 years of age, who had been brought from Africa, when a little girl) were born on the estate: like Abraham's servants, 'born in his own house.'"[17] There was, however, some transfer of family groups and gangs from one plantation to another within the district as planters built up a larger labor force. These transfers took place at the time of settling estates.

The story of R. F. W. Allston's efforts to acquire slaves for his plantations is a good example of how a labor force was acquired in Georgetown District. His father left him a boy, and a half-interest in two carpenters. His share of a residuary group was sixteen which he received in 1819. Eight or nine more were received when his brother William died in 1823, and seven the next year on the death of his mother. "Nine others having been purchased from the latter's estate, he found himself with a gang of some 42 Negroes when, in 1827, he was ready to give his whole time to planting." In 1828 he purchased two groups of slaves, one of forty-eight and another of sixteen, who had belonged to the estate of Robert Francis Withers. These were needed to clear the swamp at Matanzas in order to expand production. In 1848 he inherited fifty-eight from his aunt Mrs. Blyth; thirty-nine others were received in trust for his own sons and nephews. In 1851 he purchased fifty-one Negroes who came with Rose Bank plantation. Two more large pur-

[15] *Ibid.*, p. 25. In 1838 he received $1,500 for managing three separate plantations. Scarborough, *op. cit.*, pp. 12–13.

[16] Childs, *op. cit.*, p. 26. Allston left Bellflowers a legacy in his will. Scarborough, *op. cit.*, p. 115.

[17] William Wyndham Malet, *An Errand to the South in the Summer of 1862* (London, 1863), p. 50.

chases were made in 1859; the first consisted of forty-one individuals
from Dr. Forster for his son whom he was setting up at Guendalos and
the second of 116 from his sister-in-law. His slaves numbered 590 at
his death in 1864. Allston never sold any of his slaves except during
the Civil War when financial need forced him to do so.[18]

As an executor for others, however, he was often in the market. In
1837 he sold fifty-one slaves from the Waverly force in order to reduce
the large debt upon his brother's estate. Most of this buying and
selling, however, was within the district, and there was an attempt to
keep families together. Allston wrote his nephew on January 13, 1859:
"If you meet with an orderly gang of some planter neighbor or otherwise who would sell you at $500 rather than send away and separate his
people at a higher figure then in such case you might adventure." [19] At
the same time there was a reluctance to acquire old Negroes. On agree-
ing to buy the Negroes from Pipe Down plantation in 1859, Allston
wrote: "But I do ask to be indulged with the privilege of disposing of
O. Conkey to J. W. LaBruce who owns his wife and to have old July
(Blind-Hannah does nothing but wait on him) and old Ned, who has
been dying every night during the winter with short breath, omitted
from the list of negroes to be paid for." Although not wanting to pay
for them, Allston did agree to care for them "so long as they live, just
the same." [20]

Anthony Toomer Porter in his autobiography described how he
consulted his slaves before choosing a new master for them after he had
decided to give up planting and become a minister. He then wrote:

I sent a certified list of all of them with the doctor's certificate as to
their physical condition to Mr. Philip Porcher of Charleston, the most
respectable broker who attended to such matters, asking for the valua-
tion of them, and in due time received his appraisement. I settled on
Dr. Allard H. [B.] Flagg, of Waccamaw, as the best man I knew, and
deducted sixteen thousand five hundred dollars from their appraised
value, in order that they might all be sold to one man with no separation. This was effected in October, 1851, and the slaves were to be
delivered early in December, after the crop was disposed of. The summer passed and the time came. . . . I chartered a steamer to come to

18 Easterby, *op. cit.*, pp. 28–29.
19 *Ibid.*, p. 151.
20 *Ibid.*, p. 29.

the wharf at the barnyard, and the pilgrimage began. God knows what it cost me; my distress was greater far than those people felt. I closed up my house, and went to the negro settlement, and moved the procession. All their household goods, their pigs and chickens, their cows and calves were all put in motion, all marched down to the steamer, I followed on horseback. I saw them all on board; then drawing them all up in line, I shook hands with every one from the youngest to the oldest, and left the boat, which soon steamed away.[21]

The prices paid for slaves did not vary greatly throughout the period. In 1837 Allston got an average of $725 each for the Waverly Negroes whom he sold, but the price was considered high. In 1859 he bought two lots of Negroes for an average of $500 each. Among these a carpenter was listed at $1,200, the highest price. Allston would not buy slaves at cotton prices.[22] Slaves that were sold to the west commanded higher prices, but few were sent from Georgetown to the west. Some, of course, were. There is a letter from Mobile in the Allston collection written by a slave who had been sold west asking about his friends in Georgetown.[23] Yet, the transfers were generally such as those of Toomer to Flagg. When Mrs. Rutledge sold her Negroes in 1859, her gang was bought by Joseph Blyth Allston, the slaves being transferred from the Santee to the Waccamaw.[24] J. Motte Alston when he shut down Woodbourne sold his Negroes to Governor John L. Manning, which transfer took his slaves out of the district but not out of the state.[25]

Originally the rice fields had been cut out of the swamps, or, if the natural marsh lands were used, a great amount of time and effort were expended on ditching and dikeing. J. Motte Alston almost alone among the planters of his day had carved a plantation from virgin land, a story he tells in his autobiography.[26]

[21] Porter, *op. cit.*, pp. 79–80.
[22] Easterby, *op. cit.*, pp. 30, 351–352.
[23] He adds a postscript: "There are many people, Black and White here from Geo. Town, that gives me Some Satisfaction." *Ibid.*, p. 339.
[24] *Ibid.*, pp. 152, 414.
[25] Childs, *op. cit.*, p. 126.
[26] *Ibid.*, p. 64. Judge Smith described the reclamation of the swamplands of Hobcaw Barony in Alice R. Huger Smith and Herbert Ravenel Sass, *A Carolina Rice Plantation of the Fifties* (New York, 1936), p. 23.

Field labor was done under the task system on the rice coast.[27] Men and women were all engaged together in the planting, cultivating, and harvesting, but a task was allotted to each slave according to his age and physical ability. Thus the slaves were considered as ¼, ½, ¾, and full-task hands. Each slave had an appointed task that must be finished, and it was the duty of the overseer and the Negro foreman and drivers to see that these tasks were done. Dr. Sparkman worked his slaves eight to nine hours in the winter and ten hours in the summer.[28] A hand detailed as a cook prepared the midday meal when an hour to an hour and a half was permitted the slaves for eating and refreshing themselves. The basic diet consisted of rice, corn, peas, and potatoes with rations of molasses, salted fish, pork, bacon, and fresh beef. The fresh beef was always given out as soup which was thickened with rice and garden vegetables; each hand received two quarts daily. The rations were given out at the end of the week. Sunday was a day of rest.

The work year began as soon as the harvest was in. The late fall was occupied with ditching, embanking, and repairing the trunks. Trunks were rectangular (sometimes diamond-shaped) wooden culverts from twenty to thirty feet long, placed in the main bank along the river side, extending clear through the bank and equipped with hanging doors at each end. The water for each flow and draining swept through the trunks, which opened and closed automatically with the change of the

[27] The following description of the planting of rice has been taken from a number of sources: David Doar, *Rice and Rice Planting in the South Carolina Low Country* (Charleston, S. C., 1936); [Elizabeth W. Allston Pringle], *A Woman Rice Planter,* ed. Cornelius O. Cathey (Cambridge, Mass., 1961); Lewis C. Gray, *History of Agriculture in the Southern United States to 1860* (Washington, D. C., 1933); Smith and Sass, *op. cit.;* R. F. W. Allston, "Memoir of the Introduction and Planting of Rice in South Carolina," *DeBow's Review,* I (1846), 320–357; R. F. W. Allston, "Essay on Sea Coast Crops," *DeBow's Review,* XVI (1854), 589–615; Duncan C. Heyward, *Seed from Madagascar* (Chapel Hill, N. C., 1937); *Planter Management and Capitalism in Ante-Bellum Georgia, The Journal of Hugh Fraser Grant, Rice-grower,* ed. Albert Virgil House (New York, 1954); "Charles Manigault's Essay on the Open Planting of Rice," ed. Albert V. House, Jr., *Agricultural History,* XVI (1942), 184–193; John H. Allston to the Agricultural Society, Nov. 11, 1823, Charleston Library Soc.; Edmund Ruffin, *Report of the Commencement and Progress of the Agricultural Survey of South Carolina for 1843* (Columbia, S. C., 1843), pp. 99–118.

[28] Easterby, *op. cit.,* p. 31. "The negroes on plantations have easy work: begin at sunrise, breakfast at nine, dinner at three; by which time the taskwork is usually finished." Malet, *op. cit.,* p. 57.

tide. The trunkminder was a very important person in the plantation work force. As the fields should be level for water culture, a good deal of time was spent, certainly at first, in correcting any departures from the level noticed during the cultivation of the preceding crop. Since the fields were never absolutely level, floodings were gauged by the high and low spots. As the field must be kept dry at times, the intersecting ditches had to be cleaned. This work of ditching and embanking was generally done by the male slaves.

Since the ebb and flow of the tide was used to drain and flood the fields, rice planting was confined to those stretches of the rivers which were still fresh water yet already affected by tidal action. This tidal culture was introduced, according to U. B. Phillips, by McKewn Johnston in 1758 at his plantation along Winyah Bay and, according to David Ramsay, by Gideon Dupont in 1783 at his Goose Creek plantation.[29] When R. F. W. Allston asked J. L. Petigru to check Ramsay's assertion, Petigru replied: "I have looked" at Ramsay's note "and am much disposed to think it fabulous. The water culture of Rice must have been more or less understood from the beginning and the additions that were made to the stock of Knowledge among those who cultivated the grain, were likely to be the gradual results of experience, rather than the sudden accession of a discovery."[30] Since William Swinton's advertisement of river swamp in the *Gazette*, January 19, 1738, stated that two fields would be "over flow'd with fresh water, every high tide, and of consequence not subject to the Droughts," Petigru was wise to dismiss this question of who first adopted the tidal culture of rice.

During the winter the land was well turned by plow or hoe. If water was put on during the winter, it was changed often so that the land would benefit from the sediment. Harrowing would take place in March. Harrowing and plowing were the two processes in the planting routine requiring machinery and animal labor; all else was hand culture. Bold trenching followed, with the trenches twelve or thirteen inches apart, center to center. The seed, which was sown by hand in April, was wetted in clay and water and then dried. This was done so that the seed

---

[29] Ulrich B. Phillips, *Life and Labor in the Old South* (New York, 1929), p. 116; David Ramsay, *History of South Carolina* (Newberry, S. C., 1858), II, 116.
[30] Easterby, *op. cit.*, p. 91.

would not float to the surface during the sprout flow.[31] Sprout water remained until the grain pipped, which took from three to six days. If the sprout flow remained a day too long, until the leaf formed, then the plant would float to the surface. During the sprout flow the hands worked on high land planting corn and sweet potatoes.

After the sprout flow, the water was taken off so that the sun could cause growth to about six inches. The land remained dry until the rice could be seen the whole length of the row. Then the point flow or stretch flow was put on for three to six days. Then the land was dried for hoeing, first by a light hoeing and then as the plant strengthened by another hoeing. When the long water was put on, the rice was over-topped for three or four days to float trash off; this overtopping also destroyed insects. Then the water was lowered and kept at a general level of about six inches deep for twelve to twenty-three days. During the long flow the hands tended the provision crops on the high lands or pulled grass from the rice fields that might be seen during the long flow. The water was drawn off gradually, which permitted time for pulling out grass. A period of dry culture followed. Two additional hoe-ings were then necessary, one just after the water was taken off by a four-inch hoe and a fourth and final hoeing, light, not too deep. The harvest or layby flow was a little deeper than the long flow. There was still grass to be plucked and also volunteer rice, which was rice that came up from the refuse of the preceding year's crop and not from the seed planted in April. It was inferior in quality and could be noted by the eye. During the harvest or layby flow of seven or eight weeks, the tempo of work was reduced.

The harvest began early in September. Shortly before the rice was fully ripe, the water would be withdrawn. The next morning the reapers would be in the field cutting the grain with old fashioned sickles, known as rice hooks. Then, after a day of dying on the stubble, the sheaves were tied and stacked in the flats. The grain was then trans-ported to the threshing yards located on the highland side of the river. This was the dangerous time of the year for a freshet might coincide

[31] John Hays Allston introduced the "claying" or "water cover" or "open trunk" system of rice culture before 1826. Marjorie S. Mendenhall, "A History of Agriculture in South Carolina, 1790–1860" (PhD dissertation, Univ. of N. C., 1940), p. 152.

with the full moon. R. F. W. Allston wrote on September 6, 1860: "Look out for the weather between the 22nd Septr. and the full moon." This was also the season for hurricanes that could sweep away an entire crop, as did the hurricane of September 7–9, 1854. Mrs. Allston described the scene: "From Waverly to Pee Dee on the 8th not one head of rice was to be seen above the water, not a bank or any appearance of the land was to be seen. It was one rolling dashing Sea, and the water was Salt as the Sea. . . . Many persons had rice cut and stacked in the field, which was all swept away by the flood. . . . Mr. J. J. [I.] Middleton had 40 acres of very superior rice swept away, a total loss. . . ." [32]

Late August and early September was the season of the rice birds. The bobolinks that had come north in May from South America were at that time returning southward. When the May birds came in the spring, it was best to have the seeds under water. Bird-minding was, therefore, an important task at two seasons of the year. Allston wrote on September 6, 1860, that he was sorry to hear of rice birds as he had lost by them "over 3000 bushels of rice last year at the two places." [33]

If these dangers had been escaped and threshing had been accomplished, then the rice was sent to the mill on the plantation or to Charleston to be husked and cleaned; or, if it was to be sold in the rough, it was shipped directly to the factor's counting house. The final task of the year was the gathering of provisions, which lasted well into November.

The plantation slaves sometimes worked off the plantation or at other tasks not directly connected with the crop. The commissioners of the roads waited until after the crops were gathered before assigning work to slaves on the roads of the district. In the summer a gang, however, might be taken to Pawley's Island to rebuild the causeway. Slaves who were artisans had their special work. Carpenters built the plantation homes and the mills; coopers made the barrels for the rice, three barrels a day being average production for a cooper.

Allston used twenty carpenters to rebuild Waverly mill in 1837, hiring additional carpenters from neighboring plantations. [34] This job was done

---

[32] Easterby, op. cit., pp. 120, 165.

[33] Ibid., p. 165; A. Sprunt and E. B. Chamberlain, South Carolina Bird Life (Columbia, S. C., 1949), pp. 489–490.

[34] Easterby, op. cit., p. 341.

under the direction of David Kidd, a machinist from Scotland, "of very high character and practical ability." [35] In 1850 after the mill was converted to steam Allston hired a miller whom he paid $900 a year.[36] Allston described the milling process:

By steam power, the rough-rice is taken out of the vessel which freights it, up to the attic of the building—thence through the sand-screen to a pair of (five feet wide) heavy stones, which grind off the husk— thence into large wooden mortars, in which it is pounded by large iron-shod pestles, (weighing 250 to 350 pounds,) for the space of some two hours, more or less. The Rice, now pounded, is once more elevated into the attic, whence it descends through a rolling-screen, to separate whole grains from the broken, and flour from both; and also through wind-fans, to a vertical brushing screen, revolving rapidly, which polishes the flinty grain, and delivers it fully prepared, into the barrel or tierce, which is to convey it to market.[37]

By 1860 there were eleven rice mills in the district in which capital of $440,000 had been invested.[38] In 1790 and 1791 Jonathan Lucas had built rice mills at Fairfield, Dover, and Millbrook. By 1850 there were others at Keithfield, Weymouth, Hagley, Waverly, and Richfield.[39] The Georgetown rice mill which was sold about 1838 by John J. Green to [Benjamin] King was operated by steam power.[40] Thus, the earlier water-operated mills were adapted to steam.

The big planters milled their own rice and that of their neighbors. If they were not so big and did not have a neighboring mill, they would send their rice directly to the rice mills in Charleston. In either case, the rice went from the plantation wharf to either the rice factor's wharf in Charleston or the rice mill in Charleston. And the vessels that took the rice to Charleston brought back the supplies that were needed on the plantations. Thus, Georgetown was by-passed. This had not been the case in the eighteenth century, when there had been a prospering

[35] *Ibid.,* p. 25. The *Georgetown American,* Dec. 23, 1840, described Kidd as the most eminent millwright in the country. He died at the age of fifty-seven. *Winyah Observer,* Nov. 4, 1846.

[36] Easterby, *op. cit.,* p. 25.

[37] *Ibid.,* pp. 32–33.

[38] Products of Industry, South Carolina, Eighth Census, 1860, S. C. Archives.

[39] Easterby, *op. cit.,* pp. 113, 140; Doar, *op. cit.,* p. 22; *Winyah Observer,* Dec. 3, 1845; *SCHM,* LXIX (1968), 193.

[40] *Georgetown Union,* June 16, 1838; *Georgetown American,* Dec. 23, 1840.

group of Georgetown merchants. Although the 1854 *Southern Business Directory* lists a number of general merchants in Georgetown, none of these appear in the Allston correspondence.[41] Charles Kershaw wrote in 1819 to Allston's mother: "Whatever necessaries you may want for the Plantations under your care had better be taken up in Georgetown, the difference of the Cost will be a little more but then you can get what is wanted by degrees and at once."[42] Georgetown had become the corner store; Charleston the supermarket. The rice planters sent to Georgetown in order to fill out their needs, not to order the basic things. Gabriel Ellis, the overseer, in 1838, in order to tide over the slaves at Matanzas bought corn from Eleazer Waterman in Georgetown. The corn was priced at one dollar per bushel in town or at one dollar and 6¼ cents if delivered to the plantation. Waterman bought his corn in Cheraw and freighted it down the Pee Dee in a streamboat.[43]

The town seemed to be already turned back toward wood products for its livelihood. David Risley of Philadelphia had bought R. F. W. Allston's Waties Point plantation in 1854 in order to put up saw mills. Mr. Weston had reputedly sold his home near Waties Point for a turpentine distillery, which meant that that part of town was becoming ill-suited for residential use. Allston's comment was: "It is astonishing to see the impetus this negotiation of mine has given to the demand for property in Georgetown."[44] But it was steam saw mills and turpentine distilleries, not rice, that were changing things. Leighton and Sherman, W. S. Croft and Company, J. J. and P. Tamplet and Company had steam saw mills. Shackelford and Fraser, Taylor and Moye, and Leonard Dozier and Company were the principal commission merchants. S. B. Tunnage and J. T. and Wm. Barnes were turpentine distillers. There were also druggists, dentists, confectioners, jewelers, and carriage-makers, but Georgetown was not a thriving place.[45]

The coasting vessels were, therefore, important links between the

---

[41] *Southern Business Directory* (Charleston, S. C., 1854), I, 313.
[42] Easterby, *op. cit.*, p. 370.
[43] *Ibid.*, p. 251; "Accounts of Shipments, Steamer *Anson*, Charleston to Cheraw, 1840–1842," SCL.
[44] Easterby, *op. cit.*, pp. 118–119.
[45] *Southern Business Directory, op. cit.*, I, 313.

plantations and Charleston. During the early part of the century the coasters were schooners and sloops, capable of carrying 350 barrels of clean rice or five thousand bushels of rough rice; many coasters were Yankee vessels that brought notions and vegetables in the fall and stayed during the post-harvest season.[46] According to J. Motte Alston: "A fleet of vessels would come from the sea-ports of New England to bring the rice from the plantations on the various rivers to market in Charleston; and when the season was over would spread their white wings, like migratory birds, for their homes at the North." [47] Later in the century more of the vessels were locally owned, if the names are any indication. On November 7, 1837, Lewis and Robertson, the Charleston rice factor firm, suggested to R. F. W. Allston that he should buy a coaster as it would have full employment from the business of Weston's mill and Waverly mill. On October 20, 1838, Lewis and Robertson wrote that they had sent the *Julius Pringle* to Waverly as there was more rice at Waverly and Colonel Ward's than the *Waccamaw* could bring to town. As the price was high at that time in Charleston, time was important.[48] Francis Withers owned the *Charles Kershaw*, one-third of the profit of which he left in 1847 to John Harleston Read II for five years.[49]

The Charleston rice factor had become the principal figure in the marketing of the Georgetown rice crop. He directed the voyages of the coasters; he supervised the milling in Charleston; he watched the fluctuations in the price of rice; he sold the crop. The rice factor used his discretion since the market price fluctuated considerably from day to day.[50]

The principal Charleston rice-factor firm dealing in the Georgetown rice crop was founded by Charles Kershaw, an Englishman, who had

[46] Easterby, *op. cit.*, pp. 39–40.

[47] Childs, *op. cit.*, p. 29.

[48] Easterby, *op. cit.*, pp. 403, 408.

[49] "Will of Francis Withers," dated Nov. 24, 1841, proved Nov. 25, 1847, Charleston County Wills, XLIV, Book A (1845–1851), 268–284, S. C. Archives. The *Nina* and the *Genl. Clinch* were steam packets that ran on a regular schedule between Georgetown and Charleston. *Southern Business Directory, op. cit.*, I, 332.

[50] *Ibid.*, p. 378. Also see J. H. Easterby, "The South Carolina Rice Factor as Revealed in the Papers of Robert F. W. Allston," *Journal of Southern History*, VII (1941), 160–172.

come to Charleston after the Revolution.[51] As early as 1810 he was helping Mrs. Charlotte Ann Allston market her crop amid the restrictions of the Nonintercourse Act. By December 1823 he was associated with J. Lewis; by 1833 these two had been joined by Alexander Robertson. It was Colonel William Alston of Clifton who talked them into taking Robertson, a Georgetown boy, as a partner. Later, as the son-in-law of Dr. Paul Weston, his ties with Georgetown planters were secure. At Kershaw's death in 1835 the firm became Lewis and Robertson. After Robert Thurston joined the firm in 1838, it was known as Lewis, Robertson, and Thurston until the death of Lewis. Ultimately Robertson joined with John Freer Blacklock, the son of a Charleston merchant of British origin, to form the leading Charleston rice-factorage house of the 1850's: Robertson and Blacklock.[52]

The rice factor sold the rice and placed the profits to the credit of the planter. If the rice was sent in a rough form to Charleston, the factor would direct the coaster to the wharves of either the Bennett, Chisolm, or McLaren mill.[53] The factor served as a banker and stockbroker for the planter. Profits might be invested, as the above firm did for Mrs. Blyth, in stocks of the United States Bank or of the Charleston Bank.[54] In 1828 Major Ward already had $20,000 invested in bank stocks.[55] The factors also provided many fringe services. They would look after the children of the planter if they were in school in Charleston, providing for their expenses from time to time, would outfit a young man on his way to college as Charles Kershaw did for young R. F. W. Allston.[56] The rice factors also often served as executors of estates. Alexander Robertson was an executor of Francis Withers' estate in 1847; Robertson

[51] When he died on July 31, 1835, in his seventy-fifth year, the newspaper noted that he had been for upward of half a century a resident of Charleston. Charleston *Courier,* Aug. 8, 1835.

[52] For the letters of members of this firm with the Allston family from 1810 to 1865 see Easterby, *Rice Plantation,* pp. 357–431; Childs, *op. cit.,* p. 67; McDowell Papers, SCL. Robert Thurston died on May 20, 1841. *Winyah Observer,* May 22, 1841.

[53] Products of Industry, South Carolina, Seventh Census, 1850, S. C. Archives. Earlier Lucas and Nowell had Charleston rice mills. Easterby, *Rice Plantation,* p. 397.

[54] Easterby, *Rice Plantation,* p. 379.

[55] Mary James Richards, "Our McDowell Ancestry," typed, McDowell Papers, SCL.

[56] Easterby, *Rice Plantation,* pp. 37–38.

and Blacklock were both executors of the estates of Richard O. Anderson, Joshua John Ward, and Mrs. Benjamin Allston, Sr.[57]

The rice factors bought and sold slaves, hired out slaves, and placed some who were to learn special trades—such as a cook or serving man. They sent out plantation supplies of every variety: provisions, corn, Negro cloth and blankets, rugs, a piano—almost anything.[58]

William Ravenel and James Reid Pringle were also rice factors for the Georgetown merchants, both of them being planters at the same time.[59] Robertson and Blacklock, however, had a near monopoly of the business with the Winyah Bay area and grew extremely wealthy on this trade. The rice factor was the only person serving the planter who was on the same social level with him other than doctors, lawyers, and clergymen. All four of the above rice factors lived on as princely a scale as did the planters, as their Charleston homes would attest.[60]

The profits from rice planting were high. The price per pound varied from 4.3 to 2.9 cents per pound during the decade of the 1850's. If the Wards sold their 4,410,000 pounds of rice at 3.2 (the average price for 1859), their income would have been $141,120 for the year. A number of planters sold over a million pounds of rice during the year 1859, for which each would have received at least $32,000. Expenses would have to be deducted, but they would not have been high on the large self-sustaining plantations.[61]

The Winyaw and All Saints Agricultural Society was formed on November 17, 1842; it closed its doors on April 25, 1861.[62] The membership

[57] For Anderson's estate see *Winyah Observer*, Dec. 22, 1852.

[58] Easterby, *Rice Plantation*, pp. 253, 378, passim.

[59] *Charleston Directories*, 1849, 1852, 1855.

[60] James Reid Pringle lived at 9 Legare St.; Ravenel at what is now 13 East Battery; John Freer Blacklock at 2 Bull St.; Alexander Robertson on East Battery. *Charleston Directories*, 1849, 1852, 1855.

[61] Gray, *op. cit.*, II, 1030: Easterby, *Rice Plantation*, pp. 378, 388, 393. Freehling uses the statement—"the profits of a rice plantation of good size and locality, are about eight per cent per annum, independent of the privileges and perquisites of the plantation residence"—made by R. F. W. Allston in the early 1850's to buttress his belief that the rice planters continued to flourish. William W. Freehling, *Prelude to Civil War* (New York, 1965), pp. 28–29.

[62] "Minute Book of the Winyaw and All Saints Agricultural Society," S. C. Hist. Soc. A brief history of this society was printed in the *Pee Dee Times*, May 19, 1858. The Winyaw Farming Society had been incorporated on Dec. 18, 1824. *S. C. Statutes*, VIII, 337. In 1827 Francis Withers had been president and J. H. Read, J. W. Allston, and T. P. Alston vice-presidents. *Winyaw Intelligencer*, April 18, 1827.

duplicated those of the Waccamaw Hot and Hot Fish Club and the Pee Dee Planters Club. In fact, this society used the premises of those two clubs alternately for its meetings. Yet this organization had a more serious purpose and a slightly broader membership. Some of the older planters, who eschewed the meetings of the Hot and Hot Fish Club, were members, as well as some of the Georgetown storekeepers such as Eleazer Waterman. The purpose of the club was to encourage improvements in agriculture, in domestic economy, in the breeding of horses, mules, sheep, and cattle, to conduct experiments, and to study animal diseases. There was an annual fair sponsored by the society. Agricultural success was recognized by the award of silver medals which on one side bore the name of the society and the emblem of a plow and on the reverse the donee's name and a sheaf of rice. Under the guidance and stimulus provided by the society, the agricultural prosperity of Georgetown District reached its peak.

There were committees on the best methods of cultivating rice, corn, and potatoes, on the best manures to be used and how applied (on both high lands and old rice lands), on the best methods of preserving corn and potatoes, and on the best mode of curing, milling, pounding, and preparing rice for market. At the April 1848 meeting Colonel Ward read a report on the cultivation of rice, J. R. Poinsett on corn, Dr. E. T. Heriot on manures, and R. F. W. Allston on preparing rice for market. The society, which considered J. J. Ward, J. H. Tucker, R. F. W. Allston, and E. T. Heriot the most successful planters in the district, appointed Ward, Allston, and Heriot as a committee to find the best mode of cultivating rice and of preparing it for market. When the society handed out its awards, Ward and Tucker were the most consistent winners. In 1849 Ward's fields had the highest yields: 89½ bushels of rice per acre and 73 bushels of corn per acre. Tucker won in 1850 with 87 bushels of rice per acre and in 1852 with 82 bushels of rice per acre.[63]

[63] About 30 bushels to the acre was the average on the Pee Dee. Allston, who had won a prize for his rice as early as 1831, got 52 bushels per acre in 1858 at Nightingale Hall. *The Southern Agriculturist and Register of Rural Affairs*, IV (1831), 221; Easterby, *Rice Plantation*, p. 36. There is a prize list in the *Winyah Observer*, April 26, 1848, and another in the *Pee Dee Times*, March 31, 1858. Doar estimated that the average yield in 1850 and 1860 on the Georgetown plantations was 30 bushels per acre. Doar, *op. cit.*, p. 41. Dr. Heriot's system of manuring with rice

In 1851 it was time to publish these glad tidings to the world. At a special meeting of the Winyaw and All Saints Agricultural Society on May 1, 1851, Francis Weston, Ralph Izard, and Dr. Edward Thomas Heriot were elected delegates to attend the World's Fair in London "with authority to impart any information in their power, touching the cultivation, manufacture, or production of any articles exhibited, and coming from the aforesaid District, and to contribute any information which in their judgment may advance the object of this great and laudable communion of the Nations of the Earth." At the London Crystal Palace Exhibition Dr. Heriot won a prize medal for Carolina rice. Wade Hampton and William Seabrook won medals for cotton while McCormick won a medal for his reaping machine, Colt for his revolving rifles and pistols, and Goodyear for his India rubber.[64] Rice was Georgetown's contribution to Western civilization.

---

straw, chaff, and flour and Ward's discovery of big grain rice were the most important improvements made in the 1840's. Mendenhall, *op. cit.*, pp. 339–341.

[64] "Industrial Exhibition of 1851, American Awards," *New-York Daily Times,* Oct 29, 1851. Georgetown's rice was reputedly the best in the country. Charles Manigault, a Savannah River planter, wrote in 1852: "and I need not remark that Georgetown & its neighbouring Rivers produce the best Rice in the World. *We all look up to them.*" "Charles Manigault's Essay on the Open Planting of Rice," ed. Albert V. House, Jr., *Agricultural History,* XVI (1942), 191.

XVI

THE INSTITUTION OF SLAVERY

N otes by R. F. W. Allston for a lecture on the institution of slavery reveal that he was aware of a growing movement to abolish that institution. He jotted down a list of dates on which the slave trade had been successively suppressed: in 1792 by Denmark, in 1807 by the United States, in 1815 by the Congress of Vienna for western Europe, in 1833 in the British West Indies, in 1848 by the new Republic of France, and in 1850 in the District of Columbia.[1] Allston and his fellow rice planters of Georgetown District knew that slavery was under attack. They could only meet that attack by making slavery work in a more humane fashion. Just as Governor James F. Byrnes tried to make segregated schools more efficient on the eve of the school desegregation cases of 1954, so Governor Allston tried to make slavery more efficient on the eve of Emancipation. It was the success of the planters in this effort that permitted them to challenge the outside world and to sustain them during the long fight that followed the throwing down of the gauntlet.

The Georgetown slaves were imported into the district between the 1720's and the Revolution. They were brought directly from Africa in

---

[1] "Allston lecture" [after 1850], R. F. W. Allston Collection, S. C. Hist. Soc.

British slaving ships financed by the merchants of London, Bristol, and Liverpool. After the Revolution there were additional importations into South Carolina by the vessels of the Rhode Island traders in the 1780's and by a variety of foreign and domestic traders between 1803 and 1808. Some of the slaves imported after the Revolution may have reached Georgetown District, but after 1808 the slaves of the district had been natives and their numbers increased naturally.[2] In the fifty years from 1810 to 1860 the slaves composed 85 percent to 89 percent of the population of Georgetown District, the highest precentage of slaves in any district in South Carolina. The census gives the following figures:

1810—13,867 slaves were 88 percent of total population of 15,679
1820—15,546 slaves were 88 percent of total population of 17,660
1830—17,798 slaves were 89 percent of total population of 19,943
1840—15,993 slaves were 88, percent of total population of 18,274
1850—18,253 slaves were 88 percent of total population of 20,647
1860—18,109 slaves were 85 percent of total population of 21,305 [3]

During the 1830's the population of both slaves and whites diminished, as a few of the whites departed for the West and some slaves were sold in that direction. That was the decade in which the rice planters secured a firm hold on the district. Only in the 1850's did the proportion of slaves to whites fall below 88 percent but the decline was not significant. The problem that the whole state faced with reference to slavery was more accentuated in this district than in any other.

With such a large proportion of slaves it was necessary to keep them in check. A patrol system had been worked out by the colonial assem-

[2] Carl H. Brown, "The Reopening of the Foreign Slave Trade in South Carolina, 1803–1807" (MA thesis, Univ. of S. C., 1968). A shipload of Guinea Negroes was presumably sold in Williamsburg District in 1808. William W. Boddie, *History of Williamsburg* (Columbia, S. C., 1923), p. 332. Of the Negroes who died in Georgetown District in 1850, only two were listed as having been born in Africa. One Negro aged eighty had died of old age; another fifty-six of pneumonia. Persons who Died During the Year Ending June 30, 1850, South Carolina, Seventh Census, 1850, S. C. Archives.

[3] Slavery Schedules, Third through Eighth Censuses, S. C. Archives. The median number of slaves held in Georgetown District in 1860 was 135. The median figure indicates that approximately one-half of the slaves were in units larger than that number. This was the highest median in S. C., and not far behind the highest in the South. William K. Scarborough, *The Overseer, Plantation Management in the Old South* (Baton Rouge, La., 1966), p. 12.

bly in the acts of 1721, 1734, and 1740.[4] These acts merged the patrol system into the militia, a system which lasted until the Civil War. At every militia muster a "beat company" was ticked off from the militia lists. The beat company was composed of a captain and four other men who would ride over the plantations once a month to look for disorders and to mete out punishments. The punishments were generally whippings administered on the spot. By the 1740 law only slaveowners and overseers could serve on patrols, but after the 1816 outbreaks at Camden and at Ashepoo, Governor David R. Williams asked for additional legislation. In 1819 all white males over eighteen were subject to patrol duty; nonslaveholders were excused from this duty after they reached the age of forty-five. This regulation did not apply to incorporated towns, which were to make their own rules.[5] Georgetown, beginning in 1805, adopted a series of by-laws to control the Negro, slave and free. At the time of the Georgetown Conspiracy the town council petitioned the legislature for additional help, but only one grant of money was obtained.[6] In 1839 the legislature set up a system with general provisions for the control and regulation of patrols by municipal authorities.[7] In September 1860, R. F. W. Allston wrote his son: "Patrol duty should not be neglected, tho' the duty ought not to be done too annoyingly unless vagabond whites render it necessary."[8] One of the principal reasons for the patrol was to intimidate those who might tamper with the slaves.

There was a court for the trial of Negroes, both slave and free, who had been accused of a crime. By the 1740 law any justice of the peace who had been informed of the commission of a crime by a slave or a

[4] H. M. Henry, *The Police Control of the Slave in South Carolina* (Emory, Va., 1914), pp. 32–34. The provisions of the basic 1740 law are found in *S. C. Statutes*, III, 571–573.

[5] Henry, *op. cit.*, p. 36; *S. C. Statutes*, VIII, 538–541.

[6] See Chapter XII. "An Act to Consolidate the Two Beat Companies of Georgetown," dated Dec. 18, 1829, *S. C. Statutes*, VIII, 555.

[7] Henry, *op. cit.*, p. 37. The law was passed Dec. 21, 1839. *Acts and Resolutions of the General Assembly of the State of South Carolina, passed in December 1839* (Columbia, S. C., 1839), pp. 87–93.

[8] *The South Carolina Rice Plantation as Revealed in the Papers of Robert F. W. Allston*, ed. J. H. Easterby (Chicago, Ill., 1945), p. 165. For Plowden Weston's use of tickets (no slave was to be absent from the plantation without a ticket) see *Plantation and Frontier Documents: 1649–1863*, ed. Ulrich B. Phillips (Cleveland, Ohio, 1909), I, 116.

free Negro was to dispatch his constable immediately to arrest the suspect and summon another justice together with not less than three nor more than five freeholders within three days for the trial of the case. A quorum, which must consist of a justice and two freeholders or of two justices and one freeholder, was sufficient to convict. The sentence was fixed by the quorum according to the law, but the law allowed a wide discretion as to penalties. On one occasion in 1787 "sundry inhabitants of George Town" petitioned Governor Thomas Pinckney to pardon Abraham, who was sentenced for breaking open and robbing the store of Heriot and Grant. If the Governor would pardon Abraham, William Cuttino, his owner, had promised to send him "far away from Georgetown." [9] An 1833 act gave the accused the right of appeal from a Negro court to the circuit court for any slave or free Negro convicted of a capital offense.[10] As the court for the trial of Negroes was not a court of record, it is difficult to provide a history of this court within the state and impossible for Georgetown.

Negroes were given physical punishment rather than jail terms so that their owners would not be deprived of the profit to be derived from their property. There was a work house in Charleston where runaway slaves might be kept temporarily. If they were not claimed within a certain time after advertisement in the newspaper, they were sold. In the middle of the 1820's Charleston experimented successfully with a correctional institution which served town masters who did not wish to inflict corporal punishment on their own slaves. Such slaves were sent to the treadmill.[11] It is not known whether Georgetown had such an institution.

The most important kind of punishment meted out to the slave was that given on the plantation by the planter or by his overseer. But because such punishment was given far from the public eye, there is very little information of a reliable kind on this important aspect of slave life. According to H. M. Henry, after there had been a great number of Negro homicides in Charleston between 1800 and 1820, the Charles-

[9] Petition of Sundry Inhabitants of George Town, S. C., to Gov. Thomas Pinckney, April 4, 1787, "Thomas Pinckney," Personal Miscellaneous, LC.

[10] Henry, *op. cit.*, p. 64.

[11] Bernhard, Duke of Saxe-Weimar Eisenach, *Travels through North America During the Years 1825 and 1826* (Philadelphia, Penn., 1828), II, 9–10.

ton grand jury presented "as a serious evil the many instances of Negro Homicide, which have been committed within the city for many years." The punishment of a white man for killing a slave up until 1821 was only a fine, but in 1821 the legislature made death the punishment for the murder of a slave. The Court of Appeals in 1834 said: "This change I think made a most important alteration in the law of his (the slave's) personal protection. It in a criminal point of view elevated slaves from chattels person to human beings in the peace of society." [12]

On the distant reaches of the Pee Dee or the Waccamaw it would be difficult to know what happened. A few glimpses are given in the Allston letters. Joseph W. Allston wrote his brother Robert on September 25, 1823:

Fenmore, Mr. Tucker's driver informed me on Monday last, that . . . your Jack . . . was most dreadfully beat on Pee Dee by Swinton, General Carr's overseer, so much so that he had not been able to work since. If I had heard it immediately after it happened I should have gone to Sandy Island, for the purpose of seeing the situation of the Negro as it is Mr. Tucker's overseer is the only white person who can speak to that point, there was another white man with Swinton whose name I shall endeavour to discover and if the punishment was as severe as represented to me, I think Swinton ought to be prosecuted as nothing could justify it. . . .[13]

It was the overseer who was tempted to extremes; the master to forgive. It was said that if a Negro could reach Mrs. Blyth, the mistress at Waverly, then Ellis the overseer would be unable to punish.[14] Plowden Weston would not permit more than fifteen lashes.[15]

All evidence points to the fact that by the 1840's the slaves were submissive and content. The system, which had been worked out by the laws of the 1820's, was beginning to bring results in the sense that the slave population was passive and quiet. The institution was more firmly fixed, perhaps eradicable only by war.

There is indication that the slaves were also better cared for. At the end of the harvest each year early in November, clothes, blankets, and

[12] Henry, *op. cit.*, pp. 67–69.
[13] Easterby, *op. cit.*, p. 63.
[14] *Ibid.*, p. 34.
[15] Phillips, *op. cit.*, I, 118.

shoes were given to the slaves. Cloth was given out by the yard with buttons, needles, and thread, so that it could be made into garments. Blankets were given to the men one year, to the women the second year, and to the children the third year. Each working Negro received annually one pair of shoes. Summer clothing was provided in May. The slaves lived in family units in houses on the slave streets that were generally not far from the big house. The slave street at Mansfield is still visible. Each house had a hall and two sleeping apartments. Three days in each year were set aside for cleaning the houses. Christmas was a festive time of year when the master and mistress as well as the children of the master's family gave small presents to the slaves, perhaps a neat kerchief to the women, a cap to the men, and toys to the children.[16] As glasses of whiskey were handed around, these occasions might turn into dangerous situations. Adele Petigru Allston wrote her son Benjamin on January 1, 1857, of the doings on Matanzas and Waverly on Christmas Day, 1856. The slaves at Matanzas

made a great noise and drank the Governor's health in many a stout glass of whiskey. Many were the inquiries made after Mas Ben. All were well and in good spirits. We went to church after we finished giving out such little matters as are always given out at this season. Joe and Will went to Waverly to see Christmas given out to the negroes there, but returned here to dinner. . . . I never knew a more quiet Christmas. Accounts had been received here and in the State generally of an effort at insurrection in Kaintucky and Tennessee. It was represented as being very general and well organized, and caused a good deal of anxiety, tho very little or no talk, as every one felt it should not be the subject of general talk, Belflowers and Oliver (the overseer at Waverly) brushed up their guns and ammunition chests etc. and observed and listened, but held their tongues. No signs of organization or of serious discontent were observed as far as I am aware of.[17]

The house servants, who were of a higher status than the field slaves, were specially trained and brought higher prices. Some of the slaves were trained as domestics at the Hot and Hot Fish Club or at the Pee Dee Club House.[18] In 1838 R. F. W. Allston was offered Mrs. Benjamin

[16] Easterby, op. cit., pp. 33, 347–348.
[17] Ibid., p. 136.
[18] Ibid., p. 123.

Huger's house servants, who were to be sold as a staff.[19] All of the house servants were, of course, Negroes, although the Allstons had an Irish nurse.[20] The house servants were dressed better than the others and according to the whim of the master. R. F. W. Allston provided cotton plaids for his maid servants while his house male servants had gray mix'd cloth for their coats and tweed for their trousers.[21]

There were rewards and incentives. House servants might advance to more favored positions on the staff, being taken to Charleston at the annual removal or to Newport and Saratoga. Sowers were awarded prizes on the Allston plantations; coopers got additional pay for additional work; extra gifts were given to those who had not missed a day's work all year. And those who would tend their own small plots might have their hogs, chickens, pumpkins, or fire wood bought by the master for pay.[22]

Negroes died as frequently as whites, from chills and fever, pneumonia and pleurisy, or scarlet fever, which would seem to disprove the belief that they were better acclimated.[23] They were taken care of by the planters who hired doctors to attend their slaves. The accounts of Dr. Robert Nesbit of Georgetown, of Dr. Andrew Hasell on Waccamaw Neck, and of Dr. James R. Sparkman on Pee Dee tell the medical story.[24] Dr. Sparkman was the regular medical attendant on twenty-five to thirty plantations with slave populations of about 3,000. According to Dr. Sparkman the physician was the mutual friend of master and servant. Many planters, of course, were also doctors. The better-run plantations had sick houses, with nurses, and the doctors made frequent visits. At times slaves were even sent to Charleston to be treated by specialists.

After 1820 it was impossible to emancipate slaves in South Carolina except by a special act of the legislature, which meant that a slave was

[19] *Ibid.*, pp. 86–87.

[20] *Ibid.*, p. 117.

[21] *Ibid.*, p. 92.

[22] *Ibid.*, p. 34. Negro field hands were hired out. Isaac Carr advertised 20 to 30 field hands with their families in *Winyaw Intelligencer*, Jan. 1, 1825.

[23] Persons Who Died During the Year Ending June 30, 1850, South Carolina, Seventh Census, 1850, S. C. Archives.

[24] "Robert Nesbit's Account Book, 1796–1804," SCL; "Dr. Andrew Hasell Account Book," S. C. Hist. Soc.; Easterby, *op. cit.*, pp. 348–349.

rarely freed.[25] Many a master had freed a slave woman and her children when those children were his own. After 1820 this was not possible. W. H. Fleming of Georgetown wrote R. F. W. Allston on March 19, 1841, asking if he might be permitted to purchase Louisa and her children, the property of Mrs. Shackelford. Fleming had "private reasons for this request." He assured Allston, who was an advisor of Mrs. Shackelford, "that I will not make Louisa or her children the Slaves of any human being, and though I am aware by the Laws of this State, they cannot be emancipated yet any mode that can be adopted to make her condition free will be placed with confidence to your direction and advice." [26] A slave might be shipped out of the state and emancipated under the laws of some other state. In South Carolina the goal after 1820 was a society of free white men and slave black men.

In a perceptive book, *Methodism and Slavery*, Donald Mathews has written that Southerners, troubled by questions concerning the morality of slavery, supported two movements (one of the 1820's and the other of the 1830's) in order to ease their consciences.[27] The first was the American Colonization Movement; the second the Methodist "Mission to the Slaves." The first, an effort to send the Negro back to Africa, generated no enthusiasm in Georgetown District.

The Methodist "Mission to the Slaves," however, was of historic importance to the Georgetown District. Undoubtedly religion was a boon to the slave's soul and an alternative to the master's whip. From the time of Francis Asbury's meeting with Black Punch until the Civil War, the Methodists were continually interested in the plight of the slave. In the records of the Methodist Episcopal Church in Georgetown for 1815 there is "A correct account of the Black People in Society in Georgetown as they are divided into classes." On each plantation (at least on thirty-nine of them) there was a slave class leader who prepared the slaves for entering the church. The following list gives the

[25] John L. Bradley, "Slave Manumission in South Carolina, 1820-1860" (MA thesis, Univ. of S. C., 1964), pp. 19–20.

[26] Easterby, *op. cit.*, p. 89.

[27] Donald G. Mathews, *Slavery and Methodism, A Chapter in American Morality, 1780–1845* (Princeton, N. J., 1965), passim.

name of the class leader, where the class met, and the distance of the
meeting place from Georgetown: [28]

NAMES OF THE CLASS LEADERS	WHERE THEY MET	DISTANCE FROM GEORGETOWN
Anthony Godard	at William Waynes	Georgetown
James, Hool	at H. Rothmahlers	Georgetown
Brister	C. Kinloch	2½ miles
David	F. Kinloch	1½ miles
Tim	C. Kinloch	2 miles
Quaker	Piatt	1 mile
Billy Castles	J. Castles	Dwelling place 1½ miles
York, Wragg	at William Waynes	Georgetown
Scotland	S. Wragg	on Black River
Nero, James Hard	A. Taylors	Georgetown
Abraham, Huger	Dr. Blythe	on Wackamaw 2½ miles
Hermon	F. Weathers	Sampitt 4½ miles
Triton	F. Weathers	on Peedee 7 miles
Nead, Martin	widow Martin	on Sampit 1 mile
Jupiter	St. Fords	on Black River
Anthony, Godard	Dr. Blythes	
Ratliff, Withers	Collins	Collins plantation 10 miles
Hannal Alston	Alston	
Primus	J. Dick	on Black River 9 miles
Neptune	William Alston	Wackamaw 2 miles
Dick Leader	F. Weathers and William Shackelford	Sampit 2½ miles
Baxter, free	several places on Santee	Santee 15 miles
Jack Marcus	J. Pringle and C. Pinckney	On Black River 7½ miles
Amos	R. Weathers	Sampitt 5 miles
Peter	William Trapier	Black R. 5½ miles
John	McClendon	expelled
James	S. Smiths	Pedee 10 miles

---

[28] "Records of Methodist Episcopal Church in Georgetown, S. C., 1815," Methodist
Collection, Wofford College Library, Spartanburg, S. C.

NAMES OF THE CLASS LEADERS	WHERE THEY MET	DISTANCE FROM GEORGETOWN
Dick	Pringle	Pedee 7 miles
Doublin	B. Trapier	Black River 7 miles
Abraham Huger	B. Smith	
Stephen	General Horre	
Brister	F. Kinloch	
Adam Keith	Keith	Black River 7 miles
Ratcliffe	Weathers	Sampit 3½ miles
Joe Plateright		Wackamaw 4 miles
James Hugee		
Isaac	Tucker	

A period of probation or trial was necessary before admission to the church. After being admitted, a member might be discharged for his sins. The records show that slaves were expelled for having two wives, for leaving a wife, for swearing, for affecting to marry people, for drunkenness, for dancing, and for horse-swapping on the Sabbath. Sometimes there were transfers such as "removed to Charleston" or "removed to Stateburgh." In 1815 there were 1,677 slave members in the district. But on January 7, 1818, Samuel K. Hodges wrote: "The collered Society here is a pitiable state. Many of the Leaders are careless, & very ignorant. . . ." [29] Since instruction by slave class leaders was believed to have sparked the Denmark Vesey insurrection in Charleston, many planters believed this work should be in the hands of white clergymen. The Reverend James L. Belin began his mission to the slaves in 1819 on his own plantations and those of Robert Withers and Major Ward on the Waccamaw.[30] In Georgetown the Baptist Peter Cuttino met on Sunday afternoons with a few friends and blacks for a sermon, songs and prayers.[31]

The turmoil of the 1820's brought Charles Cotesworth Pinckney, the owner himself of Santee River plantations, to make a speech in Charles-

[29] *Ibid.*
[30] W. P. Harrison, *The Gospel Among the Slaves, A Short Account of Missionary Operations Among the African Slaves of the Southern States* (Nashville, Tenn., 1893), p. 131.
[31] Peter Cuttino to Rev. Iveson Brooks, Aug. 7, 1821, Brooks Papers, SCL.

ton in 1829 to the Agricultural Society, urging a mission to the slaves.[32] Many were shocked at the idea, which nevertheless was the seed that grew into the Methodist "Mission to the Slaves," an organized attempt by white Southern Methodist clergymen to bring the teachings of Christ to the slaves.

Charles Cotesworth Pinckney, cooperating with the Reverend William Capers, founded the mission among the Santee River slaves. The clergymen who led the mission were financed out of the General Missionary Fund of the Methodist Church. John Bunch was the first missionary on the Santee. He wrote the South Carolina conference on January 22, 1833, that as his family was leaving the state due to the "political excitement," he would like to embark on a career which would lessen the tensions in the state by preaching to the slaves.[33] In a letter of January 11, 1835, he made his report for the "North and South Santee Mission":

North and South Santee Mission has 3 branches (viz.) North and South River and the Island each of which branches has 5 appointments 15 in all including 18 Plantations. There are 595 church members the greater part of whom are worthy pious Negroes who give evidence of their 6 months probation and have been Baptized and admitted to the Sacrament of the Lords Supper. There are 400 children on this Mission capable of cathechetical instructions. . . . I sometimes catechize the grown Negroes before preaching. . . . Mr. Pinckney . . . allows me to preach at Rosetta and Fanny Mead on the Island at any time when ever the Negroes are done their task for the day hence on those Plantations I have held Class meetings myself. . . . I would further state that in visiting the sick and dying I have frequently found the slave happy in God and triumphing against the devil the world and the flesh and ready to sing. Jesus can make a dying bed full soft as downey pillows are while on his breast I leave my head and breathe my life out sweetly there. Mr. C. C. Pinckney and Mr. [James] Ladson's Negroes (I think) are profiting most by the Mission . . . that souls have gone from all the appointments on the sd. Mission to Heaven and that there are others on their way, on each Plantation imbraced by the Mission I have no earthly doubt remaining.[34]

[32] Charles Cotesworth Pinckney, *An Address Delivered in Charleston, before the Agricultural Society of South Carolina, at the Anniversary Meeting, on Tuesday, the 18th August, 1829* (Charleston, S. C., 1829).

[33] Conference Papers, Methodist Collection, Wofford College Library.

[34] "Missionary Report for N. and South Santee Mission," Jan. 11, 1835, *ibid.*

Charles Cotesworth Pinckney was so impressed by Bunch's work that he called on Capers in Charleston and urged him to continue Bunch in his mission another year. Missing Capers in town, Pinckney on January 23, 1835, wrote him from El Dorado after he had returned to the South Santee:

I find some of the Planters reluctant to contribute to the expense of the undertaking, unless their contribution belongs exclusively to the Missionary; others in consequence of short crops and low prices unwilling to contribute any sum the present year; under these circumstances I fear that most of the expence will fall on your Missionary Fund. I still think that the benefit of the undertaking will not develope itself to any great extent, until the rising generation are brought into action, and the bad example of parents counterbalanced by missionary, and other religious instruction. As far as my opportunities of observation extend, the hostility of our opponents is diminishing, and I have been asked by some, with an apparent desire of obtaining correct information, what have been the results of our experience? To these I have generally replied, that the slaves appear more attentive to morality and decorum; and if they are not less vicious, they certainly take more trouble to conceal their vices; thus the pernicious effect of evil example is partially removed.

A majority of Planters throughout the seaboard parishes north of Charleston (where revivals have not prospered) are still adverse to Missionary efforts, and give as ample cause to pray that their eyes may be opened, through the increasing influence of religion, to the awful responsibility of withholding the bread of life from famishing souls. Will you do me the favor to give the subjoined order to Mr. Bunch, with many wishes for his prosperity. I am more anxious for the success of the Mission generally, and therefore wish the proceeds appropriated to your General Missionary Fund.[35]

The mission to the slaves continued and spread through out the district. The Reverend Samuel Leard, having served the North and South Santee Mission in 1843, wrote of his experiences:

I have a lasting impression of the culture and refinement of the planters and their families, of the care they took of their slaves, of the protection furnished to them against imposition and cruelty, and the almost perfect system of plantation regulations. This last included even the negro's church going, and was most particular as to the hospital service and

[35] Ibid.

the marital relations of the sexes. I remained but one year on this very inviting but laborious field of mission work, and left it with regret, despite the arduous labors entailed.[36]

The Reverend James L. Belin was the center of similar efforts on Waccamaw Neck. In 1836, with the assistance of the Reverend Theophilus Huggins, he formed the Waccamaw Neck Mission. Belin continued this work until he was "a superannuate," but even then he boarded the clergymen who came in succession: Reverend M. L. Banks, Reverend William Carson, and Reverend J. A. Minick. Masters and overseers were cooperative. Mr. Alston provided his boat and oarsmen whenever the missionaries wanted to go to Georgetown. "Joe Hemingway, one of the overseers, had a Methodist family, and was a Methodist himself." One clergyman recalled: "I always felt at home in his family, where I knew a hospitable welcome awaited me." Belin continued to work for the slaves until he fell from his buggy and died in 1859. He left a large sum for the work of the Methodists.[37]

The Methodist Church in Georgetown was revived in 1840 while Reverend A. M. Forster was the rector. A legacy from Mrs. Blyth permitted the painting of the church, whitewashing the fence, and building a suitable cupola to install the bell, which was henceforth to be rung half an hour before every public preaching. The three stewards were Thomas L. Shaw, Eleazer Waterman, and Dr. W. R. T. Prior.[38] These leaders of the Georgetown middle class might have picked up the seeds of abolitionism and nurtured them. Waterman was a Connecticut man; Shaw and Waterman had been Unionists in 1832. Yet in 1844 they too took a stand for slavery. After the General Conference of the Methodist church had forbidden Bishop Andrews to exercise his episcopal functions so long as he owned slaves, a meeting of the Methodists was held in Georgetown on July 5, 1844. Dr. W. R. T. Prior was the chairman and R. E. Fraser was secretary. They demanded a separation from the Northern Methodist churches and defended their own church, whose ministers had become the true friend of the slaves through their labors

[36] Harrison, *op. cit.*, p. 238.
[37] *Ibid.*, pp. 181, 267–268.
[38] "Minutes of the Quarterly Conference of the Georgetown Station," Methodist Collection, Wofford College Library.

in the missionary field. It was the mission to the slaves that had convinced them of the correctness of their position on the subject of slavery.[39] In 1847 the Methodist Church of Georgetown was running a colored Sunday school with thirty children. In 1848 the stewards renewed the license of a colored man to preach. There were colored members of the church until the end of the war.[40]

Francis Withers built a meeting house for his slaves on Friendfield plantation. The South Carolina Conference of Methodists appointed a preacher whose salary Francis Withers paid. Withers' support of the Methodists may have brought him in touch with Dr. Forster, whose son married Withers' step-daughter and continued the mission to the slaves.[41]

In 1858 Dr. Sparkman, whose adult slaves attended a Methodist meeting house just outside his plantation of Birdfield, summed up the effects upon the Georgetown slaves: "The moral and social condition of the Slave population in this district has vastly improved within 20 years. The control, management and entire discipline has materially changed, crime and rebellion are much less frequent. They have learned in many instances to govern themselves and to govern each other and through this section, 'Runaways' are fewer and 'less lawless.' " [42]

This mission to the slaves was so important to the welfare of the community that the Episcopalians copied it. There was always a drift of planters from the Methodist to the Episcopal church, a church that appealed to the upper levels of Georgetown society. Dr. W. R. T. Prior resigned from the Methodist Church in 1842 and Dr. Magill in 1848 to become members of the Episcopal Church. This drain weakened the Methodist Church. If it had not been for the staunch devotion of Eleazer Waterman and T. L. Shaw, that church might not have survived. When Shaw died in 1855, his passing was noted in the Methodist records—a man "so Exemplary and devoted a member who faithfully filled the offices of Trustee, Steward, Class Leader and Superintendent of the

---

[39] *Winyah Observer*, July 20, 1844.
[40] "Minutes of the Quarterly Conference of the Georgetown Station," Methodist Collection, Wofford College Library. Also see account of Rev. Thomas Mitchell, Methodist missionary to the blacks, in *Pee Dee Times*, Aug. 5, 19, 1857.
[41] "Will of Francis Withers," dated Nov. 24, 1841, proved Nov. 25, 1847, Charleston County Wills, XLIV, Book A (1845–1851), 268–284.
[42] Easterby, *op. cit.*, p. 349.

Sabbath School." The attitude of the Methodists toward the Episcopalians is summed up in the fact that John Coachman in January 1828
was put back on trial "for marrying an unawakened Episcopalian." [43]

The man who awakened the Episcopalians was the Reverend Alexander Glennie (1804–1880), the most outstanding clergyman in the district and much beloved, as his many namesakes attest. Glennie, who
became rector of All Saints after tutoring Plowden Weston, made that
church for thirty years the center of the religious life of both the planters and the slaves. In 1832 when Glennie began his tenure there were
ten colored communicants; by 1862, 519 colored communicants had
been added.[44] In 1845 planters throughout the state sent in reports to
a meeting on the religious instruction of the Negroes held in Charleston.
R. F. W. Allston reported that of the 13,000 slaves in the parish of Prince
George 300 were Episcopalians, 3,200 Methodists, and 1,500 Baptists.
John Hyrne Tucker reported that of 4,000 slaves in the parish of All
Saints 1,100 were Episcopalians. The Charleston meeting was convinced
that after fifteen years of effort "the work must go on." [45]

A visitor to All Saints Parish in 1843 pointed out that until Glennie
started his work the clergymen as well as the planters had fled the lowcountry during the summer, leaving the slaves to forget their Christian
principles and to relapse into barbarism.[46] Glennie was fortunate in that
he moved only four or five miles from the rice swamps to the coast,
taking his church and his school with him. But he was still free to return on Sundays to catechize the slaves. On this particular Sunday
morning in 1843 Glennie and his visitor got up at an early hour for
family prayers and then drove to John Hyrne Tucker's plantation chapel.

[43] "Minutes of the Quarterly Conference of the Georgetown Station," Methodist
Collection, Wofford College Library.

[44] Henry DeSaussure Bull, *All Saints' Church, Waccamaw* (Columbia, S. C., 1949),
p. 32. Glennie described his work in a report made after the visit of Bishop T. F.
Davis to lay the cornerstone of the new church at Wachesaw in April 1855. *Southern
Episcopalian*, II (1855), 92–94.

[45] Reports were also received from A. Glennie and J. H. Ladson. *Proceedings of
the Meeting in Charleston, S. C., May 13–15, 1845, on the Religious Instruction
of the Negroes* . . . (Charleston, S. C., 1845), pp. 34–37, 52–55, 72. Also see Mason
Crum, *Gullah, Negro Life in the Carolina Sea Islands* (Durham, N. C., 1940),
pp. 173–231.

[46] "Recollections of a Visit to the Waccamaw," *Living Age*, Aug. 1, 1857, pp.
292–296.

All the slaves streamed out of their huts on the Negro street into the chapel. When asked how they were lured there, the visitor was told that roll was called and those who were not present failed to receive their extras at the end of the week. "It attacks the African in his weakest point, and appeals to his appetite for the good of his soul." Glennie then returned to the church of All Saints for a regular service for the whites. In the afternoon there was a drive to Francis Marion Weston's estate and another service held in the plantation chapel there, which had been neatly and simply constructed for almost 200 persons. Here the Negro choir, dressed alike, clean and neat, provided "a natural musical expression of joyous feeling."

Glennie was an Englishman, "anti-methodistical," who desired to emphasize content, rather than emotions. His system included more than mere catechizing, which was rote responses to routine questions. He sought answers which implied some effort at understanding on the part of the slave. But as Colonel Thomas Pinckney Alston implied, the planters were more interested in discipline than understanding, for it had been noted that the slaves were far less addicted to crime and immorality after these sessions. The disciplinary aspect is seen in the picture (drawn by the visitor) of Glennie catechizing while a Negro woman leader kept every child literally toeing the mark throughout the session, which lasted an hour.

As the catechising occupied an hour, the attention of the children, though relieved by hymns, sometimes flagged. But the lictor assumed the duty of concentrating their mental energies. Drawing a simple rod from her ample store and raising it to her shoulder like an officer's sword, she moved with noiseless step between the circles, inspecting the ranks. If any straggling toe overstepped the mark she gave an admonitory gesture, which soon brought the offender into position. If any wandering eye was raised to the ceiling or turned to the windows, she silently but positively insisted on a "front" with military exactitude. If any mouth was shut, which ought to be open in singing or answering, she stopped right before the recusant and peered into his face with a penetrating glance, which forced open the stubborn lips—or, if hints failed to arouse the sluggard, she would pass to the rear of the circle, and, with the butt of her rod, administer a reproving jog to the culprit's head, which instantly stimulated his understanding. This combination of "nurture and admonition" would have sadly hindered me; but it had no effect upon the steady nerves of the catechiser, nor did it at all distract the scholar. Nay it secured a more general attention than I have ever seen among so large a number.

The three characteristics exhibited by Glennie and passed on to the slaves were patience, punctuality, and indomitable perseverance. In a sense this system reflected the new wave of teaching. As the writer of this article remarked, it was much like the Blue Coat School in Liverpool which Mr. and Mrs. Weston had seen abroad. It was part of the universal system for teaching the lower orders. Nothing pictures the orderliness that had come over the slave society better than this.[47]

On a strip of land like Waccamaw Neck where so few whites lived and so many slaves, it was natural that the planters would see the need for a plantation chapel. There were thirteen such chapels, the most famous of which was that of St. Mary's at Hagley plantation. Plowden Weston and his wife made it a thing of beauty with stained-glass lancet windows, carved oak stalls, an English granite font, gilt cup with cover and paten, clock and bell.[48] Undoubtedly some spiritual beauty entered the lives of the slaves. The promptness with which they attended chapel, the neatness with which they dressed, along with the beauty of their own chanting that mounted up into the cathedral-like moss-hung oaks or wafted down on the rice fields were unmistakable signs that many of the slaves were happy. Religion was aimed as much at order in this world as at the hope of salvation in the next. A prayer often read in the Weston chapel was: "Give to all masters grace to keep order and discipline in their families, and to treat their servants with mercy, kindness, gentleness, and discretion; knowing that thou hast made of one flesh all the nations of the earth. Give to all servants grace to obey their masters, and please them well in all things; knowing that in thus doing they shall please thee who art the Master over all." [49]

---

[47] In the Allston papers there is an 1857 list of 27 slaves of Nightingale Hall plantation, candidates for confirmation. Easterby, *op. cit.,* p. 345.

[48] William St. Julien Mazyck, "Old Family Reminiscences," newspaper clipping of 1898 in the possession of Mrs. Mildred Weston Lewis, Charleston, S. C. Alexander Glennie in a letter published in the *Pee Dee Times,* Aug. 27, 1856, described the work of Mr. and Mrs. F. M. Weston among the Negroes of Laurel Hill plantation.

[49] Rev. William Wyndham Malet, *An Errand to the South in the Summer of 1862* (London, 1863), p. 120.

As the position of the slave became somewhat easier as the 1850's arrived, the position of the free Negro became more difficult. In the late 1850's a few free Negroes even petitioned the South Carolina legislature to permit them to find a master and to become enslaved.[50] After 1820 there were, of course, no manumissions permitted except under the rarest of circumstances and then only by special act of the legislature. The free Negroes, therefore, who lived in Georgetown itself were thus freed prior to that date or were children of free Negroes or perhaps in a few instances free Negroes from Charleston. None would have been permitted to enter the state. Those who left the state could not return. Those who stayed needed a white man as sponsor and guardian. An 1829 report of the Commissioners of the Poor simply noted the expenditure of money for "a coffin to bury free Jimmy, his benefactor's having died."[51] The Free Negroes were being squeezed out of South Carolina.

The census figures record 102 free Negroes in Georgetown in 1810, 227 in 1820, 214 in 1830, 188 in 1840, 210 in 1850, and 183 in 1860.[52] The number of free Negroes had doubled between 1810 and 1820 but after the new law of 1820 forbidding manumission the number declined over the years. Out of this group there were to come some important leaders of Reconstruction such as Joseph Rainey, whose father was a pre-war Georgetown barber. They were largely a forgotten group. They did marry and have families, as the records of the parish of Prince George indicate; indeed, even slaves married.[53] Free Negroes' occupations were among the trades or as a servant class. They were not citizens and suffered special burdens under the by-laws of the town. They were specially restricted and specially taxed. Their position in society was most eloquently described in the obituary notice in the October 21, 1825, issue of the *Georgetown Gazette* of the death of

[50] Bradley, *op. cit.*, pp. 104–106.

[51] Report of Commissioners of Poor, Georgetown District, 1829, S. C. Archives. In 1823 John Lide Wilson as guardian for Jehu Jones, owner of the Mansion House in Charleston, petitioned the state legislature asking that Jones be permitted to return to the state after visiting his family in the north. Petitions, Free Persons of Color, Legislative System, 1800–1829, S. C. Archives.

[52] Reports of the Superintendent of the Census, Third through Eighth Censuses.

[53] "Register of the Episcopal Church of Prince George Winyah, 1813–1916, S. C. Hist. Soc.

George Mitchell, a man of color, aged sixty, who had long been the sexton at Prince George Church:

George Mitchell was a man of color, but no shade of his complexion fell upon his character. He was born a slave, and bought his freedom by his merit. He felt himself a man, but was too humble to grasp at privileges which it was wrong for him to reach. . . . George was the Sexton of the Episcopal Church in this place, and truly should the pillars of that Church be clad in mourning, and her aisles return a hollow echo. The stranger shall not meet him at the door, and the pews shall be familiar with the dust and cobweb, and the priest shall look around him, and George shall not be there. . . . George was . . . a *Sailor* in his youth, and none knew better how to trim a boat or rig a Schooner. He was a good *Cook* and a *Waiting Man,* and though no citizen, in conduct and in principles he was a *Gentleman.* He *was* no citizen—he shared no civil rights—yet no man contributed more to the general weal.[54]

[54] *Georgetown Gazette,* Oct. 21, 1825.

XVII

THE COMING OF THE CIVIL WAR

The Jacksonian Revolution represented the rise of the self-made man. The average Jacksonian Democrat wanted the vote in order to crush monopolies, to cut all ties between government and business, to set up the reign of laissez-faire, to release creative energies. The Whigs on the other hand represented old wealth, vested interests, men with monopoly rights obtained from government, such as the stockholders of the second United States Bank. Since there were few self-made men in Georgetown District[1] and the planters who dominated politics were men who had inherited their plantations, the district should have been Whig. But it was not. The Georgetown planters were all Democrats.

Robert F. W. Allston summed up his views on public matters in a letter of September 5, 1838, written to his cousin John Ashe Alston. "My

---

[1] D. L. McKay, David Risley, Arthur Morgan, and Benjamin Huger Wilson may be called self-made men. McKay was first cashier (1841–1847) and then president (1848–1854) of the Bank of Georgetown. *Charleston Directories.* In 1854 R. F. W. Allston referred to David Risley as "a practical lumber man from Philadelphia." *The South Carolina Rice Plantation as Revealed in the Papers of Robert F. W. Allston,* ed. J. H. Easterby (Chicago, Ill., 1945), p. 118. Malet refers to Morgan as "an Irishman, and a very enterprising merchant." Rev. William Wyndham Malet, *An Errand to the South in the Summer of 1862* (London, 1863), p. 266. On Dec. 16, 1868, Leonard Dozier wrote to his brother Richard from Florida: "Is Risley & Morgan the only two, well-to-do men, in Prince Geo. Winyah? God save the state!" Richard Dozier Papers, SHC. Wilson is referred to as a self-made man in "Minute Book of the Georgetown Rifle Guards," pp. 96–100, SCL.

political creed is based on the principles of Thomas Jefferson, as expressed during the discussions in Virginia in 1798, and the subsequent canvass which resulted in his election as President in 1801." Allston stated that he had adopted this creed about 1825 and every year since had strengthened his belief "that a plain, honest, common-sense reading of the Constitution is the only true one, and that in legislating for the government of the United States, nothing, absolutely nothing of authority should be allowed to precedent as such. . . ." A strict interpretation of the Constitution was the rock upon which he built his political philosophy. "I believe that Congress does not, and never did possess the right to incorporate a Bank of the United States. . . ." Allston felt that posterity would bless Jackson for his veto of the bank bill.[2] The Georgetown planters were solidly in favor of the independent treasury scheme. When Martin Van Buren, the architect of that scheme, visited Joel Roberts Poinsett at his plantation on the Black River in 1842, the Planters Club of the Pee Dee made the ex-President an honorary member. R. F. W. Allston in forwarding the certificate of membership told him how much the policies of his administration had been approved by the planters of the Pee Dee.[3] John Harleston Read, a man suspected of being a Whig, perhaps because he did not always follow the main body of the planters, defended himself in a letter to the editor of the *Winyah Observer* by stating that he belonged to the Democratic Party, "the cardinal principles of which party I conceive to be a strict adherence to the constitution in its original form and meaning, and an uncompromising opposition to the favorite measures of the Whig Party viz., a Protective Tariff, a National Bank, and a Distribution of the proceeds of the Public Lands." [4]

So pervasive was the state rights view in the district that it embraced all public men with few exceptions. Eleazer Waterman, a Northern-born member of the Georgetown middle class, admired Calhoun.[5] Benjamin Faneuil Hunt, a Northern-born member of the planting class, delivered a speech in Faneuil Hall in Boston in 1841 advocating a strict

[2] Easterby, *op. cit.*, pp. 78–80.
[3] "The Secretary's Records of the Planters Club on Pee Dee," Sparkman Papers, 2732, Vol. 1, SHC.
[4] *Winyah Observer*, Sept. 17, 1842.
[5] *Winyah Observer*, Dec. 10, 1842.

construction of the Constitution.[6] These views were backed by determination. A Georgetown toast of 1841 was: the state of South Carolina, "the first to resist aggression and the last to submit to wrong."[7]

The two-party system in the United States was engulfed in the 1830's and the 1840's by a wave of humanitarian movements, one of which—abolitionism—was to disrupt the party organizations and by 1860 cause a realignment of parties. Georgetown was swept by four humanitarian movements, but not by abolitionism. The mission to the slaves has already been discussed. In 1827 Robert Heriot, whose wife had started the Ladies Benevolent Society, headed a group which organized the Bible Society as an auxiliary of the American Bible Society. The Bible Society continued to hold meetings throughout the pre-war years.[8] In 1827 the Winyaw Anti-Duelling Association was also organized with a constitution and as first president William W. Trapier. The movement to suppress duelling was supported by the clergy. The Reverends Ludlow, Postell, Keith, Winn, and Lance assisted Trapier and Robert Heriot in drawing up the constitution. Duelling, they wrote, "demoralizes society, impairs its peace, and destroys domestic tranquility."[9] This movement apparently had little success since James Hamilton who had fought fourteen duels was a local hero[10] and John Lide Wilson wrote a manual on the etiquette of dueling.[11]

The humanitarian crusade most in keeping with a national movement was the temperance crusade. The Winyaw Temperance Society was organized in May 1832 with a constitution and as first president William W. Trapier. Temperance was supported by the Methodists and the local clergy. On October 27, 1827, it was resolved at the Quarterly Con-

[6] Georgetown American, Feb. 20, 1841.

[7] Georgetown American, Feb. 27, 1841. On March 19, 1835, John Alexander Keith, Dr. W. A. Norris, John Chapman, Dr. E. B. Brown, and James Smith tendered a dinner to Calhoun, who was passing through Georgetown on his return from Washington. These men admired "the firmness with which you have, since your election to the Senate of the United States, supported the great principles of public policy, on which the welfare of the country mainly depend. . . ." Calhoun in a letter of the same date gratefully declined. Winyaw Intelligencer, March 26, 1835.

[8] Winyaw Intelligencer, Feb. 24, 1827.

[9] Winyaw Intelligencer, Dec. 5, 1827.

[10] William W. Freehling, Prelude to Civil War, The Nullification Controversy in South Carolina, 1816–1836 (New York, 1965), p. 150.

[11] John Lide Wilson, The Code of Honor; or, Rules for the Government of Principals and Seconds in Duelling (Charleston, S. C., 1838; reprinted 1858).

ference of the Georgetown Station "That this conference does not approve of a minister of the Gospel drinking toasts at public dinners."[12]

None of these movements, however, challenged the social structure of the district. They were in fact aimed at stabilizing and not at overturning society. They were respectable movements. At the head of two of them was Trapier, the planter-banker. When he died on September 27, 1832, on North Island, the newspaper noted with deep regret the passing of a man whom the edition described as "the finished gentleman."[13]

Since none of these movements represented a threat to the existing social order, the path of politics in the state should have been smooth. Allston had stated that he wanted a unified state. South Carolina was that. Allston had enough political ambition to want to be governor and then to retire,[14] but he was not in a hurry and he did not wish to electioneer. His independence is shown in December 1842 when a group in the legislature tried to push him forward at the last moment as a candidate for governor. "His friends ran him, it is said, against caucus, dictation and domination. . . ."[15] But Allston prevented this move from being successful by a "pertinacious disclaimer." He wrote his wife: "the late strenuous effort to bring me out contrary to repeated protestations to the contrary, has thrown me among a number and kind of people whom I never had been in the habit of meeting heretofore. New relations you know are what I am not apt to form." Although this was a statement of how not to be a politician, Allston's brother-in-law approved: "The circumstance that the opposition fixed on him shows that he was considered a man of weight, and his firmness in insisting that he would not take advantage of what might be considered a hasty resolve . . . shows that he deserves the influence attributed to him."[16]

It was the threat to the institution of slavery that transformed Allston into a working politician in spite of all the distaste that he had for a political role. In June 1844 a public meeting was held in Georgetown

[12] Minutes of the Quarterly Conference of the Georgetown Station, Wofford College Library; *Winyaw Intelligencer*, May 21, 1832. Also see *Winyah Observer*, Sept. 20, 1843.

[13] *Winyaw Intelligencer*, Oct. 3, 1832. His age was fifty-five years and five months. Register of Prince George Winyah Parish, 1813–1916, S. C. Hist. Soc.

[14] Allston to Mrs. R. F. W. Allston, Dec. 3, 1843, Allston Papers, S. C. Hist. Soc.

[15] Charleston *Courier*, Dec. 10, 1842.

[16] Easterby, *op. cit.*, pp. 90–91.

to discuss the annexation of Texas. Allston was called to the chair. The men present unanimously supported the idea of annexation. Annexation would be merely a continuation of the policy begun by Jefferson with the purchase of Louisiana and an endorsement of the Monroe Doctrine of 1823. Gratitude was expressed to Jackson for his support of annexation, and Polk's nomination was approved. If annexation should be a pretext for war, then let the war be "open and declared hostility." At this meeting Allston gained a valuable ally in John Izard Middleton, who offered the resolutions.[17] At the succeeding Fourth of July celebration Middleton addressed the crowd on the crisis and "the auditory was enraptured beyond expectation." When it was known that the Senate had rejected the treaty of annexation and that President Tyler at the age of fifty-five had just married a young lady of twenty-two, the *Winyah Observer* commented: "This is one of President Tyler's treaties which the Senate cannot reject."[18]

In December 1844 Allston was forced to "take part" in a debate on resolutions condemning the visit of Judge Samuel Hoar to South Carolina. The Massachusetts judge had come in an attempt to compel the abandonment of the practice of imprisoning free Negroes among a ship's crew while the vessel was in port. As Allston phrased it for his wife, the legislature took a step "which will raise a great commotion at the North." After James Hammond had written two letters to Thomas Clarkson, the English abolitionist, and had them published in the local newspapers and then reissued in pamphlet form, Allston wrote Hammond: "As a planter, also, representing others who like himself, have half their Capital invested in slaves, my warm and grateful acknowledgements for inditing and publishing the said letters."[19]

Allston supported the party of Jackson, Van Buren, and Polk, but should it embrace the abolitionist cause, Allston was ready to abandon the Democratic Party. In August 1846 David Wilmot, a Northern Democrat, offered his famous proviso—that slavery should not exist in the territories to be obtained from Mexico— thereby raising the question of slavery in the territories and in the future of America. It was this

[17] *Winyah Observer*, June 8, 1844. A meeting in favor of annexation had also been held in Williamsburg District. *Winyah Observer*, June 29, 1844.
[18] *Winyah Observer*, July 6, 1844.
[19] Easterby, *op. cit.*, pp. 93–95.

attack upon the constitutional position of slavery backed up by the growing abolitionist cry that slavery was morally wrong that drove Allston to take a public stand to stem the tide. In Allston's memorandum book there is a simple statement that "the Southern States claim for their citizens the right to settle in any part of said territory where their (African) slave labor may be profitable, or its service convenient." [20] This was a constitutional right, according to Allston, as it was to Robert Barnwell Rhett and John C. Calhoun.

Charles Sumner, who was to arouse anger among Southerners on several occasions, gave a public lecture on February 11, 1847, in which he drew unflattering comparisons between the Barbary States and the Southern states. Algiers was the wall of the Barbarian World; the Missouri line the wall of Christian Slavery. Virginia, Carolina, Mississippi, and Texas were the "American complements to Morocco, Algiers, Tripoli, and Tunis." Allston, who felt impelled to answer these strictures upon his region, pointed out that the present generation of Southerners had no responsibility for introducing slavery into America. "Las Casas the great, the good father and historian was the author of Negro Slavery in the Spanish West Indies, in place of Indians." "When the Colonists of So. Ca. petition'd the Lords Proprietors for a large supply of cattle, as the natural pastures were good, they were answer'd that they were intended to be *planters* not graziers—accordingly they were supplied after with slaves." Bristol and Liverpool had thereupon grown rich on the slave trade. And in 1760 when South Carolina had passed a prohibition act, the government in London had rejected it. Thus, at the time of the Revolution slavery had been fixed upon the South.

And then, like George Bancroft, Allston saw the hand of God in the American experiment. God's "will sanction'd the formation of the American Confederacy. Nothing but faith in His protection could have so strengthen'd the arms & nerved the energies of our Fore-fathers when contending against large odds in establishing it—Nothing but this could have sustain'd them in soul & body amidst the privations & treacheries & cool blood-shedding and countless miseries of an adverse 7 year's war." It was the goodness of God "which put it into the hearts of our great Men of old to frame our Constitution of Union, based upon

[20] "Memorandum Book. 1848–1849," Allston Papers, S. C. Hist. Soc.

justice, conciliation, & Good-Will." The Constitution was, therefore, a group of sacred compromises. God's ways were inscrutable. Faith in the justice, goodness, and power of God was increasing daily, and it would yet prevail over "all blindness & wickedness & error." "As well may the objection lie against the famine, or the pestilence, or, war." [21]

When one puts together the facts that the planters had inherited their positions, that the Constitution did contain compromises, that they were making attempts to Christianize the slaves, and that, of course, their entire economic well-being was wrapped up in the slavery question, one can see whence came their fervent belief that they were right and the abolitionists wrong.

The first editorial in the *Winyah Observer* on the Wilmot Proviso was in the August 25, 1847, issue. In defending the South, the editor pointed to the examples of Sierra Leone, Haiti, and Jamaica as bad examples of Negro republics. The first public meeting was held on November 9, 1847. Allston was again in the chair and J. I. Middleton chairman of the resolutions committee. This meeting endorsed the Mexican War and thanked the Palmetto Regiment.[22] Thomas G. Carr had died in Mexico;[23] Benjamin Huger was the local hero.[24] The war rally also adopted a resolution stating that the government of the United States "cannot of right interfere with the social or domestic institutions of any State or Territory of this Confederacy." [25]

The headlong plunge of the leading planters to endorse slavery expansion and to deny the leadership of their national party stumbled upon some local opposition in the spring of 1848, as men tried to make up their minds whether to support the Democratic candidate Lewis Cass or the Whig candidate Zachary Taylor. In December Cass had offered his own doctrine of nonintervention by Congress into the question of slavery in the territories, a straddling of the issue which apparently satisfied many of the state's leaders, although not all. On April 17, 1848, a unique public meeting was held in Georgetown. None of the large

---

[21] "Allston Lecture," Allston Papers, S. C. Hist. Soc.

[22] *Winyah Observer*, Nov. 10, 1847.

[23] He was thirty-six years old and the son of Gen. Thomas Carr. *Winyah Observer*, Dec. 15, 1847.

[24] In 1852 the S. C. General Assembly authorized the presentation of a sword to Col. Benjamin Huger for service in the Mexican War. Easterby, *op. cit.*, p. 116.

[25] *Winyah Observer*, Nov. 10, 1847.

planters were present. Leonard Dozier was called to the chair. E. Waterman, S. T. Atkinson, R. Lathers, D. L. McKay, W. P. Congdon, R. O. Bush were among the leaders who decided to send a delegate to the Democratic national convention in Baltimore to support a candidate who would be sound on the Wilmot Proviso.[26] Rhett, the editor of the Charleston *Mercury*, Calhoun, and Allston felt that no delegates should be sent. The *Winyah Observer* on May 10 contained an editorial inveighing against the *Mercury*, which "has stood confessed the very embodiment of chivalry."

The delegate selected to attend was J. M. Commander, planter, sheriff, and brigadier general of the militia, but a man of no great wealth. He did attend the convention, cast his vote (and since no other South Carolinian was present the vote of the state) twice for Levi Woodbury, and then for Lewis Cass. On his return to Georgetown he felt compelled to defend his actions and did so in a letter to the *Winyah Observer*. He challenged the *Mercury* and "the clique that has so long ruled the State. . . ." Cass was sound on "our peculiar institution." [27] Such independence could not be tolerated for very long if the drive for unity and separate state action was to continue. On July 4 at a great public gathering at the Pee Dee muster field, R. F. W. Allston condemned the April 17 meeting and all the actions, such as Commander's trip to Baltimore, that flowed from it.[28] There was never again a large public meeting in Georgetown at which the largest planters were not present.

There was some possibility of support for Taylor in 1848. There were enough Whigs in Georgetown to hold a meeting in May. C. A. Magill and R. E. Fraser were present, and Edward Gamage was elected delegate to the Whig convention. The committee of twenty-five was composed of relatively unknown men.[29] J. I. Middleton in a letter of June

[26] *Winyah Observer*, April 19, 1848.

[27] *Winyah Observer*, June 7, 1848. The Charleston *Mercury*, May 26, 1848, reported that at a local meeting in Georgetown of 8 or 10 persons J. M. Commander had been elected to go to Baltimore. He had the "unparalleled impudence" to go off to Baltimore and cast the nine votes of S. C. in the convention. D. L. McKay, the banker who "seems to be up to counterfeiting," had presided at the meeting. Also see Charles M. Wiltse, *John C. Calhoun, Sectionalist, 1840–1850* (Indianapolis, Ind., 1951), pp. 362–363.

[28] *Winyah Observer*, July 12, 1848.

[29] *Winyah Observer*, May 17, 1848.

28 weighed the relative merits of the two candidates. Cass was tainted with "Wilmotism" and was not sound on internal improvements, but the Whigs were unsound on constitutional principles. He would vote for Cass.[30]

The planters were truly in a quandary over whom to support. Gabriel Manigault, the nephew-in-law of Alexander Mazyck, would not decide but felt that Taylor was the popular man in Prince George Parish.[31] John Harleston Read was at first undecided but later wrote that he preferred Taylor since he was a Southern man and a slaveholder.[32] Allston wrote that he would have neither Cass nor Taylor.[33] There was more excitement in the elections that fall than there had been since the days of nullification. Allston won the Senate seat, while Middleton, Read, and John R. Easterling were elected to the House. Since Middleton did poorly at North Santee and well at Small Hopes and at Carver's Bay, it would seem that the large planters went for Taylor while the marginal farmers were for Cass.[34]

A letter of Rawlins Lowndes, April 17, 1849, gives the views of a North Santee planter.

The feeling hostile in the abstract to slavery of any kind, has long been steadily on the increase, and not a commotion occurs in Europe between the governors and the governed, but additional zeal is imparted on this subject to the great mass of mankind and it is in vain to expect, that a sentiment so active and so universal, should make an exception in favor of our peculiar institution. . . . domestic servitude as it exists in this Country, is the only rule by which the African can ever become civilized and fitted for a freer form of government. Such however is not the spirit of the age; but what is the spirit of the age, it is obvious, sooner or later, must lead to the emancipation of slaves in this country; unless indeed, the many evils a too hasty and inconsiderate zeal may engender, should give birth to a reaction. I however [torn] the hope, that in this country where the people are so much more enlightened, and accustomed to participate in government, that the day is *indeffinitely*

[30] *Winyah Observer*, July 5, 1848.
[31] *Winyah Observer*, July 5, 1848. Gabriel Manigault (1809–1888) married Annie Mazyck, the daughter of Dr. P. P. Mazyck of Romney plantation on the South Santee. John A. May and Joan R. Faunt, *South Carolina Secedes* (Columbia, S. C., 1960), p. 176.
[32] *Winyah Observer*, July 5, Aug. 23, 1848.
[33] *Winyah Observer*, July 12, 1848.
[34] *Winyah Observer*, Oct. 11, 1848.

distant, when a direct attack can be made upon our rights of property. That in all questions between the two sections of our country admiting of argument, such as that which now agitates the country, we must expect to find the masses of the North adverse to us, it is as well to admit; but, it could I think be a fatal error to argue, and to act upon the argument, that it is better to make a final issue upon such a question, rather than wait a more direct agression. . . . I am as little disposed to submit to robery as you can be, but in this case, where so much is at stake—I would resort to the last appeal only when the intention to rob was admitted—could no longer be questioned. I did hope that the present administration will be able to settle the present difficulty—the chance of this is derived from the President being a *Southern* man, and not a sectional Chief Magistrate. I do not yet despair of the Missouri line, but I must fear a coalition of Northern Democrats to defeat it—such is undoubtedly the game of the Free Soil Party of New York.[35]

With Taylor's victory and the possibility that the Missouri line would not be continued to the Pacific, the Southern congressmen had addressed their constitutents on the dangers brewing on the national scene. On April 9, 1849, there was a public meeting in Georgetown to respond to the Address of the Southern Delegates. Allston was in the chair, Middleton chairman of the resolutions committee, and the committee of twenty-one packed with the big planters. They agreed that the adoption of the Wilmot Proviso by Congress would be tantamount to the dissolution of the Union. Understanding revolutionary modes of action, they formed a committee of correspondence and safety composed of thirteen men. Delegates were elected to a meeting of the people in Columbia.[36]

The state meeting in Columbia was more moderate than the Georgetown one. It was admitted that peril hung over the institutions of the slaveholding states. If the Wilmot Proviso should pass, the governor should convene the legislature. South Carolina should act with the other Southern states.[37] Daniel Wallace of Union was elected to go to the Mississippi convention which met in October 1849 and made a call for a convention of the slaveholding states to be held in Nashville on the first Monday of June 1850. That body should devise some mode of resistance to Northern aggression.[38] Allston, who wrote in December 1849

[35] To Col. E. G. W. Butler, E. G. W. Butler Papers, DUL.
[36] *Winyah Observer*, April 11, 1849.
[37] Charleston *Mercury*, May 15, 16, 17, 1849.
[38] *Winyah Observer*, Jan. 19, 1850.

that the Pee Dee country intended to send him to Nashville, was ready to accept the call. "Unless the Northern people now come to be reasonable people, Revolution will be unavoidable. It were better to settle the matter now than leave it to our children." [39]

During March and April 1850 meetings of citizens were held in the parishes at which delegates were chosen, in accordance with the advice of the state legislature, to attend the conventions in each of the congressional districts by which the delegates to Nashville should be selected. On May 6 Allston was selected to represent the Georgetown–Pee Dee district.[40] On May 11 Allston wrote a public letter from Matanzas thanking the people for his selection and promising to go to Nashville, where the South would draw a line beyond which the North could not go.[41] Allston in his eulogy on Calhoun, which was "a labor of love," had stated that no Southerner could withhold his aid in promoting "a Union of the South for the sake of the Union," a phrase Calhoun had used in his famous fifth of March speech in the United States Senate. Allston twice repeated that Calhoun had died in the midst of the crisis for "Equality or Independence." [42]

The compromises which were passed at the end of the summer and have become known as the Compromise of 1850 were already being discussed in Congress long before the Nashville convention met, but there was little support for them in South Carolina. Mrs. Allston, who felt that Clay was a traitor to the South, thought that the fate of Clay's compromises would wait "to see what spirit . . . actuates the Nashville convention." [43] In Nashville Allston was pleased to find so many men like himself—of virtue and of character—and gained confidence thereby in a Southern-wide movement.[44] On July 26 Allston sat down at the sea-

[39] Easterby, op. cit., p. 99.
[40] J. R. Poinsett to E. Waterman, March 30, 1850, Poinsett Papers, Penn. Hist. Soc.; Philip M. Hamer, The Secession Movement in South Carolina, 1847–1852 (Allentown, Penn., 1918), pp. 47–48.
[41] Winyah Observer, May 22, 1850.
[42] Robert F. W. Allston, Eulogy on John C. Calhoun, Pronounced at the Request of the Citizens of Georgetown District, on Tuesday 23d April 1850 (Charleston, S. C., 1850); Winyah Observer, June 19, 1850.
[43] Easterby, op. cit., p. 101.
[44] Ibid., pp. 102–103.

shore and wrote a full report to be delivered to the reassembled convention at Marion courthouse.[45]

The passage of the compromise measures in September 1850 by the Congress of the United States was not looked upon with favor. As Philip Hamer has written: "The passage of the compromise measures served only to increase the disunion movement in South Carolina and to bring it more into the open."[46] That fall Southern Rights Associations sprang up on all sides. The Georgetown and All Saints Southern Rights Association announced in the October 9 issue of the *Winyah Observer* committees of safety for Georgetown, Black River, Sampit, Carver's Bay, Santee, Pee Dee, Sandy Island, and All Saints. At the October elections Allston and Ward were reelected senators while Middleton, Read, and Manigault were elected from Prince George and Colonel D. W. Jordan from All Saints to the House—all without opposition. When someone tried to push Dr. Heriot forward in opposition to Allston, Dr. Heriot publicly denied his candidacy.[47] At a great mass meeting on November 11, J. I. Middleton was elected president and B. H. Wilson vice-president of the Winyah and All Saints Southern Rights Association. The association was in favor of "separate State action." The Winyah Minute Men were formed under Captain J. H. Trapier. A committee was organized to meet the transient "Shaders" and "Duckers" who annually came from the North and send them home. Allston himself spoke in favor of opening up a direct trade between Charleston and Europe.[48] On December 5 a separate Southern Rights Association was organized in All Saints with J. J. Ward as president. A committee of vigilance was appointed.[49]

When the legislature met, the Georgetown men assumed prominent roles. John I. Middleton urged the state not to fill the vacant seat in the U. S. Senate.[50] J. J. Ward was elected lieutenant governor.[51] Allston

[45] *Winyah Observer*, Aug. 14, 1850.

[46] Hamer, *op. cit.*, p. 65.

[47] *Winyah Observer*, Oct. 16, 23, 1848.

[48] *Winyah Observer*, Nov. 13, 16, 1850. See also Petition against the duck hunters and shad fishers from Connecticut, 1855, Public Improvements, Wild Life, 1830–1859, Legislative System, S. C. Archives.

[49] *Winyah Observer*, Dec. 11, 1850.

[50] *Winyah Observer*, Dec. 4, 1850.

[51] *The Senate of the State of South Carolina, 1776–1962*, ed. E. B. Reynolds and J. R. Faunt (Columbia, S. C., 1962), p. 116.

was at this time first elected president of the state senate.[52] Although he won by a majority of 27 to 14, he had hoped for a unanimous election. "I feel also very sensible of the rebuke given in the 14 negatives no more than 3 of whom may be said to have been personally hostile to me. It is good for the inner man to be chasten'd sometimes. It cures vanity. . . . I feel however, that my tastes are not suited to the times even as they were in 1830-32." [53] This legislature, in which the Georgetown spokesmen were so honored, provided for elections of delegates to the Southern Congress and for elections of delegates to a state convention to consider the recommendations of that Southern Congress.

The election for delegates to the state convention was held in February 1851. Allston, Middleton, Read, and Manigault all talked of the forthcoming convention as a possible secession one: "by cooperation if we can, separately if we must." Colonel D. L. McKay read a long letter from Joel Roberts Poinsett in an attempt to stem the secessionist spirit, but the opponents were merely labeled submissionists and pushed aside.[54] The "secession candidates" won. For Prince George they were S. T. Atkinson, J. H. Read, Sr., J. H. Trapier, and B. H. Wilson and for All Saints T. P. Alston and Peter Vaught.[55] The opposition did not vote. Hamer stated that a small vote throughout the state put this convention into the hands of the secessionists.[56] The assemblying of the convention was delayed until April 1852.

With the delay of the state convention, the Southern Rights Associations elected delegates to a meeting in Charleston which was held in May. Dr. John D. Magill and John Hyrne Tucker represented All Saints Parish; Dr. Charles Williams, Dr. A. M. Forster, Dr. Edward S. Harrington, Gabriel Manigault, J. R. Easterling, and Richard Dozier represented Prince George. At this meeting the secession movement of 1850

---

[52] *Journal of the Senate, 1850* (Columbia, S. C., 1850), p. 5.

[53] Easterby, *op. cit.*, p. 107.

[54] *Winyah Observer*, Feb. 12, 1851. McKay was a Unionist in 1860. Charles E. Cauthen, *South Carolina Goes to War, 1860–1865* (Chapel Hill, N. C., 1950), p. 76. Early in December 1850 Poinsett had warned his fellow citizens that secession was revolution, that South Carolinians should consult the map and the census figures, that they should not mistake violence for power. He disapproved of the constant political violence in South Carolina for the past twenty years. J. R. Poinsett to "Fellow Citizens," Dec. 4, 1850, Charleston *Mercury*, Dec. 5, 1850.

[55] *Winyah Observer*, Feb. 15, 1861.

[56] Hamer, *op. cit.*, pp. 85–86.

and 1851 reached its peak.[57] An editorial in the *Winyah Observer*, May 14, 1851, endorsed the Charleston convention. Submission or resistance; there was no middle way.

This movement was opposed by the cooperationists, who did not want separate secession. They held a meeting in Charleston on July 29, 1851. Among those calling the meeting and designated as vice-presidents were Charles Alston, Sr., William Bull Pringle, Charles T. Lowndes, Henry A. Middleton, Allard H. Belin, and James H. Ladson. These men would not challenge the right of secession, but they wanted cooperation with the other Southern states. A committee of vigilance of 100 persons and a committee of correspondence of twenty-five were established.[58] Another meeting of this group was held on September 23, 1851, at which time the name of James R. Pringle stood in the place of Ladson's.[59]

The Southern Rights Associations organized in an attempt to elect secessionist candidates to the coming Southern Congress. Middleton presided over a great meeting in Georgetown in September and gave a secessionist speech.[60] Allston presided over a mass meeting at Morris's Ferry on the Pee Dee which the *Winyah Observer* called a "Great Secession Demonstration." [61] However, on October 13 and 14, 1851, the cooperationists won in six of the seven congressional districts in the state, losing only in the Beaufort district, the home of Rhett.[62] The battle between the two groups was then transferred to Columbia. Both sides caucused before the meeting of the legislature.[63] Allston wrote his wife that the Cooperation Party was in the majority under the persuasive leadership of Langdon Cheves. Allston, who had presided at the caucus of the Secession Party, which had been attended by eighty-five persons, was of the opinion that if the caucus yielded to his own suggestions that

[57] *Proceedings of the Meeting of Delegates from the Southern Rights Associations of South Carolina. Held at Charleston, May, 1851* (Columbia, S. C., 1851), pp. 25, 29.

[58] *Southern Rights Documents. Co-Operation Meeting, Held in Charleston, S. C.,* July 29th, 1851 (n.p., n.d.).

[59] *Proceedings of the Great Southern Co-Operation and Anti-Secession Meeting. Held in Charleston, September 23, 1851* (Charleston, S. C., 1851).

[60] *Winyah Observer*, Sept. 24, 1851.

[61] *Winyah Observer*, Oct. 15, 1851.

[62] *Winyah Observer*, Oct. 22, 1851.

[63] Hamer, *op. cit.*, pp. 126–137.

the state could be united again in less than twelve months. "But there are ambitious and restless spirits on both sides, and no one can tell what may yet be the consequence of their aspirations." [64]

The bitterness of October 1851 did give way to harmony by May 1852. The state convention, which had been postponed fourteen months, assembled in Columbia on April 26, 1852. There was a move by this convention to give the legislature of the state the power by vote of two-thirds of its members to withdraw the state from the Union, but Langdon Cheves' motion to lay the motion on the table was passed by a vote of 96 to 60, with all of the Georgetown men in the minority. The convention then agreed to an ordinance that the state had a right to secede, which was adopted by a vote of 136 to 19. [65]

The native-born Georgetown planters were secessionists; the Charleston-born Georgetown planters were cooperationists. In 1852 the cooperationists won; in 1860 the secessionists won. Did the fact that the Georgetown planters in increasing numbers secured town houses in Charleston have any effect on the final outcome? It so, secession was the final triumph of the planter over the merchant. If so, it also makes Charleston an odd choice for the setting of the national Democratic convention in 1860.

The election of Franklin Pierce, a Doughface Democrat, in the fall of 1852 brought a period of quiet to the state. E. T. Heriot wrote on April 20, 1853, from his Mount Arena plantation that "the last presidential election" has "given a death blow to the abolitionists." He urged his Scottish cousin not to believe the "fanaticks." He confessed he was tired of "answering Mrs. Stowe," but, he went on, we believe in scriptural authority for holding slaves: "it has existed for ages—and when Christ was upon Earth he neither interfered nor discountenanced it." "I have nearly 400—the majority love me and would defend my family —many will weep at my death as I have at many of theirs."[66] R. F. W. Allston visited President Pierce in May 1855 and approved of him. He wanted his son Ben to get Jefferson Davis to introduce him to Pierce

[64] Easterby, op. cit., p. 109.
[65] Journal of the State Convention of South Carolina; together with the Resolution and Ordinance (Columbia, S. C.. 1852); Winyah Observer, May 5, 1852.
[66] To Mr. Cunningham, a cousin, E. T. Heriot Letters, DUL.

upon Ben's return from a military station in the West.[67] As long as Pierce was president, slavery was safe.

The question of Kansas reopened the issue of slavery. As the editor of the *Pee Dee Times* stated, the bill organizing Nebraska "has again woke the demon of fanaticism from his fitful and feverish slumber." [68] After the passage of the Kansas-Nebraska Act in May the same paper editorialized: "Let us maintain a 'masterly inactivity'—ever vigilant, ever ready for the worst; and the North will perhaps work out our salvation for us." [69] Southerners might hope that extremism would bring a reaction. This was the thought that Rawlins Lowndes had expressed in 1849: "unless indeed, the many evils a too hasty and inconsiderate zeal may engender, should give birth to a reaction." [70] Yet the South too might be guilty of overreacting.

After the victory of the anti-Nebraska men at the polls in the fall of 1854 it was apparent that Kansas was the crucial battleground. If Kansas should be lost to slavery, then the slave power would henceforth be a a minority in the nation. The South Carolina planters had always been suspicious of the West. Thomas Lynch had worried about power moving west. John Rutledge had expressed such fears in the constitutional convention of 1787. Francis Kinloch had sensed a probable effect of the Louisiana Purchase upon the value of his rice fields. Joseph Alston may have hoped by joining Burr to solve the problem in an unusual fashion. Charles Pinckney in the House in 1819, Robert Y. Hayne in the Senate in 1830, Calhoun at Memphis in 1845, and Allston at Nashville in 1850 had sensed the power of the new West. In Kansas therefore the threat must be met. "A Rice Planter" wrote the *Pee Dee Times* in December 1855 urging the sending of men to Kansas. Kansas was the most important issue that had ever faced the rice planters of Georgetown since Georgetown of all districts in the United States was that "in which slave property is the most valuable, most necessary and that in which the black population has the greatest preponderance over the whites. . . ." [71] Allston, in March 1856, outlined the contest for his son. "We

[67] Easterby, *op. cit.*, p. 123.
[68] *Pee Dee Times*, Jan. 25, 1854.
[69] *Pee Dee Times*, June 7, 1854.
[70] To Col. E. G. W. Butler, E. G. W. Butler Papers, DUL.
[71] *Pee Dee Times*, Dec. 12, 1855.

are disposed to fight the battle of our rights with abolition & anti-slavery on the field of Kansas." Beaten there, our equality in the Union will be lost, and we must prepare for organization and defense. Otherwise, the tyranny of "king numbers" would reign. Deportation could not be practical, and emancipation could not be contemplated—"namely the giving up of our beautiful country to the ravages of the black race & amalgamation with the savages." [72]

Allston and his fellow planters decided to send men and money to aid the pro-slave forces in Kansas. According to a letter of Preston Brooks of December 31, 1855, the plan was to have a company of 100 men sent from each South Carolina district.[73] Allston sent $100 to Major Buford in Alabama, who was raising men to go to Kansas. He promised to give a Negro to any good man who would emigrate.[74] Allston was certainly one of the most active men in the state in this business, for he wrote his son in March 1856 after a large public meeting in Georgetown: "We are raising men and money here to counteract the effect of the Northern hordes sent there by the East Emigration Aid Societies. All Saints parish has raised $3000 & I suppose Winyah will do as much. I have [given] $100 to Major Buford, 100 to Major Herbert & 230 here." [75] John Rutledge Alston, the son of Colonel T. P. Alston, was to lead twenty-three men from the district to Kansas "for the purpose of making that distant Territory their permanent home." [76] John Rutledge Alston wrote home in May that the Southern railroads had given the members of his group free passes. [77] One Georgetown boy, Joseph P. Carr, was elected a delegate from Kansas to Congress in 1858.[78] After Charles Sumner had made in May 1856 his famous speech in the United States Senate on "bleeding Kansas" and Preston Brooks had taken his revenge for remarks on South Carolina by caning Sumner, the *Pee Dee*

[72] Easterby, *op. cit.*, pp. 131–132.
[73] Preston S. Brooks to Capt. E. B. Bell, Dec. 31, 1855, *ibid.*, p. 131.
[74] J. H. Means to Allston, Jan. 15, 1856; Allston to Means, Jan. 21, 1856, *ibid.*, pp. 125–127.
[75] *Ibid.*, pp. 131–132.
[76] *Pee Dee Times*, March 5, April 30, 1856.
[77] *Pee Dee Times*, May 14, 1856.
[78] Allston to Kansas Executive Committee, Feb. 18, 1858, declining invitation to complimentary dinner for Carr. Easterby, *op. cit.*, pp. 140–141.

Times approved of Brooks's actions—"blackguards have to be treated the same the world over," even in the United States Senate.[79]

The position of President became ever more important. The Georgetown men were all in favor of Franklin Pierce, but were divided on the question of whether a delegation should be sent to the national Democratic convention in Cincinnati to help nominate him. Allston and Middleton were against sending a delegation.[80] James L. Orr was the leader in the state of those desirous of sending a delegation, and in Georgetown his chief supporter was Benjamin Huger Wilson. Wilson, who had been editor of the *Pee Dee Times*, worked quite closely with Richard Dozier and Leonard Dozier and with Eleazer Waterman, Sr. and Jr., who were the proprietors of the Georgetown newspapers. The father of the Doziers, Anthony White Dozier, had opposed Allston unsuccessfully in 1834 for a seat in the South Carolina senate. These men, who had also supported J. M. Commander in 1848, came closest to challenging the political domination of Georgetown District by the planters. Wilson had said in January 1856 that it should not shame "our chivalry" to admit that knights exist in other states. Is the policy of the state never to attend a national convention? [81] At a public meeting early in March, with Eleazer Waterman in the chair, the Cincinnati idea was endorsed and a delegation consisting of B. H. Wilson, B. A. Coachman, Joseph W. Ford, and W. R. Maxwell appointed to go to Columbia in May to select a delegation for Cincinnati.[82] At Cincinnati the South Carolina delegation, of which Wilson was a member, voted for Pierce for fourteen ballots, then for Douglas, and finally for Buchanan. The delegation also voted for a plank endorsing the Compromise of 1850 and the principles embodied in the Kansas-Nebraska Act.[83] So completely did these events in the spring of 1856 seem to be a repudiation of Allston that Allston wondered if he had ruined his own chances of becoming governor in the following December.[84]

[79] *Pee Dee Times,* June 4, 1856.

[80] *Pee Dee Times,* March 5, 12, 1856.

[81] *Pee Dee Times,* Jan. 2, 1856.

[82] *Pee Dee Times,* March 5, 12, 1856.

[83] Harold R. Schultz, *Nationalism and Sectionalism in South Carolina, 1852–1860* (Durham, N. C., 1950), p. 121.

[84] Easterby, *op. cit.,* p. 132.

Back home the *Pee Dee Times* accepted Buchanan, although the paper had preferred Pierce.[85] Allston also accepted Buchanan, whom he visited that October at his home in Lancaster, Penn. Allston reported to his wife that Buchanan was in "full flesh & high spirits (for him) (he is blest you know with enviable equanimity) relying confidently on the success of his party and indeed I have never seen the actors of that party to such advantage as on this excursion." [86] Apparently, Buchanan would be another Pierce.

In the fall Wilson took his place in the Prince George delegation. Allston was sent to the senate again, and Middleton with 121 votes, Wilson with 106, and John Harleston Read, Jr., with 98 were sent to the house. Dr. Andrew Hasell represented All Saints in the senate and Plowden C. J. Weston in the house.[87] This delegation, although able and experienced, might be divided.

On November 26, 1856, Alexander Mazyck, the senator from St. James Santee, introduced in the state senate and on November 29 John Izard Middleton introduced in the house strong and defiant resolutions. Middleton resolved "That the slaveholding States cannot, with safety, continue to commit their rights and interests to the control or guidance of those who are hostile to a social and industrial organization that is vital to the former." He asked that the great, independent, and substantive powers be resumed by the states unless "such amendments be made to the federal constitution as will serve as barriers against aggression." On December 10 Mazyck's motion was tabled by a vote of 26 to 15, with Mazyck and Dr. Andrew Hasell among the 15. Allston did not vote. On December 15, on the motion of B. H. Wilson, Middleton's resolutions were tabled by a vote of 56 to 44, with Wilson and J. H. Read voting for and Middleton and P. C. J. Weston against.[88] Allston apparently did not vote, as he did not wish to endanger his chance of being elected governor of the state, which he was. The biggest planters were still the most radical men. B. H. Wilson, the self-made man, was for moderation.

[85] *Pee Dee Times*, June 11, 1856.
[86] Easterby, *op. cit.*, p. 135.
[87] *Pee Dee Times*, Oct. 22, 1856; Legislative System, Election Returns, S. C. Archives.
[88] *Journal of the Senate . . . 1856*, pp. 30, 94; *Journal of the House of Representatives . . . 1856*, pp. 103–104, 241–243, S. C. Archives.

Perhaps the clearest summation by any Georgetonian of the plight of the planters was made by Plowden Weston at a Fourth of July observance at Watchesaw in 1857. Weston was the brightest ornament of the Waccamaw rice world and, according to R. F. W. Allston, "a ripe Scholar." [89] His theme on this occasion was the fortunate fact that in South Carolina because of the difference of the two races a problem that had plagued political philosophers had been solved. In all societies there would naturally be those who command and those who obey, but in a society where all were of one race, there was the continual possibility of overturning, for no one would be quite sure of his place. In South Carolina "if a white, then a free citizen, if a negro, then a slave, at least, one without political rights." In South Carolina one carried "his testimony of citizenship . . . on his countenance." There is "this wonderful separation" which solved the core of the political problem. In one sphere there is the equality of liberty; in the other the equality of slavery. One can see why Georgetown would have been pleased with Judge Taney's decision in the Dred Scott case, for Taney said that a free Negro had no rights which a white man need respect.

Yet Plowden Weston recognized the fact that there was an attack being leveled at this perfection. It stemmed from the desire in the North and in western Europe to emancipate the slave. If it were not for the fact that the South was the agricultural core that supplied both the North and England with the needed staples, the South would have been subverted before this. Cotton and rice were still king, but a revolution was on the way. It would not be like the revolutions in South Carolina of 1719 and 1776, but more like that of France which had brought in its train many revolutions ending at that time in 1857 in the rule by a petty tyrant, Napoleon III. He saw the revolution coming, a complete overturning of society, and, without Calhoun and Butler and Cheves, South Carolina might not be able to meet the challenge. "I know that for successful agriculture a continual turning of the ground is necessary. . . . I know that the breeze is necessary to maintain the sweetness of the sea. . . . but this would be the tornado bursting over earth and ocean . . . mixing sea and shore in indistinguishable confusion.

[89] Easterby, *op. cit.*, p. 167.

. . ." [90] Weston saw with clarity his society where Negroes were 85 percent of the total and whites only 15 percent. And among the Negroes only a few were free and among the whites only a few were poor. If change did come, it would come with the force and havoc of a tornado.

When Governor Allston addressed the opening of the legislature in November 1857, he announced that he had received resolutions from Maine and Connecticut protesting the late decision of the Supreme Court.[91] Allston in replying to these resolutions revealed the core of his own position:

The political principles recognized by the decision referred to, met with the sanction of the people of South Carolina, who applaud the wisdom of the decree in which they are now judicially embodied. . . . In preserving and protecting the property of our fathers in Negro slaves, we deem ourselves entitled to the respect and aid of all good men and wise statesmen. Our ancestors, dealing with gold and silver coin, bought the negro from the capitalist of England and New England, whose thriving trade, however abused in many instances, was overruled by the Providence of God, to convert the barbarian bushman of the African coast, into the orderly domestic, the Christian black-laborer of America. There are few results more amazing in statistics than those which are produced by the fruits of this labor—a labor which could no more be dispensed with by America now, than could the commerce and manufacturers so dependent on its productions.[92]

In 1856 he had urged his son to read William Grayson's "The Hireling and the Slave." [93]

On November 23, 1858, Allston again set forth his views in a message to the legislature. He noted that a number of resolutions had been received from New England denouncing the domestic institution and the late decision of the Supreme Court, but he felt that they did not merit a response. His main regret was that parties had become national and that irresponsible conventions had been invoked. He did admit that the national Democratic Party was a barrier to many influences fatal to

[90] *An Address Delivered by Plowden C. J. Weston, before the Citizens of All Saints Parish at Watchesaw 4th July 1857* (Georgetown, S. C., 1857). Printed in *Pee Dee Times*, Aug. 5, 1857.
[91] Reported in *Pee Dee Times*, March 11, 1857.
[92] *Journal of the House of Representatives . . . 1857*, pp. 18–31, S. C. Archives.
[93] Allston to Benjamin Allston, March 16, 1856, Benjamin Allston Papers, DUL.

republican government. But he would prefer to rest upon the states. The country now lived under a fatal election every fourth year—this was "the all-absorbing topic, upon which uphappily is said to depend everything, even the integrity of the Union." He regretted too that forty millions of Southern money was spent north of the Potomac each year. Our surplus income should be "laid out in Southern securities, in improving the homestead, reclaiming and draining waste lands, cultivating grounds, and pushing railways east and west between the Atlantic and Mississippi, and still westward to the Pacific." [94]

In the fall of 1858 the moderate forces won in both parishes. B. H. Wilson defeated J. I. Middleton in the parish of Prince George while Peter Vaught defeated Andrew Hasell in the parish of All Saints.[95] Thus, both men who had voted for the extreme state rights resolution of 1856 had been beaten. Wilson, who was emerging as the dominant political figure, was the only member from Georgetown District to attend the Democratic state convention in 1860, which selected a delegation to attend the national Democratic convention in Charleston. The state convention honored him by calling him to the chair.[96] Wilson did attend the Democratic national convention in Charleston and was one of the three South Carolinians who refused to walk out of the convention, what Allston referred to as "an impracticable Douglas man." [97]

The event that tipped the scales violently in favor of secession was the election of Abraham Lincoln. Secession was obviously the course that South Carolina would take as soon as the abolitionists captured a national party and won a national election. These were the "disastrous consequences . . . from a triumph of the Seward party," [98] and nothing that a moderate like Benjamin H. Wilson could do could stem the irresistible rush to secession. John I. Middleton and Benjamin E. Sessions, both planters on the Waccamaw, were sent from All Saints to the seces-

[94] *Journal of the House of Representatives . . . 1858*, pp. 12–26, S. C. Archives.

[95] Legislative System, Election Returns, S. C. Archives.

[96] *Proceedings of the Democratic State Convention of South Carolina, Held at Columbia, on the 16th and 17th of April, 1860, for the Purpose of Electing Delegates to the Democratic National Convention, to Meet in Charleston 23d April* (Columbia, S. C., 1860).

[97] Easterby, *op. cit.*, p. 167.

[98] *Ibid.*, p. 167. A "Winyah Association of 1860" was formed in November. Cauthen, *op. cit.*, p. 43. "The 1860 Association" to F. Weston, Nov. 19, 1860, Weston Papers, S. C. Hist. Soc.

sion convention. Samuel T. Atkinson, Judge Benjamin F. Dunkin, Dr. Alexius M. Forster, and Dr. Francis S. Parker were sent from Prince George. The vote was unanimous in favor of secession.[99] So Middleton and Allston ultimately won out over Wilson, the secessionists over the cooperationists.[100]

Why did South Carolina secede? J. Motte Alston gave as good a reason as any. South Carolinians had ever been "a self-reliant people." With Indians to the west, Spaniards to the south, and pirates to the east, they had been taught to look for no outside help.[101] This spirit had animated them during the Revolution and since then had been strengthened by South Carolina's addiction to the history of her own past. To South Carolinians the Revolution had been a republican victory for freedom. not a democratic victory for equality. Francis Kinloch had written Judge Grimké in 1808: "There should be no commemoration of our independence in which the names of Marion & Sumpter—of Green—& of Governor Rutledge should not be conscious—they kept alive the flame, they watched over the embers of resistance when the holiday soldiers, the militia of the Sea Coast, who had enjoyed the frolick at first, were either dispersed or had submitted." [102]

It was Parson Weems who did for Francis Marion what he had already done for Washington. His biography of Marion which appeared in 1809 was based on a manuscript written by Peter Horry but was much embellished. Horry wrote Weems from Georgetown on February 4, 1811: "Most certainly 'tis not my history, but your romance." True or not, it was Weems' romance that the public read. And it was William Gilmore Simms who in 1842 wrote of Weems as a "person to whom . . .

---

[99] May and Faunt, op. cit., pp. 101, 103.

[100] Middleton even opposed the ratification of the Confederate Constitution by S. C. on the basis that it took out "of our hands . . . the control of our supply of labor, by a positive prohibition, giving us no efficient guaranty of the right and power of self-government at home, mingling, as it does, the National and Federative systems, and permitting the eventual accession of Anti-Slavery communities to our Confederacy by the absence of a constitutional prohibition. . . ." Quoted in Cauthen, op. cit., p. 89. Middleton and Gabriel Manigault voted against ratification. Ibid., p. 90.

[101] Rice Planter and Sportsman, The Recollections of J. Motte Alston, 1821–1909, ed. Arney R. Childs (Columbia, S. C., 1953), pp. 128–129.

[102] Francis Kinloch to Judge J. F. Grimké, April 30, 1808, Dreer Collection, Penn. Hist. Soc.

full justice has never been done, as a man of talent," implying that the picture drawn of Marion was close to the truth. Simms himself, of course, had a romantic view of the Revolution.[103]

This romantic view was fixed upon the Carolina mind in the 1820's. Lafayette's meeting with Francis Kinloch Huger, his would-be rescuer from Olmutz, brought tears to the eyes of the beholders.[104] Such a visit excited old men to relate their reminiscences before the Revolutionary stories would be lost forever. Major Alexander Garden brought out his *Anecdotes* in 1822 (reissued in 1828), in which the stories of Marion, Horry, and Maham led the parade of Revolutionary tales.[105] Sir Walter Scott received a long obituary notice in the Georgetown newspaper. It was notable that in the midst of the nullification crisis the *Winyaw Intelligencer* devoted a full page to the death of Scott.[106] The fact that some of the plantations were renamed in these years after romantic places in the English and Scottish past reveals the enhancement of these myths. Plantation names that hearkened back to Scotland and England were more common than Indian names—Caledonia, Bannockburn, Annandale, Dirleton, Waverly, Windsor, Weymouth, Arundel, Wicklow, Litchfield, Hagley, Calais, Dover are more typical than Hopsewee, Wachesaw, and Chicora Wood.[107] A visitor of 1843 who had just referred to "the lordly owners of these manors" as "descendants of king Charles's cavaliers" went on to write:

The historical associations of Georgetown District are of great interest; and many of the localities, rendered famous by feats of valor during the war of our Revolution, are still pointed out. An old soldier, whom I met by accident at the ferry-house on the banks of the Pedee, conducted me

---

[103] Quoted by A. S. Salley in his introduction to a new edition of William Dobein James, *A Sketch of the Life of Brig. Gen. Francis Marion* (Marietta, Ga., 1948), p. c.; *The Letters of William Gilmore Simms*, ed. M. C. S. Oliphant, A. T. Odell, and T. C. D. Eaves (Columbia, S. C., 1952), I, 328.

[104] Lafayette had to refuse the invitation to visit Georgetown in order to attend the dedication of the monument to the memory of de Kalb in Camden. *Winyaw Intelligencer*, March 16, 1825.

[105] Alexander Garden, *Anecdotes of the Revolutionary War in America* (Charleston, S. C., 1822), pp. 18–31.

[106] *Winyaw Intelligencer*, Jan. 5, 1833.

[107] Alberta M. Lachicotte, "Georgetown Plantation Names," *Names in South Carolina*, III (1956), 10–14.

to the spot where General Marion invited the British officer to dinner—
a scene immortalized by the pencil of White.[108]

This picture was as recognizable to South Carolinians as Washington's
crossing the Delaware was to all Americans.

The 1850 generation had not themselves earned military glory, but
almost every Georgetown family had its patriot heroes, even those
descended from British merchants. The Wards were related to Hezekiah
Maham; the Westons had borrowed the name of Francis Marion. The
Fords and Magills and Greens had fought with Marion, as had two William Allstons and James Withers. The Horrys and the Mayrants rightly
claimed connections with Peter and Hugh Horry. The Heriots, the
Tuckers, and the Trapiers were descended from patriot merchants. How
often these Revolutionary forebears were remembered can be seen in the
numerous children who bore the names of Francis Marion, Maham
Ward, and Benjamin Huger. "A Citizen of Williamsburg" reminded the
readers of the *Pee Dee Times* in January 1856 that his district had been
"rendered memorable in the history of the Revolution by the chivalric
deeds of a *James*, a *Mouzon*, a *Witherspoon*, a *Jenkins*, and a host of
others. . . ." [109]

The Santee families had even more distinguished ancestors. A Middleton, a Heyward, and a Lynch had been signers of the Declaration of
Independence. Charles Cotesworth Pinckney and Thomas Pinckney,
John and Edward Rutledge, Henry and Arthur Middleton, Ralph Izard,
John Julius Pringle, Rawlins Lowndes, Gabriel Manigault, and Dr. William Read were all notable men. This pride of past achievement was
passed on as in the names of Thomas Lynch Horry, Paul Trapier Horry,
and Christopher Gadsden Hume. Even the two Northerners who
entered this august assemblage brought family distinction with them.
Benjamin Faneuil Dunkin and Benjamin Faneuil Hunt were proud of
their Boston Huguenot patriot background, which caused them no shame
in South Carolina. The military glory and statesmanlike achievement of
their ancestors helped to set these planters apart; they wore their names

---

[108] "Sketches of South-Carolina," *The Knickerbocker*, XXII (July 1843), 3–4.
John Blake White had close family ties with Georgetown.
[109] *Pee Dee Times*, Jan. 16, 1856.

as a badge of distinction and of separation from ordinary mortals. These subtle influences were tattooed relentlessly on each new generation.

This mixture of fact and myth was at once both a strength and a weakness to the Confederate cause. Having won their freedom once from a foreign foe, they might do it again. Few communities could have been sustained by such patriotic pride. Plowden Weston, the *beau idéal* of the older generation, was called upon on May 4, 1860, to address the youthful scholars of the Winyah Indigo Society. He warned them: "We have only felt the 'whiff and wind of the fell sword;' *you* will experience its 'grinding blade.'" The stark contrast was of the "fanatic" versus the "hero." He drew upon Tennyson's "The Princess" to buttress "our state character":

> A nation yet, the rulers and the ruled:
> Some sense of duty, something of a faith,
> Some reverence for the laws ourselves have made,
> Some patient force to change them when we will,
> Some civic manhood firm against the crowd.[110]

But such pride also blinded them to the realities of the new forces at work in the world. At the firing on the *Star of the West,* J. Motte Alston asked J. L. Petigru, R. F. W. Allston's Unionist brother-in-law, how it would end. Petigru answered: "Alston, don't you know that the whole world is against slavery? So, if the South is to fight for that, rest assured it is lost, never mind which side wins." Motte added in his memoirs: "he was right." [111]

[110] Plowden C. J. Weston, *An Address Delivered in the Indigo Hall, Georgetown, South-Carolina, on the Fourth Day of May, 1860, the 105th Anniversary of the Winyaw Indigo Society* (Charleston, S. C., 1860), pp. 5, 6, 10, 11–12, 26–27, 29.
[111] Childs, *op. cit.,* pp. 128–129.

XVIII

THE CIVIL WAR

With secession came preparations for war. The state was divided into ten districts; each district was to furnish a regiment formed from the first ten companies offering their services. Georgetown with Horry, Marion, Williamsburg, and part of Charleston was the tenth district. The Tenth Regiment of South Carolina Volunteers was not filled up until May 31, 1861, and did not assemble for training at Camp Marion, White's Bridge near Georgetown, until July 19, 1861.[1] The first months of the war were, therefore, months of improvisation.

The Georgetown Rifle Guards, the first company to offer its services, elected as officers Richard Green White, captain, Archibald J. Shaw, first lieutenant, Stephen W. Rouquie, second lieutenant, and Calvin J. Coe, junior second lieutenant. The company, trained by Captain White, a graduate of The Citadel, offered its services on January 2, was accepted, and assigned to garrison duty on South Island on February 4. The first days of the war were a lark, since Plowden Weston, a private in the company, supplied his fellow soldiers from time to time with turkeys

---

[1] C. I. Walker, *Rolls and Historical Sketch of the Tenth Regiment, So. Ca. Volunteers, in the Army of the Confederate States* (Charleston, S. C., 1881), pp. 69–71.

and champagne from Hagley. They remained on South Island until after the fall of Fort Sumter; they were relieved on April 25, 1861.[2]

The main job in the early days was to build defenses along the coast and secure cannon, rifles, shot, powder, and ammunition. Georgetown could supply some engineering skills (the planters and their slaves were experts at building embankments), but the armament must be secured elsewhere, particularly from Charleston. Charles Alston, Jr., aide-de-camp to Governor Francis W. Pickens, on December 30, 1860, urged the planters to begin the work with these words:

The Governor of South Carolina asks your aid in the erection of Batteries to protect and defend the entrance to Winyah Bay and Santee River—Millions of *Property* and what is far more precious than Wealth *Life* and *Honor* will be at stake if we suffer marauding Bands to enter our ports—We have *all* some sacrifices to make in this good cause: and I doubt not that the same Patriotism which characterised your Sires burns as strongly in your Breasts now—When the History of these times is written I feel sure Carolina will make *good* the sentiment of her gallant Sons—"That she had Millions for *defence* but not one cent for Tribute." [3]

The danger was from descents upon the coast; the appeal was to emulate their forefathers. It was natural, therefore, to name the place of assemblage Camp Marion.[4]

The original plans called for defenses at the mouths of the South and North Santee, on South Island, Cat Island, and North Island. On January 4, 1861, Richard Dozier, John Harleston Read, and Plowden Weston wrote to the Board of Ordnance asking for two brass 12-pounders and two howitzers.[5] On January 7, one 18-pounder was shipped by steamer from Charleston, and on January 11 two 6-pounders.[6] On January 29 Charles Alston, Jr., reported to the Board of Ordnance that the armory and the magazine in Georgetown would be adequate after minor repairs

[2] S. Emanuel, *An Historical Sketch of the Georgetown Rifle Guards and as Co. A of the Tenth Regiment, So. Ca. Volunteers, in the Army of the Confederate States* (n.p., 1909), pp. 5–7.

[3] Board of Ordnance Papers, S. C. Archives.

[4] This was the central training depot during the war. Emanuel, *op. cit.,* p. 75.

[5] Board of Ordnance Papers, S. C. Archives.

[6] Board of Ordnance to Capt. James G. Henning [Jan. 1861], Board of Ordnance Papers, S. C. Archives.

were made. Lieutenant Louis F. LeBleux, an engineer, supervised the repairs and built the defenses on North Island. With the Georgetown Rifle Guards on South Island and Lieutenant LeBleux working at North Island the mouth of the bay was soon protected.[7] On Waccamaw Neck Captain Thomas West Daggett was in command of the Waccamaw Light Artillery, which he in March was trying to lodge in Forts Randall and Ward. Daggett, a Massachusetts man, had come to South Carolina as a young man, had been trained as an engineer, and had been miller for Francis Marion Weston at Laurel Hill. He put two 6-pounders in Fort Randall and completed the block house and magazine. He then asked whether he should bring the 12-pounders which were in the mill yard at Laurel Hill down to Fort Randall.[8] The planters exploited the facilities of their plantations in order to build the fortifications along the coast.

It was necessary to urge the men to join the volunteer companies. Two of the companies that volunteered in the spring disbanded in the summer, the Wee Nee Volunteers and the Carver's Bay Palmetto Rifle Guards. The planters may have over-persuaded these men to enlist. Benjamin Allston wrote his father on March 31 that Plowden Weston had come over to go with him to Small Hopes to review the "Carver's Bay Rifles." Although in the midst of the planting season, the prominent men gathered to furnish a dinner for the volunteers.[9]

In Georgetown itself the older men formed a "Home Guard," which included the leading citizens of Georgetown and surrounding plantation owners. W. W. Shackelford was elected captain, Samuel Atkinson, first lieutenant, and J. Tamplet, second lieutenant. They were supplied with

[7] Charles Alston, Jr., to Col. Edward Manigault, Jan. 29, 1861; Louis F. LeBleux to same, Jan. 31, 1861, Board of Ordnance Papers, S. C. Archives. The most complete statement of defense plans is in Col. Charles Alston, Jr., to D. F. Jamieson, Jan. 23, 1861, Military Affairs, 1860–1865, Legislative System, S. C. Archives. Capt. J. G. Henning wrote Gov. Pickens on March 9, 1861, that Alston had resigned and placed all volunteers under his command. Pickens Papers, S. C. Archives.

[8] Daggett to Col. Charles Alston, Jr., March 23, 1861, Board of Ordnance Papers, S. C. Archives; *Rice Planter and Sportsman,* ed. Arney R. Childs (Columbia, S. C., 1953), p. 125. Fort Randall overlooked the entrance to Little River. Was Fort Ward at Murrell's Inlet?

[9] *The South Carolina Rice Plantation, as Revealed in the Papers of Robert F. W. Allston,* ed. J. H. Easterby (Chicago, Ill., 1945), p. 173; Walker, *op. cit.,* pp. 70–72.

eighty muskets sent from Charleston aboard the steamer *Nina,* which was busily engaged in bringing supplies from Charleston.[10]

The center of interest was focused on Fort Sumter in Charleston harbor. Its fall on April 14 was the first great victory of the war, its captors heroes, destined for roles of leadership in the future. General G. P. T. Beauregard in his report of April 27 to the Confederate Secretary of War commended Captain Arthur M. Manigault of his own staff, "who did efficient and gallant services on Morris Island during the fight." He also bestowed an accolade on a group of officers, including Captain James H. Trapier, "on whom too much praise cannot be bestowed for their untiring zeal, energy, and gallantry, and to whose labors is greatly due the unprecedented example of taking such an important work after thirty-three hours firing without having to report the loss of a single life, and but four slightly wounded." [11]

James Heyward Trapier and Arthur Middleton Manigault were the two Georgetown men who became generals in the Army of the Confederacy. Trapier, born in 1815 at Windsor plantation on the Black River, was educated at West Point, where he graduated third in his class in 1838. Beauregard had been second. Trapier served in the corps of engineers and helped to build the defenses of Charleston and Savannah. After service in the Mexican War, he resigned his commission in 1848 to take up planting. For a brief period, 1851–1852, he was South Carolina's chief of ordnance. In 1853 he bought Keithfield plantation where he resided until the war. In the days just prior to the fall of Sumter he was again at work on the defenses of Charleston harbor. For this work he was promoted to major of engineers and then on October 21, 1861, commissioned a brigadier general.[12] Manigault, born in 1824, had served as first lieutenant of Company F, Palmetto Regiment, in the Mexican War. In 1856 he had moved to Georgetown District to plant family lands on the North Santee. In December 1860 he was elected captain of the North Santee Mounted Rifles, a volunteer company. After superintending the building of batteries at the mouth of the North Santee, he had gone to Charleston as a volunteer aide to General Beauregard. On May 31,

---

[10] The company roll sent with the request for arms and ammunition contains the names. April 18, 1861, Board of Ordnance Papers, S. C. Archives.

[11] *O. R., Army,* I, 34.

[12] Ezra J. Warner, *Generals in Gray* (Baton Rouge, La., 1959), pp. 309–310.

1861, Manigault was elected colonel of the Tenth Regiment, South Carolina Volunteers.[13]

The organization of the South Carolina Volunteer regiments was democratic in form but aristocratic in practice. The men volunteered, and they elected their officers. Although extremely jealous of the right of election, they usually selected aristocratic leaders. The regimental officers, elected on May 31, besides Manigault, were: J. F. Pressley, lieutenant colonel; Richard G. White, major; Captain B. H. Wilson, quartermaster; and the Reverend W. T. Capers, chaplain.[14] The Georgetown Rifle Guards, which was Company A of the Tenth Regiment, selected Private Plowden Weston to replace Captain White, as company commander. Weston proceeded to outfit his entire company at his own expense with English Enfield rifles, all gear, as well as summer and winter uniforms, treating his men somewhat as feudal retainers. Captain Weston also uniformed four of his slaves as a pioneer corps to precede the company clearing away the underbrush. Three drummers and one fifer, all colored, supplied military music.[15] On one occasion during the summer training period when there was a report of the enemy landing on Waccamaw Neck, Colonel Manigault took Company A on an expedition from Camp Marion to the beaches. It was a false alarm, but on the return march, although totally unprepared, Captain Weston entertained his entire company of 150 men at Hagley with a seated full-course meal, served in crystal and silver by the family retainers, and washed down with rare wines from his cellar. As one soldier recorded later, it was "on a par with the feudal entertainments of the great lords of Europe." [16]

On July 19, the Tenth Regiment was assembled at Camp Marion for training. By the end of the summer there were twelve companies, consisting of men from Horry, Marion, Williamsburg, and the South Santee. In August the regiment was transferred to Confederate Service, and new enlistments for longer periods were sought. The Wee Nee Volunteers and

[13] James W. Patton, "Arthur Middleton Manigault," DAB.

[14] Walker, op. cit., p. 70. When Beauregard countermanded the governor's order to hold elections, "snatching from us . . . our rights & suffrages as a free People," the privates wrote to complain to Governor Bonham from Camp Chesnut, Georgetown, Jan. 5, 1863. Bonham Papers, S. C. Archives.

[15] Walker, op. cit., pp. 70, 74; Emanuel, op. cit., p. 8.

[16] Emanuel, op. cit., pp. 9–10.

the Carver's Bay Palmetto Rifle Guards refused, however, to sign up for longer periods and were replaced by men from Marion and Horry counties. Those who remained trained at Camp Marion, which became a rendezvous for wives and sweethearts, who often came to watch the dress parades. War was still a cheerful sight. A Negro band, forever playing "Walk in the Light," stirred romantic feelings. Colonel Manigault on a fine horse followed by his two setters gave confidence.[17]

The planters were naturally full of suggestions for Colonel Manigault on how best to defend the coast. R. F. W. Allston, who paid a visit in July to President Jefferson Davis in Richmond to talk about the Carolina coast defenses, suggested a system of telegraphic communications to alert the Winyah Bay area.[18] Manigault, however, used a detachment of cavalry on duty at South Island and a guard in the Light House on North Island as lookouts for the appearance of hostile vessels. One or two mounted men could convey information in two hours from either of these points to the main base at Camp Marion. A steamer, which was sent from Charleston by General Roswell F. Ripley, along with plantation flats enabled Manigault to increase the mobility of his small force. He expected the first attack at the mouth of Winyah Bay and that forces then on South Island and on North Island could hold the enemy until reinforcements were brought up. During the summer Manigault alternated companies on South and North islands.[19] On Waccamaw Neck he relied on Ward's battery of light artillery. This battery, like Weston's company, had the earmarks of another feudal group. The captain (after Daggett) was Joshua Ward. The first lieutenant was Maham Ward, and the second lieutenant, who rushed home from his studies at the University of Edinburgh to fight, was Benjamin Huger Ward. Undoubtedly the Wards provided the necessary equipment and provisions. Throughout the war Ward's Light Artillery performed good service.[20]

General Robert E. Lee was sent to South Carolina in November 1861 to erect the defenses for the Atlantic coast of South Carolina, Georgia,

---

[17] Walker, op. cit., p. 75.

[18] Allston to Adele Petigru Allston, July 15, 20, 1861, Easterby, op. cit., pp. 178–180.

[19] Manigault to Allston, Sept. 20, 1861, ibid., pp. 183–184; Walker, op. cit., p. 75.

[20] Joshua Ward to James Speed, Aug. 12, 1865; B. H. Ward to Attorney General, Sept. 19, 1865, RG 94, National Archives. Organizational chart for Ward's Battery of Artillery is given in For Love of a Rebel (n.p., 1964), pp. 49–50.

and Florida.[21] Before he arrived the Yankees had landed on November 7 at Port Royal. They wanted a coaling, refitting, and supply station at some convenient point on the Southern coast to make the blockade of the coast already established more effective. Throughout the war the vessels blockading the mouth of the Santee and Winyah Bay when relieved generally resorted to Port Royal for coal and supplies rather than to Philadelphia or some Northern port. The capture of Port Royal therefore meant a more intensive blockade of Georgetown.

Lee established the pattern for coastal defense. Since it was impracticable to defend all of the islands and waterways, he determined to withdraw all guns and garrisons from minor, outlying positions. He then would strengthen the important avenues of entry—those at Cumberland Sound, Brunswick, Savannah, and Charleston. Finally, he would construct an interior line just east of the Savannah-Charleston Railroad, which would be far enough inland to prevent heavy Federal guns from being brought to bear upon it and yet close enough to the coast to protect the north-south lines of communication. For this purpose the governor of the state placed South Carolina troops under Lee's command. Trapier, who had been appointed on October 22, 1861, to the command of the Eastern and Middle Florida departments, would hold the southern half of Lee's line around Cumberland Island.[22] Manigault, who was designated on December 10, 1861, to command the First South Carolina District, which included the coast from Little River Inlet to the South Santee, would hold the northern end of Lee's line.[23] In both instances, however, there was the implication that troops and guns might be withdrawn to defend Savannah or Charleston, if they were needed.

General Trapier was ordered to defend the Atlantic coast of Florida and to give special care to Fernandina on Amelia Island. He was, however, unable to prevent or to thwart the descent of the Yankees on Cedar Keys on January 16, 1862, and in the evacuation of Amelia Island, ordered by General Lee, Trapier's forces lost twenty of their guns. After the citizens of East Florida petitioned their governor for his removal,

---

[21] For Lee's role see Douglas S. Freeman, *Robert E. Lee* (New York, 1934), I, 613–626.

[22] *O. R., Army,* Series I, VI, 293.

[23] *Ibid.,* p. 344.

Trapier was relieved of his duties on March 19, 1862, and sent to join General A. S. Johnston's army in Alabama.[24]

A more serious blockade of Georgetown took place in December 1861 when Admiral Du Pont stationed the *James Adger*, Commander Marchand, and the *Gem of the Sea*, Lieutenant Baxter, off Winyah Bay. (The *James Adger* was a Charleston-owned vessel which had been seized in a Northern port when the war commenced.) Since the *Augusta* stationed off Bull's Bay could view the lighthouse at Cape Romain and since the *James Adger* also kept the same lighthouse in view, the coast from Bull's Bay to North Inlet was under constant surveillance. The advantage obtained by stationing two vessels off Georgetown bar was that one could chase blockade runners while the other maintained its position.[25]

On December 24 or 25 *Gem of the Sea* chased the British schooner *Prince of Wales* (actually owned by John Fraser and Company of Charleston) loaded with salt and oranges from Nassau into North Inlet after hulling her several times. The captain set fire to his vessel as the Federals rowed in to seize her. As the Federals were trying to tow the vessel out, Captain John Hyrne Tucker's company arrived from Waccamaw Neck and after firing upon the Yankees forced them to abandon their prize. The vessel thereupon burned to her waterline. No one was wounded on either side in this encounter.[26] Twice in February *Gem of the Sea* chased schooners away from the entrance to Winyah Bay and on March 12 stopped and searched a British schooner from Nova Scotia which was carrying a cargo of fish, soap, shoes, blankets, and candles. The British schooner was sent into Port Royal. Neither the *James Adger* nor the *Gem of the Sea* ventured inside the bar during this period since they observed a steamer of about 450 tons, apparently armed, lying at anchor near the lighthouse on North Island.[27]

Colonel Manigault, with responsibility for defending this coast from raids from these vessels, concentrated on completing the defenses on Cat Island. His thinking was in line with Lee's, for he soon abandoned

---

[24] *Ibid.*, pp. 75–76, 93–94, 292–293, 412–413.

[25] *O. R., Navy*, Series I, XII, 411, 460. On Dec. 3, 1861, Robertson, Blacklock and Co. wrote to Dr. J. R. Sparkman stating that they doubted if any vessel would get from Charleston to Georgetown again. Sparkman Papers. 2791, SHC.

[26] *O. R., Navy*, Series I, XII, 459.

[27] *Ibid.*, pp. 479–480.

any attempt to strengthen a redoubt at the mouth of the North Santee River. Manigault saw a need to concentrate on interior lines and had wanted to fortify a line at least ten miles from the coast, but since this would have uncovered some of the richest plantations to the enemy, he was not free to do so. On November 14, 1861, he informed Lee that the South Island redoubt had three faces finished but was still open in the rear. The bombproof would be completed in ten days. This redoubt contained four 24-pounders, one 18-pounder, and one rifled 6-pounder. The Cat Island redoubt had its three principal faces nearly completed, although the two bastions in the rear and the curtain were entirely unfinished. There was no bombproof. The redoubt contained two 32-pounders, two 24-pounders, and one rifled 12-pounder. Together they were garrisoned with 320 men of the Tenth Regiment. There was a full supply of powder for all of the guns, but some were short of round shot.[28] Manigault during the winter completed the Cat Island redoubt.[29] A Yankee commander later described it as "a well-built fortification of quadrangular form, fitted with platforms for mounting ten guns and containing bombproofs, magazine, and furnace for hot shot."[30] The South Island redoubt was apparently never finished, although enough was done to give it the appearance of a very strong fortification. Since these redoubts were shortly to be abandoned, the work was for naught.

The redoubts were backed up by three companies of cavalry stationed on South Island and two more stationed nearer Georgetown—a total of 135 men. In Camp Marion on November 14, 1861, Manigault had 565 men of the Tenth Regiment and one company of 50 men attached to the Tenth for local duty. On Waccamaw Neck there was one section of light artillery with 40 men. Manigault, therefore, had 1,110 well-armed and well-drilled men, each equipped with 100 rounds of ammunition. With the increasing seriousness of the threat on the coast he called for 800 local volunteers, but those who trickled in during later November and December were badly armed and drilled.[31] H. J. Clifton of the Second Regiment, Pee Dee Legion, wrote his father on November 21 from Camp Harllee, about a half-mile from Georgetown: "We get

28 *O. R., Army,* Series I, VI, 321.
29 *Ibid.,* pp. 337–338.
30 *O. R., Navy,* Series I, XIII, 22–23.
31 *O. R., Army,* Series I, VI, 321.

beef and sometimes bacon, crackers, soap, candles, rice, sugar, coffee and salt. It is not too plentiful, but we can make out with it." Camp life was a "nasty life." [32] Eventually some 650 men arrived, but as their terms of enlistment were to run out on December 31, Manigault still did not have enough men to defend the coast. As the Tenth Regiment suffered greatly at this time from mumps and measles, his force by January 1, 1862, fell to 925 men. [33] With the possibility of having to retreat facing him, he sent out orders to his commanders to destroy all rice and provisions if they were forced to fall back. He also warned the planters that they should be ready to remove their Negroes 15 or 20 miles inland with provisions for one year and to hold their plantation flats in readiness to provide the necessary transportation. Troops would be at hand if planters needed force to have their commands obeyed. Since two-thirds of the rice crop of the state was in barns in this area, Manigault was trying to protect it; but, if necessary, he was ready to destroy it, rather than to let it fall into enemy hands. [34]

January and February 1862 were months of watching and waiting. W. L. Gregg wrote to his father from South Island on February 14, 1862, that his unit was guarding seven miles of beach, patrolling it two at a time. If the enemy should land and cut them off from their company, they were to come through the woods and along the banks of the rice plantations. He concluded: "send me an old wool hat for when it rains it runs down my Back." [35]

In February two disasters that struck the Confederate cause in Tennessee brought changes in South Carolina. On February 6 Fort Henry had fallen and on February 15 Fort Donelson also fell. The Confederate War Department decided to withdraw units from the sea islands to the mainland and to establish an interior line of defense with a smaller force, which change in strategy would permit reinforcements to be sent to Albert Sidney Johnston in Tennessee. [36] These changes came at the time when Lee was recalled to Virginia and replaced by General John

[32] J. L. Clifton Papers, DUL.
[33] O. R., Army, Series I, VI, 359–360.
[34] Ibid., pp. 337–338.
[35] William L. Gregg Letters, DUL.
[36] Freeman, op. cit., pp. 625–626.

Pemberton.[37] Pemberton on March 25 ordered Manigault to abandon his position on Winyah Bay. The guns were to be dismounted at night, and logs put in their positions. The guns were to be transported by light draught steamers up the Pee Dee River to the Northeastern railroad bridge and from there shipped to Charleston. Manigault should then bring his Tenth Regiment to Charleston, leaving the cavalry, light artillery, and local troops to guard the district, stationed as he saw fit before he left. Colonel Robert F. Graham was left in command.[38]

H. J. Clifton, who had been sent up the Pee Dee to guard the railroad bridge and who had spent his time catching fish and hunting ducks and turkeys, reported to his father on April 5 that there were fifteen large guns at the bridge waiting transportation for Charleston. The river itself had been blockaded with rafts of timber and was guarded by two large cannon planted twenty miles below. It was painful for him to think that the Confederate authorities had spent about $200,000 on the fortifications below and that they were now all abandoned.[39]

On April 3 Manigault arrived in Mount Pleasant with 903 men. He reported on the fifth that twenty guns were on their way by railroad to Charleston. While at Mount Pleasant the Tenth Regiment re-enlisted under the Bounty Act for three years' service. On April 10 Pemberton ordered Colonel Graham to Charleston, leaving Georgetown virtually undefended, as it was to be for the remainder of the war. The Tenth Regiment left Charleston on April 12 to join Beauregard's army at Corinth, Mississippi. Of those who went, one-half never returned to South Carolina.[40]

It is impossible in a history of Georgetown County to describe the exploits of her native sons on fields of battle in other parts of the Confederacy. The principal group to leave Georgetown for service elsewhere was Manigault's Tenth Regiment. They suffered from disease in Mississippi; they marched with Bragg in Kentucky that summer, finding a brief respite at Knoxville in October. Captain Plowden Weston left

[37] Maj. Gen. John Pemberton took command on Feb. 13, 1862. He was relieved on Aug. 29, 1862 and replaced by Beauregard.

[38] O. R., Army, Series I, VI, 417–418. Pemberton was criticized by the planters for abandoning Winyah Bay. Beauregard apparently endorsed Pemberton's arrangements. Yates Snowden, History of South Carolina (Chicago. Ill., 1920), II, 727–728.

[39] March 13, April 5, 1862, J. L. Clifton Papers, DUL.

[40] O. R. Army, Series I, VI, 425–426; Walker, op. cit., p. 76.

the Tenth in Knoxville to return to the state and take up his position as lieutenant governor, to which office he had recently been elected. The first general engagement in which the Regiment was involved was at Murfreesboro in middle Tennessee, "a gentlemanly fight" as the brigade's historian recalls it. In July 1863 at Chattanooga, Manigault was promoted to brigadier general. In September 1863 at the battle of Chickamauga and in November at Missionary Ridge the men of the Tenth fought and died. After wintering in Dalton, Georgia, they stood before Atlanta in 1864 to bar the way of Sherman. When Atlanta fell, there "fell the Southern cause." Although they knew how defenseless their homes were, they fought on with Hood in Tennessee. It was not until January 19, 1865, that the remnants of the Tenth gained permission to return to defend South Carolina. They arrived in time to oppose Sherman's crossing of the Edisto River but were forced to retreat through Columbia. Only then did 150 men desert in order to go home. The others fought on until they surrendered on April 10, 1865, in North Carolina. At first they had volunteered to defend their homes, but they learned to fight wherever the Confederacy had need of them.[41]

The departure of the Tenth Regiment and the abandonment of the redoubts were very quickly learned by the officers of the United States Navy. J. N. Merriman, the collector of the port who had been put in Georgetown jail at the beginning of the war for refusal to take an oath to the Confederacy, made his escape early in April 1862 to the *Keystone State*, then stationed off Georgetown bar. He took with him, perhaps as his guide, Prince Coit, an intelligent Negro, one of the best pilots in the Georgetown area. They brought not only news of the defenseless state of Georgetown but also of the fact that the *Nashville*, owned by John Fraser and Company of Charleston but under English registry, had arrived in Winyah Bay on March 20 and sailed on March 27 for Nassau.[42] The latter fact indicated that large vessels could cross the

[41] Walker, *op. cit..* pp. 78–129; Emanuel, *op. cit.*, pp. 10–29. Benjamin Huger (1806–1877), graduate of West Point, veteran of Mexican War, in May 1861 commanded in southern Virginia, in Oct. 1861 made major general in Confederate service and commanded a division under Lee in the Seven Days' campaign. He was later Chief of Ordnance in the West. *Confederate Military History*, ed. Clement A. Evans (Atlanta, Ga., 1899), V, 403–404.

[42] *O. R., Navy*, Series I, XII, 678–680; Charles E. Cauthen, *South Carolina Goes to War, 1860–1865* (Chapel Hill, N. C., 1850), p. 82n.

Georgetown bar safely. Additional information reached the Federal commanders from Georgetown from time to time. Early in June Messrs. Wilson and Conway escaped to the fleet. In July a Mr. Denny warned the Federals of a possible attack. In August a "Unionist"—suspected to be David Risley—wrote that General Pemberton had been in town on the third to select Mayrant's Bluff and Fraser's Point as the sites for batteries.[43] From April on, there was also a steady stream of slaves fleeing to the Federal fleet, although the information obtained from the contrabands was not considered very valuable or reliable. By the end of July there were 15 or 20 refugees and 1,700 contrabands in the navy's hands.[44] Most crucial was the defection of John E. Uptegrove, a pilot, who knew the waters of the bay and surrounding rivers.[45] With pilots who could guide the naval vessels and with many slaves apparently ready to desert their masters, the time for pushing up the rivers had come. There was also a need to curtail the activity of blockade runners. On April 3 the steamer *Seabrook* had taken on cotton at the railway bridge over the Santee and had sailed for Nassau. On April 10 the Union navy had forced the *Liverpool* of Nassau on shore at North Inlet.[46]

On April 22 Admiral Du Pont sent Commander George A. Prentiss in the *Albatross* with Lieutenant Baxter in the *Gem of the Sea* and Lieutenant Duncan in the *Norwich* to the Georgetown area. On May 21 the *Albatross* and the *Norwich* sailed over the bar, leaving the *Gem of the Sea* on watch. They found the forts on South Island and Cat Island deserted and the guns to be quakers. They landed and fired the fort on Cat Island. On May 22 they steamed up the bay to Georgetown and then steamed slowly by the wharves along the Sampit River.[47] Major W. P. Emanuel, who was then in military command of the district, ordered the brig *Joseph*, loaded with turpentine, to be burned, but its effect as a fire ship was unavailing. As Emanuel reported to Charleston: "They ordered our flag to be hauled down, but the reply

[43] *O. R., Navy*, Series I, XIII, 92–93, 192–193, 337–338.

[44] *Ibid.*, pp. 212–213.

[45] *Ibid.*, pp. 192–193, 202, 213–215. Capt. Uptegrove of the schooner *United States* had carried rice from Georgetown to Charleston. Ravenel, Stevens & Co. to Henry Cuttino, Jan. 14, 1835, Grimes Family Papers, Georgetown, S. C.

[46] *O. R., Navy*, Series I, XII, 678–680.

[47] *Ibid.*, XIII, 22–23.

was if they wished it down they would have to haul it down."[48] Prentiss informed his superior that he had sent word to the Union men in town to make no demonstrations since he was not prepared to hold the place. He could have captured it and could do so at any time the military could hold it, but he did not want to destroy the city. A woman had appeared in the belfry of the church and spread a rebel flag over the bell. Unlike the British commanders in the Revolutionary war, the Federals did not wish to occupy a place until they could hold it. In the afternoon Prentiss went up the Waccamaw River about ten miles, seizing lighters with rice and receiving on board eighty contrabands. Since there had been no sign of an enemy on North Island, on coming down the Waccamaw Prentiss occupied the North Island lighthouse. Baxter at sea reported: "On the following morning, at 8 a. m., we saw a flagstaff erected on the lighthouse, with the glorious flag of our Union attached to it." [49] The Union navy henceforth had a safe anchorage inside the bar.

Lieutenant Baxter in *Gem of the Sea* had an opportunity to explore the mouths of the Santee River. On June 5 he picked up five contrabands from A. Blake's plantation near Cape Romain. Blake, an Englishman of ancient Carolina lineage, had returned to England one week after the fall of Sumter, but the Confederates defended his plantation since it guarded the southernmost exit from the Santee via Alligator Creek and Bull's Bay to the ocean. The same day Baxter went ashore on Cedar Island, where he found abandoned summer cottages. On South Island he examined the redoubt, which was fast falling into decay. On June 9 Baxter went up the South Santee to William Lucas's rice mill situated on the north end of Murphy's Island. On this trip he learned that the steamer *Seabrook* had gotten out of the South Santee one night during a storm and that two schooners normally engaged in carrying rice from the Santee to Charleston had escaped to Nassau by way of Alligator Creek. With this news Prentiss was convinced that in order to block up the Santee exit a vessel must be stationed in the Santee above the mouth of Alligator Creek, which decision necessitated the destruction of the post at the Blake plantation. He therefore asked

---

[48] *O. R., Army,* Series I, XIV, 512–513.
[49] *O. R., Navy,* Series I, XII, 733.

Admiral Du Pont for a light steamer and a company of marines for this purpose.[50]

On June 24 with the *Albatross, E. B. Hale, Western World, Henry Andrew,* a few men from the *Gem of the Sea* on board the steam tug the *North Santee,* and a company of marines sent by Admiral Du Pont and commanded by Lieutenant Lowry, Prentiss made an ascent of the Santee. However, "with a succession of Westerly winds, low tides, intricate channels, and the very bad steerage of the two long steamers," he found it almost impossible to proceed. When the flotilla was fired upon from Blake's plantation, Prentiss landed the marines who burned the dwellings and the mill with the rice stored therein. When the Confederates counterattacked, Lieutenant Lowry retreated to the steamers, bringing along 400 contrabands who were taken back to North Island.[51]

On June 30 Prentiss sailed his four steamers up to Georgetown and demanded the wives of Wilson and Conway. The wives were permitted to board the Union vessels. Prentiss reported that a single gunboat could seize the city, but "as we can not hold it, it would be neither politic nor humane. There is some comment, I am aware, upon my course, as it may be lawfully attacked, but I should be a very unwilling agent in its destruction." [52] Admiral Du Pont approved of this humane way of fighting the war, for he later ordered one of his senior officers not to destroy buildings unless they were being used for military purposes.[53]

Prentiss continued his probing. On June 30 he had also gone thirty-five miles up the Waccamaw River to secure rice for the contrabands. On the second of July he made another attempt to reach the railway bridge on the Santee.[54] Captain John Hyrne Tucker, then commanding in Georgetown, wrote hurriedly to General Pemberton indicating the movement of Prentiss and commenting: "They have been committing great depredations in this district of late; such as burning barns, stealing negroes and rice, etc." [55] On July 3 Prentiss abandoned

---

[50] *Ibid.,* pp. 734–736; XIII, 92–93.
[51] *Ibid.,* p. 122.
[52] *Ibid.*
[53] *Ibid.,* pp. 203–204.
[54] *Ibid.,* p. 123.
[55] *O. R., Army,* Series I, XIV, 577–578.

his ascent of the Santee, because of the falling of the level of the water in the river. Prentiss then sailed for Boston, leaving Baxter in command. Baxter, who made a great deal of use of John E. Uptegrove as his pilot, on July 19 went up to Georgetown and demanded Uptegrove's family and had a talk with the mayor and provost marshal of the town who "are very bitter against the Union." [56]

On July 7 Lieutenant Duncan in the *Norwich* was sent to command the navy off Georgetown.[57] On July 21 Lieutenant Balch with the *Pocahontas* was sent to supersede Duncan. With this addition it was possible to raid the salt works along the Waccamaw beaches. On July 21 Baxter found extensive salt works on the mainland at Murray's [Murrell's] Inlet capable of making 30 to 40 bushels of salt per day. These belonged to John LaBruce, "who is a strong secessionist," and Captain Ward of the artillery.[58] The salt works were destroyed, but the Federals were driven away by a force of twenty-five men. In the last week of the month they broke up "salt boilers, stole 2 boiler heads and wantonly scatter'd the Salt into the Sand." [59]

On July 29 the Federals, with Uptegrove as pilot, went up the Waccamaw River to Laurel Hill, belonging to Colonel Jordan. They anchored further up at Doctor Magill's, "a violent secessionist, who has two sons in the rebel Army." Twenty-eight contrabands came on board, representing the doctor as an unkind master. If the Federal officer had been certain that Magill had sent for troops, as the contrabands warned, he would have thrown a ten-inch shell into the doctor's house, but he did not.[60]

Although showing some restraint, the Federals were making the lives of the leading planters miserable. They knew who were the great secessionists and where they lived. It was at this time during the late spring and early summer of 1862 that the planters began to move their slaves inland. Prentiss wrote on May 25: "The rebels are just now very much frightened, and are leaving their plantations in every direction, driving

[56] *O. R., Navy,* Series I, XIII, 123, 192–193, 202.
[57] *Ibid.,* p. 170.
[58] *Ibid.,* pp. 202–204.
[59] Allston to James H. Hammond, July 26, 1862, Easterby, *op. cit.,* p. 188.
[60] *O. R., Navy,* Series I, XIII, 213–215.

their slaves before them to the pine woods."[61] There was something like panic that spring in Georgetown. When the commissioner in equity, Samuel T. Atkinson, was requested on short notice to box up his papers in the commissioner's office and send them into the interior, he did the job so fast that by mistake he also sent off the books and papers of the commissioners of the free schools for whom he was secretary.[62] It was estimated later that three-fourths of the planters moved out, but the remaining one-fourth still planted enough to feed 50,000 men.[63]

The Fords, Lucases, and Shackelfords went to Mars Bluff. The Ford family paid $27,000 for a farm. Benjamin F. Dunkin bought a place in Cheraw for $22,500. William Bull Pringle rented a farm for $2,000 a year. Dr. Seaman Deas was at Limestone Springs in Spartanburg District. Paul T. Horry, E. S. Horry, and Charles Alston, Sr., were in Greenville. Daniel W. Jordan removed from Laurel Hill to Camden. Dr. Sparkman sent his slaves to Clarendon. Plowden Weston bought a farm in Fairfield County. William Lucas was at Aiken. The Trapiers had a place in Richland County. Mrs. Pringle sent her slaves inland.[64]

In June the Confederates began to build a fort ten miles up the Black River to bar the Federals' advance. Pemberton himself came to Georgetown on August 3 and selected Mayrant's Bluff and Fraser's Point as

[61] *Ibid.*, pp. 22–23.

[62] Report of the Commissioners of the Free Schools, Prince George Winyah, 1862, S. C. Archives. On April 17, 1862, the Executive Council in Columbia resolved "That the Clerk of the Court of Common Pleas and General Sessions: Sheriff: Register of Mesne Conveyance and Commission of Equity for Georgetown be instructed by the Chief Justice and Police to move the books and respective office and other valuable papers in their possession to the town of Cheraw, or such other safe places as may be approved by Messrs. F. S. Parker, R. F. W. Allston and R. I. Middleton or a majority of them." This was endorsed on April 22 by Francis S. Parker: "The above order is intended to include the books & records of the Ordinary's Office." *SCHM*, XIII (1912), 178–179. On April 22 Parker ordered E. Waterman, ordinary, to pack his records in one large case and one box and had them sent to the clerk of court for Chesterfield District. Georgetown County, Judge of Probate, Miscellaneous Records, 1862–1865, pp. 237–238, WPA typescript, S. C. Archives. Waterman then began to keep his records in a loose journal which survives as above. The records were removed to Chesterfield Court House. F. S. Parker to Governor F. W. Pickens, Nov. 11, 1862, Pickens Papers, S. C. Archives. Unfortunately, General Sherman passed by Chesterfield.

[63] *O. R., Army*, Series I, XXXV, Part 2, 340–341.

[64] Letters addressed to President Johnson by these planters are to be found in RG 94, National Archives; Henry A. Middleton to Harriott Middleton, Jan. 5, 1863, Cheves Collection, Middleton Papers, S. C. Hist. Soc.

the best places to fortify in order to confine the Federals to the lower bay.[65] Mayrant's Bluff, later Battery White, was to become the important fortification, but at this time it was not completed and therefore did not bar the way up the rivers. Lieutenant Balch therefore decided to go up the Black River to seize the *Nina* and a number of other vessels above Georgetown, and also to destroy the fortifications being built on the Black River.

On August 14 the *Pocahontas* and the tug *Treaty* moved up the Black River and fired on the battery which had been erected on Mrs. Sparkman's plantation. The fire of the Federal guns was returned by Ward's artillery stationed in the battery. The *Pocahontas* ran aground, and it was only with great difficulty that Baxter using the tug got the *Pocahontas* moving again and guided her downstream. Emanuel, who had brought his troops from Georgetown, followed the two boats downstream, firing upon them from every favorable place, suffering two wounded. He claimed that he killed or wounded fifty of the enemy. Balch wrote his commanding officer that the rebels had claimed to have killed fifty to one hundred, but only one man had actually been wounded. The Federals failed, however, to capture the *Nina* or any of Ward's artillery.[66] This was the deepest penetration by the Federals. J. I. Middleton, who attended in September the state convention which had been called to abolish the executive council, chided the upcountry members for their failure to rally to the defense of Georgetown.[67]

Many of the Waccamaw people had been driven to Plantersville, and all, even the Pee Dee folk, were contemplating further removals into the interior. Adele Allston wrote her son on October 30 that the Westons, Tuckers, and LaBruces had been giving parties in Plantersville, no doubt trying to keep up their spirits, but the more important news was that her husband had just come back from North Carolina where

---

[65] *O. R., Navy*, Series I, XIII, 337–338.

[66] *Ibid.*, pp. 256–259, 272; *O. R., Army*, Series I, XIV, 114–115. Henry A. Middleton wrote on Oct. 26, 1862, that Major Emanuel was "so feeble a man that—command going by elections—he does not dare give an order." The five cavalry companies in the district, therefore, "never act in concert." Cheves Collection Middleton Papers, S. C. Hist. Soc.

[67] Cauthen, *op. cit.*, p. 158. For refusal of militia to defend Georgetown see *ibid.*, pp. 146–147.

he had purchased Morven, twelve miles above Cheraw on the Pee Dee. He had paid $10,000 for 1,900 acres. "We consider this a fortunate arrangement." The same letter recounts that the Westons had recently lost "their head carpenter and 18 others of his finest, most intelligent and trusted men," who had taken a large family boat and made their escape to the enemy. "There are many circumstances connected with it that makes it very painful; and shews quite a widespread feeling not only among Mr. Weston's people, but through the neighborhood." [68]

The planters of the region in the midst of the general deterioration of the situation had to weigh individual interests against those of the state and of the Confederacy. It was natural that they should try to do everything in their power to provide protection for their region. There was a move to call home those who could help. Plowden Weston, who had just been elected lieutenant governor of the state, left the Tenth Regiment in Knoxville on October 24 and returned home.[69] General J. H. Trapier also came home from the western theater to take command of the Georgetown military district. Trapier, who complained that "the means at my command for the defense of this military district are extremely limited," planned to erect a battery at Mayrant's Bluff and then call home Manigault's Tenth Regiment from Bragg's army, as it was "composed entirely of men from this section of country, perfectly familiar with it and accustomed to the climate." [70] Trapier on November 13 asked General Harllee to use his influence in Richmond to secure the return of the Tenth Regiment. Beauregard, who was again in command at Charleston, had promised "to endorse my application for them." [71] On November 21 Beaumont, the U. S. naval commander, reported that a battery was abuilding "on Marion's plantation" and that two large guns were expected from Charleston and that another battery was be-

[68] Easterby, op. cit., pp. 189-190. J. L. Petigru had written Mrs. Allston on Jan. 25, 1862: "who knows but that Brittons Neck once the despised wilderness may become the brightest link in his [R. F. W. Allston's] possessions?" Allston Papers, S. C. Hist. Soc. Mrs. Pringle describes life at Crowley Hill, "our place of refuge during the war." Elizabeth W. Allston Pringle, Chronicles of Chicora Wood (Boston, Mass., 1940), pp. 192–199.

[69] Easterby, op. cit., p. 190; Emanuel, op. cit., p. 13.

[70] Nov. 17, 1862, O. R. Army, Series I, XIV, 681.

[71] Trapier to Harllee, Nov. 13, 1862, Gratz Collection, Penn. Hist. Soc. Beauregard assumed command on Sept. 24, 1862.

ing built on the Santee.[72] The line of defense would be Fraser's Point, Battery White, and the new earthworks on the Santee. Trapier showered Beauregard with requests and complaints during the winter. The earthworks at Santee was ready and two guns for it were in Georgetown which could be put in place in twelve hours if there were men available to remove them. Captain Warley at Battery White had only fifty-three men to man his nine guns and at Fraser's Point Captain Ward was hampered by the sickness of his men; "very many details have to be made for duty in the commissary and quartermasters departments and in the hospital, our entire population almost being in the army." [73]

Trapier on November 13 had also urged General Harllee to secure the building of an ironclad at Mars Bluff on the Pee Dee. Since the major ports were in danger of being taken in the summer of 1862, the navy yards were being removed to the interior. A wooden gunboat was laid down at Mars Bluff.[74]

With the enemy pressing ever closer the slaves did become restless. Dr. Francis S. Parker and R. F. W. Allston both wrote of the necessity of placing the Confederate troops who remained in the district in positions appropriate for preventing Negro uprisings. Pemberton had ordered Major Emanuel on June 4, 1862, to locate his troops "with a view to prevent the escape of slaves and for protection of persons and property against insubordination of Negroes." [75] One of the main reasons for the purchase of upcountry farms was to have a place where the Negroes might be sent beyond the lure of this new temptation. The other measures taken were outlined in a letter of Henry A. Middleton to his wife on November 5, 1862:

For some months back people have been in numbers leaving different plantations—and generally it has been by water—for at night there are few boats afloat—to correct this they are just about establishing a regular guard by water. I have given the best of my boats 22 feet long for this purpose—others will do the same. They will play chiefly between Frasers Point and Dover—Also of the people who went away three

[72] O. R., Navy, Series I, XIII, 548.

[73] O. R., Army, Series I, XIV, 762.

[74] Information on navy yard at Mars Bluff in Edward J. Means Letterbook, La. State Univ. Library. The Pee Dee was built at this navy yard.

[75] O. R., Army, Series I, XIV, 541, 588–589.

men, returned to the plantation of Dr. McGill and carried away their wives—the six were taken together making their way to the enemy. The men were tried yesterday by the provost martials court—they were sentenced to be hung—to day one oclock was fixed for the execution that no executive clemency might intervene—Dr. Parker came here soon after it was in the gaol yard—a strong military drawn up—there was a crowd—the blacks were encouraged to be present—the effect will not soon be forgotten. As far as I can know Dr. P. has acted with great decision and judgment.

By January 5, 1863, Middleton thought things safe enough to contemplate a visit to Flat Rock in North Carolina. There were then pickets everywhere on high land and on the water too. Yet, he wrote, "this last battle of Fredericksburg, has also had a noticeable effect even among the Negroes." [76]

Why did the slaves not rise up during the war? This is a crucial question in contemporary historiography. Asa H. Gordon, in a little-known but perceptive book, written in the 1920's, gave one answer. After admitting that the slaves did not rebel, he said: "It seems to me that the slaves acted as they did partly because of the fact that the selective process which we described above had weeded out the more warlike members of the slaves and partly because they were 'playing safe.'" [77] Pre-war conditioning and doubts about the future both played a part in helping the planters maintain control over the slaves. Yet the Georgetown planters had their doubts too.

In the spring of 1863 there was a big push on Charleston and Trapier was needed to prepare the defenses of Sullivan's Island. Lieutenant Colonel Joseph A. Yates of the First South Carolina Artillery, a Charlestonian who had commanded at Castle Pinckney, was appointed to replace Trapier in command of the Fourth Military District, a subdistrict of the First Military District. On March 8, 1863, Yates had under his command an Independent Company of Cavalry, under Captain J. H. Tucker, four companies of Rutledge's South Carolina Cavalry under Major W. P. Emanuel, the Second South Carolina Artillery under Captain F. F. Warley, and the Light Battery of Captain Ward. Ward was

[76] Cheves Collection, Middleton Papers, S. C. Hist. Soc.

[77] Asa H. Gordon, *Sketches of Negro Life and History in South Carolina* (n.p., 1929), p. 50.

at Fraser's Point supported by Tucker. Warley's men were in Battery White and on the North Santee and were backed up by Emanuel.[78]

On March 24, 1863, the English steamer *Queen of the Wave* was run ashore near the mouth of the North Santee. A Federal boarding party captured seven rebels trying to unload the cargo which contained quinine, morphine, and opium. Those captured, including Lieutenant Philip R. Lachicotte, were sent north as prisoners; Major Warley was permitted to send them letters and clothes before their departure.[79]

The attention of the U. S. Navy was drawn to Murrell's Inlet, from which five to seven vessels loaded with cotton had sailed each week ever since Christmas. On April 27 Lieutenant Braine of the *Monticello* had destroyed there a large schooner loaded with a valuable cargo and two large houses used for storing cotton. Yates thereupon sent two rifled guns from Georgetown and ordered some state troops under Captain Boykin from Little River to Murrell's Inlet. Major Emanuel with one of his companies was also present. These Confederate troops awaited the return of the Federals. The *Monticello* and *Choçura* did return on May 3 and on May 4 bombarded the port, shelling from sunrise until 11 A.M. Seven men were then sent ashore to burn the vessels. They were driven back with one man killed and three wounded. Major Emanuel mentioned Private T. G. Britton "as having behaved with great gallantry." On May 12 the *Conemaugh* with the *Monticello* returned and at a range of 2,000 yards shelled five schooners aground in the inlet. They set one on fire and damaged all the others.[80]

While this threat continued Lieutenant Colonel Yates learned that the four companies, commanded by Major Emanuel, were to be relieved of duty. He wrote asking for their retention, otherwise he would have to abandon Waccamaw Neck since he would be left with only enough men to man Battery White. To withdraw the pickets from the Neck would be to invite the enemy to take the grain and Negroes there (4,431 at the last count). He was permitted to retain Emanuel's com-

---

[78] *O. R., Army*, Series I, XIV, 797, 823. Henry A. Middleton wrote on March 10, 1863: "General Trapier left us today to join his brigade elsewhere. The satisfaction is universal in being rid of him. I heard one of his best friends express it. . . . Col. Yates and Major Warley are our strong supports." Cheves Collection, Middleton Papers, S. C. Hist. Soc.

[79] *O. R., Navy*, Series I, XIII, 687–690.

[80] *O. R., Navy*, Series I, XIV, 191; *O. R., Army*, Series I, XIV, 286–287.

panies, but he was informed "that the preservation of Murray's [Murrell's] Inlet as a port of entry for blockade runners is not regarded as of very great military importance." He was not to leave points uncovered in order to maintain the inlet as a port of entry. By May 8 he had been sent the Twenty-First Battalion of Georgia Cavalry, Major William P. White, to take the place of Emanuel's companies.[81]

On June 16 General Trapier was relieved of his duties on Sullivan's Island and sent back to Georgetown as commander of the Fourth Military District. Trapier fussed and fretted over this demotion, asking if he could hold on to Sullivan's Island as a part of his new command. Beauregard would not consent to the inclusion of Sullivan's Island in his command, but reassured him that the parishes of St. Stephen and St. James Santee were being added to the Fourth Military District. He was to watch for "negro raids" and Yankee descents upon the coast.[82]

Some of the planters were still trying to grow rice in the district in 1863. With the Yankees confined to the mouth of the bay by Battery White there was still hope that a crop could be made. Mrs. Allston wrote in January 1863 that she would prefer remaining at Plantersville to moving to North Carolina, if she only had "a tolerably comfortable house."[83] In April Ralph Stead Izard was at Weymouth arranging for the sale of his rice.[84] Charles Alston, Sr., wrote from Plantersville in June to James Reid Pringle in Charleston ordering 1,000 yards of vaucluse oznaburgs sent to him via Kingstree. At the end of the year he sold $20,000 worth of rice.[85] According to Francis S. Parker, six of the free schools with 108 scholars had been in operation during the year.[86] Alexander Glennie, though living in Plantersville, made trips to Waccamaw; he held services in both places.[87] Dr. Sparkman still practiced in the neighborhood of Plantersville, where Mrs. Sparkman gave birth to her sixth son in October.[88]

[81] *Ibid.*, pp. 921–923, 929.
[82] *Ibid.*, pp. 966–968; XXVIII, Part 2, 142–143, 159.
[83] To Elizabeth Allston, Jan. 11, 1863, Easterby, *op. cit.*, p. 192.
[84] To S. D. Doar, April 3 [1863], S. D. Doar Letters, DUL.
[85] June 23, 1863, July 19, 1864, James Reid Pringle Papers, DUL.
[86] Report of Commissioners of Free Schools, Prince George Winyah, 1863, S. C. Archives.
[87] Last baptism at All Saints during the war was April 16, 1862. Henry DeSaussure Bull, *All Saints' Church Waccamaw, 1739–1948* (Columbia, S. C., 1949), pp. 40–42.
[88] Easterby, *op. cit.*, p. 195.

Although some carried on in the district, there were additional transfers of property to the upcountry. Plowden Weston wrote J. R. Pringle in Charleston on March 27, 1863, asking that four of his slaves, who had been working for the government, be sent to him at Snow Hill in Fairfield County.[89] R. F. W. Allston had sent most of his slaves to North Carolina and would have sent his son's slaves but did not have a suitable place to send them. Four of his own slaves had been hired out to the Confederate Ship Yard at Mars Bluff. In October he was again in Plantersville, although Mrs. Allston had now moved upcountry. Books, provisions, papers, salt were sent upcountry. In October he went to Georgetown to pay his war tax of $1,236.12 and to say a word to the enrolling officer to prevent the drafting of his miller and overseer.[90] His spirit is reflected in a letter of November 11 written from Plantersville to his wife:

Ah! I am check'd by the reflection that our country suffers and is in danger of devastation. Perseverance is the quality in which as people, we are inferior to the Northern fiends. If we fail with them, it will be due less even to their superior preparation than their pertinacity and endurance. But God forbid that we should fail, the idea is intolerable. Tis sad, however and sorrowful to see that some of our people are giving away. Christian, they tell me (a man for peace on any terms) has been elected in Anson No. Ca. over Ashe, and Witherspoon over McQueen in So. Ca. I dont condemn Witherspoon but the ground of the opposition is for peace. I am for Peace as much as anybody, but Peace on honorable terms only, first of all our Independence. God grant us power to win it, and grace to administer it worthily and wisely. . . .[91]

He died the next spring, perhaps just worn out.

The cat-and-mouse game between the Federal Navy and the blockade runners continued throughout 1863. On October 19 the schooner *Rover* was driven ashore at Murrell's Inlet while running the blockade.

---

[89] James Reid Pringle Papers, DUL. The Rev. Malet has left a vivid picture of life at Snow Hill. Rev. William W. Malet, *An Errand to the South in the Summer of 1862* (London, 1863), pp. 96–97, 198–208. Mrs. Emily Weston sailed from Wilmington, N. C., for Halifax and England in the fall of 1863. She wrote Mrs. Allston, Aug. 30, 1863: "Though I am leaving it [the land], *its cause* will ever be in my heart, & in my prayers to Him who above giveth victory." Allston Papers, S. C. Hist. Soc.

[90] Easterby, *op. cit.*, pp. 194–195.

[91] *Ibid.*, pp. 197–198.

Her cargo was landed on the beach and removed behind the sand hills; the vessel was burned. The enemy, according to the Confederates, landed seventeen men in order to destroy the cargo. The Yankees reported that they had landed in order to seize another schooner a mile and a half up the inlet and to reconnoiter for water. Ensign Tillson and nine men were captured by Company B of the Twenty-First Georgia Cavalry under Lieutenant Ely Kennedy. Lieutenant Kennedy had concealed his men behind the sand hills in such a way so as to cut off the escape of the landing party, which they did with dispatch. The prisoners were sent to Richland County and then to Andersonville, where some died. Major W. P. White, commanding on Waccamaw Neck, in dispatches to General Trapier particularly mentioned Sergeant W. H. Crawford. Beauregard's reply to Trapier's report was to remind him "officers and men on outpost service, by coolness, vigilance, subordination, and resolution, may frequently render signal service by successful small encounters with the enemy." [92] Beauregard was obviously trying to inspire Trapier to greater vigilance.

On December 5, 1863, sixteen of the enemy landed on Magnolia Beach from the brig *Perry* in order to seize a blockade runner due to leave that evening, but the vigilance of the Georgia Cavalry under Captain W. H. K. Harrison was rewarded with the capture of three officers and twelve men. One of the enemy was killed in the encounter. The Confederates lost one man killed and two severely wounded. [93]

Admiral Dahlgren wrote Secretary of Navy Welles that these captures were "another of the indications that the perfect blockade of Charleston is driving speculators to the smaller ports to get cotton out and a return cargo in." [94] There may have been truth in this statement, as Trapier received on November 11 a request for information on ports that could be opened up to blockade runners. [95] On November 23 Trapier reported on the four ports along his stretch of the coast. The mouths of the North and South Santee had nine feet of water at high tide, and boats that got over the bars could usually make their way seventy miles up the river to the bridge of the Northeastern Railway. Of the three

[92] *O. R., Army*, Series I, XXVIII, Part 1, 736–737.
[93] *Ibid.*, p. 747; *O. R. Navy*, Series I, XV, 153.
[94] *Ibid.*, p. 81.
[95] *O. R., Army*, Series I, XXVIII, Part 2, 500.

channels into Georgetown harbor, one of them was eleven and one-half feet deep at ordinary high tide, which had been deep enough to permit the steamship *Nashville* to enter and repass in 1862. However, in order to discharge cargo at the Northeastern Railroad Bridge over the Pee Dee, lighters had to carry the ocean cargoes up the river. Murrell's Inlet had a nine-foot channel at high tide but all cargo landed there had to be transshipped by wagons three miles to the Waccamaw River before being sent up the Pee Dee. As the defense of his district was difficult to maintain, Trapier did not want to establish ports of entry that might provoke the enemy to attack. "It is, therefore, my duty, respectfully, but firmly and most earnestly, to protest and remonstrate against any action looking to the giving importance to this military district until better means of defense have been provided for it than it now enjoys." [96] This amazing statement was justified in part when Admiral Dahlgren organized on December 23 a retaliatory expedition against Murrell's Inlet where the Confederates had captured some men of the U. S. Navy. Fortunately, because of strong winds and high seas, the expedition succeeded in destroying only one vessel, a schooner loaded with a cargo of turpentine for Nassau. [97]

The Georgia Cavalry continued to patrol the beaches. On January 7, 1864, the steamer *Dan* from Bermuda heading for Wilmington was discovered and escaped by beaching on Dubourdieu Island 12 or 15 miles above the entrance to Winyah Bay. The crew and passengers landed safely and fired the vessel. The enemy in barges tried to reach her, but the barges capsized in the heavy surf. Three men were drowned and four officers and twenty men were captured on the beach by Major William P. White with the help of only one officer and one man. White in his report to Trapier praised Second Lieutenant Thomas Young and Private Lemuel Robertson, both of the Twenty-First Georgia Cavalry, "who gallantly charged upon 25 Abolitionists on Dubardu Beach . . . armed with cutlasses and pistols," when there was no supporting force within three-quarters of a mile. [98]

The Federals kept up the pressure all spring. On February 25 they destroyed the machinery in one of the beached blockade runners. In

[96] *Ibid.*, pp. 520–522.
[97] *O. R., Navy*, Series I, XV, 154–159.
[98] *O. R., Army*, Series I, XXXV, Part 1, 272–273

April they destroyed a rice mill on Winyah Bay. Late in April they found another salt works near Little River and broke the pans and burned the buildings. On June 2 they ran the *Rose* ashore on the south end of Pawley's Island. When the Yankees tried to drag her off, a force of seventy-five men rode up and drove the Federals off.[99] Such vigilance kept these episodes to the nature of minor irritations.

General Trapier wrote on January 26, 1864, that Battery White, which was the only cover for the Confederate naval yard at Mars Bluff, was inadequate to defend the upper bay. On February 1 he reported the desertion of the Third and Fourth South Carolina state troops under Lieutenant Colonel R. A. Rouse and Colonel J. H. Witherspoon, respectively. The officers had remained, although they said, as did their men, that their terms of service had expired. Rather pathetically on February 17 Trapier sent an unofficial note to Beauregard, confessing that it would not be safe to tell, except in a whisper, the true story about the condition of things in his district. He could not mobilize more than three hundred men at any one spot, and it would take him at least two days to do so. Beauregard had no troops to spare.[100]

On March 2 the Federal Navy landed a few troops just below Battery White and pushed back the pickets. This probing by the Federals drove Trapier on March 8 to by-pass Beauregard and write directly to Governor Milledge L. Bonham asking him for three 10-inch columbiads and one regiment of infantry. Battery White had only three old rifled 32-pounders and eight other guns of smaller caliber, which were no match for ironclads. It was only the lack of armament which made Battery White weak, for it was well situated at the gorge between the upper and lower bays where the channel narrowed to only 1,400 yards and upon a bluff that rose twenty feet above the bay, "but were it a Gibraltar, it would be useless in a conflict with plated vessels, armed as it is at present." He did not think that he was asking for too much since his district paid half a million dollars in taxes to the state treasury and still yielded foodstuffs sufficient to feed 50,000 men.[101] On March 13 Trapier addressed a similar appeal to the adjutant and inspector

[99] *O. R., Navy*, Series I, XV, 340, 409–411, 467–468.
[100] *O. R., Army*, Series I, XXXV, Part 1, 272–273, 546–547, 617–618, 621.
[101] *Ibid.*, Part 2, pp. 330, 340–341.

general in Richmond. Although his district was helping to feed General Johnston's army, he had only 558 men to protect seventy miles of coastline. General Beauregard endorsed Trapier's petition to Richmond and stated that when Colonel White's Georgia Cavalry should leave Waccamaw Neck for Virginia that Trapier's position would be even more desperate. The reply from Richmond was terse. General Lee's army was more important than Georgetown. No troops could be spared. By the end of March Trapier was considering whether he should abandon Waccamaw Neck or McClellanville after the departure of his troops for Virginia. But Beauregard pointed out that he must use his forces, small as they were, as effectively as possible to cover the coastline. Trapier suffered on, although General Ripley took over for a short time in the summer while Trapier was on sick leave.[102]

By November 1864 General Trapier's command consisted of some light artillery guarding the Santee under Captain Christopher Gaillard, a volunteer company of German Artillery from Charleston under the command of Captain Franz Melchers at Battery White, and light artillery at Fraser's Point under the command of Captain Maham Ward (Joshua Ward had resigned his commission and gone to England.) In addition there were two companies of state cavalry under Captain M. J. Kirk and one company under Captain J. J. Steele.[103] Then on November 23 General W. J. Hardee, commanding in Charleston, ordered Kirk and Gaillard to Mount Pleasant in order to prepare for a heavy attack on that city. Trapier was to hold the remainder of his troops ready to follow at a moment's notice. Only Captain Melchers' light artillery would be left to defend the district. Captain Melchers was "to defend his post to the last extremity, and if forced to retire to [save] his guns, or, if too hard pressed for that, to spike them and save his men, bringing them to Mount Pleasant." All government property was to be sent to the Pee Dee railroad bridge.[104] The final stripping of the region of all defenses had now taken place. As Grant pressed Lee before Richmond troops had been sent to Virginia, and as Sherman threatened South

[102] *Ibid.*, pp. 352–354, 380, 382, 445, 457, 593.
[103] *Ibid.*, XLIV, 875.
[104] *Ibid.*, XLIV, 890.

Carolina the last troops—saving only one company—were sent to Charleston.[105]

There was no longer safety anywhere. Dr. Sparkman wrote in December from Plantersville that he could no longer feed his Negroes (whom he had brought back from Clarendon due to the high price of food there) since the rice birds had eaten up most of his crop. All of his property was now supported by his medical practice, and he must quintuple his rates unless he could get grain at old prices.[106] On January 15 Jane Pringle wrote Mrs. Allston from White House on the Pee Dee that "it is quiet and calm here, whether merely the lull which precedes a hurricane you know as well as I." But she was planning to make salt next spring on Pawley's Island if Mrs. Allston would permit her. Frankly, she was glad she had brought back the White House Negroes and only wished she had brought back the Greenfield people. She confessed that by her presence she was trying to save something, "instead of going on the rampage refugeeing *where?* that's the question, show me a safe point and I'll go tomorrow, but no such happy Valley exists in the Confederacy and I prefer the attitude of the Roman Senators when the Gauls found them sitting in their places to a sheep-like headlong flight into perhaps a worse danger and a nearer fate." [107]

[105] On Jan. 2, 286 present; on Jan 20, 189 present; on Jan. 31, 165 present. *Ibid.*, XLVII, Part 2, 984, 1032, 1069, 1073. Capt. Franz Melchers came to S. C. at the age of 20 in 1846, edited the *Deutsche Zeitung* of Charleston, organized the German volunteers, took charge of eleven guns at Georgetown in May 1863, and stayed until 1865 when he joined the Confederate army at Kingstree and followed it to Cheraw and to Greensboro. Evans, *op. cit.*, V, 746–747.

[106] Easterby, *op. cit.*, pp. 203–204. Governor Magrath wrote Alexander Mazyck, Jan. 16, 1865, that since the lower portion of the state would be evacuated, Mazyck should make arrangements for his property. Mazyck sent S. D. Doar a copy. S. D. Doar Papers, DUL.

[107] Easterby, *op. cit.*, pp. 205–206.

XIX

RECONSTRUCTION

As 1865 dawned the residents of Georgetown District still persisted in their plantation ways, although the perfection of the pre-war days had vanished. During the war the Federal fleet had been a lure to the slaves and a threat to the planters. Many slaves did escape to the fleet, but more of them had been taken by their owners into the interior. In both instances the labor force had been disrupted. Yet along the rivers that flowed into Winyah Bay planters still worked their lands. Although farm buildings were rotting and implements had been broken, planters made use of them. Georgetown crops still fed the Confederacy, for the region had not been devastated by any invasion. The people of Georgetown, however, were waiting for the final blow, and it came late in February 1865.

Columbia and Charleston both fell to the Federal forces on February 17, 1865. General William T. Sherman took Columbia as he marched from Georgia toward North Carolina. General Quincy Adams Gillmore took Charleston and then extended his authority to the Santee and to Winyah Bay. On February 21 General Gillmore requested Admiral John A. Dahlgren, commander of the South Atlantic blockading fleet, to send gunboats up the Santee River in order to cover the movement of troops from Charleston northward over the Northeastern Railroad line. Gillmore also passed on the rumor that Battery White in Georgetown harbor had been abandoned and therefore intimated that Georgetown itself could be safely invested. On February 22 Admiral Dahlgren ordered Commander J. B. Creighton to proceed with his ship the *Mingoe* to Georgetown. Marines in the *Pawnee*, Captain Henry S. Stellwagen, were also dispatched.[1]

On the morning of February 23 the *Pawnee* with the *Mingoe* and the *Nipsic* steamed up Winyah Bay; because of the difficulty of navigation, only the *Mingoe* proceeded to Fort White. Upon approaching closely Commander Creighton could see that the fort had been abandoned. He therefore landed troops and occupied the fort which contained fifteen guns, the most formidable being two ten-inch columbiads. Plenty of shot and shell were seized, but the guns had been spiked and the powder removed. Admiral Dahlgren, who inspected Battery White several days later, felt that it could have held out for some time if it had been manned by a sufficient force.[2]

The *Mingoe*, sweeping for torpedoes as it advanced, moved up to Georgetown, which had also been abandoned by the troops of the Confederacy. On February 25 Ensign Allen K. Noyes of the *Catalpa*, which had accompanied the *Mingoe*, demanded the keys of the town hall from Intendant R. O. Bush and then ordered his men to raise the stars and stripes above it. Ensign Noyes' men climbed up to the top of the tower and raised the flag as "three cheers and a volley of six muskets" resounded over the town. As soon as the flag was raised, rebel horsemen, who had been lurking on the edges of the town, bravely dashed in, but they were driven out by men quickly landed from the two Federal vessels.[3] Intendant Bush and the four wardens meeting in the Council Chamber signed the formal submission of the town.[4] Six companies of marines under Lieutenant George G. Stoddard were thereupon stationed in the town while another company under Lieutenant Breese was placed in Battery White. In the town the United States forces occupied the Banking House. They also used the jail for their own prisoners and the Winyah Indigo Society's building for a hospital.[5]

[1] *O. R., Navy*, XVI, 260–262.
[2] *Ibid.*, pp. 268, 272, 273.
[3] *Ibid.*, pp. 276–277.
[4] *Ibid.*, p. 275.
[5] George Fox to Lt. Col. A. J. Willard, Nov. 2, 1865, RG 105, Box 525; W. R. T. Prior to Lt. Col. A. J. Willard, Nov. 27, 1865, RG 98, National Archives.

On February 26 Admiral Dahlgren arrived in the Sampit River in his flagship, the *Harvest Moon*. He immediately announced the end of slavery; henceforth all men would enjoy the fruits of their own labor. However, as the freedmen would not be able to provide for themselves for some time, their former owners must furnish them with food "of the usual description" for sixty days. Martial law was declared. Captain Stellwagen was placed in command of the town with Lieutenant Stoddard, the ranking marine officer, acting as provost marshal. The intendant and wardens, after supplying the officers with a list of the inhabitants, were permitted to continue to perform certain civic functions under the direction of Captain Stellwagen. Those persons not excluded from accepting Lincoln's amnesty of December 8, 1863, might return to their customary pursuits. Whenever a military officer should arrive, the naval officer then in command would turn over Georgetown and the neighboring posts to him.[6]

The planters, having lost their slaves, now feared that they might lose their lands if they could not qualify for Lincoln's amnesty. E. P. Coachman wrote Intendant Bush to ask if the persons and property of those remaining on their plantations would be respected. Bush suggested that the planters remain at home and keep their servants at home. He also enclosed a note from the provost marshal that Coachman might show to all planters. The note stated that all gentlemen remaining on their plantations would be unmolested in their private property. It was signed by Lieutenant Stoddard, the marine commander, whom Bush considered "a very humane man," one "disposed to be as lenient as possible." [7]

On March 1 Admiral Dahlgren ordered Captain Stellwagen to turn over the command in Georgetown to Colonel P. P. Brown, whom General Hatch had sent to occupy the town.[8] Colonel Brown of the 157th New York Volunteers commanded a brigade stationed at Georgetown, which consisted of the 54th Massachusetts Volunteers and five companies of the 102nd U. S. Coloured Troops and eight companies of the 32nd U. S.

[6] *O. R., Navy,* XVI, 274–275.
[7] Sparkman Family Papers, 1865–1866, 2791, folder 5, SHC.
[8] *O. R., Navy,* XVI, 278.

Coloured Troops.[9] The presence of Negro troops heightened tensions. Joel Williamson has pointed out in his book, *After Slavery*, that it was always more difficult to maintain law and order among the freedmen in those places where Negro troops were stationed. Georgetown was such a place.[10]

On the day the navy transferred the command of the town to the army the Admiral lost his flagship. As the *Harvest Moon* was dropping down the bay about quarter of eight in the morning, she struck a torpedo which "blew a hole through the starboard quarter, tearing away the main deck over it," which caused the ship "to sink in five minutes in 2½ fathoms water." The Admiral later wrote that he had been sitting in his cabin waiting for breakfast when "instantly a loud noise and shock occurred, and the bulkhead separating the cabin from the wardroom was shattered and driven in toward me." Fortunately only one person was killed. Admiral Dahlgren and his staff were transferred to the tug *Clover* without further discomfort. The Admiral himself reported that there had been so much ridicule of torpedoes that little caution had been taken.[11] It was ironic that the only sinking of a Federal ship by the Confederates in Georgetown waters took place after the fighting was over and by accident. But such an event must have made the Federals more watchful, perhaps less lenient in the days that immediately followed.

The soldiers and sailors of the United States forces lost no time in carrying the good news of freedom to every plantation. On March 5 and 6 marines from the naval vessels in Georgetown harbor went up the Pee Dee to the rice plantations and informed the Negroes that they were free. The Negroes began to pillage the plantation houses, to discover the wines and liquors, and to threaten the white families from the surrounding plantations who had congregated in Plantersville. The frightened

---

[9] "The Last Officer—April 1865," ed. John Hammond Moore, *SCHM*, LXVII (1966), 2.

[10] Joel Williamson, *After Slavery, The Negro in South Carolina During Reconstruction, 1861–1877* (Chapel Hill, N. C., 1965), pp. 52–53. The Memorial of the Citizens of Georgetown District to Governor Orr, Jan. 16, 1867, stated that the presence of Negro troops had excited "ideas and misconceptions." Orr Papers, S. C. Archives.

[11] *O. R., Navy*, XVI, 282–283.

whites appealed to the United States authorities. On March 6 the Reverend Alexander Glennie, Dr. James Sparkman, Charles Alston, Sr., W. Allan Allston, and Francis Weston jointly composed a memorial addressed to the military commander at Georgetown. They pointed out that thirteen white families, consisting of forty-three ladies, forty-one children, and only seven male adults, all noncombatant, had been at the mercy of a "lawless colored population" who had been stirred up by "unrelenting raiders." What had become, they asked, of the assurances given by the provost marshal to Intendant Bush and through him to the planters? [12]

The Reverend Alexander Glennie and Dr. James Sparkman also met with the naval commander, Captain Stellwagen, on board the *Pawnee* in Georgetown harbor. Glennie and Sparkman told the captain that the Negroes had been demoralized and asked that the military and naval officers exercise control over them. They professed that they had seen Admiral Dahlgren's order to supply the freedmen with sixty days' provisions which they were willing to obey, but, since the Negroes were now in control of the provisions and would not work, there was no way to replenish the larder. If the planters could not control and direct the freedmen, then the United States army and naval forces must. Since Glennie was reported later to have been thoroughly disgusted after his interview with Captain Stellwagen, few assurances must have been given at this time.[13]

The view of the planters was well put in two letters written in March by Mrs. Allston, the widow of R. F. W. Allston, to Colonel Brown in Georgetown and to Captain George U. Morris, commander of the *Chenango*. She informed the commanders that she could not return to her plantations and work them without some support from the forces. She charged that the soldiers were actually obstructing the return to normality. Some of Brown's soldiers had broken open her house, taken all they had wished, and told the Negroes to do the same. Consequently,

---

[12] Sparkman Family Papers, 1865–1866, 2791, folder 5, SHC. Jane Pringle wrote Mrs. Allston, March 2, 1865, from White House: we have lived here "as if hung by the eye lids, seeing the gun boats steaming about & daily expecting to be shelled out." Allston Papers, S. C. Hist. Soc.

[13] *Ibid.* Glennie had seen "the labors of his life time dissipated & lost in a single day." Dr. James R. Sparkman, "The Negro," *The Origins of Segregation,* ed. Joel Williamson (Boston, Mass., 1968), p. 66.

not an article was left in the house, neither bed nor sheet, table nor chair. Every lock had been taken off the doors, and the doors removed from their hinges. The meat house and the store room had been plundered. Furthermore, Brown himself had divided among the Negroes the cattle and the stock. She was ready to acquiesce in the freeing of the slaves but argued that the rest of her property should not be taken away. The Yankee officers, being gentlemen, often found the fury of the women more difficult to resist than the complaints of the men.[14]

Every planter suffered. Mrs. Francis Weston described the chaos in a letter of March 17 to Mrs. Allston. The Pyatts, she wrote, had gone at once to Georgetown, leaving everything behind and giving up at once their home to the Negroes. After Henry A. Middleton had been ordered to town, his house and buildings were burned. A faithful Negro had barely rescued for him a change of clothes. Dr. Parker went off at once, and his place was destroyed. The Trapiers were stripped of everything. They would have starved if Mrs. M. H. Lance had not sent them provisions secretly at night. Mrs. J. J. I. Pringle had had three visits from freedmen in one week. On one occasion the freedmen were so menacing that her daughter Mary Pringle had fainted. The intrepid mother had merely stooped down, seized her daughter's feet, and dragged her into the house. Astonishment forestalled further trouble. The George Fords, who had been burned out, had moved in with the Fitzsimons. Paul Fitzsimons was so unfortunate as to break his arm in a fall from his horse. Rees Ford was put under arrest for five hours and not allowed to speak to anyone because a Negro boy complained that he had switched him. Charles Alston had abandoned his plantation as the house servants refused to wash for or wait on the family. The Sparkmans and the Glennies were both talking of going away. Mrs. LaBruce wanted to go to Poplar Hill, her upcountry refuge, but her people refused to move her. Mrs. Weston stated that her own overseer had gone off at once. As for the Negroes on her plantations: "The first week they divided out our land and wanted to root up our beautiful wheat and oat and rye and pulled down fences and would obey no driver." [15]

---

[14] *The South Carolina Rice Plantation as Revealed in the Papers of Robert F. W. Allston*, ed. J. H. Easterby (Chicago, Ill., 1945), pp. 208–209.
[15] *Ibid.*, pp. 206–208.

The flight of the planters made the situation worse. The abandoned plantations became rendezvous, where the former slaves could gather to enjoy their freedom. For food they pillaged the countryside. Many families, of course, had already moved to the interior. Mrs. Weston noted that the Wards fortunately had been off in time to Marlborough District. But those who did stay wanted these refugees to return. Charles Alston, Jr., wrote to Colonel D. W. Jordan urging him to return from Camden to Laurel Hill so that he might use his influence "to keep some order and law on it" as "it is become a positive injury to all of us who are near." [16]

By the end of March the officers themselves saw a greater need to establish order. Captain Morris called upon Mrs. Weston to reassure her. He told the freedmen on her plantation that they must work in the usual manner and grow more than provisions for themselves for they must trade with the people in Georgetown.[17] Captain Stellwagen sent expeditions up the rivers to quiet the Negroes and crush the marauding bands. He sent Creighton in the *Mingoe* up the Waccamaw as far as Buck's mills. Creighton reported that "Mr. Buck, a planter on the river, thinks that the appearance of the gunboat . . . will prevent any further trouble. . . ."[18] This display of force, was not enough, however, so Stellwagen joined the *Mingoe* and proceeded as far as Conwayboro; "many small parties fled in various directions" on the approach of the naval vessels. After spreading a "salutary dread" around the region and urging blacks and whites to "prosecute planting," he withdrew to Georgetown.[19] With this show of support the planters reconsidered their thoughts about abandoning their lands. Mrs. Weston confessed that she and Jane Read were determined to stay, for they had no provisions elsewhere.[20]

The war, of course, was not yet over. The last campaign in the area was Potter's raid. General Edward H. Potter left Georgetown on April 5, taking with him many of the Negro troops stationed there. His object was to cut and destroy the railroad lines at Sumter and Camden. In this he was successful. The removal of all the Negro troops undoubtedly lessened tensions in Georgetown District. After the surrender of Robert

[16] Sept. 1, 1865, Jordan Papers, DUL.
[17] Easterby, *op. cit.*, p. 207.
[18] *O. R., Navy*, XVI, 294.
[19] *Ibid.*, XVI, 299–300.
[20] Easterby, *op. cit.*, p. 207.

E. Lee in Virginia and of Joseph E. Johnston in North Carolina brought the war to an end, Georgetown men who had been fighting with Lee and Johnston straggled home. Their arrivals heartened family after family as no other event in those days could. Jane Pringle had written Mrs. Allston on March 2: "Do hear all you can of Hamptons Cavalry—for God's sake find out if my boys are dead or alive—that is the iron in my soul. . . ." Perhaps a new life, not too remote in form from the old, could be reconstructed.[21]

The essential question was land ownership. Without their lands the planters could never hope to re-establish themselves. The Negroes, on the other hand, might have been quieter if they had been certain that they would receive land. Sherman's Field Order of January 16, 1865, had stated that abandoned lands south of Charleston should be granted to freedmen. The Freedmen's Bureau Act of March 3, 1865, confirmed Sherman's order and set aside other abandoned lands. Freedmen and loyal Unionists could pre-empt forty acres of abandoned or confiscated lands, rent them at a nominal rate for three years, and buy them at any time within this period at a price fairly appraised. This meant that those planters who remained on their lands would not lose them unless there should be wholesale confiscation in the future. Occupancy became a necessity. Jane Pringle, the mistress of Greenfield and of White House, wrote Adele Allston on April 1: "I fear that your absence from this part of the country bars your claim for the present to any of your property. . . ." But even if the lands were retained, they were useless unless the Negroes would return to work. Mrs. Pringle added: "*Here* I have over them the abiding fear of the Yankee Capts. who go out and speak sharply to them and sustain my authority," but without these frequent visits "I believe a residence among negroes would be humiliating and impossible." She warned Mrs. Allston about attempting to return and take the land away from the Negroes. "The blacks are masters of the situation, this is a conquered country and for the moment law and order are in abeyance." "I have not been in my negro street nor spoken to a field hand since 1st March." She did not know what would happen after

[21] Moore, *op. cit.*, pp. 1–14; Allston Papers, S. C. Hist. Soc. J. R. Easterling swore on March 1, 1866, that one of his former slaves had taken his horse and joined Potter's Raid. RG 98, National Archives.

the sixty days were up during which the planters were obligated to feed the blacks. All the Negroes might leave.[22]

General John P. Hatch issued an order on April 25 commanding the planters of Georgetown and Charleston districts to take an oath of allegiance to the United States, after which they were to assemble their freedmen and inform them that they were free. Equitable contracts in writing were then to be made with the freedmen. The planters must provide subsistence until the crops were gathered, at which time the freedmen were to receive one-half of the crop. These contracts must be approved by the military and naval commanders in each district. If the owners refused to cultivate the soil, colonies of refugee freedmen would be established upon the land.[23]

The planters therefore proceeded to take oaths and make contracts. Dr. James R. Sparkman and John Harleston Read took the oaths on May 24 and June 1 respectively in the form prescribed by President Lincoln in his proclamation of December 8, 1863. Captain George L. Warren, the provost marshal in Georgetown, administered the two oaths.[24] Sparkman and Read then made contracts with the freedmen still residing on their plantations.[25]

President Andrew Johnson set forth his own program of reconstruction in a proclamation of May 29 for the South as a whole and in another of June 30 for South Carolina particularly. There was to be a program of pardon and amnesty, of provisional government, and of state constitution-making. All Southerners were pardoned except special groups such as those who had held office, either civil or military, under the Confederacy and those who had owned $20,000 worth of taxable property in 1860. Most Georgetown planters were in the latter category. Johnson did, however, hold out the possibility of a special pardon for those in

[22] Easterby, *op. cit.*, pp. 209–211.
[23] Printed in Charleston *Courier*, April 26, 1865.
[24] Sparkman Family Papers, 1865–1866, 2791, folder 5, SHC.
[25] Contracts made by the following are in RG 105, Box 525, National Archives: C. J. Atkinson, A. H. Belin, E. P. Coachman, A. W. Cordes, R. Dozier, B. F. Dunkin, P. Fitzsimons, A. B. Flagg, J. Rees Ford, J. W. Ford, S. T. Gaillard, F. Green, E. P. Guerard, Dr. A. Hasell, J. H. Ladson, R. Lowndes, W. H. Mayrant, J. I. Middleton, J. L. Nowell, W. B. Pringle, J. B. Pyatt, J. H. Read, Jr., W. H. Trapier, B. H. Ward.

these excepted groups. The proclamation of June 30 designated Benjamin Perry as the provisional governor for South Carolina.[26]

There was some confusion in Federal policy. Would the agents of the Freedmen's Bureau established by Congress seize abandoned lands and turn them over to the freedmen or would the President pardon the planters and thus secure to them their landed estates? On June 7 General Rufus Saxton was appointed head of the Bureau of Refugees, Freedmen, and Abandoned Lands in South Carolina.[27] Saxton sent George C. Fox, as his agent, to Georgetown to seize abandoned plantations. According to a list of November 2, 1865, the following plantations were being managed by Fox: Hagley and True Blue belonging to the estate of Plowden Weston, J. H. Trapier's Keithfield, W. H. Trapier's Turkey Hill and Ingleside, Henry A. Middleton's Weehaw, William A. Alston's Friendfield, Strawberry Hill, and Marietta, and Forlorn Hope and Clifton belonging to the estate of Colonel W. A. Alston.[28] These plantations were tilled under the direction of the Freedmen's Bureau until December, when the rice was sold. Half the proceeds went to the government and half to the freedmen. With Saxton and Fox proceeding as they were during the summer of 1865, it became imperative for the planters to obtain pardons from the President.

Many Georgetown planters successfully sought individual pardons from President Johnson in 1865. The petitions to the President are interesting documents, for they reveal what these men had been doing during the war (their roles in the Confederate effort naturally minimized). They also give the age of the petitioner and the place where the oath was taken. The latter provides information on the dispersal of the planters about the state. B. F. Dunkin, seventy-two years old, took the oath in Cheraw on July 18. W. St. Julien Mazyck, the heir to the estate of Plowden Weston who had died in 1864, took the oath at Georgetown on July 22. Benjamin Huger Read, forty-two years a planter, took the oath in Charleston on July 31. John Harleston Read, fifty years

---

[26] *Compilation of the Messages and Papers of the President, 1789–1897*, ed. J. D. Richardson (Washington, D. C., 1907), VI, 310, 312.

[27] Martin Abbott, *The Freedmen's Bureau in South Carolina, 1865–1872* (Chapel Hill, N. C., 1967), pp. 8–9.

[28] George C. Fox to Lt. Col. A. J. Willard, Nov. 2, 1865, RG 105, Box 525, National Archives.

a planter, took the oath at Georgetown on August 3 (his second oath). Benjamin Huger Ward, twenty-four years a planter, took the oath in Georgetown on August 7. Joshua Ward, thirty-seven years a planter, who had resigned his commission and gone to Europe during the war, took the oath in Greenville on August 12. William Lucas, seventy-one at the beginning of the war, took the oath in Aiken on August 17. J. Motte Alston, who had taken no active part in the war due to ill health, took the oath in Greenville on August 18. Charles Alston, Sr., sixty-nine years old, took the oath at Darlington Court House on August 21. A. W. Dozier, sixty-four, took the oath at Kingstree on August 26. S. D. Doar, sixty, took the oath in Charleston on September 1. Paul Trapier Horry, thirty-six years a planter, and E. S. Horry, thirty-eight years a planter, both took the oath at Greenville on September 13. Seaman Deas, fifty-four years old, confessed that he had resided at Limestone Springs, Spartanburg District, since November 1861 without taking up arms. He took the oath at Spartanburg on September 29. William A. Alston, who had been a planter for thirty-one years, took the oath at Charleston on October 31. Daniel W. Jordan, fifty-six, who had removed permanently from Georgetown to Camden during the war, said he had taken no part in the struggle. Maham Ward, twenty-seven years a planter, who had gone north with his wife and two children, also applied for a pardon.[29]

The most interesting case of a planter seeking a pardon was that of Henry Augustus Middleton. He wrote Johnson on July 22 stating that he was temporarily residing in Westchester County, New York. He had never borne arms nor held civil or military office under the Confederacy. He had taken the oaths first at Columbia on May 30 and again at New York on July 21. It was true that he had owned 300 slaves in 1861, but their ancestors had been owned by his family since 1735. He had never bought or sold slaves. During the war he had resided on his plantation near Georgetown. He had received a pass with permission to proceed to the north since he had property in Newport, Rhode Island. On July 18 Mayor Cranston of Newport wrote to Secretary of State ·Seward

[29] These petitions can be found under the appropriate names in RG 94, National Archives. "Twenty-seven years a planter" must mean a planter twenty-seven years old, as it does in the case of Maham Ward.

urging that Middleton's pardon be refused since he had been an in-fluential rebel. Another Newport correspondent of July 31 had written: "It seems to me that when so many of our brave, gallant boys have been deliberately starved, frozen, and rotted by piecemeal in those accursed prison pens of the South, when an expression of love for the old flag meant death by torture, slow wasting death, that the infernal villans who are responsible for this hell born rebellion, should not be suffered to lift their heads in a loyal community." Like his fellow South Caro-linians, Middleton turned to Governor Perry for a recommendation to the President. Perry wrote to the attorney general on August 10 that he had known Middleton for ten or fifteen years "as a quiet peacible planter who never engaged in politics . . . no one in South Carolina has been more quiet . . . I have reason too to believe that his judgment prior to that event, was opposed to that movement." Middleton was pardoned on August 15.[30]

Benjamin Allston was also an interesting case. Being in an excepted class as a graduate of West Point, he had to apply for a special pardon. The provost marshal had refused to administer the oath on June 30, so Allston wrote President Johnson on July 3, informing him that he had served as inspector general in the Trans-Mississippi Department of the Confederacy for two and one-half years. Forthrightly, he said: "I felt in honor bound to bear my part with the people of my state and section—I believed that we had right and justice on our side." However, he ad-mitted war had decided the political, social, and economic questions. He was pardoned.[31]

It may be more amazing that Generals Trapier and Manigault both sought pardons from the President, being excluded under section 3 rather than section 13 of the proclamation of pardon and amnesty. Trapier wrote Johnson on August 15 that he had taken up arms in 1861 "conscientiously believing in the doctrine of State Sovereignty; and that

[30] On July 29 the Mayor had written to Attorney General Speed that he had been mistaken and that it was another Middleton who had been an influential rebel. Apparently some men in Newport thought that the mayor's change in attitude was due to his own involvement in real estate speculations. Middleton reputedly owned nearly $300,000 worth of property in Newport. "Henry A. Middleton," RG 94, National Archives.

[31] Benjamin Allston to Andrew Johnson, July 3, 1865, Amnesty Papers, S. C., RG 94, National Archives.

therefore (his allegiance being due, primarily to the state of which he was a citizen) he was in duty and in honour bound to protect and defend, with all the means in his power, the said state against all hostile demonstrations, from what quarter soever, they might come." But he was now willing to yield "to the logic of events." General Manigault wrote on December 18 stating that he had taken the oath in Charleston on that date Henry Stanbery recommended pardon.[32]

President Johnson on the advice of his provisional governor in South Carolina, Benjamin Perry, had by the end of the year pardoned many of the most prominent of the pre-war Georgetown planters.[33] A pardon was a necessary step in securing one's property, especially if it had been seized as abandoned. In September President Johnson ordered the Freedman's Bureau to restore abandoned lands to their owners. On September 12, 1865, Commissioner O. O. Howard of the Bureau issued Circular No. 15 stating that in the future all lands held as confiscated were to be restored unless they had been condemned and sold by decree of a Federal court. Those held as abandoned were to be returned to owners who offered proofs of ownership and of a pardon. A majority of the seized land was restored by December.[34] William H. Trapier had his plantations restored on January 15, 1866, and William Allan Allston his on February 20, 1866.[35] Since a pardon also meant that these men could participate once again in the politics of their state, the old planting aristocracy was being revitalized.

Under Johnson's reconstruction program, the provisional governor was to call a constitutional convention to draw up a new constitution. Elec-

[32] RG 94, National Archives. Among those who later put in claims that they had suffered damages for the sake of the Union were H. A. Middleton, F. W. Ford, Sidney S. Fraser, John LaBruce, Rev. M. H. Lance, estate of J. D. Magill, E. Jane Read, Joseph H. Risley, and H. W. Tilton. Charleston News and Courier, Nov. 24, 1873.

[33] Perry stated that he had forwarded between 2,000 and 3,000 petitions in six months. Jonathan Truman Dorris, Pardon and Amnesty under Lincoln and Johnson (Chapel Hill, N. C., 1953), p. 138. In the summer of 1868 the Georgetown men believed that "by sustaining the conservative efforts" of the Johnson administration that they would prevent the increase of evils. S. T. Atkinson to Orr, July 21, 1866, Orr Papers, S. C. Archives.

[34] Abbott, op. cit., pp. 55–57.

[35] "History of the property and plantations turned over to the planters by order of the assistant commissioner of S. C.," RG 105, Box 524, National Archives.

tions were held in All Saints and in Prince George for delegates to the South Carolina convention. Ulric Albert DeLettre, a farmer from Bucksville, was elected by All Saints.[36] Richard Dozier, lawyer, Benjamin Faneuil Dunkin, judge, and Dr. B. Clay Fishburne, physician and planter, were selected by Prince George.[37] They attended the convention that sat from September 13 to 27, 1865, in Columbia. This convention brought about some democratization of the government, such as abolishing property qualifications for holding office, equalizing representation between the upcountry and the lowcountry in the senate, and instituting the popular election of the governor, but little was done for the freedmen. The convention recognized the abolition of slavery but, since many Carolinians hoped for compensation, it attributed emancipation to "the action of the United States authorities." It was also possible under the new state constitution to draw up a "black code" which the new legislature proceeded to do in order to regulate the Negro. The men in the convention and in the legislature knew that it was important for the Negro to work, and they thought that he would not do so voluntarily.[38]

The contracts made in the spring of 1865 worked fairly well until the crops were gathered in the fall. On October 20 Benjamin Allston, Dr. F. S. Parker, Jos. W. Ford, Paul Fitzsimons, and S. S. Fraser asked Lieutenant Colonel A. Willard, the local commanding officer, to force the Negroes to work at ditching after the crop was in. Their petition was endorsed by Dr. W. R. T. Prior and Dr. R. G. White, who stated that bad drainage would be a threat to the health of the community. Colonel Willard was not willing to use force. He had only twenty men and three noncommissioned officers available in October for supervising the division of the crops.[39] Jane Pringle appealed over Colonel Willard's head to General Daniel Sickles, who had replaced General Gillmore: "Negroes

[36] DeLettre had planted no rice although he had lived on the Waccamaw River for seventeen years. DeLettre to Lt. L. Billings, Nov. 3, 1865, RG 105, National Archives; U. A. DeLettre Letters, DUL.

[37] Journal of the Convention of the People of South Carolina, held in Columbia, S. C., September, 1865, ed. J. A. Selby (Columbia, S. C., 1865), pp. 185–188. Dr. Fishburne was the second husband of Jane Rose Fraser Barnwell.

[38] The Constitution of 1865, ed. J. Harold Wolfe (Columbia, S. C., 1951).

[39] Ben Allston et al. to Col. Willard, Oct. 20, 1865, RG 98, National Archives.

must now be taught that their former masters will be protected by the U. S. authorities against all attempts to take land and life. . . . Help us General, and help *me*." [40] Sickles was, in time, to respond to such pleas.

The chief reason for the small crop of 1865 stemmed from the disruption of work patterns. The newly freed Negro would not work industriously. If he did not work according to his contract, he could be punished, but punishment for the Negro was meted out by military courts. For major crimes military commissions were formed; for lesser crimes there were provost courts, composed of one officer and two "loyal citizens." By September Governor Perry had worked out an arrangement with the military authorities whereby white men would be tried in the state courts and the freedmen in the provost courts. The latter were in fact military courts.[41] Paul Tamplet and Benjamin Huger Wilson had been appointed associate provost judges of the Georgetown subdistrict, but Tamplet resigned on November 25 and Wilson on December 11.[42] Their resignations left the provost court presided over by one officer. If a case arose involving at the same time a white man and a Negro man, there was some doubt whether the civil court or the military court had jurisdiction. The "black code" passed by the legislature late in November did not permit freedmen to testify in state courts.[43] Cases involving Negroes as a party therefore usually went into military courts. In practice, two types of jurisdiction paralleled one another. The clash of authority is illustrated by Sheriff L. L. Cooper's request on November 9, 1865, of Colonel Willard that he might use the second floor of the jail for his white civil prisoners while the military continued to use the first floor for their prisoners.[44]

Martin Abbott in his study of the Freedmen's Bureau in South Carolina states that throughout 1865 when Negroes charged whites with assault and battery and the whites were found guilty, they were fined $50. When whites charged Negroes with stealing and the blacks were found guilty, they were jailed for about two months.[45] This was true in

[40] Jane Pringle to Maj. Gen. D. Sickles, Dec. 19, 1865, RG 98, National Archives.

[41] Abbott, *op. cit.*, pp. 100–101.

[42] B. H. Wilson to Lt. Col. A. Willard, Dec. 11, 1865; Paul Tamplet to same, Nov. 25, 1865, RG 98, National Archives.

[43] Williamson, *op. cit.*, p. 74.

[44] RG 98, National Archives.

[45] Abbott, *op. cit.*, pp. 100–102.

Georgetown as it was true in the state. Three colored women were sentenced to 20 to 30 days' confinement for assaulting R. I. Middleton at Weehaw. F. S. Parker was fined $50 for assault and battery against Edward Smith, a colored man at Mansfield on February 8, 1866. Brutus swore on January 11, 1866, that Ben Allston had struck him. Jack Parker, a colored man, swore that Maxwell had hit a Negro on the head for "he gave him some sass." R. I. Middleton swore on February 13 that his watchman had caught two freedmen stealing from his barn at Weehaw. John A. Hume, agent for Mr. Horry on the North Santee, wrote January 27 that Horry's barns had been broken in. The planters would have liked to have resorted to the lash, but with the military present this could not be done.[46]

On January 1, 1866, General Sickles voided South Carolina's "black code." [47] Lieutenant Colonel B. H. Smith summed up on January 20, 1866, for his headquarters the situation in Georgetown District by saying that the civil courts were not open, that the commissioners of the poor were not caring for the poor whites, and that the roads and bridges were being neglected. Although the town council did meet, the military authorities were still doing most of the governing. It was the military authority that had levied a $25 tax on those obtaining permits for the sale of liquors in the town.[48] Order depended on the strength and vigilance of the military authorities, and at times their strength was spread very thin.[49]

In January the military once again had to supervise the making of contracts between the planters and the freedmen. When Sickles voided the "black code," he also ordered the laborers to make contracts or leave the land in ten days. When William Bull Pringle's Negroes refused to sign their contracts and were told that they must leave the plantation, they burned down his house and entrenched themselves on the place.

[46] Sworn statements, per dates above. These were cases before the Provost Court in the Fourth Subdistrict. RG 98, National Archives.

[47] Williamson, op. cit., p. 77.

[48] Jan. 16, 20, 1866, RG 98, National Archives.

[49] A Georgetown militia was organized by the white population on Dec. 4, 1865, to assist General Sickles, who was willing to remove the colored troops from the district. Roll of Members of Georgetown Militia, organized Dec. 4, 1865, Military Affairs, 1860–1865, Legislative System, S. C. Archives; R. Dozier to Gov. James L. Orr, Dec. 11, 1865, Governors Papers, S. C. Archives.

Pringle informed Sickles of this outrage on January 18, indicating that he feared the destruction of his $50,000 steam rice mill. Sickles turned the letter over to Major General Devers at Charleston, who endorsed it to Lieutenant Colonel B. H. Smith, commanding at Georgetown, as follows: Smith would "arrest all those, who can be identified, as having been connected with the burning of Mr. Pringle's house, and bring them to justice, and will take the most efficient measures that the means of his command will permit, for the quiet of that portion of his Sub Dist. In reference to the removal, of the people from the plantation Col. Smith will notify them that if contracts are offered them to the arr. plans of the Freedmen's Bureau, they must contract, or leave the premises; the single persons in ten, those with families in twenty days." [50] The officers of the Union army were supporting the planters.

On January 16 the agent on the Waverly plantation of Joseph Blyth Allston wrote to Smith that he had been the subject "of the most gross abuse" when trying to divide out the crop. "Col., My Father was a native of Portland Maine, and never took abuse unjustly from White or Black,—Shall I, his son, because I was born South . . . tamely stand up and take abuse: No, never! I shall strike the villain to the ground at all risks, and every true man will sustain the act. . . . One of my neighbors, Wm. Allan Allston his wife, and sister in law was today abused by their freed Negroes in a shameful manner. Sir, these things cannot go on so, Manhood and common sense cry no, no!" [51]

Ben Allston wrote Smith from Guendalos on January 30 that the freedmen and women at Chicora Wood had repudiated their contract.[52] W. St. Julien Mazyck wrote Smith on February 4 from Midway asking him to come up and see him and Mr. Alston as the Negroes at Hagley and True Blue were unruly.[53] On February 17 Francis Weston wrote from Hasty Point that he needed help in getting the Negroes to sign a contract.[54] On February 23 Joseph B. Pyatt informed Smith from Rosemont

[50] Charleston *Courier*, Jan. 24, 1866; William Bull Pringle to General Sickles, Jan. 18, 1866, endorsed Jan. 18, RG 98, National Archives.

[51] Edwin M. Tilton to Colonel Smith, Jan. 16, 1866, RG 98, National Archives.

[52] Ben Allston to Colonel Smith, Jan. 30, 1866, RG 98, National Archives.

[53] W. St. J. Mazyck to Colonel Smith, Feb. 4, 1866, RG 98, National Archives.

[54] Francis Weston to Colonel Smith, Feb. 17, 1866, RG 98, National Archives.

that he would not give Philis a contract as she had been disorderly.[55] Jane Pringle, once again by-passing the local commander, wrote directly to General Sickles and told him that her Negroes would not work according to the contract made with them.

All legislation goes to protect the negroes in all his rights, but the same legislation must also protect me in mine. If some more summary punishment is not divised in these cases than a case before a Provost Court, how in the name of Heaven are we to cultivate our fields? Of what earthly benefit is it to us that the men who should be laboring are thrown into prison, they can't till the land there and I assure you that a prison life is rather a pleasure to a negro than a punishment, since they are fed without working. There should be military posts at small distances for instant relief and instead of a tedious law process the punishment should be double labor on the land. A few cases of this kind would soon remedy the evil. Whereas now the idea of Georgetown and a law case is a positive frolic and inducement to offend.[56]

The most violent episode took place at Keithfield, the estate of General Trapier, who had died at the end of 1865, which F. S. Parker, Jr., was managing. According to Dennis Hazel, colored agent of Parker at Keithfield, on March 31 freedman Abram quit work and called others from the fields. They armed themselves with axes, hatchets, hoes, and poles and drove Hazel to the boat. "Sampson threw a hatchet after me which struck the water in front of the boat nearly striking me in the head." Parker sent to town for help, and later with two Union soldiers and Hazel approached the freedmen. "As soon as we entered the street the people collected with axes, hoes, sticks and bricks and pelted us with bricks and stones and poles, and took the gun away from one of the soldiers." Parker was forced to jump into the river and swim to the other side. Parker swore before Colonel Smith that no white man could control the Negroes now that they were free.[57]

In spite of such difficulties, Colonel Smith supervised during January,

[55] Joseph B. Pyatt to Capt. Woodbury S. Smith, Feb. 23, 1866, RG 98, National Archives.

[56] Jane Pringle to General Sickles, Feb. 7, 1866, RG 98, National Archives.

[57] Sworn statement of Dennis Hazel, April 4, 1866; sworn statement of F. S. Parker, Jr., April 11, 1866; sworn statement of F. S. Parker, Sr., April 3, 1866, RG 98, National Archives.

February, and March, 1866, the making of contracts by the following planters: Dr. A. M. Forster, Jos. W. Ford, Wm. H. Mayrant, W. E. Sparkman, John F. Pyatt, Dr. F. S. Parker, Wm. Bull Pringle, Stephanus Ford, Arthur Middleton, J. H. Read, Jr., Seaman Deas, J. R. Easterling, Wm. R. Maxwell, R. S. Izard, Wm. A. Allston, Paul Fitzsimons, J. Rees Ford, Ben Allston, Francis Weston, R. Dozier, Joshua Ward, D. W. Jordan, Charles Alston, John LaBruce, Ralph Nesbit, Robert Nesbit, Dr. W. J. Magill, and Mrs. Jane Pringle. The contracts provided for one-half of the rice, corn, pea, and potato crops to be given to the laborers after deducting one-fifth for plantation expenses. The planters were to furnish implements, wagons, and mules. The people were to keep in repair the fences and ditches.[58]

For the planters 1866 was the crucial year. A number had gone to Charleston, borrowed money at high rates of interest, and then returned to find that the Negroes would not work the contract that Colonel Smith himself had approved. Dr. Fishburne discovered such a situation on his Enfield plantation.[59] J. Rees Ford found that the Negroes on Waterford plantation wanted to appoint their own foremen and would not obey Ford's foreman.[60] Similar complaints were sent to Colonel Smith from Joshua Ward at Brookgreen and R. H. Nesbit at Woodstock.[61] When Smith obliged some of the planters by sending a soldier or two, the planters wanted to keep the soldiers permanently on the plantation. F. W. Heriot wrote on April 29 that he would like the private to stay a while longer at Mt. Arena.[62] The agent for Dr. Allard B. Flagg at Sandy Knowe and Oak Lawn plantations on Sandy Island wanted a detail of two soldiers for eight or ten days to "straiten them up somewhat." [63]

And yet after this immense struggle to keep the labor force together, the crop of 1866 was another failure. And with this failure gloom descended upon the planters. Benjamin Allston wrote in a discouraging

[58] The contracts, made January to March 1866, were recorded by the military authorities. RG 105, National Archives.

[59] Dr. B. C. Fishburne to Colonel Smith, March 9, 1866, RG 98, National Archives.

[60] J. Rees Ford to Colonel Smith, March 20, 1866, RG 98, National Archives.

[61] Joshua Ward to Colonel Smith, April 10, 1866; R. H. Nesbit to Colonel Smith, April 20, 1866, RG 98, National Archives.

[62] F. W. Heriot to [Colonel Smith], April 29, 1866, RG 98, National Archives.

[63] B. H. Penner to Colonel Smith, May 1, 1866, RG 98, National Archives.

vein to J. D. B. DeBow from Plantersville, on September 24, 1866: "From being one of the most wealthy Districts, I fear it will now rank as one of the most impoverished, and the vain attempts to cultivate rice under existing circumstances by many, will only complete the ruin." [64]

The story on Ralph Stead Izard's plantations was a typical one. At Milton plantation 41 hands made 806 bushels of rice, on Weymouth 47 hands made 1,045 bushels, and on Hickory Hill 49 hands made 1,502 bushels. This total of 3,353 compared unfavorably with a pre-war total of 20,000. After advances had been taken out, there was actually nothing left to divide. And Major Read, the then military commander, thought Izard "a reliable man." [65]

The planters, some of whom were borrowing money at 2½ to 3 percent per month, were willing to try again, but they could not afford to feed their workers. [66] Some freedmen were drifting to Charleston; a few even to Florida. [67] But when the young left, they left behind their old folks. In 1867 the Freedmen's Bureau began to issue rations regularly to destitute whites and blacks. Rations for 114 were issued in January, 655 in February, 3,260 in March, 1,679 in April, 4,398 in May, 14,038 in June, 15,000 in July, and 9,721 in August. These figures indicate the mounting problem. Shoes, coats, and dresses were also doled out. In this year the Bureau was also trying to set up a school. Major Read was hopeful: the freedman "are now creeping and soon will be able to walk." [68] But the 1867 crops were three-fourths destroyed by freshets. The pressures therefore mounted on laborers and planters. The former would not work on the roads, would not do their ditching, and were therefore constantly breaking their contracts. The planters, more despondent than ever, were wondering if it was worth while ever to try again.

[64] Ben Allston to J. D. B. DeBow, Sept. 24, 1866, DeBow Papers, DUL.

[65] 1st Lt. John V. Chance, Feb. 27, 1867, RG 105, National Archives. Edward Shubrick Horry, executor for the estate of Horry on the North Santee, listed the following returns for the crop of 1866: from peas $123.75, from corn $330, from potatoes $160, from rice $1,460, from cotton $1,565.14, which totaled $3,638.89. Of this, 40 percent ($1,455.55) was divided among the Negroes, which provided each hand with 19½ cents per day. Plantation Labor Account Book, 1866–1869, E. S. Horry Papers, SCL.

[66] To borrow on these terms was an act of desperation.

[67] 1st Lt. John V. Chance, Feb. 6, 1867, RG 105, National Archives.

[68] Sept. 30, 1867, RG 105, National Archives.

The successive crop failures of 1865, 1866, and 1867 were to make it almost impossible for the planters to continue planting rice. The attempt had been made with the United States army standing behind the labor contracts and forcing the Negro to work. Even with this assistance success was not possible. By the end of 1867 the planters were on the verge of bankruptcy. And in 1867 a political change loomed before them that would make their labor problems more difficult to solve. The Reconstruction Acts of 1867 put political power into the hands of the freedmen and their allies. It was, therefore, in the fall of 1867 that the planters began to look around for new possibilities. Some thought of emigrating; others of securing a new labor supply through immigration— perhaps from China.[69] It was a Northern federal official, however, who while making his way through the South that year, noticed the plight of the planters and began to offer suggestions.

Oliver Hudson Kelley stopped in Georgetown on his journey through South Carolina and met some of the local planters. He later wrote Ben Allston asking him to join his National Grange of the Patrons of Husbandry, a national organization looking for new solutions. "While I was travelling in the South I saw the unhappy state of matters and also saw plainly that the political parties never would produce a harmony of feeling. I was satisfied if all could come together as farmers and planters and keep the great interests of agriculture uppermost we could get under the vine and fig tree and wave olive branches with some meaning." As one black ball would reject a member, Kelley reassured Allston: "I fancy there will not be many 'fancy colored' members." He urged Allston not to go to California for he did not think that Allston would rid himself of the Negro by going there. In fact, Kelley believed, as did many Southerners, that the Negro would disappear because of disease and immigration. What the South needed was a large influx of immigrants. But to get immigration it was necessary to secure quiet in the region and then representation in Congress. Kelley had already urged upon

[69] The Georgetown Agricultural and Mechanical Club had endorsed a resolution to bring in Chinese labor. Wm. M. Lawton, chairman of committee on Chinese immigration of the state society, wrote Dr. Sparkman, Aug. 2, 1869, of their desire "to bring a race of People of a higher type of civilization, ingenuety, and indefatigable industry, to substitute that description, which were brought & sold to our Forefathers, through Puritan, Yankee, & British cupidity, *and then destroyed,* by their *hypocrisy & folly.*" Sparkman Family Papers, 1867–1869, 2791, folder 6, SHC.

Allston a new political path. "If the Negro predominates in your district and their vote is to carry the day, make yourself popular with them and get their votes, the color of the votes is of little consequence so long as good sensible white men are elected by them. Never mind the apathy and nervousness of your neighbors, go in for *number one*." Kelley also suggested new departures in the economic sphere. He wrote that Allston might turn his rice mill into a saw mill. "I consider your Pine land worth more money to you than all the rice lands you have in your neighborhood. . . . If I remember right, there is also a steam engine on your Mother's plantation. . . . When we see available power lying idle, we have an itching for making it work and we consider it is as poor policy to have a steam engine idle as a stable full of horses." Kelley was trying to break down the plantation image in the mind of the planters—to force them to face a new reality.[70]

This kind of talk, a jumble of plans and prejudices, was effective. The planters did form a Georgetown chapter of the Grange, which began to meet the third Sunday of each month. The leading figures were two lawyers, Richard Dozier and Benjamin Huger Wilson, who were emerging as the principal leaders of the white population in Georgetown District.[71]

The Reconstruction program as passed through Congress in 1867 was a program designed to break up what Johnson had accomplished. As the alliance of Johnson officials, military officers, and planters had been returning the Negro to slavery (at least this was the view of many Radical Republicans in Congress), this trend had to be altered. The laws of March 2, 23, and July 19, 1867, which undermined whatever hope was left in the planters, did give hope to the freedmen and a chance to rule. The first two laws made the state government as established under the Constitution of 1865 temporary and set up machinery for registering voters and calling a new constitutional convention. The machinery for calling the new convention into session must be run by those South Carolinians who could take the ironclad oath. Governor

[70] Oliver H. Kelley to Benjamin Allston, April 18, Sept. 6, Oct. 10, Nov. 30, 1867, Easterby, *op. cit.*, pp. 227–228, 232–234, 237–239.

[71] List of committees, undated, Richard Dozier Papers, SHC; also see J. H. Easterby, "The Granger Movement in South Carolina," *Proceedings of the South Carolina Historical Association, 1931* (Columbia, S. C., 1931), pp. 21–32.

James L. Orr, who had been following a course more sensitive to the demands of this growing Northern threat, wrote Richard Dozier on April 12, 1867, asking for the names of four persons to act as registrars and three persons to act as managers at each precinct. Orr stated that all of these individuals had to take the ironclad oath of July 2, 1862, before they could function as managers and registrars. To Dozier this was simply the herald of a new despotism. "Tyranny," Dozier replied, "has always endeavoured to surround itself by oaths. This is an example of the old system." [72] The ironclad oath, of course, was meant to bar the old ruling class from politics, to pave the way for a new electorate. The law of July 19, 1867, gave military officials the right to remove state officials and thereby speed up the calling of the convention.

It was the vote, not emancipation, that brought the freedmen to political life. William Sinclair, a Georgetown Negro writing at the end of the century, considered voting the crux of the Negro problem. [73] To vote was to achieve a new status, to become a human being to whom the politician must appeal, to win a place in the body politic that society must respect—and the privilege to vote was what the Negro got with the Reconstruction program of 1867. It was in November 1867 that he first exercised this new privilege. Fortunately, the books in which he registered his name for that election have been preserved. [74] These documents provide the first complete list of the names of the freedmen in Georgetown District, catching him in two acts of freedom—selecting a name and registering to vote. By these steps he asserted his individuality and his humanity.

The names themselves are important. There is scant record of how the Negroes felt about freedom, about voting, about their new role in society. This list therefore becomes an eloquent document. The voters are listed by races with 457 white voters registering and 2,922 colored.

[72] James L. Orr to Richard Dozier, April 12, 1867, Richard Dozier Papers, SHC. Dozier's remarks were written on the reverse side of Orr's letter.

[73] William A. Sinclair, *The Aftermath of Slavery, A Study of the Condition and Environment of the American Negro* (Boston, Mass., 1905), pp. 102–104.

[74] Registration books for 1867 election, S. C. Archives. On June 20, 1867, A. W. Dozier wrote his brother Richard Dozier that he hoped all the whites would register. In his own part of Williamsburg County the Negroes were still in "blissful ignorance" of the great boon conferred upon them. Dozier felt that after they were made wise upon the subject and exercised the right of voting, they would in a few years conclude that it was "folly to be wise." Dozier Papers, SHC.

For the first time the freedmen have surnames, which would be of their own choosing. Although during slavery they had had first names, many of them must have taken this opportunity to rename themselves. It seems strange that they did not take greater advantage of this opportunity, but even in this act they could not escape their past completely. Nevertheless, these documents do chart some of their hopes and fears as they enter their new life.

The Negroes overwhelmingly took for surnames the names of their former masters. This has often been said, but little proof has been given. However, if one takes the list of the planters of 1850 and 1860 who owned the largest number of slaves and then checks the planter family names against the registration role of 1867, one has an interesting series of facts. Among the 2,922 names on the role, there were more Alstons and Allstons than any other names. The surnames of the great planters of 1860 certainly predominated. Other names are those of low-country planter families, such as Moultrie, Gadsden, Vanderhorst, and Wragg, who had held slaves in this district at an earlier period. This fact would indicate that there may have been last names in use among the slaves themselves prior to the war. The Swintons had long disappeared from among the Georgetown slaveowners, yet some of the Negroes bore this name in 1867. Others carried the name of Fenwick, a family presumably never owning slaves in this district but owning many in other parts of the lowcountry. Perhaps slaves who were sold from one part of the state to another kept some designation among themselves of their former ownership. The large number of Singletons and Brockingtons in the list may imply a post-war migration of former slaves of the Singleton family from Sumter and Richland districts and of the Brockington family from Williamsburg. A study of these names on this basis might give some indication of pre-war and post-war mobility of the slave and Negro population.

It was in the choice of first names, however, that some originality was shown, although the greatest number of first names must have been carried over from slavery days. The overwhelming number of first names were the common ones found among the white population, such as Jack, Sam, Tom, and William. About one-third had distinctive first names that can be divided into the following categories: biblical, classical, literary, calendar, African, geographic, status, and historical. There were also names relating to human hopes and fears.

Biblical first names were probably no more common among the colored population than among the white. Abraham and Moses were most frequent, but names such as Israel, Lazarus, Esau, Ishmael, Isaiah, Shiloh, Job, Shadrack, Gideon, Nazarine, and Zebadee were also found. Planters had often named their slaves after classical figures. In 1867 there were 30 Caesars, 28 Scipios, 20 Hectors, 18 Cupids, 16 Pompeys, 14 Catoes, 12 Tituses, 11 Marcuses, 8 Hercules, 6 Neros, 5 Neptunes, 4 Virgils, 3 Brutuses, 2 Bacchuses, 2 Mercurys, and an Esop, Romulus, Junius, and Nimrod. Literary characters were few. There were 4 Sanchos, 1 Hamlet, and 1 Romeo.

The months of the year and the days of the week had been used by the slaves to recall their birthdates. March, June, August, and July were the favorite months, although January, April, February, and October appear on the list. There were 11 Fridays, 10 Mondays, and 1 Sunday. There were no lovelier names than Summer Gaillard or Winter Swinton.

African names have eventually been discarded, but they were not abandoned at the moment of freedom. There were 20 Cuffees, and several with each of the following: Quash, Cudjoe, Quoqua, Quaco, and Quashy. These were African words for the days of the week. Calice, Akimo, Mussau, Umbro, Mausa, Biney, Calibey, Mustifer, and Sambo were each found once. Most of the names designating the place of their origin had been lost. There were no Ebo Jacks or Calabar Sams or Angola Toms, as there were in the lists of slaves found in the inventories of the eighteenth century. There were, in fact, absolutely no surnames of African origin; to that extent the slaves had been Anglicized.

Most unusual was the use of first names denoting non-African geographical locations. It was not odd that at least 12 preferred to use the name of Mingo, which must have derived from their place of residence along Black Mingo Creek, nor that some loved their locale, such as Gabriel Black River, Winyah Gardner, and Santee Livingston. Nor that Carolina and Charleston were popular. But why should slaves at the moment of freedom have retained London, Liverpool, and Glasgow as first names, when these had been the principal slave-trading ports of England and Scotland? Perhaps it indicates that the freedmen held on to what was familiar. Only two names, however, are derived from plantations, those being Accabee Washington and Calais Tidyman. And there were a few exotics: Parish Gourdine and Roanoke Myers.

Most expected would have been names indicating a desire for rank, status, or profession. There were 34 Princes, 16 Primuses, 2 Kings and 2 Dukes, with a Minus, Governor, Boss, Major, and General. Some names must have reflected the hope for a new role in life, or merely designated a former role, recognized by master or friends: Faith Lawyer, Dandy Pinckney, Cook Read, Judge Moultrie, Essex Judge, Cuffee Doctor.

The history of great men had touched their lives for five men took Washington as first names, while one each the names of Madison, Monroe, and Lincoln. One was styled Thomas Jefferson. Among famous foreign figures LaFayette came first and Bonaparte second. The grandiloquent sound of Washington Farewell, London Washington, Pompey Washington, and LaFayette Washington appealed to the ears of a few. Only two, however, copied the aristocratic Southern habit of taking two famous planter family names. There was an Allston Pyatt and an Abram Belin Allston. The latter was a rare combination, for seldom did any freedman take a middle name.

Most revealing are the first names, indicating hope and awe at the moment of freedom. Surely some of the following must have been adopted as the freedmen assumed their new status: Deliverance Belin, Welcome Bee, Knowledge Gipson, Providence Drayton, Halcyon Nesbit, Hope Mitchell, Divine Horry, Sessamy Maginnis, and Christmas Magraw. Yet the new experiment might involve unknown risks for Chance Great, Plenty Road, Fortune Callice, Distress Ivins, Hardtime Road. Hardtime was a particularly popular first name. Some stand out as just reflecting the sheer exuberance of being free and making a choice: Sigh Golden, Trumpeter Wineglass, Card One, and Purdaza Wilks.

All in all, in the name-taking, there was more of tradition than there was of new departure, but where a few struck out the path was clear. What was true of name-taking must have been true of much of the freedmen's activities. Only here in these documents, however, are these feelings brilliantly trapped.

The Negro voters were six times as numerous as the white voters. On

November 19, 20, 1867, the people elected Franklin F. Miller, Henry W. Webb, and Joseph H. Rainey to represent Georgetown District in the constitutional convention to be held in Charleston from January 14 to March 17, 1868.[75] Among these three, Rainey took the most active part in the convention. Later, as the first Negro to be elected to the national House of Representatives,[76] he represented Georgetown and her congressional district in Congress for four years. He was a good example of the new man turned up by the social revolution.

Rainey was born in Georgetown on June 21, 1832, of slave parents. His father, a barber, bought his own freedom. The son, after receiving a limited education, also became a barber. During the war Rainey was at first forced to work on the Confederate fortifications in Charleston but escaped to the West Indies and remained there until the end of the war. He was, like the Negro leadership of the 1868 convention, not from the rice and cotton fields, but a free Negro who had had some education and experience beyond the shores of Carolina. In 1874 a St. Louis newspaperman described Rainey as

a light mulatto with regular features; bright genial eyes; pleasant expression; broad, clear brow; and a profusion of silky hair. He was of medium height, with a graceful and easy carriage and with very small hands which he used effectively in gesturing. He was courteous and suave rather than aggressive, but could defend himself well if necessary. As a speaker he was fluent and even eloquent on occasion, moderate but earnest, and held his own with opponents even in impromptu debate.[77]

The 1868 convention restored the designation of county for the districts that had existed since 1800. Each county was to have one member in the state senate, while the house was to be based for the first time on population alone. Georgetown County henceforth would have one

[75] *Proceedings of the Constitutional Convention of South Carolina, held at Charleston, S. C., beginning January 14th and ending March 17th, 1868. Including the Debates and Proceedings,* reported by J. Woodruff (Charleston, S. C., 1868), p. 8. H. W. Webb to Maj. Read, Nov. 17, 1867, accepts nomination as delegate, RG 98, National Archives. F. B. Simkins and R. H. Woody, *South Carolina During Reconstruction* (Chapel Hill, N. C., 1932), p. 72.

[76] He was elected Nov. 15, 1870. New York *Times,* Nov. 21, 1870.

[77] Quoted in Samuel D. Smith, "The Negro in Congress, 1870–1901" (PhD dissertation, Univ. of N. C., 1930), pp. 86–87.

senator and three representatives. The governor, who was elected for a two-year term and who could be re-elected once, was given a veto, yet one which could be overridden by a two-thirds vote of the legislature. Those whites, disfranchised by the proposed Fourteenth Amendment, were forbidden to vote in the state until Congress should remove such disability. The suffrage would therefore be dominated by the Negro vote. The court system was overhauled with trial justices at the local level being appointed by the governor.[78]

Although this convention drew up a constitution that insured the rule of the Negro (with his allies) for some time to come, Rainey himself was not vindictive toward the white population. He asked for leniency for debtors who had purchased slaves before the war and still owed money, even though the slaves had now been freed.[79] He was opposed to any confiscation of lands [80] and moved that the convention request Congress to remove from the citizens of South Carolina the political disabilities imposed by the Fourteenth Amendment.[81] A social revolution was not incorporated into the new constitution, neither through confiscation of landed property, nor through forced integration of the races. However, the way for the advancement of the Negro race was opened with the establishment of a free school system guided by a state superintendent of public instruction. There was to be compulsory education for six months of each year.[82]

The year 1868 saw the advent of Negro rule. In the elections for the new state officials in March 1868 many whites, feeling hopeless, refrained from voting, with the result that the Republicans won quite easily the control of state offices.[83] General E. R. S. Canby superintended

[78] *Constitution of the Commonwealth of South Carolina, Ratified April 16, 1868* (Columbia, S. C., 1883).

[79] *Proceedings of the Constitutional Convention, 1868, op. cit.*, p. 42.

[80] *Ibid.*, p. 213.

[81] *Ibid.*, p. 880.

[82] *Constitution of . . . 1868, op. cit.*, pp. 41–44.

[83] Simkins and Woody, *op. cit.*, p. 109. "The freedmen from their respective plantations assembled *en masse* to participate in the selection of their representatives in the general assembly. Prior to the meeting, groups were to be seen in every direction on Bay Street, holding their caucuses and discussing the merits and demerits of the respective candidates for nomination. The shrill shriek of the fife, however, soon summoned them to their rendezvous where a hot contest ensued between the friends and supporters of the several candidates." *Ibid.*, p. 106.

on July 6, 1868, the changeover from the administration of Governor James L. Orr to that of the newly elected Robert K. Scott.[84] As the four congressional districts were gerrymandered so that the full weight of the Negro vote in the lowcountry could be felt, the Republicans captured control of the congressional delegation as well.[85] Thus, by the end of the year 1868 the federal, state, and county offices were in the hands of the new men. With the ratification of the Fourteenth Amendment in December 1868 and the ratification of the Fifteenth Amendment in February 1870, both of which were designed to insure the continuance in power of the Negro, the revolution was complete.[86]

At each level Negroes filled offices for the first time. Rainey would be shortly elected to Congress from the First District.[87] He had been the first state senator under the new constitution, serving from 1868 to 1870. J. F. Beckman (1870–1872) and William H. Jones (1872–1876) followed him.[88] The state representatives during this period were Henry W. Webb, Franklin F. Miller, William H. Jones, J. A. Bowley, Thomas D. McDowell, R. M. Harriet, Charles S. Green, and Bruce H. Williams.[89]

Under the constitution of 1868 the sheriff, coroner, solicitor, and clerk of court were to be elected for four-year terms and the justices of the peace, constables, probate judge, school commissioner, and the three members of the board of county commissioners were to be elected for two-year terms. In the town the intendant and four wardens were still elected annually. The treasurer and auditor were county officials appointed by the governor. During Reconstruction the officials elected to county offices were quite often Negroes whereas the town officials remained generally in the hands of the white citizens of Georgetown. Since the Republicans controlled the federal government, the appointments to local federal offices were given to Negroes. The postmaster, the collector of customs, and the lesser customs officers were, therefore, gen-

[84] *Ibid.*, pp. 112–113.
[85] *Ibid.*, pp. 117–119.
[86] The federal laws to control the Ku Klux Klan which were passed in 1870 and 1871 and the Civil Rights Act of 1875 rounded out the federal measures.
[87] He was elected Nov. 15, 1870, and took his seat on Dec. 12, 1870.
[88] *The Senate of the State of South Carolina, 1776–1962,* ed. E. B. Reynolds and J. R. Faunt (Columbia, S. C., 1962), p. 154.
[89] These names have been compiled from the Journals of the House of Representatives, S. C. Archives.

erally Negroes. The pilots and the medical doctor for the port were also Negroes.[90]

The power of this group was strengthened by two changes that took place at this time. During 1868 and 1869 the Freedmen's Bureau was bringing to a completion its work in the county. This welfare organization had supplied rations and medical help as well as the beginnings of a rudimentary school system for the freedmen and their families.[91] These needs would now be met by the local officeholders, who would therefore have no rivals for the affection of the people. As the United States army was withdrawn, the moderation of a Sickles or of a Canby would be felt less frequently. A Negro militia was organized to maintain order.[92]

The permanent revolution could come only through the economic advancement of the Negro and through education. The Negroes did improve their economic status during Reconstruction, but they never managed to undergird their political position with a firm economic base. After the attempt to re-establish the task system of work with a crop division at the end of the year had failed, wages in money had to be paid. Wages were pitifully small, but they did provide a step toward greater independence. When the lumber industry began to pay higher wages than the planters, labor was drawn off the plantations. The rice economy was dealt another blow. In 1883 wages were 50 cents a day.[93]

Did the Negroes become landowners? The abandoned lands had been returned to the owners at the end of 1865. The constitutional conven-

[90] The papers of Governors Scott, Moses, and Chamberlain, S. C. Archives, contain many letters from the Georgetown officeholders. See Rainey, Jones, and Webb to Scott, Oct. 12, 1868; citizens of Georgetown to Scott, March 25, 1870; Bowley et al. to Moses, July 24, 1873; petitions to Chamberlain, Dec. 6, 28, 1874, Jan. 4, 1875. Concerning appointments to the positions of treasurer and auditor see petitions from Georgetown to Chamberlain, Dec. 4, 7, 1874, and Charles H. Sperry to Chamberlain, Dec. 14, 1874, Chamberlain Papers, S. C. Archives.

[91] There was a sale of medical and hospital property in December 1868. Also see "Register of Out Patients—Refugees, Georgetown, S. C.," RG 105, National Archives.

[92] J. Harvey Jones, George Pawley, and Brass Richardson were instrumental in securing "An act to incorporate the Winyah Guards, of Georgetown, South Carolina," March 9, 1871, *Acts and Joint Resolutions of the General Assembly of the State of South Carolina, 1870–1871* (Columbia, S. C., 1871), pp. 653–654. On the Negro militia see J. Harvey Jones to Moses, July 31, Sept. 10, 1873, Moses Papers, S. C. Archives.

[93] *South Carolina, Resources and Population, Institutions and Industries* (Charleston, S. C., 1883), p. 70.

tion of 1868 did not confiscate lands for the Negro. A South Carolina Land Commission was set up in 1870 to purchase lands and redistribute these lands among the Negroes, but the commission did little business in Georgetown County.[94] If the Negroes became landowners, it was by purchase of a few acres here and there. In 1883 the price of uplands was $1 to $15 per acre and of rice lands $3 to $50 per acre.[95] The price of uplands was low enough for some Negroes to make purchases. By 1910 there were in Georgetown County 519 Negro-owned farms, totaling 19,223 acres (of which 5,198 acres were improved land) and valued at $207,476. But in 1910 Beaufort County had 4,197 Negro-owned farms, totaling 87,541 acres (of which 60,501 were improved), valued at $1,860,687. Beaufort County had the greatest number of farms in the state owned by Negroes; Georgetown County the smallest number.[96] Beaufort Negroes had benefited from the long Yankee occupation and also from Sherman's Order of 1865.[97] In Georgetown County the Negroes made very little progress toward economic independence. In 1883 there was not one Negro businessman in the town.[98]

High hopes were placed in education; but these hopes were blighted. The Constitution of 1868 and the School Act of 1870 established the basis for free public education in South Carolina, perhaps the most lasting contribution of Radical Reconstruction. The first state superintendent of education, Justus K. Jillson, who held the job from 1868 to 1876, put the new school plans, which called for compulsory attendance of all children between the ages of six and sixteen, into operation in February 1870. The results in Georgetown County were, however, close to total failure.[99]

[94] Carol Rothrock Bleser, *The Promised Land, A History of the South Carolina Land Commission, 1869–1890* (Columbia, S. C., 1969). The Land Commission purchased two tracts in Georgetown County: one of 713 acres from B. H. Rutledge and one of 5,310 acres from Risley and Dozier. Of the 6,023 acres purchased, 5,235 acres had not been sold as late as 1883.

[95] *South Carolina, Resources and Population, Institutions and Industries* (Charleston, S. C., 1883), p. 70.

[96] Department of Commerce, Bureau of the Census, *Negro Population, 1790–1915* (Washington, D. C., 1918), pp. 665–666.

[97] Willie Lee Rose, *Rehearsal for Reconstruction, The Port Royal Experiment* (Indianapolis, Ind., 1964), pp. 397, 406.

[98] "The Trade and Industries of Georgetown, S. C.—1883," *Georgetown Enquirer*, Sept. 1, 1883.

[99] Williamson, *op. cit.*, pp. 223–229.

In the report of 1876, Georgetown County was one of seven counties in the state to show a decrease in school population and one of nine to show a decrease in the number of free common schools. At that time Georgetown County had the smallest number of free common schools in the state (31) and the fewest teachers employed (34). There were only ten school districts in the county. The average session of the free school ran for four and one-half months, with the average wage for the male teacher at $30.40 per month. No local or school district taxes were raised in the county or in the town. State funds alone supported the system.[100]

One of the reasons for the failure was that children of the well-to-do white families opted out of the free school system. Scarcely any of the old families managed to retain tutors. In the town, however, those who could afford to do so sent their children to the Winyah Indigo School, which was held in the society's building. This school provided a good education for a few. Some of the graduates were able to enter the best American universities. Walter Hazard went to Princeton upon graduation.[101] In 1883 there were only two public schools in Georgetown itself—one was for white children and the other for colored.[102]

Students of both races attended the post-war state university. By an act of February 1874, 124 scholarships were provided, which were to be proportioned among the counties on the basis of representation in the legislature. Each scholarship paid $200 a year and was awarded on the basis of competitive examinations. The first examinations were held in March 1874. Most of those, however, who were awarded scholarships were Negroes. William A. Sinclair and Julius J. Holland were in the sub-freshman class in 1875, studying Latin, Greek, arithmetic, algebra, and history. By 1876 the student body of the university was almost entirely Negro.[103]

It was ironic that the seeds of segregation were planted during Re-

[100] Reports and Resolutions, 1876–1877, pp. 338–344.

[101] "Walter Hazard," J. C. Hemphill, Men of Mark in South Carolina (Washington, D. C., 1908), II, 197–199.

[102] South Carolina, Resources and Population. Institutions and Industries, op. cit., p. 686.

[103] D. W. Hollis, College to University (Columbia, S. C., 1956), pp. 71–73; Report of the Chairman of the Faculty of the University of South Carolina . . . 1875 (Columbia, S. C., 1875), p. 15.

construction. A physical separation of the races began to appear which in a sense had not occurred before. The regime in the state did not force racial mixing by law, although there was no prohibition against racial intermarriage. The pattern of legal segregation did not come until the 1890's, but in the 1870's a spontaneous trend in that direction set in. The best example of this separation was to be found in the churches. Before the war the slaves had been gathered into the plantation chapels and in Georgetown had sat with the whites in the Episcopal, Methodist, and Baptist churches. By the time of a state survey in 1883 there were three white churches in Georgetown, Episcopal, Methodist, and Baptist, and two colored, Methodist and Baptist.[104] By that time racial lines had been clearly drawn between the churches.[105]

The most thorough analysis of religious groupings can be found in the religious census for 1906. At that time in Georgetown County there were 9,616 Protestants and 77 Catholics out of a population of 22,846. The largest Protestant grouping was the African Methodists with 5,235 members. The African Methodists consisted of four churches: African Methodist Episcopal Church, African Methodist Episcopal Zion Church, Colored Methodist Episcopal Church, and Reformed Methodist Union Episcopal Church. The census did not distinguish between white and Negro Baptists, for 2,442 members were listed as in the Southern Baptist and National Convention (Colored) Baptist denominations. There were 279 Methodists, 213 Episcopalians, and 75 Presbyterians—all presumably white. There were 315 others of various Protestant denominations.[106] Not listed in the census was a small Jewish congregation. Separation therefore had taken place among the Baptists, Methodists, and Episcopalians.

The two largest Methodist groups among the Negroes were the Afri-

---

[104] *South Carolina. Resources and Population. Institutions and Industries, op. cit.,* p. 686.

[105] The records of the Salem Presbyterian Church on Black River (not, however, in Georgetown County) tell this story. On March 29, 1868, the clerk was directed to issue letters of dismission to the colored members who wanted to connect themselves with a new church forming in the vicinity. On Nov. 16, 1869, letters were issued to the eleven colored members still left. On May 5, 1871, the names of colored members who for several years had ceased to attend the church were erased. Records of Salem Presbyterian Church, Black River, III, 91, 96, 102, 114, typed copy in SCL.

[106] Department of Commerce and Labor, Bureau of the Census, *Religious Bodies: 1906,* Part I (Washington, D. C., 1910), p. 353.

can Methodist Episcopal Church and the African Methodist Episcopal Zion Church, both of which had been established in the North many years before the war and merely took the opportunity afforded by Reconstruction to expand into the South. Two chaplains with the Union army, W. H. Hunter and H. M. Turner, began work among the freedmen, winning many to these churches. The Zion Church had great success at first in North Carolina. The Colored Methodist Episcopal Church was composed of the Negro Methodists who did not leave the white Southern Methodist Church after the war. However, in 1866 this Southern white church set up separate Negro churches and in 1870 a special conference was held in Jackson, Tennessee, to organize the Negroes as a separate church. All three of these denominations had churches in Georgetown County.[107]

The Reformed Methodist Union Episcopal Church was born in 1884 and 1885 after a split in the AME Church. The Reverend Samuel Washington, who had come from Nevis in the West Indies in 1874 to Carolina, served for four years as the pastor of the AME Church in Georgetown, and three more as presiding elder for the Georgetown District. In 1883 he was reassigned to the Morris Brown Church in Charleston. On his departure from Georgetown the *Enquirer* testified to "his intelligent conversation, his liberality of opinion, his dignified and courteous demeanor and his zeal and fidelity in the performance of the sacred duties of his office." He was well-educated and had supplied superior leadership to the Georgetown Negroes.[108] At the conference of the AME Church held in Georgetown in February 1884, Washington had W. E. Johnstone suspended because of insubordination. When Washington charged Hayne in Charleston with insubordination also, Johnstone and Hayne joined forces to form a new church. They accused Washington, their chief target, of sending large sums of money to Northern churches. The AME Church had split on a question of discipline.[109]

The most significant break was in the Episcopal Church, which contained the remnants of the planting class that had provided the pre-war leadership. The crucial debate in the Episcopal Church occurred in

---

[107] *Ibid.*, II, 446–449, 455–457.
[108] Charleston *News and Courier*, May 6, 1884.
[109] *Georgetown Enquirer*, Feb. 1884.

Charleston in May 1876 over the question of whether the congregation of St. Marks in Charleston should be admitted. St. Marks, representing the elite among the Charleston Negroes, was composed of Negro families who had been free before the war. The majority report, written by the Reverend Richard S. Trapier, then rector of St. Michael's Church in Charleston, and two laymen, opposed admission. "In the Southern States," the majority report stated, "are two races with broad distinctions. To Force these two into union we believe both impossible and unlawful, why commence this work of thwarting God's law in the church?" The clergy voted 17 to 9 for admission; the laity, voting as churches, voted 12 to 17 against. Prince George Winyah and Prince Frederick Pee Dee were both against admission. Complete separation in all of the Georgetown churches had taken place.[110]

Without an economic base to prop up Negro society and without significant advances in Negro education, Negro rule could not last forever. With growing segregation the Negroes would also be left to their own devices. Leadership was provided for some time from the outside and as long as that lasted, Negro power would be buttressed. But with Rainey in Congress and the Reverend Samuel Washington gone to Charleston and the lesser Negro leadership being split by personal rivalries, the period of Negro rule was limited. Rainey saw the dangers and worked for permanent gains before the day of white power returned.

A key point in the career of Rainey in Congress came in the debate over the general amnesty bill which General Benjamin Butler reported from the judiciary committee on May 13, 1872. This bill was designed to remove white Southerners from the exclusions of the Fourteenth Amendment; its passage would mean the reappearance of the old planting class in politics. Rainey was willing to see the bill pass if Charles Sumner's civil rights bill, designed to abolish discrimination in public places, could pass with it. The quid pro quo was the removal of political disabilities in return for the denial of segregation in public life. When the amnesty bill came before the House Rainey, speaking for the colored race, said:

[110] Charleston *News and Courier*, May 13, 1876; Albert S. Thomas, *A Historical Account of the Protestant Episcopal Church in South Carolina, 1820–1957* (Columbia, S. C., 1957), p. 399.

It is not the disposition of my constituents that these disabilities should longer be retained. We are desirous of being magnanimous; it may be that we are so to a fault. Nevertheless we have open and frank hearts towards those who were our former oppressors and taskmasters. We foster no enmity now, and we desire to foster none, for their acts in the past to us or to the Government we love so well. But while we are willing to accord them their enfranchisement and here to-day give our votes that they may be amnestied, while we declare our hearts open and free from any vindictive feelings towards them, we would say to those gentlemen on the other side that there is another class of citizens in the country, who have certain rights and immunities which they would like you, sirs, to remember and respect. . . . We invoke you, gentlemen, to show the same kindly feeling towards us, a race long oppressed, and in demonstration of this humane and just feeling, I implore you, give support to the Civil-rights Bill, which we have been asking at your hands, lo! these many days.[111]

The amnesty bill was passed in 1872; the civil rights bill, sponsored by Charles Summer, in 1875. When Sumner died in 1874, Rainey was asked to deliver one of the funeral orations. In this oration Rainey tried to wipe out the legacy of Preston Brooks, the South Carolina congressman who in 1856 had beaten Sumner over the head thirty times with his gutta percha walking stick until Sumner collapsed to the floor of the Senate. Rainey, as a South Carolina congressman and a legitimate successor of Brooks in that body, praised Sumner, the champion of civil rights.[112]

The Georgetown rice planters wanted to regain their political power and throw over the Negro hierarchy, but as long as a federal force remained in South Carolina there was little chance of doing so. The private sphere was therefore alone left to them. This had traditionally meant rice planting, but after three years of post-war failures, this way of life was evaporating. The planters must either restore prosperity to rice planting or find new avenues to wealth. Otherwise they would have no economic base from which to regain power.

Dr. Sparkman was a good example of a planter who tried. He was fortunate in that he could support his family by his medical practice

[111] *Congressional Record* (42nd Cong., 2d Sess.), pp. 1439–1440, 1442–1443, 3382–3383. Rainey was willing for power to pass into the hands of the white population, if the civil rights of the freedmen could be secured.

[112] Speech on April 27, 1874. *Congressional Record* (43rd Cong., 1st Sess.), Part 4, pp. 3412–3414.

while he experimented. In January 1868 he proposed to Francis Withers Johnstone that the two of them should cultivate Dirleton on shares, using permanent and transient labor. Dr. Sparkman would furnish the necessary plantation utensils and tools and pay the wages of the workers. The permanent laborers were to receive $8 per month plus two pounds of bacon, or one quart of molasses weekly, with one peck of corn as rations which was the equivalent of $11 per month. Transient labor would receive fifty cents per day. Johnstone would have entire control of the hands, assigning them tasks and directing their labor. In order to finance this operation, Dr. Sparkman would borrow $3,000 in New York at 10 percent interest. At the end of the year the net profits were to be divided equally between Sparkman and Johnstone after deduction of seven specific items of plantation expense. This plan was agreed to, but at the end of the year there was a deficit of $839.32. This, so far as can be judged, was a typical effort of these years.[113]

The great burden was the need to borrow at high interest rates with the ensuing need to repay by the end of the year. For example, in 1869 many planters had to hurry through with their threshing in order to get the crop to market in order to obtain funds with which to meet the factor's advances, thereby losing one of the most beautiful seasons on record for ditching since the rivers were very low that November and December. Until there was proper drainage there was no chance of using animal power or machinery. But the credit system and the slovenly work done for the wages paid made this impossible. What was needed for rice planting was "a cash capital." Dr. Sparkman in an estimate of the rice crop in 1870 thought that there was "skill and experience and energy sufficient to revive the Carolina Rice Crop. . . ." There was labor which understood the needs of planting. If the fiscal year began in October, labor might be insured for a succeeding crop just as soon as the growing crop was harvested. Then when the rivers were low, ditching could be done, and when the rivers were high, the crop could be prepared for market. There was still "money in the old mud banks of So. Ca. as well as in Northern Rail Roads and corporations," but only an experienced rice planter who understood "our peculiar people" and

[113] J. R. Sparkman to F. W. Johnstone, Jan. 13, 1868; expenses, etc., Dirleton Plantation, 1868, Papers of Mrs. Witte, Columbia, S. C.

their particular way of asserting their privileges as freedmen could hope to succeed. No theoretical planter would. The high rates of interest and the annual difficulties in renewing labor contracts held the planter back. Dr. Sparkman, "no theoretical planter," was not succeeding.[114]

In 1874 Dr. Sparkman wrote a report on the rice crops since 1859 for Frederick Watts, the U. S. Commissioner of Agriculture. Up to 1860 about 46,000 acres of rice had been planted annually. The crop of 1859, the largest ever grown, yielded 95,127 tierces of clean marketable rice, estimated at 600 pounds to the tierce—that would give upwards of 1,200 pounds to the acre. The records of the years 1860 to 1868 could not be obtained, but for the period 1868 to 1874 the figures were:

1868	12,143 acres		
1869	16,100		
1870	15,133	13,636 tierces	540 lbs. per acre
1871	17,439	13,500	464
1872	16,900	15,175	562
1873	17,100	13,126	460
1874	16,232		

The decline in 1871 was due to "an almost unprecedented wet harvest, by reason of continued rains when the crop was on the stubble." In 1873 a heavy and protracted freshet from August to mid-October proved disastrous. Not 5 percent of the rice estates were able to pay the expenses of cultivation. "Most of the planters had to give liens upon the present growing crop to cover deficiencies of the last year, and the usurious rates of interest demanded by money lenders, and those who furnish advances in the shape of plantation supplies, leave so small a margin of profit for the producer, there is no wonder that the area of cultivation had decreased." The 1874 crop was grassy and would not produce as much per acre as the previous year. The control of labor was as difficult as ever, so until political and fiscal changes came about there would be no real chance for success.[115]

[114] Dr. J. R. Sparkman, "The Rice Crop of 1870, Georgetown County," Papers of Mrs. Witte, Columbia, S. C.

[115] "Report on Rice Crops in Georgetown County, written in 1874 to Hon. Freck. Watts, Commissioner," Papers of Mrs. Witte, Columbia, S. C.; rice crops, 1868–1875, Sparkman Papers, 2791, folder 7, SHC.

Despair settled upon the rice planters. Bankruptcies were common. In March 1868 R. G. White, Seaman Deas, and E. G. Hume, all of Georgetown County, declared themselves bankrupt.[116] General Sickles wrote Governor Orr, September 21, 1867, stating that his general order staying prosecutions in over 30,000 suits for debts had been responsible for his dismissal.[117] Many thought of moving to Florida, or to Texas, or to California. Richard Dozier's two brothers were attracted to new regions. A. W. Dozier wrote his brother Richard on February 10, 1868, that his children were going to California: "I am feeling rather sad today . . . some of my children left my house this morning, bound to a distant land, from which it is not probable that all of them—if any— will ever return; and there being as little probability that I shall ever be able to follow them there, the separation seems to be for all time. . . .This separation from her children, with so little prospect of ever meeting them again, is a terrible trial to my poor wife, who, I am afraid, is fast breaking down under the accumulating privations and afflictions of the times." [118] By November 1868 A. W. Dozier had decided to go to California and was willing to sell his lands, as cheap as $2.25 per acre for the Snow's Island tract where Marion had camped, in order to raise the money for the trip.[119] By the fall of 1869 A. W. Dozier had joined his children in California whence one had written that San Jose was handsomer than any city he had seen, except Kingstree. One Dozier

[116] Charleston *Daily News*, March 9, 1868. Just as this volume was going to press the author discovered through the assistance of Mr. A. K. Johnson, Jr., and Mr. Edward Weldon that the following Georgetown men were petitioners in bankruptcy proceedings under the provisions of the U. S. Act of 1867: Benjamin Al[l]ston, R. O. Bush, E. P. Coachman, Geo. R. Congdon, Quintus L. Cooper, Seaman Deas, Fred. W. and Joseph W. Ford, Stephen Ford, Edw. G. Hume, Simons E. Lucas, J. D. and W. J. Magill, B. H. Read, S. W. Rouquie, Moultrie Weston, R. G. White, Benj. H. Wilson. The author did not have time to investigate the case files which are deposited at the Federal Records Center, East Point, Ga., under U. S. Courts, S. C. District, Bankruptcy Records, Act of 1867.

[117] Orr Papers, S. C. Archives. J. I. Middleton wrote to General Sickles, April 20, 1867, asking if he might salvage the iron in a vessel beached on the shore in January 1863. This might be a small request, "but to those in the predicament of the undersigned this is the day of small things, & small things are important to those who have been suddenly deprived of almost everything like capital. . . ." RG 98, National Archives.

[118] A. W. Dozier to R. Dozier, Feb. 10, 1868, Richard Dozier Papers, SHC.

[119] A. W. Dozier to R. Dozier, Nov. 24, 1868, Richard Dozier Papers, SHC.

became a school teacher, another a dairy farmer, another a warehouse manager, and one attended a commercial college in San Francisco.[120]

Leonard Dozier, who had gone to Florida during the Civil War, kept urging Richard to sell his lands and come to Fernandina, the "land of the flowers," because Georgetown was "ded as the devil." There was not a spark left in her; all of her citizens were broke. "Where are the Waccamites—the Pee Deeites—the Black riverites? All 'gone up'?" In 1872 Leonard wrote that his children were doing well; his son was a railroad agent, and his daughters had married enterprising young men.[121]

Alexander Mazyck of the South Santee moved to London, Ontario, where he swore allegiance to Queen Victoria and became a British subject. Fortunate investments eased his exile. He took his niece Annie Mazyck Manigault and her husband Gabriel Manigault with him.[122] Manigault, a belletrist, revealed his pessimism concerning the trend of mankind in *A Political Creed: Embracing Some Ascertained Truths in Sociology and Politics,* which was published in New York in 1884. In this work, subtitled "An Answer to H. George's 'Progress and Poverty'," he extolled the rightness of the pre-war Southern society.

Many letters indicated that there was a desire to get away from the Negro. Francis Withers Johnstone wrote Dr. Sparkman on February 7, 1869, that he was afraid the planters would do no better in that year. "My business as rice planter is plaid out." His only hope was that his children could do something else in life so that they would not be cursed with the Negro forever.[123] In 1870 Dr. Sparkman received two letters urging him to migrate to Texas. Bishop Alexander Gregg wrote from Galveston, and Benjamin Allston, whose wife was a Texan, spoke of the prospects in Austin. Yet in many ways Allston was not impressed with the country "especially coming from an old and refined Society like our own—there are many things that grate on the nerves and sensibilities of one habituated to the civilization of more than a century."

[120] A. W. Dozier to R. Dozier, Sept. 22, 1869; A. W. Dozier, Jr., to R. Dozier, Sept. 27, 1869, Richard Dozier Papers, SHC; Genealogy and Life Sketches of the Dozier Brothers, Dozier Family Papers, SCL.

[121] Leonard Dozier to R. Dozier, Dec. 16, 1868; April 7, 1872, Richard Dozier Papers, SHC.

[122] John A. May and Joan R. Faunt, *South Carolina Secedes* (Columbia, S. C., 1960), pp. 176, 179–180.

[123] Sparkman Family Papers, 1867–1869, 2791, folder 6, SHC.

He might still decide to return to the Pee Dee "after all I may prefer the somewhat effete civilization of Georgetown, to the rude—half formed thing here, but growing day by day." [124]

Unless a new source of wealth was discovered, the white population would disappear. Fortunately, there was some turning to new avenues of business. At first there was talk of a railroad. Northern capital might build a railroad from Charleston to Wilmington. There was a rumor that an English company might buy land on the Santee for the production of rice and sea island cotton by a white labor force. But nothing came of these two projects. The rumors did prove, however, that outside capital was needed and even desired. Some men like David Risley turned to pine forests, and as lumbering became important again Negro labor was drawn from the declining rice fields. The Franco-Prussian War stimulated a need for spirits, and turpentine interests for awhile reaped profits.[125]

A few men built up small capital resources in the town and thus laid the foundations for a new white economy. Merchants supplied the plantations with necessities and secured first liens on crops. In February 1876 Heiman Kaminski held $86.60 worth of "tickets or due bills" which William C. Johnstone had issued to his laborers on Estherville plantation. The Negroes had used this scrip to buy goods at Kaminski's store in town. Kaminski wrote the sheriff that these tickets had a prior claim on the crop and should be satisfied before Joseph Sampson & Company's lien on the crop itself. Kaminski and Sampson were both accumulating funds while the planters decayed. In the 1880's such capital would spark an economic revival.[126]

One "very remarkable woman," Penelope Weston, a daughter of Francis Weston, "received a present of a small sum of money from a relative in England, which she invested in supplies that every one was in need of, opened a small store, and as fast as she sold our reinvested the money. . . ." Through her own exertions at her store in Plantersville,

---

[124] Bishop Alexander Gregg to Sparkman, Feb. 17, 1870; Benjamin Allston to Sparkman, March 18, 1870, Sparkman Family Papers, 1870–1875, 2791, folder 7, SHC.

[125] T. P. Bailey to T. J. McKie, March 8, 1872, March 26, 1873, T. J. McKie Papers, DUL.

[126] Documents in the possession of Mrs. Charlotte K. Prevost, Georgetown, S. C.

she educated her sisters and brothers and eventually paid off the mortgage on the family plantations.[127]

The letters of a local Georgetown druggist and doctor, T. P. Bailey, reveal the underlying political hopes of the displaced whites. The first hope was for a political triumph for the Democrats in the North. Thus, almost any measure to maintain the unity of the national Democratic Party was good. Bailey wrote: "I wish no affiliation with niggers & a platform acknowledging the right of the negro to vote and hold office simply disintegrates the Democratic Party and discourages the efforts of the Northern Democracy—The *privilege* may be *allowed the negro at this time* to vote &c but it is certainly not a *right*." [128] On February 20, 1871, he wrote that he wanted the white people to stand firm and not be trampled by Governor Scott and his minions, for firmness would "teach the misguided Africans to stand in the subordinate position nature intended." As "forbearance has ceased to be a virtue," he was "exceedingly delighted at the Union & York 'outrages'—I think an occasional raid of the kind strikes terror in the hearts of the Rads. . . ." As for Georgetown,

the Negroes certainly behave very well & the truth is they have things pretty much their own way, but the politicians are in the town, & the country negro is getting very tired of these rascals—& it seems as if their very segregation on the plantations has been rather salutary than otherwise—as is usually the case there has been some difficulty about contracts when January dawned upon us, but I believe the planters generally have arranged for the year—There is one pestilential fellow a Northern nigga named Jones who stirs up the negroes and goes on the plantations & renders them dissatisfied with the terms of their contracts. I believe if he could be Ku Kluxed we would have very little trouble.[129]

In these two letters of 1870 and 1871 the ways in which the whites could regain power and retain it are foreshadowed. Bailey expressed the dominant feeling at the end of the second letter: "I feel that it is impossible for an inferior race to rule the superior, that things must drift back to first principles based on the eternal foundations of truth."

[127] Patience Pennington [Mrs. Elizabeth W. Allston Pringle], *A Woman Rice Planter* (Cambridge, Mass., 1961), pp. 68–69, 86.

[128] T. P. Bailey to T. J. McKie, May 12, 1870, McKie Papers, DUL.

[129] Same to same, Feb. 20, 1871, McKie Papers, DUL.

During that spring there were disturbances in Union and York counties which forced Grant, "our asinine President" as Bailey called him, to issue a proclamation establishing martial law. The Negroes in Georgetown County were "as a general thing" quiet, but Bailey did mention that the Negroes in town had been of late "quite outrageous." [130] The only hope was for a complete change in Washington. But even the Northern Democrats were now admitting the legality of Reconstruction. As Bailey said, however, in a letter of June 9, there "would be no bar to undoing it at some future time *if* the *people* so desire." [131] In 1872 Bailey voted for Greeley "with all his isms" for anyone was better than Grant, but he was finding it very hard to eke out a living in "this rice and negro country." [132]

On January 22, 1874, Bailey complained that taxes had become "practically confiscation." [133] This was the final and ultimate burden of the times. Even without a paying crop most planters could have held on if taxes had not been confiscatory. This was the one element of vindictiveness in the Reconstruction government of the state. Tax the planters and force them to sell. It was this pressure that brought about the two taxpayers' conventions, the first in 1871 and the second in 1874. Benjamin Huger Wilson was the Georgetown delegate to each convention.[134] The sponsors of the convention wanted to highlight the corruption in the state government in order to win support in the national arena for a change. The first convention had not succeeded, but Bailey hoped for some good the second time. Concerning the meeting of 1874 Rainey was disdainful. He wrote General Babcock on February 24, 1874:

---

[130] Same to same, March 27, 1871, McKie Papers, DUL.
[131] Same to same, June 9, 1871, McKie Papers. DUL.
[132] Same to same, May 29, 1872, McKie Papers, DUL.
[133] Same to same, Jan. 22, 1874, McKie Papers, DUL.
[134] *Proceedings of the Tax-Payers' Convention of South Carolina held at Columbia, beginning May 9th, and Ending May 12th, 1871* (Charleston, S. C., 1871), p. 8; *Proceedings of the Tax-Payers' Convention of South Carolina, held at Columbia, beginning February 17, and ending February 20, 1874* (Charleston, S. C., 1974), p. 7. At the second convention Wilson was joined by W. W. Walker, Col. L. P. Miller, Col. B. M. Allston, and Robert E. Fraser. As early as Sept. 4, 1867, Daniel, Joseph, and Henry M. Tucker, Francis Weston, and Mrs. J. H. Read had written to Governor Orr requesting a stay of tax executions "owing to an unprecedented freshet of six weeks duration, causing a *total* loss of our crops." Orr Papers, S. C. Archives.

"please read where I have marked, and judge of the class of men which composed the late Taxpayers' Convention of South Carolina." [135]

The whites were aided in this movement to regain power by divisions among the Negro leaders. The most serious rivalry in 1874 was that between James A. Bowley and William H. Jones. Bowley, a native of Maryland, had come to South Carolina in 1867 when he was about twenty-three years old. At first he had worked harmoniously with Jones, who was two years his elder. In 1868 Jones had been elected a member of the state legislature and Bowley school commissioner. They first split during the campaign to elect B. F. Whittemore to Congress. Whittemore, a minister of the Methodist Episcopal Church who had served as a chaplain in the Union army, had been sent by the Freedmen's Bureau to organize schools in the eastern part of South Carolina. He had established about sixty schools and many churches and thus had a vast influence among the colored people.[136] Jones had been for Whittemore and Bowley against him. By 1872 Jones, who was at that time elected to the state senate, was working with Rainey. Jones and Rainey tried to prevent Bowley's re-election to the state legislature. By this time according to *The Nation* both Jones and Bowley were rich and using their money to build up local political machines. Jones spent money lavishly and gained support among the rice-field workers. Bowley, who was reputedly rich by virtue of being chairman of the state committee of ways and means, spent his funds in Georgetown.[137] In 1873 Bowley with the assistance of R. O. Bush was editing the *Georgetown Planet*.[138]

In 1874 Jones was trying to defeat Bowley's attempt at re-election by sending his supporters to the Bowley meetings and breaking them up by rowdyism. Bowley claimed that Jones was "a political incendiary." He also charged Captain Harvey Jones, a cousin of Jones, as having got up KKK documents and sent them to local officials to undermine him. In August a veritable civil war broke out between the two factions. Sheriff S. R. Carr, Intendant Congdon, and Congressman Rainey wrote

[135] S. C. Papers, DUL.

[136] Charleston *Daily News*, March 9, 1868.

[137] Bowley was indicted for accepting a bribe from the superintendent of the penitentiary for including in the appropriation bill an allowance of $80,000 for that institution.

[138] *Georgetown Planet*, May 31, 1873, was issue Vol. I, No. 10.

the Governor, August 16, 1874, that the Bowley faction had made a "dastardly assault" upon the home of Jones. Two hundred shots had been fired by rifles and revolvers at the house; three were wounded inside. "This confusion grew out of a factious spirit of opposition, composed of the country people on the one hand and the town people on the other; consequently taliation and retaliation is rampant." [139] The Jones crowd managed to put Bowley, Peter Woodbury, and twelve of Bowley's supporters in the jail, threatening their lives also. As the town itself was threatened with fire the U. S. steam cutter *Moccasin* was sent from Charleston, arriving in Georgetown on August 17. The Bowleyites were removed from jail and taken to Charleston. The white population for the first time since the war felt that they had a government now willing to protect them.[140]

The division among the local Negro leaders, who after all were outsiders, the corruption in office, and the failure of these leaders to provide adequate educational opportunities (one of the banners at the Hampton rally in 1876 proclaimed: "No free schools for the last nine months") gave the new white leaders in Georgetown a chance to regain control.[141] Yet it was still impossible for the white people of Georgetown County to regain political control without the help of the white people elsewhere in the state. This is evidenced by the fact that Negro officeholders held on longer in Georgetown County than in any other county in the state. Bailey, the druggist, wrote T. J. McKie of Edgefield County on February 10, 1875, that he did not condemn the Edgefield people for the recent disturbances there. "I believe a unanimous cooperation in this way is *the* true solution of our political difficulties." [142] This unanimous cooperation came from the statewide Hampton movement of 1876.

[139] Chamberlain Papers, S. C. Archives.
[140] Charleston *News and Courier*, Aug. 24, 1874; *The Nation*, Aug. 27, 1874. Jones had tried very hard to extend the corporate limits of Georgetown so as to add 30 votes to the voting population of the town. Bowley had blocked these moves to amend the charter of the town in the state legislature. The intendant, George R. Congdon, and the white population of the town opposed Jones. Congdon to Chamberlain, Feb. 8, 10, 1875, Chamberlain Papers, S. C. Archives.
[141] Charleston *News and Courier*, Nov. 3, 1876.
[142] T. P. Bailey to T. J. McKie, Feb. 10, 1875, McKie Papers, DUL.

The revival of the Georgetown Rifle Guards was a sign of resurging militancy among the whites. On August 20, 1874, at a meeting of the white citizens of Georgetown at the Winyah Indigo Society Hall there was organized "a Club for self defense." Article II of their constitution stated that the object of the club "shall be the promotion of Social inter-course and the enjoyment of the members by means of target shooting and such other amusements as they may determine." Heiman Kaminski was to secure rifles and uniforms in New York. The uniform was a grey single-breasted frock coat edged with green cord and faced with green with a single row of palmetto buttons down the front and three smaller buttons on each sleeve. A feather was to be worn in the cap. B. A. Munnerlyn was president, George R. Congdon was first vice president, Sol Emanuel was second vice president, and the Reverend Alexander Glennie chaplain. The flag given by Plowden Weston in the spring of 1861 to Company A, the Tenth Regiment, was turned over to the Guards. And in June 1776 the Georgetown Rifle Guards went off to Charleston to help celebrate the 100th anniversary of the Battle of Fort Moultrie.[143]

The visit of Hampton to Georgetown on October 31 was the high point of the fall election campaign. Hampton and his party arrived from Charleston on board the new steamer *Planter*. They were met by S. S Fraser, the Democratic county chairman, and a committee including Colonel Richard Dozier, Trial Justice C. R. Anderson, B. A. Munnerlyn, Colonel L. P. Miller, A. McP. Hamby, F. W. Arnholter, and A. P. Haz-zard and escorted to the hall of the Winyah Indigo Society where before a mixed crowd of white and colored they were formally welcomed. Hampton stayed overnight in the home of Richard Dozier, which was decorated with ivy leaves spelling out "Hail to our Chief!" The next morning there was a great parade from White's Bridge, through the town, past the decorated homes, to an open lawn known as Greenwich. There were mounted men from Williamsburg and Horry counties as well as a guard of honor led by Colonel R. Nesbit. The speakers stand stood on the ruins of a palatial home of Dr. Francis S. Parker. "In the rear of it stood the remains of a chimney, surmounted by a palmetto tree

[143] "Minute Book of the Georgetown Rifle Guards Club. Organized Aug. 20, 1874," SCL.

and covered with the Stars and Stripes. It represented the Prostrate State rising above her troubles, and clothed once more in the mantle of purity and justice."

Hampton spoke to the colored folks directly, asking them to move to the front so that they could hear. He spoke of peace. He promised to protect the "rights of the colored men," saying that they could not be taken away. Then Major T. G. Barker, Mr. E. W. Moise, and S. L. Hutchins, a colored man from Indiana, spoke to the crowd. Hampton seemed to be promising Rainey's program. While this rally was going on, School Commissioner S. P. Gipson was trying to hold another, but Peter Woodbury, Bowley's lieutenant, lured some of the crowd away to the *Planter* where a pro-Hampton Negro meeting was held.[144]

In the ensuing election Hampton eventually won. The final decision was not known, however, until the spring of 1877. The *Georgetown Comet*, April 11, 1877, described the joy of the local citizens when Hampton took over the state government. The newspaper column was headed, "Our Town Runs Wild." The homes of T. P. Bailey, B. I. Hazard, C. R. Anderson, and many others were brightly illuminated.[145] Hampton had won, but would the promises be kept?

[144] "Hampton in Georgetown," Charleston *News and Courier,* Nov. 3, 1876.

[145] A clipping of this issue of the *Georgetown Comet* can be found in the W. D. Morgan Scrapbook, Winyah Indigo Society Collection, Georgetown County Library.

XX

POST-RECONSTRUCTION, 1876 TO 1900

The twenty-four years from 1876 to 1900 fell between a period of black domination on one hand and white domination on the other. It was a period in which, according to C. Vann Woodward, one could find the origins of the "solid South" which existed after 1900.[1] The New South was built upon an economic structure which the more enterprising whites erected after Reconstruction. Property in land was no longer the basis for power, but instead property in railroad companies, public utilities, banks, lumber companies, and rice mills. Eventually the holders of new money would wrap themselves in the old plantation myth through marriage alliances, patriotic societies, and an emulation of a style of family living that hearkened back to antebellum times. This, the classic pattern in the South, was the pattern in Georgetown County with only minor variations, notably in the length of time during which, in spite of growing white economic power, political power was shared with the Negro population. It is this sharing of political power which sets the limits for this period in Georgetown County, for it was not until after the riots of September 1900 that the Negroes were shut out of political

[1] C. Vann Woodward, *Origins of the New South, 1877–1913* (Baton Rouge, La., 1951).

power and the "solid South" of the 1900 to 1954 period ushered in.[2] This was the third time in its history that the individuals residing in Georgetown County had sorted themselves out into a well-ordered, hierarchical society, with the Negro once again relegated to the lower levels.

The new economic leadership had emerged by the 1880's. These men were the directors of the railroad and the lumber companies, the rice mills, the steamship lines, the distributing businesses, along with a few lawyers and bankers. These men were not the sons of the pre-war Georgetown planting families. Only Richard I. Lowndes, president of a local rice mill, represented the survival of the old elite. Many of the Georgetown planting families who had homes in Charleston chose to make their way in that city rather than to remain on the land or to try business in Georgetown. The leadership of Georgetown in the 1880's was drawn from the middle ranks of the pre-war society or from the ranks of entirely new men.

The year 1883 is a good one in which to analyze the new group, for it was on July 1 in that year that the Georgetown and Lanes Railroad Company commenced operations.[3] This, the first railroad to reach Georgetown after more than forty years of abortive projects, was a signal achievement of the new leadership.[4] The railroad did not tie

[2] Patton has written that "the real forces which brought about the disintegration of South Carolina Republicanism took fashion in the years between 1876 and 1895." James Welch Patton, "The Republican Party in South Carolina, 1876–1895," *Essays in Southern History,* ed. Fletcher M. Green (Chapel Hill, N. C., 1949), p. 92.

[3] The following information on Georgetown in 1883, unless otherwise noted, comes from "The Trade and Industries of Georgetown, S. C.—1883," Georgetown *Enquirer,* Sept. 1, 1883.

[4] The Georgetown and Lanes Railroad Co., incorporated Dec. 20, 1881, constructed 36 miles of broad gage road from Georgetown to Lanes during 1882 and 1883. Operations commenced July 1, 1883, and continued to July 1, 1885, when a receiver was appointed who operated the company until May 27, 1887. The property was sold under foreclosure to C. O. Witte on Oct. 5, 1886, but deed and possession was not taken until May 27, 1887. C. O. Witte operated the company from May 27, 1887, to June 9, 1887, when title was transferred to the Georgetown and Western Railroad, which had been incorporated June 2, 1887. In 1888 the broad gage was changed to standard gage. This company was in receivership from Dec. 15, 1902, until April 15, 1912. On May 15, 1915, it was sold to the Carolina, Atlantic and Western Railway (later the Seaboard Air Line Railway Co.). At that time there were 68.6 miles of track (36 Georgetown to Lanes and 32.6 from Andrews to the Pee Dee) as well as 40 miles of logging spurs. Interstate Commerce Commission, Val. Docket No. 1031, Seaboard Air Line Railway Co. This note was supplied by William H. Patterson, the author of "Through the Heart of the South,

Georgetown directly to Charleston and Wilmington along the coast but provided a line thirty-six miles into the interior, where at Lanes it joined the line from Charleston to Florence. A railroad to the interior had always had more support from local men, as it had long been understood that Georgetown would only be a way-station on a road from Charleston to Wilmington. In 1883 Philip R. Lachicotte was president of the Georgetown and Lanes Railroad Company with B. I. Hazard, R. Dozier, L. S. Ehrich, D. Risley, B. A. Munnerlyn, R. E. Fraser, and H. Kaminski as directors. P. E. Braswell was the superintendent, and Major G. W. Earle the engineer in charge of construction. A number of these same men had also brought telegraphic communication to Georgetown. R. E. Fraser was president of the Georgetown Telegraph Company; his brother S. S. Fraser was its secretary and treasurer. The directors were B. I. Hazard, H. Kaminski, L. S. Ehrich, and B. A. Munnerlyn.

The failure of the Palmetto Lumber Company had given the local economy a temporary set-back in June 1883, but O. M. Deysher, who had been the superintendent of that company, soon established a planing mill. W. T. Braswell also established a planing mill. Since both Deysher and Braswell had started out as mechanics, they were proving that new men could find opportunities in the community.

There were two rice mills in the county. The Waverly Mill on Waverly plantation was operated by P. R. Lachicotte and Sons. Their Georgetown agent was Congdon, Hazard and Company. The Georgetown Rice Milling Company, which was located in the town itself, had been set up in 1879 as a joint-stock company. Its president was R. I. Lowndes; its directors H. Kaminski, G. R. Congdon, W. M. Hazzard, E. W. Hazzard, and B. A. Munnerlyn. L. S. Ehrich of the firm of J. Sampson and Son was the mill superintendent. In 1883 this corporation declared a dividend of 35 percent.[5]

A History of the Seaboard Air Line Railroad Company, 1832–1950" (PhD dissertation, Univ. of S. C., 1951). Also see *Georgetown, South Carolina, As It Was, As It Is, As It Will Be* (Charleston, S. C., 1888), pp. 29–30.

  [5] This mill represented an attempt of the planters and merchants to work together. In 1880 R. I. Lowndes was president. The directors consisted of four planters (W. M. Hazzard of Santee R., C. P. Allston of the Pee Dee, E. W. Hazzard of Black R., and B. H. Ward of the Waccamaw) and four merchants (B. I. Hazard, L. S. Ehrich, H. Kaminski, and B. A. Munnerlyn). *Georgetown Rice Milling Company, Georgetown, S. C.* ([Charleston, S. C.] 1880). Copy in SCL.

The railroad and the river steamers brought cotton from the interior for export. The lumber companies and rice mills provided naval stores and rice. The lumber products went mainly to the West Indies; the cotton and rice to Charleston or to New York. The vessels that came for these items brought in merchandize and fertilizers. Thus, the port of Georgetown was the scene of renewed activity. The value of the goods going in and out in 1883 were:

cotton	23,100 bales	$1,050,000
rice	14,960 tierces	493,680
rice flour	43,616 bushels	10,900.
naval stores:		
spirits	27,500 casks	440,000
rosin	145,000 bbls.	290,000
tar	850 bbls.	1,700
lumber	15,000,000 feet	270,000
shingles	5,000,000	55,000
fish, oysters, game		25,000
wholesale and retail trade		1,000,000
mdse. and fertilizers for river landings		850,000
misc.		30,000
		$4,516,280

In the year ending August 31, 1883, 292 domestic and 3 foreign vessels were engaged in the trade of Georgetown. There were 187 schooners, 103 steamers, 4 brigs, and 1 bark; this was the transition period between the days of sail and of steam. Three of the largest vessels were on the New York to Georgetown run. One of these was owned by Mulredy and Jones. Congdon, Hazard and Company were agents for the *B. I. Hazard* of 305 tons and the *G. R. Congdon* of 458 tons. J. Sampson and Company and H. Kaminski and Company were agents for the other New York lines.[6] Among the local companies Cole and Cordes (B. A. Munnerlyn was the Georgetown agent) had five steamers plying between

[6] The three-masted schooner *Linah C. Kaminski* was built in the 1880's in New York and owned jointly by Heiman Kaminski, Captain Stephen E. Woodbury, and William L. Buck (an owner of mills on Waccamaw River in Horry County). Georgetown *Times*, Aug. 19, 1965.

Charleston, Georgetown, and the upper Pee Dee. On the Waccamaw the steamers of Burroughs and Collins carried the trade between Conway and Georgetown. On the Black River, Rhem and Kellahan operated steamers. In the port itself each of the rice mills owned a steam tug, and Congdon, Hazard and Company owned two.

In 1886 the Board of Pilot Commissioners consisted of B. I. Hazard, L. S. Ehrich, C. Gilbert, W. D. Morgan, A. A. Springs, and W. J. L. Uptegrove with Hazard as chairman and Ehrich as secretary and treasurer. The pilots were W. J. L. Uptegrove, G. H. Watts, Frank Woodbury, J. W. Rumley, K. Morse, Prince Coit, Peter Woodbury, J. E. Uptegrove, and Addison Wilson. The new leadership of the town had therefore not removed the Negro pilots from their jobs.[7]

With increased water traffic there was a revival of interest in river and harbor improvements and in canals. The main effort was to remove obstacles to river navigation and to build jetties at the mouth of the bay. There was also interest in the Estherville Minim Creek Canal, a project to join Winyah Bay and the Santee River.[8] The correspondence of W. D. Morgan, who was intendant and then first mayor of Georgetown between 1891 and 1906, is filled with the story of his efforts to secure federal aid for these projects.[9] Sol Emanuel wrote Morgan in 1896 that he was "the sentinel at the outpost" in all of this work.[10] These efforts were successfully supported by federal grants; the work was done under the direction of the United States Corps of Army Engineers. In April and May 1898 at the beginning of the Spanish American War fortifications were once again constructed at the mouth of the bay.[11]

[7] *Acts of the Legislature Relating to the Port and Harbor of Georgetown, S. C., and Rules and Regulations Governing the Pilots of Said Port*, 1886 (Charleston, S. C., 1887). Copy in SCL.

[8] Reid Whitford to W. D. Morgan, Feb. 26, 1892, Box 2, W. D. Morgan Papers, SCL.

[9] W. D. Morgan Papers, SCL.

[10] Feb. 9, 1896, Box 4, W. D. Morgan Papers, SCL.

[11] The Board of Trade of Georgetown, *The Rivers of South and North Carolina entering Winyah Bay, So. Ca.* [Georgetown, S. C., 1896]. Copy in SCL. Maj. E. H. Ruffner to Gen. J. M. Wilson, April 4, 6, May 14, 1898, RG 77, 25316, National Archives. The author has not been able to explore the nearly 70 cubic feet of book records kept by the collectors of customs at Georgetown between 1849 and 1943, which are now lodged in the Federal Records Center at East Point, Ga. "Included here are such multifarious items as letters, import manifests, and coastwise clearances, crew lists, masters' oaths, lighthouse service activities, cash books and accounts

Georgetown's population, which had been stationary, expanded slightly, particularly as the Negroes moved off the land into the town:

1850	604 whites	1,024 Negroes
1860	786	934
1870	683	1,397
1880	746	1,811

In 1883 all property in the town, real and personal, was valued at $800,-000. The annual taxes on this property were only $7,000. There were five churches in the town, a courthouse, jail, and market, as well as the hall of the Winyah Indigo Society. There were three boarding houses, but no hotel until the Lafayette Hotel opened.[12] There were fourteen miles of streets paved with stone, brick, or wood. The houses were supplied with water from wells and cisterns; four main drains with lateral connections carried the surplus into the Sampit River. (There were no public water works nor public electric plant when Morgan wrote his mayor's report at the end of 1895.) [13] Bricks for the public buildings came from Port's Creek, eight miles from town; heart of pine for dwellings came from the local forests. Houses rented for $60 to $300 per year. Skilled laborers got $1 to $2 per day while unskilled laborers received from 25 cents to 75 cents per day. Since eggs cost 12 to 15 cents per dozen and beef or mutton from 10 to 12 cents per pound, living was cheap. It was still more of a rural setting than an urban one. However, some enterprising members of the community were already thinking in terms of growth. In January 1883 the Georgetown Land Association was formed with capitalization of $15,000 as a joint-stock company to purchase J. B. Pyatt's Serenity plantation. The plantation was made a subdivision of the town. There was a complaint that the new streets in the subdivision were to be only sixty-six feet wide while those in the old city were seventy-five feet. R. Dozier, the leading lawyer in the town, was president with R. E. Fraser, G. R. Congdon, P. E. Braswell, T. M.

current with both the U. S. and C. S. A. government, statements of the marine hospital, statistical abstracts, and records of wreck reports." Edward Weldon (Director, Regional Archives Branch) to the author, Nov. 24, 1969.

[12] Clipping, Mrs. C. W. Rosa's scrapbook, pp. I and J, Winyah Indigo Society Collection, Georgetown County Library.

[13] Report, Jan. 23, 1896, to the City Council of Georgetown, Box 4, W. D. Morgan Papers, SCL.

Merriman, W. W. Taylor, and General H. Heath of the Corps of Army Engineers as directors. This same group in 1886 established the Georgetown Building and Loan Association. G. R. Congdon was president, W. D. Morgan vice president, LeGrand G. Walker secretary and treasurer, W. Hazard attorney, G. R. Congdon, W. D. Morgan, L. S. Ehrich, T. M. Merriman, W. W. Taylor, J. B. Steele, G. R. Congdon (of Williamsburg), W. O. Bourke, and Fritz Young directors.[14] Amid this revival of trade and commerce there were no Negro capitalists, nor with the exception of R. I. Lowndes any sons of the pre-war planters.

Philip Rossignol Lachicotte (1824–1896) was one of the most successful of the new men. His ancestors had fled from Santo Domingo to Charleston in 1792. He was first employed in the Charleston engine and boiler works of the McDermid, Carron, and Mustard Company and later connected with the West Point Rice Mill, where his brother Jules was superintendent. He was superintendent of a rice mill at Dean Hall on the Cooper River, before he came in 1857 to Brookgreen to operate a rice mill belonging to the Wards. During the war he served as a lieutenant in Ward's Light Artillery on Waccamaw Neck. On March 24, 1863, he was captured while trying to save the cargo of the blockade runner *Queen of the Wave* and sent north in the *Quaker City* as a prisoner. In May 1871 he bought Waverly plantation from Joseph Blyth Allston and began to develop the rice mill there. When he died in 1896, he left Waverly and the mill to his two sons, St. Julien M. Lachicotte and Francis W. Lachicotte.[15]

Richard Dozier had taken the place of his law partner Colonel Benjamin Huger Wilson, who had died in 1876, as the "politician of the county."[16] Richard Dozier, after being educated in the Winyah Indigo Society school and at Yale, was admitted to the bar in December 1844 and opened a law office in Georgetown in January 1845. He married the daughter of John Exum and, therefore, on the eve of the war had

---

[14] *Charter and Constitution of the Georgetown Building and Loan Association, Organized July 28, 1886* (Charleston, S. C., 1886). Copy in SCL.

[15] *Genealogy of the Rossignol-Lachicotte Family. With Historical Notes of Localities. Investigations by Henry A. Lachicotte* (Douglas, Ga., 1950); O. R., Navy, XIII, 687–690.

[16] T. P. Bailey to T. J. McKie, Aug. 22, 1878, McKie Papers, DUL. Wilson died at Charleston on May 16, 1876, in his fifty-eighth year. See eulogy in "Minute Book of the Georgetown Rifle Guards Club. Organized Aug 20, 1874," pp. 96–100, SCL.

become a Black River planter. He had been a member of the constitutional convention of 1865 and state senator from 1865 to 1868. From 1868 to 1876 he practiced law privately in Georgetown. He had worked with Wilson throughout Reconstruction, led the Georgetown forces for Hampton in 1876, and in the 1880's lent his name and legal talents to all the projects to rejuvenate Georgetown. From 1876 to 1882 he was chairman of the Democratic Party in Georgetown County.[17]

Robert Ellison Fraser (1816–1895) and his brother Samuel Sydney Fraser (1829–1904) were sons of a family long-established in Sumter and Darlington counties. They were not of the Georgetown planting Frasers. Robert E. Fraser, who was thirteen years older than his brother, had come to Georgetown before the war and served as cashier of the bank until he resigned after a difference of opinion with the president over the management of the funds. In order to support his family during the war he had held the office of receiver under the Sequestration Act passed by the Confederate government. Because of rheumatism and his official position, he had not served in the Confederate army. His brother had been a commission merchant in Georgetown prior to the war and during the war a collector of Confederate taxes. Because they had both been civil officeholders under the Confederacy, they had to petition President Johnson for a pardon in 1865. S. S. Fraser had been appointed county treasurer in 1876 and held that office for nine years. S. S. Fraser married first a daughter of Hugh Wilson of Wadmalaw Island and second (in 1883) a daughter of James Rees Ford of Plantersville, which marriages gave him ties to the older planting families. The two brothers were prominent in almost every big business transaction of the 1880's, including the establishment of the Georgetown Ice Company.[18]

George Reynolds Congdon (1834–1909) and Benjamin Ingell Hazard were partners in the firm of Congdon, Hazard and Company, a business with many ramifications in the 1880's. Both were of Rhode Island fami-

---

[17] Charleston *News and Courier*, Dec. 2, 1888; "Genealogy and Life Sketches of the Dozier Brothers," bound volume, 1833–1936, Dozier Family Papers, SCL.

[18] "Samuel Sydney Fraser," *Cyclopedia of Eminent and Representative Men of the Carolinas of the Nineteenth Century* (Madison, Wis., 1892), I, 419–420; S. S. Fraser to Andrew Johnson, Aug. 16, 1865, R. E. Fraser to Andrew Johnson, n.d., RG 94, National Archives; notes in possession of Mrs. Catherine Overton, Georgetown, S. C.

lies whose members had been drawn to Georgetown by the coasting trade. Congdon was the son of William P. Congdon (1806–1880), who had come from Newport, Rhode Island, as a boy of thirteen or fourteen to work with Joseph Thurston and John Stevens. He had strongly opposed nullification and had left the region during the Civil War only to return and establish himself in trade once again.[19] Benjamin Ingell Hazard, whose wife was a native of Taunton, Massachusetts, had come to Georgetown in 1848 from Rhode Island. He was in the mercantile line before the war and during the war engaged in the manufacture of salt at Murrell's Inlet. After the war he joined first with W. P. Congdon and then with G. R. Congdon in the firm of Congdon, Hazard and Company. From his profits he was able to provide his son Walter with the best possible education. After attending the Winyah Indigo School, his son went to Princeton, returned to read law in the office of Richard Dozier, and was admitted to the bar in 1881.[20]

Elliot Waight Hazzard (1842–1896) and William Miles Hazzard were scions of a Beaufort rice-planting family. William Miles had married in 1864 a daughter of George Alfred Trenholm, who invested his blockade-running profits in plantations on the North Santee. After the war the Hazzard brothers tried to plant rice on the North Santee and the Black Rivers, and as rice planters they had become interested in the milling of rice.[21]

Louis S. Ehrich had married Cornelia Sampson and thereby became a partner in the firm of Joseph Sampson and Company. The Sampsons, one of the first Jewish families in Georgetown, had a thriving mercantile business in Georgetown prior to the war. Louis S. Ehrich was intendant from 1886 to 1889, at which time he was characterized as a "bustling, active, and energetic young man." [22]

The Munnerlyns, although a county family, had never risen to the level of the great planting group. They had held minor offices in the county. Benjamin Allston Munnerlyn (1835–1908) had served as a major

[19] SCHM, XXXI (1930), 206; Obituary of W. P. Congdon, Georgetown *Enquirer*, Oct. 13, 20, 1880.

[20] "Walter Hazard," J. C. Hemphill, *Men of Mark in South Carolina* (Washington, D. C., 1908), II, 197–199.

[21] SCHM, XVI (1915), 153; XXXI (1930), 313.

[22] *Georgetown, South Carolina, As It Was, As It Is, As It Will Be.* (Charleston, S. C., 1888).

in the Confederate army, had married Anna Jane Wilson, and was a steamboat agent. From 1892 until his death on May 28, 1908, he was president of the Winyah Indigo Society.[23]

Heiman Kaminski, born in Posen, Prussia, May 24, 1839, came to Charleston as an immigrant in 1854. He attended high school there and in 1856 became a clerk in a merchant house in Georgetown. He fought as a volunteer throughout the war in Company B of the Tenth South Carolina Regiment. Upon dismissal from service at the end of the war, he returned to Georgetown with only two silver dollars in his pocket and started his own business. Heiman Kaminski and Company (his partners were Sol Emanuel and W. W. Taylor), housed in a three-story brick building, were wholesale merchants and Clyde Ship agents. Before his death in 1924 he had the most diversified of business interests. He was in 1907 president of the Kaminski Hardware Company, Willow Bank Boat and Oar Company, Pee Dee Steamboat Company, Taylor-Dickson Medical Dispensary, vice-president of the Bank of Georgetown, and director of the Georgetown Rice Milling Company. He married first Charlotte Virginia Emanuel of a prominent Jewish family of Georgetown and second (in 1885) Rose Baum of another South Carolina Jewish family. There were three sons of the first marriage: Edwin, who died a bachelor; Joseph, who married Esther Sampson (1882–1961); and Nathan, who married Julia Baum. Harold (1886–1951), the son of the second marriage, married Julia B. Pyatt in 1926, thereby merging a new family and an old family.[24]

David Risley (1825–1895), a New Jersey native, began in the lumbering business in Maryland at the age of nineteen. He came to Georgetown in 1855 and bought Waties Point plantation from R. F. W. Allston. During the war he was suspected of being a Unionist, since he left Georgetown and traveled extensively in the West Indies and in South America. With the end of the war he returned to Georgetown, where he

---

[23] *SCHM*, XXXI (1930), 190; "Tribute to Benjamin Allston Munnerlyn, late President of Winyah Indigo Society," Winyah Indigo Society Collection, Georgetown County Library.

[24] "Heiman Kaminski," Hemphill, *op. cit.*, I, 202–203; "Harold Kaminski," David D. Wallace, *History of South Carolina* (New York, 1934), IV, 640; notes in possession of Mrs. Charlotte K. Prevost, Georgetown, S. C.

helped to promote railroading and lumbering. Although there was much jealousy (Leonard Dozier in 1868 had written: "Is Risley and Morgan the only two, well-to-do-men, in Prince Geo. Winyah? God save the state!"), Risley had been elected intendant before his death.[25]

These new men fall into no single pattern. Some were entirely self-made men like Heiman Kaminski. Others were holding on to a pre-war status such as the Hazzard brothers and Lowndes had had. Most, however, were moving up the economic ladder a notch or two, such as Congdon, Hazard, Munnerlyn, Lachicotte, and the Frasers. This was particularly true of the Georgetown Jewish families: the Ehrichs, Sampsons, and Emanuels. Together, no matter what their origin, they represented a new economic power. They cooperated with each other in each new economic venture. Socially they banded together in the Palmetto Club, which was organized in 1883 and incorporated in 1885. This club subscribed to newspapers and journals, bought a billiard table, and held annual banquets. The Palmetto Club's banquet in 1896 in honor of President Grover Cleveland was the culmination of the rise to wealth and respectability on the part of the new elite.[26]

The intellectual leadership of the community was shared by Walter Hazard and William Doyle Morgan. Hazard, the lawyer, with an M.A. from Princeton, a student of the Bible, English literature, sociology, and of the sermons of Frederick D. Maurice and Charles Kingsley, was editor of the Georgetown *Enquirer* from 1880–1889. In the first issue of the newspaper on October 13, 1880, Walter Hazard, the editor and proprietor, expressed his democratic principles: "He must identify himself with the elements of wealth, respectability, honesty and intelligence." He was elected to the state legislature in 1882 but was defeated in 1884. He refused to run in 1886 (he had many personal enemies probably stirred up by his Christian socialism), but he sat again in 1888 and 1890. In 1889 he sponsored a bill to end the use of convicts in phos-

[25] "David Risley," *Cyclopedia of Eminent and Representative Men of the Carolinas,* I, 421–422; D. Risley to W. D. Morgan, Oct. 10, 21, 1891, Box 1, W. D. Morgan Papers, SCL.

[26] *Constitutions and By-Laws of the Palmetto Club of Georgetown, S. C.* (Georgetown, S. C., [1897]), copy in SCL; clippings, W. D. Morgan scrapbook, pp. 122, 222, 298, Winyah Indigo Society Collection, Georgetown County Library.

phate mines and to provide agriculture work on prison farms instead. In 1890 he was a delegate to the anti-Tillman convention. On December 2, 1890, he wrote Morgan from Columbia: "The Tillmanites are swinging partners here in high glee & we are in the *cold!*" In 1892 he was elected to the state senate.[27]

William Doyle Morgan (1853–1938) came from Ireland via New York with his parents John and Mary Morgan. His father died in 1886. He started his career as a bookkeeper but in 1891 organized the Bank of Georgetown, of which he was president until January 1927 when the bank was reorganized.[28] He was a notable intendant and mayor of Georgetown, and he prodded Walter Hazard to introduce a bill in the state legislature incorporating Georgetown as a city. Hazard as corporation counsel continued to advise Morgan and the City Council.[29] Morgan not only sponsored economic and civic improvements but he also founded the Catholic Church in Georgetown. Ultimately, he left his fine library to the University of South Carolina and his scrapbooks, which contain many memorabilia about the history of the region, to the Winyah Indigo Society. When Morgan wrote his history of the Palmetto Club, it was Hazard who passed judgment on the performance.[30]

The new Georgetown elite had supported Wade Hampton in 1876. Hampton had promised that he would protect the Negro's voting rights. These men were willing to honor the spirit of Hampton's promises by working in cooperation with the Negroes in the political sphere. They did so on a fusion basis for at least twenty-four years. As long as the Negro was permitted to vote and did vote, these men could not control absolutely the political power in the county. In 1880 the Negroes were 82 percent of the population of the county. In 1910 they were still 72.3 percent.[31] Since the white population was a distinct minority and as the

[27] "Walter Hazard," Hemphill, *op. cit.*, II, 197–199; "A Brief Sketch of the Life of Walter Hazard by his Daughters," Winyah Indigo Society Collection, Georgetown County Library, Hazard to Morgan, Dec. 2, 1890, Box 1, W. D. Morgan Papers, SCL. The Georgetown *Times* was edited by Josiah Doar during the 1880's.
[28] "William Doyle Morgan," Hemphill, *op. cit.*, I, 278–282.
[29] Hazard to Morgan, April 30, Nov. 29, 1892, Box 2, W. D. Morgan Papers, SCL.
[30] Hazard to Morgan, Oct. 28, 1896, Box 5, W. D. Morgan Papers, SCL.
[31] Samuel D. Smith, "The Negro in Congress, 1870–1901" (PhD dissertation, Univ. of N. C., 1930), p. 4; Department of Commerce, Bureau of the Census, *Negro Population, 1790–1915* (Washington, D. C., 1918), p. 829.

pledge of Hampton was kept, a fusion program was worked out with the Negro leaders.

The agreement to agree in order to disagree was seen in the election of April 6, 1879, for the position of intendant of Georgetown. In that election R. E. Fraser was elected intendant on the "Railroad Ticket" over Dr. Henry F. Heriot on the "Peoples' Ticket." On both tickets the names for wardens' positions were the same. B. A. Munnerlyn and G. R. Congdon were the white wardens named on both tickets and John F. Davis and Van R. Harrison the colored wardens.[32] This agreement to divide offices between the members of the two races was carried over into the countywide elections in 1880. In 1880 the Democrats agreed with the Republicans that each party would nominate certain officers and that there would be no contest in the general elections. The Democrats were given the right to nominate candidates for sheriff, clerk of court, coroner, two county commissioners, and one representative. The Republicans could nominate the senator, one representative, probate judge, school commissioner, and one county commissioner. All of the Republican nominees were Negroes except a white probate judge (R. O. Bush), who served until replaced by a Negro in 1894. George E. Herriot who helped to arrange the fusion was county school commissioner for twenty-two years and county chairman of the Republican Party for many years.[33]

During the period of fusion the Negroes who served in public office were local Negroes, not carpetbaggers.[34] This may help to explain why the policy of fusion worked. Bruce H. Williams, a Negro, was state senator from 1878 to 1888. Along with Thomas J. Reynolds of Beaufort, he was one of the last Negroes to sit in the South Carolina Senate. Williams was succeeded by Richard Dozier in 1888 and by Walter Hazard in 1892. Williams had been born in slavery in Georgetown District. After the war he attended high school in Raleigh, North Carolina, and was then ordained to preach in the African Methodist

[32] Charleston *News and Courier*, April 10, 1879.
[33] Maham W. Pyatt to George B. Tindall, Nov. 21, 1949, quoted in George Brown Tindall, *South Carolina Negroes, 1877–1900* (Columbia, S. C., 1952), pp. 61–64.
[34] Bailey wrote his friend McKie on March 22, 1879: "There is certainly a great change in the negro population, & it is refreshing to be rid of the political scoundrels that have been such pests to our peace & general security. I think their political aspirations are nearly if not entirely at an end." McKie Papers, DUL.

Episcopal Church. After being assigned to Georgetown, he gained great popularity with the people there.[35]

William J. Moultrie, a Negro, was elected state representative in 1880 and 1882. In 1886 he was named postmaster.[36]

Jonathan A. Baxter was elected in 1884, 1886, and 1888. He had been born free in Charleston in 1858, the son of a shoemaker. His family had moved to Georgetown during his infancy. He was educated in the public schools of Georgetown, became a teacher, and in 1878 served as a commissioner of elections.[37]

Robert B. Anderson was a Negro who had been born and reared in Georgetown County. He was there educated and became a school teacher. On November 25, 1890, the *News and Courier* commented that he "has never taken any officious part in politics." He served for a time as one of the town wardens before serving four terms in the state legislature, being elected in 1890, 1892, 1894, and 1896. After being a member of the state constitutional convention of 1895, he was appointed postmaster at Georgetown. In this position he "avoided any friction with the white employees and the public generally. He served out his term of office and retained the respect of the community." [38]

John W. Bolts was the last of the Georgetown Negroes to serve in the state legislature, being elected in 1898 and 1900 but defeated in 1902. Bolts, the last Negro to sit in the state legislature, was an obscure figure who "did nothing during his term of office to cause any friction between the whites and blacks."[39]

Fusion had worked longer in Georgetown County than in any other South Carolina county because of the willingness of the white population to continue the arrangement and also of the Negro community to supply the necessary leadership. The latter depended upon the educational opportunities provided.

The important fact for the success of fusion was that the Negro office-

[35] Charleston *News and Courier*, Dec. 1, 1884.

[36] Clipping, W. D. Morgan scrapbook, p. 46, Winyah Indigo Society Collection, Georgetown County Library.

[37] Charleston *News and Courier*, Dec. 1, 1884.

[38] Charleston *News and Courier*, Nov. 25, 1890; Maham W. Pyatt to George Tindall, Nov. 21, 1949, quoted in Tindall, *op. cit.*, p. 61.

[39] Tindall, *op. cit.*, p. 61.

holders were all after 1876 locally produced. Under the School Act of 1878, which revised the free public school system in the state, the county school commissioner was still elected, but the other two members of the county board were to be chosen by the state board.[40] These three then named the trustees for each school district. Although the strides were never great, G. E. Herriot obviously looked after the education of his fellow Negroes. In the scholastic year 1882 there were forty-four schools in the county with sixteen white teachers and thirty colored teachers. The average salary for a male teacher was $27.05 per month. The school year was an average of four and one-half months. There were 412 white and 1,785 colored students.[41] Although during the period from 1878 to 1895 the expenditure per white child increased whereas that for the Negro child fell, the state did try to live up to Hampton's promises with respect to education for the Negroes. The state did retain and consolidate the system which originated during Reconstruction, but it was not extended markedly. Between 1880 and 1900 there was a decrease in Negro illiteracy from 78.5 to 52.8, proof that some progress was being made.[42]

Most important was the continuation of Negro leadership provided by the preachers and teachers. Robert B. Anderson, a good example of a Georgetown Negro who supplied leadership while carrying on his profession as a teacher, served in the state legislature and in the constitutional convention of 1895 while living on his salary as a school teacher. In the convention of 1895 Anderson introduced a resolution for the compulsory attendance at school of all children seven to twelve, but his proposal ran headlong into growing white supremacy sentiment and was lost.[43] Anderson also spoke against leaving the control of the industrial and normal school at Claflin under the Methodist Episcopal Church North. He objected to the school's being under the control of a board of Northerners who did not teach the students to be in sympathy "with the great interests of the South." Anderson wanted his race

[40] Statutes at Large, XIV, 23–25, 339–348, 574–584.
[41] South Carolina, Resources and Population. Institutions and Industries (Charleston, S. C., 1883), pp. 545–546.
[42] Joel Williamson, After Slavery (Chapel Hill, N. C., 1965), p. 238.
[43] Journal of the Constitutional Convention of the State of South Carolina . . . 1895 (Columbia, S. C., 1895), pp. 127, 308.

to be educated, but he wanted an education that would fit the Negro into a Southern Society.[44]

The year 1895 was a dividing line in the field of education within the state. Tillman saw a need to educate the whites while shortchanging the Negroes. It was after 1895 that the discrepancy grew between the education provided for the two races, a policy that continued until the 1950's when Governor James F. Byrnes established a crash program to bring about an equality of condition in the separate school systems.[45]

The policy of fusion was ultimately undermined in the same way that Wade Hampton's politics and prestige and power were undermined, by an erosion of public opinion that took place in the state. The erosion began with the passage in 1882 of the eight-box election law, which made the voting procedure more complicated and thereby permitted election officials the opportunity for fraud. When the state courts failed to prosecute white officials for frauds in 1883 and 1884, another step toward Negro disfranchisement had been taken. Through such methods the Republican vote in the state was cut from 91,870 in 1876 to 13,740 in 1888. The decline in Georgetown County Republican votes was not as sharp.[46]

The 1880's was a decade of extreme election turbulence. The story can be followed in the records of the national House of Representatives, for on at least five occasions the elections of South Carolina congressmen were challenged before the House. In every case the national House awarded the election to the Republican claimant. As the decisions were always made late in the session, these South Carolina Negro congressmen became less and less effective. In 1878 John S. Richardson defeated Rainey for the seat from the First Congressional District. In 1880 the state board of canvassers declared Richardson elected over Samuel Lee, but a congressional investigation was held. Lee had charged that in

---

[44] *Columbia Daily Register,* Nov. 17, 1895.

[45] Simkins and Woody state that during the scholastic year 1894–1895 thrice as much was spent by the state for the maintenance in school of each white child as was spent for each Negro child. By 1927 the expenditures for white schools had become eight times greater than those for Negro schools and the per capita expenditure nine times greater. F. B. Simkins and R. H. Woody, *South Carolina During Reconstruction* (Chapel Hill, N. C., 1932), p. 443n. Their information came from *Reports and Resolutions, 1897,* pp. 262, 274–275; *ibid., 1927,* II, 69, 77.

[46] Tindall, *op. cit.,* pp. 69–73.

Georgetown County the commissioners of election had illegally refused to count the votes at the Upper Waccamaw, Lower Waccamaw, Santee, Sampit, Choppee, and Pee Dee polls; only the Georgetown box had been counted. J. W. Tarbox, the Democratic chairman of the county board of commissioners, swore that these boxes had been thrown out because they had either been stuffed or had been delivered without a written certificate authorizing delivery by the bearer. Lee was declared elected.[47] In February 1882 the state was gerrymandered; all the Negro areas were lumped into one congressional district, the Seventh. This was the strangest gerrymander of them all, for it wound along the coast from Beaufort to the Santee River, omitting Charleston, and then included the Santee River basin, a part of Sumter District, and part of Georgetown County. In 1882 a white Republican, E. W. M. Mackey, was elected; in 1884 the Negro Robert Smalls. In 1886 William Elliott of Beaufort was declared the winner after additional charges of fraud in Georgetown County.[48] There was another contested election case in this district in 1888, but apparently on this occasion there were no charges of fraud in Georgetown County.[49]

The trend to disfranchise the Negro was made permanent in the 1890's when the Tillman movement in the state succeeded in rewriting the constitution in 1895. Mississippi in 1890 had incorporated into her new constitution an "understanding clause" as a requirement for voting. She had then declared her constitution in effect although it was never presented to the voters of the state for ratification. When the call came for a South Carolina convention in 1895, many saw that the results in South Carolina would be similar.[50]

[47] House Miscellaneous Documents, *Cases of Contested Elections in the House of Representatives, Forty-Seventh Congress from 1880 to 1882, Inclusive*, IX (47th Cong., 2d Sess., 1882–1883), 526–531.

[48] House Miscellaneous Documents, *Digest of Contested-Election Cases arising in the Forty-eighth, Forty-ninth, and Fiftieth Congresses*, IV (50th Cong., 2d Sess., 1888–1889), 670–671, 721–724.

[49] House Miscellaneous Documents, *Digest of the Contested-Election Cases in the Fifty-first Congress*, XVI (51st Cong., 2d Sess., 1890–1891), 505–580. For a good general account of the significance of these congressional changes see William Cooper, *South Carolina Conservatives* (Baltimore, Md., 1967), pp. 103–108.

[50] Georgetown voted 35 for and 1,164 against the convention. Charleston *News and Courier*, Nov. 14, 1894.

The Republicans called a meeting for Columbia on February 6, 1895. The ministers of the Negro churches throughout the state organized a registration campaign during the spring in order to rally the Negro voters.[51] One of the few voices raised by a white man was that of Colonel John J. Dargan of Sumter, who wrote to the Columbia *State*, March 16, 1895, urging a continuation of what had been Hampton's program and pointing to Georgetown as the most encouraging example of the success of that program. He wrote that Hampton himself in Congress had held up Georgetown and Beaufort as two examples of what his policies had succeeded in doing for South Carolina.[52]

Georgetown elected once again a fusion ticket to represent the county in the convention: Robert B. Anderson with two white men, E. F. Mathews (a farmer at Sampit) and John Harleston Read III.[53] There were only six Negroes in the convention, and they led the attack upon the report of the committee on suffrage, which dealt with the most critical issue. Miller of Beaufort who led off for the Negroes referred to the words of Henry Laurens and Charles Pinckney for vindication of the rights of the Negro race. Anderson spoke of the progress that had been made during the preceding thirty years: "I am constrained to raise my voice in protest against the passage by this convention of the political scheme . . . proposed by the committee on suffrage. A scheme that will forever rivet the chain of disfranchisement upon the colored people of South Carolina. A scheme that was conceived in equity [iniquity?] and born in sin." [54] The final vote on the "understanding clause" was 116 for and 7 against, with only two white men voting with five of the Negroes.[55] One of the white men was John Harleston Read III, who explained his vote in this fashion:

My reason for voting "no" on the question of adopting the Constitution as a whole is: I have been from the beginning opposed to the understanding clause in the Article on Suffrage, believe it will be upset if tested in the United States Court, believe it opens the door for fraud,

[51] Charleston *News and Courier*, Feb. 7, May 4–9, 1895.
[52] Quoted in Tindall, *op. cit.*, pp. 78–79.
[53] *Journal of the 1895 Convention*, pp. 5, 738. See also George Brown Tindall, "The South Carolina Constitutional Convention of 1895" (MA thesis, Univ. of N. C., 1948).
[54] Quoted in Tindall, *op. cit.*, pp. 83, 85.
[55] *Ibid.*, p. 725.

and think it unnecessary, in as much as other provisions in the Article, which are beyond suspicion of unfairness, will accomplish the desired end, i. e., securing white supremacy.[56]

Read was undoubtedly trying to live by the idea of fusion, to remain true to the forces that had sent him to the convention. The Constitution of 1895 was declared in force without submission to the people.

By October 1896 it was reported that under this constitution 50,000 whites had registered to vote, but only 5,500 Negroes. Only in Georgetown County did the Negroes have a majority, and there it was only 861 to 814, a majority shortly to be wiped out.[57] In the face of these facts, the Republicans tried to organize and fight back. A meeting was held in Columbia in April 1896, which George E. Herriot attended for Georgetown County.[58] In 1897 George Murray presented a memorial to the state legislature signed by 355 citizens asking that the "so-called" Constitution of 1895 be re-examined.[59] But after the United States Supreme Court in 1898 in *Williams* v. *Mississippi* had given its approval to the Mississippi constitutional provisions, there was little hope that the Negroes could prevail against the South Carolina constitutional changes.[60] South Carolina Negroes would have to wait until 1947 when Judge Waties Waring in the case of *Elmore* v. *Rice* restored the importance of their voices by admitting them to the Democratic primaries.[61]

Although there had been little violence in Georgetown since Reconstruction, there was always tension that could erupt into violence. The eruption occurred on Saturday, September 29, 1900. In suppressing this eruption the dominant local white element also put an end to the policy of fusion. On that Saturday Deputy Sheriff J. C. Scurry had called on John Brownfield, a Negro barber, in his shop to collect the poll tax. Brownfield shot Scurry, who died shortly thereafter. Brownfield was

---

[56] *Ibid.*, p. 727. John Harleston Read II had written before the war a masterly report against efforts to interfere with the liberty of free colored persons. Charleston *Courier,* Sept. 3, 1866.

[57] Tindall, *op. cit.,* p. 88.

[58] Charleston *News and Courier,* April 15, 1896.

[59] Tindall, *op. cit.,* p. 90.

[60] "Williams v. Mississippi," 170 U. S. 213 (1898).

[61] "Elmore v. Rice," 72 F. Supp. 516 (1947). See V. O. Key, Jr., *Southern Politics in State and Nation* (New York, 1949), pp. 628–629.

apprehended by a Negro policeman and lodged in the local jail. When rumors spread among the Negroes that the whites intended to lynch Brownfield, they gathered on Sunday to the number of 1,000 and walked through the streets shouting "Save John," threatening at the same time to burn down the town if any harm befell him. The colored women, armed with hoes and rice hooks, were particularly menacing. Mayor W. D. Morgan, with Colonel J. R. Sparkman and Alderman Jonathan Baxter, tried to calm the Negroes and urged them to disperse. Captain S. M. Ward and the Georgetown Rifle Guards were held in readiness in the Armory but were not used. Some thought the failure to show force on Sunday permitted the repetition of a large gathering on Monday which was as threatening as that of the day before. The Mayor issued a proclamation commanding all to stay at home and consulted with the Negro leaders: Alderman Baxter, School Commissioner Herriot, William Woodbury, and J. L. Mitchell. He also met with a group of the "best citizens," referred to in the dispatches as an advisory board, consisting of Colonel J. R. Sparkman, Major B. A. Munnerlyn, Captain S. M. Ward, S. S. Fraser, J. B. Steele, H. H. Gardner, G. R. Congdon, L. S. Ehrich, Senator LeGrand G. Walker, Alderman Mark Moses, and F. G. Tarbox. The latter group unanimously urged the Mayor to wire the Governor for four companies and a Gatling gun. They wanted an overwhelming display of force to produce a moral effect upon the local Negroes. The Governor promptly issued orders to the Sumter Light Infantry to proceed to Georgetown and placed three companies in Charleston under the orders of the Mayor of Georgetown. The Sumter company arrived that evening and was met by the Georgetown Rifle Guards under Captain Ward and the Hampton Imperial Guards, a cavalry group of Sampit, under Captain B. O. Bourne. The next morning Major Schachte arrived from Charleston on the train via Lanes with Hotchkiss and Gatling guns. A parade was planned for 11 o'clock on Tuesday morning to show "that the white man was in the saddle." After the parade a mayor's court tried six women and three men as ringleaders of the movement, and they were sentenced to pay fines or to serve on the chain gangs. The main point made on that October 2 was that the white population of Georgetown could depend upon overt support from the white population of the rest of the state. Fusion was dead.[62]

In spite of the fusion, there had always been a feeling among most of the whites that the white man alone should rule. This feeling reappeared again and again in the letters of the Georgetown doctor and druggist, Thomas Pearce Bailey (1832–1904). On March 15, 1878, he had written to his upcountry friend, T. J. McKie of Edgefield County, that the white men must rule America and that the Negro would become a cipher. This could only come about in South Carolina if the upcountry helped the lowcountry. In union within the state there was strength.[63] A letter of August 22, 1878, indicated that Bailey was a great admirer of General Gary's "straightoutism," that is, the whites should not cooperate with the Negroes in political movements. "The late course of the Radical Convention is so disgusting that I think the coalition party are surely convinced by this time, that it is all color line, and there is no hope except in uncompromising Democratic principles—I think our own Hampton must have changed his views somewhat ere this—Poor old Georgetown is in a hopeless condition—We are like a ship without a rudder and are hopelessly negroized I fear." When Colonel Wilson died, he wrote: "We have no leader and many of the whites, I regret to say are *unbound* i. e. they are not Democratic enough for me." [64] On April 7, 1880, he was hoping that "S. C. has crushed and will for all time wipe out negro government." [65] On July 29, 1880, upon Jefferson Davis's reappearance in public life, he commented: "Our cause is lost but the principles for which we fought must reassert themselves at some future day. . . . Are we not about to realize these utterances?" [66] They were realized ultimately, but in 1900, not in 1880. In 1889 Dr. James R. Sparkman wrote down his views on the "Negro question." He was quite convinced that the civilizing tendencies of slavery had been stripped

[62] Charleston *News and Courier*, Oct. 2, 3, 1900; Columbia *The State*, Oct. 1, 2, 3, 1900; Yorkville *Enquirer*, Oct. 6, 1900; copy of proclamation, Oct. 1, 1900, Box 11, W. D. Morgan Papers, SCL.

[63] T. P. Bailey to T. J. McKie, March 15, 1878, McKie Papers, DUL.

[64] Same to same, Aug. 22, 1878, McKie Papers, DUL.

[65] Same to same, April 7, 1880, McKie Papers, DUL.

[66] Same to same, July 29, 1880, McKie Papers, DUL.

away and that the Negro was reverting to his natural barbarous state.[67] This was a pessimistic mood permeating that group which had believed most in paternalism. With such sentiments as those of Bailey and of Sparkman being nurtured by the new imperialism of the 1890's, it is amazing that fusion lasted so long. In the end, of course, it was the rest of the state that restored white rule to Georgetown, as Bailey had predicted.

After 1900 the county was, like the rest of the state, in the hands of the white population, even though in Georgetown county a few federal offices remained in Negro hands. Anderson continued as postmaster. In the face of such a large majority of Negroes, the whites had to maintain a solid front, which meant a one-party political system with primaries barred to the Negroes. When the national Republican Party in 1904 endorsed a plank urging a reduction in representation in Congress when discrimination against Negroes occurred (that is, to enforce the second section of the Fourteenth Amendment), the state turned more ardently to the Democratic Party. The national Democratic convention of the same year adopted the following plank: "The race question has brought countless woes to this country. The calm wisdom of the American people should see to it that it brings no more. To revive the dead and hateful race and sectional animosities in any part of our common country means confusion, destruction of business, and the reopening of wounds now happily healed. North, South, East, and West have but recently stood together in line of battle, from the walls of Peking to the hills of Santiago, and as sharers of a common glory and a common destiny we should share fraternally the common burdens."[68] Thus, the politics of a solid South Carolina emerged.

[67] Dr. James R. Sparkman, "The Negro," *The Origins of Segregation*, ed. Joel Williamson (Boston, Mass., 1968), pp. 64–70.

[68] Quoted in a book by a Georgetown Negro. William A. Sinclair, *The Aftermath of Slavery, A Study of the Condition and Environment of the American Negro* (Boston, Mass., 1905), pp. 305–306, 311.

XXI

THE RICH YANKEES

In 1925 Francis Pendleton Gaines wrote *The Southern Plantation, A Study in the Development and the Accuracy of a Tradition.* The theme of the book is that American society in the late nineteenth century developed a plantation myth. There were several factors at work both in the South and in the North that nourished the myth. As a flood of immigrants came from abroad, the old American stock sought more eagerly for their roots. In the South that search quite naturally led back to the plantation past. It was in the 1890's that so many of the memory groups were born, including not only the Daughters of the American Revolution but also the United Daughters of the Confederacy. The Arthur Manigault Chapter of the U. D. C. was founded in Georgetown on May 2, 1896. That year this group joined with the Confederate Veterans to celebrate Confederate Memorial Day (May 10), which celebration established a pattern for the annual observances. The day began with the tolling of bells. In the afternoon there were public addresses, the singing of the "Bonnie Blue Flag" and "Dixie," and a parade, made up of Marion's Men of Winyah, the Hampton Imperial Guards, and the Georgetown Rifle Guards, who marched to the Confederate monument which had been erected at the very center of the town in the cross roads of Broad and Highmarket streets. The local chapter of the U. D. C. assumed the task of locating and marking the graves of Confederate soldiers. The aim of such a group was to glorify the antebellum South.[1]

It was ironic that the North helped to nourish and to transform the plantation myth into a new reality. The Northern industrialists were rich and in search of status. There was money enough to buy anything. Lord Duveen has told the story of how he sold old masters to the new millionaires after they had bought horses and yachts and magnificent homes.[2] Cleveland Amory in *The Last Resorts* has vividly described the life in the "cottages" of Newport, the Berkshires, and Palm Beach.[3] But where could an American millionaire find an aristocracy? Louis Hartz has written that the Yankee millionaire in seeking to find an aristocracy had several alternatives: "He might go to Europe outright and possibly end up in the House of Lords as William Waldorf Astor did, or he might marry off his daughter to purchasable European nobility as Collis P. Huntington did. He might even follow the path of Carnegie and buy an Old World castle, or the path of William Randolph Hearst and bring one all the way home."[4] Some, however, merely settled for Southern plantations.

The tendency to look backward was stimulated by the centennial of the founding of the nation. The phenomenon began with the 1876 celebration in Philadelphia. It was continued by other festivities, culminating with those of 1889. A great ball was held in New York City to honor the one-hundredth anniversary of Washington's inauguration. Ward McAllister, the social arbiter of the Four Hundred, in a planning session for the ball with Mrs. Cornelius Vanderbilt, discovered that they were both descendants of the Marion family of South Carolina and that McAllister was a connection of the Wards of Waccamaw. The result of this conversation was not only a ball in New York but also the marking of Marion's grave in South Carolina.[5] This story was typical of the day when new families were searching for old roots.

[1] *For Love of a Rebel* (Charleston, S. C., 1964), pp. 190–192. The Confederate monument has since been moved to the Baptist cemetery on Church Street.

[2] Samuel N. Behrman, *Duveen* (New York, 1952).

[3] Cleveland Amory, *The Last Resorts* (New York, 1952).

[4] Louis Hartz, *The Liberal Tradition in America* (New York, 1955), p. 221.

[5] Newspaper clippings in W. D. Morgan scrapbook, Winyah Indigo Society Collections, I, 175, 182, Georgetown County Library. In 1889 the Eclectic Club of Georgetown celebrated the 100th anniversary of the inauguration of George Washing-

A happy accident also drew attention to Georgetown. President Grover Cleveland, who was fond of hunting ducks, paid a visit in 1894 to General Edward Porter Alexander, who had acquired South Island. General Alexander with his interests in railroading was representative of the New South. While hunting the President was tossed from a duck hunter's skiff by a stiff gale. This gale proved to be no ill wind for Georgetown, for it also carried news of the President's rescue. The nation thereby became informed of the fine duck shooting available in Georgetown waters.[6] The rich Yankees began to fall in love with the ready-made plantations, all with historic pasts and with appropriate settings for their gentlemanly sports.[7]

The desire of the rich Yankees for Southern plantations coincided with the final decline of the rice industry. There had been a slight revival of the rice industry toward the end of the century. A few men had seen the possibility of putting a number of the plantations together and operating them under the direction and financial control of joint-stock companies. In the 1880's Philip R. Lachicotte tried this method on the Waccamaw, using Lachicotte and Sons as the corporate device.[8] James Louis LaBruce formed the Guendalos Company to work Pee Dee River plantations,[9] while Samuel Mortimer Ward formed the S. M. Ward Company to work those on the North Santee.[10] These three companies accumulated plantations from the hands of those tired of the effort. These companies, which combined planting with rice milling in order to cut costs, along with a few notable individuals, principally Mrs.

---

ton. On that occasion the members thanked William Elliott (the Congressman for the Seventh District) for getting the club a set of the *Official Records of the War Between the States*. "Constitution and Minutes of the Eclectic Club of Georgetown, 1883–1889," pp. 143–145, SCL.

[6] Clippings in W. D. Morgan scrapbook, Winyah Indigo Society Collection, I, 234–241, Georgetown County Library.

[7] The following article had also drawn attention to this section of South Carolina. Coyne Fletcher, "In the Lowlands of South Carolina," *Frank Leslie's Popular Monthly*, March 1891, pp. 280–288.

[8] In 1896 on the death of the father Francis Williams Lachicotte and St. Julian M. Lachicotte took over as equal partners. Alberta Morel Lachicotte, *Georgetown Rice Plantations* (Columbia, S. C., fourth printing with revisions 1967), pp. 33–36.

[9] There were three original partners: Louis Claude Lachicotte, Francis W. Lachicotte, and James Louis LaBruce, the son of Joshua Ward LaBruce. After 1899 LaBruce bought out the two Lachicotte brothers. *Ibid.*, p. 111.

[10] There were three partners in this firm: S. M. Ward, St. Julian M. Lachicotte, and A. A. Springs. *Ibid.*, p. 178.

Pringle at Chicora Wood, kept alive the rice industry until after the turn of the century. Mrs. Pringle in *A Woman Rice Planter* has summed up these loving efforts in a dying rice world.[11]

These efforts, however, ultimately failed. The generation of Negroes who grew up after slavery did not understand the intricacies of rice culture, nor did they have the patience. By the end of the century there was also competition from the states of Louisiana, Texas, and Arkansas. There was thus an overproduction of rice. Nor did the planters of the Southwest suffer from freshets in the streams and storms along the coast. The draining of fields and the destruction of forests in the upper part of the state caused freshets to rise higher and become more frequent and therefore more damaging. Duncan Clinch Heyward, who wrote the final chapter on the South Carolina rice industry in his *Seed from Madagascar*, described the storms that hit the Carolina coast as the ultimate blows.[12]

The hurricanes of August 27 and October 13, 1893, September 26, 1894, September 28, 1898, September 20, 1906, October 19, 1910, and August 27, 1911, provided the *coup de grâce* to the industry. The 1893 storms were the most violent to hit the Carolina coast. During the October 1893 hurricane the Arthur Belin Flagg family was washed out to sea.[13] The other storms were almost as severe. The cost of rebuilding the dikes was prohibitive. Mrs. Pringle wrote after the September storm of 1906: "I fear the storm drops a dramatic, I may say tragic, curtain on my career as a rice planter." At the end of the year and the end of her book she wrote: "The rice-planting, which for years gave me the exhiliration of making a good income myself, is a thing of the past now—the banks and trunks have been washed away, and there is

[11] Patience Pennington [Mrs. Elizabeth W. Allston Pringle], *A Woman Rice Planter* (Cambridge, Mass., 1961). C. J. Huske had written to A. P. Butler, Commissioner of Agriculture, Jan. 16, 1884, suggesting that the rice fields be turned into carp ponds to supply a cheap source of food. "Minute Book, State Board of Agriculture," pp. 124–131, S. C. Archives.

[12] Duncan Clinch Heyward, *Seed from Madagascar* (Chapel Hill, N. C., 1937), pp. 213–214, 220, 239–245.

[13] *Family Records of the Descendants of Gershom Flagg . . .*, compiled by N. G. Flagg and L. C. S. Flagg (Quincy, Ill., 1907), p. 128; newspaper clippings in W. D. Morgan scrapbook, Winyah Indigo Society Collection, I, 272–274, 317, Georgetown County Library.

no money to replace them." [14] Thus the rice economy collapsed between 1893 and 1911. Symbolic of this collapse was the decline of the churches of Prince Frederick on the Pee Dee, All Saints on the Waccamaw, and the Church of the Messiah on the North Santee. The last was abandoned during this period.

The purchase of rice plantations by outsiders which began in the 1890's went on until the 1930's. In the years after 1900 the rich Yankees came to seek what their fathers had destroyed. This, the second Yankee invasion of Georgetown county, strengthened the national myth about the glories of the Southern plantation past, a movement of which the film *The Birth of a Nation* was an early teaser and *Gone With the Wind* the final statement. It was under this blanket of national public opinion that the solid South was put together. These Yankees had no desire to reform the South in any way.

Bernard Baruch, a native South Carolinian, led the way in the purchase of the plantations. He had made a great fortune through speculations on the New York stock market. Through his mother's family, the Wolfes, he was connected with the Kaminskis and more indirectly with the other Georgetown Jewish families. By 1905 he had put together all of the plantations at the foot of Waccamaw Neck, recreating what he called Hobcaw Barony. His 17,000 acres were, however, more extensive than the original barony. He eventually built a spacious new dwelling in the white-columned manner. [15]

Between 1906 and 1931 Dr. Isaac E. Emerson bought Bannockburn, Oak Hill, Prospect Hill, Clifton, Forlorn Hope, Rose Hill, and Fairfield. Fairfield was the last of the Alston properties to pass out of the family's hands. This new estate with the home at Prospect Hill as its center was called Arcadia. In 1936 it became the property of Dr. Emerson's grandson George Vanderbilt. [16]

In 1930 Mr. and Mrs. Archer M. Huntington bought Laurel Hill, Springfield, Brookgreen, and The Oaks, which they combined and called Brookgreen. Huntington built a winter home on the ocean side of his property in a modified Spanish style. From the beach this low-

[14] Pennington, *op. cit.*, pp. 399, 446.
[15] Lachicotte, *op. cit.*, pp. 9, 13–16; *News and Courier*, May 17, 1931.
[16] Lachicotte, *op. cit.*, pp. 18, 21–26; *News and Courier*, Aug. 28, 1930.

lying (towers did obtrude), brick, and cement structure looked like a
Moorish castle amid the sands of Africa. The name of the home is
Atalaya, which in Spanish means "a tower overlooking the sea." On the
Waccamaw side of the property the sculptress Anna Hyatt Huntington
created a formal garden, where Joshua John Ward's had once stood, in
which she displayed her sculpture and those of her American contem-
poraries. Together the Huntingtons forged a new and unique estate
which at the death of Huntington became the property of the people of
South Carolina, supported by a non-profit corporation which he had
established, called Brookgreen Gardens, which is a society for the
study of southeastern flora and fauna. Brookgreen has become the most
frequented tourist attraction in South Carolina, drawing over 300,000
visitors annually.[17]

In 1925 Dr. Henry Norris of Pennsylvania bought Litchfield plantation.
Dr. Norris and his wife were more permanent residents than the other
Northern owners, often remaining until June on their plantation.[18] In
1926 William S. Ellis of Bryn Mawr, Pennsylvania, bought Turkey Hill,
Oatland, and Willbrook. The property, which included two miles of
ocean frontage along Magnolia Beach, was used for duck and quail
hunting.[19] In 1926 Dr. J. D. Paxton of Lynchburg, Virginia, bought the
lower half of Waverly plantation, the St. Julian Lachicotte home on the
site which had the best view commanding the Waccamaw River.[20]

An estate almost as large as that of Baruch's was assembled along the
Pee Dee and on Sandy Island by Jesse Metcalf, the nephew of Senator
Jesse Metcalf of Rhode Island. In 1927 Metcalf bought Bates Hill,
Glenmore, Holly Grove, Hasty Point, Breakwater, and Belle Rive. He
later added Sandy Knowe, Oak Lawn, Pipe Down, Taylor Hill, Ruin-
ville, and Oakhampton on Sandy Island. And still later he bought
William Ellis's estate on the Waccamaw. At Hasty Point he erected a
brick hunting lodge with stables and kennels for his polo ponies, fox

[17] Lachicotte, op. cit., pp. 55, 59, 61–62; News and Courier, June 7, 1931.
[18] Lachicotte, op. cit., pp. 43–44, 50; News and Courier, Aug. 16, 1931.
[19] Lachicotte, op. cit., p. 52.
[20] News and Courier, July 26, 1931. After Dr. Paxton's time, the Ancrums and
the Ruffs owned this plantation and called it Rossdhu. Now under the current ownership of Theron Hines this half is called Lower Waverly. The northern half which
contained the rice mill remained in the hands of the Lachicotte family. Lachicotte,
op. cit., pp. 27–29.

hounds, and bird dogs. He sped between his many plantations in a luxurious speed boat capable of making forty-five miles per hour. An international sportsman, he raced his horses in the Grand National at Aintree, England. In 1936 he sold his properties because of his unwillingness to abide by the local prohibition laws.[21]

Thomas G. Samworth of Newcastle, Delaware, purchased Exchange plantation, but sold it in 1945 when he acquired Dirleton.[22] Dirleton had been bought in 1915 by three Upton brothers of Norfolk, Virginia, who wanted to try truck farming, but they soon became interested in the recreational aspects of their property. In 1932 they sold the plantation to Louis Laval Hamby, a Washington attorney, whose wife was a granddaughter of Dr. James R. Sparkman, who had built the home at Dirleton before the Civil War.[23]

In 1916 Jacqueline S. Holliday of Indianapolis, Indiana, bought Nightingale Hall. She built a two-story frame house which she used during the quail-hunting season.[24]

In 1935 Walker Inman, half-brother of Doris Duke, bought Greenfield plantation on the Black River, where he built a handsome home. He preferred Georgetown, among Southern winter resorts, because of its excellent airport where he expected to construct a hangar for his two planes.[25] There were two other hunting estates along the Black River. William E. Fertig of Titusville, Pennsylvania, was at Ponemah.[26] Winea (pronounced wee-nee) Lodge, at the site of the first Anglican church, was owned in 1931 by Carl L. Amos of Syracuse, New York, and H. B. Mebane of Knoxville, Tennessee.[27]

[21] Lachicotte, op. cit., pp. 52, 54, 131; News and Courier, March 22, 1931. "Jesse Metcalf to Leave State," 1936 newspaper clipping in possession of Mrs. Richard G. White, Charleston, S. C. Williams Furniture Company of Sumter, S. C. eventually bought all of the lands that had been owned by Metcalf. In 1960 Williams Furniture Company sold the present Hasty Point house with a few surrounding acres to Philip van Every, former mayor of Charlotte, N. C., the rest of the property being retained for timber harvesting.

[22] Lachicotte, op. cit., pp. 108, 128.

[23] Lachicotte, op. cit., p. 108; News and Courier, May 3, 1931, March 2, 1932.

[24] Lachicotte, op. cit., p. 101.

[25] Lachicotte, op. cit., pp. 89, 92–93; News and Courier, April 12, 1935.

[26] C. S. Murray, "Ponemah," clipping in possession of Mrs. Richard G. White, Charleston, S. C.

[27] C. S. Murray, "Wee Nee, Black River Lodge," News and Courier, 1931, clipping in possession of Mrs. Richard G. White, Charleston, S. C.

Dr. E. W. Hitchcock of Auburn, New York, bought Beneventum in 1916 and sold it after fifteen years to Cornelius J. Rathbourne of Harvey, Louisiana, and Westbury, Long Island. Although a senior at Yale, Rathbourne was a well-known polo player, a friend of James Paul Mills, the son of Paul D. Mills who lived at Windsor lower down the Black River. Rathbourne and young Mills hoped to make Georgetown a center for polo comparable to Aiken and Camden, other South Carolina winter resorts.[28]

In 1912 Charles W. Tuttle, of Auburn, New York, bought Mansfield plantation, which in 1931 he sold to the Philadelphia banker Robert L. Montgomery, the owner of a large hunt stable. Mrs. Montgomery in 1944 bought Maryville and in 1969 is still living at Mansfield.[29]

Robert Goelet purchased Wedgefield in 1935. He, Walker Inman, and Bernard Baruch also owned quail preserves near Kingstree.[30]

In 1929 Paul D. Mills of New York city purchased Windsor plantation. Mills owned kennels of both fox hounds and deer hounds.[31]

In 1932 Herbert Pulitzer purchased the rice fields of Richmond and leased the hunting rights of Rosemont. Pulitzer came to shoot ducks. William A. Kimbel later bought Richmond Hill and Wachesaw.[32]

In 1930 Radcliffe Cheston of Philadelphia purchased Friendfield, Silver Hill, and Midway on the Sampit River. Since the old house had burned in 1926, he built a new home on the old foundations. Mrs. Cheston, a relative of Paul D. Mills, was the owner of the famous Sacandaga, twice winner of the Maryland Hunt Steeple Chase. Mr. and Mrs. Cheston re-created the beautiful gardens that the Withers family had first planted.[33]

In 1929 Mrs. Henry M. Sage of Albany, New York, signed a ten-year lease to Belle Isle. Mrs. Sage, after her lease expired, bought Dover plantation which she still uses as her winter home.[34]

In 1918 John A. Miller, president of Pennsylvania-Dixie Cement Company bought Estherville. He created a 50-acre deer park and

---

[28] Lachicotte, *op. cit.,* p. 88; *News and Courier,* Feb. 1, May 4, 1931.
[29] Lachicotte, *op. cit.,* pp. 78, 82–84; *News and Courier,* March 1, 1931.
[30] Lachicotte, *op. cit.,* p. 77; *News and Courier,* April 12, 1935.
[31] Lachicotte, *op. cit.,* p. 74; *News and Courier,* Dec. 22, 1929, Sept. 27, 1931.
[32] Lachicotte, *op. cit.,* pp. 67–68; *News and Courier,* April 19, 1932.
[33] Lachicotte, *op. cit.,* p. 138; *News and Courier,* Aug. 2, 1931.
[34] Lachicotte, *op. cit.,* pp. 147, 149, 152–154.

helped to form the Winyah Gun Club. This property was later purchased by George L. Buist of Charleston, the first Charlestonian in some time to buy a Georgetown plantation.[35]

South Island, which had been the property of General E. P. Alexander, by 1911 was in the hands of W. H. Yawkey, the owner of the Boston Red Sox, who built two comfortable club houses and a stable and entertained the great of the baseball world, Ty Cobb, Tris Speaker, and others. He also acquired Cat Island and left the entire estate, which consists of some 20,000 acres, to his son Thomas A. Yawkey.[36]

In 1927 Mrs. William Gouverneur Ramsay of Wilmington, Delaware, purchased Cat Island and Belle Island, the latter later becoming the estate of her daughter Mrs. William E. Phelps.[37]

In 1924 R. E. Reeves of Summit, New Jersey, bought Hopewell, Hopeland, and Annandale. This plantation is now operated as a cattle ranch.[38]

In 1912 the Kinloch Gun Club was formed, composed of wealthy Wilmington, Delaware, men. This club bought Wicklow, Pleasant Meadow, Richfield, Milldam, Camp Main, White Oak, and Newland plantations on the North Santee. T. Cordes Lucas was the manager of the Gun Club; a clubhouse was built in 1923. In 1930 the lands were purchased from the club by Eugene Du Pont.[39]

In 1926 William N. Beach bought Rice Hope and the next year added White Oak, LaGrange, and Fawn Hill. In 1935 he acquired Prospect Hill, Retreat, a large part of Dover, and parts of Belle Isle and Mount Hope. The Beach properties later passed in 1956 and 1961 to the Koppers Company and the Williams Furniture Company.[40]

The Santee Gun Club was formed in 1898 on the South Santee. The club bought twelve former rice plantations, amounting to 20,000 acres in the Santee delta.[41]

[35] Lachicotte, *op. cit.*, pp. 155, 158, 173; *News and Courier*, Feb. 15, 1931.
[36] Lachicotte, *op. cit.*, pp. 164, 166; *News and Courier*, Feb. 8, 1931.
[37] Lachicotte, *op. cit.*, pp. 163, 164, 176.
[38] Lachicotte, *op. cit.*, pp. 169–170; *News and Courier*, Dec. 12, 1966.
[39] Lachicotte, *op. cit.*, pp. 178, 181, 183, 190; *News and Courier*, Oct. 3, 1938.
[40] Lachicotte, *op. cit.*, pp. 152, 183, 186, 189–190; *News and Courier*, June 14, 1931.
[41] Clipping undated.

Susan Lowndes Allston in 1929, when writing about the recent purchase of Windsor plantation, asked: "And who could wonder at these purchases?" She gave her answer:

Given the means to make it possible, people of taste and intelligence always want to be able to leave the cities' whirl and go to "the retreat of coot and tern." And no more heavenly retreat could be afforded than that of this South Carolina coast. Woods and marshes teem with wild life. Rivers and creeks spread their crystal paths through enchanting scenes. Once more their waters are preferred for travel and jaunts, even as in the early days of the country—with the difference that, instead of the rhythm of the rowing crew, which burst into song, anon of joy, anon of sadness (Song so exquisite that the writer can never, never forget the thrill of it as a child),—instead of anything like that, now a variety of wonderful mechanisms cause the parting of the waters and, when released, the swift little speed boats plunge and dash like race horses. Besides the hunting, the lovely climate and the natural beauty, unencumbered by too much humanity, there is a trace of the grace and romance left by the old regime on the plantations.[42]

By 1931 there was scarcely a plantation left in the hands of native South Carolinians. The final spate of purchases had taken place after the stock market crash of 1929. Money in land was safer than money in stocks. The Yankee owners had become such an important group in the community that the Charleston *News and Courier* ran a series throughout the year 1931 telling the story of these purchases. Their comings and goings became matters of local interest. The *News and Courier* for November 25, 1931, noted that many of the Georgetown plantation owners had already arrived for the winter. Their improvements were watched. Both the Huntington and Baruch homes were ready for occupancy that November, and each had electricity.

In every instance these people wanted to create something beautiful, something reminiscent of an older way of living that had gone out of style in other parts of the country. Here in an almost eighteenth-century backwater they could recover the past. Entertaining could be simple, yet patrician in style. Bernard Baruch entertained Winston Churchill and Franklin D. Roosevelt as well as prominent members of every admini-

[42] *News and Courier*, Dec. 22, 1929.

stration from Wilson to Eisenhower.[43] Robert Goelet and Paul D. Mills
had their homes designed in a neo-colonial style by Simons and Lapham
of Charleston.[44] Dr. Emerson collected coaches and carriages of a by-
gone age which seemed not out of place on the country lanes.[45] The
Norrises of Litchfield provided a new brick wall for the restoration of
All Saints Church.[46] In 1920 Henry Ford disassembled the rice mill at
Fairfield and reassembled it at his museum near Detroit.[47] Mrs. Henry
M. Sage bought the one-hundred-year-old Mendenhall house in New-
berry County and moved it to Belle Isle on the banks of Winyah Bay.
At the expiration of her lease, Mrs. Sage wished to move her home from
Belle Isle to Dover. Although she was not able to do so, she did take
with her the fine wallpaper (on one side of the room the paper depicted
an Indian skirmish and on the other young colonial couples amid a
rustic setting) and the handsome staircase. In 1949 the present house at
Dover was put together from three sources. The residence came from
Woodlawn plantation in St. John's Berkeley which had to be removed to
make way for the flooding of Lake Moultrie; the main doorway, Palladian
window, and balcony came from the Hunter house of Savannah, Georgia;
and the wallpaper and staircase from the Mendenhall house of Newberry.[48] The Montgomerys added touches to Mansfield that were in
keeping with the traditions of that plantation.[49] Most noteworthy of all
was the re-creation of the gardens at Brookgreen.

This Yankee invasion occurred in all parts of the Carolina lowcountry.
These new plantation owners formed in the 1930's the Carolina Plantation Society, which was an "organization consisting primarily of a
group of men from other parts of the country who, in recent years, have

[43] Bernard M. Baruch, *Baruch, The Public Years* (New York, 1960), pp. 167, 177,
190, 299, 315–316. Roosevelt spent the month of April 1944 at Hobcaw. "He finished
and cruised the Pee Dee and Waccamaw Rivers, visited some of the show-place
gardens in the neighborhood, sat in the sun, and managed to sleep ten to twelve
hours every night. He had intended to stay only two weeks, but he enjoyed his visit
so much that he extended it to a month." *Ibid.*, p. 316.

[44] Albert Simons and Samuel Lapham have long been the leading restoration archi-
tects of the Charleston and lowcountry areas.

[45] These are put on display at the time of the spring tours.

[46] Lachicotte, *op. cit.*, p. 25; Henry DeSaussure Bull, *All Saints' Church, Waccamaw* (Columbia, S. C., 1949), p. 55.

[47] Lachicotte, *op. cit.*, p. 25.

[48] Lachicotte, *op. cit.*, pp. 147–154.

[49] Lachicotte, *op. cit.*, pp. 82–84.

acquired these plantations and are trying to restore them somewhat to their former grandeur." [50] Among those who were members in the 1930's from Georgetown County were William N. Beach of Rice Hope, George L. Buist of Estherville, Radcliffe Cheston, Jr., of Friendfield, Eugene Du Pont of Kinloch, Robert Goelet of Wedgefield, Robert L. S. Manigault of Winyah, Robert L. Montgomery of Mansfield, and William E. Phelps of Cat Island.[51]

Without this group the county might not have survived the depression of the 1930's, for they brought a little "New Deal" to Georgetown. Although none of these plantations produced staples, they did provide jobs. Many owners built new homes; all needed staffs. Huntington consciously provided jobs for Negroes by building far more brick walls than any home needed.[52] Metcalf estimated he spent $20,000 a year in the county.[53] Dr. Norris established an infirmary in the Negro village near his plantation where the Negroes might be treated free.[54] These men, however, did not advocate social change. This Yankee Reconstruction was vastly different from that of 1868 to 1877. A paternal attitude was adopted toward the Negroes, not much different from that of the old planters for their slaves. Baruch in his autobiography declared that one reason for establishing his second home was to "do something for the Negro." [55] Although Baruch did not have many Negro tenants, he always tried to strengthen the desire among individual Negroes to stand alone in business or in agriculture. He did believe that the Negro was climbing "both the educational and economic ladder," [56] and from time to time he assisted his efforts.

This invasion quickly came to an end with World War II.[57] The plantation as a reality is disappearing and probably for all time. The International Paper Company and other lumber concerns have bought the pine lands. Georgetown itself has spread over Maryville, Serenity, Richmond,

---

[50] David Doar, *Rice and Rice Planting in the South Carolina Low Country*, ed. E. Milby Burton (Charleston, S .C., 1936), p. 6.

[51] *Ibid.*, pp. 69–70.

[52] *News and Courier*, June 7, 1931.

[53] Newspaper clipping, dated 1936, in possession of Mrs. Richard G. White, Charleston, S. C.

[54] *News and Courier*, Aug. 16, 1931.

[55] Bernard M. Baruch, *Baruch, My Own Story* (New York, 1957), p. 261.

[56] *Ibid.*, p. 274.

[57] *News and Courier*, May 29, 1944.

Willowbank, and Greenwich. Hagley, Lower Waverly, and Litchfield on the Waccamaw are being divided into one suburban development and Windsor on the Black is being divided into another. Annandale has become a cattle farm.[58] Wedgefield and Beneventum are egg farms. Belle Isle is a tourist attraction. Brookgreen is run by a nonprofit foundation and Hobcaw Barony by the Belle W. Baruch Foundation. Litchfield Beach is now famous for its inn and golf course. Mrs. Robert Balding, who inherited Arcadia and Dubourdieu Beach, is in the process of subdividing the latter into beachfront lots with a system of canals and a golf course behind the beach. But the myth of the plantation is still appealing and difficult to destroy. Every spring the Georgetown tours represent a noble effort by the women of the parish church of Prince George Winyah to make the myth an enduring one.

[58] *News and Courier,* Dec. 12, 1966.

XXII

MODERN GEORGETOWN COUNTY

In the New South the factory was considered to be the fulfillment of Southern dreams. A factory would provide jobs, security, prosperity—a way up for the entire community. When the factory did come, according to Wilbur J. Cash in *The Mind of the South*, it was the Southern plantation in a new form.[1] Thus, the pattern of Southern life did not change. There is much truth in such a statement when one looks at the two giant corporations which sparked the economic growth of twentieth-century Georgetown. The twentieth century in Georgetown County has belonged to wood products as the nineteenth century had belonged to rice. The story of the Atlantic Coast Lumber Company covers the first three decades, the story of the Southern Kraft Division of the International Paper Company the years since 1936.

Georgetown businessmen, when searching in the 1880's for alternatives to the culture of rice, had redeveloped the lumbering business, which extended back to the naval stores industry of the 1720's. In 1889 a group of Georgetonians with several men from Atlanta, Georgia, set up the Georgetown Lumber and Manufacturing Company, a forerunner

[1] (Garden City, N. Y., 1954), p. 206.

of the Atlantic Coast Lumber Company.[2] The latter company, formed in May 1899, began to buy up pine lands. On August 21, 1903, the Atlantic Coast Lumber Company was incorporated at a capitalization of one million dollars. The capital to start a Southern business came from lumbermen in other parts of the country. The general manager after 1901 was Ohio born and Pennsylvania educated; he had married the daughter of a lumberman of Minneapolis, who was a leading stockholder in the company.

The principal capitalists behind the venture from Boston and New York in July 1912 sent to Georgetown a Canadian to be president and general manager of the company. What was needed was some system in the operation. A disastrous fire of April 21, 1913, which destroyed two of the mills, made it both obligatory and possible to build a new plant. The new steel-and-concrete plant, which had cost three-quarters of a million to build and was then the largest lumbering manufacturing plant on the east coast, began operations on July 5, 1914. In 1916 the company owned or controlled timber rights on 250,000 acres "bearing about 2,000,000,000 feet of lumber, broad measure," enough "virgin stumpage" for fifty years. This timber was located in eight South Carolina counties and consisted of 75 percent short-leaf yellow pine, 10 percent cypress, and 15 percent other hardwoods, including white oak. The company appointed foremen to run six camps, each of which was equipped with skidders, snakers, and cableways. There were also forty mule and horse teams in scattered areas. Ten percent of the logs were rafted down the rivers to the mill on the Sampit River; the rest were shipped by rail. The central logging railroad was the Georgetown and Western Railroad, which ran to Lanes 36 miles away. In addition to 217 miles of mainline railroad, there were 70 miles of logging roads.

The plant covered fifty-six acres in a bend of the Sampit River. Within the plant, nine miles of standard gauge electric railroad tied the plant operation together. There was a central power plant, three sawmills, dry kilns, planing mill, rip mill, machine shop, dry sheds, turpentine still, car shops, foundry, pattern shop, boiler shop, blacksmith shop, electrical

---

[2] The following account has been drawn from two sources: "Efficiency in the Production of 'Atlantic Coast Soft Pine,' . . . A Story of a System," *American Lumberman* (Jan. 8, 1916), 43–67; Papers of the Atlantic Coast Lumber Co., 1716–1946 (containing about 16,000 Mss. items), SCL.

headquarters, warehouse, and administrative building. An alcohol plant owned and operated by the Du Pont Company bought sawdust from the Atlantic Coast Lumber Company from which alcohol was made.

This company provided the basis for an economic revival which was further stimulated by World War I. Many young Georgetown men joined the armed forces. During the summer of 1917 the Masonic Temple was converted into a barracks. Yates Snowden in his *History of South Carolina* has described South Carolina's contribution to the military victory in France. Although there was no division composed entirely of South Carolinians, individuals did distinguish themselves. Colonel Holmes Buck Springs (1879–1951), who had been born at Bucksville, graduated from The Citadel, and later became a Georgetown business-man, was mentioned in dispatches. First Lieutenant Richard G. White of Georgetown ancestry won the distinguished service cross for "extra-ordinary heroism" at Soissons.[3]

The speculative fever of the nation was shared in Georgetown County during the immediate post-war period. The story of the town of Andrews illustrates the hopes and disappointments. *The Andrews News* in its first issue of January 31, 1918, stated that the town, then eight years old, had 2,000 inhabitants.[4] In 1900 the land upon which Andrews stands had been owned by Edwin Harper, who had already laid out the town of Harpers.[5] About 1905 he sold 600 acres to the Rosemary Land As-sociation, a group of men who intended to create a town situated around the junction of the Georgetown and Western Railroad and the spur track of the Atlantic Coast Lumber Company, known as the Marion branch. In 1912 the two towns of Harpers and Rosemary were consolidated into one town, which was renamed Andrews after Captain Walter Henry Andrews, who had come to Georgetown with the railroad and later became a business and political figure. Through the agency of Andrews, who was the first mayor of the town, and his associates the Seaboard Railroad Company (which had bought the Georgetown and Western

[3] Yates Snowden, *History of South Carolina* (Chicago, Ill., 1920), pp. 1116, 1143; *Independent Republic Quarterly*, II, No. 3 (1968), 20–21.
[4] A file of the *Andrew News* from Jan. 31, 1918, to Sept. 9, 1921 is in the Winyah Indigo Society Collection, Georgetown County Library.
[5] Paul Harper, "The Growth of the Town of Andrews," in the possession of Mr. Samuel Harper, of Andrews, S. C.; "Walter Henry Andrews," *South Carolina and Her Builders*, ed. Ralph E. Grier (Columbia, S. C., 1930), pp. 13, 232.

in 1915) opened a sea level route from Hamlet, North Carolina, to Savannah, Georgia, which passed through Andrews. The railroad shops of the Seaboard and the Atlantic Coast Lumber Company plus wartime prosperity sparked a boom period in the town.

In 1919 in preparation for continued expansion electric light, water, and sewage systems were planned. A tri-county fair of Georgetown, Williamsburg, and Berkeley counties was established as an annual event. The Andrews Bank and Trust Company was organized to help finance the expansion. But then in 1928 misfortune struck when the Seaboard shops were closed and the mechanics and their families were offered jobs elsewhere. Some 700 persons left the town at this time. In 1932, when the shops of the Atlantic Coast Lumber Company were also shut down, the town reached the economic bottom. No town suffered more during the depression.

Georgetown passed through similar phases. The early optimism can be seen in the growth of the banks. The Bank of Georgetown had been founded in 1891 by W. D. Morgan, who was its president throughout its life. Jonathan Ingell Hazard, the brother of Walter Hazard, was the vice president and cashier. In 1904 the Peoples Bank of Georgetown was established by H. W. Fraser, who was its president. Holmes B. Springs had been the organizer in 1913 of the Farmers and Merchants Bank, of which he was the first president. And then in 1919 F. A. Bell became president of the Planters and Mechanics Bank. These banks proceeded to lend money for development secured by mortgages on land. Georgetown's hopes were spelled out in the "Development Edition" of the Georgetown *Times*, August 17, 1923, published in four large sections.[6] By the end of 1929, however, all of the banks had failed.[7] The old Bank of Georgetown (commonly called the "Morgan Bank") was reconstituted in 1929 as a branch of the Peoples State Bank. When the latter failed in 1933, the old Bank of Georgetown went down again with it.[8] The closing of the banks was the greatest blow to the people of the county

[6] Also see Lockwood, Greene & Co., *Industrial Survey of Georgetown, S. C.* (Atlanta, Ga., 1924). Copy in SCL.

[7] The story of the Georgetown banks has been drawn from *The State* ("Bankers' Special"), April 23, 1908; Georgetown *Times*, Aug. 17, 1923. The Andrews Bank and Trust weathered the depression crisis.

[8] Morgan had retired on Jan. 2, 1932. "William Doyle Morgan," *Men of Mark in South Carolina*, ed. J. C. Hemphill (Washington, D. C., 1909), I, 278–282.

since the defeat in 1865. The ensuing unemployment and poverty of all ranks of people were unbelievable, even for the United States of that day. It was in 1929, 1930, and 1931, that the final sale of the plantations took place. In 1932 the Atlantic Coast Lumber Company stopped cutting timber and not only closed its shops in Andrews but also its plant in Georgetown.

To talk to any person who lived through the years 1932 to 1937 in Georgetown is to secure first-hand accounts of depression experiences. There can be no doubt that these people welcomed the advent of Franklin D. Roosevelt to the presidency. In 1932 and in 1936 the people voted overwhelmingly for Roosevelt.[9] Paul Harper of Andrews has written of his visit with other Georgetown County leaders to the new federal administrator of relief in South Carolina. Meeting with the administrator in his office, they secured $19,000 in relief for Georgetown County for the month of October 1933. "With the cooperation of the state highway depart., who loaned us shovels, axes, picks, trucks, and other things, we were able to start work on the morning of October 19th, and by the end of that week there were 4200 men at work on relief in Georgetown County. The people wanted something to eat and a little something to wear and actually struggled with each other for implements with which to work." During this period of hardship, Harper's wife and daughter "worked at the grading tables where cucumbers were sorted for pickling, at the going price for such labor."[10] Later, the local Public Works Administrator L. H. Siau cooperated with the state highway department and the Lafayette bridge was built across the Black and Waccamaw rivers. The bridge was opened in July 1935.[11] The New Deal agencies had provided a stopgap. Soon people had enough to begin saving again but for a while they only trusted the Cash Depository. Later they used the South Carolina National Bank which had opened a branch in the town.[12] The opening of the Palace Theater in November

[9] *Georgetown, South Carolina, Public Schools, A Survey Report* (Nashville, Tenn., 1967), pp. 16–17. (Hereinafter *The Peabody Report.*) This Peabody survey contains the most recent assessment of school conditions in Georgetown County.

[10] Harper, "The Growth of the Town of Andrews," *op. cit.*

[11] "Bridge Edition," Georgetown *Times,* July 19, 1935.

[12] The S. C. National Bank opened its branch in 1939.

1936 brought moving pictures to a large audience and a cheap form of entertainment.[13]

It was the paper mill and World War II that brought returning prosperity, however, to the region.[14] During the depression of the 1930's, the Seaboard Railroad went into receivership. Warren T. White, industrial agent for the railroad, brought the Seaboard Company and Georgetown County together to cooperate in the setting up of a paper mill. The county would furnish the site and water lines. In October 1936 the construction of the mill began on a 525-acre site, bordered on one side by the Sampit River. It was completed in nine months; the first pulp was made in June 1937. Late in June the No. 2 paper machine made its first reel of paper. A month later the first reel of paper also rolled off the No. 1 machine. On July 16, 1937, the first cargo of kraft (*kraft* means "strength") board made in the Georgetown mill was loaded aboard the steamer, S. S. *Orizaba,* and shipped to Philadelphia and New York.

In February 1942 the giant No. 3 paper machine began production. With this machine in operation the mill became the largest kraft paper mill in the world. The three machines consume 2,100 cords of wood, mostly pine, per day, again drawing as did the earlier mill on the vast resources of timber in the counties which surround Georgetown.

In 1942 the Container Plant was established to make shipping containers. During the war the plant manufactured weatherproof "V" grade boxes exclusively. These boxes were used by the armed services for packaging and shipping supplies overseas. In 1946 further diversification came with the completion of the Chemfibre (semi-chemical) pulp mill. Chemfibre is a corrugating medium, developed first at International's Bastrop, Louisiana, plant, which has made the corrugated container industry what it is today; 1,350 tons of kraft and chemfibre board were then produced daily. In 1961 further diversification came with bleaching facilities. Now bleached kraft is produced for cartons, tabulating cards, paper cups, etc.

The presence of the International Paper Company has transformed the

[13] Jean Harlow in "Libeled Lady" was the first film shown at the "magnificent and modernistic" Palace Theater. Georgetown *Times,* Nov. 13, 1936.

[14] The following account is drawn from various newspaper articles; *The Intapco Bulletin,* XIV, No. 6 (July 1962); and information supplied by the company.

county. In July 1962 it employed 1,700 persons in the mill, 400 in the Container Plant, and 250 in its Woodlands Division—a total of 2,350 employees. As there were only 34,798 persons resident in the county in 1960, the importance of the mill to the local economy can be measured. Through its Woodlands Division, which helps farmers to farm scientifically, the mill has brought about a revolution in farming in the area. Through the need to export its products the mill helped to revive the port. The company has had a marine terminal for thirty years. Most of the products of the mill leave by the one railroad and the twenty trucking firms which serve Georgetown.

The paper mill by its higher wages and fringe benefits has become a model for other employers. The company provides a recreation park at Brown's Ferry, a plantation on the Black River for executive-level guests, and a golf course.

During World War II the young men of Georgetown once more went forth to war. As in World War I, they did not fight in units composed entirely of Georgetown men but as part of a national army. However, the National Guard unit fought the entire war as a unit. The nucleus of the Naval Reserve division went through the war as a group on one ship. Units of the National Guard and the Naval Reserve still use their armories in Georgetown. The returning World War II veterans, as did those of World War I, brought home a different view of the world.

The period from 1945 to 1968 has seen far-reaching changes in the county. There has been economic diversification. Andrews since 1928 had been trying to secure other industries. The Odum Manufacturing Company was established in the 1930's. The Brooks Veneer Company has been in operation since the 1940's, the Santee Pine Company since 1955, and Oneita Knitting Mills since 1958. The S. C. Howe and Company makes furniture. The West Virginia Pulp and Paper Company maintains a lumber yard to collect lumber from its extensive timber holdings in the county. But the majority of income for the people of Andrews comes from the International Paper Company. Many residents commute to Georgetown to work in the plant, and many local dealers produce for the International Paper Company. This business enterprise is reflected in the fact that the Lions Service Club was founded during World War II and the Rotary Club was founded in 1967.

Although the paper mill still dominates the economy, the construction of new port facilities opens up a future. Georgetown is the second port of the state. In 1940 Major Reading Wilkinson made a full report to the United States Corps of Engineers on the status of Georgetown as a port.[15] By annual dredging, the Corps of Engineers maintains a channel of twenty-seven feet at mean low water from the jetties to Sampit River. By 1959 the South Carolina State Ports Authority had constructed a single-berth facility of a 500 foot dock and 60,000-square-foot transit shed. Both of these are run in order to stimulate ocean transportation in and out of Georgetown. There has been a steady increase in the use of these facilities. Five ships used them in 1960 and seventy-eight in 1967. In 1968 the authority envisaged adding another 500-foot dock and a second transit shed of about 75,000 square feet.[16] Over the same period there has been an increase in the use of the Georgetown dock of the International Paper Company. In 1960, 55 ships were handled and 109 in 1967.[17] Georgetown's imports have been mainly fuel oil; her exports paper and paper board.[18]

A great new boost to the economy will result from the completion of a steel mill which is being built on the banks of the Sampit River by a German-American steel corporation. The Korf Industries have created a subsidiary, the Georgetown Steel Corporation, which will build a 150,-000-square-foot manufacturing structure between South Fraser Street and the Sampit River on the main shipping channel. The basic raw material will be scrap iron brought by rail, truck, and barge, which will be made into steel to be used by the Korf Industries' plants in North Carolina and Mississippi. The plant is scheduled to begin operations in the summer of 1969 and to employ 200 persons at the start. This will be the most important addition to Georgetown industry since the establishment of the International Paper Mill.[19]

[15] Report of Maj. Reading Wilkinson to Corps of Engineers, Jan. 23, 1940, RG 77, 7145, National Archives.

[16] Charleston *News and Courier*, April 12, 1968; statistics supplied by Mr. Donald V. Richardson, S. C. State Ports Authority, Georgetown, S. C.

[17] Statistics supplied by Mr. Bobby Alford, International Paper Company, Georgetown, S. C.

[18] Statistics supplied by Mr. James M. Tobias, S. C. State Ports Authority, Charleston, S. C.

[19] "Special Edition," Georgetown *Times*, Oct. 13, 1967.

Perhaps the most important contemporary change is in the development of the recreational and tourism aspects of the county. This has been made possible by the building of roads and the coming of the automobile. The man who heralded these changes was James Henry Rice, Jr., who came to Georgetown with the Atlantic Coast Lumber Company but who stayed to edit a newspaper in Georgetown and to boost the region.[20] He was one of the developers of the Horry County region, which includes Myrtle Beach. On September 19, 1924, he made a speech in Conway on the glories of the Carolina coast. The birds had drawn down the Yankees and the lumber the paper mills, but the coast itself, the beaches, were yet to be exploited. He urged the people "from out of the wreck of bygone splendor . . . to restore and perpetuate their richest heritage, the South Carolina coast." This was at the time that John T. Woodside of Greenville, South Carolina, had bought a portion of Myrtle Beach and had begun to develop the "grand strand." Rice printed his speech in extended form in *Glories of the Carolina Coast* in 1925.[21] In 1934 he published *The Aftermath of Glory*, which first portrayed the glory that had been.[22] Plowden Weston was the grandee of the old glory; Huntington, Emerson, and Baruch of the new. But Rice envisaged a new future opening up as roads and bridges were built. The Yauhannah Bridge was constructed over the Pee Dee in 1925. By 1935 when the Lafayette Bridge over the Waccamaw was opened, there were bridges over the Black, the Sampit, and the North and South Santee. Since the Cooper River Bridge at Charleston was completed in 1929, a direct connection had been established between Charleston and Myrtle Beach by 1935. The toll was removed from the Lafayette Bridge in 1937.[23] As the automobile was just reaching the average family, more people would be thinking in terms of highways, fewer in terms of waterways. And yet as the inland waterway was cut through the region,

[20] "James Henry Rice, Jr.," Hemphill, *op. cit.*, IV, 299–300. Also see large collection of uncatalogued James Henry Rice, Jr., Papers, DUL.

[21] James Henry Rice, Jr., *Glories of the Carolina Coast* (Columbia, S. C., 1925).

[22] James Henry Rice, Jr., *The Aftermath of Glory* (Charleston, S. C., 1934).

[23] "Bridge Edition." Georgetown *Times*, July 19, 1935; Charleston *News and Courier*, Sept. 27, 1931, April 11, 12, 1936; Charleston *Evening Post*, Jan. 5, 1934. After the death of Louis Harrell Siau in 1939, former chairman of the Board of County Commissioners, the Lafayette Bridge was renamed the "L. H. Siau Memorial Bridge." In 1967 a more modern bridge replaced the old span.

pleasure craft would pass through. For the first time in its history, the people of Georgetown County would have to think geographically in a different fashion.[24]

Pawley's Island [25] and Murrell's Inlet,[26] Garden City and Litchfield Beach have become the summer vacation spots. The planters had built summer homes on North Island, Dubourdieu Beach, and at Pawley's, but only Pawley's had been accessible across a causeway, which in recent times was made to sustain a hard-surfaced road. Houses had been built in the eighteenth century on these islands; some still remain that were constructed before the Civil War; but the extension of new building after World War II to the south end of Pawley's was washed away by hurricane Hazel on October 15, 1954.[27] But the occasional hurricane cannot keep the people of Georgetown County or of the state from these magnificent beaches. The island, with its firm beach, clear water, and back creek, affords the finest surf bathing along the Carolina coast and some of the finest crabbing and shrimping. It has retained something of its family atmosphere with no public place of rendezvous except the pier, which is strictly for fishing, and the pavilion (there have been four within the memory of the oldest generation) which sits on the edge of the back marsh. Out of the pavilion in the thirties came the Big Apple, the most important forerunner of the modern dances. Just behind the creek the Lachicottes for many years provided the necessaries and the frills in their all-purpose store. Some members of the family still own and operate the Hammock Shop and Nursery, where maps and books and mementos of the past can be bought.

Murrell's Inlet has less unity of living and perhaps a greater diversity of clientele. There is deep-sea fishing in the Gulf Stream; the vessels

[24] The rapid growth of this region has been labeled a "recreation explosion." James R. Fussell and Richard G. Silvernail, "The Impact of Recreation on Coastal South Carolina," *Business and Economic Review* (published by the Univ. of S. C.), XIII (1966), 3–8.

[25] Pawley's Island was named after the Pawley brothers, George, Anthony, and Percival. For the story of the island as told through pictures see Sally Edwards and Jean Erwin, *Pawley's Island* (Charlotte, N. C., 1960). Also see Celina McGregor Vaughan, *Pawley's . . . As It Was* (Columbia, S. C., 1969).

[26] Murrell's Inlet was named after John Morrall, who purchased 610 acres on the inlet in 1731. "Will of John Morrall," dated Sept. 16, 1769, proved Jan. 18, 1771, Charleston County Wills, XIV, Book A (1767–1771), 574, S. C. Archives.

[27] *News and Courier,* Oct. 14, 15, 16, 17, 1954.

make their way in and out through the same inlets that the blockade runners used during the Civil War. There are road-side eating places renowned for their sea food. But there are also quiet homes for year-round living where a good deal of writing can be done. Julia Peterkin in the twenties found an escape at Murrell's Inlet and at Brookgreen. Sandy Island was the locale of her story *Black April*.[28] Mickey Spillane has lived at Murrell's Inlet for many years although his mystery thriller novels make no use of the local scene.

Some of the family traditions have served as background for Charleston writers. This is certainly true in the works of Katharine Drayton Mayrant Simons [29] and in the little volume of verse published in 1932 by Alston Deas, entitled *Charleston Boy*. Julian Stevenson Bolick has tried to capture some of the folklore of the region in his successive works: *Georgetown Houselore, Waccamaw Plantations, Georgetown Ghosts,* and *The Return of the Gray Man and Georgetown Ghosts.* Susan Lowndes Allston in her many sketches of the old plantations [30] and Alberta Morel Lachicotte in *Georgetown Rice Plantations* have also tried to pin down the historic past. But none have equaled the slightly earlier works of Elizabeth Waties Allston Pringle.

When her mother died in 1896 Mrs. Pringle, who had inherited White House plantation from her husband, bought in Chicora Wood, the last of her father's plantations remaining in possession of the family, and determined to carry on in the old way. Her valiant attempt beautifully recorded in her two works reveal the strengths which she had inherited and must have been a part of every plantation mistress. Her love for all humanity is shown in a letter she wrote to Mayor W. D. Morgan on January 30, 1897, on mourning stationery, in which she inquired concerning the inmates of the local jail whom she had heard had no blankets. From her pittance she was willing to supply their needs.[31] She

[28] Julia Mood Peterkin, *Black April* (Indianapolis, Ind., 1927).

[29] Katharine Drayton Mayrant Simons, *The Red Doe* (New York, 1953); *White Horse Leaping* (Columbia, S. C., 1951).

[30] Susan Lowndes Allston, *Brookgreen, Waccamaw, in the Carolina Low Country* (Charleston, S. C., 1935); *Early Sketch of St. John in the Wilderness and Flat Rock, North Carolina* (n.p., [1964]); *Sketches Along the Peedee River* (n.p., n.d.); and numerous newspaper articles.

[31] Box 5, W. D. Morgan Papers, SCL.

struggled on between her need to be stern and her sympathy for the weakness of humanity. The day-by-day account for the years 1903 through 1906 of her failure is etched in *A Woman Rice Planter*, which she dedicated in 1913 to her father. The heritage that gave her strength is recorded in *Chronicles of Chicora Wood*, which was published in 1922. Together these works portray the depths and the heights of the struggle to preserve the rice industry. That failure brought forth the best in local literature.[32]

The local chapter of the U. D. C. has published *For the Love of a Rebel*. Clark M. Wilcox has added to the knowledge of the region in *Musings of a Hermit*. The Reverend Henry DeSaussure Bull's *All Saints' Church, Waccamaw, The Parish, the Place, the People, 1739–1948* (published by the Winyah Press in 1948 and again in 1968) is a valuable account of one of the most important local institutions. His *The Family of Stephen Bull of Kingshurst Hall, County Warwick, England and Ashley Hall, South Carolina, 1600–1960* was also published in Georgetown, in 1961.

The Georgetown County Library, the Georgetown Historical Society, and the Winyah Indigo Society assist in many ways with their records and their meetings those who write the story of the region. The service clubs and the Chamber of Commerce publicize the local accomplishments.

Tourists are deliberately drawn to the region by spring and summer tours. Each spring since 1947 the church of Prince George Winyah has sponsored three successive days of tours during which the plantations on all the rivers and the town houses are thrown open to visitors. In the summer the parish of All Saints sponsors a tour of the oldest beach cottages. The Johnstone family, which now owns Belle Isle Gardens on which Battery White stands, keeps this tourist attraction open all year round. These tours still give a glimpse of the olden times. There is, however, very little of the old planting world left. Miss Susan Lowndes Allston wrote James Henry Rice from Windsor plantation in 1922: "It is a horrid, materialistic age. Society does sound at times . . . something

[32] *A Woman Rice Planter* was reprinted in 1961 by the Belknap Press of Harvard University Press and *Chronicles of Chicora Wood* in 1940 by the Christopher Publishing House of Boston, Mass.

like a pig sty. . . . There is less fineness of manners but perhaps less humbug." [33]

The population of Georgetown County has begun to grow. During the 1950's the town doubled its population from 6,000 to 12,000 persons. The population of the county in 1960 was 34,798, of whom 16,652 were white and 18,146 were nonwhite. Although the Negroes still outnumber the whites, the percentage of Negroes in the population has continually slipped during the twentieth century. During the period from 1910 to 1920 the Negroes declined by 1,649 while the whites increased by 1,096. In 1940 the Negroes represented 58 percent of the total; in 1960 only 52 percent. As there are only two towns (Georgetown with 12,261 in 1960 and Andrews with 2,995), the population is still 56 percent rural. [34]

Modern Georgetown County has never recovered the prominence that it had in the state in the 1850's when it supplied the state with a governor and a lieutenant governor. Although it is beginning to grow wealthier, it is still not the rich county that it was in 1860. The county is thirty-first among the forty-six counties of the state in per capita income. The state average in 1960 was $1,538 whereas in Georgetown County the average was $1,042. [35]

LeGrand G. Walker (1850–1920), a native-born, Princeton-trained lawyer, who became active in the Hampton campaign of 1876 and who was counsel for the Atlantic Coast Lumber Company, first qualified for the senate on November 27, 1894, and held his seat in the South Carolina senate until his death on October 26, 1920. He was president pro tempore of the senate from 1915 to his death. [36] Herbert L. Smith served until 1923 when he resigned upon his appointment as clerk of court. Samuel Mortimer Ward (who qualified on January 23, 1924) sat until 1940. Ward, who was a descendant of J. J. Ward and whose wife was a LaBruce, was for many years chairman of the senate Finance Committee. [37] Dr. Olin Sawyer, senator from 1940 to 1948, had formerly been

[33] Dec. 19, 1922, James Henry Rice, Jr., Papers, DUL.

[34] *The Peabody Report,* pp. 3–9.

[35] Recent survey for Ports Authority.

[36] "LeGrand G. Walker," Snowden, *op. cit.,* III, 261; *The Senate of the State of South Carolina, 1776–1962,* ed. E. B. Reynolds and J. R. Faunt (Columbia, S. C., 1962), p. 154; obituary, Georgetown *Times-Index,* Oct. 26, 1920.

[37] There is information about the father in "Samuel Mortimer Ward, Jr.," Snowden, *op. cit.,* IV, 289–290.

doctor for the Atlantic Coast Lumber Company.[38] Senators James B. Morrison and Cecil Claymon Grimes have been the most recent incumbents.

The present form of city government was established in 1892 when the city was reincorporated.[39] The corporate limits ran from Serenity plantation on the west to Willowbank on the north and Greenwich on the east. The Sampit was the southern boundary. Henceforth, there would be a mayor and four aldermen, elected every second year beginning on the third Monday of January 1894. The new city corporation might make ordinances "relative to the streets, roads, bridges, markets, public squares, parks, public buildings, public scales, weights and measures, fire department, water supply, harbor, wharves, pavements, sewers, lights, drains, police and health of said city as they may deem necessary and proper, and all such ordinances as may tend to preserve the quietude, peace, safety, good order and health of the inhabitants thereof, and the protection, security and enjoyment of their property." They might prohibit the cultivation of rice within the city limits. William Doyle Morgan was the first mayor of Georgetown, holding the office until January 1906. By the end of his term of office, the town had a good telegraph and telephone system, three good newspapers one of which was a daily, an abundant and pure water supply drawn from the Black River and from artesian wells, a modern sanitary sewerage system, fine electric lights, broad streets which were macadamized and shaded with oak and elm trees, cement sidewalks, and, as the *Handbook of South Carolina* for 1908 said, "the flavor of colonial life, culture and tradition, mingled with the snap and vim of twentieth century progress. . . ." Mayor Morgan stepped down in 1905 at the time of the centennial of the incorporation of Georgetown as a town. The citizens presented him with a handsome silver bowl for his work in the civic

[38] Olin Sawyer had supported Cole L. Blease until Blease had attacked Wilson and World War II. Frank E. Jordan, Jr., *The Primary State, A History of the Democratic Party in South Carolina, 1896–1962* (n.p., n.d.), p. 66; Reynolds and Faunt, *Biographical Directory of the South Carolina Senate*, pp. 303–304.

[39] "An act to Charter the City of Georgetown," dated Dec. 22, 1892, *Acts and Joint Resolutions of the General Assembly of the State of South Carolina, Passed at the Regular Session of 1892* (Columbia, S. C., 1892), pp. 260–274.

improvements and his success in the improvement of the harbor and the building of the jetties at the ocean entrance to Winyah Bay.[40]

The county is run by a large number of elected county officials. A listing of these includes: a sheriff, county attorney and coroner, a treasurer and auditor, a probate judge, clerk of court and magistrates, and a school board and superintendent. In the past, the chief power in the county was held by the state senator and the members of the legislative delegation. They appointed a five-member board of county commissioners. This system has been slightly changed due to changes within the state with reference to reapportionment. As it may be possible in the near future that Georgetown will not have a senator resident in the county (since Georgetown and Horry counties have now been joined in one senatorial district), there have been some changes in the direction of more elected officials and thus the maintenance of local control. Members of the Board of Education and of the Board of Commissioners after 1968 will all be elected to office.[41]

Georgetown has had a succession of newspapers in the twentieth century. *The Outlook* was begun on January 25, 1901, by E. W. Wolfe and J. Walter Doar. It was a weekly that supported the Democratic Party. The *Carolina Field* first issued on May 3, 1905 was a weekly published by James Henry Rice, Jr., which was designed to advertise the industries, resources, and climatological advantages of eastern Carolina. The Georgetown *Daily Item* started as a daily on May 1, 1907. The *Progressive Democrat* appeared on November 13, 1913, with Thomas W. Barfield as owner and publisher, who promised to give his readers a "square deal." The editor was Arthur L. King, federal postmaster. The Georgetown *Times-Index*, which began on September 1, 1920, was to appear twice weekly under the direction of the editor E. N. Beard. The *Coastal Chronicle* was first published on November 23, 1922, and was to be managed by Archie P. Lewis on sound Democratic principles.[42]

[40] "William Doyle Morgan," Hemphill, *op. cit.*, I, 278–282; *Who's Who in South Carolina, 1934–1935*, ed. Walker S. Utsey (Columbia, S. C., 1935), pp. 318–319; *The State*, Dec. 18, 1905; *News and Courier*, Dec. 19, 20, 1905; *Handbook of South Carolina for 1908* (Columbia, S. C., 1908), p. 568; manuscript notes for report, dated Jan. 23, 1896, Box 4, W. D. Morgan Papers, SCL.

[41] *The Peabody Report*, pp. 14–17.

[42] Copies of these newspapers can be found in the Winyah Indigo Society Collection, Georgetown County Library.

The Georgetown *Times* founded in the post-Civil War period has passed through the hands of a succession of owners. Adelbert T. Wendt, Cecil Davis, and Percy LaBruce were editors in the 1930's. Today the paper is owned and operated by Thomas Petigru Davis. The citizens of Georgetown, however, still subscribe to the Charleston, Columbia, and Charlotte newspapers as dailies.[43]

There is now much greater diversity in local business and churches in Georgetown today as the yellow pages of the phone book reveal. Besides the paper mill, the lumber companies, the banks, the railroads, there are many smaller establishments, retail stores, or public services. Aside from the paper mill, the major industries are clothing, nylon carpet stock, lumber, and laboratory equipment. Minor industries produce such items as chemicals, soft drinks, hammocks, paper plugs, meat, and candles. Laws have recently in 1968 been changed to make it even more advantageous for industry to locate in Georgetown.

More and more of the farms are residential or part-time farms. Flue-cured tobacco has been one major introduction into the farm economy. Tobacco farming, however, is on a modest scale combined with off-farm work. Small-scale cotton farming is common. Grains, vegetables, fruits, melons, and nuts are also produced. Irish potato and sweet potato growing bring in some income. Livestock raising, chiefly cattle and hogs, seems to be on the up-grade. In 1959 the value of farm products sold was $2,870,000 while that of livestock was $615,000. But, as one recent report stated, "the average level of living of farmers is among the lowest in the nation."[44]

Besides the pre-war Episcopal, Methodist, and Baptist churches there are now many others. A Presbyterian church has been established. In 1905 a Jewish congregation was formed and served by Dr. Barnett A. Elzas from Charleston.[45] There have been Catholics in the community since the early nineteenth century. After the war mass was said in the home of Arthur Morgan until his death in 1878, after which mass was celebrated in the home of his nephew, W. D. Morgan. The cornerstone of

[43] The most complete file of the Georgetown *Times* is in the Georgetown County Library.

[44] *The Peabody Report*, p. 10.

[45] Barnett A. Elzas, *The Jews of South Carolina* (Philadelphia, Penn., 1905), p. 244.

the Church of St. Mary of Ransom was laid on November 30, 1899; it was dedicated on January 5, 1902.[46]

There are also pentecostal and Christian churches as well as Negro churches. The Reverend A. T. Fisher is pastor of the Bethel AME Church. The Reverend W. A. Johnson is pastor of the Bethesda Baptist Church. These are the largest of the Negro churches.

As the state maintains no constitutional mandate for a system of public schools, there is a great deal of variation on the local level among school systems. In Georgetown County the system is classified as a county school district, which is controlled by one board of education, known as the Georgetown County Board of Education. This board consists of nine citizens who since 1966 have been elected, four every four years. The county superintendent, also elected, is the ninth member. The board is therefore composed of citizens who sit for four-year terms. They have the responsibility of final adoption of a school budget and the levy of sufficient taxes to furnish the local funds needed. The superintendent holds an elected position for a four-year term.[47] In 1965 a newly formed Winyah Academy opened as a private school.

Changing national conditions have brought about a change of political allegiance in the county for most of the whites. In 1948 nearly 60 percent of the vote was cast for Strom Thurmond, who ran on the third-party ticket. In 1956 52 percent of the vote was cast for neither of the two major party candidates. In 1964 58 percent of the vote was cast for Goldwater. This would indicate a departure from the Democratic Party for most members of the white community. This therefore represents a marked conservative bent among the voters.[48]

As the Peabody Report summed up the local situation:

It is altogether probable that history at once has been kind and unkind to Georgetown County. It has enjoyed and descended from the proud, genteel and often vibrant plantation culture. It has inherited also the burdensome history of social inertia and economic bondage. These "two histories," apparently at a juncture during recent years, have come into focus around various problems of social change. School integration, however preoccupying it may be of the community mind, is surely only

[46] *The Saint Anthony Guild*, V (1904).
[47] *The Peabody Report*, pp. 20–33.
[48] *The Peabody Report*, pp. 16–17.

one aspect of this situation. Many of Georgetown's problems are not of its own making, but rather stem from the forces of the larger society. But they can no less be avoided. The general problem seems to be one of discovering ways of compromising old values with new goals for a genuine course of progress. Change for progress must be perceived as being more desirable than stability for the status quo. Change will not come easily for Georgetown County because of economic constraints and political conservatism. But it is not possible for a community of people to remain static or to move sideways for long. Eventually it will either move forward or drift backward. Whither Georgetown?[49]

[49] *The Peabody Report,* pp. 18–19.

I

MEMBERS COMMONS HOUSE OF ASSEMBLY[*]

2nd Assembly—began February 23, 1725.
Prince George—James Nicholas Mayrant, Richard Smith.

3rd Assembly—began January 31, 1728.
Prince George—William Waties, George Pawley.

4th Assembly—began July 9, 1728.
Prince George—Meredith Hughes, John Tompson.

5th Assembly—began September 17, 1728.
Prince George—Meredith Hughes, George Pawley.

6th Assembly—began January 15, 1729.
Prince George—James Brown, John Bullen (Bulline).

7th Assembly—began August 6, 1729.
Prince George—John Bulline, Thomas Bonny.

8th Assembly—began December 2, 1729.
Prince George—John Bulline, Tweedie Somerville.

9th Assembly—began January 20, 1731.
Prince George—Richard Smith, Richard Pawley.

10th Assembly—began November 15, 1733.
Prince George—William Waties, Richard Smith.
(William Swinton was chosen on April 16, 1735, in place of Richard Smith deceased.)

[*] The members of the Senate and the House of Representatives from the Georgetown area can be found in Emily Bellinger Reynolds and Joan Reynolds Faunt, *Biographical Directory of the Senate of South Carolina, 1776–1964* (Columbia, S. C., 1964) and in a forthcoming posthumous work of Joan Reynolds Faunt, a biographical directory of the S. C. House of Representatives.

11th Assembly—began November 9, 1736.
Prince George—William Whiteside, William Poole.
Prince Frederick—Thomas Henning, Maurice Lewis.

12th Assembly—began September 12, 1739.
Prince George—Robert Austin, Joseph Huggins
Prince Frederick—James Abercromby, John Bassnett

13th Assembly—September 14, 1742.
Prince George—Isaac Mazyck, James Abercromby.
Prince Frederick—Noah Serre, Daniel Crawford.

14th Assembly—September 10, 1745.
Prince George—Elias Horry, Alexander Vander Dussen.
Prince Frederick—Isaac Mazyck, David Hext.

15th Assembly—began September 10, 1746.
Prince George—John Ouldfield, George Pawley.
Prince Frederick—Anthony White, John White.

16th Assembly—called for September 2, 1747, but never met.

17th Assembly—began January 17, 1748.
Prince George—William Waties, Paul Trapier.
Prince Frederick—Isaac Mazyck, Daniel Crawford.

18th Assembly—called for January 10, 1749, but never met.

19th Assembly—began March 28, 1749.
Prince George—John Ouldfield, Elias Foissin.
Prince Frederick—Isaac Mazyck, a vacancy never filled.

20th Assembly—began November 14, 1751.
Prince George—Paul Trapier, George Gabriel Powell.
Prince Frederick—William Buchanan, Thomas Lynch.

21st Assembly—November 12, 1754.
Prince George—William Allston, George Gabriel Powell.
Prince Frederick—Joseph Cantey, Richard Richardson.

22nd Assembly—October 6, 1757.
Prince George—Paul Trapier, Thomas Waties.
Prince Frederick—Thomas Lynch, John Waties.

23rd Assembly—October 6, 1760.
Prince George—Thomas Lynch, Thomas Waties.
Prince Frederick—Thomas Lynch, James Crockatt.

24th Assembly—March 25, 1761.
Prince George—George Gabriel Powell, Thomas Lynch.
Prince Frederick—George Gabriel Powell, James Crockatt.

25th Assembly—February 6, 1762.
Prince George—Elias Horry, Thomas Lynch.
Prince Frederick—John Moultrie, William Moultrie.

26th Assembly—October 25, 1762.
Prince George—Thomas Lynch, Alexander Rose.
Prince Frederick—James Moultrie, John Murray.

27th Assembly—October 28, 1765.
Prince George—Thomas Lynch, Daniel Horry.
Prince Frederick—William Moultrie, Samuel Clegg.

28th Assembly—October 25, 1768.
Prince George—Thomas Lynch, Elias Horry, Jr.
Prince Frederick—Charles Cantey, Theodore Gaillard.
All Saints—Thomas Lynch, Joseph Allston.

29th Assembly—March 21, 1769.
Prince George—Thomas Lynch, Elias Horry, Jr.
Prince Frederick—Charles Cantey, Theodore Gaillard.
(Both refused to sit, Cantey because of ill-health. Benjamin Farar
took his seat on December 5, 1769.)
All Saints—Joseph Allston, Benjamin Young (both refused.)

30th Assembly—April 2, 1772.
Prince George—Thomas Lynch, Elias Horry.
Prince Frederick—no members listed in *Gazette*, April 9, 1772.
All Saints—no members listed henceforth for this parish.

31st Assembly—October 8, 1772 (met in Beaufort).
Prince George—Thomas Lynch, Elias Horry, Jr.
Prince Frederick—Theodore Gaillard took his seat on Oct. 22.
Benjamin Farar was elected but did not take his seat at Beaufort
because of illness.

32nd Assembly—January 1, 1773.
Prince George—Thomas Lynch, Elias Horry.
Prince Frederick—Benjamin Farar, Theodore Gaillard, Jr.

33rd Assembly—February 23, 1773.
Prince George—Elias Horry, Jr., Thomas Lynch.
Prince Frederick—Benjamin Farar, Theodore Gaillard, Jr.

II

ALLSTON AND ALSTON GENEALOGY

John Allston (-1750)
m. Sarah Belin

1. John (-1751)
   m. Esther Marion
   a. Martha
      m. Benjamin Young

2. Martha
   m. Benjamin Marion

3. Josias (1731-1776) of Turkey Hill
   m. three times and had eleven children
   a. Francis (1753-   )
   b. John (1756-   )
   c. William (1759-1776)
   d. Benjamin, Sr. (1765-1847)
      m.
         i. Martha
            m. John F. Pyatt (1790-1820)
   e. Josias (1777-   )

* The genealogical information to be found in Joseph A. Groves, *The Alstons and Allstons of North and South Carolina* (Atlanta, Ga., 1901), is unreliable. The above charts are the author's attempts at clarification.

4. Samuel

5. William, Jr. (1738-1781) of Brookgreen
   m. (1) (1763) Anne Simons
     a. Benjamin, Jr. (1766-1809)
       m. Charlotte Anne Allston
         i. Elizabeth Ann (1790-1822)
           m. John Hyrne Tucker
         ii. Charlotte Atchison (1793-1847)
           m. John Coachman
         iii. Mary Pyatt (1795-1836)
           m. William H. Jones
         iv. Joseph Waties (1798-1834)
           m. three times
         v. Robert F. W. (1801-1864)
           m. Adele Petigru
         vi. William Washington (1804-1823)
   m. (2) (1776) Rachel Moore
     b. Mary (1779-   )
       m. (1) Thomas Young
         (2) William Algernon Alston
     c. Washington (1779-1843)
     d. William Moore (1781-   )

        William Allston (1698-1744)
          m. (1721) Esther LaBrosse de Marboeuf
          (1704-1781)

1. William, Sr. (1724-   )
   m. Sabina Atchison
     a. Charlotte Anne (-1824)
       m. Benjamin Allston, Jr. (1766-1809)
     b. Elizabeth Frances
       m. Joseph Blyth

2. Esther (1726-   )
   m. Archibald Johnston

3. Elizabeth (1728-   )
     m. Thomas Lynch

4. Joseph (1733-1784) of The Oaks
     m. (1755) Charlotte Rothmahler
         a. William Alston of Clifton (1756-1839)
         b. Thomas (1764-1794)
             m. Mary Allston (his first cousin)

5. Anne (1735-   )
     m. Thomas Waties

6. Mary (1737-   )
     m. John Waties

7. Frances (1739-   )
     m. Robert Pawley

8. John (Captain Jack) (1741-   )
     m. Mary Faucheraud
         a. Mary
             m. Thomas Allston and then Benjamin Huger

                William Alston (1756-1839) of Clifton
                (the first of the single "l" Alstons)
                    m. (1) (1777) Mary Ashe

1. Maria (1778-   )
     m. Sir John Nesbit

2. Joseph (1779-1816)
     m. (1801) Theodosia Burr
         a. Aaron Burr Alston (1802-1812)

3. John Ashe (1780-1831)
     m. Sarah McPherson (1785-1812)
         a. Sarah McPherson (1807-1878)
             m. John Izard Middleton

4. William Algernon (1782-1860)
    m. Mrs. Mary Allston Young (-1841)
        a. Joseph (-1861)
           m. Helen Mason of New York
             i. William Algernon (1830-1867)
        b. John Ashe
           m. Fanny Fraser
        c. Mary Ashe
           m. Seaman Deas
        d. Anna Louise
        e. Charlotte

5. Charlotte
    m. John Lide Wilson

        m. (2) (1791) Mary Brewton Motte (1769-1838)

---

6. Rebecca
    m. Robert Y. Hayne

7. Thomas Pinckney (1795-1861)
    m. twice and had nine children

8. Elizabeth
    m. Arthur P. Hayne

9. Charles Cotesworth Pinckney (-1881)
    m. Emma Pringle and had three children

10. Mary Motte
    m. William Bull Pringle and had nine children.

11. Jacob Motte (1797-1818)

III

FAMILY ESTATES

	1850[1]		1859[2]	
	Cash value of farm	No. of Slaves	Value Charleston real estate	No. of Slaves
J. J. Ward	527,050	1,092	20,000	15
Pyatt family	380,950	768	18,000	24
F. M. Weston	316,250	196		
W. A. Alston	200,000	84	36,000[3]	17
J. H. Tucker	145,000	201	22,900	22
A. J. Allston, Est.[4]	140,000	166		
R. F. W. Allston	130,000	401	35,000	10
Charles Alston, Sr.	124,000		22,000	16
R. S. Izard	120,000	187		
J. I. Middleton	110,000	318[5]	Rented	
R. O. Anderson	100,000	384		
H. A. Middleton	100,000	303	13,000	17
A. Johnston	100,000	230		

[1] From 1850 census.
[2] From Charleston Taxpayers List for 1859.
[3] Four members of the W. A. Alston family had Charleston homes.
[4] This may be the estate of John Ashe Alston.
[5] Number of slaves in 1860.

	1850 [1]		1859 [2]	
	Cash value of farm	No. of Slaves	Value Charleston real estate	No. of Slaves
La Bruce family	96,000	150	25,000	11
J. H. Read I and II	90,000	323	50,000 [6]	30
B. F. Hunt	90,000	234		
J. W. Allston, Est.	90,000	84		
B. F. Dunkin	84,000		11,000	6
F. Withers, Est.	80,000	506		
Mary Nesbit	80,000			
W. B. Pringle	76,000	281	18,000	34
W. H. Trapier	75,000	118	Rented	17
Robert Hume	75,000	135		
Francis Weston	70,000	225	25,000 [7]	37
C. C. Pinckney	60,000			9
J. H. Ladson	60,000	201	———— [8]	2
J. R. Pringle	55,000	143	12,000	16
M. H. Lance	54,000	263	Rented	
W. R. Maxwell	50,000	157		
Mrs. P. Rutledge	50,000	302		
F. Shaffer	50,000	97	15,000	18
P. W. Fraser, Est.	50,000	133		
A. B. Flagg	50,000		11,000 [9]	9
F. W. Ford	49,000	55		
S. D. Doar	48,000	97	14,000	11
E. Horry, Est.	45,000	150		
J. D. Magill	40,000	200		
R. H. Lowndes	40,000	147		

[6] Two Charleston houses.
[7] Two Charleston houses, one belonged to the estate of Weston's father.
[8] Apparently Ladson did not own the house he lived in at No. 4 Meeting.
[9] This was owned by his mother, Mrs. M. E. Flagg.

	1850 [1]		1859 [2]	
	Cash value of farm	No. of Slaves	Value Charleston real estate	No. of Slaves
Rawlins Lowndes	40,000	109		
J. G. Shoolbred	40,000	121		
William Lucas	40,000	72	25,000	13
Alexander Hume, Est.	40,000	183	16,000 [10]	7
Robert Pringle	40,000	142	5,000	5
B. F. Trapier, Est.	40,000	207		
E. T. Heriot	37,000	370 [11]		
H. E. Lucas	35,000	72		
J. R. Poinsett	30,000	103		
Eliza Pinckney	30,000	84	16,000	2
Thomas Pinckney, Est.	30,000			
W. H. Mayrant	30,000	121		
P. Tidyman, Est.	30,000	130	8,000	8
T. L. Horry	30,000	101		
S. Deas, Sr.	30,000	103		
S. Deas	30,000	66		
M. A. E. Sparkman	30,000	102	Rented	
J. Manigault, Est.	28,000	151		
Elias Doar	27,000	85		
F. W. Johnston	26,000	90		
T. L. Bulow	25,000	62	66,100	19
J. St. J. Pringle	25,000	78		1
Ravenel and Pringle	25,000	76	34,000 [12]	10
J. H. Lucas	25,000	178	2,000	5
Stephen Ford	25,000	140		

[10] This was owned by T. M. Hume, son of Alexander Hume.
[11] Number of slaves in 1854.
[12] This was the home of William Ravenel.

| | 1850[1] | | 1859[2] | |
	Cash value of farm	No. of Slaves	Value Charleston real estate	No. of Slaves
F. S. Parker	25,000	122	6,500[13]	4
J. Exum	25,000	87		
Simons Lucas	23,000	70		
S. C. Ford	22,500	54		
W. P. Vaux	22,400			
Hugh Fraser	22,000	67		
Thomas Lowndes, Est.	22,000	111		
C. K. Huger	21,000	64	15,000	1
Heriot Huggins	20,000	61		
J. R. Sparkman	20,000	87		
J. P. Ford	19,000	99		
Coachman and McKay	18,000	40	8,000	7
J. R. Ford	15,000	54		
W. G. Linerieux	15,000	48		
J. M. Commander	15,000	36		
S. T. Gaillard	15,000	71		
C. J. Atkinson	14,000	70		
J. R. Easterling	10,000	65		
J. J. I. Pringle	10,000	62		
J. W. Ford	9,000	16		
Francis Green	5,000	49		
J. J. Green	3,700	35		
T. P. Alston[14]		274		9
A. H. Belin[15]		246	20,000	11

[13] Parker acted as trustee.
[14] There is no entry for T. P. Alston in the Georgetown census for 1850.
[15] Ditto for A. H. Belin.

IV

INTENDANTS AND MAYORS OF GEORGETOWN *

1806—John Keith	1824—Thomas Carr
1807—Paul Trapier	1825—Thomas Carr
1808—Savage Smith	1826—Abram Myers
1809—Paul Trapier	1827—Abram Myers
1810—Thomas Chapman	1828
1811—John L. Wilson	1829—Eleazer Waterman
1812—John L. Wilson	1830—A. W. Dozier
1813—Thomas Carr	1831—A. W. Dozier
1814—Thomas Carr	1832—William Chapman
1815	1833—William Chapman
1816	1834—A. W. Dozier
1817	1835—A. W. Dozier
1818—Solomon Cohen	1836—John Harrelson
1819—Robert Heriot	1837—Solomon Cohen
1820	1838—J. W. Coachman
1821	1839—Thomas L. Shaw
1822—John Wragg	1840—Eleazer Waterman
1823—John Porter, Jr.	1841—John F. Lesesne

* This list is based upon the lists drawn up by William D. Morgan but corrected according to the signers of the Ordinances, the names of whom can be found in the Book of Ordinances, 1806–1848, City Hall, Georgetown, S. C.

1842—John F. Lesesne

1843—B. T. Cuttino

1844—J. M. Commander

1845—O. M. Roberts

1846—Eleazer Waterman

1847—Leonard Dozier

1848—Benjamin H. Wilson

1849—Benjamin H. Wilson

1850—Benjamin H. Wilson

1851—Benjamin A. Coachman

1852—Benjamin A. Coachman

1853—Benjamin A. Coachman

1854—Benjamin A. Coachman

1855—Benjamin A. Coachman

1856—G. W. Christie

1857—William S. Croft

1858—W. J. Howard

1859—W. J. Howard

1860—W. J. Howard

1861—W. J. Howard

1862—W. J. Howard

1863—W. J. Howard

1864—W. J. Howard
     (died in office)
     succeeded by R. O. Bush

1865—no election

1866—R. O. Bush

1867—R. E. Fraser

1868—H. F. Herriot

1869—H. F. Herriot

1870—R. O. Bush

1871—W. K. Heston

1872—George R. Congdon

1873—R. O. Bush

1874

1875—J. W. Tarbox

1876—Sol Emanuel

1877—Sol Emanuel

1878—R. E. Fraser

1879—R. E. Fraser

1880—R. E. Fraser

1881—David Risley

1882—David Risley

1883—David Risley

1884—David Risley

1885—R. E. Fraser

1886—L. S. Ehrich

1887—L. S. Ehrich

1888—L. S. Ehrich

1889—David Risley

1890—David Risley

1891—William D. Morgan

Mayors

1893-1905—W. D. Morgan

1906-1911—H. W. Fraser

1912-1914—W. H. Andrews
     (resigned)

1915-   —H. W. Fraser

1916-1919—Olin Sawyer

1920-1923—J. W. Wingate

1924-1929—C. B. Colbert

1930-1935—Harold Kaminski

1934-1945—H. L. Smith

1946-1947—J. Lee Wilson

1948- —William J. Miller
(deceased)

1948-1961—Sylvan L. Rosen

1962-1965—Lester L. Weed

1966- —O. M. Higgins

ALPHABETICAL INDEX

This index has been compiled according to the letter-by-letter mode of alphabetizing. Headings are treated as single words, ignoring spaces and commas. In many cases where dates are necessary for identification, the date is alphabetized according to its usual spoken form.

Example: Middleton, Arthur (1832 – —)   (Eighteen thirty-two)
             Middleton, Arthur (1742 – 1787)   (Seventeen forty-two)

"Jr." appears (alphabetically) before "Sr."; however, proper names with roman numeral designations are listed in chronological order beginning with the roman numeral sequence:

Horry, Elias, I
Horry, Elias, II
Horry, Elias, III
Horry, Elias, IV
Horry, Elias, V

but:

Waties, William, Jr.
Waties, William, Sr.
Waties, William, III

THE HISTORY OF GEORGETOWN COUNTY,
SOUTH CAROLINA

The typeface of this volume is Linotype Caledonia composed by the R. L. Bryan Company and printed by off-
set lithography by the T JM Corporation on Warren's
University Text, an acid-free bookpaper noted for its
longevity. The paper has been specially watermarked
with the University of South Carolina Press colophon.
The binding is by the Nicholstone Book Bindery using
a natural finish cloth furnished by the G. S. B. Fabrics
Corporation. The book was designed by Robert L.
Nance.